For Reference

Not to be taken from this room

The Judicial Branch of State Government

People, Process, and Politics

Other Titles in ABC-CLIO's
ABOUT
STATE GOVERNMENT
Set

THE JUDICIAL BRANCH OF STATE GOVERNMENT

People, Process, and Politics

Edited by
Sean O. Hogan

A B C C L I O

Santa Barbara, California   Denver, Colorado   Oxford, England

Library of Congress Cataloging-in-Publication Data

The judicial branch of state government : people, process, and politics / edited by Sean O. Hogan.
        p. cm. -- (About state government)
    Includes bibliographical and references and index.
    ISBN 1-85109-751-1 (hardcover : alk. paper) -- ISBN 1-85109-756-2 (ebook) 1. Courts--United States--States. 2. Court Administration--United States--States.
I. Hogan, Sean O..
KF8736.J58 2006
347.73'3--dc22

2006018461

09   08   07   06   10   9   8   7   6   5   4   3   2   1

This book is also available on the World Wide Web as an eBook. Visit abc-clio.com for details.

ABC-CLIO, Inc.
130 Cremona Drive, P.O. Box 1911
Santa Barbara, California 93116-1911

Production Team
    Production Manager: Don Schmidt
    Acquisitions Editor: Alicia Merritt
    Media Editor: Karen Koppel
    Media Resources Manager: Caroline Price
    Production Editor: Martha Ripley Gray
    Editorial Assistant: Alisha Martinez
    Associate Production Editor: Kristine Swift

Text Design: Darice Zimmermann, ZimmServices

This book is printed on acid-free paper ∞ .
Manufactured in the United States of America

For Jane

Thank you for everything

CONTENTS

FOREWORD

Most Americans have some familiarity with the role and structure of the federal government. At an early age, we are taught in school about the president of the United States and the roles performed by the three branches of the federal government: the legislative, the executive, and the judicial. In civics classes, we are often given a skeletal picture of how the nation's government works; we are told that Congress writes the laws, the president executes them, and the Supreme Court acts as the interpreter of the U.S. Constitution. Outside of the classroom, the media repeatedly remind us of the important duties that all three branches play in the nation's political system. Through television news, radio talk shows, newspapers, magazines, and web blogs, the media draw our attention to the major political battles in Washington, D.C., building our knowledge of the president, Congress, and the U.S. Supreme Court.

While most Americans have some knowledge of the federal government, they tend to know far less about their state governments. Our schools frequently teach us about the governments in our own states, yet what we learn about state government does not become as deeply ingrained as what we learn about the federal government. The media do little to improve our knowledge about the states. With their attention primarily drawn to conflict in the nation's Capitol, the media tend to devote little attention to the politics in our state capitols.

The lack of knowledge about state government is unfortunate because state governments today play a major role in American politics. Certainly, one cannot dismiss the importance of the federal government. The president, Congress, and the Supreme Court routinely address some of the most vital political issues confronting the nation today, from the health of the economy to the advancement of civil rights to whether the nation will go to war or seek peace. Yet on a day-to-day basis, the state governments may have an even greater effect on our lives, for they tend to be directly responsible for establishing most of the laws under which we live and for providing the everyday services that we need to survive. The importance of state governments can be seen by simply noting three facts.

- State legislatures produce more laws than the U.S. Congress. Combined, more than 20,000 new laws are passed each year across the states, with an average of more than 400 new laws per state. Congress tends to adopt fewer than 300 laws in a given year. State laws are essential because they constitute most of the rules governing criminal behavior in the nation and help shape such things as the character of our schools, the strength of the states' economies, the type of help that is provided to the needy, the quality of our roads, and the health of the environment.

- State governments are large and growing. Their growth has been outpacing that of the federal government for the past several decades. In fact, the expansion of government bureaucracy over the past three decades has come primarily at the state and local level, while the number of federal employees has seen little change. As of 2004, more than 5 million people were working for state governments compared with 2.7 million for the federal government. Another 11 million people are employed by local governments, many of whom handle responsibilities determined by the state government.
- Far more cases are heard in state courts each year than in the federal courts. In an average year, more than 93 million cases are filed in state courts. This compares with approximately 2.6 million cases filed in the federal courts.

Not only does state politics matter, but state governments are in many ways different from the federal government. The three branches of government are common to both the national and the fifty state governments, yet beyond this rather cosmetic similarity, significant differences exist. One of the most central is that while the executive branch of the national government is led by one individual—the president—the executive branch of state governments is led by several executives. Beyond the governor, who is the state's chief executive, the fifty states have other elected executives who have their own independent responsibilities and sources of power, including such figures as the lieutenant governor, the secretary of state, the attorney general, the treasurer, and the superintendent of public instruction.

The state legislatures also vary considerably from Congress. Some of them, most notably the California and New York legislatures, look a lot like Congress, meeting year-round, with full-time staff and well-paid members. Yet other legislatures, such as those in Wyoming and South Dakota, meet only briefly every year or every other year, have minimal staff support, and pay members very little. The legislature in Nebraska, unlike Congress or any other state, has only one chamber and is the only nonpartisan legislature in the nation. With 400 representatives, the house of representatives in the state of New Hampshire has almost as many members as the 435-seat U.S. House. The boundaries for all state senate districts in the nation are based on population so that each district in a given state has approximately the same number of residents, whereas population does not affect the number of members each state elects to the U.S. Senate. All states elect two U.S. senators, even though the states vary widely in population.

The state courts are similarly distinctive. One of the most significant differences between the state and federal courts is that all state court judges are selected through some type of election, whereas federal judges are appointed by the president with Senate approval. Thus, state court judges are more directly beholden to the public. State courts are also affected by variations in state constitutions, some of which grant more extensive rights and liberties than what is set forth in the U.S. Constitution. Thus, important differences may exist across the states in what the state supreme courts will consider constitutional and unconstitutional.

These differences across the states and between the states and federal government affect how politics is practiced, who wins and who loses, the substance of state laws, the extent to which government pays attention to voters, the ability of government to fulfill its responsibilities, the types of rights and liberties we enjoy, and the type of people who are elected to public office. Learning about state government provides a means for understanding different ways in which democratic government can be structured and how those differences affect us.

Part of the reason that Americans know so little about state government is likely a result of the strong emphasis placed on the federal government by the media and the schools, but some of it also reflects the lack of available resources on state governments. Numerous books are devoted to the national government generally and to each of the three branches of the national government, yet there are very few places where you can turn to find information about the structure and character of state governments. If you want to understand how government and politics works in the states, it is just not easy to do so. The few scholarly books available on state governments can be difficult to locate, narrow in scope, or hard for someone unfamiliar with government studies to understand. A few general reference books on American politics touch on topics related to state government, but these often provide only a bit of the picture of how state government works. You can also find books on the governments of individual states, but these tell you little as to how the structure of government and character of politics in those states compare with the government and politics in other states. Simply put, there is no reference work available that focuses solely on explaining the workings of state government across the nation.

About State Government is designed to help fill this gap by providing a comprehensive source of information on state government for high school students, college undergraduates, and the general public. The *About State Government* reference set consists of three volumes, with each volume devoted to a different branch of state government: the legislative, the executive, and the judiciary. All three volumes provide general information about the states, explaining major trends found across the states, while also pointing out important differences that make some states unique or unusual. The books explain how each branch of state government has changed over time, what roles the three branches play in state politics, how the three branches are structured, who serves in them, and how these individuals are selected. The books also describe the character of politics in the states today, the relationship among the different branches of government, some of the major problems confronting state government, and modern proposals for political reform. Each volume also includes a lengthy chapter providing information on the governments state by state, including a description of how each state government is structured, an overview of how the elected officials are selected, and some insights into the character of politics in each state. All three books include a glossary of terms, a comprehensive index, and an annotated bibliography to provide direction for further study.

This set will not make everyone in the nation as familiar with state government as they are with the federal government. But it should provide a good starting place for those who have questions about government in the nation's fifty states and are looking for a book to provide them with answers.

Richard A. Clucas
Portland State University

PREFACE AND ACKNOWLEDGMENTS

Though often described as "the least dangerous branch," the judiciary plays a significant role in state government. Moreover, state courts are at the cutting edge of many of today's most contentious social issues such as gay marriage, cessation of medical care for the terminally ill, liability reform, law enforcement powers, and business regulation. Like other state governing institutions, though powerful, state courts are subject to a variety of limitations. Many of these limits are spelled out in constitutions, state law, and tradition. The limits on courts also are the result of the self-restraint exercised by judges themselves, the influence of interest groups, and the process of selecting judges. Judges also rely on the support of other actors in government and in many cases voters to support their decision making. Most important, though, the notion of due process of law lays out each of the stepping stones along the way to a judicial decision and limits the behaviors of the actors involved in the judicial process.

Understanding the ways in which courts can and must address issues of social concern can be particularly vexing to the nonlawyer. Courts are perhaps the most poorly understood of the three branches of government. This is a result of the way courts conduct themselves in public. On important issues, courts issue written orders or judgments to express their decisions; they do not take questions about their written decisions. Meanwhile, a governor holds press conferences and explains his or her plans to an assembly of news reporters, thereby expanding public familiarity with the governor's decision making. Instead of direct appeals to popular sentiment, courts rely on the compliance of lower judges and lawyers to win public acceptance. Legislators initiate action on their agendas, while judges take only the cases handed to them. Unlike legislators or executive agents, judges vest themselves in robes, express themselves in Latin, and retire to their "chambers," rather than an office. Despite the picture many have of courts as being aloof and monastic, judges, courts, and law can, and should, be understood by people who do not directly interact with them. It is the intention of this volume to make the legal systems of the states more easily understood to the layperson.

This volume explores the common features and the unique qualities of state courts. It also can serve as a reference for the reader who may be mystified by the general nature of courts, their use of Latin, their support agencies, and their formal routines. The first several chapters of the book discuss the topics of law, judicial behavior, and courts in broad focus. This includes discussions of central legal tendencies and competing perspectives on law, courts, and legal ideals; summaries of the work of leading legal scholars, court judges, and political scientists; and, a list of readings and case citations at the end of each chapter. The final chapter details the court system in each state individually, in the form of an encyclopedia of the state judicial systems of the United States. The goal is to provide readers with a comprehensive overview in the opening chapters, and more specific information on the individual states in the final part.

Case citations are provided in this book to help interested readers locate source materials. Full case citations will be found at the end of each chapter. In the main body of the text, most citations will mention only the case name and the year in which it was decided, to avoid distracting readers from a central topic of discussion. However, at times a contributor has provided readers with citations in the main text, whether to highlight certain cases of particular importance, or because a case is rarely cited in other works, is hard to find, or stands out in some significant way. The "Court Case Citation" sidebar (p. 7) gives an element-by-element explanation of case citation.

Throughout the book the reader will also find informational sidebars and tables that are intended to provide a fuller insight into the American state legal process. In most instances, these sidebars have direct relevance to the text of the chapter in which they appear. In a few instances, however, we have chosen to include additional information that relates only indirectly to the text, but which provides additional information that we believed the reader might find interesting and useful.

• • • • • • • • • • • • • • •

Each state court has important characteristics about its judicial structure and powers, the culture in which it operates, and the resources available to it, which differentiates it from other states. There are also differences in the laws that state legislatures authorize the courts to apply. While there are great differences among the courts, there are also growing similarities. The courts rely on written opinions for guidance, most of which descend from British legal principles. However, there are hints of colonial France and Spain in some states' traditions. American courts universally rely on an adversarial system of presenting cases. The judges also operate within the context of our national union, its political philosophies, and moments in history. So, each state court is a product of both its unique qualities and the national identity.

Because of the small amount of research on the courts of all fifty states, this volume favors description over scholarly analysis. State courts have long been observed closely by local groups interested in advancing policies close to home. Political parties, state bar associations, and business groups, for example, have long kept close eyes on their courts for what should be obvious reasons. This makes it easy to find information on an individual state's courts, but only recently have scholars tried to study state courts so they can make generalizations about state courts in aggregate. These efforts will help us figure out the how much local and national influences independently affect the decision making of state courts.

A growing number of researchers are taking interest in the decision-making habits in state courts, the influence of court decisions, and the forces giving shape to those decisions. Organizations such as the National Center for State Courts systematically collect and publicize information related to state court caseloads, finances, and administrative abilities. Another recent, and welcome, addition is the State Supreme Court Data Project. This is a joint venture of Rice University and Michigan State University to collect and make data available about the outcomes of state high court decisions, judges' voting records, and case characteristics. Rutgers University at Camden is home to the Center for State Constitutional Studies. This research center produces studies comparing court decisions pertaining to state constitutional principles. Government agencies are also interested in state court activity, and provide information on these courts. For example, the U.S. Department of Justice's website (http://www.ojp.gov/bjs/welcome.html) makes data available on the work of state courts. State courts themselves are publicizing information on their decisions and histories, upcoming cases, personnel, funding, and workloads.

Throughout this book, the information sources just mentioned prove valuable in discussing the role of state courts. The development of these sources and this growing body of literature provide a clear indication that legal experts are taking a new look at state courts and are realizing the scope and effects of state courts on public life in the United States.

This volume treats courts and judges similarly to the ways the sister volumes treat governors and legislatures: as part of a political process. This is to say that the courts are a part of a system by which our government seeks to reach decisions and resolve disputes. State courts and judges are a significant part of this dispute-resolution process. Also, like the other volumes in the set, this book may be best read like a cookbook, rather than a novel. In this way readers can look up succinct discussions, definitions, or descriptions of some element of state court systems and then put the book back on the shelf.

As an examination of state court systems, this book systematically covers topics concerned with judges and lawyers, parties to legal action, and the bureaucracy that supports resolving legal disputes. Moreover, readers will find discussions of the core elements of legal procedures. The contributors believe it is important to introduce readers to both legal reasoning and social scientific theories of judicial behavior in order to pique the readers' interest in these intellectually stimulating fields. The text discusses the relationships between state courts and the federal courts and explains some of the ways states influence each other's legal theory and ways in which state and federal laws interact. Readers also are exposed to brief discussions of the development of law in the states through significant social and economic transitions.

Readers will also find a consideration of the role of police, prosecutors, executive agencies, and governors, but only as they interact with the judicial systems of the states and as they influence the scope and direction of law. Since this volume is just one of three in the *About State Government* set, readers are encouraged to consult the companion volumes on the respective executive and legislative branches to gain a more complete picture of the workings of state government.

CONTRIBUTORS

Sean O. Hogan is a survey research director for the Research Triangle Institute (RTI-International). His research interests include opinion and behaviors of decision makers, such as medical professionals, elected officials, lawyers, and judges. He has conducted survey research on behalf of state and federal agencies and for groups concerned with state judicial selection reform and tort innovation. His research on the decision making of state supreme court justices, Chicago aldermen, and voters has appeared in peer-reviewed publications. His book contributions include chapters on state judicial systems and the field of survey research and survey methods. Hogan earned is Ph.D. in public policy analysis from the University of Illinois at Chicago.

Mathew Manweller is an assistant professor of political science at Central Washington University in Ellensburg, Washington. Direct democracy, tort reform, and constitutional law are among his research interests, and his work has been published in *American Research Politics*, *American Review of Politics*, *Business and Politics*, the *Independent Review*, and the *Journal of Socio-Economics*. His book, *The People vs. The Courts: Initiative Elites, Judicial Review and Direct Democracy in the American Legal System*, was published in 2004. He sits on the research advisory board for the Seattle-based Washington Policy Center. Manweller earned his Ph.D. in political science from the University of Oregon.

James L. Walker earned a bachelor's degree from Santa Clara University and a Ph.D. from the University of California at Berkeley. For 33 years, he was professor in the department of political science at Wright State University in Dayton, Ohio, before retiring in 2002. He is coauthor with Michael Solimine of *Respecting State Courts: The Inevitability of Judicial Federalism*. He is also author or coauthor of several articles on the state and federal judiciaries.

Ruth Ann Watry holds a Ph.D. in political science from the University of Delaware. She is an associate professor of political science and public administration at Northern Michigan University. Watry is the author of *Administrative Statutory Interpretation: The Aftermath of Chevron v. Natural Resources Defense Council* (2002). Her research and teaching interests include state courts, state and federal level administrative law, women and politics, and constitutional law.

Other Contributors

Kwame Badu Antwi-Boasiako
Stephen F. Austin State University

Sara Buck
University of Southern Misssissippi

Doug Goodman
Mississippi State University

Vicki Lindsay
University of Southern Mississippi

Lana McDowell
University of Southern Mississippi

Elizabeth Corzine McMullan
University of Southern Mississippi

James A. Newman
Idaho State University

Lisa S. Nored
University of Southern Mississippi

Barbara Patrick
Mississippi State University

John David Rausch Jr.
West Texas A&M University

La Shonda Stewart
Mississippi State University

R. Alan Thompson
Old Dominion University

1

AN INTRODUCTION TO STATE COURTS AND LAW

Sean O. Hogan

Some 93 million lawsuits are filed in state courts every year. That number represents one case for every three people in the United States. This workload seems especially daunting when compared with the relatively smaller number of lawsuits brought to U.S. federal courts. Only about 2.6 million new cases are filed each year in federal district courts, according to the Administrative Office of the U.S. Courts. In other words, 97 percent of the judicial workload of the United States passes through state courts and only 3 percent of it passes through the federal judicial system. This means the state courts have many more opportunities than federal courts to shape law and directly affect individuals.

This encyclopedia introduces the reader to a variety of topics essential to understanding the work of state court systems. Despite the fact that most cases in the United States appear in state courts, scholars have long neglected studying them and the laws they help create. The development of law in the United States and the work of U.S. courts can only be understood properly when one appreciates the volume and nature of the work of state courts. This book is designed to explain in clear language what we know about state courts, their histories, routines, work, and personalities, and to put into context the vital role state courts play side-by-side with federal courts in the U.S. legal system.

State courts are, at once, very far reaching and very close to home. To imagine how close the work of state courts is to the public, consider that each of those 93 million new cases involves at least two parties, courthouse staff, perhaps two lawyers, and a judge. Many cases, though not all, will have a few witnesses, a court stenographer, a newspaper reporter, and jurors on hand. Judicial decisions, and the anxiety created by being involved in legal proceedings, directly or indirectly affect the employees, customers, children, or students related to the parties named in the suit. Add to this the fact that many of us will one day be called for jury duty, be involved in an auto accident, or pay a traffic ticket, and the scope of local court systems becomes clearer and closer to home. The work of state courts concerns each of us as citizens; it affects our personal lives, and it influences the conduct of our business affairs.

The sheer volume of litigation passing through the courts presents state and local judges with abundant opportunity to exert power and influence behavior. In addition to the volume, the nature of the cases brought to state courts puts them in a position to help shape our society in many ways. The kinds of cases state courts must resolve can be mundane or complex; they can be small claims or involve enormous sums of money. State courts distribute rights, and have lasting effects on businesses, families, and communities. It is no exaggeration to say the state courts deal with life and death issues. Such cases include discontinuing life support for comatose patients, affirming death sentences, and deciding rights at the earliest stages of the life cycle in cases arising from disputes over frozen embryos, abortion, and the prerogatives of surrogate parents.

A case in point was a prominent trial in Tallahassee, Florida, that began in the fall of 2003 and continued well into 2005. A 39-year-old woman named Terri Schiavo had been in a comatose condition for more than a decade after a serious potassium imbalance stopped her heart (Cotterrell 2003). Though her heart was revived, she suffered severe brain damage and was not expected to recover. She was fed through a tube and was minimally responsive to sensations. Her husband asked that life support be discontinued and that she be allowed to die. Meanwhile, her parents wanted the hospital to continue life support. Governor Jeb Bush was soon involved in the controversy, along with legislators and interest groups representing the "right to die," and advocates from the "right to life" movement.

The normally quiet and routine work of local Florida courts now received national attention. Two local judges had to wrestle with a plethora of procedural issues. On top of the technical issues, Florida courts had to resolve fundamental questions of state law governing life support and medical treatment. The Florida courts had to determine which family member—husband or father—should have the final say in deciding on medical care for the loved one who could not speak for herself. This case presented questions about political power, such as the scope of the governor's authority to intervene; and the separation-of-powers issues involved when the governor ordered life support be continued following a court's order to the contrary.

The drama of cases involving life-ending issues or, more recently, over gay marriages, stands in stark contrast to the day-in and day-out work of most state and local courts. About 56 million garden-variety traffic tickets are filed each year. In addition, the state courts participate in uncontested wills, divorces, and petty criminal cases. The management of most felony cases could even be construed as routine. That is because 97 percent of all felony convictions are resolved through plea agreements, where the prosecutor and defendant make a deal, usually allowing the defendant to plead guilty in exchange for a lighter sentence.

Despite the abundance of no-contest divorces and plea agreements, these cases, too, call on judges to consider our society's core issues of fairness and distribution of wealth. In affirming a felony plea agreement, judges must consider the possibility that the defendant's plea was not voluntary. Though divorce cases are often uncontested, a judge will put the authority of government behind a decision about how much time children will have with their father or mother. In dividing marital property or signing off on an agreed alimony settlement, a judge will put governmental authority behind an agreement about the value of a homemaker's contribution to family wealth. In signing off on these decisions, courts go beyond merely placing a price tag on these services. In any such case, judges are using the power of government to allocate personal wealth between divorcing couples.

Local judges intimately affect quality of life for their neighbors when their job responsibilities force them to resolve disputes between property owners about community development issues. Multimillion-dollar injury cases and authorization for local government to forcefully take ownership of land are brought before state courts, too.

Some Fundamental Issues in Understanding State Courts

To understand state courts, it is helpful to start by introducing some of their fundamental aspects. Among the most important qualities of state courts that need to be introduced at the outset are the distinctions among judges, courts, and law. *Courts* are governmental institutions that have legal and constitutional authority to resolve disputes between two or more competing parties over matters of law, rights, or compliance with law. As institutions, they are staffed by personnel with specific roles to play in the organization. As a branch of government, courts are viewed by most people as having legitimate authority to issue decisions that the parties involved should obey, or be forced to obey by governmental power.

A *judge* is an individual who has power, by virtue of his or her place in the institution of the court system, to hear evidence, resolve arguments over points of law, make binding judgments in those cases, and see that the judgment is enforced. The court of law is the forum from which the judge issues a decision. It is also the governing body that puts the judge's decision into effect. A judge's decision is supposed to stem from the law and available evidence in particular cases. When decisions do not stem from these sources, appellate courts may overrule lower court decisions, and in some cases errant judges may be disciplined or removed from office through some institutional process. While the judge's institutional role entitles the judge to make certain decisions about policy and behavior, the institution conditions the judge's choices.

Another term worth taking some time to clarify is *law*. One may define *law* as the body of formal rules, rights, and regulations that people expect government to protect and enforce through the exercise of coercive power. One element of this definition is the threat of governmental coercion, or *force*. Not all legal scholars agree that the threat of force is a necessary component of law. Some find a law exists when individuals feel compelled to behave in some way, with or without the threat of force. This approach encompasses morality, cultural norms, courtesy, and other social pressures that regulate individual behavior. These forces certainly are important in society, but unless there is an expectation that government will enforce a behavior, it is beyond the scope of this discussion. Of concern is the collection of rights and norms of behavior that come through governmental channels and that will be enforced by government officials.

With these distinctions in mind, the remainder of this chapter consists of three parts. First is a further discussion of law, courts, and judges. The law is a concept more abstract than courts or judges. Still, a proper appreciation of the work of courts and judges requires some background in the law they must analyze. This discussion moves from coverage of law at its most abstract to more concrete terms.

Next, this chapter introduces fundamental characteristics of state court systems and judging. This will enable the reader to have a rudimentary understanding of state courts to enable further appreciation of the discussions of subsequent chapters.

The second part of the chapter then provides a brief overview of key historical developments in state court practices and politics. Finally, this chapter introduces readers to the coming chapters to help readers find relevant materials for individual interests.

LAW: ITS ORIGINS, AUTHORITY, AND NATURE

To help analyze law, scholars try to categorize types of law that seem to have common attributes, much the way biologists try to sort plants into categories of kingdom, phylum, genus, and species. In the same spirit, law can be organized into classifications by its distinguishing features.

The Sources of Law

There is considerable debate about the sources of authority that permit courts to rule as they do. It is important for readers to understand the sources of authority cited in U.S. courts. Not all laws are created equally. There is a pecking order in the American system that determines which law should prevail if two legal principles come into conflict. This discussion gives an overview of how competing legal authority is typically prioritized.

Natural Law

Some theorists, particularly those interested in the philosophy of law, turn to the study of nature to find parallels with the ultimate origins of law. *Natural law* is often associated with theological concepts, but not always. In short, the natural law theory suggests that a natural or divine source instilled in the human imagination creates certain norms of behavior that cause most people to respect the dignity of themselves and others without legislation having to insist on it. This same ultimate source of human behavior instills in individuals a common sense of certain self-restraints or duties. To natural law scholars, law that is common to all societies can be observed through appropriate scientific methods, just as the use of appropriate scientific tools allows one to observe chemical or biological phenomena. Much of human behavior, in this school of thought, is a natural occurrence.

Natural law scholars find that almost all societies oppose incest and killing other humans, and that most individuals have a sense of self-preservation and act in their self-interest. Therefore, at some minimal level, a divine or natural force makes some rules common to all societies, regardless of culture, climate, or dominant religion. In the United States, much has been made about the phrase in the *Declaration of Independence* that all people are "endowed by their Creator with certain unalienable rights" to argue that natural rights–natural law reasoning is at the core of American political philosophy. Many natural law theorists would agree with the sentiment among the American revolutionaries that when the laws of a government are unjust, reasoning people have no moral obligation to conform, a precept of natural rights thinking.

Positive Laws: Laws Made by People

Many political scholars are interested in natural law theory, but in general, its relevance to understanding the day-to-day work of American state courts is limited. This is because U.S. courts rely on written civil authority to justify rulings. Without written civil authority, a judge's decision making would be seen as arbitrary, or pressing up against the constitutional separation of church and state. Rather, the laws enforced by government are referred to as positive law. Here, the word *positive* means that a government asserted regulatory authority to put rules into words and then into force, regardless of what is motivating them to do so.

There are seven main types of positive regulations that make up the law that is enforced by American courts. These are: constitutional laws, statutes, ordinances, regulations, executive orders, common law rulings, and contracts. There are two main factors that help differentiate the types of laws. The first is the authorship of the law. Each type of law or rule is written by a different authority. The second is the order of importance of these laws and rules.

Constitutions in the U.S. tradition are the highest form of law. Any act of government found to be in conflict with the U.S. Constitution or that state's constitution must be ruled invalid. Among the state and federal courts, the federal Constitution is supreme. In the states, however, courts show similar respect for their constitutions that the U.S. Supreme Court shows to the national charter.

A constitution's principal function is to establish a government, determine who in that government should make which decisions, set out the process of making binding rules, and resolve disputes within a society. Just as noteworthy, constitutions in each of the states say there are certain things government cannot do, such as prohibit religious worship, limit the expression of political opinions, and keep people from traveling. Some state constitutions severely limit certain taxing powers, or limit the number of terms of office for some leaders, protect important industries, and, recently, prohibit same-sex and polygamous marriages.

Because of the number of amendments addressing local concerns, state constitutions can be quite wordy. Alabama's runs 315,000 words and has more than 740 amendments. California voters, for example, are quite fond of the voter initiative, where ordinary citizens put proposed constitutional amendments to a vote on statewide ballots. Constitutional rules can make the amendment process quite easy or very difficult. Due to the weight of numerous amendments, forty states introduced new constitutions after 1960.

Constitutions at the federal and state levels refer primarily to procedural aspects of law. That is constitutional law dictates how decisions should be made, who should make them, and, in general terms, how a society will choose its political leaders. The U.S. Constitution requires that each of the states have a *republican* government, or one in which elected leaders make decisions, usually by majority rule.

Procedural aspects of constitutions can be contrasted with the substantive elements of constitutions. Substantive features of law refer to specific rights or duties. For this reason, some law is ruled invalid because it was passed in an invalid way, not necessarily because the law itself violated some fundamental right of a citizen. For example, many state constitutions have single-subject rules that require each bill coming through the legislature to deal with only one topic. Congress, by contrast, often finds it necessary to pass omnibus bills that carry many subjects to please many audiences. State courts have struck down otherwise valid laws because they violate their state's single-subject clause. (Further discussion of specific constitutional requirement of courts to prioritize sources of authority is discussed in Chapter 2.)

Statutes, also referred to as *acts*, are rules enacted by legislatures. Ordinances are similar to statutes, but the term generally refers to the acts established by local legislatures like city councils and county boards. Statutes and ordinances become law primarily through deliberative bodies, though some states and cities allow voters to enact legislation directly through what is called the initiative process. (The volume on state legislatures in this encyclopedia set provides a detailed discussion of how legislation is enacted in state legislatures.)

Regulations, which are rules made by regulatory agencies, have the same force as statutes. Agencies, however, cannot create regulations of their own volition. Rather they must find statutory authority to create particular rules. In other words, a statute will authorize an agency to create specific regulations to achieve some general goal. For example, a state legislature may authorize the state natural resources department to regulate airborne pollutants for the public good. In doing so, the legislature delegates to the agency's scientific and legal staff the responsibility to define "pollutant" and "public good." This then leads to the limits on the fumes that cars or factories can emit into the atmosphere. As legislatures can grant authority to create rules, they also can limit the scope and process of bureaucratic rule making.

Executive orders are rules or commandments issued by the governor, a mayor, or the heads of bureaucratic agencies to inferior administration agents. This may be the case when the governor orders a hiring freeze or cancels travel during financial crises. Formally, the executive order is thought of as an internal issue, between the boss and sub-

---

Court Case Citation

***Serrano v. Priest* 20 Cal.3d 25 at 31 (1977)**[1]

Serrano is the petitioner, and is asking the Court to review the case.

v. stands for *versus*, suggesting that the two parties have competing interests that the court must resolve.

Priest is the respondent, and is answering claims made by Serrano in the California Supreme Court.

20 Cal.3d means this decision is found in volume 20 of the *California Reports*, 3rd edition. Published cases are gathered and bound into large volumes called reports.

Regional reports issue from various parts of the country and cover both federal district and federal appeals courts and published state rulings from that region. Examples include the *Northeast Report*, represented by the initials NE, the Southwest, by

SW, and the *Lawyers Edition*, by LE. State reports cover published decisions within individual states. Because of the variety of reports issued, an individual court case may appear in several reports. No report is considered superior to another, given that these books include almost no commentary except written court rulings, concurrences, and dissenting opinions.

1977 is the year the decision was published.

25 is the first page of the case decision in the cited report.

31 ("25 at 31" or "25, 31") is the page of a given quotation in the cited report.

[1] In this volume, this format appears in the main text; for cases in the References the format is ***Serrano v. Priest*. 1977. 20 Cal.3d 25, 31.**

---

ordinate, but the effects may be felt outside the agency. (Additional details on the politics and process of executive orders and regulatory policy making are included in ABC-CLIO's *The Executive Branch of State Government: People, Process, and Politics.*)

Case law, also called common law, is the reasoning consistently applied by courts in the resolution of disputes. Case law finds its origins in the courts (see box, above, to learn how to cite a case). Case law not only creates a command; it also provides a way of thinking about a problem so that similar situations can be addressed with similar legal logic. For example, in the absence of statute, superior courts have developed standards to be used by lower courts when they hear cases. Supreme courts in each state have established standards regarding the responsibility of different parties when an injury occurs in a workplace or elsewhere, which the trial judges must consider when ruling in personal injury cases. In this way, courts devise reasoning about how to handle responsibility when someone claims she or he was hurt while on the job, when using a manufactured product, or in other situations.

The individual may claim the injury was caused because of reasonable use (for example, the injured party stood on a chair to change a light bulb). The character of the case, however, may require that the judge consider a higher standard of intended use of the product. In this way, the higher court creates a rule that gives rise to outcomes by governing the decision-making process and the selection of what items are worthy of consideration in a hearing.

Constitutional law can be considered a type of case law. Only some of what is written in a constitution is straightforward. Courts are left to give meaning to high-minded phrases such as "equal protection" or "high-quality education," since constitutional authors seldom define these expressions in the text of a state charter. While state constitutions provide the foundation for constitutional law, state courts must give meaning to ambiguous terms. State supreme courts issue decisions related to the powers of government, decision-making processes, civil rights and liberties, and other concerns incorporated into the constitutions.

Contracts are enforceable agreements by which individuals or organizations submit to rules of their own creation and by their own volition. This type of law is the work of parties who freely choose to submit to the terms of the contract to receive the benefits of the duties performed by the other party. Government's coercive power comes into effect only when courts are called on to enforce these agreements. In some cases, courts are bypassed altogether in favor of alternative dispute systems such as arbitration. (Alternative dispute resolution is discussed in Chapter 3.) State law, federal law, and court decisions place some restrictions on the content of contracts, but in general, contracts represent a distinct type of rule in the sense that they only directly affect the people who entered into the agreement.

A Hierarchy of Law

Law can be organized according to a hierarchy, or by order of importance. It is very much a part of the American legal tradition that some sources of political power outweigh others, and the law from one source can outweigh another.

For those who subscribe to the ideas of natural law, God's law or the laws of nature have precedence over all other types of law. This approach is advocated not only by religious scholars, such as Thomas Aquinas, but secular observers like Sir William Blackstone, whose treatise *Commentaries on Laws of England* is cited quite widely today in American courts. Blackstone argues that:

> This law of nature, being coeval with mankind and dictated by God Himself, is of course superior in obligation to any other. It is binding over all the globe, in all countries, and at all times. No human laws are of any validity, if contrary to this; and such of them as are valid derive all their force, and all their authority, mediately or immediately, from this original. But in order to apply this to the particular exigencies of each individual, it is still necessary to have recourse to human reason; whose office it is to discover, as was before observed, what the law of nature directs in every circumstance of life; by considering, what method will tend most effectually to our own substantial happiness. (Vol. 1, 1735.)

Even if one does not subscribe to the ideas of natural law, there still remains a hierarchy of laws within any states' political system. When one legal obligation or right is in conflict with another, the superior source of authority prevails. In general, the hierarchy of American law ranges from the U.S. Constitution at the top to local ordinances

TABLE 1.1   HIERARCHY OF LAW IN THE UNITED STATES

Federal hierarchy	State legal hierarchy
U.S. Constitution	U.S. Constitution
Acts of Congress	Acts of Congress and federal treaties not in violation of the Tenth Amendment
Executive orders, treaties, regulations, and common-law decisions	State Constitutions
Contracts	State legislative acts
N/A	Executive orders, regulations, and state common-law decisions
N/A	Local ordinances and contracts

Source: Public data compiled by author.

and contracts at the bottom. Table 1.1 displays the hierarchy for both federal and state law. From the supremacy clause of the U.S. Constitution, the national charter acquires power superior to all other positive law at work in the United States (for further discussion of the supremacy clause and related decisions see Chapter 2). Since local governments acquire their power from state legislation, local rules and regulations are lower in authority.

Within individual states, state constitutions have a place analogous to the federal Constitution. This allows state courts to overturn state statutes when the statutes are contrary to the state's constitution. Statutes are next in importance. Bureaucratic regulations, case law, and executive orders can be modified or reversed by an act of the legislature. Local ordinances can be overridden by state authorities since under the U.S. system, state government authority is sovereign, with local governments existing as instruments of the states. Contracts have the least authority, since these are instruments between private parties and the public good usually outweighs individual need.

The Public and Private Nature of Law

Public law refers to the rules that affect the prerogatives of governmental officials and the rights of citizenship. Like their colleagues on the federal courts, the 31,000 state judicial officers are presented with demands to consider issues related to the government's role in society, its power to tax, spend money, and control behavior. They determine the scope of individual rights under federal and state constitutions. Public law includes questions about voting, public speech, legislative deliberations, and the monetary value of court awards. They also review the work of state regulatory agencies.

Public law, in short, is concerned with public-policy making, citizenship, society, and the relationship between government and the individual. An individual court decision that affects the law governing the conduct of public affairs is a decision in public law.

Within this genus of public law are various species. Constitutional law is the body of doctrines that define the meaning of the federal or state constitutions, the rights guaranteed to individuals, or the powers granted to government through these documents. Another species of public law is criminal law, which deals with violations of law, enforcement powers, arrest processes, and investigation, prosecution, and the punishments that may be meted out as a result of conviction. Another form of public law is administrative law. This is a complex area of law that is concerned with the authorities of bureaucratic agencies, ranging from their powers to develop regulations to the rights of agency staff in relation to their employer. Since many agencies have executive enforcement powers as well as quasi-legislative rule-making power and quasi-judicial powers, administrative law contains a hybrid of other forms of public law.

Private law refers to cases between individuals, corporations, or other nongovernment entities. In private suits, parties seek peaceful resolution of a quarrel between the parties at hand, and have no immediate implications for public affairs. Within the confines of private law one can find tort law, which is more frequently than not related to personal injuries. Another type is contract law, which deals with the agreements that individuals freely make with each other and the extent to which courts can, or will, enforce them. Family law deals with marriage, children, adoption, and the like. State courts determine private issues such as adoption and child custody, personal injury claims, conflicts over contracts, property ownership, and the organization of businesses. By dealing with private law, state courts determine ownership of a disputed piece of property, including creative works and other intellectual property. In this way courts can bring a nonviolent solution to private conflict.

While called private law, state supreme courts play a vital function in shaping the rules by which individuals resolve their disputes. Even in cases that are not contested, the lawyers advising clients in private negotiations are familiar with the boundaries set by state supreme courts. With this in mind, it becomes evident that when negotiating a contract, or making amends for personal injury, informed parties are influenced by the decisions already made by local and state level courts.

Criminal and Civil Law

Another way to distinguish types of law is between criminal and civil law. The public versus private distinction is of limited help here, being a somewhat more academic organizational framework used in the study of law and the philosophy of law. Criminal law always involves public issues, but a case brought in civil law can be either public or private. The civil–criminal distinction is more frequently used in organizing court systems and assigning cases in American courts.

Criminal cases are brought for the protection of society at large. A crime is a behavior that a society decides is so harmful that government must act to prevent it, or punish those who commit a crime. From this definition, come several characteristics that help identify a criminal complaint. First, criminal complaints always are filed on behalf of the community. Second, only specific governmental officials have authority to file criminal complaints. Third, in the American tradition, proving guilt requires the government to meet a high standard of "beyond a reasonable doubt."

Criminal acts may be classified further as misdemeanors, which are petty crimes. Punishments for misdemeanors include jail terms usually shorter than a year, and fines usually under $2,000. Felonies, on the other hand, are major offenses such as serious violent crimes or large-scale narcotic sales. Punishments for felony offenses involve higher monetary fines, longer imprisonment, and community service.

Civil cases usually involve an individual asserting his or her rights and legal privileges. Civil cases do not require the government to be a party, though sometimes individuals make a claim against the government. The burden of proof is the lower standard of "the preponderance of evidence." Civil rights cases are a special type of civil action in which an individual or group seeks court protection for ensuring equal rights, so that they are not discriminated against based on their race, ethnicity, gender, religion, age, disabilities, or sexual orientation. Several standards of evidence are used in civil cases, though they are also generally less demanding than beyond a reasonable doubt.

Civil courts never find guilt. Rather the courts may use less malignant words like *liable*, or *culpable* to describe the obligations of the losing party. Both ordinary individuals and governmental agencies may file and defend themselves against civil claims. Civil claims typically seek to determine who should bear some responsibility or enjoy some privilege. The claims never result in a prison sentence. Money may change hands, but this is not a fine, rather the exchange is to provide the successful plaintiff with what is due to him or her.

The Nature of Law: Process and Substance

There are two other categorizations of law: procedural law and substantive law. Procedural law is concerned with the rules of the court decision-making system. Procedural law controls how law is to be enforced, understood, argued, made, or changed. It is the rules of the game, so to say.

Substantive law refers to the actual right, responsibility, or norm of behavior that is in dispute. In the U.S. system, a procedural rule is that our courts use an adversarial system where opposing lawyers argue before a neutral judge. The substantive argument may be over whether Jones owes Johnson money. The procedure may be friendlier to the debtor, or the creditor, by requiring that creditors file claims within very tight or very relaxed deadlines, which in turn affects how long someone has to make the substantive claim to money. These concepts are described in full detail in Chapter 3.

COURTS: TRADITION, ROUTINES, AND CUSTOMS

Like their British ancestors, American courts pay respect to tradition. Beyond the reliance on Latin, the American legal culture has developed rigid expectations about actors in the court system. These traditions have evolved into formal rules, which have ramifications for court decisions. This culture affects how a case is discussed, which reasons and evidence are persuasive to the decision-making process, and who is entitled to plead a case. The sections that follow discuss these cultural characteristics.

State Court Structures

One of the most important characteristics of courts is their basic structure. The state court culture values positions of authority in addition to expertise. This culture also respects hierarchy. Some states have fairly simple structures, with only two layers, but more typical is three tiers. In either structure, one court has higher authority than

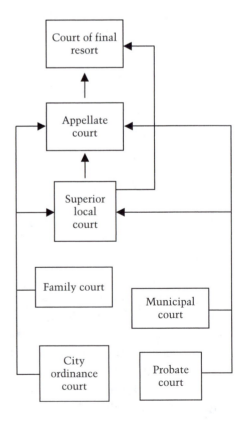

FIGURE 1.1   TWO MODELS OF COURT STRUCTURES IN THE STATES

another to review and resolve arguments. This lends certainty to decisions. The culture also thrives on percolation, or the opportunity for many lower courts to disagree with each other on a point of law before the higher court has to choose from competing ideas.

The hierarchical structure of courts encourages this idea vetting (see Fig. 1.1, opposite). The first tier in the structure is the trial court, which is authorized to hear all manner of trials from complex civil litigation, to heinous felony trials, to small claims. Above the trial court is an appeals court, which reviews trial cases for errors in legal judgment. At the apex is the court of final resort, usually called the supreme court. This three-layer model, where cases pass from low to middle to high court, is often called a unified court system. In more complex systems there are multiple limited jurisdiction courts. Each of these courts has jurisdiction over a focused type of case, like traffic court or juvenile court. In two states there are multiple supreme courts, authorized to review either criminal or civil cases. In these courts, the route of an appeals case is state-specific. Court structure is important because it affects a judge's breadth of knowledge and expertise, with the more complex systems allowing judges to develop legal specialties. The court structure also affects the workload of courts and the ease with which cases reach higher levels of judicial review. In each structural framework, judges and lawyers consider the opportunity for appeal and the likelihood of success. The structure of the court system either helps encourage or limit litigation, which in turn, affects the judges' time to consider a case.

Cases and Controversies

Institutional norms of behavior are also important in determining whether a case will ever come before a judge at all. One such custom is the adversarial structure of a trial. This means there are no friends in court. Rather opposing sides bring forward a case or controversy for the judge to resolve. In this way, courts avoid being bogged down resolving academic legal questions or testing hypothetical situations. Similarly, the court will not hear a case until after an injury has occurred, a quality called *ripeness.* If an issue is resolved elsewhere, it is considered moot by the court. Finally, many courts shy away from political questions, which are better left to the legislative or executive branches of government to resolve. The political-question criterion is very ambiguous. These are general rules, and some exceptions are discussed in Chapter 2.

Inputs to Court Decisions

In the other branches of government, the elected and appointed officials are very open about which issues they choose to bring up for a decision. The character of state court politics is different from the policy-making habits of the other branches. In the courts, litigants choose the arguments to put before the courts. For this reason, courts are called the passive branch of government. While judges may decide that some evidence is irrelevant to the decisions they have to make, it is the lawyers who do the most important legwork in providing the information that goes into making a ruling. On the other hand, governors and state legislators are expected to be policy leaders and identify problems and then advocate the policy outcomes they favor.

Lawyers play a key role in determining the nature of the input on which courts will make rulings. Unlike the lobbyists in other branches of government, the culture of the courts presumes that formal legal training is a requirement for preparing an effective presentation in court. Like other lobbyists, attorneys are skilled in understanding the mechanics of how decisions are made in the branch of government they stand before. Ordinary people usually can represent themselves in court (after overcoming some hurdles to show they are capable), but few laypersons can match a licensed attorney's familiarity with methods of questioning witnesses or ability to efficiently comb through documentary evidence. Nor will a layperson have the mastery of the regulations governing the way evidence is to be presented and the lawyer's grasp of what points must be raised at trial to preserve rights to appeal.

Once the case is in court, all parties have to be before a judge when any information is presented. It is illegal for individuals to attempt *ex-parte* communication, which is communication between the judge and only one side in the case. Lobbyists cannot privately persuade judges during the decision-making process, as they would when lobbying a legislator. While the First Amendment's right to petition government protects this type of lobbying of legislators, it can be grounds for a contempt-of-court citation when the judge is the target. Courts are duty bound to involve all parties in all communication that is presented to the court. Judicial tradition expects to produce decisions based on the record of facts and arguments presented in trial.

Announcing Decisions

Judges announce their decisions only after all the evidence is presented. Governors and legislators, meanwhile, are free to predispose themselves in public before, during, and after legislative debate. This same type of action by a judge brings scorn from all angles of the legal profession. Justice Antonin Scalia in 2004 was pressured into recusing himself from a gay-rights case because he delivered a speech to the Philadelphia Urban Family Council, an "anti-gay" organization, though the organization was not represented in the case and Justice Scalia did not even mention the case or legal theory at work in it. The organization, which Scalia praised, was actively opposing a domestic-partnership ordinance the Philadelphia City Council had been considering (Serrano and Savage 2004).

Only after both sides rest their cases do judges announce decisions, and usually in writing. The customs of court do not approve of holding press conferences to explain judicial decisions. None of this is to say that one decision-making process is better, or that another necessarily is corrupt. It is to say that the culture of the courts has somewhat different expectations of its decision makers.

In the public eye, judges are regarded poorly unless they act, write, and speak like judges: that is, appear dispassionate in their relation to the parties, scholarly in their writing, and certain of their decisions. For this reason, judges often seem stoic, even when presiding over very emotionally charged cases. Displays of emotion may be fine for a governor, for example, when he or she reveals humanity or concern. But the norm of judicial restraint, or the exercise of strict self-control, advises judges to conceal their emotional reactions, to choose their words with care, and to apply the law as it is written, no matter how they personally feel about it.

Growing Workload in State Courts

There are two important trends that are occurring in criminal courts. One of them is the growing use of negotiated settlements to resolve cases and the other is the growing number of criminal cases being filed. The vast majority of felony cases being handled in the United States go through state court systems. That is about 14 million criminal cases, with some of the most rapid growth in felony filing rates coming in many of the midwestern states (Strickland and Otto 2003). By comparison, about 115,000 criminal charges were filed in 2002 in the federal court system, excluding military courts, according to the U.S. Department of Justice.

What happens to these cases after they enter the court system? In general, the legal culture of the states encourages negotiated settlements over trials. Plea agreements are negotiated settlements between the parties and affirmed by a judge. The judge, in a plea agreement, remains a neutral third party, free to accept or reject the settlement. The trend toward more plea agreements is true even in states in which there is greater public opposition. Various studies on state courts have found a fairly constant trend in the proportion of cases being settled across the nation, despite some public outcries.

Court observers often believe negotiated settlements eliminate uncertainty for both the prosecutor and the accused. Settlements are defended as a way to bring a case efficiently through an otherwise expensive and seemingly endless system of trial and appeal. The interdependence between regular actors in the court system fosters shared local ideas about which cases should be tried and those that should be settled. That is to say, defense attorneys often know the going rate that a defendant will see in minimized punishment in exchange for a guilty plea. Attorneys may find it in their personal interest, as well as that of the client, to urge some suspects to accept or reject a settlement given the current economy for a guilty plea.

Despite the tendency of the states to look for negotiated settlements, the workload of the criminal courts has been growing since the mid-1980s. This increased burden has been attributed to stricter law enforcement in the areas of domestic violence, illicit drugs, and gang-related crimes. In addition, teenagers accused of serious crimes increasingly were processed in adult criminal, rather than juvenile, court systems (Puzzanchera 2001). The U.S. Justice Department reports that between 1989 and 1994 the number of cases waived from juvenile to adult courts rose from about 8,000 to 12,000. By the late 1990s, this number began to recede, returning to 1989 levels.

Civil Case Workload

While criminal activity may garner much of the space in news coverage about state and local courts, the bulk of the courts' work falls under the civil category. As recently as 2001, 52 percent of the work in state trial courts was devoted to civil actions, as opposed to 38 percent that was concerned with criminal allegations. These civil cases are relevant, because they often involve large sums of money, rights of tenants, claims of unfair treatment in the workplace, and the authorities of local units of government.

State courts have been encouraged to take part in monumental legal decisions. In 2003 the Illinois trial court awarded a $10 billion verdict to smokers who alleged that Phillip Morris USA and its parent firm Altria Group, Inc., misled them about the dangers of smoking light cigarettes. The Illinois Supreme Court has agreed to hear the firm's appeal. A Florida trial court imposed a $145 billion verdict against several cigarette makers like Altria, R. J. Reynolds Tobacco Co., and Liggett Group, Inc. (see *Liggett Group Inc. et al. v. Engle et al.*).

Similarly the Arkansas courts recently have been swamped with documents in an ongoing complaint against several of the country's most prominent accounting firms in a suit alleging fraudulent billing (Weil and Bryan-Low 2003). Just preparing to come to court can be a complex and expensive enterprise. One firm reported having spent $25 million to prepare for trial. If the accounting firms are found liable, the court then will order a redistribution of enormous value far above the costs of preparation for trial.

In one of the most closely watched political dramas in history, the Florida Supreme Court was drawn into a high-stakes election-law dispute, with the presidency of the United States hanging in the balance. Between November and December of 2000, the Florida court system was forced to decide the meaning of a handful of ballots, where the voters' choices in the 2000 presidential election was obscured by "dimpled" or "hanging" chads. The outcome of the presidential election was a virtual tie and Florida was a critical "swing state." With the country's eyes on Florida, the presidency would be decided on the meaning that the state court would give to fewer than 400 disputed ballots.

On a second appeal, the U.S. Supreme Court ultimately agreed to take up the central issues of the case. The U.S. Supreme Court ultimately reversed the outcome of the state court (see *Bush v. Palm Beach Canvassing Board* [2000] and *Bush v. Gore* [2000]), but not until the Florida Supreme Court sat at the center of national politics for a time.

Civil filings rarely are as dramatic as those, and the growth rate in this area is not as rapid as is the change in criminal court filings. Between 1987 and 2001, the number of civil case filings rose roughly 23 percent. However, when controlled for population growth occurring at this time, civil claims rose by about 3 percent, with peak filings coming in the early 1990s, according to the National Center for State Courts (NCSC).

While the state of New York may have led the pack in new civil filings with 1.4 million in 2001, it was fifth on a list of per-person case filings. Maryland, with about 832,000 new civil cases had more than 15 new cases per 100 people. By comparison, New York had about 7.5 new civil cases per 100 residents.

While civil cases may have risen during this time, the NCSC indicates that tort filings (primarily personal injury and property damage cases), declined by about 7 percentage points.

Judicial Federalism: The Relationship between Federal and State Courts

It is not accurate to say the United States has *a* judicial system. Rather it has many judicial systems. Each of the fifty states has a judiciary, and no two states have systems that are exactly the same. Parallel to the state systems is the federal judicial system, beginning with a trial court (federal district courts), leading to an appellate court (usually the circuit court of appeals), and ending with the U.S. Supreme Court. State court systems can have even simpler structures, with only a trial and a supreme court. Other states may have more complex judicial systems with a variety of special purpose courts, or two separate supreme courts, one to review civil cases and another for criminal cases.

The relationship between these two court systems is sometimes referred to as judicial federalism. Federalism is the distribution of power and responsibility between the national government and the individual states. The state courts play an important role in American federalism because they are given considerable legal decision-making powers and responsibilities. In addition the state courts are significant because they serve to bring new legal issues and ideas into the nation's court system and they act to apply U.S. Supreme Court rulings to the states. In recent decades, state supreme courts have emerged as even more important players within judicial federalism as these courts have discovered the use of state constitutions for deciding rights cases. Chapter 2 more formally describes issues related to judicial federalism but it is mentioned here to place the concept in a broader context. Judicial federalism is both a cause and consequence of American law, national politics, and the structure of the federal system.

At the top of the U.S. federal court system is the U.S. Supreme Court. The Supreme Court's decisions, in particular, receive the most attention in popular news coverage, high school civics courses, and law school reading assignments. The great attention devoted to the Supreme Court reflects the Court's authority to decide the most profound legal issues confronting the nation. Before many of the cases reach the Supreme Court, however, they first pass through state court systems. The opinions of state supreme courts help the U.S. Supreme Court think through emerging, thorny legal issues. Professor Howard Gillman's observations suggest a vital role for state high courts in American judicial federalism, by helping to define and direct national legal trends.

Despite the slim chance that any case will be brought to the U.S. Supreme Court, Professor G. Alan Tarr finds that state noncompliance with federal Supreme Court decisions is uncommon. The compliance of state courts to the U.S. Supreme Court's decisions reinforces the high court's stature and indicates to all who enter a state courtroom where final authority rests in American judicial federalism. Sometimes one decision may become the source of new legal questions. When that happens, states may pioneer novel legal theories, or more commonly distinguish a case from an issue already decided by the U.S. Supreme Court. In this way, state courts play an important role in defining issues for the U.S. Supreme Court, and redefining issues. State supreme courts are at the intersection of U.S. law, filtering cases and ideas up to the U.S. Supreme Court, and interpreting them for the trial courts closer to home.

One of the most important trends in judicial federalism has been the increased reliance by state supreme courts on state constitutions in making rights rulings. This increased reliance on state constitutions has been labeled "the new judicial federalism." While some observers think the U.S. Supreme Court of the 1990s and early 2000s is more "conservative" than the Court of the 1960s and 1970s, and has become less supportive of civil rights and liberties suits, many state courts have expanded personal rights based on their own constitutions. Supreme Court Justice William Brennan (1977) was one of the first advocates for expanding individual rights through state constitutional interpretation. In recent years state courts have used their authorities to do exactly that. Even prior to Brennan's advocacy, Oregon Supreme Court Justice Hans Linde argued that the state constitutions, rather than the federal Bill of Rights, were "first in right and first in logic" (Linde 1980).

It is from Linde's theory that state courts have turned to their own state constitutional provisions to find rights unlikely to be found from the U.S. Supreme Court. These include a right to educational funding (see, for example, *Tennessee Small School Systems v. McWherter*), to low-income housing (see *Southern Burlington County NAACP v. Township of Mount Laurel*), and to firearm possession outside the home (*State of Wisconsin v. Hamdan*). In 2003, the Massachusetts Supreme Judicial Court declared that homosexual couples should enjoy the same right to marriage as heterosexual couples (*Goodridge v. Dept. of Public Health*). It did so based on the "equal protection clause" of its state constitution, not the parallel clause in the Fourteenth Amendment of the U.S. Constitution. The U.S. Supreme Court, as a rule, refrains from upsetting the state courts' interpretation of state law, even when they would come to contradictory conclusions about the meaning of very similar language.

The emergence of the new judicial federalism is important because it means that the state high courts do not have to rely solely on the interpretations of the U.S. Supreme Court when they issue rulings. They may be responsive to local state political concerns, state history, and faithful to the text of state constitutions.

Even when federal issues are involved, the U.S. Supreme Court increasingly has turned in favor of states' rights. This places state courts in a more central decision-making position. With the decision *United States v. Lopez*, the U.S. Supreme Court reasserted the unique qualities of the state in decision making, ending a sixty-year history of acquiescing to congressional claims of authority. One final aspect of judicial federalism is the relationship each state has with other states. Often states deal with many of the same issues and they borrow ideas from one another. This sharing among state court opinions is referred to as "horizontal federalism." States such as California and New York are considered to have among the most innovative court systems in the nation, and their opinions are widely cited by the courts of other states (Caldiera 1985). State supreme court judges also frequently refer to judges with whom they share a point of view.

JUDGES: DISCRETION, REASON, AND POLITICS

Judges, like other governmental actors, make choices when issuing their decisions. Like other citizens, judges have individual policy preferences. The impulse for judges to act solely on these policy preferences when making choices is kept in check by institutional expectations, and by the knowledge that they are being watched by their peers, and the larger legal profession. The language of relevant law and political pressure help shape how judges rule. These pressures include such factors as elections, prevailing policy preferences among lawyers, and the persuasiveness of legal argument (Brace and Hall 1990; Hogan 2000). Chapters 4 and 5 discuss in detail some of the personalities in state courts and the politics surrounding them. In this chapter the subject is introduced to put politics in a broad context and in combination with law, court structure, federalism, and history.

Even though there are constraints on how they act, judges do have some discretion when making decisions. New and novel cases are frequently brought to the courts, whether they are about life-prolonging medical treatment, gay marriages, or something else. In these cases judges are forced to think and rethink how the law applies. In some cases the law has not been tested, and judges must for the first time resolve a problem. In these and other situations, a judge may be able to shape the direction of future legal interpretations. For example, one interesting question being raised today relates to the nature of the Internet. Judges are finding themselves being asked whether when an individual buys a product over the Internet, did that transaction take place on the buyer's home computer, or on the seller's computer system? A court's answer to that question could have important implications for which state gets to impose a sales tax. The logic applied here could then be transferred to apply to other legal and illegal activity.

Politics and Judging

Political scientists view the application of governmental authority as an act of politics. Consequently, the use of judicial power is by definition a political issue. On a more basic level, judges in all cases come into contact with other political actors, such as the governors who appoint them, the parties that support their elections, or the voters who select them. These facts of life place burdens on judges to account for political considerations, either because they are explicitly brought into the reasoning in rulings, because the case is highly charged and permeates the background of the decision, or because the decision affects voting, campaign finances, and other political activities.

One of the most prominent forces influencing the judges are the bar associations, which are the professional association for attorneys in each state. These groups have special status in the politics of judging in a number of ways. First these associations establish guides and codes of conduct for lawyers and judges. They are vocal when structural reform efforts, like the merit selection of judges, are discussed. Bar associations assert themselves in framing legislation that affects the discretion of judges. Bar associations also take a very keen interest in who gets appointed or elected to the courts. Almost always, prominent members of bar associations are appointed to serve on the commissions that help select judges in states that use the merit plan. In states where judges are elected, the bar associations publicly announce their ratings of the judicial candidates. These associations are also influential in shaping rules of procedure for courts and in setting licensing standards for prospective lawyers.

Other groups are also important in judicial politics. Manufacturers and physician associations have led civil reform efforts to limit personal injury litigation. Interest groups petition courts to file *amicus curiae* or friend-of-the-court briefs to influence the decisions rendered by courts of final resort. Other interest groups sponsor litigation. Though they do not often have the right to sue in their own name, interest groups identify parties who themselves have a right to sue. Then interest groups influence courts by providing their clients with the legal representation and technical support to move issues through the courts.

Thus, even though the courts are often seen as being above politics, they are actually very political.

HISTORICAL DEVELOPMENT OF STATE COURTS

The traditions, character, and structures of the state court systems are rooted both in the national and local histories. The laws of individual states grew out of their colonial or territorial experiences, industrial and technological evolutions, and their internal political struggles. The earliest colonial courts were quite different in many ways from modern state courts, and often different from each other. Over time, as new political issues arose, and new demands confronted the states, the state courts had to adapt and become able to address these new issues and demands. These demands caused both structural and doctrinal reforms. As the loosely connected states of a new nation became more economically and politically integrated, courts began adopting some more uniform qualities and laws to help facilitate economic evolution. In American law there is a constant tension between continuity and change; between the stability and wisdom that tradition promises and the opportunities and innovation hoped for through progress. To understand today's law and courts it is helpful to reflect on their origins.

American national law and court systems contain many elements of British legal traditions and doctrines. These British customs were not entirely welcome or appropriate for the remote and rustic conditions of the colonists. At the same time, this was the only law familiar to them. Following the American Revolution, British legal and judicial traditions were rejected just as surely as the hereditary monarchy. Later, as the United States advanced, and revolutionary tempers cooled, American courts turned again to their British origins for advice.

The Colonial Courts

During the colonial era, the structure of the courts differed vastly among the thirteen colonies. This is because the colonies themselves were established under differing charters. Some were created by edict of the Crown (like Virginia), some were owned by corporations (like Massachusetts Bay), and others initially were the private property of an individual (like Pennsylvania). Thus, the systems of justice in each colony evolved to serve the political needs of different masters. This helps explain some surviving disparities in court structures and doctrines across the states.

Since the courts evolved from different grants of power, judges gained their power from various sources of selection. In this way, they were responsive to the one who selected them. Perhaps most notably, the British monarch appointed many judges either directly, or authorized their very existence, in a colony's charter. This ensured that Crown-appointed judges displayed sympathy for the king.

In Virginia, for example, two colonial courts sat. The general court included the governor and the council, or colonial senate. In his official capacity, the governor himself served as a judge in many colonies resolving business disputes. Since the Virginian governor was the king's appointee his economic decisions reflected the king's interests in trade disputes.

The Colonial Judge

During the colonial and early days of the new republic, lawyers and judges typically were not products of law schools. Rather they had served as apprentices for established lawyers before going into practices of their own. Their studies often focused on political theory and philosophy, of which law was one part. Judging in the colonial era was a part-time job. Judges often were responsible for overlapping local chores. In addition to their judicial duties, justices of the peace administered local government, levied and collected taxes, and made local appointments in the way modern mayors and city councils would. On top of these duties, justices of the peace ran their own businesses and farms. This is to say, judicial responsibilities for them was a part-time job that did not pay particularly well. They were usually prominent and upright members of their communities and tried to reflect the sensibilities of their communities, as consistent with the demands of the colonial charter. They meted out punishment for cursing, failure to attend church, horse theft, treason, and murder.

While governors sat as judges, so too did legislators. In Virginia, members of the senate could hear criminal cases when it convened as the Court of Oyer & Terminer. Royal grants permitted some measure of local responsiveness in this way. Another way of accommodating the separation between London and the American colonies, was a grant of authority to governors to appoint prominent, landowning, white, Protestant men of their own choosing to serve as justices of the peace. The selection of judges in the colonies more closely resembles the way in which federal judges are selected with legislative approvals. Today, in many states judges must face some type of election. As had become the custom in England, judges were appointed in many of the colonies to serve during "good behaviour" (Friedman 1985).

The American Revolution and the Courts

As the American Revolution drew near disputes between royally appointed governors and locally elected legislators escalated. So too did tensions related to establishing court systems, punishments, and crimes. In addition, the government in London frustrated attempts to continue giving judges life tenure. Parliament also demanded that many types of cases would be taken from colonial courts and transferred to London. The debate over the terms of judges and the demand that increasing number of cases be heard in England became important points of contention leading up to the American Revolution. The Crown complained that its prerogatives were undermined by life terms for judges, since it created fewer vacancies for the king to fill with like-minded judges. The colonial revolutionaries, meanwhile, said transporting trials across the Atlantic Ocean took justice out of the hands of those closest to the events and denied defendants, witnesses, and victims an opportunity to follow trials. The nature of administering justice was at the core of the American Revolution and its identity after independence was won.

Liberty and Justice for Some

Protestant free men were able to serve as justices of the peace. Usually it was a justice of the peace who resolved disputes and meted out punishment for crime during the Colonial and Founding eras. The character of these courts was considerably different than modern courts in many ways, other than the gender and race of the decision maker alone. First, only Protestant, landowning, white men were eligible for decision-making positions. As parties to a case, white Protestant men could appeal their cases to the higher judicial authorities, including the governor, his council, or the state legislature. For white men convicted of a felony and who hoped to escape harsh capital punishment, there was the option of appealing to the "benefit of clergy." This meant they could turn their case over for a church trial and punishment. In some instances, the punishment was spent in a convent or monastery, rather than the stockades, whipping, or hanging.

For women, slaves, and Native Americans, the story was different. They were not permitted to sit on a jury or to enjoy the prerogative of having cases heard beyond the local justices of the peace. The benefit of clergy for slaves and women was often contested, and this privilege turned on the mood of the colony (or state), whether the slave practiced Christianity, or whether the defendant could read the Bible. When a woman was in court, she was usually as a witness and seldom as the plaintiff. For free or enslaved Africans appearing in court almost always meant being tried for an offense. Blacks in most places through the mid-1800s enjoyed none of the protections enjoyed by British subjects or U.S. citizens. As witnesses, blacks could not testify against whites, only against other blacks.

State Courts in the New Republic

As the new republic emerged, the former colonies struggled openly about the role and function of courts. Many of the courts wanted to establish new traditions and legal reasoning that were more appropriate for a republic, as opposed to a monarchy. One of the most important changes to emerge is that the courts began to rely less frequently on British common law, and began to develop law more suited to American needs. Change was often slow in coming. For example, the New York Constitution of 1777 explicitly kept the British-style court system intact during the Revolution, with the caveat that the legislature could make revisions as necessary. For the first forty years of the new state's history, the New York high court remained untouched, save for the elimination of the king's name as authorizing its orders. Yet in other colonies change was more rapid. For example, Judge Thomas Jefferson of the Virginia Supreme Court in 1788 urged his colleagues to break an earlier tradition and to begin publishing opinions, quite unlike the British.

After Jefferson left the court to serve in President George Washington's administration, a mentor and friend of Jefferson came to the Virginia Chancery Court and gave the United States a remarkable new theory of justice. Now a bedrock concept of constitutional law, in 1782 Virginia Chancery Judge George Wythe first announced the concept of judicial review. This is the legal theory that courts have the duty, and the authority, to interpret the meaning of a constitution and nullify any legislative or executive act that conflicts with it.

In *Commonwealth v. Caton* (4 Call 5 Va. 1782), Judge Wythe wrote: "Pointing to the constitution, [I] will say, to them [state legislators], here is the limit of your authority; and, hither shall you go, but no further." The idea of judicial review was born in a state court and was enshrined as federal constitutional law in the U.S. Supreme Court's 1803 decision *Marbury v. Madison*, from which the national high court today claims this power.

Almost as soon as its British roots left American legal tradition, so too did the charters that created local courts and authorized justices of the peace. Constitutions would take their place and through the rest of U.S. history they would be adopted, amended, and replaced in various ways. Another quality quickly abandoned was the French legal heritage in what is now much of the Midwest, and Spanish colonial law in the Southwest. With the Northwest Ordinance, the French common law was imposed between Pennsylvania and the Mississippi River.

Without law, though, early state courts realized elements of British tradition were better than chaos. The common law would be reintroduced, and modified to address citizens, rather than subjects and an economy based on landowners rather than tenants. State legislatures also hastily passed statutes rescinding British legal principles that were repugnant to the revolutionary spirit; often later realizing some had utility.

Postrevolutionary Law and Constitutions

Seeing the utility of decisions in British law, New York in 1821 adopted colonial regulations that did not otherwise contradict the state constitution. Courts also got in the act, claiming that the new republic had adopted the common law. There were, of course, loud outbursts of anxiety about turning to a foreign system, and the British in particular, for legal advice. The Kentucky legislature abided in this revolutionary zeal. As New York was allowing British tradition to seep back into state law, Kentucky declared that "reports or books" containing British decisions, "shall not be read or considered" in its courts (Friedman 1985). For the laws and courts of the new republic, this would be a checkered part of their history. Thus, much of the tension among the industrial, rural, and frontier states remained until after the Civil War.

At this time, no two state constitutions were exactly alike and no one was completely unique. State constitutions became more divergent during much of this era, generally reflecting tension over suffrage, apportionment, and trade. For example, Rhode Island narrowly defined voting rights as a prerogative that existed for property-owners despite violent outbursts from tenants. What was common among these charters was the deference paid to legislatures. Executive power generally was kept in check and held in some contempt. With *Marbury v. Madison*, even courts grew in constitutional powers of judicial review, though this was employed with great caution. Suffice it to say, that what these loosely united states held in common was a core faith in representative government, with voting rights available to a broader section of the public than elsewhere in the world.

Courts and Judges of the Jacksonian Era

Colonial judges were often beholden to executive authorities, and in fact were executives themselves. However, during the eighty years between the Founding Era and the Civil War, the doctrine of separating political powers spread rapidly in the individual states as it was in the central national government. The idea of the part-time lay judge receded into memory as well. Modern staffing is described in Chapter 4; however, it is useful to contrast it here with the ebb and flow of historic events that affected the nature of the separation-of-power cases that courts would be called on to decide.

Americans of this era placed emphasis on political control from below, not from above. Judges would be selected by vote in many but not all counties in the new republic. In the wake of Andrew Jackson's presidency, however, the appointed judge became extinct. In 1777 Vermont began this march, requiring the popular election of judges. The rest of the states followed suit, with New Yorkers finally adopting popular election of their supreme court judges in 1846. The theme of popular control of government remained powerful until the turn of the next century, when faith in the voter was shaken as waves of immigrants sided with scandalous political machines, and merit selection of judges gained fashion.

Also falling by the wayside between the Founding and Civil War eras was legislative and executive interference in the business of state judiciaries. While governors in New Jersey and Connecticut retained high judicial authority in the Founding Era, this slowly faded into history as New York and Rhode Island constitutions in the 1840s took their governors off their courts of last resort.

Other Americanisms emerged during the antebellum era affecting the courts' personnel. The federal Constitution remained true to the executive appointment of judges. It also maintained lifetime tenure, another theme antithetical to Jacksonian democracy. Whereas federal judges could be forced out only by impeachment, usually for serious offense, states like Pennsylvania and South Carolina made it easy to fire judges for misdemeanor infractions.

Industrialization and Rugged Individualism in the Progressive Era

After the Civil War two intertwined events—the industrialization of the United States and massive immigration to the United States cities from impoverished parts of Europe and China—ushered in new ideas about law and courts between the 1880s and 1920s.

The shift in attitudes toward injury and responsibility began in the mid-1800s, but became more prominent early in the twentieth century. By that time, industrialization, railroading, and immigration brought about the adoption of wage and work safety regulations. Among these laws were limits on the hours and conditions that pregnant women and children could toil in strenuous work environments. Industrial innovations introduced rapidly moving, extremely hot, dusty, and heavy equipment that would be used in agriculture, railroading, and manufacturing.

With economic innovation came the need to evaluate how law responded and understood the dangers and opportunities in the marketplace. Courts and legislatures adapted to the industrial revolution by putting forward political ideas similar to the way they had 100 years before by purging and reintroducing common law traditions in the Founding

Era. Legal innovation came in fits and starts. Courts in California, Illinois, and Pennsylvania held tightly to rugged individualism as an organizing ideology despite legislative language attempting to address harsh labor conditions. Courts such as these argued against many types of legislative interference in employment regulation on two primary principles: first, regulation undermined a right to a contract, which was premised on the dignity of the rational individual who should decide for himself whether to accept dangerous employment conditions. Second, it treated all workers or certain types of laborers as a class, separate and unequal in the law only because of membership in that class.

Employers generally had little obligation to the safety of their workers, and consumers had high hurdles to surmount to sue for faulty manufacturing in courts such as these. Judges trained by mentors educated at the time of the Civil War considered and placed high value in the individual's right to contract, and denied legislatures' rights to interfere in the private relationship between employer and employee. In other words, the courts denied that an omniscient government could deny a man the right to work twelve-hour days, six days a week in a hot, dusty coal mine for a paltry wage. Using similar logic for the consumer, the legal motto *caveat emptor* (let the buyer beware) was in effect. The right to contract, or purchase, was not to be upset by unnecessary common law or regulation. The federal courts and Congress generally took a laissez faire (let it be) attitude toward American enterprise.

Progressive Era (1880s–1930s) reformers and journalists shed light on the economic power held by monopolies in the petroleum, rubber, steel, and mining industries and the deplorable living and workplace conditions of urban laborers. A new generation of state justices revisited legal theories in light of new realities about economic forces, productivity, and human safety. Judges were also moved by the forces of political organization. Emerging labor unions pointed out the value of friendly judges on the bench with respect to forming unions and addressing labor conditions. The influence of urban political machines in New York, Boston, Albany, Illinois, and Kansas City thrived on the support of working-class voters as well. Democratic machines were able to keep courts staffed with judges favorable to worker-friendly legislation, and patronage for lawyers, government attorneys, and would-be judges.

By the end of this era, courts had had a change of heart. New York Supreme Court Justice Benjamin Cordozo led the way in the 1920s by articulating modern ideas of product liability. Under this new legal doctrine, state courts across the nation began to hold manufacturers responsible for injuries that occurred from their products. This change has been slow and deliberate. Between the 1930s and 1990s, California, New Jersey, and other states' judges shifted the burdens of product liability from caveat emptor to *caveat venditor* (let the seller beware). The changes in legal thought on issues of liability are one of the most profound transformations in legal philosophies since the founding of the nation. It redefined the position of different groups within society. Plus the transformation demonstrates how broader changes in society affect the courts.

Other underdogs gained the attention of influential members of society. The poor, the immigrant, and the mentally disabled had been unnoticed in the law. Worse, housing for orphans and the poor was despicable. Champions of the poor, such as Jane Addams's and emerging women's rights movements, urged legal reforms to protect those who were unable to defend themselves, such as widows and children. Laws were enacted empowering state agencies to represent the interests of wards of the state. Laws for the poor distinguished between worthy and unworthy. Vagrants and drunks were afforded no quarter, while the disabled, veterans, widows, and orphans should be provided subsistence. In concert with this sensitivity, came common law adjustments. For example, changing economic realities recognized in other avenues of society brought awareness to judges of how courts should think about the legal relationship between a vulnerable worker or illiterate consumer and a powerful, well-educated manufacturer.

Elements of Liability at the End of the Progressive Era

The debate over liability and responsibility continues, however. In recent years, state courts have faced a steady backlash from politicians and groups representing the manufacturing, medicine, and insurance industries that contend that the awards for personal injury cases have gotten too large. Recent high-profile cases involving cigarettes, spilled coffee, medical care, and other consumer goods or services have raised public awareness of high awards and put the issue of liability and responsibility back onto reformers' agendas. Before looking at this more modern debate, it is important to continue to explain other historical changes in the state courts during these earlier periods.

Selection Method Reforms at the End of the Progressive Era

Since the early 1900s, many reformers have sought to have judges appointed, rather than elected. Since political machines controlled the tools of election campaigning, it was thought that the partisan elections led to scandalous judging and patronage staffing of justice systems. Reformers, both in industry and in the American Bar Association worried that unqualified party loyalists were unable to decide fairly. The principles of popular control remained strong in the United States, however. During the 1980s, progressive activists still supported nonpartisan elections, which became a custom in the Midwest and parts of New England. On the other hand, trusted progressives like President Woodrow Wilson advocated a government run by technicians, or well-qualified administrators. In this political environment merit selection methods, most notably the Missouri Plan, reintroduced executive influence to the selection process, while trying to keep some semblance of popular control. Missouri Plan states have a committee that sends the governor a list of qualified candidates. The governor makes a nomination from this list, with some type of legislative approval. At the next election, voters decide to keep or remove the judge. The judge faces no opponent in the election. Details of this selection method and its uses are discussed in Chapter 5.

After the Great Depression

The Second World War put a pause on interest in state courts, as did growing national power to regulate commerce. After the 1937 *NLRB v. Jones-Laughlin* case in the U.S. Supreme Court, doctrinal issues receded and structural issues became the focus on reform in the state courts.

In particular, court reformers have wanted two things. The first thing they sought was the merit selection of judges and consolidation of the courts. They also wanted to remove the idiosyncrasies and confusion that was created because there were so many different types of limited-jurisdiction courts in each state. The reforms have sought to streamline judicial systems so that they look more like the federal court structure, making the court structure more rational and easier to understand by the public. The efforts to reform, however, have often been difficult to achieve because many local governments and court employees object to state intrusion into their territories. In the past, local political machines had used court staffing for patronage, and their opposition made reform efforts difficult. Local lawyers, who navigated these systems more effectively than outsiders, had an advantage over out-of-town lawyers, and fought reform.

The Illinois court system is said to have been the first to adopt a *unified system*. A unified system models the structure of the United States federal judicial system. Under the Illinois structure, there are no limited-jurisdiction courts. Rather there is a single local circuit court at the county level. In heavily populated areas, such as Cook County, the court may assign judges to hear specific case types. Still, it remains a single court jurisdiction. Above the circuit court, Illinois has five district appellate courts, each with jurisdiction over some region of the state. Finally, there is a single supreme court with statewide jurisdiction.

Over the past few decades, most states have made an effort to unify their court systems, though not all have mirrored Illinois's reforms. Some states retain limited jurisdiction courts, and others have separate appeals systems for criminal and civil litigation. For example, Wisconsin reduced its special-function courts to the municipal courts, which hear cases arising from the violation of city laws. In states such as Arkansas, Massachusetts, and Rhode Island, officials have opted to keep a broader array of special-function and appellate courts. New York's government has decided to stay with many limited duty courts and multiple appeals courts.

In addition to efforts to consolidate court structures, there has also been an effort to improve the appellate process. While many states historically had a wide variety of low-level courts, they had few appellate courts. As of 1960, only fourteen states had middle-level appellate courts. Without this buffer, supreme courts were swamped with cases that had little or no broad social impact. The state's supreme courts were forced to play a supervisory role, overturning poor trial decisions, rather than a policy-making role of interpreting laws and constitutions, as the U.S. Supreme Court does. Much of that has changed over the past few decades as all but eleven states now have intermediate appellate courts. Even in some of the states that do not formally have intermediate courts, the superior trial courts can hear appeals from limited-jurisdiction courts. This provides a buffer between the trial court and the state supreme court. In Delaware's court system, for example, this alleviated pressures on the final court. Though the appellate courts are considered higher in the structure of the court system, they have little control over who actually occupies judicial offices in trial courts. The higher courts are able to set aside bad decisions, but cannot control bad judges by firing or suspending them for violating higher court orders or issuing rulings contrary to precedence. States have distinct disciplinary procedures for judges who are accused of serious misconduct. But removing judges for disagreeable rulings is not common.

Modern Reform Efforts

In recent years, perhaps the four most visible efforts to reform law and the courts at the state level have been (1) movements to ease the burden of punitive damages on parties found liable in tort law, (2) stringent sentences for criminal offenders, (3) continued emphasis on consolidating court systems, as discussed earlier, and (4) selection methods of judges (T1.2, p. 30). The selection method questions have been extended since the Progressive Era. States where political parties exerted greater influence than reform movements maintain partisan election methods. More watered-down versions, in parts of the South and Midwest, have led to nonpartisan elections. The Missouri Plan remains the selection method of choice among most bar associations and reform movements.

The merit selection, or Missouri Plan, is used in almost half the states. Another twenty states have elected judicial systems, with only six making them nonpartisan affairs. Six other states function somewhat like the federal system, with executive appointment and legislative approval.

The push to reduce legal liability began in the 1980s and has continued to generate debate. Claiming that high-priced punitive damages are detrimental to businesses and health care, physician groups, insurance companies, hospitals, and manufacturers have sought to limit the dollar amount of awards in personal injury cases that judges and juries can assign. Between 1986 and 1997, eleven state legislatures enacted limits on awards for non-economic damages. Also during that time span, seventeen states placed limits on the amounts that plaintiffs can collect in punitive awards. New Hampshire prohibited awarding punitive damages altogether. Other states insisted on more stringent courtroom findings before punitive awards could be issued. Undoubtedly, many state governments found the issues surrounding tort law to be of critical concern. Central to these concerns are unresolved arguments about the question of fairness in the civil litigation, the economic effect of civil litigation, and the influence of various pressure groups.

Critics also say civil fines are so high they drive up the market price of goods and services, which harms consumers. However, there is reason to think that several of these initiatives will be reversed. By the end of the 1990s, eleven state supreme courts dismissed these limitations for failure to comply with the constitutions in these states.

Some eighty-seven decisions in these states have found that liability limitation statutes, at least in part, violate plaintiffs' state constitutional rights to recovery and interfere with the prerogatives of the judiciary.

Consumer advocates and trial lawyers say that in order for punitive awards to work they should "hurt" the party causing the damage (see for example Philips 1970 and Poukas 1992). The threat of civil penalty would make businesses cautious only if the fine is steep enough to take away the profit motive of bringing a defective product into the marketplace. They also say these penalties help the economy, by giving consumers confidence in the products they buy. Some state courts' judges have charged that dam-

TABLE 1.2   SELECTION METHODS FOR STATE JUDGES

Partisan elections	Nonpartisan elections	Merit commission*	Gubernatorial or legislative appointment
Alabama	Arkansas	Alaska	California†
Louisiana	Georgia	Arizona	Maine
Ohio	Idaho	Colorado	New Hampshire§
Pennsylvania	Kentucky	Connecticut	New Jersey
Texas	Michigan**	Delaware†	South Carolina§
West Virginia	Minnesota	District of Columbia	Virginia
	Mississippi	Florida†	
	Montana	Hawaii	
	Nevada	Indiana	
	North Carolina‡	Iowa	
	North Dakota	Kansas‡	
	Oregon	Maryland	
	Washington	Massachusetts	
	Wisconsin	Missouri+	
		Nebraska	
		New Mexico	
		New York‡	
		Oklahoma	
		Rhode Island	
		South Dakota†	
		Tennessee‡	
		Utah	
		Vermont	
		Wyoming	

Source: Adapted from *Judicial Selection in the States,* American Judicature Society, 2004, (http://www.ajs.org/selection/sel_stateselect.asp).

*In Delaware, Maryland, Massachusetts, and New Hampshire commissions are established by executive order; in other locations commissions are required by state statute or the constitution.

†Certain lower court judges or limited jurisdiction court officials are chosen by nonpartisan election.

‡Some lower court judges are chosen by partisan election.

§Nominee must be approved by a nominations commission.

**Supreme Court justices are elected in partisan elections.

age caps are counterproductive, and have resisted legislative efforts to impose these rules (Glabberson 1999).

In 1996, the U.S. Supreme Court entered the debate over punitive damage awards by imposing strict guidelines on the prerogatives of state courts. In its decision *BMW of North America Inc. v. Gore,* the Court gave its first hint that it had grown concerned with punitive awards. Punitive awards hope to punish deliberately harmful behavior by causing the culpable party to pay the victim more than enough to compensate for lost wages, medical expenses, and repair of damaged property. In 2003 the Supreme Court went further in restraining the state courts' ability to issue large penalties. The divided Court ruled that punitive damages that were 145 times greater than the actual damages were excessive (a violation of the Eighth Amendment's restriction against excessive penalties and the Fourteenth Amendment's due process clause), because civil process is less demanding than a criminal process. The Court, however, stopped short of giving clear guidelines about the size of punitive awards.

The Court has been reluctant to identify concrete constitutional limits on the ratio between harm, or potential harm, to the plaintiff and the punitive damages award; but, in practice, few awards exceeding a single-digit ratio between punitive and compensatory damages will satisfy due process (*State Farm Mutual Automobile Insurance v. Campbell* [2003]).

The Campbell decision did not end the debate. Rather, President George W. Bush, delighted with the outcome, two years later mustered congressional support for legislation to impose stricter liability limits, especially for suits against drug manufacturers and physicians. His legal reform program also made it easier for tort defendants to move cases out of state courts and into less plaintiff-friendly federal courts.

Along with pressures on the courts to limit punitive damages, there has also been an effort to impose stricter sentences on criminal offenders. During the later part of the 1980s and early 1990s, concerns about drug-related violence grew, as the rates of assaults, robberies, homicides, and incarcerations rose dramatically (Langan and Farrington 1998). The rising crime rate led to demands for reform from both the political Right and Left. For those on the Right, the rising crime rate led to concerns that violent offenders were being treated lightly and allowed to repeat their offenses. For those on the Left, there were concerns over the uneven sentencing of defendants convicted of similar crimes. As a result of these concerns, many states adopted new guidelines as to how judges should sentence felons. Among these were three-strikes rules requiring long-term sentences for certain repeat offenders, and minimum sentencing guidelines for a variety of offenses. Justice Sandra Day O'Connor's dissenting opinion in *Blakely v. Washington* provides a succinct history behind sentencing guidelines.

The get-tough-on-crime movement ran into turmoil in the early 2000s. For starters, then Governor George Ryan of Illinois suspended executions in the state. This came after a group of enterprising undergraduate college students and a private investigator demonstrated that police brought faulty, if not fictional, evidence against thirteen defendants who were convicted for murders that they did not commit. Moreover, state and federal sentencing guidelines were found unreasonable with the *Blakely v. Washington* decision. Here the U.S. Supreme Court held that: (1) "aggravating" factors that might lead to harsh sentences must be proven at trial, not merely presented at sentencing. (This might include the actual weight of some drug being sold.) (2) Legislatures could not give judges authority to "enhance" sentences based on unproven evidence. This ruling has left state and federal prosecutors trying to recraft legislation to impose sentences appropriate to the level of a crime.

Contemporary Judicial Authority

After having sharpened current national debates over economic issues such as punitive damages, as well as hot social topics such as assisted suicide, same-sex marriage, crime, and election law, state courts sit at the heart of current events in the United States. It would be an exaggeration to think they alone are determining the outcomes of these controversies. Rather, with fifty states, courts in each of these states continue to raise and revise cutting-edge legal theories. Therefore, it benefits the observer of news, politics, and policy to understand how these vital institutions function, how judges reason, and how their environments place pressures on them. Students of state courts only recently have begun to systematically examine the structure, function, and politics of state courts as a group. Some 400 years after the first local courts were established in the American colonies and more than 200 years after Virginia's Judge Wythe established the power of a state court to exercise judicial review, our state courts have begun to receive something more than local attention.

Today's state judges are better organized, educated, and paid than any of their predecessors. Constant training opportunities and electronic communications allow judges across the country to be familiar with common legal topics and arguments. Similarly, the supporting casts for judges, clerks, and legal research staff enjoy similar organization and training. This allows state courts to function at a higher level of efficiency and competence. Just the same, judges are subject to the environments in which they serve. This environment includes elections, interest group activity in the courts, media attention, and pressures from other actors in government, who also enjoy improved information and research.

MAJOR TOPICS IN STUDYING STATE COURTS

Courts may hold power in defining the meaning of provisions in their state constitutions, but they depend on other branches of government for enforcement and authority to render judgment in other areas. They also depend on others to bring cases to the courts. Unlike state legislators who bring issues before the legislature, judges depend on litigants, often state officials, to bring cases and to define the issues that judges are to decide. Courts also depend on other branches of government for their funding, which has important implications for staffing, record keeping, research facilities, and other resources that allow judges to make "independent" decisions.

Within a state's governing apparatus, the courts can play a critical role in shaping policy and checking the powers of the legislative or executive branches of government. Some observers (see for example Baar 1982) think state courts act more aggressively in this respect than the federal courts do toward Congress, federal agencies, or the president. Baar recounts an instance where one colorful judge in Wayne County, Michigan, called the county commissioners into court. He was angered over a lack of funding for the local judiciary. Those who supported the court's budget requests were dismissed, while the others were held in contempt of court.

Courts also are using their powers beyond the garden-variety exercise of judicial review. Normally courts striking down statutes stop when they have identified the constitutional violation. More recently, some have advocated particular policies within their rulings, and offered specific advice on how to draft the law. For example, a Wisconsin Supreme Court's decision included a page in which justices wrote to "urge the legislature to thoughtfully examine . . . the possibility of a license or permit system for persons who have good reasons to carry a concealed weapon" (*State of Wisconsin v. Hamdan* 2004).

This chapter has tried to explain some of the fundamental aspects of state courts that are helpful for understanding the role, structure, and character of these courts. The chapter has also provided background on the historical development of these courts and important judicial trends. Yet there is far more to state court politics that will be explored in the following chapters.

References and Further Reading

Baar, Carl. 1982. "Judicial Activism in State Courts: The Inherent-Powers Doctrine." In *State Supreme Courts: Policy Makers in the Federal System*, eds. Mary Cornelia Porter and G. Alan Tarr. Westport, CT: Greenwood Press.

Baum, Lawrence, and Bradley C. Canon. 1982. "State Supreme Courts and Activists: New Doctrines in the Law of Torts." In *State Supreme Courts: Policy Makers in the Federal System*, eds. Mary Cornelia Porter and G. Alan Tarr. Westport, CT: Greenwood Press.

Blackstone, William. 1979. *Commentaries on the Laws of England: A Facsimile of the First Edition of 1765–1769.* Chicago: University of Chicago Press.

Brace, Paul, and Melinda Gann Hall. 1990. "Neo-Institutionalism and Dissent in the State Supreme Courts." *Journal of Politics* 52, no. 1 (February): 54–70.

———. 1995. "Studying Courts Comparatively: The View from the American States." *Political Research Quarterly* 48 (March): 5–29.

Brennan, William J. 1977. "State Constitutions and the Protection of Individual Rights." *Harvard Law Review* 90, no. 3 (January): 489–504.

Caldiera, Gregory A. 1985. "On the Reputation of State Supreme Courts." *Political Behavior* 5, no. 1: 83–108.

Carp, Robert A., and Ronald Stidham. 1996. *Judicial Process in America.* Washington, DC: CQ Press.

Church, Thomas W. 1995. "Plea Bargaining and Local Legal Culture." In *Contemplating Courts*, ed. Lee Epstein. Washington, DC: CQ Press.

Cotterrell, Bill. 2003. "Bush Given Power in Case." *Tallahassee Democrat*, October 22, 2003, Tallahassee.com.

Dailey, Debra. 1998. "Minnesota Sentencing Guidelines: A Structure for Change." *Law and Policy* 20, no. 3: 311.

Elazar, Daniel J. 1966. *American Federalism: A View From the States.* New York: Thomas Y. Crowell.

Fino, Susan P. 1987. *The Role of State Supreme Courts in the New Judicial Federalism.* Westport, CT: Greenwood Press.

Flango, Carol A, Victor E. Flango, and H. Ted Rubin. 1999. *How Are Courts Coordinating Family Cases?* Alexandria, VA: State Justice Institute report 96–12C-B-222.

Friedman, Lawrence M. 1985. *A History of American Law.* New York: Simon and Schuster.

Gillman, Howard. 1993. *The Constitution Besieged.* Durham, NC: Duke University Press.

Glabberson, William. 1999. "State Laws Limiting Injury Suits Are Falling like Dominoes." *New York Times,* July 16, 1999.

Hall, Melinda Gann. 1987. "Constituent Influence in State Supreme Courts: Conceptual Notes and a Case Study." *Journal of Politics* 49: 1117–1166.

———.1994. "The Vicissitudes of Death by Decree: Forces Influencing Capital Punishment in State Supreme Courts." *Social Science Quarterly* 75 (March): 136–151.

———. 1999. "State Supreme Courts and Their Environments: Avenues to General Theories of Judicial Choice." In *Supreme Court Decision-Making,* eds. Cornell W. Clayton and Howard Gillman. Chicago: University of Chicago Press.

Hall, Melinda Gann, and Paul Brace. 1993. "Integrated Models of Judicial Dissent." *Journal of Politics* 55, no. 4 (November): 419–435.

Heinz, John P., and Edward O. Lauman. 1982. *Chicago Lawyers: The Social Structure of the Bar.* Chicago and New York: Russell Sage Foundation and American Bar Foundation.

Hogan, Sean O. 2000. *Continuity and Change in the Common Law: The Illinois Supreme Court's Tort Doctrine 1970–1996.* Unpublished Ph.D. diss., University of Illinois–Chicago.

Klaversma, Laura G., and Daniel J. Hall. 2003. *Organizational and Administrative Review of the Fulton County, Georgia, Juvenile Court.* Denver: Court Services Consulting.

Langan, Patrick A., and David P. Farrington. 1998. *Crime and Justice in the United States and in England and Wales, 1981–1996.* Washington, DC: U.S. Department of Justice.

Linde, Hans. 1980. "First Things First; Rediscovering the State's Bill of Rights." *University of Baltimore Law Review* 3: 379–394.

———.1995. "Are State Constitutions Common Law?" In *Intellect and Craft: The Contributions of Justice Hans Linde to American Constitutionalism,* ed. R. F. Nagel. Boulder, CO: Westview Press.

Mecham, Leonidas Ralph. 2002. *Judicial Business of the United States: 2002 Annual Report of the Director.* Washington, DC: Administrative Office of the U.S. Courts, Government Printing Office.

Mikeska, Jennifer L. 2000. "Court Consolidation: Reinventing Missouri State Courts." Institute for Court Management, Court Executive Development Program, Phase III Project. [N.p.], MO: McDonald County Circuit Court.

National Center for State Courts. 2001. "Customer Service and Court Consolidation: Are Consolidated Courts Better Able to Serve Their Customers?" Report to Institute for Court Management, May 2001.

———. 2002. "Civil Justice Reform Initiative: Advancing Civil Justice Reform." Examining the Work of the State Courts: Caseload Highlights. Williamsburg, VA: National Center for State Courts.

Philips, John G. 1970. "Collateral Source." *Illinois Bar Journal* 58: 288.

Pinello, Daniel R. 1995. *The Impact of Judicial-Selection Method on State Supreme Court Policy Innovation, Reaction, and Atrophy.* Westport, CT: Greenwood Press.

Poukas, Erick P. 1992. "*Loitz v. Remington Arms Co.:* The Illinois Supreme Court Sets a Tougher Standard for Reviewing Punitive Damage Awards in Product Liability Cases." *John Marshall Law Review* 25, no. 2 (Winter): 427.

Puzzanchera, Charles M. 2001. "Delinquency Cases Waived to Criminal Court, 1989–1998." *OJJDP Fact Sheet,* Office of Juvenile Justice and Delinquency Prevention, vol. 35. Washington, DC: U.S. Department of Justice.

Sarat, Austin. 1977. "Studying American Legal Culture: An Assessment of Survey Evidence." *Law and Society Review* 11, no. 3 (Winter):427, quoting Lawrence Friedman, "Legal Culture and Social Development." *Law and Society Review* 4 (1969).

Serrano, Richard A., and David G. Savage. 2004. "Scalia's Talk to Anti-Gay Group Spurs Ethics Debate." *Boston Globe*, March 8, 2004.

Steiger, John. 1998. "Taking the Law into Our Own Hands: Structured Sentencing, Fear of Violence and Citizen Initiatives in Washington State."*Law and Policy* 20, no. 3 (July): 333–356.

Strickland, Shauna M., and Brenda G. Otto. 2003. *State Court Caseload Statistics, 2002.* Williamsburg, VA: National Center for State Courts.

U.S. Department of Justice. 2000. *Compendium of Federal Justice Statistics.* Washington, DC: U.S. Bureau of Justice Statistics, Department of Justice.

Weil, Jonathan, and Cassell Bryan-Low. 2003. "Audit Firms Overbilled Clients for Travel, Arkansas Suit Alleges." *Wall Street Journal*, September 17, 2003, A-1.

Cases

Blakely v. Washington. 2004. 542 U.S. 296.

Bush v. Gore. 2000. 531 U.S. 98, 121 S. Ct. 525.

Bush v. Palm Beach Canvassing Board. 2000. 531 U.S. 70.

Commonwealth v. Caton. 1782. 4 Call 5 Va.

Goodridge v. Mass. Dept. of Public Health. 2003. 798 N.E.2d 941.

Liggett Group v. Engle. 2003. 853 So.2d 434 at 445; Fla. 3d DCA.

Marbury v. Madison. 1803. 5 U.S. 137.

NLRB v. Jones & Laughlin Steel Corp. 1937. 301 U.S. 1.

Southern Burlington County NAACP v. Township of Mount Laurel. 1975. 67 NJ 151.

State Farm Mutual Automobile Insurance v. Campbell. 2003. 538 U.S. 408.

State of Wisconsin v. Hamdan. 2003. 665 NW2d 785.

Tennessee Small School Systems v. McWherter. 1993. 851 SW2d 139.

United States v. Lopez. 1995. 514 U.S. 549.

Natural Law

Aquinas, Thomas. 1988. *On Law, Morality and Politics.* Indianapolis: Hackett.

Finnis, John. 1980. *Natural Law and Natural Rights.* Oxford: Clarendon.

George, Robert P., and Christopher Wolfe, eds. 2000. *Natural Law and Public Reason.* Washington, DC: Georgetown University Press.

On the Web

General Readings in State Courts and Judges

American Judges Association, http://aja.ncsc.dni.us/.

American Judicature Society, http://www.ajs.org/cart/storefront.asp.

Center for State Constitutional Studies, Rutgers University–Camden, http://www-camlaw.rutgers.edu/statecon/.

Compendium of Federal Justice Statistics, Bureau of Justice Statistics, U.S. Department of Justice, http://www.ojp.usdoj.gov/bjs/.

Conference of State Court Administrators, http://cosca.ncsc.dni.us/.

National Center for State Courts, http://www.ncsconline.org/.

State Supreme Court Data Project, http://www.ruf.rice.edu/~pbrace/statecourt/index.html.

Criminal and Civil Court Activity

National Association of Drug Court Professionals, http://www.nadcp.org/home.html.
RAND Corp. Institute for Civil Justice, http://www.rand.org/icj/.
U.S. Justice Department's National Criminal Justice Reference Service,
    http://www.ncjrs.org/.

2

THE ROLES, FUNCTIONS, AND POWERS OF STATE COURTS

Mathew Manweller

State courts and judges perform a variety of functions for state governments and their citizens. State courts resolve private economic disagreements like contract and tort disputes, as well as personal disputes such as divorce and child custody cases. State courts also mediate public disagreements including school funding claims, procedures for criminal defendants, and other state constitutional issues. To carry out these functions, state courts are invested with specific political, legal, and constitutional powers. The courts in each state use these powers to enforce their rulings, as well as to shape the state's political landscape. However, state courts do not exist in a vacuum. State judges must navigate a complex legal environment that includes federal courts and federal law, state constitutional and statutory restrictions, mandates, and sometimes even international law. As a result, state courts and judges must make and enforce their decisions while respecting other political institutions and competing bodies of law, using the specific and limited powers at their disposal.

Chapter 2 examines several basic questions about state courts. First, the chapter looks at where state courts get their power or authority. Political actors, even judges, must have a basis for their authority. In the case of state courts, their power comes from state constitutions, legislative statutes, common law, and in some cases, federal law. Second, the chapter examines what state courts do with their authority. State courts perform different tasks than federal courts. State courts spend much more of their resources dealing with issues such as torts, contract law, family law, and local issues like traffic violations, petty crime, and small claims. However, state courts must also deal with issues of public law such as death penalty appeals, statutory interpretation, and constitutional interpretation. Third, the chapter looks at the specific powers state judges have to enforce their decisions. It is one thing for a judge to issue a ruling on paper. It is quite another to ensure that the judgment is enforced in the real world. State judges have a variety of powers at their disposal. These include, but are not limited to, issuing writs of enforcement, garnishing wages and property, empowering special masters (officials appointed by the court to carry out investigative and administrative tasks for the court), invalidating state laws, and directing state law enforcement officers to carry out legal orders.

JUDICIAL FEDERALISM

State courts coexist with other jurisdictions. Federal and international law, as well as the rulings from other state courts, impact the discretion and authority of state judges. Later sections of Chapter 2 look at how state courts interact with other legal environments. The interaction of state courts with federal courts is called vertical judicial federalism. The relationship can be complex. The federal Constitution's supremacy clause requires that state courts enforce federal law. Yet, at the same time, state supreme courts are the final arbitrators of state law. Therefore, in some cases, state courts must obey federal courts, but in other cases, state courts are free to develop their own bodies of law independent of federal courts.

State courts interact with courts from other states. This relationship is called horizontal judicial federalism. Sometimes, state courts use precedents issued by other state courts to decide cases. At other times, because of the U.S. Constitution's full faith and credit clause, state courts are required to enforce decisions issued by other state courts. By the end of the chapter, it will be clear that state courts have a host of functions to perform and a variety of powers to enforce their decisions. However, in conjunction with these functions and powers there are a number of boundaries imposed by other institutions and legal jurisdictions.

THE FOUNDATIONS OF STATE COURT AUTHORITY

The authority of state courts comes from several different sources. Primarily, state courts get their authority from state constitutions. Constitutional grants of authority can be supplemented by legislative statutes that are authorized by state constitutions. State courts also have federal sources of authority. The U.S. Constitution is an indirect source of state authority, and therefore, an indirect source of authority for state courts. The supremacy and the full faith and credit clauses, as well as the Tenth Amendment, carve out roles for state courts in America's federalist system. Both federal and state constitutions, as well as state legislatures, establish limits to state court authority.

Constitutionalism

Constitutionalism is the idea that the powers of government should be limited by certain fundamental principles. These principles are typically established in a written document, or constitution. A constitution declares the limits of government power and sometimes establishes the rights of citizens that cannot be violated by government.

State Constitutions and Federalism

Students of law typically assume that all state constitutions were drafted in the early stages of our history. In fact, this is not always true. The Montana State Constitution was rewritten in 1972 when over eighty delegates met in Helena. The Montana Constitution is considered one of the most progressive constitutions in the United States. It contains an extensive bill of rights that includes a "right to participation," a "right to know," a "right to privacy," and a "right to a clean and healthful environment." In 1999, the Montana Supreme Court began enforcing the clean and healthful environment clause by issuing several rulings that preemptively limited the ability of mining companies to pollute.

Constitutionalism grew out of the Enlightenment but has roots in history prior to that period. During the Middle Ages, the notion of the divine right of kings meant that monarchs ruled as the representative of God. Therefore, there were no limitations on the political power of the monarch. However, the Magna Carta of 1215 established written limitations on the powers of the English king. During the Enlightenment, political writers such as Thomas Hobbes and John Locke further explored the idea of constitutionalism. They argued that monarchs and government were limited by a social contract between the rulers and the ruled.

In the United States, constitutionalism gained greater prominence after the American Revolution. While America was a colony of the British Empire, ultimate sovereignty rested with the Crown. However, after severing all political and legal ties to Britain, America's leaders needed a new source of ultimate authority. On a theoretical level, Americans decided to place ultimate sovereignty in the people. Constitutions were drafted to represent the will of the populace. After the Revolution, constitutions became more than simply rules by which citizens and legislators had to abide. Instead, state constitutions became the embodiment of popular sovereignty.

The authority of American courts is closely tied to the concept of constitutionalism. Both the United States and every individual state have written constitutions that delineate the powers and limitations of the government. More important, the existence of constitutions highlights the fact that governments are not the highest form of authority. Instead, the will of the people, as expressed in the written constitutions, supercedes the will of government officials. Therefore, courts can limit the acts of government officials by establishing that those acts are forbidden by the state or federal constitution. In a constitutional system, courts are responsible for insuring that governments do not violate the constitutional rights of individuals or exercise powers not granted to them in the given constitutions. The courts act to ensure the governments stay within the established constitutional bounds. Because each state court has the power to enforce the written provisions of its state constitution, state courts have considerable authority to dictate to the elected and administrative branches of their state.

State Constitutions

All state courts, with varying degrees, get their authority from state constitutions. Either the state constitution establishes the entire judicial system, including minor bureaucratic details, or the state constitution establishes general guidelines and grants of power while leaving the details to the state legislature to establish. The Washington State Constitution exhibits characteristics of both. In terms of the state supreme court, the Washington Constitution prescribes specific details about its jurisdiction and powers. Article IV, Section 4 of the Washington Constitution, in part, states,

> The supreme court shall have original jurisdiction in habeas corpus, and quo warranto and mandamus as to all state officers, and appellate jurisdiction in all actions and proceedings, excepting that its appellate jurisdiction shall not extend to civil actions at law for the recovery of money or personal property when the original amount in controversy, or the value of the property does not exceed the sum of two hundred dollars ($200) unless the action involves the legality of a tax, impost, assessment, toll, municipal fine, or the validity of a statute. The supreme court shall also have power to issue writs of mandamus, review, prohibition, habeas corpus, certiorari and all other writs necessary and proper to the complete exercise of its appellate and revisory jurisdiction.

In comparison, the establishment and the allocation of power for lower courts is left to the state legislature by the Washington Constitution. Section 12 of Article IV simply reads, "The legislature shall prescribe by law the jurisdiction and powers of any of the inferior courts which may be established in pursuance of this Constitution."

It is important to realize that state constitutions tend to be much longer than the federal Constitution. Article III of the U.S. Constitution establishes the power and jurisdiction for the U.S. Supreme Court. Yet, Article III is one of the shortest articles in the Constitution and speaks with sweeping generalities. Furthermore, the federal Constitution was constructed primarily, although not entirely, as a document of limited government. That is, the purpose of the federal Constitution was to limit the federal government's scope of power. Therefore, much of the U.S. Constitution addresses what the federal government cannot do. Finally, it is very difficult to amend, and therefore it is hard to add clauses to the federal Constitution. Despite thousands of attempts, Americans have only been able to add twenty-seven clauses to the U.S. Constitution in over 200 years.

For a variety of reasons, state constitutions, in contrast, are very long and detailed documents. State constitutions are comparatively easy to amend. As a result, state constitutions can include relatively mundane clauses. The Alabama Constitution, for example, has a prohibition against taxing wharfs. The Colorado Constitution has a clause banning the general assembly from prescribing textbooks for high schools. The Missouri Constitution has a provision mandating a department of mental health.

Alan Tarr (1998) argues that there is a reason why state constitutions dedicate so much text to seemingly mundane legislative areas. He notes that state legislatures have plenary power. This means that laws passed by the state legislature are assumed to be constitutional unless there is a specific proscription against such authority in the state constitution. In contrast, the federal Congress can only legislate in areas in which the federal Constitution specifically authorizes them to do so. Therefore, state legislators have a much freer hand than members of Congress. Because state legislatures are less constrained, drafters of state constitutions spend much more effort detailing specific limitations of authority for their legislatures.

In addition to constitutional clauses limiting state legislative power, state constitutions cover more policy areas and include affirmative grants of power that are absent in the U.S. Constitution. For example, many state constitutions mandate that the state guarantee a free, public, and adequate education. Likewise, many state constitutions establish fundamental guarantees of privacy, equal rights for women ("little ERAs"), and environmental quality. Such provisions empower state governments to pursue certain policies. There are no similar clauses in the federal Constitution.

What is often overlooked by policy analysts is the fact that such constitutional guarantees also expand the scope of state judicial power. Consider the case of educational funding. Both federal and state governments contribute to the funding of education. However, state courts have much more power to impact state funding of education than federal courts have to impact federal or state spending. The reason for the disparity in power is that federal courts cannot point to any provision in the U.S. Constitution that establishes jurisdiction over education funding. There are no federal guarantees to a public education. As such, plaintiffs unhappy about federal education funding cannot claim that any of their federal rights have been violated. State constitutions, and therefore, state courts, do not face such a dilemma. Since most state constitutions promise their citizens a public education, state citizens can go to state court and claim their state constitution is being violated. The existence of state constitutional education provisions gives state courts the authority to ensure minimum levels of education spending and an equal distribution of education spending across the state.

The above scenario is not just a legal hypothesis. In 2003 the Nevada Supreme Court ordered the Nevada legislature to fund education at higher levels. The Nevada legislature faces a variety of procedural hurdles before enacting a law. The legislature must balance the budget, but cannot raise taxes unless there is a two-thirds vote. Because of these dual requirements the legislature was unable to agree on an appropriations bill for the state school system. In response, the governor sued the legislature in the Nevada Supreme Court. Because Article 11, Section 6 of the Nevada Constitution "compels the Legislature to support and maintain the public schools," the Nevada court ordered the legislature to ignore the two-thirds vote provision and "fulfill its obligations under the Constitution of Nevada by raising sufficient revenues to fund education while maintaining a balanced budget" (*Guinn v. Legislature of Nevada* [2003]). Because the Nevada Constitution explicitly requires the funding of education, the Nevada courts had the power to order the legislature to raise taxes and then require that the funding be spent on education. Federal courts, lacking such specific authoritative grants of power, do not have the ability to influence public policy so directly.

The Nevada Supreme Court is not alone in challenging legislative autonomy over school financing. Alan Tarr (1992) records that between 1973 and 1994, twenty-two state courts accepted constitutional challenges regarding school finance, and in ten of those cases, the state courts demanded significant changes to the funding system.

Judicial Gatekeeping

The power of state courts is also enhanced by liberal standing requirements established in most state constitutions. *Standing* is the judicial requirement that individuals show they have been directly harmed before gaining access to the courts. The federal requirements for standings are relatively high. For example, federal taxpayers cannot challenge federal statutes simply because they are taxpayers. Many state constitutions, however, do not limit their court's jurisdictions to cases where plaintiffs meet federal standing requirements. In fact, many state constitutions explicitly provide for suits by taxpayers. Tarr and Porter note that thirty-four states provide for taxpayer suits against the state government and almost all states allow for suits against local governments.

Liberal standing criteria enhances the power of state courts because it provides state courts with a venue to impact state policies. If state courts are unable to hear cases because plaintiffs lack standing, those state courts cannot issue rulings that will alter state policy. However, if it is easy to access state courts, state judges will be able to hear all types of cases covering all areas of policy, and subsequently issue rulings that alter those policies.

State courts also have the authority to issue common law decisions. Common law is established through judicial rulings, not legislative enactments (statutory law) or constitutional amendments (constitutional law). Common law relies on precedents to bind lower courts to previous decisions handed down by higher courts. The purpose of common law is to fill in the gaps of vaguely written statutory law. Some well-known examples of federal common law include the Miranda rights, the exclusionary rule, and even privacy rights that ensure abortion rights. State judges also have the power to craft common law by issuing decisions that interpret state statutes or constitutions. The power to fashion common law comes from state constitutions. When state courts are granted jurisdiction by state constitutions, those courts also acquire the inherent and concurrent authority to issue rulings regarding their areas of jurisdiction and such rulings become part of common law.

At the state level, significant amounts of property, contract, and tort law, as well as corporate and criminal law, are created by common law. The power to craft common law is tantamount to the power to craft legislation. Even though state constitutions only grant state courts judicial power, the reality of common law is that state courts have the power to act like legislative bodies and write their own laws. Furthermore, in

Courts Make Policy by Defining Constitutional Rights

Some of America's most well-known laws were never enacted by the U.S. Congress or any state legislature. Instead, they were written by judges. Most Americans who have watched a television show about police officers know that citizens must be read their rights before being interrogated. These rights, which include "the right to remain silent," are known as Miranda rights. In *Miranda v. Arizona* (1966), the Supreme Court issued a ruling that all police officers must read defendants a list of rights. If the police failed to do so, the courts could throw out defendants' incriminating testimony.

Previously, in the 1961 case *Mapp v. Ohio*, the Supreme Court created new common law known as the exclusionary rule. The exclusionary rule requires police officers to obtain a legitimate warrant before collecting evidence against a defendant. If a warrant is not obtained, the courts may exclude the incriminating evidence from being presented at trial.

Ernesto Miranda was convicted of a rape-kidnapping after confessing during a police interrogation with no attorney present. In Miranda v. Arizona *(1966), the U.S. Supreme Court overturned his conviction and established the now commonly used "Miranda Warning." This is an example of how courts affect policy. (AP/Wide World Photos)*

the landmark case *Erie v. Tompkins* (1938), the U.S. Supreme Court ruled that federal courts must follow state common law when deciding issues that relate to state governance. The impact of this case was to grant state courts considerable power over, and autonomy from, federal judges.

State Statutes

State constitutions are not the only source of law within a state. State legislatures, as empowered by state constitutions, have the authority to draft statutes. In fact, an overwhelming majority of all laws are statutory laws, not constitutional laws. Legislative statutes may be as mundane as speed limits or as complicated as regulating property rights. All state statutes, regardless of complexity, have the force of law and therefore are enforceable by state judges.

State statutes outline the basic rules by which citizens live. As such, statutes form the basis for almost all judicial decisions. Courts are responsible for ensuring that laws are fairly applied and that punishments are distributed if laws are broken. Furthermore, state statutes can be as general as some constitutional provisions. Whenever statutes are vaguely drafted, courts must employ their interpretive methods to apply the law to individual circumstances. Other than rare federal and state constitutional grants of authority, all state judicial power flows from legislative statutes.

For example, the primary role of the legislature is to write the statutes the courts must interpret and enforce. Therefore, judges cannot simply punish individuals who engage in objectionable behavior. They must confine themselves to enforcing the laws the legislature has passed. In the early 1980s state courts were powerless to punish individuals for the act of stalking. Despite the fact that many women were being terrorized by ex-spouses and obsessed strangers, the courts had no power to prevent such behavior because, at the time, no antistalking statutes existed. It was not until the early 1990s, after states drafted new antistalking criminal statutes, that state judges could intervene on behalf of women who were victimized.

The Federal Constitution

State courts and judges also obtain authority from the U.S. Constitution and federal common law. When the Constitution was written in 1787, the states that participated in the process jealously guarded their sovereignty. Many Framers sought to delegate as few powers to the federal government as was necessary to conduct foreign affairs, regulate interstate commerce, and maintain domestic stability. The result was a constitution that limited the powers of the federal government to the eighteen enumerated powers identified in Article I, Section 8 of the U.S. Constitution. All other powers were reserved for the states. The concept of reserved powers for the states was formalized with the passage of the Tenth Amendment two years after the ratification of the Constitution. The reserved powers for the states include police powers, which typically encompass the authority to regulate all criminal behavior, domestic relations such as marriage and family law, and business relations within a state such as contract, tort, and corporate law.

Over time, the federal government has expanded the scope of its authority, at the expense of state authority, to address the challenges of various economic and military crises. Despite the gradual encroachment of federal power, the U.S. Supreme Court continues to protect the authority of state governments and state courts to adjudicate significant areas of public policy. For example, in two recent cases, *United States v. Lopez* (1995) and *United States v. Morrison* (2000), the U.S. Supreme Court rejected attempts by federal authorities to intrude on traditional state areas such as police powers and criminal law. The impact of these cases was to maintain state power, and concurrently, the power of state courts.

The U.S. Constitution also formalizes the relationship between federal law and state courts. Article VI or the supremacy clause states, "This Constitution, and the Laws of the United States which shall be made in Pursuance thereof; and all Treaties made, or which shall be made, under the Authority of the United States, shall be the supreme

Lopez: A Reemergence of State Sovereignty?

Both the *Lopez* and *Morrison* cases limited the scope of Congress's ability to interfere with state police powers. The *Lopez* decision invalidated sections of the Gun-Free Zone Act. The congressional act made it a crime to possess a gun within a school zone. However, the Supreme Court ruled that firearm regulation was traditionally a state responsibility and Congress's commerce powers did not include the power to regulate internal state criminal codes. A few years later, the U.S. Congress passed the Violence Against Women Act, which allowed victims of sexual assault to sue their assailants in state civil courts. The Supreme Court rejected this part of the law with the same reasoning as *Lopez*.

Law of the Land; and the Judges in every State shall be bound thereby, any Thing in the Constitution or Laws of any State to the Contrary notwithstanding."

The indirect result of the supremacy clause is that state courts have the power of judicial review over any state law that violates the U.S. Constitution. Judicial review is the ability to invalidate laws that conflict with constitutional law. This means that state courts have the power to reject the laws passed by their state legislatures if they feel those laws conflict with the U.S. Constitution or any other federal laws.

The California Supreme Court provides some examples of how the supremacy clause is used by state courts. In 1995, the California Supreme Court used the supremacy clause to reject state legislation regarding credit card interest rates. In *Smiley v. Citibank*, the Court ruled that certain California rules relating to interest rates were invalid because they conflicted with federally mandated rules about interest rates. Eight years later, in *White v. Davis*, the same court ordered the California state government to pay all its nonexempt employees despite its failure to pass an appropriations bill

Fearing the Power of the Federal Courts

In 1788, after the Constitution was drafted in Philadelphia, the document was sent out to the respective states for ratification. During the ratification debates, a group of citizens known as the Anti-Federalists were opposed to the adoption of the new constitution. The supremacy clause was one of many reasons the Anti-Federalists opposed the Constitution. The Anti-Federalists argued that the supremacy clause would be used by the U.S. Supreme Court to overrule the decisions made by state courts. Robert Yates, writing under the pseudonym "Brutus" claimed, "The powers of these [federal courts] are very extensive. It is easy to see, that in the common course of things, these courts will eclipse the dignity, and take away from the respectability, of the state courts. These courts will be, in themselves, totally independent of the states . . . they will swallow up all the powers of the courts in the respective states." While Yates' fears about the impact of such a development are open for debate, there can be no denying that federal courts have used the supremacy clause to contravene the will of state courts.

For more on Yates and his alter ego, the Anti-Federalist Brutus, see Anti-Federalist #17 (Oct 18th, 1787), http://press-pubs.uchicago.edu /founders/documents/v1ch8s13.html (accessed March 29, 2006).

authorizing payment. The court reasoned that the federal Fair Labor Standards Act required the payment of the employees and the supremacy clause empowered the state supreme court to enforce the federal mandate, regardless of existing state rules.

Grants of Jurisdiction

Jurisdiction is the power to hear and determine a case. State courts are granted jurisdiction by either state constitutions or state statutes. Without jurisdiction, courts have no legal authority to compel parties to carry out any action or any authority to interpret statutes. There are several types of jurisdiction, and each type confers a specific amount of authority.

In Personam

In personam jurisdiction is based on geography. Courts have in personam jurisdiction over a defendant simply as a result of the defendant's physical presence in the state. For example, Montana state courts have jurisdiction over Montana residents simply because those residents live in Montana. In personam jurisdiction also includes nonresidents who have met the minimum contacts test. The minimum contacts doctrine states that if an individual has had sufficient contacts with entities within a state, even if the person does not live in that state, that person is under the jurisdiction of that state. Common actions that establish minimum contacts are doing business within a state, advertising within a state, or accepting insurance payments from a state. Individuals can also establish in personam jurisdiction through their own consent. Residents of one state may choose to file suit in another state. By choosing to file in a state in which one is not a resident, the law assumes that one has consented to that jurisdiction. And finally, in personam jurisdiction can be established through long arm statutes. Long arm statutes establish jurisdiction over nonresidents if the cause of action affects local plaintiffs. The most common use of long arm statutes is to give local courts jurisdiction over defendants from other states who have been involved in local auto accidents.

In Rem

State courts also have *in rem* jurisdiction. The court obtains in rem jurisdiction as a result of property being located within its state. Individuals may live in one state but own property in another. In these and other cases, state courts have in rem jurisdiction over such local property regardless of the residency of the owner. State courts often use their in rem jurisdiction to issue liens, foreclose property, or garnish income.

Legal Culture and Approaches to Interpretation

State constitutions and state statutes grant state courts their jurisdictions and powers of enforcement. However, individual justices interpret those grants of power differently.

The way a judge interprets his or her grants of power will affect the level of authority state courts possess. Some justices prefer to interpret their powers very narrowly and limit their use of judicial power. Other justices prefer to take a broad interpretation of their grants of authority and wield their judicial power more comprehensively.

Judicial Restraint

Judges who impose a self-limitation on their use of judicial power follow a philosophy of "judicial restraint." Judges who adopt this interpretive philosophy believe that courts should try to limit their roles in governance. They feel that democratically elected representatives should have the primary responsibility for creating laws in their state. Judges who believe in judicial restraint will only interfere in the lawmaking process if a state legislature has clearly violated its own constitution, or written a law so vaguely that judges must interpret it for the law to have any effect. Additionally, judges who believe in judicial restraint feel that judges should interpret the law, but not write the law. Therefore, they refrain from drafting common law. Courts create common law when they establish new legal requirements in their written opinions. And finally, judges who follow judicial restraint fervently believe in the concept of separation of powers, and therefore try to avoid dictating to the other branches of government.

State courts with a legal culture of judicial restraint will exercise less authority. The very concept of judicial restraint is to limit the power of courts. By deferring to the elected branches, and resisting the tendency to write common law, courts with a culture of restraint will be less intrusive into the governing process.

Judicial Activism

In contrast, judges who take a greater role in the governing process advocate a philosophy of "judicial activism." Judicial activists feel that judges need to assert themselves into the political process in three ways. Activist courts are more likely to invalidate legislation (judicial review), write their own laws (common law), and create new constitutional rights such as privacy.

Voters and the Limits of Judicial Activism

State judges who adopt an activist approach to legal interpretation sometimes suffer electoral reprisals at the hands of voters. Whereas federal judges are appointed for life most state constitutions have recall provisions and require judges to face periodic retention elections. In 1986, California voters recalled three sitting supreme court justices including the Chief Justice Rose Bird. The voters were reacting to a variety of activist decisions, the most salient of which were repeated refusals to implement the state's death penalty statutes and onerous business regulations. The successful recall had a direct impact on the way the California Supreme Court applies the death penalty. After the recall, the new judges were much more likely to uphold death penalty sentences.

Each time a judge or a court invalidates legislation the judge is replacing the will of the legislature with the will of the court. Courts that are more willing to use the power of judicial review exercise more authority over a legislature than restraintist courts. (A more detailed analysis of judicial review appears on p. 66.)

Activist judges reject the notion that only legislatures should write law. Activist judges believe that constitutions outline broad goals and visions, but courts must craft specific details and legal procedures when they issue written opinions.

Activist judges also create new rights that are not expressly delineated in the state constitution. For example, many courts have declared that individuals have a right to privacy even though their state constitutions do not specifically register a "right to privacy" anywhere in the text. Some activist judges use judicially created common law to grant other rights. For instance, the Massachusetts Supreme Court established the right of homosexuals to marry. The court did this by interpreting, very broadly, the text of its constitution, in addition to previously established common law.

State courts with a culture of judicial activism may exercise more authority than courts with a culture of restraint. Activist courts often see their role as protecting the individual against the tyranny of the majority. To protect minorities from electoral majorities, they insert themselves into the political process by limiting the power of the elected branches of government. Therefore, a court with a culture of activism is more likely to use its judicial powers to dictate to other branches of government.

Limits of State Court Authority

Just as state constitutions, the federal Constitution, and state legislatures empower state courts, they also serve to limit the power of state courts. State legislatures limit the discretion of judges, state constitutions limit the jurisdiction of state courts, and the U.S. Constitution mandates that state courts enforce federal law.

Legislative Limits on State Courts

State legislatures are typically responsible for determining the basic nuts-and-bolts aspects of state courts. Legislatures determine how many judges will make up a court, the judges' salaries, and the structure of the public defender system.

Judges are also limited in the punishments they can dispense. Whereas judges have considerable discretion over what types of evidence and testimony can be heard in their courtrooms, state legislatures have more control over the punishment phase of trials. Legislatures, not the courts, have the power to determine which crimes are classified as misdemeanors or felonies. Misdemeanors carry smaller punishments than felony convictions. Concurrently, legislatures determine the range of punishments that are available for judges to impose on the guilty. State judges have some latitude when it comes to punishment, but the upper and lower limits are set by the legislature.

Recently, state legislatures and citizens have moved to further limit the discretion of courts in the punishment phase of trials. Many state legislatures, or citizen ballot measures, have imposed mandatory minimum sentencing laws. These laws require that judges impose a certain level of punishment regardless of the opinions of the trial judge. In 1994, California voters and the California legislature separately passed the Three Strikes and You're Out initiative that requires judges to impose a life sentence on criminals after they have committed a third felony. By 1995, twenty-four states had added three-strikes laws to their criminal statutes. Many state judges object to mandatory minimum sentences. They argue that judges are sometimes forced to impose unfair sentences and that court dockets and state prisons are becoming overwhelmed. In fact, some judges, in protest, have resigned over mandatory minimum sentence legislation.

Federal Limitations on State Courts

The federal government also imposes some limitations on state court power. The most fundamental limitation on state courts from the federal government is the requirement that state judges enforce federal law. In this respect, the supremacy clause is a double-edged sword. From one standpoint, the clause empowers state judges to invalidate state laws. However, the supremacy clause also mandates that state judges abide by constitutional standards and federal statutory law. Such a requirement inherently limits the discretion of state courts. For example, in the late 1950s, before the U.S. Supreme Court began incorporating the Fourth, Fifth, and Sixth Amendments into the states, many state courts and judges had considerable latitude on issues such as admission of evidence and testimony, providing counsel to defendants, sanctioning interrogation techniques, determining the make-up of juries, and other criminal procedures. However, with landmark cases such as *Mapp v. Ohio* (1961), *Gideon v. Wainwright* (1963), and *Escobedo v. Illinois* (1964), the Warren Court established new mandates on criminal procedures that state courts were required to enforce. At the time, many state judges criticized the federal court for intruding on state court prerogatives. Despite some initial resistance, all state courts now accept these federal mandates. The interaction between federal and state courts is called judicial federalism and is discussed in more detail on p. 83.

Federal law can also limit the power of state courts through a doctrine known as *preemption*. Preemption doctrine states that when the U.S. Congress passes legislation, that legislation takes precedence over, or preempts, state law on the same topic. Therefore, when state law conflicts with federal law, federal law triumphs. Another way to view preemption doctrine is to see it as a seizure of jurisdiction. As noted earlier, one of the sources of state court power is the constitutional grant of jurisdiction. Preemption is the federal government taking jurisdiction away from state courts. Therefore, every time the federal government enacts laws that preempt state laws, state courts lose the jurisdiction to resolve claims that fall under the scope of that legislation.

Once Opposed, Supreme Court's Defendants' Rights Rulings Gain Local Acceptance

In *Gideon v. Wainwright* (1963) the Supreme Court ruled that not only are defendants entitled to an attorney, but that the state must provide attorneys to defendants who cannot afford to pay for one. In *Escobedo v. Illinois* (1964) the Supreme Court went a step further and mandated that states must make attorneys available to defendants as soon as the interrogation process begins as opposed to after a defendant is formally indicted. At the time, both of these decisions attracted the ire of many state supreme courts. However, today, these cases are generally accepted as fundamental tenets of criminal due process.

Danny Escobedo sits in a police station after his arrest in the fatal shooting of his brother-in-law. The Supreme Court threw out his conviction because he was denied access to an attorney at the police station. (UPI–Bettmann/Corbis)

Two areas in which preemption doctrine has limited the power of state courts are labor law and medical law. In terms of labor law, many plaintiffs file suit in state court when they feel their labor rights have been violated. Often, there are specific state statutes that encourage plaintiffs to file in state court. However, Congress's passage of the National Labor Relations Act (NLRA) and its subsequent amendments has preempted much labor law away from states and therefore state courts. In *Burton v. Covenant Care* (2002), an employee filed suit in a California court after she was fired for discussing her wage information with other employees. However, the California appellate court refused to rule on the case because it had no jurisdiction to do so. The NLRA had preempted that authority away from state courts.

The same situation has confronted state suits regarding medical care provided by health maintenance organizations (HMOs) and managed care organizations (MCOs). Many of these suits are rejected by state courts because they lack the authority to hear such cases. The Employee Retired Income Security Act of 1974 (ERISA) shifts the jurisdiction for these types of cases to federal court. Therefore, when plaintiffs attempt to sue for malpractice in state courts, HMO defendants usually move the case to federal court under the preemption doctrine.

THE ROLE OF COURTS AND JURIES

There are many different types of state courts. Some state courts, called limited juris-diction courts, deal only with specific issues. For example, there are traffic courts, pro-bate courts, small-claims courts, and juvenile courts. Hawaii even has a water court to hear cases just about water rights. Each of the aforementioned courts adjudicates only those disputes that fall within their jurisdictions and areas of law. In contrast, other state courts, called general jurisdiction courts, hear all types of cases. In addition, gen-eral jurisdiction courts address larger issues such as the interpretation of state statutes and the state constitution.

State court systems also rely on juries to help adjudicate conflicts. In some courts, such as small-claims courts, judges rely on their own judgment to determine the out-come of a case. However, in other courts, judges rely on juries to determine the guilt or innocence of a defendant. As there are different types of courts, there are also different types of juries, each serving different legal purposes. State courts use both grand juries and petit juries. Grand juries decide whether the state has enough evidence against a de-fendant to issue an indictment, but petit juries decide questions of fact, such as the guilt or innocence of a defendant.

Although a more detailed discussion of state court structure appears in Chapter 3, it is important to briefly introduce the topic here. The structure of state courts impacts the roles different state courts perform in our legal system.

Courts of Original Jurisdiction

Legal disputes are originally heard in courts of original jurisdiction. These courts admit evidence and hear testimony from participants in the case. It is said that courts of orig-inal jurisdiction hear questions of fact not questions of law. This means that original ju-risdiction courts decide issues such as: Is the defendant guilty? Who should have cus-tody of the child? Who is responsible for the property damage and how much should they pay? Courts of original jurisdiction do not entertain questions such as: Is this law constitutional? How should this vague statute be interpreted? Does the governor have the power to do that? These are questions of law and are left to courts with appellate jurisdiction.

State court systems typically have two types of original jurisdiction courts. Limited jurisdiction courts only hear certain types of cases. As noted earlier, traffic courts only hear cases involving traffic accidents. They do not hear child custody cases or corporate tort cases. Their jurisdiction is limited to traffic cases. Many states also have general jurisdiction courts. These courts hear all types of cases; from criminal cases to tort cases to family law cases. As long as the issue deals with a question of fact a general ju-risdiction court has the authority to adjudicate the case.

Courts of Appellate Jurisdiction

Appellate courts entertain questions of law. In other words, they accept as true all the issues of fact that have been determined by courts of original jurisdiction. Appellate courts accept appeals from lower courts only if there is a question about the validity or interpretation of statutory law or constitutional law. For example, criminal suspects are found guilty or not guilty in a court of original jurisdiction. The defendant's innocence or guilt is a question of fact. On appeal, a convicted defendant can raise issues of law, but may not revisit questions of guilt or innocence. An appellant may challenge a lower court's interpretation of a statute or the constitutionality of a statute. An appellant may argue that his Fourth Amendment or other procedural rights were violated. But these questions do not address the guilt or innocence of the defendant; they simply question the validity of the law or its interpretation.

Typically, legislatures draft generally worded or even vague statutes. Legislators cannot foresee every circumstance for which the law may need to apply. Vague or general statutes may not be specific enough to provide sufficient guidance to courts that are asked to apply such statutes to specific circumstances. The role of appellate courts is to draft common law that will provide specific ways to interpret vague statutes. For example, many states require that special education students be educated in the least restrictive environment. However, many lower court judges have a difficult time determining what constitutes a "least restrictive environment." It is the role of appellate courts to create specific criteria to determine what schools need to provide to create a least restrictive environment. The common law developed by appellate courts is then implemented by lower courts of original jurisdiction. In a legal sense, appellate courts write the rules and original jurisdiction courts enforce the rules.

Appellate courts can also invalidate statutes passed by the legislature. As noted earlier, this is the power of judicial review. Original jurisdiction courts do not have the power of judicial review. Lower courts must enforce statutes as they are written. However, appellate courts may nullify laws in their entirety or just selective provisions of the law. Some states, such as Alabama and Tennessee, have two appellate court systems—one for criminal appeals and a second for civil appeals. Such a system allows judges to specialize in one field of law.

Courts of Last Resort

Every state has a supreme court, or what is termed a court of last resort. Supreme courts are so termed because there are no further appeals after a case is heard in a court of last resort. Not all states refer to their court of last resort as a supreme court. For example, Maryland simply refers to its highest court as the court of appeals. In Oklahoma, there are two supreme courts: one for criminal appeals and one for civil appeals. Supreme courts are a special type of appellate court (supreme courts have limited original jurisdiction in select areas of law). If a defendant or plaintiff loses a case in a lower appellate court, he or she can appeal to the state supreme court. Other than being the highest court in the state, supreme courts function just like other appellate courts.

State supreme courts have either mandatory jurisdiction or discretionary jurisdiction. Supreme courts with mandatory jurisdiction must accept and adjudicate appeals cases. In cases where the court's jurisdiction is discretionary, it has the option of refusing to hear the case. In general, state supreme courts have mandatory jurisdiction in some areas of law and discretionary jurisdiction in other areas of law. Although the rules regarding mandatory and discretionary jurisdiction change from state to state, there exist some general patterns. Typically, smaller states, where the volume of cases is low, have supreme courts with mandatory jurisdiction. In larger states, where the case volume is higher, mandatory jurisdiction is usually reserved for civil cases exceeding a certain value, death penalty appeals, felony convictions, and administrative agency decisions. Supreme courts often have discretionary jurisdiction over appeals from cases dealing with small claims, minor criminal offenses, and many types of juvenile cases.

When studying state court systems it is important to remember that no two states conduct their judicial affairs exactly alike. States take different approaches to creating limited jurisdiction courts, appellate jurisdiction courts, and courts of last resort. The structure of the state court system influences what roles and functions the different types of courts perform. In states with limited jurisdiction courts, judges can specialize in one field of law. Because states create both original and appellate jurisdiction courts, some judges concentrate on questions of fact while other judges concentrate on questions of law.

In states with mostly discretionary jurisdiction, courts have the ability to set the legal agenda. Courts with discretionary jurisdiction can refuse to hear some cases but select others. The ability to set the legal agenda is often an underestimated power of courts. Agenda-setting power is the ability to determine which political and legal issues the state will focus on. Courts can signal to politicians, attorneys, and potential litigants which issues the court considers important, and which issues it does not. For example, a court may refuse to hear any business regulation cases, but accept all civil rights cases. In doing so, the court sets the agenda. The court signals to society at large that certain issues will command the court's attention and others will not. As a result, it is possible that some litigants will elect not to bring their cases to court; others, seeing that the court has signaled its interest in a specific field of law, will. In this way, the court can serve as a catalyst for pushing some areas of law and atrophying others.

Grand and Petit Juries

The American legal system uses two different types of juries. The petit jury is the most familiar to the casual legal observer. Petit juries determine issues of fact in criminal and civil proceedings. Simply put, petit juries declare the guilt or innocence of criminal defendants or determine the liability or lack of liability for civil defendants. In some states, and in some cases, petit juries impose sentences on guilty defendants. In other states, juries may only recommend sentences but the presiding judge makes the final determination. In civil trials, petit juries can impose damages.

Petit Juries

Petit juries typically consist of twelve members of society who are required to sit for the duration of one case. In some rare cases, state judicial systems allow six-person juries. To find a defendant criminally guilty, almost all states require that the jury be unanimous. However, the United State Supreme Court has held nonunanimous jury verdicts constitutional.

Grand Juries

Grand juries serve a different legal purpose. Grand juries determine if the state has the legal authority to issue indictments. Grand juries serve as a check on the discretion of state prosecutors and police officials. In the American legal system, police officers collect evidence and turn that evidence over to a prosecuting attorney. The prosecuting attorney decides if there is enough evidence to justify a trial. However, in cases when a more serious crime has been committed, the prosecuting attorney may not make that decision alone. The prosecuting attorney must present the evidence before a grand jury and request an indictment. The grand jury examines the evidence and even hears witnesses. If, after hearing the state's evidence, the grand jury decides there is enough evidence to justify a trial, it will issue an indictment. Issuing an indictment does not indicate that the grand jury believes the defendant is guilty. It simply indicates the grand jury felt there was enough evidence to merit a trial with a petit jury.

Grand juries are so called because they impanel more jurors; typically twenty-three people compose a grand jury. Grand juries meet and hear evidence in secret for several reasons: (1) to ensure that individuals whose indictment is being considered will not flee; (2) to prevent subornation of perjury or tampering with the witnesses who may testify before the grand jury and later appear at the trial of those indicted by it; (3) to encourage honest disclosures by witness; and (4) to protect the reputations of innocent individuals who grand juries refuse to indict.

The Fifth Amendment to the U.S. Constitution mandates that grand juries be used in the federal legal system. The Fifth Amendment states, "No person shall be held to answer for a capital or otherwise infamous crime, unless on a presentment or indictment of a Grand Jury, except in cases arising in the land or naval forces, or in the Militia, when in actual service in time of War or public danger . . . ." However, unlike most provisions in the Bill of Rights, the grand jury provision has never been incorporated to the states. Therefore, state court systems are not required by the Constitution to use grand juries but most do.

THE WORK OF STATE COURTS

In the United States the federal courts, especially the U.S. Supreme Court, get most of the attention. The national media tend to focus on issues that affect all Americans and legal decisions handed down in one state rarely qualify. The reality, however, is that state courts do most of the heavy lifting in America's legal system. State courts hear more cases, hand down more decisions, and adjudicate a wider field of legal questions than federal courts.

To begin with, the sheer size of the state court system dwarfs the federal system. State courts have more judges and hand down more decisions. In 2001, the federal courts employed 665 district judges, 167 appeals court judges, and 9 Supreme Court justices for a total of 841 judges. All combined, those 841 judges were confronted with approximately 2.6 million filings. In contrast, according to the National Court Statistics Project, during that same year, 15,555 state courts with over 29,000 judges processed 93 million court filings. A majority of the work was done in the 13,515 limited jurisdiction courts in comparison to the 2,040 general jurisdiction courts. The number of state judges has grown by about 1 percent a year since 1990.

In one aspect, the data are misleading. Traffic cases account for a significant number of the state court filings. The data in Table 2.1 (p. 56) shows that 55.7 million of the 93 million cases filed dealt with relatively simple traffic issues. However, even extracting the traffic cases, state courts still handled over 37 million filings. Recent studies indicate that the number of traffic filings has been falling since 1987 and other types of filings have been increasing. Again, Table 2.1 illustrates the numbers of non-traffic-related-cases and provides some selective comparisons to federal caseloads.

Sometimes, aggregate data can be overwhelming. In the case of state court filings, per capita data can offer a more nuanced perspective. For example, the data in Table 2.1 note that there were 15.8 million civil filings in 2001. However, in terms of per capita data, the number of civil filings represents about 6,000 filings for every 100,000 citizens. This means that about 6 percent of American citizens filed some type of civil suit in 2001. Not all state courts face the same rates of litigation. In Maryland, the state with the most prolific filing was about 15,000 per 100,000 citizens, whereas in Tennessee, the least prolific state in terms of civil filings, it was only 1,200 per 100,000.

Not only is the sheer size of the state court systems larger than the federal court system, state courts adjudicate a wider range of legal issues. State courts deal with private conflicts such as torts, contracts, death penalty appeals, attorney discipline, custody hearings, small claims, probate, divorce applications, criminal trials, and juvenile trials. To better understand state court systems, it is helpful to categorize state court workloads into four general divisions. State courts adjudicate criminal proceedings, civil proceedings, family law, and appeals. In recent years, the overwhelming number of private disputes has led courts to encourage alternative methods for resolving

TABLE 2.1   FEDERAL AND STATE COURT FILINGS, 2001

	Type	Filings	Change since 2000 (percent)
Federal Courts	**Criminal**	62,708	–0.1
	Civil	250,907	–3.3
	Bankruptcy	1,437,354	13.9
	Magistrates	873,948	8.2
	Total	2,624,917	9.7
State Courts	**Criminal**	14,054,945	–0.1
	Civil	15,792,277	5.6
	Domestic	5,300,114	2.2
	Juvenile	1,997,403	–0.4
	Traffic	55,685,616	–0.1
	Total	92,830,355	0.9

Source, state court data: Ostrom, Brian, Neal Kauder, and Robert LaFountain. 2002. *Examining the Work of State Courts, 2001: A National Perspective from the Court Statistics Project.* Williamsburg, VA: National Center for State Courts.

Source, federal court data: Judicial Business of the United States: Annual Report of the Director, 2001. Washington, DC: Administrative Office of the U.S. Courts.

disputes. Therefore, a complete study of state courts includes an examination of alternative dispute resolution methods that have arisen in the past few decades.

State courts do more than just hear private disagreements. State courts also hear public law cases. Public law is an area in which the courts must rule on the law itself, not a citizen's violation of the law. For example, state courts can use their powers of judicial review to invalidate legislative acts, interpret vague clauses in state laws, and even write new laws known as common law. State courts can use these same powers to invalidate or interpret laws passed by the people themselves. Many state constitutions allow for direct democracy where citizens can write state ballot measures enacting their own laws. Just like legislative acts, these new laws must be interpreted by state courts. Every time a state court invalidates a law, interprets a law, or writes new common law, it makes public policy.

Criminal Proceedings

Criminal law is predominantly the responsibility of state courts. Because the federal Constitution was designed to impart only specific and enumerated powers to the national government, states were left relatively undisturbed in the area of criminal law. Beginning with the New Deal and accelerating during the civil rights movement, the federal government started using its commerce clause powers as a vehicle to create federal police powers. Despite these trends, state courts still adjudicate most criminal law.

Criminal law can be subdivided into two categories: felonies and misdemeanors. A felony is a more serious crime than a misdemeanor. Felonies typically include crimes such as murder, rape, robbery, and arson. One cannot be charged with a felony unless a separate grand jury allows the prosecutor to file charges. Those convicted of a felony usually serve serious prison terms. Misdemeanors are lesser crimes and typically include petty crimes that inflict less than a certain dollar amount of damage. Prosecutors can file misdemeanor charges without the approval of a grand jury. Sometimes crimes once identified as misdemeanors become felonies. Many states once listed driving under the influence (DUI) as a misdemeanor, but after drunk driving became a salient issue, many states began to classify DUIs as felonies.

Judges within a state criminal court system are responsible for a variety of functions. Criminal proceedings usually begin with a preliminary hearing or a grand jury indictment. Absent a grand jury indictment, state judges can hold preliminary hearings to decide if there is enough evidence to warrant a trial. If the judge decides there is enough evidence to warrant a trial, the defendant is arraigned. At the arraignment, defendants are informed of charges against them and the judge asks for a plea. After entering a plea, judges either set bail or remand the defendant to jail to await trial.

Before the trial begins, judges entertain pretrial motions. During this stage of a criminal proceeding attorneys can make discovery motions, move that evidence be suppressed, and defense attorneys inform the judge of their defense strategy. For example, defense attorneys inform the judge they plan to argue insanity, self-defense, or some other legal defense.

Once a trial begins, judges serve as an umpire between the prosecution and defense attorneys. They ensure that all evidence is submitted according to the rules of law. They rule on objections from attorneys. They make sure witnesses are only asked questions that conform to the rules of evidence. After all the evidence and testimony have been introduced, it is the judges' role to inform the juries about the nature of the law. Judges instruct juries on what criteria must be met in order to return a guilty verdict. If juries become deadlocked the judge will work to overcome the stalemate without directly participating in the deliberations.

If the jury returns a guilty verdict, the judge is responsible for imposing a sentence. In some cases, the judge is solely responsible for the punishment phase of the trial. In other cases, juries recommend sentences to the judge.

As one can expect, the amount of time courts dedicate to criminal filings fluctuates with the overall crime rate. Between 1987 and 2001 the number of criminal filings rose 28 percent. However, remember that the population has also grown between 1987 and 2001.

Criminal law consumes more time and resources from state courts than civil matters. The reason is that criminal defendants are guaranteed certain procedural rights in state and federal constitutions. For example, criminal defendants are guaranteed attorneys, jury trials, and an appeals process. Civil litigants do not have such procedural guarantees. One of the ways state courts overcome the burden of criminal trials is to use a procedure called plea bargaining. Plea bargaining is a process in which attorneys for the defendant and the state compromise on charges and penalties. Typically, the attorney for the state or city offers to reduce the charges and promises to seek less serious penalties in return for a guilty plea from the defendant. If the defendant pleads guilty, a jury trial is not needed and the process can move directly to the penalty phase. According to empirical data, only 3 percent of all criminal cases actually end up before a jury. The other 97 percent are decided by plea bargains or a dismissal of the charges.

Civil Proceedings

Civil proceedings unfold analogous to criminal proceedings. However, civil proceedings employ different legal standards and impose different sanctions. Because civil proceedings don't deal with criminal statutes, there are no arraignments, grand juries, and bail proceedings. Instead, civil proceedings begin with a pleading stage. During the pleading, parties inform the court of the nature of their dispute. The plaintiff in the case issues a complaint and the defendant offers a reply.

Like criminal proceedings, civil proceedings have pretrial motions where attorneys make discovery requests, move for summary judgments, and indicate who they plan to depose. Once the trial begins, civil trials are similar to criminal trials. Witnesses are called, evidence is introduced, and judges make rulings on the appropriateness of each.

A significant difference between criminal and civil proceedings is that civil proceedings have a much lower burden of proof standard. Criminal juries are required to find defendants guilty beyond a reasonable doubt. However, civil juries are held to lower standards. They may find a party responsible for damages simply based on a preponderance of the evidence. Second, civil juries do not impose prison sentences; they award monetary damages.

Tort Cases

When individuals or businesses feel they have suffered harm by another individual or business they can file a lawsuit seeking compensation. These types of suits are called torts. Tort cases are civil filings. A civil filing seeks monetary damages, but not criminal punishment. In the past decade, national and state politicians have turned their attention to the tort system in America. A few high profile cases, in which large damages were awarded for seemingly trivial accidents, have made America's tort system a political issue.

Because the national and local media often highlight astronomically high tort awards, or frivolous cases, it is commonly assumed that state courts are overburdened by tort filings. The data, although not comprehensive, suggests qualified support for this contention. Between 1975 and 1986, tort filings in 16 of the more populous states shows a jump from about 200,000 filings to more than 300,000 filings per year. One contributing factor to the increase in tort filings was the liberalization of standing requirements. Courts require that a plaintiff have standing before he or she can file a suit. Prior to the 1970s, individuals had to show that they had personally suffered direct harm before they could file a suit. Such a standard prevented taxpayers or special interest groups from suing the government over public policy. However, in the 1970s, many states, by statute or constitutional amendment, eased their standing requirements to allow more legal suits.

In addition, in the 1970s courts began to liberalize the use of punitive damages. Before the 1970s, punitive damages were only awarded for intentional torts. These were torts where the defendant intentionally harmed another individual. Eventually, the courts lowered the standard to gross negligence. Under this standard, plaintiffs did not have to prove a tort was intentionally committed; they only had to show that defendants acted without regard for others. When the legal standard was lowered, the number of tort filings began to increase.

Yet since 1996, tort filings have shown a modest decline. Many scholars attribute the decline since 1996 to the host of tort reform measures that swept the states in the early 1990s. In fact, in a study of thirty states between 1992 and 2001, there was an average decline in tort filings by 15 percent. One of the reasons people sometimes misinterpret the tort filing data is that they fail to take into account an increase in population over time. Simply totaling the number of medical malpractice suits between 1992 and 2001 shows a 24 percent increase. However, if population increases are accounted for, the number of malpractice filings per 100,000 citizens actually fell 1

Nation Responds to Local Court's Award

Calls for state tort reform often follow high-profile cases in which juries have awarded seemingly astronomical awards for trivial offenses. For example, in 1992, 79-year-old Stella Liebeck of Albuquerque, New Mexico, spilled a cup of McDonald's coffee in her lap while riding in her grandson's sports car. Claiming the coffee was too hot, she successfully sued the restaurant for $200,000 in compensatory damages and an additional $2.7 million in punitive damages. Critics argued that Liebeck was responsible for spilling the coffee on herself, and regardless of fault, the award was too high. The story was picked up by the national media and repeated so often that if has become part of American pop culture. Incidents like those of Liebeck contribute toward a general dissatisfaction with state tort systems.

TABLE 2.2   GROWTH RATES OF TORT FILINGS IN 30 STATES, 1991 TO 2000

State	Filings per 100,000 Population 1991	2000	Percent Change 1991–2000
Unified Courts			
Kansas	163	203	24
North Dakota	84	96	15
Connecticut	494	543	10
Puerto Rico[1]	242	261	8
Missouri	412	341	–17
Wisconsin	179	144	–20
Minnesota	164	113	–31
California	376	210	–44
General Jurisdiction Courts			
Indiana	147	229	55
New York	364	413	13
Utah	98	103	6
Alaska	147	148	0
North Carolina	128	124	–4
Idaho	121	114	–6
New Jersey	949	885	–7
Florida	333	308	–7
Ohio	315	266	–15
Washington	227	191	–16
Nevada	457	374	–18
Tennessee	267	209	–22
Arkansas	215	165	–23
Maine	137	98	–28
Oregon	277	198	–29
Hawaii	208	141	–32
Michigan	340	224	–34
Maryland	335	220	–34
Texas	254	164	–35
Colorado	186	119	–36
Arizona	412	239	–42
Massachusetts	229	126	–45
Average	**275**	**232**	**–16**
Median	**235**	**201**	**–15**

Source: Ostrom, Brian, Neal Kauder, and Robert LaFountain. 2002. *Examining the Work of State Courts, 2002: A National Perspective from the Court Statistics Project.* Williamsburg, VA: National Center for State Courts.

[1]Unincorporated U.S. Commonwealth governed by U.S. law.

percent in that nine year period. Table 2.2 highlights the growth rates of tort filings in thirty states between 1991 and 2000.

Contracts

Contracts are promises, or a set of promises, between two participants in which both participants agree to certain obligations. Contracts can be written or oral. People who write and sign contracts devote considerable effort to ensuring that contracts anticipate every possible contingency. Despite that effort, there are unforeseen circumstances that contracts do not anticipate. When that happens, judges must interpret contracts and decide which parties to the contract bear certain obligations.

In other circumstances, the guidelines of the contract are perfectly clear, but one or more parties to the contract refuse to meet their obligations. In these cases, when asked, judges step in and require that delinquent parties meet their obligations. Sometimes, this requires that a judge seize property or other assets to compensate individuals who have entered into a contract.

State courts are also called on, in appropriate cases, to declare contracts void. In certain instances, contracts can be entered into without the legal consent of one of the parties. Courts have held that consent is absent when one of the parties was under duress or undue influence. Courts also void contracts where one of the parties was subject to fraud or misrepresentation.

Surprisingly, contract cases typically account for more of a state court's workload than tort cases. For example, in 1987 there were 369,000 contract filings in state courts (in a seventeen-state study) but only 221,000 tort filings. However, contract cases rarely attract media attention. By 2001, tort filings increased 20 percent from 1987 and contract filings had decreased 14 percent in that same time frame. However, contract cases still outnumbered tort cases by several thousand.

Unenforceable Contracts: Examples from Minnesota Law

Minnesota contract law states that contracts are unenforceable for the following reasons:

A mutual mistake by both parties to a contract on an important issue makes the contract unenforceable. However, a mistake by only one party does not necessarily make the contract void.

Duress is the use of force or pressure by one party to make the other party agree to the contract. The force does not have to be physical—one could be put under mental duress. The use of duress makes the contract voidable by the party under duress.

Fraud is the intentional misrepresentation of an important issue of the contract. The presence of fraud in a contractual proceeding makes the contract voidable by the party upon whom the fraud was perpetrated.

For more on Minnesota contract law visit: "Guide to Minnesota Law: Minnesota Contract Law," http://www.weblocator.com/attorney/mn/law/contract.html (accessed March 29, 2006).

Family Law

Family law is different from criminal and civil law in that the main purpose of family law is neither to punish nor to award damages. Family law is more concerned with overseeing the legal aspects of marriage, mediating family disputes, and insuring that family members are protected. Judges involved in family law grant marriages and divorces, award child custody after divorce, regulate adoptions, and decide paternity responsibilities.

Domestic Relations

Domestic relations include most of the laws that regulate relationships between families. In fact, many people refer to domestic relations law as family law. State courts deal with a lot of types of domestic relations. Courts grant divorces between married couples, decide custody issues when the parties to the divorce have children, resolve paternity claims, establish child support payments, and regulate adoptions. In 2001, there were over 5.2 million domestic relations cases filed in state courts. Paternity hearings are the most common type of domestic relations case. Because of recent federal laws streamlining child support laws, child support cases have fallen considerably in the last few years and now account for the smallest proportion of state court dockets.

Juvenile Cases

Juvenile courts are special courts of limited jurisdiction. Such courts are designed to adjudicate cases in which a minor has committed a crime or when a minor needs protection from abusive or neglectful guardians. Usually, anyone under the age of seventeen is eligible for juvenile court. In most cases, juvenile records are kept sealed until the minor reaches adulthood, at which point they are expunged. The rationale is to allow children who have committed crimes to have a fresh start when they enter adulthood. However, as it has become more common for minors to commit serious offenses such as murder, many states have lowered the age at which a person can be considered an adult.

Juvenile (In)justice: Trying Children as Adults

Deciding when a child should be considered an adult and prosecuted in adult courts is becoming a controversial issue in many state courts. In 1999, twelve-year-old Lionel Tate killed six-year-old playmate Tiffany Eunick. Tate's attorneys claimed that it was an accidental death resulting from Tate trying to mimic professional wrestlers. Florida prosecuting attorney Ken Padowitz decided to try Tate as an adult in criminal court. After Tate's mother and attorney rejected a plea offer, the Florida jury found Tate guilty of first-degree murder and the judge sentenced Tate to life in prison. The idea that a twelve-year-old minor could be sentenced to life shocked many Floridians.

In 2004 a Florida appeals court overturned Tate's conviction. The court reasoned that Tate was too young, and therefore not competent, to participate in his own defense.

Judges who work for juvenile courts often take a greater interest in the background and environment of the child than they would if they were overseeing an adult case. Many juvenile court judges see their role differently than judges in criminal courts. Juvenile court judges rely heavily on officers of the court, such as probation officers, doctors, and psychologists, for information about the juvenile case before them. Judges in juvenile court typically use the information to craft a ruling that is designed to reform the child. Juvenile courts are less interested in punishment than they are in protecting and molding minors. For example, it is common for juvenile court judges to require defendants write letters of apology, or earn money to compensate victims of their crimes. Sentences often include community service or mandatory counseling. Only in extreme circumstances do juvenile court judges confine minors to detention institutions.

For the past decade, juvenile court filings have averaged just fewer than 2 million per year. Approximately 60 percent of those filings involve some type of delinquent act by the minor. About 20 percent of the cases confront child protection issues such as delinquent or abusive guardians. The remaining cases typically deal with issues that are unique to minors. For example, only a minor can be charged with truancy, or being a runaway.

Appeals

Like the federal court system, state court systems include appellate courts that entertain questions of law. Tort, contract, criminal, domestic, and juvenile cases are heard in trial courts that only entertain questions of fact. However, participants in trial courts often disagree with the rulings or procedures as they were conducted in the trial court. Such individuals can seek a remedy in appellate court. Appellate court judges review lower court trials and decide if the participants' procedural rights were protected. If they find errors by the lower courts, appellate courts can craft remedies and refer the cases back to the trial courts. Appellate court judges also reexamine how lower court judges have interpreted statutes or constitutional provisions. If an appellate court disagrees with the way a lower court has interpreted a statute, it can remand the case to the lower court. The remand usually comes with instructions on how the lower courts should have interpreted the statute or constitutional provision.

Appellate courts hear both mandatory and discretionary appeals. Appellate courts must accept mandatory appeals, but can elect not to hear discretionary appeals. All death penalty appeals are mandatory appeals. For the past decade, total appellate filings in state courts have hovered around 300,000 per year: 68 percent of the cases appellate courts hear come from mandatory appeals while the remaining 32 percent come from discretionary appeals. The composition of these appeals cases depends on the type of appellate court. Civil cases make up about 47 percent of the cases intermediate appeals courts (appeals courts one level below supreme courts) hear, and criminal cases make up an additional 40 percent. Other administrative cases and writs for *habeas corpus* make up the rest of the caseload. Habeas corpus writs ask courts to determine the legality of a detainee's confinement. If courts find that an individual has been illegally detained, they can issue such a writ demanding that the individual be released.

State Supreme Courts

Although a state supreme court is just a special type of appellate court, these courts deserve special attention because they are courts of last resort. In addition, it is valuable to compare the workload of the federal Supreme Court with the workloads of state supreme courts.

State supreme courts are the final arbitrators of questions dealing with state law. The U.S. Supreme Court can only review a decision by a state supreme court if the case addresses some type of federal constitutional question. State supreme courts hear many more cases that the U.S. Supreme Court but state supreme courts have much less discretion over their dockets.

In the 1999–2000 session, the U.S. Supreme Court received 8,445 applications for appeal. Informally, judicial scholars refer to this process as "granting cert," or *certiorari*. The word means to become informed, or to be made certain. So, when the Supreme Court takes an appeal, it issues a writ of certiorari, which orders a lower court to inform the Supreme Court by sending up the case records.

Of the more than 8,000 applications, the Court only granted certiorari to 73 cases during the 1999–2000 session. Unlike state supreme courts, the U.S. Supreme Court has almost complete control over the cases it decides to hear. Therefore, the U.S. Supreme Court can grant cert or deny cert if it chooses. Most state supreme courts have mandatory jurisdiction and therefore, must grant an appeal to a variety of cases. Although there are no data analyzing the rates of certiorari for every state, limited comparative data exists. For example, in the 1996–1997 session a busy court such as the Florida Supreme Court granted certiorari to 1,699 cases. The Minnesota Supreme Court granted certiorari to 488 appellants. Regardless, both states heard considerably more cases than the 73 heard by the U.S. Supreme Court.

There are three factors that contribute to higher caseloads for state supreme courts. State statutes and constitutions may require mandatory jurisdiction for many types of cases. In contrast, after the Judiciary Act of 1925 and subsequent amendments in 1988, the U.S. Supreme Court has very few mandatory cases. Therefore, state supreme courts are required by state law to hear more cases than federal law requires of the U.S. Supreme Court. In addition, all states grant mandatory jurisdiction in death penalty cases. Therefore, states that have the death penalty also tend to have supreme courts with higher caseloads. Last, most states give their supreme courts original jurisdiction in a variety of cases. For example, Colorado, like many other states, gives its supreme court original jurisdiction over any controversies arising from reapportionment. Almost all states grant original jurisdiction in cases of attorney discipline. And many other states, such as Ohio and Kansas, grant their supreme courts original jurisdiction in *quo warranto* (see p. 79), *mandamus* (see p. 75), and habeas corpus proceedings.

Alternative Dispute Resolution

The evidence is overwhelming that state courts perform a significant amount of work for state governments. They adjudicate millions of legal claims and disputes each year that cover an extensive range of public policy issues. However, on many levels, state courts are becoming overburdened by the amount of filings they face each year. As a consequence of their workloads, fewer and fewer legal conflicts are resolved by an actual trial.

According to the American Bar Association's Vanishing Trials Project, over the last twenty-five years, the percentage of cases decided by a trial has diminished in both state and federal courts. In 1976, 34 percent of cases in state court were decided by a trial. By 2001, that percentage had fallen to 18 percent. As court systems become clogged with so many cases, judges look to other ways to resolve conflicts. Often, judges encourage attorneys to reach out-of-court settlements so a trial will not be necessary. State prosecutors offer plea bargains to criminal defendants to avoid the need for a trial. To further reduce the caseload, courts have begun to encourage the use of alternative dispute resolution (ADR). ADR is a mechanism available for the resolution of a conflict without using the court system. ADR includes mediation, voluntary or mandatory arbitration, and settlement conferences.

Mediation is the process of using a neutral third party (a mediator) to assist differing parties in finding a resolution. Mediators have no formal power; they can only suggest options and help facilitate communication between parties. Arbitration is similar to mediation, except that the neutral third party (an arbitrator) has the power to enforce, or bind, the parties to his or her decision. Parties that elect to use arbitration engage in it voluntarily. Parties that are required to use arbitration, either by a signed contract or a state statute, engage in mandatory arbitration. Settlement conferences are also similar to mediation except that arbitrations typically convene and administer a settlement conference.

Not all state courts view ADR with the same degree of approval. While most courts accept that ADR reduces caseloads and is a cost-efficient method of conflict resolution, there is no consensus on the appropriate role of ADR as a replacement for legal proceedings. Most of the concern has focused on the legality of mutual arbitration agreements, sometimes called *cram down arbitration*. In response to increasing litigation costs, many employers require that new employees sign contracts in which employees waive their rights to resolve employment disputes in court. Instead, the employee agrees to mandatory arbitration. The U.S. Supreme Court, in *Gilmer v. Interstate/Johnson Lane Corp* (1991), upheld mandatory arbitration agreements in cases of age discrimination claims. Some state supreme courts have followed the U.S. Supreme Court's lead. For example, the New Jersey Supreme Court has taken steps to encourage ADR. The New Jersey court held that disability discrimination suits were subject to mandatory arbitration agreements. The Texas Supreme Court also held that employers must accept mutual arbitration agreements and that the decision of the arbitrator carries the same weight as a legal decision from a court. However, other state supreme courts have been more suspicious. California courts, for example, have shown some resistance to mandatory, or cram down, arbitration. In several cases, the California courts have ruled that certain cram down, arbitration agreements are unconscionable, and therefore unenforceable. Because alternative dispute resolution is relatively new to state courts, there will most likely be a period of adjustment in which state legislatures and state courts craft a body of law that promotes efficiency while at the same time protects individuals' civil rights.

State Courts Make Public Policy

Discussions about public policy typically focus on the role of the legislative and executive branches. Legislatures are most visible when they are drafting, debating, and enacting legislation. Governors are most prominent when they are signing bills into law or using their veto power to reject legislation. However, state courts also play a significant, but sometimes more subtle, role in crafting public policy. There are two main avenues by which state courts create public policy. State courts have the power of judicial review and the right to develop common law.

Judicial Review

Judicial review is the power of courts to invalidate any law enacted by the state if the court finds the law conflicts with the state or U.S. Constitution. The power of judicial review gives courts the ability to act as a check on the power of other elected officials. However, courts cannot use the power of judicial review indiscriminately. First, courts must wait for a citizen to challenge a law before they may invalidate it. Because state courts with the power of judicial review have only appellate jurisdiction, they can only invalidate a law after it has become subject to a constitutional challenge. Governors, on the other hand, may veto a bill before it becomes a law. Second, governors may veto a law for any reason including a simple dislike for the proposed legislation. Courts, however, are supposed to invalidate only those laws that expressly violate the state or federal Constitution. Courts are not supposed to use their personal dislikes for a law as grounds for invalidating it. When courts invalidate laws quite frequently, or use their own values to reject legislation, they are often called judicial activists.

Political debates in the United States about judicial activism are as old as the republic. Ever since Chief Justice John Marshall established the use of judicial review in American federal courts, there have been debates on how courts should use such power. Some argue that courts should defer to the legislature since the legislature is elected by the people. Individuals who advocate such a stance promote the concept of judicial restraint. Judicial activists believe that courts need to protect civil and other rights by invalidating any law that seems unjust, even if there are no specific provisions in the state or federal Constitution that are violated. These arguments were previously outlined in the section Legal Culture and Approaches to Interpretation.

Despite the centuries-old conflict about the legitimacy of federal judicial review, state courts adopted the practice of judicial review early in American history and without much controversy. In the 1780s, the same decade the U.S. Constitution was ratified, five state courts confronted issues of judicial review. In four of those cases, the state supreme courts ruled they had the power to invalidate unconstitutional state legislation. By 1820, state supreme courts in ten of the original thirteen colonies had invalidated acts of their legislatures. One reason state courts may have been more comfortable with the process of judicial review was their history as royal or charter colonies of the British Crown. Prior to the American Revolution, legislative acts of a colonial legislature could be repealed by an Act of Parliament, the king, or even a Privy Council. If colonial legislatures became too rebellious, the king or Parliament could revoke their colonial charter. Therefore, state legislatures had ample experience with judicial review prior to the establishment of post-revolutionary state constitutions or the drafting of the federal Constitution. In many ways, state supreme courts simply replaced English Privy Councils, but maintained their same function.

Reversing a Decision: Justice Gibson and the Early Years of Judicial Review

Pennsylvania Supreme Court Justice John Gibson occupies a unique place in history with respect to the debates over judicial review. While a state supreme court justice, he offered a stinging critique of Chief Justice John Marshall and his decision in *Marbury v. Madison*, the federal case that granted the U.S. Supreme Court the power of judicial review. Gibson, in an 1825 Pennsylvania Supreme Court case, *Eakin v. Raub*, argued that "it is the business of the judiciary to interpret the laws, not scan the authority of the lawgiver." He argued that neither the Pennsylvania nor U.S. Constitution granted courts the power of judicial review. However, later in his life, Judge Gibson changed his mind. Twenty years after the *Eakin* decision, Judge Gibson would come to support judicial review on the grounds that "experience had proved that great wrongs may undoubtedly be perpetuated by legislative bodies."

Chief Justice John Marshall developed the federal courts' power to exercise judicial review. Justice John Gibson of the Pennsylvania Supreme Court wrote one of the most compelling counterpoints in Eakin v. Raub. *(Collection of the Supreme Court of the United States)*

State Courts and the Development of Judicial Review

The use of judicial review by state courts actually predates the U.S. Constitution. While still being governed by the Articles of Confederation, each state printed its own currency. At the time, the currency printed by Rhode Island was depreciating in value and local citizens were refusing to accept it. In response, the Rhode Island legislature passed a law imposing fines on those who refused to accept the state's money. In 1786 Weeden was convicted under the statute, but the Rhode Island Supreme Court, in *Trevett v. Weeden*, granted him an acquittal on the grounds that the currency law was unconstitutional. The court wrote, ". . . these legislators derive their power from the constitution; how then can they change it, without destroying the foundation of their authority."

Despite early historical debates about judicial review, today, all courts use the power of judicial review to eliminate laws. Such an act has a profound effect on public policy. In the past, state courts have invalidated death penalty statutes, tort reform measures, changes to the criminal justice system, school funding legislation, restrictions on gay rights, and many other laws. Judicial scholars have shown that state supreme courts are most protective of civil liberties. State laws that infringe on civil liberties are the most likely to be overturned.

Craig Emmert has studied how state courts use the power of judicial review. He has found that state supreme courts hear, on average, thirteen challenges to the constitutionality of a state statute each year. Subsequently, about two laws per year, per state, are invalidated by state supreme courts. Although that number may seem low, taken together, state supreme courts invalidate about one hundred twenty state laws per year. In comparison, the U.S. Supreme Court only invalidates about twenty-two state laws per year.

Common Law

There are two aspects of common law. First, courts are needed to interpret vague or undefined constitutional provisions. Legislatures cannot address every possible area of potential conflict. They need judges to follow general directives set forth by the legislature and fill in the gaps on their own. Second, courts are needed to create new law when they encounter a controversy without any statutory, administrative, or constitutional guidelines to follow. Sometimes issues arise that need to be adjudicated immediately, but the court has no guidance from the typical sources: precedent, statutes, and the state constitution. Sometimes judges need to be judicial innovators.

Interpretation of Statutes and Constitutions.   State courts also have the authority to interpret all state statutes and constitutional provisions. Yet, constitutional clauses and legislative statutes often include vague terminology. Legislatures cannot foresee every possible conflict that may arise. For example, what is a *reasonable* search and seizure? What exactly constitutes *cruel and unusual* punishment? What type of behavior must one commit to be guilty of *gross negligence?* All these terms lack specific criteria. As a result, courts must issue judicial opinions that clarify vague terms.

The power to interpret laws is akin to the power to write laws. A constitutional provision may require "adequate spending" on education, but courts would then have the power to determine what exactly constitutes adequate spending. Under such a provision courts would have the power to interpret such a law and then require specific levels of funding either per school district, or even per pupil. A legislature may pass a law holding contractors liable for injuries caused in work that is "inherently dangerous." But it will be the state courts who decide which types of work qualify as inherently dangerous.

In 1996 the Oregon legislature passed a comprehensive disability law protecting the rights of disabled workers. The statute read, in part, that it was the purpose of the law "to guarantee disabled persons the fullest possible participation in the social and economic life of the state, [and] to engage in remunerative employment." Specifically, the statute requires employers to make "reasonable accommodations" and/or transfer disabled employees to other jobs in which they are "otherwise qualified." However, the law failed to specifically define a "reasonable accommodation" or how one determined if an employee was "qualified." After a number of lawsuits by dismissed employees, the Oregon court issued many rulings that specified the rights of employees and responsibilities of employers.

While the Oregon legislature may have established the overall goal of equality for disabled workers, and created the legal authority for employees to pursue such rights, it was actually the Oregon courts that established the specific guidelines employers must follow. Although state courts do not actually draft law in the same manner as other officials, their rulings interpreting statutes have the same force as law.

Judicial Innovation.   Common law is a system of jurisprudence that is based on judicial precedent rather than statutory laws. Sometimes, however, courts encounter controversies in which there is little to guide them to a legal solution. Either the legislature has not anticipated the issue, administrative agencies have not drafted any rules concerning the issue, or courts have never created any precedent on the issue. These types of cases are often called cases of first impression. In cases such as this, courts need to draft their own laws.

An example of judicial innovation would be the Massachusetts Supreme Court's ruling legalizing gay marriage. In 2001, several homosexual couples in Massachusetts applied for, but were denied, marriage licenses. The existing marriage statutes in Massachusetts were silent on the issue of gay marriage. The statutes simply establish minimum standards for obtaining a license such as health and age as well as banning marriage between relatives and those who are already married. However, the statute did not explicitly mention that marriage was only between a man and a woman, nor did the statute expressly forbid issuing a license to people of the same gender. Furthermore, the Massachusetts Supreme Court had no precedent from the state body of common law directly relating to gay marriage. Therefore, the court had to examine the state constitution and craft new law from scratch. The court, citing general constitutional clauses and some tangential precedents, decided that marriage between people of the same sex was protected by the Massachusetts Constitution.

Advisory Opinions.   State supreme courts sometimes offer advisory opinions to state legislatures. There are times when a state legislature does not know if a proposed statute will comply with the state's constitution. In such a case, the legislature will ask the court to give its opinion as to whether a yet unpassed law would be upheld if it were subjected to a constitutional challenge. Legislatures seek advisory opinions to save time and anticipate the possible objections of the state supreme court. For example, in 2003, the Massachusetts Supreme Court held unconstitutional the state practice that only authorized marriage licenses for heterosexual couples. In confronting this ruling, the Massachusetts legislature was unsure if a new law that allowed civil unions, but not marriage licenses, for homosexual couples would comply with the court's ruling. In

Federal Supreme Court Turns Down Advisory Role

The first advisory opinion was issued by the Massachusetts Supreme Court in 1781. The State House of Representatives and Senate were unclear on a technicality regarding which branch had the authority to initiate money bills. The Supreme Court agreed to mediate the problem prior to the legislature actually passing a bill.

In contrast, the first U.S. Chief Justice John Jay refused to issue advisory opinions. President George Washington requested that the Supreme Court advise him on some foreign-policy decisions and how they might conflict with the Constitution. Jay refused, stating that he could only rule on actual cases or controversies.

John Jay, the first chief justice of the United States, refused President Washington's request for an advisory opinion on the grounds that the Constitution granted the Supreme Court power to resolve only actual "cases and controversies." Many state surpreme courts are permitted by their constitutions to provide this type of legal advice. (Collection of the Supreme Court of the United States) an advisory opinion, the Massachusetts court indicated to the legislature that such a compromise would not be upheld by the court. After receiving the advisory opinion, the legislature abandoned its work on the civil unions bill.

Advisory opinions exist under the *nonbinding doctrine* that means that such opinions have no force of law and carry no weight of precedent. They are simply advisory. In many states, it is not the court itself that issues the opinions, but the judges. This way, it appears as if the opinions are coming from an individual, and not an institution.

In general, state supreme courts avoid issuing advisory opinions. Many jurists feel that it is inappropriate for judges to rule on hypothetical cases, or to so directly participate in the legislative process. Currently, only eight states have constitutions that authorize their supreme courts to issue advisory opinions. Two states authorize advisory opinions via a legislative statute. However, even in states where courts are specifically permitted to issue advisory opinions, the justices resist.

State Courts and Direct Democracy

Twenty-six states in the United State have some form of direct democracy. Direct democracy includes the right to draft and vote on ballot measures (initiatives), recall elected officials, and ratify or reject legislative bills (referendums). American states first started experimenting with direct democracy during the Populist Era of the late 1800s, but the movement gained wider acceptance during the Progressive Era of the early 1900s. Therefore, many Western states, which joined the Union after the Populist Era, have some form of direct democracy as part of their constitutions. Recently, some Eastern states have begun to adopt forms of direct democracy.

Direct democracy presents unique issues for state courts. Political activists who use direct democracy have to follow different rules than legislators. To qualify an initiative for the ballot, activists must collect signatures, draft ballot titles, and follow specific guidelines unique to the initiative process. Supreme courts almost never interfere with the internal mechanisms of a legislature, but state courts frequently oversee the initiative process. For example, most states require that ballot measures only address a *single subject.* This means that ballot measures may not change both the tax system and a completely unrelated criminal statute. Like other legal terms, single-subject is prone to many interpretations. It is very common for opponents of ballot measures to appeal to state courts claiming that a ballot measure addressed two subjects and then demand that the measure be invalidated.

Furthermore, many state ballot measures challenge basic civil rights that are protected by state constitutions or common law. For example, ballot measures have sought to limit abortion rights, homosexual rights, the rights of immigrants, and the rights of criminal defendants. Most state courts are very protective of civil rights. Therefore, state courts nullify a much greater percentage of ballot measures than legislative statutes.

Courts Nullify State Constitutional Amendments

Unlike federal and state statutes, state ballot measures suffer an extremely high rate of judicial review. Ken Miller (1999) demonstrates that about 50 percent of all ballot measures are eventually challenged in court, and approximately 50 percent of those challenges result in partial or complete nullification of the statute. The data in Tables 2.3 and 2.4 illustrate how often courts have invalidated state ballot measures in the past forty years in California, Colorado, and Oregon.

TABLE 2.3   RATES OF INITIATIVE CHALLENGE

Decade	Initiatives Challenged in Court*	Percent Challenged
1960s	3 of 6	50
1970s	10 of 20	50
1980s	21 of 41	51
1990s	35 of 60	58
Totals	69 of 127	54

Source: Miller, Ken. 1999. "The Role of Courts in the Initiative Process: A Search for Standards." Paper presented at Annual Meeting of the American Political Science Association, Atlanta.

*Data are for California, Oregon, and Colorado only, states that historically have used the initiative process more than others.

TABLE 2.4   RATES OF INITIATIVE INVALIDATION

Decade	Initiatives challenged	Invalidated in part	Invalidated in full	Percent invalidated
1960s	3	0	3	100
1970s	10	5	0	50
1980s	21	6	4	48
1990s	35	8	7	58
Totals	69	19	14	54

Source: Miller, Ken. 1999. "The Role of Courts in the Initiative Process: A Search for Standards." Paper presented at Annual Meeting of the American Political Science Association, Atlanta.

Many ballot measures are drafted by people who have little or no experience with politics or the law. When these types of measures are passed by the electorate, state courts become responsible for fixing them. State courts fix initiatives by invalidating small parts of the initiative, or using legal decisions to rewrite parts of the initiative that conflict with the state constitution, preexisting statutes, or previous common law. Legal scholars refer to this process as narrowly tailoring an initiative to comply with existing law.

Direct democracy also makes it easier for citizens to overrule a state court decision, even a state supreme court decision. One of the only ways to overrule a U.S. Supreme Court decision is to pass an amendment to the U.S. Constitution. That process is very difficult; so difficult, in fact, that it has only been done twenty-seven times. However, at the state level it is relatively easy to amend the state constitution via the initiative process. Therefore, when interested political groups disagree with a state supreme court decision, they can draft and pass constitutional initiatives overruling the court.

THE ENFORCEMENT POWER OF STATE COURTS

It is often said that courts have neither the power of the purse nor the sword. Alexander Hamilton used those words to describe the U.S. Supreme Court in 1788 when he wrote *Federalist 78*. Hamilton was suggesting that because the Court lacked an army or the power to tax and spend, it would be the "least dangerous branch" of government. To some extent, Hamilton was right and his comments about the U.S. Supreme Court are equally applicable to state courts. However, if courts lack any real power, as Hamilton suggested, then they would have a difficult time enforcing their decisions. Yet, citizens have considerable faith in the court system to bring about justice, both criminally and civilly. Though Hamilton was right when he said that the courts lacked an army and spending power, it would be incorrect to assume that state courts lack all types of coercive and financial power. Every day, state courts issue rulings and those rulings are enforced. In truth, state courts have considerable power to use the police powers of their state and to direct the flow of money.

In some respects, state courts do have the power of the "sword." State judges can use the services of law enforcement officers in their state. Judges can order police officers to seize individuals, property, and carry out other types of judicial orders. Courts can also hold law enforcement officers at bay by withholding search or arrest warrants. Hamilton may have been right when he argued that courts do not have an army, but state courts definitely have armed individuals at their disposal. Additionally, state judges have the power to seize money and property from defendants. Through a variety of legal procedures, discussed in the following sections, state judges can transfer wealth from one party to another. Again, state courts may not have the power of the purse, but they do have the power to seize financial assets and transfer those assets to other individuals.

Judicial Orders

Before addressing the specific powers courts have to enforce their decisions, it is important to understand the types of orders judges issue. Judges issue temporary or permanent orders, and self-executing or non-self-executing orders.

Temporary and Permanent Orders

The difference between temporary and permanent orders is intuitive. Temporary orders impose some type of restraint on an individual for a limited amount of time. For example, a judge may issue a temporary injunction or a temporary restraining order. A temporary injunction or restraining order is a judicial order that temporarily bars a legal party from doing or continuing some type of action. A permanent injunction would ban such actions permanently. Judges usually employ temporary orders to buy the court some time. Often, courts intervene in the middle of an ongoing process. If courts are

---

Court Case Made for TV

In 2003, the TNN television network launched a new station called Spike TV. The new station was billed as the "first network for men." The lineup of shows included *Baywatch, Miami Vice,* and *The A-Team.* Before the station could go on the air, director Spike Lee sought an injunction to enjoin TNN from using the name "Spike." He argued before a New York state judge that allowing TNN to use his name would harm his reputation. Furthermore, if Lee were required to wait for a trial, TNN could continue to use his name while the lawsuit was pending. The judge granted Lee's petition and issued a temporary injunction on the use of the term "Spike" until a trial could be held. While the injunction was in effect, TNN was not allowed to use the name "Spike TV." Eventually TNN and Lee reached an agreement that was not made available to the public. On reaching the agreement, a New York Supreme Court justice lifted the temporary restraining order.

---

forced to conduct an entire trial before taking any action, harmful behavior could continue. For instance, an individual being illegally evicted needs immediate relief from the court. It would not benefit society to allow illegal acts to proceed and then, afterward, declare them illegal. Temporary orders allow the court to hear evidence and testimony and then make decision. Once a final decision has been reached, the court will issue a permanent order.

Self-enforcing and Non-Self-enforcing Orders

Some orders by state courts are self-enforcing, but others need external police power to carry them out. Judges do not personally seize assets or take people to jail. They need the assistance of police officers or other state-empowered officials. When a judge grants damages to a plaintiff, he or she simply issues the defendant a piece of paper. The paper itself does not facilitate the transfer of funds. A state officer must physically seize the defendant's assets. Orders such as these are non-self-enforcing. In contrast, some judicial orders take effect simply because the judge issues an order. These types of orders are self-enforcing. Sometimes participants in a political or legal conflict do not know their rights. They may seek a declaratory judgment from a court. A declaratory judgment simply explains an issue of law or indicates what rights an individual has. There is no need for an official of the state to enforce this type of decision.

Political Remedies

State courts essentially have two types of powers: they can seize money and assets from defendants, or they can order a defendant to cease a certain type of behavior. It is helpful to think of the first type of action as a civil remedy and the second type of action as a political remedy. Political remedies take many forms. The following sections identify and detail the most common political remedies.

An Example of a Writ of Prohibition

The following is a hypothetical application for a writ of prohibition disqualifying a judge from hearing a case:

Judge Smith, of Jefferson Court, respondent named in the petition lost all jurisdiction to continue with the action pending before him by reason of his bias and prejudice as established by the petitioner duly served and filed, pursuant to state statute 01.23.45, a copy of which affidavit is attached, marked Exhibit A and incorporated by reference or as the case may be. Nevertheless, the judge refuses to disqualify himself although required so to do, and has persisted and will continue to persist, unless prohibited and restrained by this court, in presiding over the action in which petitioner is defendant.

Extraordinary Writs

There are two types of extraordinary writs: writs of mandamus and *writs of prohibition*. A writ of mandamus is a legal command from a court. In fact, mandamus is Latin for "we command." Courts issue a writ of mandamus to compel an official to carry out some ministerial act that the court recognizes as an absolute duty. Often, administrative or elected officials have a certain amount of discretion as to how they perform their duties. Courts may order officials to carry out specific tasks with a mandamus order. Writs of mandamus are also used by higher courts to order lower courts to take some type of action. In very rare cases, defendants cannot wait for the appeals process. Instead, they need a higher court to order a lower court to engage in some proceeding prior to the lower court making its final decision.

A writ of prohibition is similar to a writ of mandamus. Instead of ordering a specific action, a writ of prohibition bars a specific action. Writs of prohibition can be issued by judges to prevent, for example, the state from suspending someone's drivers license or liquor license, preventing a city council or county commissioner's ordinance from going into effect, and even dismiss another judge from hearing a case if there is evidence he or she may be biased against the defendant.

Declaratory Judgments

A declaratory judgment is a ruling by a court that establishes the rights of parties engaged in a legal dispute, or expresses the opinion of a court about a question of law. Declaratory judgments simply inform; they do not order any specific action. Often, parties who are bound by a legal contract or subject to a state statute do not know their rights or responsibilities under the contract or statute. In such a case, they can appeal for a declaratory judgment. The court will then examine the contract or statute and deliver an opinion regarding the demands of the statute or contract.

The court also informs each party of its duties or rights. For example, the Maine statute on declaratory judgments states, "Courts of record within their respective jurisdictions shall have power to declare rights, status and other legal relations whether or not further relief is or could be claimed. No action or proceeding shall be open to objection on the ground that a declaratory judgment or decree is prayed for. The declaration may be either affirmative or negative in form and effect. Such declarations shall have the force and effect of a final judgment or decree."

The purpose of a declaratory judgment is to address disputes before they require further legal action. Often, legal disputes result from the fact that contracts or statutes are vague or fail to address an unforeseen event. In such a case, parties simply do not know what is required of them, or there is a disagreement between parties as to the obligations of each. Declaratory judgments can clarify the law before the need for further legal action.

Contempt Citations

One of the most powerful tools state courts have is the ability to hold individuals in contempt of court or issue contempt citations. Courts can hold individuals in *direct* contempt if they resist a court order while in the presence of that court. Courts can hold individuals in *constructive* contempt if individuals fail to comply with a court order while outside the actual courtroom. Individuals can be held in *civil* contempt if they fail to abide by a court's order to remedy some financial debt. Typically, in civil cases, the losing party is ordered to pay the winning party some type of damages. If the losing party fails to pay, it can be held in civil contempt. Courts can also hold people in *criminal* contempt. People who obstruct the administration of justice can be held in criminal contempt.

The penalties for contempt are either a fine or imprisonment. Courts can imprison those held in contempt for an indefinite period. The purpose of contempt imprisonment is to compel an individual to carry out a court-ordered action. For example, a state judge may order an individual to testify or turn over evidence to a court. If the individual refuses, he or she can be held in contempt, and then imprisoned until he or she complies. But contempt imprisonment cannot be perpetual. Judges may only use contempt im-

---

Courts Attempt to Compel Testimony with Contempt Citation

Judges can use contempt citations to compel testimony from witnesses. It is common for investigative newspaper reporters to have crucial evidence regarding criminal trials. Because reporters often promise confidentiality to their sources, they typically resist providing such testimony. For example, in 1997, *Miami Herald* reporter David Kidwell interviewed murder suspect Walter Zile. On learning about the interview, Kidwell was subpoenaed by the prosecuting attorney. Kidwell refused to testify. The trial judge threatened to issue a contempt citation against Kidwell and eventually carried out such an action. Because Kidwell refused to testify, he was given a seventy-day jail sentence and a $500 fine.

prisonment to coerce individuals to act, not to punish. Once it becomes clear that the imprisonment will not result in an acceptance of the court's demands, the defendant is freed. Judges have wide discretion in determining when such a time arrives.

Injunctions

Injunctions are the courts' method of preventing or interrupting damaging or illegal activities. An injunction is similar to a writ of prohibition. The purpose of an injunction is to prevent or guard against future injuries. Most of the time, courts award damages after an injury has already been committed. Courts can use injunctions to prevent such injury from ever occurring.

Courts can issue temporary and permanent injunctions. A temporary injunction, sometimes called an *interlocutory* injunction, prevents any further action until a trial court can make a final determination. Because court proceedings can be lengthy, courts may want to prevent an action while the hearing is taking place. Otherwise, the offending party would be able to continue its harmful actions while the court carried out its business. A temporary injunction halts potentially harmful action until the court can decide if the action is, in fact, harmful. If the court determines the action was not harmful, the temporary injunction is lifted and the defendant is allowed to resume his or her business. A *permanent* injunction is issued after a trial court has reached a final decision. The permanent injunction enforces the will of the court. Those who violate injunctions can be held in contempt and imprisoned.

One reason injunctions are such powerful tools is that there are almost no limitations on how a judge may use an injunction. A judge can use an injunction to prevent any behavior he or she wishes. The only way to overturn an injunction is for a higher court to overrule the injunction imposed by the lower court, but this rarely happens.

During the late 1800s, when the labor movement was gaining influence, state courts regularly used injunctions to prevent strikes and protests, claiming they violated conspiracy and antitrust laws. When workers ignored the courts and proceeded with their strike plans, they were held in contempt and jailed. Furthermore, once courts had issued injunctions and held workers in contempt, they also facilitated the participation of governors and other police officials to enforce the injunction. Therefore, acting on the authority of the courts, many governors would call out state militias to break up strikes and protests. After the passage of the Wagner Act in 1935, courts could no longer use their injunction powers to prevent collective action by unions.

Judicial Review of Administrative Decisions

Just as state courts have the power of judicial review to invalidate state laws, courts also have the power to invalidate administrative decisions. As with any governmental system, elected officials rarely administer the programs or laws they enact. Bureaucratic officials manage the day-to-day business of the state. Administrative agencies make decisions about unemployment compensation, marriage licenses, environmental rules, welfare benefits, and much more. State courts have the power to overturn most administrative decisions. Moreover, state courts have the power to direct administrative agencies to take specific actions. As a result, state courts have considerable influence over how state benefits are distributed and how rules are enforced.

Special Masters

Special masters, sometimes called masters in chancery, are officials appointed by the court to carry out investigative and administrative tasks for the court. Many appellate courts need information before they can administer the law. Special masters can be directed to collect testimony, investigate conflicts, and then report their findings back to the court. Special masters can also be used to investigate civil cases by computing damages, determining the holdings of a defendant, auditing individuals and firms, and taking affidavits. In family courts, judges often appoint special masters to act as custodial referees. In this role, the special master interviews children and parents, visits the home, and arbitrates family conflicts. The special master then refers the findings to the court where a final decision is made.

Special masters enhance the power of courts by giving force to judicial decrees. It is one thing for a court to order that a defendant declare his or her assets. It is quite another for a court to order a special master to determine those assets. Often courts suffer from the principle-agency dilemma. This dilemma arises from the fact that courts must often rely on a party to the case to carry out the decision or order of the court. Many times, the preferences of the party so ordered are at odds with the court's commands. Therefore, courts are often faced with ordering the fox to watch the chicken coop. Special masters alleviate this problem. Special masters also ensure that information given to the court is impartial.

Arkansas School Case Relied on Special Masters

In 2002 the Arkansas Supreme Court, in *Lake View School District No. 25 v. Huckabee,* held that the state was in violation of Article 14 of the Arkansas Constitution. According to the court, Article 14 mandated that the state provide an equitable education to all students regardless of geographic location. However, the court did not have the administrative capabilities to examine the spending levels, teacher hiring practices, and curriculum development processes of every school district within the state. Lacking that information, they had no way to determine if their ruling was being met by the state legislature. To ad-

dress the problem, the Arkansas Supreme Court appointed two special masters to collect school district data on all the relevant issues addressed in the court's ruling. The special masters conducted interviews, examined recent school-funding legislation, and visited various school districts. They compiled a 128-page report for the state supreme court summarizing their findings.

It was not the job of the special masters to determine if the state had met its constitutional burden. Their job was simply to inform the court so that it could make such a determination.

In addition to collecting information, special masters can oversee the enforcement of a judicial decree. Judicial decisions often impose a variety of restrictions on a party, or impose a variety of commitments. Special masters are given the power to ensure that those commitments are met. For example, a judge may issue a ruling that demands that an administrative agency reduce the amount of toxic materials in a public waterway. A judge may not have the ability to direct the day-to-day events of the administrative agency. Instead, judges can empower a special master to oversee the enforcement of the decree.

Quo Warranto

Quo warranto is Latin for "by what authority." State attorneys general can file writs of quo warranto when an elected official usurps a power that he or she does not legally posses. In a quo warranto proceeding a state supreme court asks an elected official "by what authority do you take this action?" If the state officer cannot legally justify the action, the court can order the official to stop. Quo warranto proceedings can also challenge the actions and authority of a corporation within a state. Quo warranto proceedings are very rare.

Civil Remedies

In addition to arbitrating conflicts in the political arena, state courts also arbitrate civil disputes. When adjudicating civil disputes, the most versatile tool state courts have is the power to award and collect damages. State courts can award many different types of damages and have a variety of methods at their disposal to collect those damages. Awarding and collecting damages is the state court's "power of the purse."

Compensatory Damages

State courts award three types of damages: compensatory, punitive, and nominal. Compensatory damages are awarded to compensate a plaintiff for such things as property damage, personal injury, pain and suffering, mental distress, loss of wages, and injury to reputation. The purpose of compensatory damages is to award plaintiffs enough to return them to the situation they were in before they suffered harm by the defendant. In some cases, perfect disgorgement is easy to compute. If a plaintiff has suffered $2,000 in damage to an automobile, then the court will award $2,000 and sometimes attorney fees. However, in a case such as mental anguish or physical deformity it is more difficult to establish a monetary figure that represents perfect equity. To succeed plaintiffs must prove to the court they have suffered some harm due to the tortuous conduct of a defendant.

Punitive Damages

In some situations, state courts can award punitive damages (sometimes referred to as exemplary damages). Punitive damages are designed to go beyond merely making the plaintiff whole; they are intended to punish. In addition to punishment, punitive damages have two other functions. They serve as a deterrent against future misconduct, and high punitive awards are one way juries express their outrage at a defendant who shows disregard for others. For example, corporations may not be deterred from producing products with a known defect if the only consequence is paying compensatory damages. However, if additional punitive damages are awarded, a financial incentive is created to correct its reckless or deliberate misbehavior. Punitive damages not only create incentives for the current defendant, but also for potential future defendants. Punitive damages can range from a few thousand dollars to several billion dollars. Textbook legal theory suggests to succeed in winning a punitive award, plaintiffs must show that the defendant acted deliberately to cause harm, or in such a way that the misbehavior was likely to cause harm.

Achieving equity can be complicated when there is more than one defendant, or when the plaintiff bears some of the blame. For example, in car accidents involving multiple cars, a plaintiff may sue several defendants who caused the wreck and an automaker who sold a car with a defective braking system. At the same time, the plaintiff may bear some blame for exacerbating the injury by failing to wear a seatbelt. In this

---

Intentional Tort

To win monetary damages in a civil case, a plaintiff must prove that the defendant acted in a sufficiently egregious manner as to be liable for the damages. However, legislatures and courts have established different standards that plaintiffs must prove in order to receive damages. The legal standard that must be met is typically identified in the statute.

An intentional tort occurs when someone purposefully injures another party. To recoup damages from an intentional tort, the plaintiff must prove, in court, that the defendant intended to cause harm. For example, in assault and battery cases, the plaintiff can usually prove that the defendant intended to cause harm.

In other torts, the plaintiff does not have to prove that the defendant intentionally caused harm. Instead, the plaintiff is held to lower standard and must only prove that the defendant acted with negligence. For example, in most personal injury lawsuits, including medical malpractice and car accidents, a plaintiff can prove negligence if he or she simply shows the defendant acted in

a manner counter to how a reasonable person would act. It typically falls to the jury to decide how a reasonable person would act.

In some cases, statutes require that a plaintiff prove that the defendant acted in a reckless manner. This standard of proof is slightly harder to prove. In such a case, the plaintiff must show that the defendant acted more than just carelessly but in a manner that showed a conscious disregard of substantial and unjustified risk. To be reckless, a defendant needs to be conscious of the danger associated with his or her actions and follow through with those actions anyway.

To win punitive damages, plaintiffs typically need to show the defendant acted in a willful and wanton manner, which is a slightly higher standard of proof than recklessness. A wanton action is usually described as acting with extreme carelessness that exhibits a reckless disregard for the rights of others. When someone acts in a willful and wanton manner, he or she knows that the actions will result in harm to others.

respect a court will have to assign blame to several parties, including the plaintiff. Awards can be adjusted to account for the proportion of injury the plaintiff allowed to occur by not exercising sufficient care. (The methods for apportioning blame among multiple parties are discussed in the sidebar "Violent Crimes, Property Crimes, and Victimless Crimes" in Chapter 3, p. 109).

The data in Table 2.5 illustrate that median punitive damage awards remain relatively low. However, the percentage of punitive damage awards that are over $2.5 million, although still rare, is rising.

When compensatory and punitive damages are inappropriate, courts award nominal damages. Nominal damages are awarded when a defendant breaches a legal duty, but no damages were suffered by the plaintiff. In such a case, courts cannot award compensatory damages because there is no harm to compensate. Nominal damages are often awarded when someone's rights have been violated. For example, if one's privacy rights are violated, it is difficult to monetarily quantify the harm inflicted. If punitive damages are not legally permitted, the court can award nominal damages.

In state courts, judges rarely determine the amount of damages a plaintiff receives. Juries typically perform that duty. However, state judges do have the power of *additur* and *remittitur*. When judges feel the damages awarded by a jury are insufficient, courts can add to the award by granting an additur. This increases the damage award. Conversely, if the trial judge or appellate court feels the award is too high, courts can grant a remittitur and lower the award value. In high-profile tort cases, appellate judges often grant a remittitur. Although it is common for the media to highlight extremely high

TABLE 2.5   PUNITIVE DAMAGE AWARD TRENDS

Year	Median (dollars)	Mean (dollars)	Awards above $2.5 million (percent)	Highest settlement (dollars)
1993	20,000	217,000	1	40 million
1994	18,000	168,000	1	33 million
1995	20,000	199,000	2	13 million
1996	23,000	256,000	2	30 million
1997	29,000	280,000	3	48 million
1998	50,000	475,000	3	280 million
1999	100,000	609,000	5	27 million

Source: Jury Verdict Research Services. 2000. *2000 Current Award Trends.* Horsham, PA: LRP Publications.

punitive damage awards, they rarely publicize subsequent remittiturs that lower the award significantly.

After courts award damages they have several means to collect those damages. The following sections discuss methods state courts use to collect damages. It is important to remember that the following methods consist of more than simply issuing a piece of paper. The issuance of these orders empowers state police officers to enforce them.

Writs of Attachment and Execution

A writ of attachment is a process by which the court seizes the property of a defendant. The attached property can be sold so that damages awarded by the court can be paid. Or, the court can hold property until the damages are paid, after which the property is returned. At one time, courts could attach property during judicial proceeding on the chance that the plaintiff might prevail. However, the U.S. Supreme Court has limited the practice. Now, courts must provide due process before they seize property prior to a judgment.

Writs of execution are similar to writs of attachment. They empower police officers to seize property from someone who has been directed to pay damages. However, writs of execution can be general or specific. A general writ of execution instructs an officer to seize property without identifying any particular property. A specific writ of execution instructs an officer to seize a particular or set of particular items.

Garnishments and Liens

Judges do not always seize property. Damages can be collected by garnishing wages. Courts can issue a writ of garnishment that gives the court the authority to seize a percentage of a defendant's salary. States do not allow courts to seize an entire paycheck but only a limited percentage. Each state has different rules about the maximum percentage to be garnished.

Garnishments apply to a third party. Writs of attachment take property from the person who actually owes a fine or court-ordered damages. Garnishments seize property or money from a third party who owes the debtor. The most common use of a garnishment occurs when courts order an employer (third party) to turn over funds that were destined for the debtor. Instead, those funds are re-routed to the plaintiff who was awarded the damages.

A lien does not immediately seize property. Instead, a lien declares that once a piece of property is sold, the owner is not entitled to the funds acquired. Rather, once the property is sold, the lien holder has the first rights to the profits. If there is any money left over, then the owner of the property gets to keep the remaining funds. For example, if a homeowner refuses to pay required association dues, the courts can put a lien on the home. When the home is sold, the court seizes the payments and allocates the appropriate funds to the homeowner association. The remaining funds are then granted to the owner of the house. Liens are typically placed on property. However, courts can also place liens on tax returns and business inventories.

Receivership

State courts can appoint a person (a receiver) to act as a custodian for contested property during the length of the trial. Receivership serves civil disputes in the same manner that temporary injunctions serve political disputes. The court appoints a receiver to ensure that no harm comes to the property or either party to the suit during the length of the trial. In most cases concerning property, the owner of the property maintains ownership until the court decides the legal controversy. Such an arrangement leaves the nonowners of the property vulnerable to the acts of the owner while the trial proceeds. For example, legal disputes sometimes challenge the way a pension plan is being administered. There can be charges of embezzlement or fraud. During the length of the trial, the embezzlement or fraud can continue. To prevent that from occurring, courts can appoint a receiver to manage the pension fund while the trial takes place. If it turns out no tortuous activity was proven, the receiver returns control of the property to its rightful owner.

Rescission and Reformation

Rescission and reformation typically apply to contract law. There are times when individuals enter into a contractual agreement, but because of ambiguous language, mistakes, or outright fraud, the contract does not reflect the agreement of the two parties. In such cases, courts can use their powers of reformation to rewrite parts of the contract to bring the contract in line with the intended agreement.

Rescission occurs when a court simply invalidates a contract. There are times when parties use coercion, such as threats or other types of illegal pressure, to make people sign contracts. Or, one party simply lies about the nature of the contract. Rather than rewrite the contract, a court will declare it void.

JUDICIAL FEDERALISM

The United States has a federal system of government. In a federal system of government, political and legal power is shared between a central political authority and decentralized subunits of political authority. In the United States, there is one national government, based primarily in Washington, D.C., and fifty state governments. Because federal systems share political power, there are constant tensions between the different levels of government. It is common for the United States's national government to impose burdens or demands on state governments. As can be expected, state governments often resist these burdens and demands in an effort to protect their autonomy.

The courts play a role in federalism. The national government maintains the federal court system and each state maintains its own state court system. In some respects, each court system is isolated from the others. The national courts interpret the U.S. Constitution and all federal laws. The state courts each interpret their own state's constitution and body of state laws. However, the court systems are not completely independent of each other. The supremacy clause of the U.S. Constitution, requiring state courts to enforce federal law and apply federal court decisions, causes an intermingling of the court systems. Therefore, state courts often find themselves enforcing the decisions and interpretations of federal courts. Sometimes state courts do so willingly. At other times, state courts try to thwart the impact of federal court decisions. Just as state and national governments sometimes conflict with each other, so do state and national court systems. The interaction of state and federal courts is called vertical judicial federalism.

State courts also interact with other state courts. Decisions in one state court are not binding on courts in other states. However, sometimes one state court borrows from the experiences of other state courts. For example, it may be that Michigan has never had a case dealing with euthanasia. If such a case arises, the Michigan court may look to other states that have had such experiences. The Michigan court may borrow the logic and legal interpretation of a different state court and use it as its own. The interaction of state courts with other state courts is called horizontal judicial federalism.

Vertical Federalism

State supreme courts are the final arbitrators and interpreters of state law. Federal courts cannot dictate to state courts how to interpret their own state constitutions or state statutes unless those laws interfere with federal laws. The concept that federal courts will not interfere in a state court's interpretation of its own law was established by two U.S. Supreme Court decisions, *Rooker v. Fidelity Trust Co.* (1923) and *District of Appeals v. Feldman* (1983), and has come to be known as the Rooker-Feldman doctrine. The Rooker-Feldman doctrine is fundamental to protecting the autonomy of state courts. Because of the doctrine, federal courts cannot meddle in the affairs of state law unless those laws explicitly violate the U.S. Constitution or other federal statutes.

The Rooker-Feldman doctrine was an issue in the historic case of *Bush v. Gore* (2000), which arbitrated the disputed presidential election of 2000. Lawyers for then Governor George Bush challenged the State of Florida's vote-counting procedures. When appealing to the Supreme Court, Justice O'Connor's first question was, "Why are we here?" Justice O'Connor asked that question because voting procedures are covered by state constitutions, state law, and the Supreme Court of Florida had already issued a ruling. To many court observers, the Rooker-Feldman doctrine should have applied and the federal Court should have refused to hear the case. However, lawyers for Governor Bush claimed that the voting procedures established by the Florida Supreme Court violated the Fourteenth Amendment of the U.S. Constitution. The Rooker-Feldman doctrine does not apply if state laws or state supreme court decisions violate the U.S. Constitution or other federal laws.

If the U.S. Supreme Court in *Bush v. Gore* had not agreed that there was a federal legal question presented to the Court, it would have been unable to hear the case. Furthermore, once the Supreme Court agreed to hear the case, it was limited to adjudicating only the federal Fourteenth Amendment questions. It was not allowed to revisit the

Florida Supreme Court's interpretation of the Florida statutes regulating election procedures. The U.S. Supreme Court could only rule as to whether those election statutes or Florida court decisions violated federal law.

The supremacy clause empowers federal courts to dictate to state courts in areas of federal law. However, even when state courts are legally required to comply with federal courts, state courts are not powerless to frustrate the will of federal judges. Civil rights law has been one area of law that has historically led to tensions and disagreements between state and federal courts.

Beginning in the 1950s federal courts started taking a leading role in the protection of civil liberties. *Brown v. Board of Education* (1954) was the most notable of many cases that started the process of insuring civil rights to African Americans. Numerous other cases expanded the rights of the accused. In a series of decisions by the Warren Court, defendants were guaranteed attorneys, interrogation protections, Miranda rights, search and seizure protections, and much more. The Warren Court was in the process of selective incorporation.

Selective incorporation is the process of applying particular amendments in the Bill of Rights, or even particular clauses from one amendment to state governments. Ever since the 1834 decision in *Barron v. Baltimore,* state governments had not been bound by the restrictions of the Bill of Rights. In his last decision, Chief Justice John Marshall reasoned that because the First Amendment states that *Congress* "shall make no law respecting . . ." that the Bill of Rights only applied to the federal government. Following the Civil War, however, Congress passed, and the states adopted, the Fourteenth Amendment, which limited the autonomy of state lawmaking by barring state legislatures from passing laws that "deprive any person of life, liberty, or property, without due process of law; nor deny to any person within its jurisdiction the equal protection of the laws." Once states were prevented from denying any of its citizens liberty without due process, the Supreme Court eventually determined that "liberty" included the provisions of the Bill of Rights.

Slowly, between the 1920s to the 1970s, the U.S. Supreme Court reversed the *Barron* decision and required that state lawmakers respect the mandates of the Bill of Rights. However, in the process of incorporating the Bill of Rights into the states, the Court met resistance from state supreme courts. The Warren Court was considered an activist court and not all of the rulings handed down by the Warren Court were popular at the time. States with a more conservative ideology did not like many of the Warren Court incorporation cases.

In response, many state supreme courts took actions to resist mandates from federal courts. In some cases, state supreme courts simply ignored federal rulings. In other cases, state supreme courts used the ambiguous or vague language of federal decisions to carve out legal exceptions in their states. In the same manner, state supreme courts could use vague language to argue that the federal precedent did not apply to their particular states' laws. David and Francine Romero (2003) have shown that state courts remained very hostile to civil rights for African Americans even after *Brown* was decided.

After *Brown*, 74 percent of all federal court civil rights rulings supported the protection of civil rights for African American citizens. However, in comparison, only 31 percent of state supreme court decisions protected civil rights for African Americans. State courts also resisted the expansion of rights for criminal defendants.

Neil Romans (1974) has examined how state supreme courts resisted the mandates of *Escobedo v. Illinois* (1964) and *Miranda v. Arizona* (1966). Both *Escobedo* and *Miranda* were U.S. Supreme Court decisions that expanded the rights of criminal defendants. However, most criminal defendants are tried in state courts, not federal courts. Romans shows that although the state supreme courts were bound by federal precedent, many state supreme courts justices took the narrowest possible view of federal decisions to maintain long-standing state law enforcement practices.

New Judicial Federalism

Surprisingly, following personnel changes on the U.S. Supreme Court in the 1970s and 1980s, the tension between state supreme courts and the U.S. Supreme Court reversed itself. When the U.S. Supreme Court was dominated by liberal appointees in the Warren Court, the federal courts were seen as the primary defenders of civil liberties. However, with the retirement of Earl Warren and the appointment of his successor, Warren Burger, the U.S. Supreme Court began to hand down a new line of civil rights cases. In many cases, the Burger Court rescinded or narrowed the application of many of the Warren Court decisions. As a result, many state supreme courts began to rely on their own state constitutions to protect civil rights that were no longer protected by federal precedent. Scholars have referred to this movement as new judicial federalism. Although it is no longer new, the term highlights the fact that federalism provides multiple access points to the political system. If proponents cannot get what they want at one level of government (federal level), they are free to try at a different level of government (state level). Now, when litigants attempt to secure more rights in state courts than are recognized by the federal Supreme Court, it is known as relying on independent state grounds.

State supreme courts can rely on independent state grounds because each state has its own constitution and therefore its own set of civil liberties protections. Because of vertical judicial federalism, state courts cannot offer fewer protections of civil rights than the federal courts mandate. However, the reverse is not true. State supreme courts are free to offer greater protections than offered by federal precedent. As the Burger Court began to rein in the precedents of the Warren Court, state supreme courts responded by expanding protections of civil liberties by relying on state law instead of federal law.

For example, Alan Tarr (1998) points out that in 1973 the U.S. Supreme Court reversed course and declared that illegally obtained confessions can still be introduced in court for the purposes of impeaching witnesses. To many legal activists, this decision was seen as a rollback of Fourth Amendment protections. However, in response to the

1973 decision, four state supreme courts declared that their state constitutions forbid the introduction of illegally obtained confessions. Thus, what the U.S. Supreme Court took away, several state supreme courts returned. Many times, the conflict between federal and state courts is a function of ideology. When the U.S. Supreme Court is dominated by liberal appointees, supreme courts from conservative states try to resist the mandates of the federal court. When the U.S. Supreme Court is dominated by conservative appointees, supreme courts from more liberal states try to use their own state constitutions to go beyond what the federal court has mandated.

It is the ideologically driven nature of new judicial federalism that fuels much of the criticism of this doctrine. Some judicial scholars have objected to judicial federalism because it appears to be opportunistic rather than theory driven. Critics argue that using state constitutions to thwart the decisions of the U.S. Supreme Court is typically an ends-driven policy rather than a sincere interpretation of state constitutions. As such, judges appear to be playing politics and imposing their personal values as much as fairly interpreting state law.

However, state supreme courts often sincerely disagree with the precedents set by federal courts. In some cases, state judges feel the federal courts have gone too far and try to impede the will of federal courts. In other instances, state supreme court justices feel the federal courts have not gone far enough and seek to use state constitutions to offer more protections to their citizens. The following cases provide recent examples illustrating how the process of vertical judicial federalism works both ways.

In 1976 the U.S. Congress passed the Hyde Amendment, which restricted the use of federal tax dollars for abortions. A year later, the U.S. Supreme Court, in *Maher v. Roe* and *Beal v. Doe*, upheld the congressional policy and further ruled that state governments are not required to fund abortions. Having lost the battle at the federal level, many abortions rights organizations focused their attention on state governments and state courts. Eventually, several state supreme courts ruled contrary to the U.S. Supreme Court. The states of Massachusetts, New Jersey, California, Vermont, and Connecticut all declared that their state constitutions required the state funding of abortions as part of state medical plans.

In *Lawrence v. Texas* (2003) the U.S. Supreme Court faced a sodomy case. Texas statutes criminalized sodomy, but several plaintiffs argued the Texas law violated their rights of privacy. The U.S. Supreme Court agreed and invalidated the sodomy statute. However, the Court did not endorse the concept that privacy rights also guaranteed homosexuals the right to marry. Later in that same year, the Massachusetts Supreme Court, citing the *Lawrence* precedent and relying on the Massachusetts Constitution, declared that homosexuals did have the constitutional right to marry, at least in Massachusetts.

The case of *Zelman v. Simmons-Harris* (2002) arbitrated a disagreement over the use of school vouchers. Opponents argued that vouchers violated the establishment clause of the First Amendment. Supporters argued they were permissible under the First Amendment. The U.S. Supreme Court ruled that school vouchers did not violate the concept of separation of church and state and were therefore constitutional and permissible. However, a year later, courts in both Florida and Colorado ruled that vouchers violated their state constitutions' prohibitions against mingling church and state. Therefore, even though the U.S. Supreme Court authorized the use of vouchers, two separate state courts barred their implementation.

Using the doctrine of independent state grounds, state supreme courts have been willing to challenge the rulings of the U.S. Supreme Court. In some cases, state supreme courts have expanded the rights of individuals beyond what the federal courts require. In other cases, they have further limited the options of individuals. In 1983 the U.S. Supreme Court intervened to establish rules for when courts may use the doctrine of independent state grounds. In the case of *Michigan v. Long* (1983), the U.S. Supreme Court ruled that if state supreme courts want to rely on independent state grounds to contravene federal precedents, they must use only state legal precedents.

Prior to *Michigan*, state supreme courts were using federal precedent to support the rejection of federal precedents. State courts were arguing that state constitutions protected individual rights beyond those protections established by the federal Court, but were then using federal precedents to buttress their cases. The *Michigan* ruling rejected that process. After *Michigan*, state courts must clearly indicate that they are relying on "bona fide separate, adequate, and independent grounds" and in doing so, must only cite state common law to buttress their decisions. State supreme courts can still mention federal law and precedents, but they must include a plain statement clause ensuring the U.S. Supreme Court that the decision was based on state law. For example, in a Montana case, the Montana Supreme Court noted, "While we have devoted considerable time to a lengthy discussion of the application of the Fifth Amendment to the United States Constitution, it is to be noted that this holding is also based separately and independently on [the defendant's] right to remain silent pursuant to Article II, Section 25 of the Montana Constitution" (*State v. Fuller* [1996]).

By including such a statement in the decision, the Montana court has signaled that the decision was based solely on Montana constitutional law and therefore is beyond the review of the U.S. Supreme Court. In contrast, the U.S. Supreme Court has made it clear that if "a state court decision fairly appears to rest primarily on federal law, or to be interwoven with the federal law" (*Michigan*, 463 U.S. at 1040) the U.S. Supreme Court can take jurisdiction and contravene the state court's decision.

The development of the independent state grounds doctrine does not necessarily mean that state courts universally offer greater civil rights protections than federal courts. Often, state courts are seen as too responsive to local politics. During the initial stages of the civil rights movement, state courts regularly ignored the rights of African Americans. Their only recourse was to appeal to federal courts. A more recent example stems from the beating of California resident Rodney King in 1991. Arrested after a high-speed chase, King was repeatedly beaten by Los Angeles police officers, who were caught on tape in the act. After the incident received national attention four police officers were tried in a California criminal court. After a year-long trial, the jury surprised many court analysts and returned with a not-guilty verdict. In response to the verdict, federal officials indicted the police officers for violating federal civil rights laws. At the federal trial, two of the four officers were convicted.

Horizontal Federalism

Horizontal judicial federalism is the manner in which state courts interact with other state courts. Some of the interaction is voluntary. Courts can elect to use precedents from other states to help them resolve disputes in their own states. Some of the interaction is mandatory. The U.S. Constitution's full faith and credit clause mandates some cooperation between state judges.

Diffusion

Diffusion is the process by which a precedent developed in one state court is adopted by courts in other states. State courts are not bound by any decision or ruling in other states. However, at times, state courts voluntarily adopt, as precedent, rulings that come from other state supreme courts. Gregory Caldeira (1985) has studied the process of judicial diffusion. He found that diffusion was a function of geography, the size of a state's caseload, and the prestige of the court. State supreme courts are more likely to adopt precedents from other states if they are geographically close. Second, the number of cases a supreme court decides impacts how often that court will be cited by other state courts. Last, some state supreme courts have a higher level of prestige. Because some state courts are more respected than others, they are also more likely to be cited. Research shows that the California, New York, and New Jersey courts have the highest reputation among all the other supreme courts. Wyoming, South Dakota, and Hawaii have the lowest reputation scores. Having a low reputation score does not mean a court makes bad decisions; it simply means their rulings do not have the same impact on other jurisdictions as other courts.

A recent example of judicial diffusion is the Oregon Supreme Court's *Armatta v. Kitzhaber* (1998) decision. In *Armatta* the Oregon court ruled that state ballot measures voted on by the people may only amend one clause in the Oregon Constitution. The court reasoned that without the *Armatta* separate vote rule, ballot measure drafters could change multiple parts of the constitution with only one vote. Soon after the *Armatta* case was decided, the supreme courts of Montana and Washington adopted the separate vote rule. Despite the fact that neither the Montana nor Washington constitutions required a separate vote, nor were there any in-state precedents supporting such a decision, both supreme courts accepted the Oregon ruling as binding in their respective states.

Full Faith and Credit Clause

Because in our federalist system each state has jurisdiction over its own laws, no state is bound by the constitutions or statutes of other states. Such a legal environment invites problems. Defendants could escape the judgments of state courts by fleeing to other states. A couple married in Virginia who moved to New York could be denied marital status. In response to these possibilities, the Framers drafted the full faith and credit clause, in Article IV of the U.S. Constitution, which reads, "Full faith and credit shall be given in each state to the public acts, records, and judicial proceedings of every other state. And the Congress may by general laws prescribe the manner in which such acts, records, and proceedings shall be proved, and the effect thereof."

According to Justice Harlan Stone in *Milwaukee County v. M. E. White Co.* (1935), the full faith and credit clause "was to alter the status of the several states as independent foreign sovereignties, each free to ignore obligations created under the laws or by the judicial proceedings of the others, and to make them integral parts of a single nation throughout which a remedy upon a just obligation might be demanded as of right, irrespective of the state of its origin." The full faith and credit clause is regularly used to enforce child support decisions, extradition rulings, and to make sure civil damages are paid to successful plaintiffs even if the defendant moves to another state. The clause also prevents defendants from forum shopping. Once litigants have reached a judicial settlement in one state, they may not move to another state and relitigate the same conflict.

Recently this clause has experienced a revival of interest in connection with the controversies surrounding gay marriage. Because one section of the clause seeks to ensure that all states respect the marriage licenses issued by other states, when Massachusetts started issuing marriage licenses to gay couples in 2004, other states questioned whether they would be required to accept such marriages. Anticipating such a question the U.S. Congress preempted the debate by passing the Defense of Marriage Act (DOMA) in 1996. DOMA stated, "No State, territory, or possession of the United States, or Indian tribe, shall be required to give effect to any public act, record, or judicial proceeding of any other State, territory, possession, or tribe respecting a relationship between persons of the same sex that is treated as a marriage under the laws of such other State, territory, possession, or tribe, or a right or claim arising from such relationship." There are, however, questions as to whether DOMA violates the full faith and credit clause. Although the Supreme Court has not yet heard any cases challenging the constitutionality of DOMA, it is probably only a matter of time before it will.

STATE COURTS AND INTERNATIONAL LAW

On rare occasions, state courts must navigate international law. The most common areas in which international law and state courts intersect are cases that concern the death penalty for minors, child abduction from foreign nations, diplomatic and sovereign immunity, commerce with belligerents during times of war, and civil claims that involve foreign plaintiffs or defendants. The intersection of state courts and international law is governed by the U.S. Constitution. The supremacy clause binds state judges to enforce all federal laws and all federal treaties.

Before the Constitution was drafted, U.S. treaty obligations were enforced in separate state courts. Often, state courts favored the inhabitants of their own state. As a result, foreign citizens had a difficult time obtaining justice under treaty obligations. In response, foreign investors were reluctant to invest their capital in the United States. When the Framers met in Philadelphia, they sought to fix this problem with the supremacy clause. The supremacy clause requires state judges to enforce international

---

State Courts in International Law: A Case from NAFTA

In 1993, the United States, Mexico, and Canada passed the North American Free Trade Agreement (NAFTA). Chapter 11 of NAFTA created international tribunals that hear appeals from defendants who feel that a foreign court has subjected them to unfair damage awards. In 1995 a Mississippi jury awarded two Americans $500 million from a Canadian company for breach of contract. After paying a reduced amount of $175 million, the Canadian company, claiming an abuse of due process, filed a suit for $725 million against the United States in a NAFTA tribunal. The tribunal rejected the claim noting that the Canadian company had become a U.S. company and that NAFTA tribunals only allow foreign companies to sue.

The use of NAFTA tribunals is rare and amounts to about twenty cases in the first ten years of the agreement. However, these courts indicate the ever increasing overlap between state courts and international law.

President George H.W. Bush attends the North American Free Trade Act (NAFTA) initialing ceremony in October 1992. Among NAFTA's many provisions is a system for tribunals to review some international consumer and business disputes. In the United States, this is an area of law dominated by state courts. (George Bush Library)

treaties in their courts. In 1920 the State of Missouri sought to challenge the right of the federal government to impose treaty obligations on states. In *Missouri v. Holland,* the U.S. Supreme Court upheld a treaty protecting the migration of birds between Canada and the United States against Missouri's assertions that the Tenth Amendment insulated the state from treaty regulations.

State courts are increasingly called on to settle international disputes. There are three reasons for the increase. First, the federal government continues to sign more international treaties, thus increasing the amalgamation of domestic law with international law. Second, treaties used to focus on the relationships between two state actors. Today, it is common for international treaties to focus on the relationships between states and individual citizens. As a result, state courts must adjudicate individual claims of foreign citizens rather than just resolving disputes from foreign government actors. Third, globalization has led to an increase in international commerce. Mundane contract and tort cases are now more likely to involve at least one foreign corporation or a foreign citizen. Because international commerce is controlled by both domestic laws and international treaties, state courts must look to many sources of law before resolving a dispute.

The Convention on the Civil Aspects of International Child Abduction illustrates how international law overlaps with federal and state law. The convention was passed at The Hague in 1980. The international treaty requires that children who are abducted from their home country be returned to their country of origin. After signing the treaty, the United States made it enforceable domestically by passing the International Child Abduction Remedies Act. The act requires that state courts, with some minor exceptions, enforce the international treaty and return abducted children to their homeland.

In different instances, state courts are expressly released from the obligations of international treaties. In 1992, the United States ratified the International Covenant on Civil and Political Rights. One of the provisions in the covenant is a prohibition on the execution of minors. However, the United States Supreme Court has upheld the right of states to execute minors. Therefore, there appears to be a conflict between state law and international law. Foreseeing this problem, the U.S. Senate included a reservations provision when it ratified the covenant. The U.S. Senate uses reservations provisions when it feels international treaties will interfere with existing domestic law—in this case, the right of state courts to uphold death penalty sentences to minors.

The use of international treaties to protect the procedural rights of foreign criminal defendants in U.S. courts is a relatively new area of law. The U.S. Supreme Court has yet to speak definitively on this subject. Recently, the ability of states to prosecute and punish foreign nationals has come under international attack because the United States is a signatory of the Vienna Convention on Consular Relations. This international treaty requires that arrested foreign nationals have the right to meet with representatives from their country. As of 2004, over fifty Mexican nationals have been convicted of capital crimes in eight different states in the United States. In each of those cases, the defendants did not meet with representatives of the Mexican government. The International Court of Justice ruled that state courts could not order the execution of these individuals. However, state courts are not required to follow the dictates of the International Court of Justice. In most cases, the United States ratifies treaties with non-self-executing provisions. These provisions state that the clauses of the treaty are only enforceable after the U.S. has enacted specific laws to make them enforceable. Whereas U.S. Congress specifically passed the International Child Abduction Remedies Act to make the Convention on the Civil Aspects of International Child Abduction enforceable in the United States, no such law was passed with respect to the Vienna Convention on Consular Relations. Until the Supreme Court speaks definitively on the use of international treaties in state courts, disputes about their applicability will be common.

REFERENCES AND FURTHER READING

Atkins, Burton, and Henry Glick. 1976. "Environmental and Structural Variables as Determinants of Issues in State Courts of Last Resort." *American Journal of Political Science* 20 (February): 97–115.

Baum, Lawrence. 1994. "What Judges Want: Judges' Goals and Judicial Behavior." *Political Research Quarterly* 47, no. 3 (September): 749–768.

Beiser, Edward. 1974. "The Rhode Island Supreme Court: A Well-Integrated Political System." *Law and Society Review* 8, no. 1: 167–186.

Buehler, Cheryl, and Jean Gerard. 1995. "Divorce Law in the United States: A Focus on Child Custody." *Family Relations* 44, no. 4: 439–458.

Caldeira, Gregory. 1983. "On the Reputation of State Supreme Courts." *Political Behavior* 5, no. 1: 83–108.

———. 1985. "The Transmission of Legal Precedent: A Study of State Supreme Courts." *American Political Science Review* 79 (March): 178–193.

Canon, Bradley. 1972. "The Impact of Formal Selection Processes on the Characteristics of Judges—Reconsidered." *Law and Society Review* 13: 570–593.

———. 1973. "Reactions of State Supreme Courts to a U.S. Supreme Court Civil Liberties Decision." *Law and Society Review* 8, no. 1: 109–134.

Canon, Bradley, and Dean Jaros. 1970. "External Variables, Institutional Structure and Dissent on State Supreme Courts." *Polity* 4: 185–200.

Canon, Bradley, and Lawrence Baum. 1981. "Patterns of Tort Law Innovations: An Application of Diffusion Theory to Judicial Doctrines." *American Political Science Review* 75 (December): 975–987.

Champagne, Anthony, and Judith Haydel, eds. 1993. *Judicial Reform in the States*. Lanham, MD: University Press of America.

Cohen, Jeffrey, and Charles Barrilleaux. 1993. "Public Opinion, Interest Groups, and Public Policy Making: Abortion Policy in the American States." In *Understanding the New Politics of Abortion*, ed. Malcolm Goggin. Newbury Park, CA: Sage Publications.

Emmert, Craig. 1988. "Judicial Review in State Supreme Courts: Opportunity and Activism." Paper presented at the Midwest Political Science Association Meeting, Chicago.

———. 1992. "An Integrated Case-Related Model of Judicial Decision Making: Explaining State Supreme Court Decisions in Judicial Review Cases." *Journal of Politics* 54, no. 2: 543–552.

Esler, Michael. 2003. "Federal Jurisprudence, State Autonomy: *Michigan v. Long:* A Twenty Year Retrospective." *Albany Law Review* 66 (March): 835–856.

Forer, Lois. 1992. "Justice by the Numbers." *The Washington Monthly* (April): 12–14.

Glick, Henry. 1991. "Policy Making and State Supreme Courts. In *The American Courts: A Critical Assessment*, eds. John Gates and Charles Johnson. Washington, DC: Congressional Quarterly Press.

Glick, Henry, and Kenneth Vines. 1969. "Law-Making in the State Judiciary: A Comparative Study of the Judicial Role in Four States." *Polity* 2, no. 1: 142–159.

———. 1973. *State Court Systems*. Englewood Cliffs, NJ: Prentice-Hall.

Goggin, Malcolm, and Christopher Wlezien. 1993. "Abortion Opinion and Policy in the American States." In *Understanding the New Politics of Abortion,* ed. Malcolm Goggin. Newbury Park, CA: Sage Publications.

Halva-Neubauer, Glenn. 1993. "The States after *Roe:* No Paper Tigers." In *Understanding the New Politics of Abortion,* ed. Malcolm L. Goggin. Newbury Park, CA: Sage Publications.

Handberg, Roger. 1978. "Leadership in State Courts of Last Resort: The Interaction of Environment and Procedure." *Jurimetrics* 19: 178–195.

Justice at Stake Campaign, http://www.justiceatstake.org/ (accessed March 29, 2006).

Kagen, Robert, Bliss Cartwright, Lawrence Friedman, and Stanton Wheeler. 1977. "The Business of State Supreme Courts, 1870–1970." *Stanford Law Review* 30, no. 1: 121–156.

McConkie, James. 1976. "Decision-Making in State Supreme Courts." *Judicature* 59 (February): 337–343.

Miller, Ken. 1999. "The Role of Courts in the Initiative Process: A Search for Standards." American Political Science Association, Atlanta, GA.

National Courts Statistics Project. "Tort and Contract Caseloads in State Courts," http://www.ncsconline.org/D_Research/csp/CSP_Main_Page.html (accessed March 29, 2006).

Nelson, William. 1972. "Changing Conceptions of Judicial Review: The Evolution of Constitutional Theory in the State, 1790–1860." *University of Penn Law Review* 120: 1166–1185.

Ostrom, Brian, Neal Kauder, and Robert LaFountain. 2002. *Examining the Work of State Courts, 2001: A National Perspective from the Court Statistics Project.* Williamsburg, VA: National Center for State Courts.

Phillips, Thomas. 2003. "State Supreme Courts: Local Courts in a Global World." *Texas International Law Journal* 38, no. 3: 557–568.

Romans, Neil. 1974. "The Role of State Supreme Courts in Judicial Policy Making: *Escobedo, Miranda* and the Use of Judicial Impact Analysis." *Western Political Quarterly* 27, no. 1: 38–59.

Romero, David, and Francine Romero. 2003. "Precedent, Parity, and Racial Discrimination: A Federal /State Comparison of the Impact of *Brown v. Board of Education.*" *Law and Society Review* 37, no. 4: 809–827.

Slotnick, Elliot. 1977. "Who Speaks for the Court: The View from the States." *Emory Law Journal* 26, no. 1: 107–147.

Songer, Donald, and Susan Tabrizi. 1999. "The Religious Right in Court: The Decision Making of Christian Evangelicals in State Supreme Courts." *Journal of Politics* 61 (May): 507–526.

Tarr, Alan. 1992. *Constitutional Politics in the States: Contemporary Controversies and Historical Patterns.* London: Greenwood Press.

———. 1998. *Understanding State Constitutions.* Princeton: Princeton University Press.

Tarr, Alan, and Mary Porter. 1988. *State Supreme Courts in States and Nations.* New Haven, CT: Yale University Press.

Topf, Mel. 2001. "State Supreme Court Advisory Opinions as Illegitimate Judicial Review." *Detroit College of Law at Michigan State University Law Review* 1, no. 1: 101–137.

The Vanishing Trial: Papers from Symposium on Civil Justice Initiatives Task Force, American Bar Association, http://www.abanet.org/litigation/taskforces/cji/nosearch/home.html (accessed March 29, 2006).

Walsh, Joseph. 2003. "The Evolving Role of State Constitutional Law in Death Penalty Adjudication." *New York University Annual Survey of American Law* 59, no. 2: 341–353.

White, Penny. 2003. "Legal, Political, and Ethical Hurdles to Applying International Human Rights Law in the State Courts of the United States." *University of Cincinnati Law Review* 71 (Spring): 937–975.

Cases

Armatta v. Kitzhaber. 1998. 327 Ore. 250; 959 P.2d 49.
Barron v. Baltimore. 1833. 32 U.S. 243.
Beal v. Doe. 1977. 432 U.S. 43; 97 S. Ct. 2366.
Brown v. Board of Education. 1954. 347 U.S. 483.
Burton v. Covenant Care. 2002. 99 Cal. App. 4th 1361; 122 Cal.
Bush v. Gore. 2000. 531 U.S. 98; 121 S. Ct. 525.
District of Appeals v. Feldman. 1983. 460 U.S. 462; 103 S. Ct. 1303.
Erie v. Tompkins. 1938. 304 U.S. 64; 58 S. Ct. 817.
Escobedo v. Illinois. 1964. 378 U.S. 478; 84 S. Ct. 1758.
Gideon v. Wainwright. 1963. 372 U.S. 335; 83 S. Ct. 792.
Gilmer v. Interstate/Johnson Lane Corp. 1991. 500 U.S. 20; 111 S. Ct. 1647.
Goodridge v. Department of Health. 2003. 440 Mass. 309, 323.
Guinn v. Legislature of Nevada. 2003. 71 P.3d 1269.
Lawrence v. Texas. 2003. 539 U.S. 558; 123 S. Ct. 2472.
Maher v. Roe. 1977. 432 U.S. 464; 97 S. Ct. 2376.
Mapp v. Ohio. 1961. 367 U.S. 643; 81 S. Ct. 1684.
Michigan v. Long. 1983. 463 U.S. 1032; 103 S. Ct. 3469.
Milwaukee County v. M. E. White Co. 1935. 296 U.S. 268.
Miranda v. Arizona. 1966. 384 U.S. 436; 86 S. Ct. 1602.
Missouri v. Holland. 1920. 252 U.S. 416.
Rooker v. Fidelity Trust Co. 1923. 261 U.S. 114; 43 S. Ct. 288.
Smiley v. Citibank. 1995. 11 Cal. 4th 138; 900 P.2d 690; 44 Cal.
State v. Fuller. 1996. 915 P.2d 809, 816.
United States v. Lopez. 1995. 514 U.S. 549; 115 S. Ct. 1624.
United States v. Morrison. 2000. 529 U.S. 598; 120 S. Ct. 1740.
White v. Davis. 2003. 30 Cal. 4th 528; 68 P.3d 74; 133 Cal.
Zelman v. Simmons-Harris. 2002. 536 U.S. 639; 122 S. Ct. 2460.

3

THE STRUCTURE AND PROCESS OF STATE COURTS

Sean O. Hogan

This chapter explains the structure and processes of each level of the court systems at work in the American states. It also explains, in general terms, how a case is filed, negotiated, tried, appealed, and announced. The first part describes judicial structures beginning with the most local and limited levels of judicial decision making. The discussion follows the court system, ascending to the most general and authoritative courts in the states. Since no two state court systems are exactly alike, this chapter provides a general overview of common characteristics and important differences. Chapter 6 provides a state-by-state explanation of each state's court structure.

The second part of the chapter explains the judicial process. It begins with an examination of the elements necessary to make a claim in court and goes on to explain how a case would proceed through the court system. It provides insight to the nature of evidence and argument, general filing requirements, and some detail into how the decision makers in state appeals and supreme courts discuss, negotiate, and resolve cases out of the public view.

STRUCTURE OF COURT SYSTEMS

It may be appealing to think of courts in the hierarchical structure of the federal judicial system. The general structure of the federal judicial system is drawn to look like a pyramid. It begins with trial courts at the foundation, appellate courts in the middle, and a court of last resort at the apex. Thinking of the state courts in these terms, however, would be a serious mistake. Only four states—Illinois, Iowa, Minnesota, and South Dakota—have this type of three-step judicial system: trial court of general jurisdiction, an intermediate court of appeals, and a single court of last resort. Each of the remaining forty-six states has its own variety of courts of limited jurisdiction. Two states (Oklahoma and Texas) have more than one court of final resort. The states with courts of limited jurisdiction have distinct appeals processes, sometimes requiring more steps between the trial court and court of final appeal than would be the case in the federal system. Some state court systems do not have the intermediate appellate court, which means that appeals of trial court decisions proceed directly to a court of last resort.

All of this is to say that no one diagram accurately describes the structure of state court systems. Rather, it is more accurate to think of the variety of court systems that exist. Despite the variety of structures, the Fourteenth Amendment of the U.S. Constitution insists on some characteristics of *due process* that make some of the procedures and structures common to all states. One of the most important due process features that affect structure is the principle that a trial decision may be reviewed by an appeals court. In other words, in every state, no matter how simple or complex in structure, there is a court of origin in which cases are initially filed (originates) and where trials are held. There is also at least one court of review, or a court of appeals, which is authorized to accept, reject, or require modifications to the legal decisions made in lower courts. This section begins with an explanation of the courts of most narrow and limited authority. It then progresses to a discussion of trial courts with general authority and finally moves through the appeals process.

Courts of Limited Jurisdiction

Courts of limited jurisdiction are those trial courts authorized to resolve cases of a special and focused nature. This contrasts with courts of general jurisdiction, in which any type of case, with any level of significance, can be filed.

Organized either by a state constitution or by an act of legislation, courts of limited jurisdiction may have geographic jurisdiction. A common type of limited jurisdiction court is a municipal court, which serves the needs of an individual city. In other cases, these courts are limited by subject matter, such as drug courts, family courts, and in some Western states, water courts. Some are limited by the gravity of the issues that may be brought before them, such as small-claims courts, which are limited by the dollar value of the awards they can issue.

It is perhaps the limited jurisdiction courts that distinguish the state judicial systems from one another. In the United States, there are 13,515 of these limited jurisdiction courts. What makes the judicial systems so distinctive is that there are so many types of limited jurisdiction courts across the nation. Moreover, even when states have the same type of limited jurisdiction courts, there can be important differences in how these courts function and the work they do. New York and Georgia, for example, have eight separate limited jurisdiction courts. Some of these courts may have jury trials, while others are not allowed to use juries. Some of the limited jurisdiction courts are active in specific locations, such as Atlanta or New York City, while others are found in every part of these states.

Massachusetts, for example, has six types of limited courts. In Massachusetts one special court, *probate and family* court, deals with divorce and adoptions, while the *ju-*

venile court handles other domestic matters such as domestic battery. New Jersey has a tax court, where residents are able to contest local tax bills. Other states have specific duty courts to deal with the environment, water rights, wills, or children. Despite these important differences, there are eight main types of limited jurisdiction courts. These are described in the following sections. Read the individual state entries in Chapter 6 for details about each state's court system.

Administrative Agency Courts

Administrative agency courts are designated to hear cases emerging from disputes with particular governmental bureaucracies, or on narrowly defined subject matter. Administrative courts are independent from the executive branch of government. Before accepting cases, these courts typically require that all avenues for resolving the conflict through commissions and agencies have been attempted. It is only when the bureaucracy has failed to find a resolution that is satisfactory to the parties involved in the dispute that the court will take up a particular case. Selection of judges, their terms of service, and qualifications for office vary by state. Appeals of the decisions made by administrative agency courts go directly to intermediate appeals courts, or in some states, to the highest court.

There are different types of administrative courts across the nation. The development of particular administrative courts is closely connected to the particular culture, history, industry, and natural environment of individual states. For example, there are water courts in arid Western states, such as Montana and Colorado, which are often subject to drought and forest fires. The water courts allocate access rights to rivers, lakes, and underground aquifers. In Arizona, where many residents prefer limited governmental intervention, there is a special *tax court* to review complaints about property tax assessments.

Chancery Courts

Chancery courts are judicial offices where chancellors rather than judges are empowered to substitute equity for law in rendering a decision. The point of a court of equity is to afford a *fair* ruling when the common law might render a harsh verdict.

A decision in equity often takes the form of commandment for some party to act, or stop performing some act. These injunctions and orders typically attempt to balance financial considerations with other values not easily understood in the common-law tradition. Common-law traditions would care only about the ownership of some property, ignoring the historic, natural, sentimental, or spiritual value of that property to nonowners. For example, a real estate developer with a proper deed to land may discover that he is building on an ancient Native American burial ground. The sentimental and spiritual value of this parcel to a Native American tribe may be argued in a court of equity. The tribe may seek *equitable* relief, or an order to refrain from upsetting holy ground, without any demand for money to change hands.

As venues for resolving dispute, *courts of equity* handle disputes that are concerned with business, finances, tax, contracts, shareholders, and property. In some states, such as Arkansas and Mississippi, chancery courts have jurisdiction in civil areas like wills, family, juvenile, and insanity cases.

Chancery courts have existed in Europe since feudal times. Chancellors hear cases either alone, or on panels that usually consist of three people. While the United States inherited many English legal traditions, the importance of chancery courts in the United States has diminished over time. The clear distinction between law and equity has faded and the two principles may be pleaded in the same court. Through adoption of the U.S. Constitution in 1789, federal courts were authorized to hear both law and equity cases. Most states followed suit and abandoned the use of a distinct chancery court. However, Arkansas, Delaware, Tennessee, Mississippi, and, to a lesser extent, New Jersey, maintain distinct chanceries in their state court systems.

Originating as clerical offices of European monarchs, chanceries eventually gained from the Crown the power to waive common-law judgments. The ancient chanceries were organized to provide ministerial support, maintain official records, and provide formal communications for European kings, princes, and bishops. Chancellors later were given power to resolve disputes outside common-law systems.

Today some chanceries still perform support functions by providing notary services and record keeping.

Drug Courts

Drug courts are among the most recent types of limited jurisdiction courts in the nation, and have become one of the busiest. The creation and growth in drug court activity reflects changes in laws during the 1980s. At this time the "war on drugs" meant state and federal officials tightened laws against the trafficking and possession of illegal substances. Many misdemeanor offenses were reclassified as felonies, drug laws were enforced more rigorously, and punishments became more severe. With stricter laws, the caseloads of the state trial courts swelled. In 1997 more than one-third of the nation's prison population was made up of individuals who had been convicted on drug offenses. This compares with about 7 percent in 1980 (Garrison 2002). With this burgeoning activity in court, states established special venues to handle the traffic in drug cases.

These courts are unique in that they generally have broader geographic jurisdiction than most state trial courts. Where most state courts have geographic jurisdiction boundaries, drug courts operate without these to avoid questions about *venue*, or where a trial must be held. Drug courts also are encouraged to refer cases to federal courts when federal penalties are higher or when a case involves interstate drug trafficking.

Drug courts rely both on traditional punishment as well as rehabilitation, counseling, and education programs to discourage offenders from using drugs in the future. In states with drug courts, a special division of the local court system receives most drug cases. Drug case judges receive additional training and have social service agencies in close contact but remain in the general jurisdiction court systems.

Family Courts

Family courts, sometimes called *domestic relations* courts, deal strictly with family matters. There are ten states that have formal family courts. In these courts, a specially trained family law judge hears domestic abuse, juvenile delinquency, and divorce cases. Family law concerns adoptions, incest, domestic violence, juvenile delinquency, disposing of wills, divorce, institutionalization of someone mentally unfit to care for him- or herself, and paternity–child custody issues.

Family-court judges are afforded additional personnel and liaisons with social service agencies uniquely suited to dealing with the sensitive domestic issues beyond the typical scope of the legal dispute. Family courts have extra latitude to look at social rehabilitation in addition to incarceration and penalties when criminal behavior is involved. In some states, such as Delaware, judges are required to have specialized training and practice in domestic law matters prior to serving as a family court judge, while most other states do not formally recognize family law as a subspecialty.

Justice of the Peace Courts

Justice of the peace courts may be best known for providing civil marriage ceremonies. Once a fixture in every state, today justices of the peace (JPs) have judicial duties in only seven states: Arizona, Arkansas, Delaware, Louisiana, Montana, Wyoming, and Texas. These JPs are magistrates in petty criminal offenses and small-claims civil cases; they are notaries and they administer oaths of office. Several other states continue to select JPs but do not grant them any formal court authority. Rather, in states such as Vermont, JPs serve on local election commissions, hear tax abatement petitions, and preside at weddings. Unlike other judicial officers, JPs advertise their wedding services and earn income this way. JPs usually are chosen in local elections and are not required to have a law license. The idea of justice of the peace courts came to colonial America from England. British monarchs appointed JPs to serve a variety of local judicial and administrative purposes in rural government. Most of the early JPs in America were volunteer judges and police officers, and were not trained in law.

Juvenile Courts

In recent decades, the juvenile courts in many states have been absorbed into family courts. Where they are active, juvenile court is another name for family court. Juvenile courts began in Chicago in 1899 and service two types of youths: abused and neglected children, and young criminal suspects. The reason for special juvenile criminal courts is three-fold. First, some crimes, such as truancy and curfew violations, apply only to youths. Second, U.S. society generally has come to accept the idea that young offenders should be given a second chance at a career and social life without the baggage of an adult criminal record. So, teens may be tried in a specially designated juvenile court. Third, juvenile courts are often equipped to coordinate traditional legal intervention with social and developmental resources to modify the behavior of young offenders and to place abused or neglected children in foster care.

The use of juvenile courts provides states with a means to address these concerns. Moreover, the use of these courts also helps keep the names of juvenile offenders secret and the court proceedings closed to the public. By concealing juvenile offenders in this manner, it helps protect the juveniles' reputation and the reputation of their families, which can help reduce recidivism. Abused children similarly benefit from this type of discreet court system.

Juvenile court processes often automatically trigger evaluations of a young person's needs for education, substance abuse treatment, or family counseling; whereas adult criminal courts do not necessarily do so. During the late 1980s and 1990s, however, a rash of gang-related violence prompted prosecutors to bring teenagers charged with violent and serious drug crimes to adult courts, where they would be punished as adults rather than as children. Today, twenty-eight states require that older teens charged with

---

Arbitration

In arbitration, a neutral decision maker called an arbitrator takes information and recommends a solution. The arbitrator may take testimony or make a decision after only reading documents. If there is a hearing, the setting can be informal and closed to the public, unlike a trial. Arbitration can be binding or advisory. A mediator is like an arbitrator, but gives only advisory opinions, while an arbitrator's decisions are said to have more binding power.

Begun principally as a means of resolving labor disputes, arbitration is increasingly used in real estate, insurance, and other contract cases. Some thirty-five states have laws that govern arbitration, as does the federal government. Though arbitrators are not government officials, state laws frequently give them limited power to issue subpoenas and to render binding decisions. State law also sets out the rights of parties to have an attorney, fees arbitrators can charge, how they must communicate their rulings, and the appeals process. States also decide what parts of an arbitration's record can be presented in court. Usually, laws state that arbitrators themselves cannot be questioned in court and evidence is shielded from use in the judicial process.

Arbitration begins when there is a dispute, and one party files an *arbitration*

claim with the arbitrator. The arbitrator notifies the other side and informs both of hearing dates. Arbitration can relax some of the trial procedures, rules of evidence, or witness questioning. However, most states insist that evidence is shared before hearings, much like a discovery. Law usually requires both parties to have an opportunity to be heard and to cross-examine adverse witnesses. Where judges are prohibited from meeting with only one side of a dispute, in arbitration this can be different. Arbitrators are not necessarily licensed lawyers and they do not necessarily follow the tradition of consulting written legal opinion to support their decisions. Better arbitration services make known their rules of procedure and the principles on which their arbitrators should make judgments.

Some law firms specialize in this type of practice, rather than the more conventional practice of giving advice and advocacy. Fees for this service, and which party must pay for the service, are set out in a contract. There is neither a uniform standard of qualifications to act as an arbitrator, nor is there a national association of career arbitrators. Since there is no professional association of arbitrators little is known for certain about the amount of arbitration, the variety of cases handled, or number of arbitrators in practice.

violent crimes be processed in adult courts. The specific age at which teens are now being charged as adults depends on the state, but it ranges from ages fifteen to seventeen. In other jurisdictions, a court order is required to try teens in adult court. Nationally, for every 1,000 formal delinquency cases, an average of eight were waived to adult criminal court between 1989 and 1998 (Puzzanchera 2001). The number of waived cases has declined since 1994 to 1.2 percent of all juvenile criminal cases.

Municipal Courts

Municipal courts (city courts and alderman's courts) typically have jurisdiction over cases involving local regulations. These courts decide local liquor-license issues, complaints about land-use violations, city ordinance violations, misdemeanor traffic and parking violations, and other minor complaints. In many states, such as Delaware, local elected officials, including the mayor or city council members, preside over these courts as part of their official duties. In Montana the municipal courts have jurisdiction in small claims, with maximum awards ranging from $3,000 to $15,000. The Montana courts often include a jury. Meanwhile, municipal courts in Arkansas and New Jersey have no juries, but presiding officers handle initial felony appearances. The existence and particular powers of these courts vary, even within individual states.

Small-Claims Courts

Small-claims courts are those with jurisdiction to hear cases with very limited financial implications, generally valued up to $15,000, or with a maximum as low as $5,000. Small-claims courts generally have less rigorous procedures and they are venues that encourage individuals to represent themselves, without the assistance of a lawyer. In many instances the small-claims courts have been absorbed into municipal courts where a magistrate assists the trial court by setting bond and still satisfying demands for justice claimants of modest means.

Courts of General Jurisdiction

Moving up the judicial ladder are courts of general jurisdiction. Unlike courts of limited jurisdiction, courts of general jurisdiction exist in every state. However, like limited jurisdiction courts, these courts are designed as trial-level courts. The general jurisdiction courts are the first step in the judicial process for felonies and larger civil disputes in all states, even if there is a limited jurisdiction court for the cases of lower financial value or criminal gravity. Their jurisdiction is called *general* because there are very few limitations on the nature of the cases that may come to their attention.

They have authority to try facts and apply law in both civil and criminal affairs, regardless of their magnitude. In states using courts of limited jurisdiction the general jurisdiction courts serve dual roles. Their first role is to serve as the trial court for most felonies and civil cases with higher amounts of money at issue. A second role for general jurisdiction courts is to hear appeals from limited jurisdiction courts. Discussions of both these functions follow.

Courts of general (superior) original jurisdiction are trial-level courts that hear a wide range of criminal and civil cases, from misdemeanors to felony offenses and from small-claims cases to large-sum civil suits. In less populated communities, an individual judge will hear a broad array of case types, while in court systems in heavily populated areas, such as the Cook County Circuit Court in the Chicago area, judges are assigned either to a civil or criminal court, but not both.

These courts go by various names. In California, New Jersey, and Rhode Island they are called *superior* courts; in Illinois, Kentucky, and Michigan, *circuit* courts; and in Iowa, Louisiana, and Montana, *district* courts. In New York the supreme court is the general jurisdiction trial court and the court of appeals is the court of last resort, but the court structure is even more complicated than this. The supreme court in New York City hears both criminal and civil complaints, but in the rest of the state the supreme court hears only civil suits, while the county court hears criminal cases.

Indiana has both superior courts and circuit courts, with almost identical duties. However, Indiana's superior courts are created by the state legislature and circuit courts by the constitution. The selection process of superior court judges varies from place to place within the state. Indiana's circuit courts, however, were created by the state constitution; the state circuit judges are chosen by election.

Powers of General Jurisdiction Courts

In addition to their role in hearing these types of cases, general jurisdiction courts frequently are the first level in the appellate process in states with limited jurisdiction courts. Land-use cases contested in municipal courts often are good candidates for rehearing in the more rigorous superior courts. Once a case has been decided in a limited court, the dissatisfied party may seek review in the general court. A single judge, assigned randomly in most cases, will preside during the presentation of arguments and reexamination of evidence.

Courts of general jurisdiction have the authority to set bail. In states where a limited jurisdiction court initially sets bail, the general jurisdiction court can modify the bail. In many jurisdictions, judges can modify jury sentences and remedies. These courts have power to determine which evidence may be excluded from trial, stop a lawyer from posing particular questions, or rule that an argument is not germane to the trial. These courts also have power to weigh the value of that evidence. Courts of general jurisdiction also have authority to review the actions of other coequal branches of government and set those actions aside if they do not meet with principles of the state or federal constitutions. This is a power called *judicial review,* and this power is described in greater detail later.

Finally, these courts have authority to make binding judgments. Sides are obliged by law to comply with the orders of a court of general jurisdiction. The decisions of trial courts rarely are set aside, and usually never come to review. Recent statistics from the National Center for State Courts indicate that barely 278,000 final trial decisions are challenged with an appeal.

Intermediate Appellate Courts

The American legal tradition favors the idea that, in law, each party is entitled to a fair trial and a fair review of that trial. The next step in that ladder, in all but eight states and the District of Columbia, is an intermediate court of appeals. These courts exist to ensure that each side had an adequate opportunity to present its case, challenge opposing evidence, and have a ruling from a decision maker with no stake in the outcome. A panel of three judges usually makes the decisions of appellate courts.

Appellate courts are not designed to retry cases. Evidence is not presented and witnesses are not called to testify. Instead, appellate judges assume that lower courts correctly decided the *facts* of the case, and only those facts presented at trial can be discussed on appeal. What is of interest to the appeals court is the legal meaning that the lower court gave to the facts. Rather than trying to prove guilt or innocence, lawyers filing an appeal usually try to prove there was an error in the trial process, that the law was not properly applied, or that the law itself is illegitimate. Appellate courts assume the trial was conducted fairly. However, if the process or the law was in error, the case outcome should be reversed on appeal.

When bringing a case to appeal, the process shifts the burden of proof to the one pressing the appellate case, no matter his status at trial. Appellate courts presume the lower court's verdict was correct; that the trial court properly applied the law, and that it met the constitutional requirements for ensuring that the defendant's due process rights were protected.

Among the primary justifications for the creation of appellate courts is to reduce the workload on courts of final resort and to afford parties dissatisfied with the trial outcome an opportunity for a higher court to review the lower court's ruling. States like Tennessee, Texas, and Oklahoma have separate intermediate courts for criminal and civil matters. Delaware, Maine, Montana, Nevada, New Hampshire, North Dakota, Rhode Island, Vermont, West Virginia, and Wyoming do not have separate intermediate appellate courts. However, their courts of general jurisdiction can review the decisions of lower limited jurisdiction courts. When the general jurisdiction courts of these states are the court of origin, appeals are made directly to the court of last resort.

In ten jurisdictions, only a trial court and a final court, with no intermediate court, make up the judicial process. In Oklahoma, criminal cases can be appealed to the court of criminal appeals, which is the final state court for a criminal case. However, there is a middle-tier court of civil appeals. In other words, only civil cases get an intermediate level of review. This again demonstrates that the duties and structures of appellate jurisdiction can be as varied among the states as are the courts of origin.

The Powers of Appellate Courts

For a detailed explanation of appellate powers, see Chapter 2. While quite varied, typical powers of appeals courts include issuing or rescinding restraining orders or injunctions. In rare cases they can decide to reject an appeal. More likely, they may set aside a final trial decision, or exercise judicial review.

The authority of the intermediate appellate courts is established by state law and varies considerably. State constitutions and statutes determine which court may receive appeals, or whether appellate courts have discretion in taking cases. State law establishes whether intermediate courts can issue various types of orders to individuals and governmental agencies. Laws and constitutional provisions establish whether appellate courts may alter a lower-court's judgment on criminal sentences or civil remedies. Law and custom decide whether these courts will remand a case—that is to return it to the trial court for new proceedings—or whether the outcome for the parties is determined at the appeal level.

Courts of Final Resort

At the end of the judicial system in each state is a court of last resort (COLR). This is the final court in a state's judicial system and the one empowered with the greatest authority to give meaning to the law in each state. Most commonly, these courts are called the state supreme court. In some states, however, they go by other names. In New York, the highest court is the court of appeals. In Oklahoma and Texas, there are two final courts: one for criminal appeals and another for civil decisions. Almost all final courts sit *en banc*, but in Connecticut, Mississippi, Montana, Nebraska, Nevada, and New Mexico, three- to five-member panels of the COLR review cases from the lower courts.

Membership in the COLRs ranges between five to nine justices, with all final courts having an odd number of justices. Odd-numbered courts avoid tied decisions. When there is a vacancy causing an even number of judges on the COLR, ties may occur. In such a case, the lower court ruling would stand. In general, COLRs sit en banc, that is to say all the judges on the court, not just a panel, hear cases. As is the situation with trial and appellate courts, the final courts in the American states differ in their structure, size, and authorities.

Courts of last resort are reviewing panels and almost never hear trials. In some situations they are authorized to do so, but in general they delegate trial duties to lower courts, or to an especially appointed master. The COLR, then, reviews the evidence and written decision of the master.

Since these courts usually are not reviewing facts, the questions from judges focus more on how law applies. This type of hearing is almost identical to that of the intermediate appeals court process. The process of these hearings is described in the coming pages.

Complete discussion of appellate powers is explored in Chapter 2. However, to understand the process it is important to recall ways in which those powers emerge from the COLR's place in the American judicial process. In certain cases like death penalty cases, the COLR may be forced into the process, whereas in other areas of law, it may have a choice to withhold judgment. Unlike the intermediate and trial courts, courts of last resort have significant control over their dockets.

Often state COLRs are required to hear *certified questions,* in which lower court judges ask the higher court for clarification on matters of law or procedure needed to allow a trial to proceed. State constitutions also force high courts to hear cases involving judicial review, budget matters, or separation-of-power cases. Supreme courts may also find themselves authorized to try cases of mandamus, where the court is asked to order an office holder from another branch of state government to fulfill some official responsibility. Additional powers of these courts may include the discipline of wayward lawyers, setting rules of procedure for all courts in the state, filling certain judicial vacancies, and handling other administrative matters. However, their most important power is serving as the state's final authority in the judicial process. These courts decide matters of federal and state constitutional law, death penalties, and rules that affect millions of dollars at stake in civil litigation.

JUDICIAL PROCESS

The structure of the court system itself implies a process. In this process few and fewer cases are brought up to higher levels of authority for review. Only after another decision has been made can a case go up the hierarchy for further review. The judicial process in the American states is intended to ensure fairness, although it can be somewhat mystifying. Essential elements of this process are explained in the following sections.

Types of Claims

Once an injury or a crime is to be presented to a court for a decision, the first step is to make the complaint known to a court. Filing a claim, or synonymously a petition, initiates the judicial process. A criminal claim often is called a *complaint* or a *charge.* The party who feels injured by the other party files the claim. The responding party files an *answer.*

Before going further, it is important to distinguish between two types of claims: civil and criminal cases. Civil and criminal complaints carry with them different procedures and expectations. A thorough examination of the distinctions between civil and criminal proceedings can be better understood once the nature of civil and criminal activity is explained.

While the purpose of both civil and criminal law is to bring order to social behavior, the distinction between the two is substantial. From the often-subtle distinctions flow very important expectations about precisely the type of behavior the court is asked to help control, who is involved in the judicial process, and the tools available to the court for accomplishing social control. The criminal-civil distinction affects who may bring a case, the rigor applied to the process, and the nature of the court's response to behavior. As is explained in further detail, if one is responding to a suit, this distinction indicates whether the government seeks to label someone a criminal and penalize a suspect as such, or whether one is being called on to repay a debt or perform a promised service. The distinction suggests whether one can require the government to hire the respondent an attorney (if unable to pay), or whether one must rely on his or her own resources to get legal advice. It also determines whether the court has authority in law to sentence the defendant to prison, or merely order the defendant to comply with the terms of a contract.

Criminal Cases

A criminal act is considered a disruption to the community as a whole, not just to the individual victim. As a consequence, only the government, acting on behalf of the community as a whole, can file criminal cases. Our society has given limited authority to government to use regulated violence to impose the community's will. Acting on behalf of their respective communities, the 2,341 state and local prosecutors' offices across the United States file their criminal complaints in the name of such parties as "the state of Arizona" or "the people of the state of Illinois." More than 14.5 million criminal cases were filed in state courts during 2000, according to the National Center for State Courts (NCSC) annual caseload statistics (2002). While the government alone files criminal cases, the government itself is never the suspect in a crime. Still, all too often governmental officials are charged with crimes because they personally abused

---

The Attorney General Addresses Public Corruption

The U.S. Attorney General's *Performance and Accountability Report of 2002* (U.S. Department of Justice, 2003) says the federal government won 631 convictions or "pretrial diversions" in public corruption cases. It collected some $28 million in restitution and an additional $25 million in fines. According to the *Accountability Report*:

Public corruption is a serious crime against both the individual and society as a whole. All public corruption offenses, regardless of the type, share a common objective: to pervert our representative system of government and replace it with a government of special interests. Furthermore, the higher the office or level of government tainted by the corruption, the broader the nega-

tive effects. The Department, therefore, places a high priority on attacking public corruption by senior government officials. The Public Corruption Unit of the FBI believes a significant amount of corruption is untouched. . . . There is a growing trend of law enforcement corruption cases involving law enforcement officers actively participating in criminal acts, rather than merely protecting such actions. The single greatest obstacle to a law enforcement corruption investigation is the fact that police departments throughout the country regard their own corruption issues as their own "dirty laundry" not to be taken outside the agency. (Section 2.4c) the authority society loaned to them. When this happens, they are prosecuted through the same system in the name of the community.

General Characteristics of Criminal Law

The key features of criminal law are that the government forbids an act, government enforces and prosecutes violations, and the law sets the terms of punishments. These punishments may include probationary periods, fines, prison terms, and even death. For an act to be considered criminal, it first must have been forbidden by an act of the legislature. Under the U.S. Constitution's ex post facto provision, the act must have occurred while a law forbidding the action was in effect. Horrible as some act might be, someone cannot be prosecuted for a crime unless a law was in existence to make that act illegal. Similarly, even with illegal acts, the Constitution prevents government from increasing the level of punishment after the act has taken place. In the U.S. tradition, foreknowledge of the punishment should deter criminal behavior, or at least allow ordinary people a way to weigh the risks of performing an illegal act before they commit it.

Felonies and Misdemeanors

Within the criminal justice system, two levels of offense are prosecuted: felony and misdemeanor. The process of each is very similar, but there are a few notable differences. To understand this it is necessary to clarify the difference between criminal and misdemeanor events.

The most offensive crimes are called felonies. This category of serious crime includes offenses such as homicide, arson, rape, large-scale drug distribution, treason, and so on. Official FBI statistics refer to many of these as index crimes. Punishments in these

---

Violent Crimes, Property Crimes, and Victimless Crimes

Criminal acts can be divided into categories of violent crimes, property crimes, and victimless crimes. Violent crimes are those acts that involve real or threatened physical harm to a person. Some 5.7 million violent crimes were estimated to have occurred in 2001, according to the DOJ Crime Victimization Survey (2005a). Also, crimes are quantified in the FBI's Uniform Crime Report, which summarizes criminal activity made known to state and local police agencies. These two reports show different levels of crime occurring. The difference between these two reports is that some crime—including violent crime—goes unreported to law enforcement agencies but gets picked up in the Crime Victimization Survey. This

is a household survey, in which an interviewer asks respondents about crimes committed against him or her.

Property crimes involve either stealing or damaging something that belongs to someone else. More than three-quarters of the 24 million crimes reported to the DOJ were property crimes. A third category, victimless crimes, includes those unlawful acts where the parties most immediately involved have given their consent. For example, prostitution, sodomy, illegal gambling, and drug possession are considered illegal in many jurisdictions. Opponents of these behaviors have argued successfully that society is diminished by these actions and should prohibit them.

types of cases usually require heavy monetary fines and can remove convicts from general society by placing them in a state penitentiary for more than a year or by putting them to death. State courts convicted 928,000 people of felony offenses in 1998, according to U.S. Department of Justice (DOJ) statistics (2005b).

Misdemeanors are minor offenses like traffic violations, minor drug possession, littering, or various boisterous behaviors. Though not as morally offensive as felonies, misdemeanors upset public peace and so they are prosecuted by the government's law enforcement agencies. Misdemeanor punishments usually require the payment of smaller fines, detention in a local jail for less than a year, or the performance of some community service.

Civil Cases

Where criminal law requires recognition of an act of the state legislature, only some of the civil law draws its authority from legislation. Courts have a greater hand in defining civil law. Another important difference is in the variety of cases. In criminal law there are felonies and misdemeanors. In civil law, there are many, many types of cases and a simple scale of severity like misdemeanor and felony cannot be applied in civil law.

Civil law finds its origins in Imperial Rome, and relies on edict, legislation, and other written regulations. The lion's share of modern civil law is intended to provide a means of peacefully resolving disputes when private individual parties believe they have been wronged. Unlike criminal cases, private parties initiate the vast majority of civil cases and a civil violation may take place even where there is no legislation to label an act illegal. Though legislatures may (and often do) create types of civil actions, courts themselves declare behaviors a violation of some interest. Even individuals can create their own expectations that civil courts can enforce, as is the case in contracts law for example. Rather than meting out punishment to offenders, the aim of a civil action is to give to each his own.

General Characteristics of Civil Law

According to the National Center for State Courts (NCSC), almost 20.3 million new civil cases were filed and about 10 million had finished their courses in state courts during 2000 (NCSC 2004). This is a much more active area of law than is criminal law, even when traffic tickets are added to the equation. Most civil cases advance private interests, but this body of law covers a huge variety of cases including divorce, child custody, personal injuries, rights to property, and contractual obligations. Civil cases generally are separated into these categories: torts, property, probate (or succession), family law, equity, contracts, and constitutional law.

Though civil cases are initiated to advance the narrow interests of an individual or firm, they may advance larger social interests as well. A civil case can advance a social interest when it is used to change the scope of the government's authority, or the balance of power between various levels of government. Civil suits also can affect whole societies by ruling on matters related to the quality of life in a neighborhood, land development, constitutional rights, pollution, and the like. Similarly, they can affect the larger society when private suits cause big interests like hospitals, drug companies, equipment makers, and other firms to modify the way they conduct business under the threat of liability suits.

Civil law may be distinguished from common law, which originated in English social customs. In the common-law tradition, judges make law. Rather than referring to legislation, common-law rulings were based on widely held expectations about relations between common, or ordinary, people. English common-law judges would explain their reasoning to establish a precedent. This precedent made explicit some social expectation and established logic that would give lawyers a basis for advising their clients. The precedent would provide other judges with principles to guide their thinking in later cases. In the American legal experience, many common law doctrines come under the umbrella of civil law. In modern law, however, the common law is considered a subset of the civil law.

Level of Proof

While the level of proof needed in criminal law is beyond a reasonable doubt, in civil law it is typically the preponderance of the evidence. Though a reasonable doubt is a flexible term, the government must put to rest any doubt that the juror of ordinary intelligence could have before there can be a finding of guilt. Though not mandatory, unanimous jury decisions have indicated the lack of a reasonable doubt. Even if the evidence is strong, if there is a small but reasonable doubt about the evidence, the doubt should decide. In civil law, the preponderance of the evidence standard allows a reasonable juror to have doubts about the evidence, but to still find for the plaintiff when the weight of the evidence seems to point in favor of the plaintiff's case.

Findings and Judgments

Another important distinction between criminal and civil law is that in a criminal case a suspect is either guilty, or not guilty. There is no in-between with criminal case outcomes. Civil cases, on the other hand, are not either-or propositions. Rather, civil courts often try to resolve the degree to which someone has a right, or an obligation, or a liability (see sidebar, p. 114). This way courts decide the amount of time and conditions surrounding visits between noncustodial parents and their children, rather than assigning exclusive custodial rights to one parent. In personal injury cases, a civil court can assign each of several drivers in a traffic accident some degree of liability for the injury suffered. This way a jury can assign some degree of fault to a plaintiff for not fastening her seatbelt, and a proportional share to the other drivers.

A further distinction is in the outcome of a case. While maximum criminal sentences are fixed in law, civil remedies, including financial payments, often are much more flexible. A court might require the liable party to pay a fair share to repair damaged property, to replace a defective product, or the courts might order someone to stop doing something. In this way, a judgment may go up or down depending on the degree of harm proven by the plaintiff. In criminal law, the corresponding court order is to label someone guilty and the penalty is usually fixed by statute. This choice of words indicates a greater degree of social indignation toward the guilty criminal than with the liable civil party. Moreover, a guilty party pays his or her debt to society; whereas with civil liability, the wrongdoer pays a private party.

Overlapping Boundaries between Civil and Criminal Law

There is plenty of overlap between criminal and civil law, and so a single event may be the genesis of both a criminal indictment and a civil complaint. An example might help bring clarity. Former football star O. J. Simpson was tried in Los Angeles for the murder of his estranged wife and another man who was with her at the time. The police arrested Simpson and developed the information used against him at trial. In the criminal proceedings, the county prosecutor sought to convict him. This is punishable by death or prison under California law. The court returned a verdict of not guilty, and he was released from the government's custody.

After the criminal process ended, his wife's family initiated civil proceedings against Simpson for his wife's wrongful death. The family's lawyers, rather than the government, were responsible for assembling the information to be presented to the court this time. They claimed, among other things, they endured great emotional despair because he brought about her untimely death. This contrasts with the government's interest in protecting society from murderers. In the civil process, Simpson was found liable and ordered to compensate the family in cash for their grief.

Making a Claim

Regardless of whether a claim is civil or criminal, a case does not exist until one is filed with the right court. A claimant, or plaintiff, is the party who files a civil case with a court, claiming that he or she suffered some type of injury. In criminal law the claimant is referred to as the prosecution, or the state.

Courts of Origin

The first stage of a case is with a court of origin, commonly called the trial court, which is where a case originates. The complaints are written by a lawyer, or law clerk, and filed in the office of the local court clerk. Nonlawyers may prepare some small-claims and no-fault divorce cases by using preformatted documents available in a number of office supply stores. In criminal cases, the local prosecutor's staff files after approving of the police evidence. Once filed, the court clerk's assistants decide if the written complaint is accompanied by appropriate filing fees and whether it meets requisite formatting. If it is properly filed, then it is given an identification number and random lot, the assistant then assigns it to a judge for the next phase.

For a case to be filed properly, the plaintiff must identify the party who caused the harm. In criminal cases, a defendant is usually a person. In civil cases the respondent is the person or institution that will answer a claim. In this way, a governmental agency can be accused of a civil violation such as exceeding the authority the state assembly granted to it, or denying a person his or her constitutional rights.

Very early in the process, courts will decide whether the parties have standing. To have standing the plaintiff must show that he or she has in fact suffered some injury, or have other authorization to file. Also, the plaintiff must show that the government recognizes the injury, or crime, as something a court can act on. Finally, a plaintiff must usually demonstrate that the respondent, or defendant, is a potential source of the injury. In both civil and criminal cases, the party who initiates the case bears the burden of proving these things.

THE CRIMINAL TRIAL PROCESS

Whether an infraction is major or minor, when it comes to trial the U.S. Supreme Court has ruled that certain requirements are fundamental to saying the suspect has been afforded his or her constitutional rights to due process of law. The fundamental outline is:

- The right to be informed of the charges;
- The right to legal representation;
- The right to know and challenge the government's evidence, including the right to cross-examine adverse witnesses;
- The right to a neutral decision maker; and
- The right to an appeal.

The burden of proof is on the government. In addition, elements of the Bill of Rights (for this discussion Fourth, Fifth, Sixth, and Eighth Amendments) are incorporated into state trial procedure through the U.S. Constitution's Fourteenth Amendment's due process clause. These requirements include the defendant's right to keep evidence gained from unwarranted searches out of the process, the right to be free from coerced confessions, the right to be free from torture while in custody, the right to legal representation, and the like.

Misdemeanor Process

Criminal cases begin with the infraction, followed by an investigation and arrest. Courts define an arrest as the point at which police restrict a person's movements, even if this restriction is implied and not explicitly announced (see *United States v. Martinez-Fuerte* [1976] and *Terry v. Ohio* [1968]). The restriction may come by creating an environment where a reasonable individual would feel no alternative but to stay. Following an arrest, a suspect often will be released on a signature bond, which means he or she promises to attend the court hearing. In other misdemeanor cases, bail is made by surrendering a driver's license or a small sum of cash until the hearing is held or the fine is paid.

In minor cases there is no bond hearing in court. Rather, the arresting officer receives the signature bond, driver's license, or some down payment. With more serious misdemeanors, such as drunken driving or weapons violations, a suspect may be jailed until bail is paid, or a judge orders the release. At the bond hearing the suspect is informed of dates for future hearings. With traffic citations there is an arrest and a trial, with no other intervening hearings.

With higher misdemeanors, suspects follow judicial processes much more like the felony process. These include various types of hearings. The first is the preliminary hearing, at which the judge decides if prosecutors have enough evidence to continue pressing charges. For the sake of efficiency, the preliminary hearing usually combines other elements of the judicial process, such as the arraignment and bond hearing into a single visit.

At arraignments, the suspect may enter a plea, which is to either claim to be guilty, not guilty, or in some jurisdictions *nolo contendere,* meaning no-contest. If the suspect

---

Liability

In personal injury law, courts sometimes measure the fault of both respondent and plaintiff, so the respondent pays only a pro rata share of the award. This practice is called comparative negligence. For example, John is speeding and crashes his car into a car driven by Joan, who failed to wear her seat belt. When Joan sues, courts abiding in this doctrine will reduce the amount of the award John must pay by the extent to which Joan hurt herself by not wearing her seatbelt. Each party's proportion of fault would be a fact established by trial evidence.

The comparative negligence rule evolved out of an older principle of contributory negligence. If the plaintiff's misbehavior contributed anything to his or her own injury, plaintiffs would collect nothing. In the example, Joan would be responsible for all of her hospital expenses and John would pay nothing. Courts once thought that if the plaintiff's hands were even a little bit dirty, he or she should not benefit. Later, as this policy became viewed as unfair, courts started shifting the burden to a more equitable pro rata formula.

Still, legal reformers are challenging courts to deal with the apparent unfairness of the joint-and-several-liability doctrine. Under this theory, where there are many liable respondents (joint tortfeasors), any one of them can be held responsible for the full dollar amount of the court award. Our example of Joan's injury could be expanded to include a truck driver who dropped part of his load in front of Joan's car and a city bus driver who read-ended her all in the same accident. In states using the joint-and-several rule, the bus driver may have caused only a small part of Joan's injury, but because the city government has the deep pocket it could be forced to pay its and the other respondents' parts of the award. Some say this unfairly burdens big businesses and governments, and creates incentives to sue. Plaintiff's lawyers, on the other hand, argue that it's better for a guilty party to pay more than its fair share, than for the injured party to be uncompensated for harm she did not cause to herself.

pleads not guilty the case proceeds, otherwise the judge accepts or rejects the plea and then issues a sentence. If a judge thinks the suspect is incapable of understanding his or her legal rights at this time, the court may temporarily reject a guilty plea until the suspect can consult with a lawyer.

By this point most misdemeanor and felony cases are resolved. When the prosecutor and defendant wish to negotiate the outcome, they ask the judge to ratify their plea agreement. Plea agreements require the suspect to enter a guilty plea, while prosecutors may reduce a charge to a lesser offense, or ask for mercy in sentencing. Plea agreements are entered because they benefit both parties. Both sides avoid the uncertainty of the trial or sentencing process. Defendants and their families avoid the embarrassment from public attention and law enforcement can move on to other cases.

If the case has not resolved, next step for lawyers is to file *motions,* or requests of the courts. Motions seek permission for additional time to collect and analyze data, to suppress some evidence, or to reconsider previous decisions. Motions may ask the court to order someone to turn over information or demand that a witness testify. If someone objects to a motion, the judge may hear arguments on the issue.

There may be a period of *discovery* in which sides exchange information and the names of witnesses that will form the evidence for a trial (see sidebar, p. 117). This process of discovery can be quite extensive, especially in white-collar crimes, where prosecutors must sift through volumes of business documents, financial records, correspondence, and other sorts of information to find relevant papers. With more serious cases the attorneys may seek a pretrial conference with the judge to discuss whether a plea bargain is an option and the various sentencing guidelines. If the case goes to trial there could be hearings for the selection of jurors.

In many jurisdictions, associate judges, justices of the peace, or magistrates will decide minor criminal cases. These judges serve shorter terms of office and their job is to take the burden off trial-level judges who have somewhat higher responsibilities. In some states like Illinois, elected trial court judges from a local jurisdiction appoint the associate judges or magistrates to fill these short-term appointments. Magistrates and justices of the peace in many jurisdictions do not have law school training or a license to practice law.

Plea Bargains

Courts will not automatically accept plea bargains. Judges still must be sure that there is a reasonable basis for the charges. Also, courts need to be assured that the defendant entered the guilty plea voluntarily and without threats or delusions about the re- duced sentence a judge might, or might not, issue. Finally, the defendant needs to understand the consequences of the plea and understand the evidence against him or her. All the while, the defendant is entitled to the advice of an attorney.

Some states do not make formal distinctions between its misdemeanor and felony courts. Other states do delegate misdemeanor cases to courts of limited jurisdiction. In Delaware for example, these courts may hear only certain types of cases, such as drug or local ordinance violations. Low-level courts may also accept guilty pleas or hand down sentences in related felony cases. In some jurisdictions these courts may issue search-and-arrest warrants. With more serious and complex legal proceedings, judges with higher stature than magistrates will preside at trial and decide if evidence should be admitted to the trial process. However, in misdemeanor cases the court of limited jurisdiction hears the trial, issues a verdict and, if necessary, sentences a guilty party usually in a single hearing.

Felony Process

In felony cases, more stringent procedures are followed even before the arrest. However, if a law-enforcement officer witnesses a criminal event, he or she must attempt to make an arrest on the spot. Also, if a law officer has probable cause that someone committed a crime, the officer may make the decision to arrest. Otherwise, the investigating officers seek an arrest warrant. To do this, the officers present their evidence first to the local prosecutor's office, which works with police to present the evidence to a judge who will either approve the warrant, or reject it.

In most jurisdictions a local prosecutor may file charges, which is to say the prosecutor reviews the evidence and decides whether someone's behavior fits the definition of a crime. This decision may rest on witness testimony, documents, videotapes, or physical evidence like fingerprints or a weapon. In many serious and very complex criminal cases, prosecutors instead may call for grand jury hearings before pressing charges.

A grand jury is a committee of citizens (usually 15–25) that examines testimony and evidence from the government's side only. In many jurisdictions, defense lawyers or a suspect are not present, except when called to give testimony. The grand jury holds hearings in secret, to shield the reputations of innocent subjects and to avoid disrupting the work of detectives.

The grand jury holds these hearings to decide if law enforcement agencies have enough evidence to proceed with a full trial; it is not asked to decide guilt. If the grand jury finds there is enough evidence to charge a suspect with a crime, it says so in a formal document called an *indictment* or a *true bill*; the opposite finding is announced in a *no bill*. At that point the grand jury is finished investigating an individual for a particular offense. Even after a no bill, the grand jury may continue investigating the same person and other people for related offenses. The grand jurors' term of service and compensation are set in each state by law.

The modern grand jury hearing is a part of the judicial process in that it checks the power of prosecutors. The grand jury screens cases before they go to trial. At the same time, an investigation is part of the prosecutorial process. Grand juries investigate passively, relying on career law enforcement agents to do the work. Grand juries can issue court orders, like subpoenas, which demand witness testimony, or the submission of digital or written documents, photographs, or sound recordings. In effect, they help build cases for law enforcement agents this way.

The origins of the grand jury come from twelfth-century England, where local informants reported to the king about crimes and who committed them. When a grand jury refused to indict the enemies of King Charles II it was seen as able to protect the ordinary people against the strength of the government (Kadish 1996). The grand jury concept was imported to the United States through the Fifth Amendment of the U.S. Constitution. This requires that "No person shall be held to answer for a capital, or otherwise infamous crime, unless on a presentment or indictment of a Grand Jury . . . ." This requirement applies to the U.S. government, and most local jurisdictions follow this model.

When charges are filed, warrants issued, and a suspect is in custody, the process continues with hearings much like the misdemeanor. There is opportunity for a bond hearing and preliminary hearings, which may combine several procedural steps into a single appearance. If the prosecutor's charges come to court without the grand jury's involvement, a judge will hold a preliminary hearing to determine whether there is enough evidence to continue charging someone with a crime. The arraignment, or advisement, is the point of the process when the judge informs the suspect of the charges and likely penalties. The judge also asks if the suspect understands the charges and whether he or she can afford a lawyer, or if the court should appoint one. States usually check someone's finances to be sure that person is eligible for a public defender.

The felony bond hearing is the same procedurally as in misdemeanor court, but the stakes are higher. Most commonly, the bond requires a cash deposit with the court. The bail is the amount deposited and is a fraction (typically 10 percent) of the bond. The full

---

Discovery Phase

The discovery phase has several parts. Discovery begins with an exchange of written questions and sworn answers called *interrogatories*. Parties can press each other to make their answers more specific. Each side may also require witnesses to participate in formal face-to-face interviews, called *depositions*. The deposition is recorded and typically takes place in a lawyer's office.

Depositions can be collected from anyone the parties want, and interrogatories are collected from the parties named in a suit. Lawyers may also consult with clients as they prepare responses to either. Though depositions may have a broad focus, a trial judge should limit courtroom use of transcripts to witnesses and statements central to the trial issues.

Since these are sworn statements, if a witness dies or is incapacitated before trial, courts can accept relevant passages as though the witness was in court. The honesty of a witness will be challenged if he or she gives trial testimony conflicting with his or her deposition or interrogatory. Some courts allow lawyers to hire actors to sit in the witness stand and read the deposition answers of absent witnesses while the lawyers repeat their questions.

bond is forfeited if the suspect flees justice before the end of the trial. Bond is higher, and out of reach for many suspects, when an accused is at a high risk for fleeing. Judges may also issue no-bond orders if convinced that a suspect is likely to flee.

In addition to posting bail, conditions of release may include orders that the suspect not leave the court's geographic jurisdiction until the end of court proceedings. Other typical obligations are to avoid contact with witnesses or victims of a crime, or an order not to carry weapons, or go near certain places like schools or playgrounds pending the outcome. Failure to abide by these requirements may mean the court system will keep the cash deposits and put the suspect in custody until the outcome is finalized.

As with misdemeanor processes, there is opportunity for pretrial hearings, motions, discovery, and plea bargains. In fact, 95 percent of felony convictions in state courts during 2000 came by a plea rather than a trial (Durose and Lanagan 2003).

Prior to the trial defendants will inform the court that they want a jury or a bench trial, where a judge alone decides both the facts and the law. If a defendant wants a jury, a pool of prospective jurors, called the venire, is selected from the local adult population. Court clerks usually draw prospective jurors at random from names on voter registration and drivers license records. Once called, prospective jurors are screened for eligibility and interviewed by lawyers during a process called *voir dire.*

Various states have stipulations about who may opt out of service due to such conditions as age or occupation. In the voir dire process, lawyers look for indications that a prospective juror is predisposed to decide the verdict in some way and they then seek that person's exclusion from the jury. If this is the case, lawyers can ask the court to dismiss an unlimited number of prospective jurors if there is cause. Lawyers also get a limited number of peremptory challenges, which allow them to disqualify a juror without explanation. More typically, they try to find statements from a prospective juror suggesting that he or she has begun to form opinions about the case.

Lawyers also consider various traits like race, religion, gender, age, or occupation that they think may be correlated with certain sympathies (see sidebar p. 121). However, the U.S. Supreme Court has ruled repeatedly that it is a violation of the Constitution to exclude jurors by using race alone as a crude indicator of attitude. In capital cases it may be necessary to ask prospective jurors if they could be fair to a defendant of another race (see for example *Powers v. Ohio* [1991] and *Ristaino v. Ross* [1976]).

Defense lawyers also may suggest that pretrial news coverage has affected opinions of the pool of jurors. If this is the case defense attorneys may ask for a change of venue, so the trial is held out of town, where prospective jurors are less likely to have come across inflammatory news coverage of the case. This also imposes additional costs to prosecuting the case. Even when there is a great deal of pretrial news coverage, local courts have a great deal of latitude in deciding whether the trial needs to leave town to get jurors who are not predisposed (see for example *Mu'min v. Virginia* [1991] and *Aldridge v. United States* [1931]).

After jurors, and substitutes (called alternates), are chosen, the trial begins. If there is a jury, jurors decide which testimony and evidence to believe. Meanwhile, the judge

Coroner's Inquest

Another pretrial investigating hearing is the coroner's inquest. In many, but not all, jurisdictions the local coroner's office is the agency that provides the medical evidence needed to determine the cause of an unnatural, or suspicious, death. A coroner's inquest produces a legal determination, rather than a scientific one, about whether the cause of death was due to an illness, or an unnatural source like suicide or homicide.

Coroners are the chief administrator of the office, and staff medical examiners perform autopsies. Once the work of morticians, autopsies today are conducted by scientists trained in medical schools. The autopsy is a process of examining the body, organs, and blood for evidence of the cause of death. An autopsy report is presented publicly at a coroner's inquest. A jury reviews the coroner's evidence and listens to testimony, and votes to determine the cause of death.

rules on which principles of law and procedure apply. During trial, judges admonish jurors to avoid discussing the proceedings with anyone, especially the press or people involved directly in the case. There are standing orders for jurors to avoid paying attention to news coverage of the case during trial. In cases with extremely high levels of news coverage, judges can sequester juries, which is to put them up in a hotel during the course of the trial so the court can manage their access to news coverage and other outside influences.

The trial begins with an introduction from the prosecution's attorney and the defense attorney. The government is obliged to present a case, which is its evidence, witnesses, and rules of law supporting the accusations against the defendant. The defendant, in the U.S. legal system, has the right, but not the obligation, to present a case.

The government's case usually involves direct questioning, during which the government's lawyers pose questions to witnesses hoping to get answers supporting their argument. Witnesses may be eyewitnesses who personally watched an event. They may be expert witnesses, like detectives, medical examiners, handwriting analysts, and crime scene technicians who collect and evaluate evidence. The defense has an opportunity to cross-examine these witnesses, hoping to draw out testimony weakening the government's arguments. In civil cases, expert witnesses are called because of their knowledge of some relevant issues.

After the government's case is presented, defense lawyers have an opportunity to ask for a directed verdict. This is a motion that asks the judge to declare that the state's evidence is too weak to continue charging the accused. Normally, this is not successful and the defense attorney then may bring in witnesses supporting the defendant. At this time, the defense would pose the direct questioning and the state would cross-examine the defendant's witnesses. This is followed with the summation, also called closing arguments, from each side. Opposing lawyers typically summarize the high points of the testimony and evidence presented to the judge or jury and they ask for a verdict favoring their side.

If there is a jury, the judge presents directions for the jury. Typically, both sets of lawyers give the judge recommended instructions and the judge can modify them. The jury instructions tell the jurors the basic rules of law, and the weight of evidence that they should consider and the possible verdicts they can return. The instructions typically tell jurors that it is up to them to decide whether a piece of evidence or testimony is believable, but that they are not to decide the fairness, or the constitutionality of the law itself. In this way, judges decide law, jurors decide facts.

After this, the jury retires to a room in which all deliberations take place. There they select a foreperson, who serves as a chairman of the committee. The foreperson records the jury's votes and formally communicates with the judge. During deliberations various forms are provided to the jury. These forms are prepared in advance, so the jury can return any one of the possible decisions that it may reach.

During deliberations, jurors can ask questions of the judge. These questions are made known to attorneys for both sides and the judge may give some additional guidance. Judges have discretion in how long they will allow a jury to deliberate before ruling that a hung jury cannot reach a decision. Judges may ask the foreperson if he or she thinks the jury is making progress toward a verdict. An inability to decide will prompt the judge to declare a mistrial, which would mean the jury is dismissed and the process goes back to the pretrial motions. The verdict is the finding that the defendant is guilty or not guilty on any, or all of the possible charges. In felony cases, the jury usually must agree unanimously to the outcome of each charge.

When a verdict is reached, the jury foreperson announces the verdict, or passes the verdict papers to the judge to announce in court. Defense attorneys may elect to poll the jury, or to ask each juror to restate in public his or her vote on each charge.

Posttrial Proceedings

When a suspect is found guilty at trial, the next step is to decide on a punishment. If the suspect is found not guilty, his or her release from the charges comes with a formal declaration from the judge, usually on the same day. Following a guilty verdict, the judge, or sometimes jury, must decide what punishment to impose. To persuade the court, the prosecutor will present aggravating evidence, which is intended to demonstrate how horrible the crime is and how society has suffered from it. This often involves testimony from loved ones of a murder victim, for example. Most states require an opportunity for victims to give impact statements that become part of the decision-making process.

The defense attorney will present mitigating evidence, which is intended to show there may have been grounds for committing an evil offense. This is done without challenging the guilty verdict. Mitigating factors might involve showing that a crime victim was not entirely innocent. The victim may also have been a competing drug dealer, or may have previously hurt or threatened the defendant. Recent U.S. Supreme Court

Discrimination and the Courts

Before concluding that lawyers cannot discriminate in their peremptory challenges, the Supreme Court had to break barriers that local court systems put in the way of minorities (see *Carter v. Jury Commission* [1970]) and women (see *Taylor v. Louisiana* [1975]) ever becoming part of the venire.

Now, there is a more contemporary, and philosophical, debate over whether it is better that a jury be impartial, or representative. That is to ask: is it better to have a jury that is neutral, or one that resembles the racial, religious, and income characteristics of the community?

The U.S. Supreme Court held that the juries are "instruments of public justice [and] that the jury [should] be a body truly representative of the community" (*Smith v. Texas* [1940]). However, the Court refined the cross-section requirement by applying it only to the venire. "The fair cross-section requirement is a means of assuring, not a representative jury [which the Constitution does not demand], but an impartial one [which it does]" (*Holland v. Illinois* [1990]).

rulings determined that those aggravating factors must be proven during trial if they are going to be used during the sentencing phase (see sidebar, p. 122).

In capital cases, the jury is called on to make two separate choices. The first is to determine whether the nature of the crime makes the defendant eligible for the death penalty, and second whether the jury actually recommends a death sentence. While the guilty or not-guilty verdict must be unanimous, the sentencing decision does not require unanimity though many state laws make this a requirement.

Following the jury's sentencing deliberations, it formally announces the decision and the judge ratifies it at a later time. When there is a suggestion that the jury was improperly influenced, a judge may set aside the verdict and sentence. Without a jury, and at some time soon after trial, a sentencing hearing is the formal announcement of the sentence. In every state, death penalty sentences are automatically appealed to the state's highest court (see Von Drehle 1995). These courts alternatively review the sentence alone, or the entire court process. In lesser offenses, defendants have an opportunity to appeal to a reviewing court. The review process is discussed later in this chapter.

THE CIVIL TRIAL PROCESS

As with criminal cases, civil cases can be organized by the nature of claims. Civil matters, however, are far more complex than criminal matters. Due to the complexity of civil cases, many states offer more courts of limited jurisdiction in civil matters than they do for criminal ones. Unlike criminal cases, the Sixth Amendment does not guarantee a speedy trial in civil cases. Instead, with more than 15 million civil cases processed in the state courts each year, civil trials typically take more than two years to complete. Many additional claims are settled without a suit being filed.

The civil trial process is similar to the criminal process. However, there is nothing in the civil process akin to the grand jury process and there is no bond hearing. During the

---

The Sentencing Phase

As in the verdict phase, the sentencing phase involves jury instructions that can be a bone of contention. Jurors need to know what will happen to the convicted defendant if they decide against death (see *Kelly v. South Carolina* [2002]). They also need to be able to give effect to mitigating circumstances, that is the jury forms must allow them to vote against the death penalty (see *Penry v. Lynaugh* [1989]). In addition, the Court has held that it violates the cruel and unusual provision of the Eighth Amendment to apply the death penalty to mentally retarded defendants (*Atkins v. Virginia* [2001]), but not to minors.

1980s and 1990s, however, with complaints of rapidly increasing numbers of personal injury cases, some state legislatures put up hurdles to frivolous claims. Often this involved review of cases by a panel of experts to advise courts whether there was evidence that a person in a responsible position lapsed in judgment.

There may be steps that a plaintiff must go through before filing suit in court. In a case where an individual is challenging a decision by a government body, such as terminating welfare benefits, expelling a student from school, or a disciplinary process for a governmental employee, courts may require the plaintiff to show he or she has used all appeals available in the administrative process before filing suit. A growing number of contract and insurance cases are expected to be resolved through arbitration. In this alternative dispute resolution arbiters other than judges hear cases in a quasi-judicial, but private, setting to resolve civil complaints out of court. Contractual provisions in insurance policies or employment agreements frequently require alternative dispute resolution processes.

APPEALING DECISIONS

Once the decision is made, the unhappy party has the opportunity for an appeal. Generally, this opportunity comes after a final disposition, meaning the conclusion of the trial. In several situations the decisions of trial courts may be appealed when a court is asked to decide a procedural question that would affect the outcome, such as the admission of evidence, or have long-lasting effects, such as the placement of children during custody hearings.

The process of trying to overturn a trial decision is done through the appellate courts. The process of presenting arguments on appeal is very different from the trial process. In fact, many outstanding trial lawyers will turn over cases to colleagues better versed in presenting appellate cases. The decision-making process of a trial is most rigorous for felony-criminal processes, holding the prosecution to a standard of proving guilt beyond a reasonable doubt. Somewhat less stringent are misdemeanor processes. The civil process, while very rigorous, holds the plaintiff to a standard of the preponderance of the evidence. At the conclusion of the trial, it is generally presumed that the defendant/ respondent has been afforded due process of law. Thus, the burden of overcoming the decision of a trial court rests with the party asking for review in the appellate court.

After the trial the unhappy party has the opportunity for a case to be reviewed and overturned. Perhaps it is better to say, the dissatisfied party has the opportunity to appeal those parts of the trial that may have been conducted in error. By appealing the case to a higher court, the unhappy party can hope to reverse a trial judgment, or at least some part of it. The civil and criminal processes in appeals courts virtually are indistinguishable, except in states such as Oklahoma and Texas, which separated the two very formally at the appellate stages. More routinely, the formal process is the same, though deadlines may be altered to accommodate the needs of time-sensitive cases. For purposes of this discussion, criminal and civil appeals processes are not distinguished.

Appellate Process

When arguing about the rules of the game, parties can ask reviewing courts to intercede from the outset. Trial courts must make decisions about relocating high-publicity trials to ensure suspects have an unbiased jury. Trial courts must decide whether to freeze bank accounts during financial cases, and decide whether to permit progress on demolition of a building when neighborhood or preservation societies contest the plans. These are intermediate decisions that can affect the course of a trial and have long-lasting effects on parties if a trial takes an extended period of time. Consequently, parties argue fiercely about such decisions and appeal these intermediate court rulings.

Appeals courts routinely take interlocutory appeals, which are hearings made during the course of trial proceedings. This is often one of the first times an appeals court will come to know of a specific trial case. Interlocutory hearings go before the appeals court on short notice, because they challenge a trial judge's temporary, rather than final, court orders. They challenge the rules of the trial, suppression of evidence, allowing a witness, exclusion of a juror, and so on, rather than the final outcome like a finding of guilt.

Interlocutory appeals also are made to challenge temporary restraining orders (TROs), which are used during the judicial process to prevent a party from doing something that would be irreversible. A typical TRO would order a party to wait until the court's final order is issued to spend money, receive a nonemergency medical procedure, remodel an historic building, or alter the natural environment. Parties argue over whether waiting for a trial outcome to continue with some activity is a great burden.

Other short-term decisions are challenged on interlocutory appeal. These affect children or wards of the state. Their concerns are often appealed on an expedited basis. These often involve custody of children during divorce or involuntary hospitalization of the mentally ill. The admission of evidence or witnesses may be challenged prior to the trial process also. If judicial processes drag on, temporary orders can have long-term consequences. Thus, they are afforded instant decisions.

In the interlocutory appeals process, all parties are bound to very strict deadlines. These deadlines apply first to the party wishing to contest the trial court's order and the opponent's reply. Second deadlines apply to the appeals court itself. Once filed, an appellate court is under guidelines to hold a hearing, typically within three to five business days of the filing. This pushes aside other tasks on the desks of judges, and pushes the interlocutory appeal ahead of others on the agenda. With interlocutory appeals, the reviewing court is almost always under deadlines to provide rapid feedback. This type of deadline varies across the states, but usually a decision is due in a business week, or at the most thirty days. Failure to do so could cause further delays in a trial, seriously burden parties to the trial, or render moot one of the parties' cases.

Review of Final Orders

It may be more customary for news consumers to read or hear about an appeal on a final order. The process of appellate review typically begins after a trial court gives its final decisions in a case. Then the unhappy party (the appellant) may seek review in the higher court. It is common for some lawyers to first file a motion with the appeals court. The first is the petition for a stay of judgment, which puts on pause the trial court's remedy until the appeal is completed. This is then followed with the formal petition to the appellate court to review the decision.

More often than not, state appellate courts have little choice but to accept a case for review. When they do use discretion, appeals courts can accept the case by issuing an order to lower court officers requiring them to send the case record to the higher court. Most appeals come through a petition for leave to appeal (PLA). This is the formal request made by appellant for review of a trial decision. On the other hand, when a court has discretion, it may deny the petition usually without explanation. If granted, parties are free to reach negotiated settlements before the higher court hears the case or announces a ruling.

When the losing party files the PLA and any court fees, the opposing party is formally notified with a copy of the PLA and is given time to file an answer. Each state has deadlines and strict format guidelines for filing PLAs and answers. These format requirements ensure that certain statements are made on the cover to identify the case and the author of the document. Format guides give details for maximum length of the document and the rules for making a table of contents and table of cases. They also might require certain font style and size for print, color, and size of paper, and may even demand certain colors for the cover page so judges can identify documents by the color codes. A set number of stapled photocopies are acceptable in some jurisdictions, while other places have fancier duplication and binding requirements.

Closer to the substance of the issues before the court, a PLA must explain the jurisdictional authority (or duty) of the court to take the case, cite precisely the legal authority being questioned in the appeal, explain how specific trial errors adversely affected the client, and state how the appellate court should respond. Appellate courts will reject appeals that do not cite specific trial errors for review. It is not enough for a party only to be dissatisfied. Appellate courts routinely reject cases unless it is claimed that there were both errors in trial court judgment and that those errors led to an adverse outcome. They also reject cases when they are outside the court's authority.

Appellate Case Processing

In most states, the appellate court clerk's office first examines the appellate filing to make sure it conforms to rules about length and formatting specifications. The clerk's office also collects any filing fees and verifies that the responding party gets a copy of the PLA. Once that is verified, the clerk's office sends the PLA to a panel of three judges. All of the appellate judges in a jurisdiction constitute the court. In most appeals, however, a panel of three judges is chosen by lot from all the available appellate judges in that jurisdiction to review the case. On occasion, all of the judges in an appellate court will sit en banc to decide the case. Courts sit en banc after two different panels from the same court have reached conflicting opinions on some topic.

This system of randomly assigning cases serves four purposes. First, it averts judge shopping by lawyers, who might hope to know in advance whether they will have a sympathetic or hostile panel. Second, random assignment minimizes specialization on the appeals courts. Many judges resist specialization on their courts out of fear that they would get cozy with litigants frequently before a specialized court. Third, it is expected that the random selection method keeps the law more coherent, since judges participate in deciding cases across many areas of law, rather than only in a specialized field. Finally, it helps distribute the workload more evenly among all judges in a jurisdiction. This way the chief judge cannot keep all the glamorous cases for himself while sending an overwhelming number of dull cases to a disfavored colleague.

In many jurisdictions, the lottery will further assign one of the judges on the panel to be the case administrator. In other jurisdictions the judge with the greatest number of years of service will be the presiding judge for the case. The administrator will make sure there is proper communication with parties and superintend the scheduling of hearings and announcement of a decision. This judge-administrator is involved in the decision.

If accepted for appeal, a new set of briefs will be filed with the court. Appellate judges want lawyers to summarize only those trial elements that they claim are in serious error and successful lawyers are skilled at explaining trial errors and appropriate law succinctly. Appellate courts may be reviewing dozens of cases at a time and almost never have the time to review a case in its entirety. The whole case transcript and documents, however, may go to the court for reference.

After the appellant files a case, the opposing party is notified formally of the appeal and may file its own answer to the briefs. After both are filed, judges begin reviewing the documents. In some cases the judges may write to both parties and ask them to revise their documents and address, or to avoid discussing, certain legal authority or theory.

A judge's law clerks play a vital role at this point as well. Law clerks are advanced law students or lawyers early in their careers who assist judges in their legal research and writing. These individuals must be distinguished from court clerks who are administrators, responsible for the accurate keeping of vital court documents. Law clerks analyze the case formally and informally for their employers. Law clerks will prepare memoranda verifying lawyers' interpretation of prior court decisions, examine case records, and do other research under the direction of a judge. Law clerks find out how, or if, other appellate courts in the state or in neighboring states deal with similar issues. In this way, clerks help the judge understand how an individual case fits into the overall landscape of the law.

Oral Arguments and Decisions on the Records

Most appellate decisions are made by reviewing briefs and case records without any discussion from lawyers. This is customary and most lawyers expect, and often ask for, no oral hearing. When novel legal issues are brought up, or when lawyers request it, appeals courts will invite lawyers to give short question-and-answer presentations called oral arguments. Judges at this level do the questioning and lawyers are the ones who answer. This is quite to the contrary of the trial experience where lawyers do questioning and judges have a relatively more passive role.

By the time of oral arguments, judges have reviewed the case and have become aware of legal developments on the point. Therefore, they probably have formed some initial opinions. At minimum, they have formed opinions about whether the lawyers have focused on the interesting issues, or have made compelling written arguments. Judges want oral arguments to be focused discussions, but oral arguments give judges an opportunity to clarify issues by posing hypothetical situations about the consequences of legal innovations (Hogan 2000). Judges listen for direct, complete, logical, and thorough answers to their questions. Floundering and illogic indicate uncertainty in a lawyer's argument, or at least a lack of preparation. Oral arguments generally last about an hour or less.

Oral arguments take place before the three-judge panel. Each lawyer has an opportunity to present arguments. Their time is limited and consumed with the questions of judges. Lawyers must be thoroughly prepared, since judges are free to ask any question about the case, its facts, or any element of law any of the three judges thinks needs explanation. Judges may be energetic in this questioning, or sit passively and listen to arguments. This is a matter of a judge's personality and the nature of the case before the court.

Scholars say that lawyers should be cautious in reading a judges' questioning for clues about a case outcome. Judges variously use questioning to get lawyers to say something that will influence other judges on the panel, to gain information central to their own decision making, to play devil's advocate, and to unmask weaknesses about their own tentative decisions. The precise questioning may depend greatly on the nature of the case. When the court is asked to review novel issues courts may be animated and judges may interrupt with frequent questions. With more mundane issues, a cold court might sit passively as lawyers deliver oral arguments.

Oral arguments make up a relatively small amount of the appeals judge's working day. In geographically large states, judges and lawyers may have to travel for hours to reach the courthouse, so oral hearings are scheduled well in advance. Courts in these states may hear oral presentations for a few weeks during each season of the year and then return to their hometowns to write opinions and read newly filed cases. In smaller states it is easier for appeals judges to hold court more frequently.

Forming Decisions

After the oral presentations, judges on the panel hold a conference to discuss the case in private. If there are no oral arguments, judges can deliberate either in person, by conference phone call, through e-mail, or through memoranda. Even before the conference, judges have read the lawyers' material and done independent research. This allows them to form some initial impressions about the case. During deliberations, however, judges also have the opportunity to persuade each other, analyze the case, and gain additional information. Usually an impression vote indicates a judge's views on a case, but this vote is not binding until the decision is made public.

Decisions require a majority vote to modify or overturn the trial court's decision. Unlike a lone trial judge, judges on appellate courts must reach conclusions by building consensus both in terms of which party should win, and in terms of the reasons for the outcome. To do this, appellate judges must work in close consultation with each other to make rulings. As a result, judges learn the thought processes of their colleagues, they learn to persuade one another, they learn to accommodate one another, and they learn to debate and negotiate satisfactory outcomes with each other. They learn to swallow disagreements, and they learn to express their disagreements so that they can continue to work together in a professional environment.

Judges discuss cases either immediately after each oral argument, or they take up discussions after the full day's oral arguments are done. In private, the case administrator may summarize the issues as he or she understands them and opens the topic for discussion. After the discussion, if there is any, judges will take an impression vote.

If the case supervisor is in the minority, he or she will trade writing responsibilities with a colleague who will write the majority opinion. Otherwise the vote is recorded with the basic rationale each judge thinks important to supporting the decision. Typically, the judge-administrator for the case writes the ruling. During the decision process, judges compose their written opinions with the aid of their law clerks. Drafts are distributed usually through a secure e-mail system and then shared with the rest of the panel. Colleagues on the panel will give the author input. Colleagues may ask for spelling corrections, or they may request substantial changes in rationale, construction, statements of relevant facts, or citations.

Judges may change their minds after making an impression vote and deliberations may continue over the course of several days. Votes count only when the court's decision is announced to the parties. However, Marvell (1978) estimates that judges change their minds between the initial vote and the announcement in fewer than 15 percent of the cases. Hogan (2000) found judges said this is rare, but it does happen and is hardly an alien idea.

Sources of Information

In addition to the formal filed paperwork and oral arguments of litigators, judges have several sources of information to help them decide cases. In addition to the formal processes, judges may encounter news coverage, friends, or staff members who have something to say about a case. Only some of those informal sources are discussed here. There are far too many potential sources to cover them all; moreover, the means by which state appellate judges arrive at decisions is just beginning to be explored.

The Role of Law Clerks in the Decision Process

In the process of writing opinions, law clerks play an important role. There may also be a legal research staff appointed by the court; however, the clerks of individual judges work under the direction of individual judges, and are the employees of individual judges. The extent to which the work of law clerks finds its way into the formal opinion of the court varies from case to case and from judge to judge. H. W. Perry's book *Deciding to Decide* illustrates the vital role law clerks play in drafting opinions for the U.S. Supreme Court. Marvell and Hogan, meanwhile, see much more diversity in the way that state appellate judges apply the work of law clerks.

As a case enters the court system, law clerks may be asked to prepare bench memos, which further reduce the central questions, authority, and issues before the court decides to take an individual case. Clerks also frequently discuss cases with their employers as they prepare for oral arguments. Finally, clerks play varying roles in the preparation of the court's final orders.

On one extreme is the law clerk who has little role in the substance of the outcome. This clerk finds citations for a judge and checks his or her punctuation. At the other extreme is the clerk whose memoranda become the court's opinion. The typical law clerk will not draft memoranda during the first few months on the job. When they do, judges may dictate the memo. In others the judge may tell the clerk what rationale to use and which cases to cite, but leave the writing to the clerk. Other clerks will have more latitude, depending on the confidence the judge has in them. All the while, it is the judge, not the clerk, who has decision-making power. Some judges fear becoming lazy or dependent on law clerks for their reasoning, while others prefer to delegate.

Law clerks also serve other informative roles. By discussing cases clerks may debate outcomes with their supervisors. As lower employees, the clerks may bring to light relevant side issues that do not get into the published opinion. In addition, clerks may help write speeches for the judge, keep the judge's personal law library and subscriptions current, or act as a chauffeur. In any event, law clerks provide research, ideas, and services judges would not otherwise get.

Consultation with Other Legal Professionals

In addition to the prescribed routines of holding oral arguments and reviewing official case documents, judges have told researchers that they may turn to outside sources of information when deciding a pending case. Marvell said this type of consultation is the exception. Similarly, Hogan's research found that on rare occasions an appeals judge might consult with fellow judges who are not on the same appeal panel. Marvell writes that judges looking for some guidance prefer to direct clerks to discreetly contact their professors about points of law. Otherwise a judge may discuss the case, in the abstract, with a trusted friend or relative about the practical implications of some decision. However, it is taboo for judges to discuss the specifics of any pending litigation.

Seeking outside information does not give parties to the litigation opportunity to challenge it. For this reason, judges tell Marvell that they find it unfair to receive input this way. Judges who might seek consultation typically couch these discussions in abstract, or hypothetical, form. Or they may ask about where to go for further information to avoid revealing details or their thoughts of a case before them.

Consultation with Party and Interest Group Leaders

When contacted by party officials about charged cases, judges told Hogan that they quickly change the subject. Even among elected judges who attend party functions, none admitted to discussing pending litigation with state or local legislative or executive officials. In addition, none acknowledged with certainty that any colleagues shared information on pending litigation. This custom is so strict that one Illinois Appellate Court judge with whom Hogan spoke said her husband (also a lawyer) learned that she had decided a high-profile case only by reading about her opinion in the local newspaper. Local professional culture and the court's customs will dictate the extent to which judges feel free to consult with outside sources, but it is forbidden to forward third parties case outcomes or the leanings of a court prior to formal announcement.

Some public officials and interest groups may attempt vicariously to communicate with judges about pending litigation. Holding a press conference to discuss cases may have this effect. However, many lawyerly publications decline to publicize news related to pending cases. It is more customary, and acceptable, for elected officials and interested third parties to communicate with judges by filing formal friend of the court briefs. In this way, public officials and policy advocates legitimately can communicate political information through the judicial process.

Announcing Appellate Decisions

When a majority is satisfied with the written opinion (both a decision and, if needed, a dissent), it is announced through the court clerk's office. In most jurisdictions, the appellate court is expected to announce rulings within a fixed time frame. Since these rulings represent a binding governmental decision, appeals courts issue written rulings following standardized and formal writing routines. Like the lawyers' briefs, court opinions adhere to conventional writing techniques to easily identify case parties, issues under consideration, legal authority, and the court's final ruling.

Setting Precedence

Unlike trial courts, appellate courts are much more likely to issue rulings that explain the court's reasoning in writing. For more routine issues, decisions are issued in memoranda sent only to the affected parties. When there are more issues of larger concern, decisions can be made public by being published in a volume called a reporter, and more recently on the Internet. The importance of written opinions is to set precedence, which is to establish reasoning that gives guidance to other courts deciding a case on the same point of law. This tradition of following precedence, also called *stare decisis*, requires that lower courts within a reviewing court's jurisdiction abide by that reasoning, until it is modified or rejected by a higher court. Only a few appellate decisions have precedential, or law-making value. No statistics are kept, but most rulings merely decide disputes and are of little interest except to the parties (Marvell 1978).

Many times appellate-level judges would like to see precedent overturned. Some appeals judges have devised strategies to impress upon higher courts the urgency for this. Appellate judges may use what Stanley Fish calls the rhetoric of regret. In this way they write that despite their own misgivings, duty binds them to apply a cruel law (Fish 1999). Hogan's interviews with Illinois Appellate Court judges revealed that on selected cases, appeals judges work together to form a majority opinion applying current law as it is, but they will also help a colleague write an even more compelling dissent to urge Illinois Supreme Court reconsideration of some issue.

Judges are intelligent readers of current events about their colleagues, but do not tend to reverse higher court rulings until given formal direction to do so. Some judges and scholars have tried to anticipate changes in state and U.S. Supreme Court direction by counting each justices' public statements, as opposed to the opinions, to estimate whether the state or U.S. Supreme Court was ready to reverse precedent. In the U.S. Supreme Court's decision *Agostini v. Felton* (1997), justices both changed policy and reminded readers that they should not jump to conclusions that a decision is overruled based on writings justices make outside the Court. "The statements made by five Justices . . . do not, in themselves, furnish a basis for concluding that our (First Amendment) jurisprudence has changed. . . . The views of five Justices that [a] case should be reconsidered, or overruled cannot be said to have effected a change in [the] law."

SUPREME COURT PROCESS

The last stop in a state's judicial system is with its court of final resort. The only possible venue after the state supreme court is the U.S. Supreme Court and it will refuse cases that do not have a claim made in federal law. The decision process of the state supreme courts is very similar to that of intermediate appeals courts. Differences are highlighted in the discussion that follows, though the section on intermediate appeals courts offers helpful insights to the process of preparing for appeals, and hearing and deciding them.

The process for bringing a case to courts of last resort typically follows one of two paths. When filing a petition to appeal, lawyers must be careful to identify which of these avenues they wish to pursue, and explain in a few words why this is the correct legal path to the high court.

The first route is by petitioning for a petition for leave to appeal as a mandatory appeal, which says the court is obliged to review the lower court's decision. The other is through a writ of certiorari, also called a discretionary appeal. This is where the court accepts the case as a matter of choice. All states require their high courts to hear some types of cases. The most commonly used mandatory appeal is the automatic right all states grant criminals who have been sentenced to death. In addition, many state constitutions require high courts to review decisions related to the use of a writ of mandamus, certain budget cases (namely those where a trial court has declared a tax or budgetary item in violation of the state constitution), and cases where public officials are expelled from office through the judicial process.

Filing Process

As with other courts, the state supreme court has a court clerk who receives the case and advises the parties about whether it was filed within deadlines and according to appropriate format requirements. In most states, cases meeting proper deadline and format requirements are screened to see if any of the justices have a conflict of interest in the case.

Once approved by the clerk's office, in most states the case is randomly assigned to a justice to usher the case through the court. This justice summarizes the case and puts it on an agenda with other cases that the court will consider for review. If accepted, this judge usually is the author of a written decision. The judge discusses whether there are any legal merits to reviewing the case and the court decides as a group if the case is ready, or worthy, for court review. Given that hundreds of cases are brought to high courts for review in any year, justices find that they can only do a good job by taking those with the most important legal matters at hand. In a vast majority of cases, the supreme courts will decline to take discretionary cases.

Courts will reject cases if there is no showing that a lower court was in error. Courts also reject cases if the case has resolved itself or has been settled before oral hearings (*moot*). Supreme courts will decline cases if the court finds no novel legal issues at stake, or if they find that a litigant is challenging a law that has not gone into effect (these are considered not *ripe*). Less commonly, the court may find out during oral arguments that a case they accepted was not what they expected. If this is the case, the court can declare the case dismissed as improvidently granted without issuing an opinion. This leaves the lower court decision in tact.

Once the court accepts a case, it is placed on its docket for review. Review may be by private discussion among judges, or with oral arguments. When justices grant oral arguments, lawyers will be given information about when the case will be heard and they will be told how much time will be allotted to present cases. During oral arguments, lawyers very often will be interrupted with pointed questions from the court. This can be unnerving to inexperienced lawyers. Again, as a reviewing court, there will be no witnesses or evidence presented. Rather the case facts are accepted as the trial court found them. The higher courts use the real case facts as real-world examples of how the law is being applied. This gives them feedback to make adjustments to earlier supreme court rulings, or to decide whether an act of the legislature is in violation of the constitution.

Deciding to Accept a Case

Though dramatic to lay observers, death penalty cases have in some respects become routine for state supreme courts. This is because the core legal questions have been resolved. On the other hand, serious doubts recently have been raised about the death penalty process in states like Illinois.

Through the petition for writ of certiorari the court uses its own discretion to take a case. In this process lawyers must be more persuasive. Using this process, courts accept cases when lawyers succeed in raising more serious questions about the meaning of a law or by arguing that a constitutional principle is being looked at in a new light. Evidence that the court needs to resolve a case is seen clearly when lower state courts express confusion over the proper interpretation of a supreme court decision.

Two examples might help explore this point. In some cases, several appeals panels may have examined the same legal question, with a similar fact set, but have reached opposing decisions. Clearly, then, the law cannot be applied fairly when reasonable people come to wildly different conclusions about the meaning of a law. In this way, there is an unfairness in the law when the same case is getting different outcomes.

Another indicator of confusion comes in an individual case when the trial court judge and one appellate judge see the rule of law one way, but the other two appellate judges think differently. These types of cases indicate to supreme court justices that legal experts are confused about how they should decide court cases. With this sort of situation, a state supreme court can be persuaded that it needs to put its authority behind one way of thinking, so lower courts can apply a uniform standard to future cases.

Making Rulings

There is nothing in the current literature on state courts that would distinguish the process of preparing for and holding oral arguments in a supreme court with an intermediate appeals court. Readers are referred to that section of this chapter for discussion of preparing for and holding oral arguments. Similarly the process of engaging in conference deliberations and impression votes is very much the same.

Much more is known about small group consensus building on the U.S. Supreme Court. However, some scholars think much of that knowledge can be translated to the state courts. The knowledge, intellectual capacity, sense of humility, a desire to "do the right thing," and a sense of humor of individual judges has helped propel courts during tense moments. Within state final courts, personality of judges is a subject of some interest. Henry Glick, in interviewing a variety of state supreme court judges, found that many judges learn to bite their tongues to preserve a friendly work environment. "Such things as arrogance, pride and a loss of temper were condemned" (Glick 1991).

How Does the Difference in Court Structure Matter?

The structure of a court and its size play important roles in several aspects of its internal function and decision-making routines. Generally, smaller courts with special functions attract lawyers with particular specialties. These attorneys, in turn, gain valuable insight to the thinking of judges and court routines simply by having regular contact there. This type of intimacy would frustrate outside lawyers trying to win decisions there. Meanwhile, more formalized and bureaucratic court systems are built for efficiency, uniformity, and lawyers who are able to thrive in a more formalized work environment.

Consolidated Courts

Satisfaction among court personnel is seen as being higher in consolidated courts than in multiple limited jurisdiction courts, according to Mikeska (2000). Remember that consolidated courts are those structured in the same way as the federal court system. They have a simple structure with a single trial-level court, though the trial court may hold sessions in many locations. In comparing local court structure, Mikeska found that staff in consolidated courts reported greater levels of teamwork, fewer political pressures, less interpersonal conflict, and a fairer distribution of workloads than the staffs in multiple special jurisdiction systems. In exploring resistance to efforts to move to consolidated forms, court clerks in limited jurisdiction venues voiced fears of greater political influence, loss of their own influence or prestige, and heavier work burdens.

Part of the efficiency courts gained through consolidation came through combining numerous bank accounts used to collect and distribute funds. This simplified record keeping. Furthermore, consolidated courts had more standardized operating procedures in the clerical, personnel, and financial departments. This made operations easier to follow to users who had business in the courts. Under consolidation, rules for case filing, accepting payment by check, decisions about disclosing court records to the public, and the rates charged for certain types of court services did not vary from court to court within a single county as they did in local judicial systems of multiple limited jurisdiction courts. This undermined the value of insider knowledge.

A recent study of family court services by NCSC reported that success in service delivery did not depend entirely on a court system being either oriented toward limited jurisdictions or organized in a consolidated fashion. It was the efficient and effective delivery of legal representation for children, case processing, and cooperation with human service agencies that are the better measures of judicial effectiveness some observers believe (Flango et al. 1999).

Flango et al. do indicate that the consolidated system can be more approachable for ordinary users. This is because an individual may look at many cases as a single case, when they stem from one event. For example, a court could assign components of a case separate case numbers and court dates for a domestic battery case (felony court), child custody case (juvenile court), and divorce case (another civil court). Meanwhile, the individuals involved may regard the three cases as having arisen from a single family and the same event. Many individuals will find it frustrating to work through the idiosyncrasies of three limited jurisdiction courts.

Consolidated courts make tracking case progress easier for court users with a one-stop-shopping sort of approach. Unified courts may also find it easier for judges to share information across cases, when they can be flagged as being related. However, some jurisdictions in Oregon and Delaware tried overcoming this by creating liaisons that alert judges when a single family may have relevant cases in several divisions of the local court system. This allows some families with overlapping litigation to bundle their cases into a single case.

Small Jurisdictions

Small jurisdictions, meanwhile, had some interesting qualities of their own. On one hand, a study of Fulton County Georgia's juvenile court system found that the system's two full judges could work collaboratively and share authority well (Klaversma and Hall 2003). To accomplish this, the two judges revealed high degrees of confidence in each other's decision-making abilities. However, much of their time was divided between managing the day-to-day administration of the court system and resolving disputes. Associate judges, who had less institutional authority, also lacked resources such as legal research and secretarial staff and could not be counted on to alleviate the administrative burdens of the full judges.

Large Jurisdictions

Large jurisdictions tend to have more bureaucratization and specialization. These districts, such as the Cook County Circuit Court surrounding Chicago, has multiple locations, hundreds of judges, clerks, and other staff. They have many institutional resources such as libraries and record-keeping facilities. For judges in these systems, division of labor is highly rigorous. The judges of the civil division do not hear criminal cases, unless they seek reassignment. This occurs despite the fact that Illinois has a unified, or consolidated, court system. Functions, by necessity, are distributed. Appointed associate judges in these large court systems may do little more than hear traffic violations all day long, while senior judges are swamped in complex and challenging litigation.

Differences in Selection

Differences in selection remain a matter of controversy. Some think that elected supreme court justices will be interested in the separation-of-power questions if they are appointed by governors and approved by legislatures. This is because these judges depend on other actors for their jobs. On the other hand, judges who are elected directly will connect the law to popular demands and be sensitive to the policy implications in preparation for future elections (Comparato 2003).

The jury is still out, so to speak, on the implications of judicial selection and policy implications. At the same time there is no real consensus on the effects of selection on representation on the courts. Women, Latinos, and African Americans are underrepresented in the courts; that is there are more white men sitting as judges (Alozie 1990). What has yet to be determined is the degree to which selection methods best meet prevailing social sentiments (ideological representation), or whether there is advantageous group representation for underrepresented groups to be had by greater numbers of female and minority judges.

Party Control

Party control of state government affects the latitude judges may feel. Where the governor and legislature are divided over a policy, courts may enjoy more latitude. Where both of the other chambers of government are in unison on a policy, they may bring resources, cooperate with interest groups in filing friend of the court (amicus curiae) briefs, and bring public pressure on courts to rule a certain way.

Courts with greater resources of their own and a tradition of independence may shrug off this sort of pressure. *Institutionalism* has to do with the resources of a branch of government and its members. Institutionalism or partisanship within other branches of government provide courts an opportunity to carve out a middle ground, or even take sides, while finding at least some support from a peer institution of state government (see, for example, Langer 2003). On the other hand, where both of the political branches are of one mind, the potential for retribution against the courts is high. In such cases, judges have an incentive to suppress their true policy goals and avoid costly political battles.

REFERENCES AND FURTHER READING

Alozie, Nicholas O. 1990. "The Distribution of Women and Minority Judges." *Social Science Quarterly* 71, no. 7 (June): 321.

Comparato, Scott A. 2003. *Amici Curiae and Strategic Behavior in State Supreme Courts.* Westport, CT: Praeger.

Durose, Matthew R., and Patrick A. Lanagan. 2003. "Felony Sentences in State Courts, 2000." *Bureau of Justice Statistics Bulletin* (June): 1–12.

Fish, Stanley. 1999. *The Trouble with Principle.* Cambridge, MA: Harvard University Press.

Flango C. E., et al. 1999. *How Are Courts Coordinating Family Cases?* Williamsburg, VA: National Center for State Courts.

Garrison, A. H. 2002. "Drug Treatment Programs: Policy Implications for the Judiciary." *Court Review* 38, no. 4 (Winter): 24–35.

Glick, Henry. 1991. "Policymaking and State Supreme Courts." In *The American Courts: A Critical Assessment,* eds. John B. Gates and Charles A. Johnson. Washington, DC: Congressional Quarterly Press.

Hogan, Sean O. 2000. *Continuity and Change in the Common Law: Illinois Tort Law 1971–1996* (unpublished Ph.D. diss., University of Illinois at Chicago).

Kadish, Mark 1996. "Behind the Locked Door of an American Grand Jury: Its History, Its Secrecy and Its Process." *Florida State University Law Review* 24 (Fall): 1.

Klaversma, Laura G., and Daniel J. Hall. 2003. *Organizational and Administrative Review of the Fulton County, Georgia, Juvenile Court.* Williamsburg, VA: National Center for State Courts.

Langer, Laura. 2003. *Judicial Review in State Supreme Courts: A Comparative Study.* Albany: State University of New York Press, 2003.

Marvell, Thomas B. 1978. *Appellate Courts & Lawyers: Information Gathering in the Adversary System.* Westport, CT: Greenwood Publishing.

Mikeska, Jennifer. 2000. *Court Consolidation: Reinventing Missouri State Courts.* Williamsburg VA: National Center for State Courts.

National Center for State Courts. 2002. "Civil Justice Reform Initiative: Advancing Civil Justice Reform." Examining the Work of the State Courts: Caseload Highlights. Williamsburg, VA: National Center for State Courts. http://www.ncsconline.org/WC/Publications/Res_CtComm_CJRIPub.pdf (accessed April 7, 2006).

Puzzanchera, Charles M. 2001. "Delinquency Cases Waived to Criminal Court, 1989–1998. " *OJJDP Fact Sheet,* vol. 35 (September). Washington, DC: Office of Juvenile Justice and Delinquency Prevention, U.S. Department of Justice.

U.S. Department of Justice. 2003. *Performance and Accountability Report of 2002.* Office of the Attorney General, http://www.usdoj.gov/ag/annualreports.html, (accessed March 20, 2006).

———. 2005a. "Crime Victimization Survey." Bureau of Justice Statistics, Washington, DC, http://www.ojp.gov/bjs/abstract/cvusst.htm. Last updated July 7, 2005 (accessed March 20, 2006).

———. 2005b."Criminal Sentencing Statistics." Bureau of Justice Statistics, Washington, DC, http://www.ojp.gov/bjs/sent.htm. Last updated December 22, 2005 (accessed April 6, 2005).

Von Drehle, David 1995. Symposium "The Death Penalty in the 21st Century." *American University Law Review* 45: 239.

Cases

Agostini v. Felton. 1997.521 US 203.
Aldridge v. United States. 1931. 283 U.S. 308.
Atkins v. Virginia. 2001. 533 U.S. 976.
Carter v. Jury Commission. 1970. 396 U.S. 320.
Holland v. Illinois. 1990. 493 U.S. 474 at 480.
Kelly v. South Carolina. 2002. 534 U.S. 246.
Mu'min v. Virginia. 1991. 500 U.S. 514.
Penry v. Lynaugh. 1989. 492 U.S. 302.
Powers v. Ohio. 1991. 499 U.S. 400.
Ristaino v. Ross. 1976. 424 U.S. 589.
Smith v. Texas. 1940. 311 U.S. 128, at 130.
Taylor v. Louisiana. 1975. 419 U.S. 522.
Terry v. Ohio. 1968. 392 U.S. 1 at 20.
United States v. Martinez-Fuerte. 1976. 428 U.S. 543 at 554.

4

THE PEOPLE WHO SERVE IN STATE COURT SYSTEMS

Ruth Ann Watry

A huge system of decision makers enters into the judicial processes of the American states. Judges are perhaps the most visible and the individuals most immediately associated with the court systems. Judges are not the only important decision-making actors in the state courts. This chapter introduces the reader to the characteristics of state court judges, and also to the lawyers and court support staff including court clerks and law clerks who make up the court systems in the fifty states. The first section discusses judges, the characteristics of lawyers, and judicial support personnel. Finally, this chapter describes the characteristics of jurors.

JUDGES

There are many types of people who are called to be judges. Some of the characteristics of judges are imposed by the rule of law. In other cases, there are requirements that are not written into the law. This chapter describes the formal and informal qualities of judges, the methods by which judges are selected, their earnings, and some of what is known about judicial selection and judicial outcome.

Characteristics of Judges

State judges "are overwhelmingly older, white male and Protestant. They tend to be home-grown fellows who are moderately conservative and staunchly committed to the status quo. They believe in the basic values and tradition of the legal and political communities from which they come" (Carp and Stidham 1996, 244). Over time, some of these qualities of the judges in the state courts have changed, but this change has been gradual.

One group that has been growing as a proportion of the population of judges is women. The first woman to serve on a state court was Florence Allen in 1920. By 1980, women represented 4 percent of state court judges, and by 1991, that percentage had increased to 9 percent. In May of 2003, there were 233 female judges on intermediate courts of

Florence Ellinwood Allen

Although Florence Allen was not the first female lawyer in the United States, she was the first assistant prosecutor, appointed as an assistant city prosecutor in Ohio in 1910. She also became the first female judge, after being elected as a judge in 1920. She beat nine male opponents. One year later in 1921 she was the first female judge to preside over a murder trial with women on the jury, and the first female judge to sentence a man to death. In 1922 she became the first female state supreme court justice, after being elected as a justice of the Ohio State Supreme Court.

Source: Russ, John A., IV, "Florence Ellinwood Allen," http://law.stanford.edu /library/wlhbp /papers/flo.html (accessed February 20, 2005).

Florence Ellinwood Allen (Library of Congress)

appeal (23.2 percent of all judges) and 92 women justices on state courts of last resort (typically called supreme courts). Nineteen of the fifty courts of last resort were headed by women (GGG). Although the percentage of female judges and justices does vary by state, women now represent approximately 20.5 percent of state judges and justices (AJS).

Racial minorities are gaining representation on state courts and at the bar, as well. Minorities now represent more than 10 percent of law school graduates. As a general rule, the percentage of minority judges is significantly below their percentage of the population. For example, although Texas is 32 percent Hispanic, and African Americans are 12 percent of the population, they are only 13 percent and 2 percent of the state's judges, respectively. Nationally, 6.2 percent of state judges are African American, 2.9 percent are Hispanic, 0.1 percent are Native American, and 1.1 percent are Asian or Pacific Islander (AJS).

While it is certain that there are more women and racial minorities on the state courts now than at any time in U.S. history, the degree to which demographic changes have affected ideological commitments or the use of discretion in the state courts is much less certain.

Selection of Judges: Some General Criteria

Many states have requirements for service as a judge. These typically involve age and residency requirements, and certain career experience. One of the first criteria for being selected as a judge is education. To be a judge in the state courts of the United States, one must be a licensed lawyer, which generally means that one has graduated law school. The one exception to this is some justices of the peace and judges in courts of limited jurisdiction who are required to have at least a high school education. If one of these nonlawyer judges hears a case, the parties involved must have the opportunity to have the case reheard in front of a law-school-trained judge if they are unhappy with the first trial's outcome.

The necessary qualifications to be a judge are discussed in state law or the state constitutions. Generally, states require that judges be licensed lawyers. The Supreme Court ruled in the 1970s that if a judge is not a lawyer, due process requirements are met only if an individual has the right to a later trial in front of a judge who is trained in the law. Often, states also require that judges have been a member of the state bar for a certain number of years and require that judges be citizens of the United States and residents of the state, and possibly the jurisdiction in which they would preside. Many states also have mandatory retirement ages, requiring that judges can only serve until the age of seventy. Beyond being qualified, an individual must also be selected to be a judge. In the state courts of the United States, there are five methods of judicial selection: appointment by governor, appointment by state legislature, merit selection, nonpartisan election, and partisan election.

Appointment by Governor

During the Founding Era (1776–1830s), state judges were either chosen by state legislatures or by the governor. There are currently four states that use appointment by governor as their primary method of judicial selection: California (supreme court and court of appeals judges only), Maine, New Hampshire (also requires approval by a five-member executive council), and New Jersey. It is worth noting that in most states using partisan or nonpartisan elections, interim vacancies generally are filled through gubernatorial nomination. Statistics indicate that as many as one-half of all judges initially reach the bench through gubernatorial appointment.

One of the criticisms of appointment by governor is that the governor is likely to select individuals who have been active in the governor's political party—not necessarily a glowing recommendation for a judge. The concern is that these individuals are chosen to serve as a judge not because they are qualified to be a judge, but rather, because of a political favor. Daniel Pinello found, when looking at state supreme courts, that gubernatorially appointed judges were more likely to prefer business over the individual and the states, and to prefer the individual over the state.

Appointment by Legislature

As was mentioned previously, selection by state legislature was one of the ways that state court judges were chosen during the Founding Era. Currently two states, South Carolina and Virginia, have state judges chosen by state legislatures. Since 1997 South Carolina's general assembly has used a ten-member nominating commission to screen judicial candidates. The South Carolina General Assembly can only select candidates found qualified by the Merit Selection Commission (AJS). Virginia's legislature does not use a nominating commission, but the governor can make recess appointments when the legislature is not in session.

One of the criticisms of appointment by legislature is that state legislatures tend to turn to former members of the legislature when appointing judicial candidates (Carp et al. 2004). The concern is that individuals are appointed to trial and appellate courts because they have friends and colleagues in the state legislature, rather than being appointed because of ability. Pinello found, when looking at state supreme courts, that legislatively selected judges tended to favor government (Pinello 1995).

Partisan and Nonpartisan Elections

Election of judges became popular during the time of Andrew Jackson's years as president, an era when his supporters sought to make the political process more democratic. By 1860, twenty-four of the thirty-four states elected some or all of their judges, and every new state admitted into the country from 1846 to 1912 elected some or all of its judges (Lozier 1996). Unfortunately, strong (and often corrupt) "political party machines" in many large urban areas had "party bosses" selecting incompetent party members for judicial positions (Lozier 1996). Since the party machine controlled elections, the result was an incompetent judiciary in many parts of the country. Today, partisan elections are used in fewer states than nonpartisan elections. In a partisan election, judicial candidates must be endorsed by a political party (unless they are running as independents) and the candidate's party affiliation appears on the ballot during the general election. States that select judges in this manner include Alabama, Arkansas, Illinois, Pennsylvania, Texas, and West Virginia. States that select some of their judges in this manner include Indiana, Kansas, Missouri, and Michigan (AJS).

States that use nonpartisan elections hold judicial elections, but do not allow party affiliation to appear on the ballot or to appear in campaign materials. It is difficult to say exactly how many states use partisan elections since many states use more than one method to select their judges. There are approximately twelve states that use nonpartisan elections to choose judges, and an additional eight states that use nonpartisan elections to choose some of its judges, or as one stage in their selection processes.

For example, though Michigan has nonpartisan elections of judges at the general election stage, judicial candidates are chosen during partisan primaries. Also, the state of California chooses its supreme court and court of appeals judges through appointment by governor, but chooses its superior court judges through nonpartisan elections.

Prior to the 1970s judicial elections were generally uncontested. A judge running for reelection (in Pennsylvania, Illinois, Indiana, and New Mexico, elected judges face a retention election after serving their first term) was often not running against another candidate. This has changed in recent decades and this change has caused concern. Judicial candidates are spending money to win elections, and increasingly, it is lawyers who are making contributions to these campaigns (Carp et al. 2004). Critics say the problem with lawyers contributing to campaigns is twofold. First, some fear that lawyers contribute to campaigns in hopes that a judge will treat them more favorably. The second concern focuses on judges soliciting contributions from lawyers. If a sitting judge approaches a lawyer for a campaign contribution, lawyers may feel pressured to contribute to the judge's campaign.

There are additional concerns surrounding the financing of judicial elections. One source of campaign funds is interest groups. As much as there is concern that a lawyer contributing to a campaign will receive favorable treatment from the bench, there is concern that interest groups making contributions will receive similar benefits. By putting judges in a position where they have to solicit campaign contributions, some suggest that judges are placed in a position that threatens their ability to be impartial decision makers. Groups supporting various economic interests or social causes have the resources to make large contributions to judicial candidates, and this worries some observers.

One way around campaign contributions is to have candidates use their own money, or public funding, to pay for campaign expenses. The downside to this is probably obvious. If we begin to expect candidates to pay for their own campaigns, we are restricting judgeships to those who have the personal resources to pay for publicity and can afford to take time off of work to campaign. If it is publicly funded, then state treasuries are forced to provide scarce funds for candidates or parties. Moreover, many taxpayers object to seeing their taxes support the messages of candidates and causes with which they may disagree.

An additional criticism of nonpartisan elections is that voters are not likely to be familiar with candidates running for judicial office. Press coverage of judicial races is far less intense than for executive or legislative races, so the lack of party identification on the ballot will leave voters with one less clue about the candidate. Voters will be left to decide not to vote in that particular race, or to vote for the candidate with the most familiar sounding name. Such strategies are not in concert with selecting the most qualified candidate in the judicial race, or the one who is most sympathetic to a voter's interests.

In a state with partisan elections, there is a strong likelihood that voters will select the candidates endorsed by their favorite party, even though they know little or nothing about the judicial candidate (Anderson 2004). In addition, if a state uses partisan elections, and one of the political parties dominates the state, the majority of judges will probably be members of that party. This is a problem in West Virginia, a state that uses partisan elections, and a state that is predominantly made up of Democrats. It is estimated that at any given time, 80 percent of judges in West Virginia are Democrats. Pinello found, when examining state supreme courts, that elected judges were more likely than other judges to be influenced by public opinion, more likely to favor the state over individuals and business, and in cases where the state is not a party to the suit, to favor individuals over business.

Merit Selection

The most common method of judicial selection in the state courts is merit selection. Thirty-two states use this approach to select some or all of their judges (AJS). Merit selection, also referred to as the Missouri Plan, is a three-step judicial selection process. It involves a nominating committee (or commission), the governor, and the voters. The first step involves a nominating commission or committee. The make-up of the committee is determined by the state constitution or by state law. The nominating commission typically is comprised of lawyers and nonlawyers appointed by the governor. Law may place a limit on how many commission members can be from any one political party. Law may also dictate that members of the commission must come from certain geographic parts of the state.

Commission members typically serve set terms, with a few commissioner terms coming up each year. When a judicial vacancy occurs, it is the job of the commission to review potential judges and to forward to the governor a list of the candidates who they feel are best qualified. The governor is then required to select a name on that list

Judges Disqualify Themselves from Case due to Conflict of Interest

On April 16, 2003, South Dakota Representative Bill Janklow ran a stop sign, killing a motorcyclist. Janklow, who was also a former governor of South Dakota, was found guilty of second-degree manslaughter and reckless driving. Janklow appealed the decision to the South Dakota Supreme Court. All five justices of the supreme court disqualified themselves from hearing the case; four had been appointed by Janklow to the supreme court and one had been appointed by Janklow as a circuit court judge. South Dakota uses the merit system to choose its judges and justices. The appeal was heard by five circuit court (trial court) judges who had not been appointed to their position by Janklow.

Source: Kafka, Joe. 2005. "Janklow's conviction in motorcyclist's death upheld by state supreme court." *Minneapolis Star and Tribune,* February 24.

William Janklow, who served as governor of South Dakota (1978–1986, 1994–2002) and U.S. representative (2002–2004) was convicted of manslaughter after running a stop sign. The "merit system" of selecting judges meant the state supreme court could not review the case, since he appointed most of the justices. (Office of Governor William Janklow)

and to appoint one of those individuals to the judicial vacancy. Once individuals have been appointed to the bench, they serve for at least one year, and then during the next scheduled general election, they are put up for a retention vote. The retention vote involves putting the judge's name on the ballot and asking the voters to essentially vote yes, retain the judge, or no, don't retain the judge. Typically, if judges receive a majority vote, they serve a set term (determined by individual state law), and at the end of that term, once again face a retention election.

Merit selection is supported by many scholars because it is believed that this method of selection produces the best qualified judges. Opponents of merit selection argue that the members of the nominating commission are often friends of the governor and that this method does not differ significantly from gubernatorial appointment.

Critics also point out that in most states that use this method, judges almost always survive the retention election—possibly because voters are not informed enough about them to vote them out of office. Additional criticisms of the merit selection system include that it takes away the right of citizens to elect government officials, that the nominating commissions do not represent the entire community, that voters do not understand retention elections, and that those chosen as judges do not represent a cross-section of the community.

Arguments in favor of merit selection include research that indicates that it is beneficial for women and minorities trying to get on the bench. Eight states that use merit selection have provisions providing for diversity of applicants and ten states (including two of the previous eight) have rules against discrimination (AJS). Those in favor of merit selection also argue that in states where it is used, more highly qualified judges have been the result. In addition, several states that use merit selection for some courts and elections for others have found that judges selected through the merit selection method are much less likely to face disciplinary charges than judges chosen through election (Lozier 1996). Many argue that in addition to giving us a more diverse judiciary, merit selection gives us the best of both worlds: a judge chosen based on merit, and retained in office through the votes of the citizens.

Becoming a Judge

Once an individual has been appointed or elected, he or she needs to make the transition from lawyer to judge. For many years, it was assumed that judges would be able to do this on their own. The belief was that lawyers had seen what judges did while arguing cases in the courtroom; that was seen as sufficient training. Increasingly, states are now requiring additional education for their judges. This may be as simple as a judicial orientation course to a requirement for continued education if an individual wants to continue to serve as a judge. The National Center for State Courts, the American Judicature Society, and many law schools provide training for first-time judges and continuing educational seminars for experienced judges.

One resource that has been very useful for states is the Federal Judicial Center, which offers courses for both federal and state court judges. Courses cover topics ranging from jury selection to criminal practice to torts. In addition to training judges on substantive areas of law, many training programs also cover technological advances, case management, security, and personnel management. More recently, the not-for-profit National Association of State Judicial Educators was formed in 1975 and is entirely devoted to the education of state court officials. Many states also offer their own judicial education programs. For example, Vermont has shifted from using nationally offered programs for education of state court judges to offering its own one-week judicial college (Morse et al. 1997). By providing its own program, it is able to address issues specific to Vermont courts.

Compensation and Tenure

Salaries for state judges vary by state and by judicial position. At the bottom of the pay scale are justices of the peace, whose entire income comes from fines collected or fees charged to perform weddings. At the other end of the pay scale would be supreme court justices in the more populous states. A survey conducted by the National Center for State Courts (see T4.1, below) found that on average, state supreme court chief justices earn $130,000 per year, supreme court justices earn $126,000, intermediate appellate court judges are paid $123,000, and trial court judges earn $114,000.

Although these salaries may seem high at first glance, for many lawyers becoming a judge, even at these salaries, involves taking a pay cut. In Minnesota, the salary for a district court judge is $118,141; there are first-year associates in Minnesota law firms who are paid more than that amount (Soule 2005). In Texas, Chief Justice Wallace B. Jefferson's 2005 "State of the Judiciary" message mentions that Texas is losing good judges because of the relatively low salaries earned by judges. A Texas court judge who returns to private practice is likely to double or triple his or her salary. Those who choose to go into education or move on to the federal bench are likely to see a 40 percent increase in pay.

TABLE 4.1   STATE JUDICIAL SALARIES

Position	Mean	Medial	Range
Chief justice, highest court	$130,461	$125,500	$95,000–191,483
Justice, highest court	$126,159	$112,500	$95,000–175,575
Judge, appellate court	$122,682	$117,850	$94,212–164,604
Judge, trial court	$113,504	$110,330	$88,164–158,100

Source: Data from "Survey of Judicial Salaries," National Center for State Courts, www.ncsconline.org/D_KIS/Salary_Survey (accessed March 26, 2006). Williamsburg, VA: NCSC.

Once an individual becomes a judge, there is a very high likelihood that he or she will remain a judge for as long as he or she wants to serve in that position. Supreme court justices and court judges serve terms ranging from four years to fourteen years, to life. Mandatory retirement at age seventy may be the only way to remove a judge, depending on which state he or she is in (see T4.2, p. 148).

Terms of office vary quite dramatically. An individual on the Kansas Court of Appeals has a term of four years, while an individual on the Massachusetts Supreme Court or court of appeals is appointed for life, with mandatory retirement at age seventy. At the trial court level, judges are typically looking at terms of four to twelve years. At the end of their terms, judges who were appointed by a governor or a state legislature must be reappointed, judges selected through partisan or nonpartisan elections must be re-elected, and judges chosen through merit selection must stand for another retention election.

Leaving the Court

Judges can leave the court in a voluntary or involuntary manner. Some judges at the end of their terms, or even in the middle of their terms, decide that they no longer want to be judges. Some choose not to stand for retention. They resign from their judicial positions and are replaced by others. Many states also have mandatory retirement ages for judges. In these states, a judge is required to resign when he or she reaches that age. In some states judges may complete their terms of office after reaching the retirement age.

Judges may also leave the bench against their will. This typically happens when a judge is found guilty of illegal activity (for example, accepting a bribe), abuse of power (for example, using one's power as a judge to issue a warrant when evidence does not support the warrant), or found to be incapable of doing the job due to incompetence or senility. Many states hope that a mandatory retirement age will reduce the number of cases where age leads to senility or loss of stamina needed for the job.

There are two major avenues by which judges are forced out of office. One is by impeachment by the state legislature. The other is through a hearing, typically involving a state judicial disciplinary board and the state supreme court. Almost all state constitutions allow legislatures to intervene by impeaching a judge by vote of the state legislature. If the legislature finds against a judge, he or she may be removed from office by a vote of the state senate. This approach is rarely used.

More commonly, if a judge abuses his or her power or commits an illegal act, someone will file a claim with a state judicial disciplinary commission. There are variations among the states, but all states follow some combination of these general guidelines. The agency or commission will investigate the complaint. Staff investigators will compile a file and present the data. Appointed officers, who make up the voting members of the commission, will first decide if the complaint is valid, and if it is the commission holds a formal hearing. At the end of that formal hearing, if the commission finds the judge guilty of the charges, the judge will be disciplined either by the commission

TABLE 4.2   MANDATORY RETIREMENT AGE OF JUDGES

State	Age	State	Age
Alabama	70	Montana	n/a
Alaska	70	Nebraska	n/a
Arizona	70	Nevada	n/a
Arkansas	n/a	New Hampshire	70
California	n/a	New Jersey	70
Colorado	n/a	New Mexico	n/a
Connecticut	n/a	New York	70
Delaware	n/a	North Carolina	72
Florida	70	North Dakota	n/a
Georgia	n/a	Ohio	70
Hawaii	70	Oklahoma	n/a
Idaho	n/a	Oregon	75
Illinois	75	Pennsylvania	70
Indiana	75	Rhode Island	n/a
Iowa	72	South Carolina	72
Kansas	70	South Dakota	70
Kentucky	n/a	Tennessee	n/a
Louisiana	70	Texas	75
Maine	n/a	Utah	75
Maryland	70	Vermont	70
Massachusetts	70	Virginia	70
Michigan	70	Washington	75
Minnesota	70	West Virginia	n/a
Mississippi	n/a	Wisconsin	n/a
Missouri	70	Wyoming	70

Source: Data from U.S. Department of Justice, Bureau of Justice Statistics (BJS), 2000.

or by the state supreme court. Discipline can involve anything from a formal reprimand to removal from the court.

The American Judicature Society (AJS) collected data on judicial discipline for 1999 and found that ninety-nine judges were disciplined in that year. Eight received suspensions and seven were removed (CJA). AJS estimates that there are in excess of 10,000 complaints filed each year, with 1 percent (or 100) resulting in disciplinary action by the various state disciplinary bodies (CJA).

Supreme Court Chief Justice Removed from Office

Roy Moore, Alabama's supreme court justice, was removed from office on Thursday, November 13, 2003, for defying a federal court order. A federal judge had ordered him to remove a monument containing the Ten Commandments from the judiciary building. As a judge, he had a legal responsibility to obey the order from the federal court. A nine-member judicial ethics panel, made up of judges, lawyers, and nonlawyers, voted unanimously to remove Moore from the Alabama Supreme Court.

Source: "Ten Commandments Judge Removed from Office," November 14, 2003, http://www.cnn.com/2003/LAW/11/13/moore.tencommandments/ (accessed February 28, 2005).

Alabama Supreme Court Chief Justice Roy Moore. (Alabama State Law Library)

ATTORNEYS

Judges are just one group of actors found within state court systems. Another group of actors is attorneys. This group includes attorneys who represent the state government as well as attorneys who represent individuals and nongovernmental institutions such as businesses or nonprofit agencies.

According to the American Bar Association (2005), 74 percent of attorneys work in private practice, 8 percent work for government, 8 percent work in private industry, 5 percent are inactive or retired, 3 percent work in the judiciary, and 1 percent each work in education, legal aid/public defender, and for a private association. According to the Bureau of Labor Statistics (BLS), the mean salary for lawyers working for state governments was $73,970 in 2005. In Britain and Ireland the lawyers who practice in courtrooms are called barristers, while those who provide legal advice outside the courtroom are called solicitors. In the United States there is no such formal distinction, but there are some lawyers who specialize as a matter of preference.

Attorneys for the State

The companion volume *The Executive Branch of State Government* provides complete details about the workings of attorneys general and local prosecuting attorney offices. Because these agencies work so closely with the courts it is essential that their role be mentioned here as well. Each state has an attorney general who acts as the chief legal official for the state. It is the job of the attorney general to see that the laws of the state are enforced. This individual, who is an elected official in most states, manages an office of attorneys who handle civil cases and statewide criminal cases involving the state. The office of the attorney general can participate in statewide criminal investigations, institute civil suits, represent state agencies, and handle criminal appeals. This office defends state laws when they are questioned on constitutional grounds. Most state attorneys general offices also employ many additional attorneys. Of greater interest in the area of courts is the role of the prosecutor. Prosecutors include state prosecutors, district attorneys, county attorneys, and assistant and deputy county and district attorneys. By 1981 more than 1,200 of the more than 14,000 state court lawyers were women (GGG).

District attorneys (often called county attorneys or state's attorneys) typically are locally elected. The job of a district or county attorney involves prosecuting cases on the government's behalf. Jurisdiction is determined by law, and may involve anything and everything from traffic tickets to capital murder, to advancing a county's interests in civil proceedings. So state's attorneys' offices usually have civil divisions that acquire property for road projects, defend the county's land-use policies, or respond to tort claims against the county. The job of a prosecutor involves reviewing evidence, pertinent court decisions, laws, polices, and regulations, and then deciding whether there is sufficient evidence for indictment and prosecution. Things that go into the prosecutor's decision of whether or not to prosecute can include the chance of winning the case in front of a jury, the nature of the evidence against a suspect, and whether resources exist to support prosecution of the case. The decision to prosecute also includes the decision concerning which charges to pursue and the applicable law.

The prosecutor also has discretion concerning whether a defendant can enter into a negotiated outcome, such as a plea agreement. As this is an elected position in most states, voters can remove a district or county attorney if they do not agree with his or her decision concerning the prosecution of a case. In cases including eminent domain, land use, and civil rights, state law determines whether the attorney general acts alone, whether county attorneys act alone, or whether the two work together. For example, in Minnesota, the attorney general acts in conjunction with county attorneys in cases involving the use of public lands.

Assistant county attorneys, deputy county attorneys, assistant district attorneys, and deputy district attorneys work for the county or district attorney. These are not elected positions. These individuals are trial attorneys and prosecute cases as assigned. They do not have discretion as to whether to bring charges in a case, and typically need the approval of the county or district attorney to enter into a plea agreement. The prosecutor is responsible for participating in preliminary and probation hearings, and bench and jury trials. This includes the need to interact with the public, identify and question witnesses, and understand relevant laws and policies.

Attorneys for Activists

There are many activist groups that use the courts to bring about social change, and there are lawyers who specialize in these types of cases. Scheingold and Sarat (2004) call this "cause lawyering." They see this group of lawyers as including everyone from property rights lawyers to right-to-life lawyers to environmental lawyers. Lawyers take cases in these and other fields not by accident, but because they have an intent to bring about change in some particular policy area. Groups that come to mind when one thinks of cause lawyers include the American Civil Liberties Union (ACLU) and the National Association for the Advancement of Colored People (NAACP). These groups hire lawyers and provide legal services for parties in cases related to the cause supported by the group.

These groups rarely are listed as the plaintiff or respondent in their most profound suits. Rather, they provide legal or financial support to the people or groups who are named in a case. For example, though the NAACP was not the litigant, it provided the legal staff that succeeded in desegregating the Topeka, Kansas, schools in *Brown v. Board of Education*.

Brown v. Board of Education

When the Supreme Court heard *Brown v. Board of Education* in the early 1950s, it was actually considering eight different cases. Louise Brown was the young student involved in the actual *Brown* case. The legal expenses for the case were paid for by the National Association for the Advancement of Colored People (NAACP) and the case was argued by NAACP attorney Thurgood Marshall.

Lawyers for the National Association for the Advancement of Colored People (NAACP) celebrate outside the U.S. Supreme Court building after successfully challenging school segregation in Brown v. Board of Education *(1954). From left to right are George E. Hayes, Thurgood Marshall, and James Nabrit. (Library of Congress)*

Attorneys for Criminal Defendants

In 1963, in a case called *Gideon v. Wainwright,* the U.S. Supreme Court ruled that the Sixth Amendment right to an attorney included an attorney at the expense of the state, if a criminal suspect could not afford an attorney on his or her own. In 1972, in *Argersinger v. Hamlin,* the Supreme Court ruled that an individual cannot be sentenced to jail if he or she had not been provided with the opportunity to have an attorney. If an individual can afford to hire an attorney, there are many attorneys available in most communities who specialize in defending individuals in criminal cases. Private defense counsel is available either for an hourly fee or for a set amount of money for a certain type of case. Although paying for an attorney can be a hardship for some, unless defendants can show that they are indigent (destitute and in need of help from others), they must pay for an attorney on their own. On the other hand, if individuals are indigent and cannot afford an attorney, one is provided for them by the state.

The first step taken by an individual who cannot afford an attorney typically is an application for indigent defense services. Individuals can show that they are indigent by showing that they do not have property that can be converted into cash, showing that they have excessive debt, or by demonstrating through past and present financial history that they do not have the resources necessary to hire an attorney. The judge then makes a ruling on whether an individual is indigent. It is also possible for an individual's status of indigence to change over the course of a trial. If individuals are indigent, legal assistance will be provided for them in the form of assigned counsel or a public defender.

States and localities provide indigent defendants with defense attorneys. Some local governments turn to private attorneys who take cases for indigent defendants. These assigned counsel attorneys are paid by the government to do this as part of their regular work. Some states have entire agencies dedicated to defending the poor. Public defenders are government lawyers outside the attorney general's chain of command, who represent poor criminal defendants at trial and on appeal. Most states use a combination of assigned counsel and public defenders, with assigned counsel being more common in rural areas, and public defenders more common in urban areas. Lawyers may or may not have a choice as to whether they will serve as assigned counsel, and if assigned to a case, lawyers must accept the compensation set by state law, even if that compensation is less than they would receive through private practice. For example, although attorneys may typically charge $100 per hour for their legal services, they may only get compensated $50 per hour on a case where they are an assigned counsel.

There are multiple criticisms of the system of assigned counsel. Some argue that states place cost containment above quality. There is also concern that attorneys are assigned to cases that they may not be well qualified to deal with. Some states offer incentives to lawyers who plead a case rather than take the case to trial and some states conduct little or no monitoring of assigned counsel. In states that contract out for indigent defense services, some reward low bids, placing more emphasis on hiring an inexpensive, rather than highly qualified, legal service. Critics do acknowledge that some states do a better job with assigned counsel than others. States that have effective systems related to assigned counsel are more likely to require minimum attorney qualifications, offer compensation in line with local fees, and provide some type of oversight mechanism. The state of Indiana for instance has a Public Defender Council, a state agency whose responsibility is to be a support center for assigned counsel.

Approximately 25 percent of states use a public defender system to provide counsel for all indigent parties, and many other states use it to provide counsel for some indigents. With a public defender system, a state agency hires attorneys to defend indigent criminal defendants. For example, in Maryland, all indigent suspects who are involved in a criminal case carrying a possible jail sentence or a fine greater than $500 can be provided with an attorney through the public defender's office. Although there are states that use just public defenders, a more common situation is a state like Ohio that uses both public defenders and assigned counsel. The office of the public defender in Ohio both provides legal representation in the form of public defenders and oversees appointed counsel in its county courts. Ohio has an interesting division of responsibilities in that it uses primarily assigned counsel at the trial level and public defenders at the appellate level. In some parts of California assigned counsel is used, while more populous counties such as Orange County have public defenders.

Some of the criticisms of public defender systems include the complaint that lawyers work with very heavy caseloads but lack the experience or resources necessary to compete with staff and resources of the state's attorney's office, especially in death penalty cases. States have been responding to these criticisms, successfully in many cases. Public defenders in Maryland now must have at least five years prior experience in litigating criminal cases. Alaska also has a statewide public defender system, with sixty-five public defenders employed in thirteen offices throughout the state. Finally, Colorado is another state that has a public defenders office that serves the entire state. Colorado has separate trial and appellate public defenders. In addition, Colorado has trial-level public defenders who specialize in death penalty cases. Most individuals hired as public defenders in Colorado are hired directly out of law school, although many have clinical or clerking experience.

Attorneys for Civil Defendants

The Sixth Amendment right to have an attorney provided if one cannot afford one is a right that is present only in criminal cases. The Constitution does not discuss the right to an attorney in a civil trial. As a general rule, if one desires to have an attorney in a civil trial, one pays for one's own attorney. In most civil cases, if one cannot afford his or her own attorney, one must proceed without an attorney. This may not seem significant, unless one realizes that civil cases include divorce and custody issues. There are, however, three developments that have made an attorney in a civil case more affordable to a middle-class litigant.

The first of these is flat fees. There are some lawyers who offer basic legal services, such as an uncontested divorce, for a flat fee. The second advancement is prepaid legal services. Individuals are enrolled in prepaid legal services typically through their employer as part of a benefit package, or through a plan offered with a credit card or credit union or other similar entity. Basically, a job benefit, or credit union benefit might be a set number of hours of legal assistance in a given year. The plan normally provides a list of attorneys that an individual must choose from. A third development that has made legal assistance more accessible for the middle class is the use of contingency fees. The way that contingency fees work is that an attorney will agree to take a case on contingency, meaning that his or her compensation in the case is based on the amount of the settlement. If the attorney loses the case, the individual pays nothing; but if the attorney wins the case, he or she is sometimes reimbursed for expenses, and then also receives some percentage (typically around 33 to 50 percent) of the remaining settlement.

In some states, such as Wisconsin, contingency fees are limited by law (Kritzer 2002). In his 1995 study of contingency-fee practitioners, Kritzer found that contingency fees did not have the negative impact on the legal practice feared by many scholars. He found that contingency fees are adequately governed by the market, that contingency fees are generally competitive, and that although there are some extremely large contingency fees paid to lawyers, as a general rule, they are reasonable (Kritzer 2004). Furthermore, Larry E. Coben finds that over the past thirty years, there is no real evidence that contingency fees have been harmful to the public (Coben 2004).

Free Legal Services for the Poor

Legal services for the poor in civil cases are difficult for many to find. It is primarily provided in three ways: as *pro bono* work, through legal clinics provided by law schools, and through legal services programs. Pro bono work refers to legal services provided by an attorney for free. The American Bar Association's Model Rules of Professional Conduct suggests that attorneys have an obligation to perform pro bono work. Some attorneys satisfy this obligation by representing poor individuals in civil cases. Law schools often provide clinical experiences for their third-year students. Although clinics exist in many legal fields, clinics focusing on issues such landlord-tenant disputes and family law can provide affordable legal assistance for the poor. Legal services programs, historically funded by federal, state, and local funds, involve setting up offices in cities and neighborhoods to provide legal services for indigent clients. Funds went to pay attorneys providing the legal services. Recent budget cuts at the state and federal level have resulted in a reduction in legal services programs.

SUPPORT STAFF

State trial courts and appellate courts would not function without court clerks, law clerks, and other support staff. These are the individuals who assist judges in carrying out their duties, as well as taking care of the administrative responsibilities involved in a smoothly functioning court system. Some of these individuals are elected, some are appointed, and some are hired. Some serve terms set by state law or the state constitution, while others serve at the pleasure of the individual who hired them. Without these support personnel, the state courts would come to a grinding halt.

Court Clerks

The clerk of a court is an elected or appointed official. A court clerk is responsible for docketing cases, arranging jury selection, maintaining court records, and collecting court fees. This is the individual who handles the day-to-day functions of the court.

Court clerks are different than a judge's law clerks, who assist judges in their legal research. A clerk of a court will frequently have responsibility for one or more courtrooms while the court administrator may run an entire courthouse. Appointed clerks frequently serve at the pleasure of the individual or court who appointed them, while elected clerks typically serve terms of two, four, or six years and are accountable to the voters, rather than judges of the court. Appointed clerks may be appointed by the court, a chief judge, a county board, some other local governing body, or the governor. In Hawaii, the clerks of trial courts actually have civil service tenure.

Appellate Court Clerks

Clerks play an important role in appellate courts, and are provided for either by state law or in the state constitution. The majority of clerks of appellate courts are appointed by the judge(s) of the court that they are working for. In Indiana, Montana, and Ohio (court of appeals only) they are elected. In Rhode Island they are appointed by the governor. Most clerks serve at the pleasure of the court; however, in some states, such as Arkansas, Indiana, and Kansas, clerks of appellate courts serve set terms. Clerks of appellate courts frequently have staffs who work for them.

Responsibilities of the clerks' offices in the appellate courts include day-to-day operations of the courts physical plant, management of the court's docket, oversight of the state bar, and support for the judges of the court. These functions include accounting, accounts payable, administrative meetings, oversight of the state bar, budget preparation, oversight of commissions and boards, maintenance of court statistics, data processing, facility management, legal research, liaison with state legislature and other courts, payroll, property control, purchasing, records management, planning, and technical assistance to lower courts. It is their responsibility to keep the court operating in every manner imaginable. In many states, there is no minimum qualification if one wants to serve as the clerk of an appellate court, but in some, an individual must be a lawyer and admitted to the state bar, and in some, an individual must have experience in court operations (BJS 2000).

Trial Court Clerks

The clerk of court for a trial court differs significantly from a clerk of court for an appellate court. Whereas the majority of clerks of court for appellate courts are appointed by the court, many clerks of court for trial courts are elected, in either partisan or nonpartisan local elections. Legislation typically provides a clerk of court for each court, so it is not uncommon within a given state for there to be more than 100 clerks of court. Much like clerks of appellate courts, clerks of trial courts often have staffs who work for them. Responsibilities of trial court clerks are set by law. In some states, such as Minnesota, clerks of the court are called court administrators. Clerks of trial courts are responsible for the day-to-day operation of that particular court. Every state now has something resembling an administrative office of the courts. This agency performs a variety of administrative tasks including judicial education, budgeting, research, personnel management, facility management, and public information.

Responsibilities of the administrative office of the courts in a trial court can include day-to-day operations of the court's physical plant, management of the court's docket, oversight of the state bar, and support for the judges of the court. These functions include accounting, alternative dispute resolution, assignments for sitting and supplemental judges, alternative sanction programs, budget preparation, facility management, foster care review, judicial education, law libraries, legal research, representation and general counsel, legal services, liaison with the state legislature, oversight of adult and juvenile probation, public information, purchasing, research and planning, and technical assistance to the courts (BJS 2000).

As an example, the Trial Court Services Division of the Alabama Administrative Office of the Courts provides assistance for Alabama trial courts in the areas of court automation, case management and time standards, jury management, judge case assignments, education support, municipal courts, uniform traffic ticket complaints, the unified judicial system magistrate program, and municipal court clerk and management certification. For instance, in the area of judge assignment, this division handles all temporary judge assignments. In the area of case management and time standards, this division monitors the processing of cases in all state trial courts and works with individual court staff to more efficiently schedule cases and utilize court staff.

The National Center for State Courts (NCSC) is a research and training resource for both court clerks and for trial court administrators. One of NCSC's functions, carried out through its Institute on Court Management, is providing education and training for court personnel, with the goal of helping courts to better serve the public. NCSC offers a Court Executive Development Program and a Court Management Program. In addition to participating in one of the two programs previously mentioned, state court clerks and state trial court administrators can take courses in person or online, on topics covering everything from managing court financial resources, to introduction to case flow, to emergency management and court security. NCSC offers a course corresponding to most of the functions mentioned previously.

Law Clerks

The use of law clerks at the appellate court level has allowed appellate courts to increase their efficiency in handling their caseloads. State law typically provides that each supreme court justice or appellate court judge has one to three law clerks. Law clerks are different from court clerks in that law clerks provide legal assistance while court clerks are administrative assistants. These individuals have legal backgrounds, work for a specific individual justice, and may be a short-term or long-term employee. In addition, state law may provide for some number of central law staff for a court. Central staff attorneys typically have a legal background, work for the appellate court as a whole, have limited ties to individual justices, and often work in the office of the clerk of the court. This individual may be referred to as a research attorney, a commissioner, a staff law clerk, or may have another title. Law clerks are either individuals still in law school or are individuals with a law degree.

When one thinks of law clerks working in the appellate court environment, the function that initially comes to mind is that these individuals assist judges and justices in preparing their opinions in cases that the court has considered. Law clerks assist the court in many more ways. Law clerks can assist the court by helping conduct and manage settlement conferences and they can assist in handling cases by helping screening, preparing memoranda, scheduling the case for oral argument, or other aspects of case management. They can also assist the court by helping train new staff, conducting research on motions and writs, and preparing memoranda on discretionary petitions. Functions performed by law clerks can also include developing databases, tracking information, indexing cases, and making recommendations to a judge concerning questions that should be asked during oral argument. Any work that can be handled by a law clerk frees up a judge or justice's time to focus on other more important tasks.

Law clerks also play a role at the trial court level. Trial court law clerks may assist judges by assisting in legal research and court management, processing motions, attending conferences, mediating small-claims cases, and summarizing information for the judge.

Court Reporters and Courtroom Deputy

Court reporters are courthouse staff who create word-for-word transcripts of what occurs during legal proceedings. Often using stenography equipment to take transcriptions, it is their responsibility to make sure that there is a complete and accurate record of the trial. This is important because the transcript of the trial created by the court reporter is the record on which any appeal is built. In addition to providing a transcript of a trial, court reporters may also take pretrial depositions from witnesses involved in a case, or take transcripts during other hearings during the process. The National Court Reporters Association provides training for court reporters. Depending on the type of certification required, this training, on average, takes two to four years. According to the Bureau of Labor Statistics, there were approximately 10,800 court reporters employed at the state level in 2002.

The courtroom deputy position is one that goes by many names—deputy clerk, bailiff, deputy sheriff—but whose function is the same: courtroom security. Specific job functions differ from one courtroom to the next, but essentially, the bailiff is responsible for maintaining order and security in the courtroom and for ensuring the protection of judges, juries, and courtroom participants. This individual announces the entrance of the judge and jury, prevents persons from entering the courtroom while a judge is instructing a jury, escorts the judge outside of the courtroom when necessary, and removes individuals who disrupt court proceedings. When a jury is sequestered, bailiffs may escort jurors to restaurants and to their hotels. Individuals who work as bailiffs typically have police academy training, have arrest authority, and often are employed through a sheriff's department. According to the Bureau of Labor Statistics there were approximately 16,690 individuals employed as bailiffs in 2003.

JURORS AND THE JURY

Although there are tens of millions of felonies and misdemeanors in the United States each year, only 300,000 cases or so are actually decided by a jury (Abraham 1998). Although an individual is guaranteed a jury trial in the U.S. Constitution's Sixth Amendment, many individuals waive that right and opt for a bench trial (a trial in front of a judge) rather than a jury trial. Despite this low number, the jury (also called *trial jury* or *petit jury*) plays an important role in the American judicial system. The jury system as it is used here in the United States is a legacy of our English common law tradition. The right to a jury trial dates back to antiquity and the jury trial as we understand it has been part of the Western tradition since the Magna Carta. In the United States, an individual has the right to request a jury trial if he or she faces a sentence of more than six months in jail.

Civil Rights

The Supreme Court, in *Strauder v. West Virginia*, in 1880, declared that blacks had the right to serve on juries. Despite that decision, blacks were kept off of juries in many parts of the country until the civil rights movement and beyond. In 1970, in *Carter v. Jury Commission*, the Supreme Court ruled that jury pools must be constructed in such a manner that black citizens are included in the pool. In 1986 in *Batson v. Kentucky*, the court ruled that peremptory challenges cannot be used to keep blacks off juries.

Sources: *Batson v. Kentucky* 476 U.S. 79 (1986); *Carter v. Jury Commission* 396 U.S. 320 (1970); *Strauder v. West Virginia* 100 U.S. 303 (1880).

Women on Juries

Historically women were denied many political rights. Although women were granted the right to vote in 1920 with the Nineteenth Amendment, their right to automatically be considered as potential jurors came much later. In 1975, in *Taylor v. Louisiana*, the Court looked at the Louisiana jury selection system, which excused all women from jury service unless they filed a written declaration asking to be considered for jury service. The Court found this unconstitutional and a legal requirement to be in violation of an individual's right to a jury selected from a representative cross-section of the community.

Source: Taylor v. Louisiana 419 U.S. 522 (1975).

Women take to the streets with signs in support of the suffrage movement in 1917. Though the right to vote was secured for women in 1920, it would take another 55 years to have equal treatment for jury service. (Library of Congress)

The first step in jury selection involves the creation of a master jury list, which includes a representative cross-section of the community. States use multiple sources in creating these lists. States may use city or county directories, driver's license lists, motor vehicle registrations, telephone directories, tax rolls, lists of utility customers, voter registration lists, or some combination of these. Most states allow a person to serve on a jury on reaching the age of eighteen, although Alabama and Nebraska require

TABLE **4.3**   STATES WITH A MAXIMUM AGE FOR POTENTIAL JURORS

State	Maximum Age	State	Maximum Age
Alaska	70*	New Hampshire	70
Florida	70	New Jersey	75
Georgia	70*	North Carolina	65
Idaho	70*	Oklahoma	70
Maryland	70*	Oregon	70
Massachusetts	70	South Carolina	65
Michigan	70	Tennessee	65
Minnesota	70	Texas	65
Mississippi	65	Virginia	70
Nebraska	65	West Virginia	65
Nevada	70**	Wyoming	73

Source: Data from U.S. Department of Justice, Bureau of Justice Statistics (BJS), 2000.

* Request for exemption must be made in writing

** Age is sixty-five if the person lives more than 65 miles from court

that a potential juror be at least nineteen, and Mississippi and Missouri require that potential jurors be at least twenty-one years of age. Many states disqualify convicted felons from serving on juries and some require that a potential juror have been a resident of the jurisdiction for some amount of time, although residency requirements are not to exceed a year (BJS 2000). The U.S. Supreme Court has ruled that women *(Taylor v. Louisiana* [1975]), blacks *(Strauder v. West Virginia* [1880]) and Mexican Americans *(Castaneda v. Partida* [1977]) cannot be systematically kept off juries simply due to race or gender. This is one valuable legacy of the civil rights and women's movements. Women and blacks, who were systematically kept off of juries for years, are now allowed to serve.

The next phase in jury selection is venire, or the drawing of a jury pool from the master jury list (see also Chapter 3). Clerks of the court randomly select a group of names from the master list and send a survey to those individuals asking questions concerning their eligibility to serve on a jury. Some states exempt potential jurors who are senior citizens (see T4.3, above).

States may also exempt a person from serving on a jury if he or she is in a specified profession including judicial officer, public official, elected legislator, physician, or attorney. If people are in an exempt category, they will not be allowed to serve on a jury, even if they want to.

In addition, some states will excuse potential jurors if serving on a jury would pose undue hardship or extreme inconvenience, or if public necessity or physical or mental disability should preclude this person from serving on a jury (BJS 2000). These include

Judge and Jury

Marlborough, Massachusetts, District Court Judge Thomas Sullivan Jr. wouldn't be expected to recognize everyone showing up for jury duty. But he was a bit surprised to find the name of local resident Stephen Breyer on the jury list. "When I looked at the slip I said, 'Oh, my God,'" Sullivan said in a telephone interview with the Associated Press. U.S. Supreme Count Justice Stephen Breyer, not one to ignore a court order, appeared in Judge Thomas's courtroom with jury summons in hand in January 2005 and was ready to decide a drunk driving case. According to Sullivan, the defense attorney said, "The last thing I need is two judges on the case."

Breyer said it was important to do his civic duty and report to the courthouse. "It proves that everyone can participate, and in a democracy that is important," Breyer said. Sullivan was impressed. "If anyone could have made a phone call and gotten out of it, he could have. He really wanted to sit on the case," Sullivan said. "That might put some other people to shame who were planning to try to get out of jury duty."

Source: Associated Press, Jan. 4, 2005.

Stephen Breyer is a current associate justice of the U.S. Supreme Court, where he is considered a moderate liberal. (Collection of the Supreme Court of the United States)

cases where a person's absence from work or family would adversely affect public health, safety, welfare, and interest. For example, some state law makes it easy for lawyers, public officials, police officers, and news reporters to be excused from jury service. Potential jurors who are not exempted or excused will eventually receive a summons directing them to appear at the courthouse on a given date to possibly serve on a jury.

Voir dire is the final step in jury selection. Potential jurors are asked questions concerning their ability to be an impartial juror in a particular trial. The complexity of this process is often influenced by the nature of the case involved. At one end of the spectrum was the O. J. Simpson case where 250 potential jurors were asked to complete a 79-page, 294-question questionnaire. At the other end would be a misdemeanor state trial where a jury of six can be selected in an hour or two. For example, if one was charged with writing a forged check in California, it would be a misdemeanor offense, and that person would be facing up to a year in jail, giving them a right to a jury trial. Chances are that a jury would be chosen rather quickly.

Jury Selection and the O. J. Simpson Trial

One of the highest profile cases of the 1990s involved a California case where O. J. Simpson was accused of murdering his wife, Nicole Brown Simpson, and a friend of hers, Ron Goldman. Jury selection in the case began on September 24, 1994 with 250 potential jurors present. The jury pool was 40 percent white, 28 percent black, 17 percent Hispanic, and 15 percent Asian. Jurors were asked to complete a 79 page, 294 question questionnaire. Answers to the questions determined if jurors would be removed for cause. During selection, every time the prosecution team used a peremptory challenge to remove a black as a potential juror, the defense challenged that they were using the challenge specifically to keep the person off of the jury because of race. Jury selection took until November 3, and the jury was comprised of eight blacks, two Hispanics, one half-Caucasian, half-Native American, and one Caucasian female.

Source: "The O. J. Simpson Trial: The Jury", http://law.umkc.edu/faculty/projects/ftrials/ Simpson/Jurypage.html (accessed January 15, 2005).

At the voir dire stage, a potential juror can be excused in two ways: removal for a challenge for cause or removal through use of a peremptory challenge. A juror is removed for cause if his or her personal attitude, personal experiences, or knowledge of the case results in the judge believing that an individual has a bias that would prevent him or her from being an impartial juror. Each party is also given a limited number of peremptory challenges, which can be used to remove potential jurors without giving a reason. The Supreme Court has ruled that these cannot be used to systematically keep a person off of a jury due to race *(Batson v. Kentucky* [1986]) or gender *(JEB v. Alabama ex rel. T.B.* [1994]).

Some state law requires that the voir dire interviews be conducted by the judge, some require that they be conducted just by the attorneys, but in the majority of states, they are conducted by both the judge and the attorneys. The number of peremptory challenges given to the two parties varies by state, with the severity of the crime, and by party. In some states, the defense receives more peremptory challenges than the prose-

Use of Peremptory Challenges in Selection of Michael Jackson Jury

During jury selection in the 2005 Michael Jackson child molestation trial, the prosecution used peremptory challenges to remove two black women as potential jurors. The defense objected, but the judge upheld the removal of both. Although Jackson is black, the jury contained no blacks. Of the eight alternates, one was black. Santa Bar-bara County, where the trial was held, is 2.3 percent black.

Source: CBS News, "Jury Selected for Jackson Trial," http://www.cbsnews.com/stories/2005 /02/23/entertainment/main675898.shtml (accessed March 26, 2006).

cution. As a general rule, more peremptory challenges are provided in a capital felony case than in a regular felony case, which normally has more peremptory challenges than a misdemeanor case (BJS 2000).

Jury selection in a capital (death penalty) case differs from jury selection in general in two ways. First, the defense may be provided with additional peremptory challenges. When a defendant's life is at risk and his attorney has a "gut feeling" that a particular juror may be hostile to the defendant, the attorney is able to use a peremptory challenge to keep that person off of the jury. An additional difference is something referred to as *death qualification* of a jury. The prosecution is allowed to ask potential jurors whether they feel that they could impose a death sentence if the defendant is found guilty. Asking this type of question is not seen as a method of creating a jury that is pro–death penalty. Instead, it is a way of ensuring that if a person is on the jury, he or she can fairly apply the law to the case at hand.

Increasingly, attorneys are using scientific jury selection, where professional jury consultants are brought in to pinpoint the type of juror who is most likely to side with their client. In addition to assisting attorneys during jury selection, professional jury consultants can also assist attorneys in developing trial presentations targeted at the specific types of individuals on the jury.

Jury size and the number of votes required to reach a verdict also differ by state. The U.S. Supreme Court has ruled that a jury in state trial can have as few as six members (*Williams v. Florida* [1970]), that the vote of the jury need not be unanimous (*Johnson v. Louisiana* [1972]), but that in order to allow a nonunanimous vote, the jury must have at least twelve members (*Burch v. Louisiana* [1979]). The one exception to this rule is Oregon, which has a five of six rule concerning juries of six in some of its courts. States have been moving away from requiring a unanimous jury verdict. If one requires a five of six or a nine of twelve vote, there is less likelihood of a hung jury than if unanimity is required.

Most states require a jury of twelve in felony cases, but Alabama, Connecticut, Florida, Indiana, Massachusetts, and Utah allow for juries of six or eight members in some or all noncapital felony cases. All states, with the exception of Louisiana and Oregon, require a unanimous vote by the jury in a felony case. Louisiana will allow a

Scientific Jury Selection

A high profile case that involved scientific jury selection was the court case between Oprah Winfrey and the Texas Cattleman, concerning comments that Oprah had made regarding beef. Oprah hired Courtroom Sciences, Inc., a consulting firm cofounded by Dr. Phil McGraw, to assist with jury selection. The jury, picked with Dr. Phil's assistance, found Oprah not liable for comments she made during her show about eating beef.

Source: Petersen, Karen S. "Dr. Phil dishes advice right in your face." *USA Today,* October 14, 2002, http://www.usatoday.com/life/2002–10–14–dr-phil–1acover_x.htm, (accessed February 15, 2005).

ten of twelve vote in cases where punishment is hard labor and Oregon allows a ten of twelve vote in all cases not involving a murder. Jury size for cases involving misdemeanors also varies by state. In civil cases, jury sizes range from six to twelve jurors, with some states requiring that a judgment be unanimous, some states employing a five of six rule, and others employing a three of four rule (BJS 2000).

The Grand Jury

Although the Fifth Amendment of the U.S. Constitution provides "[N]o person shall be held to answer for a capital, or otherwise infamous crime, unless on a presentment or indictment of a Grand Jury," this has never been interpreted as applying to the states. As a result, not all states require grand jury indictment in felony cases. Some states require a grand jury indictment for all felonies, some states require a grand jury indictment only if the death penalty and/or a life sentence is being requested, and some states use the grand jury primarily for criminal investigations. In many states, grand jury indictment has been replaced by a document called criminal information that is drawn up by the prosecutor and presented directly to a magistrate or judge. An *information* is essentially a legal document that lays out the evidence that the prosecutor has that a crime has occurred. An information is a more efficient method of processing a criminal complaint, but for complex criminal problems such as public corruption and fraud, the grand jury is still the preferred route. If the judge or magistrate believes that there is probable cause that an individual has committed a crime, the judge will issue the necessary search and/or arrest warrant.

The grand jury functions very differently from a trial jury. The job of the grand jury is not to determine guilt or innocence; rather, it is to determine if there is sufficient evidence to arrest an individual and to bring him or her to trial. A grand jury is convened when a prosecutor has a case he or she wants the grand jury to review. The pros-

Applying the Bill of Rights to the States

As written, the first eight amendments of the Bill of Rights were not intended to apply to the states. The first Congress resoundingly rejected wording that included the states. You may be asking yourself, why then, do they seem to apply today? Since the late 1800s, the Supreme Court has interpreted the due process clause of the Fourteenth Amendment ("nor shall any State deprive any person of life, liberty or property, without due process of law") to include many of the rights included in the first eight amendments to the Constitution. Thus, an illegal search and seizure is seen as a violation of due process, so states must abide by that portion of the Bill of Rights. There are several clauses in the first eight amendments that have not been applied to the states through the due process clause; one of these is the right to a grand jury indictment in a felony case (provided by the Fifth Amendment).

ecutor presents the state's case, and then witnesses are called to testify in front of the grand jury.

The accused and his or her attorney are not present in the room, and suspects are often not aware that they are the target of the investigation. In many states, the only individuals allowed in the grand jury chamber are the jurors, the prosecutor, and a single witness who has been called to testify. The individuals testifying can have their attorneys outside the room, and can consult with their attorneys whenever they feel the need. Some states also allow the judge to be present during testimony, and in some states, witnesses are allowed to have their attorney present during testimony. In addition to the prosecutor asking questions of the witness, jurors are also allowed to ask questions.

Witnesses who have testified in front of a grand jury are prohibited from discussing their grand jury testimony with others. The grand jury investigation is kept secret so that the grand jury can faithfully do its job without risk that witnesses will be tainted, witnesses will be threatened by the targets of the investigation, or that the investigation itself will be compromised.

If a grand jury believes that the state has a compelling case, the grand jury issues an indictment, which allows the state to bring charges against an individual. Unanimity is not required to issue an indictment; most states allow for a majority, two-thirds, or three-fourths vote. In some states grand juries are primarily employed to help conduct criminal investigations. A single grand jury may hear evidence in more than a single case, unlike a petit jury that dissolves at the end of the individual trial for which it was assembled.

Selection of grand juries has many similarities with selection of trial juries. The same master list is used, and venire is often the same. At this point, there is not questioning by attorneys or use of peremptory challenges, as one would see at the voir dire stage with a trial jury. Instead, the judge will empanel those for whom service on a grand jury would not pose an undue hardship. One significant difference between trial juries and grand juries is that in many states, grand jurors may be asked to serve as long as eighteen or twenty-four months, and during that period of time, the grand jury may hear multiple cases.

Grand jury sizes range from a low of five to seven jurors in the state of Virginia to a high of as many as twenty-three in eleven states. Due to the hardship faced by jurors serving terms of up to two years, in some states, grand juries can conduct business with a quorum (Kansas requires a grand jury of fifteen members, but has set a quorum at twelve), and some states, such as Pennsylvania, have alternate jurors. Individuals serving on a grand jury are not sequestered. In addition, the grand jury generally meets from 9 A.M. to 5 P.M., allowing jurors to go home at night, and generally does not meet every day, allowing jurors to go to their jobs. In some states grand jurors serve a set term, while in others the grand jury is convened to address a particular case, and is dismissed by the judge when that task is complete (BJS 2000, 283–285).

Jury Compensation and Characteristics

Jury compensation varies by state. Some states require an employer to continue to pay a juror while on jury duty, while the majority of states compensate jurors. Some states provide for jury compensation through state law, while in other states, jury compensation is a local or county matter. Compensation ranges from as little as $4 per day to as much as $50 per day (or more if jurors' employers must pay them while on jury duty). In some cases, jurors may also receive compensation for mileage, parking, and other expenses.

Financial hardship is often offered as a reason that people do not want to serve on juries. As many of 60 percent of individuals who receive a questionnaire concerning their eligibility to serve as jurors try to get their name removed from the list of eligible jurors (Neubauer 1997). There has been a recent trend to increase compensation for jurors, with several states matching or exceeding the rate of $40 paid by federal district courts.

There is concern that juries are not representative of the population at large. A study of juries in Vermont revealed that people selected for jury service tend to be wealthier, older, white collar, and better educated than the community at large (Nelson 2005). This stands to reason, since these same characteristics apply to those who vote most regularly and voter rolls are an important source of juror selection lists. This raises concern over groups that are systematically kept off of juries. As mentioned in the discussion of venire, groups that may be exempted from jury duty include convicted felons, judicial officers, public officials, elected legislators, physicians, and attorneys.

Some states will also keep members of additional groups off of juries (through excusal) if serving on a jury would pose an undue hardship on the individual or the community. These groups include schoolteachers, hospital employees, firefighters, police officers, those active in the military, and those who do not read and write in English (BJS 200). The exemption and excusal of large groups of people might result in the tacit denial to a defendant the jury of his or her peers, as guaranteed in the Sixth Amendment.

An additional concern is that low compensation for jurors is also keeping many potential jurors off of juries. In states where jury compensation is low, compensation may not even be enough to cover gas, parking, and lunch, let alone enough to make up for wages that a person will not receive from their employer for that day or days spent serving as a juror. Approximately 40 percent of states have juror compensation of $15 per day or less. There are very few states that require employers to pay jurors their regular salary while serving as a juror. Scholars examining the jury system in Florida found that individuals with good paying jobs were likely to ask to be excused from jury service. In addition, they found that Florida courts often excused professionals and parents with child care expenses, as well as laborers and salespersons (Rebein et al. 2003). They found that those who typically remained in the jury pool, after excusal for hardship, were those who were not employed and those whose employers continued to pay their salaries while they served on a jury. Increasingly, a jury of one's peers has become a jury of the retired and unemployed (Schwartz et al. 2003), creating concern as to whether defendants are truly being judged by a jury of their peers.

TABLE 4.4   JUROR COMPENSATION

State	Compensation (per day, unless otherwise noted)
Alabama	$10
Alaska	$5 for the first half day, $12.50 per half day after that
Arizona	$12
Arkansas	$15 minimum if not selected, $35 minimum if selected
California	$15 (minimum; county can stipulate more)
Colorado	$50; employer pays regular salary first three days, state compensates jurors on day four and after
Connecticut	$50; employer pays regular salary first five days, state compensates jurors on day six and after
Delaware	$20
Florida	$15 first three days, $30 day four and after
Georgia	$5–$35, determined at the county level
Hawaii	$30
Idaho	$5 per half day (if traveling from more than 30 miles, compensation is $10 per half day)
Illinois	$4, $5, $10, or amount set by county
Indiana	$17.50 if not selected, $40 if selected
Iowa	$10
Kansas	$10
Kentucky	$12.50
Louisiana	$16 in civil cases, $25 in criminal cases
Maine	$10
Maryland	$10–$20, determined at county level
Massachusetts	$50; employer pays regular salary first three days, state compensates jurors on day four and after
Michigan	$12.50 per half day for first day of service, thereafter $20 per half day
Minnesota	$30
Mississippi	$25
Missouri	$6
Montana	$25
Nebraska	$35
Nevada	$40 per day once sworn in
New Hampshire	$10 per half day
New Jersey	$5 first three days, thereafter $40
New Mexico	State minimum wage (paid per hour)
New York	$40
North Carolina	$12 first five days, thereafter $30
North Dakota	$25 first day, thereafter $50
Ohio	$20
Oklahoma	$20
Oregon	$10 first two days, thereafter $25
Pennsylvania	$9 first three days, thereafter $25
Rhode Island	$15
South Carolina	$10–$25, determined by county
South Dakota	$10 if not selected, $50 if selected
Tennessee	$10 minimum
Texas	$6–$50, set by county
Utah	$18.50 first day, $49 each subsequent day
Vermont	$30
Virginia	$30
Washington	$10–$25, set by county
West Virginia	$40
Wisconsin	$8 per half day minimum
Wyoming	$30 first four days, thereafter $50 per day at discretion of the court

Sources: Data from "Jury Management: Juror Pay in the States," National Center for State Courts (NCSC), http://www.ncsconline.org/WC/Publications/StateLinks/JurManPayStateLinks.htm (accessed April 18, 2006); U.S. Department of Justice, Bureau of Justice Statistics (BJS), 2000; and state government websites.

REFERENCES AND FURTHER READING

Abraham, Henry J. 1998. *The Judicial Process*. 7th ed. New York: Oxford University Press.

American Bar Association Lawyer Demographics (ABA), http://www.abanet.org /marketresearch/lawyerdemographics-2005.pdf (accessed February 15, 2005).

American Judicature Society (AJS), Center for Judicial Selection, http://www.ajs.org/selection /index.asp (accessed February 15, 2005).

Anderson, Brian P. 2004. "Judicial Elections in West Virginia: 'By the People, for the People' or 'By the Powerful, for the Powerful?' A Choice Must Be Made." *West Virginia Law Review* 107 (Fall): 235.

Carp, Robert A., and Ronald Stidham. 1996. *Judicial Process in America*, 3rd ed. Washington, DC: Congressional Quarterly Press.

Carp, Robert A., Ronald Stidham, and Kenneth L. Manning. 2004. *Judicial Process in America*, 6th ed. Washington DC: Congressional Quarterly Press.

Citizens for Judicial Accountability (CJA), http://judicialaccountability.org/ (accessed May 2, 2005).

Coben, Larry E. 2004. "Contingency Fees: If It's Not Broken, Why Fix It?" *Arizona Attorney* 41 (September): 44.

Gender Gap in Government (GGG), http://gendergap.com.governme.htm, June 21, 2004 (accessed February 16, 2005).

Jefferson, Wallace B. 2005 "The State of the Judiciary in Texas," http://www.texasweekly .com/documents/SOTJ2005.pdf (accessed February 23, 2005).

Jonakait, Randolph N. 2003. *The American Jury System*. New Haven: Yale University Press.

Kritzer, Herbert M. 2002. "Seven Dogged Myths Concerning Contingency Fees." *Washington University Law Quarterly* 80 (Fall): 739.

———. 2004. "Advocacy and Rhetoric vs. Scholarship and Evidence in the Debate over Contingency Fees: A Reply to Professor Brickman." *Washington University Law Quarterly* 82 (Summer): 477.

Lozier, James E. 1996. "Is the Missouri Plan, a/k/a Merit Selection, the Best Solution for Selecting Michigan Judges?" *Michigan Bar Journal* 75 (September): 918.

Morse, James L., Stephen B. Martin, Lee Suskin, and Marna Murray. 1997. "The Vermont Experience: A Small State's Story in Educating Judges." *Vermont Bar Journal and Law Digest* 23 (April): 35.

National Center for State Courts (NCSC), http://ncsconline.org/ (accessed February 25, 2005).

Nelson, William. 2005. *Vermont Criminal Practice*, http://defgen.state.vt.us/lawbook /ch19.htm (accessed February 14, 2005).

Neubauer, David W. 1997. *Judicial Process: Law, Courts, and Politics in the United States*. New York: Harcourt Brace.

"The O. J. Simpson Trial: The Jury", http://law.umkc.edu/faculty/projects/ftrials/Simpson /Jurypage.html (accessed January 15, 2005).

Pinello, Daniel R. 1995. *The Impact of Judicial-Selection Method on State-Supreme-Court Policy: Innovation, Reaction and Atrophy*. Westport, CT: Greenwood.

Rebein, Paul W, Victor E. Schwartz, and Cary Silverman. 2003. "Jury (Dis)Service: Why People Avoid Jury Duty and What Florida Can Do About It." *Nova Law Review* 28 (Fall): 143–156.

Scheingold, Stuart A., and Austin Sarat. 2004. *Something to Believe In: Politics, Professionalism, and Cause Lawyering*. Stanford, CA: Stanford University Press.

Schwartz, Victor E., Mark Behrens, and Cory Silverman. 2003. "The Jury Patriotism Act: Making Jury Service More Appealing and Rewarding to Citizens." American Legislative Exchange Council, www.alec.org/meSWFiles/pdf/0309.pdf (accessed February 14, 2005).

Soule, George W. 2005. "Protecting an Independent and Qualified Judiciary." *Bench and Bar of Minnesota* 62 (April): 34.

Tarr, G. Alan. 2003. *Judicial Process and Judicial Policymaking*, 3rd ed. Belmont, CA: Thomson-Wadsworth.

Texas Politics. 2003. "Profiling Texas Judges." University of Texas at Austin, http://texaspolitics.laits.utexas.edu/html/just/features/0403_01/judges.html (accessed March 26, 2006).

U.S. Department of Justice, Bureau of Justice Statistics (BJS), Office of Justice Programs. 2000. "State Court Organization 1998." Report prepared by the National Center for State Courts, Court Statistics Project, http://www.ojp.usdoj.gov/bjs/pub/pdf/sco98.pdf (accessed March 26, 2006).

U.S. Department of Labor (BLS). Bureau of Labor Statistics Data, Occupational Employment Statistics, http://www.bls.gov/data/ (accessed June 15, 2006).

Cases

Argersinger v. Hamlin. 1972. 497 U.S. 25.
Batson v. Kennedy. 1986. 476 U.S. 79.
Burch v. Louisiana. 1979. 441 U.S. 130.
Castaneda v. Partida. 1977. 430 U.S. 482.
Gideon v. Wainwright. 1963. 372 U.S. 335.
JEB v. Alabama ex rel. T.B. 1994. 511 U.S. 127.
Johnson v. Louisiana. 1972. 406 U.S. 356.
Strauder v. West Virginia. 1880. 100 U.S. 303.
Taylor v. Louisiana. 1975. 419 U.S. 522.
Williams v. Florida. 1970. 399 U.S. 78.

5

THE POLITICS OF STATE COURTS

Jim Walker

Most Americans have been accustomed by their political culture and its mythology to draw a clear distinction between politics and courts. To people at large, politics is seen as full of compromises, passion, and doubt. Courts are seen as bastions of rigor, intellect, and certitude. It is somehow thought untoward to mention the two in the same paragraph, much less the same breath. This is mainly because politics may have a negative sense, particularly when applied to the internal workings of institutions. To say that a decision was reached for political reasons may imply, or at least some may infer, that those reasons were more motivated by venal interests or even corrupt intentions than by rationality, or appreciation of the common good.

But to those who have a broader experience with both politics and courts, it is not only seemly but also important to examine the close connection between them. Courts, after all, comprise the third branch of government in both the state and federal systems, and government is nothing if not the handmaiden of politics. Although it is sometimes tempting to view courts as unbiased arbiters of the political system, standing above the fray with dignity and detachment, one must not be fooled into thinking that the trappings of the judicial branch truly insulate it from the total struggle of politics.

In the American system of state government, there are many ways for groups favoring particular policies to achieve access to political power. Those who fail to get their way with the legislature, the bureaucracy, or the executive can still turn to the courts for redress, thus drawing the third branch into the political process. Most of the time, those who go to court are dissatisfied with a policy adopted by some other branch of government or by a citizen initiative or referendum. They may ask the courts to find the policy in violation of some other law or some part of the state constitution, or even of the federal Constitution. Sometimes they will ask the courts to limit the scope of the law to a domain smaller than its authors had intended.

It is even possible, although rare, for groups to petition the courts to cause policies to be adopted that the legislative and executive branches have ignored. This is more difficult, of course, mainly because the courts cannot directly tax or appropriate money to fund policy initiatives. However, if courts find that laws or state constitutions require certain action on the part of state government, they may order that these actions be taken.

The groups that are most likely to seek political power through the courts are those that are less politically influential with the legislative and executive branches. Among these are racial, religious, and ethnic minorities, and politically unpopular groups such as public utilities and real estate developers. But whatever the issue, or the group pressing it, the conclusion is that the courts are partners in the political process.

Yet another way to understand the political role of the courts is to focus on the life of the judge. No judge, no matter what his or her background or training, can come to the bench without political attitudes and philosophies. Scholars differ greatly on how much a judge's partisan background, view of life, or for that matter religious upbringing may ultimately affect the decisions that are made. But no one, not even the judges themselves, claims that they have no impact.

In fact, if it really made no difference which otherwise-qualified candidate is on the bench, that once donning the robe the judge simply puts all past experiences and views out of mind and looks only at the facts before the court, then judges might as well be chosen by a blind draw, a proposition that has not gained much purchase over the years. Judges have political leanings and those leanings have effects on the decisions of the courts. In fact a good citizen must pay careful attention to the background of a judicial candidate. Americans know this. They are well aware that a vote for a Republican more likely is a vote for a conservative, law-and-order judge. Likewise, electing a Democrat typically means that a more liberal, civil-libertarian judge will be on the bench.

Politics has a variety of definitions. "Politics" is anything that affects the distribution of public goods, or as one commentator remarked, "the authoritative allocation of values" (Easton 1953). Another common, perhaps more lighthearted way of putting it is "who gets what, when and how" from government (Lasswell 1958). No matter which definition of politics is chosen, however, even the most casual look at the operation of the courts serves to show that courts are influenced by politics and in turn courts influence the politics of the states and of the nation. Thus it is unrealistic to assume that courts are not fundamentally political institutions.

But it would be overstating the case to claim that everything the courts do is political. This would have the effect of rendering the analysis meaningless. Therefore, this chapter explains the political workings of the courts by concentrating in turn on four general areas where politics and the courts are connected. These are:

- *The Electoral Process.* Not only are almost all state judges elected, and therefore must at some point campaign for office, state courts are often involved in the direction and implementation of all state elections.
- *The Structure and Relationships of Courts in the States.* Just as important as the selection of judges to serve on the courts is the structure of those courts. The number, types, and jurisdictions within the states is a political decision,

made by state legislatures and governors, or, less often, by a provision in a state constitution. Each state court is also linked to every other court in that state and to the federal courts. These relationships can be affected by the political cultures of the states and of the nation and have an important effect on subsequent political decisions.

- *Reform, Rules, and Procedure.* Each state has a different political culture, and on this culture rests the political choices of how state courts operate, that is, their procedures. Although there have been attempts, with some success, to standardize the procedures across the country, ultimately they are the result of political bargains within the states. Most of what are known as judicial reforms are specifically aimed at judicial procedures, broadly defined.
- *Policy Decisions and the Diet of Cases.* Different political cultures and environments lead to a whole different diet of cases in the various states. Jurisdiction and access to courts are both heavily dependent on state politics. Thus, what a court does not decide may be as important as what it does decide. The output of politics is policy. Courts make policies, and thus serve as political actors in the same way as executives issuing orders or legislators making laws.

JUDGES, POLITICS, AND ELECTIONS

Elections are at the heart of politics in any democratic society, and the state judiciary is intimately connected to elections in the United States. To begin with, the great majority of state judges are elected. There are thirty-one states that choose some or all of their appellate and general jurisdiction judges through some form of election. Others, where judges are initially appointed, require justices and judges to run in retention elections. Elections play a role in more than 80 percent of jurisdictions. These elected justices and judges write most of the legal opinions.

Even where judges are not elected, they are almost always appointed by an elected official. The selection of the judge is almost always the result of constituent preference. That is, a judge is going to be chosen, either directly or indirectly, by a group of voters who must be satisfied with his or her performance, or an appointing official must ultimately satisfy his or her constituents that the right kind of judges have been appointed.

The politics of judicial elections in the states is more complicated than that of the legislative and executive branches. When the people elect a representative or a governor, they expect that their wishes and needs will be attended to, usually by creating new laws and policies. If they aren't, and the officeholders become too independent, they may very well be voted out of office. This elective process obviously promotes accountability over independence.

Judges, on the other hand, are expected to follow the existing law and to be faithful to the U.S. Constitution. Judicial independence means that they must do this despite the needs and wishes of other governmental entities or of influential groups in society.

An independent judiciary, that is one that is not beholden to the other elected branches of government or to a particular faction in society, is a hallmark of all democratic systems. All developing democracies seek such an independent judiciary, not just for the protection of individual rights, but also for stability in property and business laws, in order to encourage investment and economic growth.

In theory, an elected judge must strike a balance between attending to the needs and desires of those who put him or her in office, and being faithful to the laws and the constitution of the state. But many judges would recoil at such a suggestion, and might even take extreme offense. They would claim that the election is one thing and the decisions on the bench quite another. They would say they are not accountable to the people once elected, and that there is no balancing to be done.

As can be seen in the following discussions, however, that position has come under intense scrutiny, and is no longer tenable given the current realities of judicial politics in the states. Judges, who are elected, especially at the highest levels, are expected to make decisions that, in general, favor the interests of those who supported their elections. The reason is that a huge amount of money is being poured into judicial campaigns all over the country. It would be naive to think that the millions of dollars contributed to elect judges by various interest groups have no other motive than putting the most qualified people on the court. These contributions and the brutal campaigns that they finance are a clear indicator that people expect results from the judges they elect, not just adherence to the rule of law. This is why the American Bar Association (ABA) has called for the public financing of judicial campaigns in the states, in addition to reiterating its preference for the merit selection of judges rather than elections.

In any event, three facts are clear. The first is that people generally prefer to elect their judges than to have them appointed. National public opinion surveys demonstrate the amount of popular support for judicial elections. One survey asked respondents to choose whether elected or appointed judges are more likely to be fair and impartial. The results indicated that 75 percent of respondents chose elected judges, while only 18 percent chose appointed judges. In a survey of voters conducted by the Justice at Stake Campaign in 2001, 76 percent favored electing judges. When respondents in still another survey were asked to choose between judicial elections and a system of initial appointment followed by retention elections, 54 percent favored elections and 42 percent the appointment-retention option (Justice at Stake 2001).

On the other hand, when voters are given more details about alternative plans, they do sometimes indicate a preference for those plans over elections. For example one sample of citizens was asked to choose between a system of nomination by a broad-based, nonpartisan commission, appointment by the governor, legislative confirmation, retention elections; and the simple statement "judges in my state should be elected to office." Seventy percent chose the detailed plan, while only 26 chose the simple declaration. Experts on polling caution that the outcome might be heavily dependent on the level of detail in the alternative because survey respondents tend generally to choose more detailed answers over simpler ones (Justice at Stake 2001, 2004a).

Rose Bird and the Short Hoe

Rose Bird, a former chief justice of the California Supreme Court, was the first female chief justice of the court, and also the first to be removed from that office by a majority of the state's voters. Bird was removed in the November 1986 election. Much was made of Bird's consistent opposition to capital punishment. Justices Cruz Reynoso and Joseph Grodin were voted off at the same time, ostensibly for their anti–death penalty stance as well.

However, there were much deeper reasons for Bird's dismissal by the voters—most important were the campaigns waged against her by business and agricultural interests. They had waged a heated campaign to try to block Bird's confirmation as chief justice. They then embarked on a decade-long drive to remove her from the court, finally convincing voters. It was under her leadership as agriculture secretary that the state had banned use of the short-handled hoe, a tool that most growers had abandoned. However, California's lettuce growers insisted that it was needed for speed and efficiency. They had prevailed during previous administrations that had allowed them to continue to use what the United Farm Workers called "this despised tool" (Meister 2004). Growers and their allies were also outraged at Bird. They were even angrier over her work in helping draft the Agricultural Labor Relations Act that granted union rights to the state's farmworkers.

The interests who financed the effort to remove her were concerned mainly with the court's pro-labor stance. Among the decisions that angered them was that state and local government employees had the right to strike as long as they did not endanger public health and safety. Only firefighters were specifically excluded. Business interests attacked the decision as judicial presumptuousness and antibusiness bias of the state high court.

California Supreme Court Chief Justice Rose Bird, with Justices Cruz Reynoso (left) and Joseph Grodin, were voted off the court in November 1986. (Judicial Council of California)

The three major groups opposing Chief Justice Rose Bird raised $3,337,179 in 1985: Californians to Defeat Rose Bird, $2,504,847; Crime Victims for Court Reform, $406,983; Law and Order Campaign Committee, $425,394. Chief Justice Bird's reelection committee (Committee to Conserve the Courts) raised $1,122,100. After Bird's removal, she remained so controversial she could not get a job in the law of any kind. She eventually let her membership in the bar lapse and she retired to Palo Alto to take care of her mother. Rose Bird died in 1999 of breast cancer at the age of sixty-three.

Although public opinion is necessarily fluid on this issue, most citizens want to retain the electoral connection to the judiciary in the states. Movements to alter electoral systems to appointed ones always face an uphill battle. Recent attempts to eliminate judicial elections in Florida and South Dakota, for example, failed to attract a majority of voters in those states. Second, judges who offend public sensibilities, or who make decisions that fly in the face of strong public opinion, are sometimes removed from office, even when their decisions are clearly justified by the law. Examples range from local judges who are perceived as being lenient in sentencing, to justices of state supreme courts who render decisions opposed by major interest groups.

It is somewhat ironic that the constitutional amendment that created the right of the people to vote on the retention of their state supreme court justices had the original intent of removing political influence from the court. The original proponents in 1934 said the court should give only the "honest, intelligent, and fearless service they have a right to expect; and the voter would have a power . . . of casting a vote for or against one particular candidate on the basis of his fitness for office" (Von Klemsmed and Robinson 1934). Although intent of the law was to divorce the judiciary from partisan political influences, there is nothing in the law that can prohibit people from voting or campaigning against the justices for any reason.

Finally, there is a connection between judicial selection systems and outcomes in actual cases, but usually it is an indirect one. Here again, research is somewhat clouded on the issue. Some studies have claimed to find no difference between the elected system and the appointed system in terms of the outputs or decisions that they produce. But there are demonstrable differences between appointed judges and elected judges. These include ethnicity, party affiliation, political attitudes, and, to a somewhat lesser degree, socioeconomic status and education. These attributes, in turn, have been shown to have a significant impact in decisions in a variety of subjects. Among these are criminal sentencing, tort liability, property disputes, labor law, and environmental regulation.

However, it must be noted that to this point there has been no comprehensive, systemwide comparison of the outcomes in elective and appointive jurisdictions. Instead there are some specific topics where differences are detected. For example, elected judges are much more likely to avoid cases involving abortion, a very politically sensitive topic, than are appointed judges.

Opponents of judicial elections cite many reasons for their stance. They believe that judicial independence is much more important than accountability and that elections cannot help but lessen independence or, at a minimum, the appearance of independence. Additionally, they contend that voters are not able to evaluate a judge's credentials, tending to concentrate on things that are irrelevant to the duties of a judge, such as name recognition and ethnicity.

Additionally, if the election is partisan, that is if the candidates run with a party label, opposition or support for a candidate will be based on party affiliation, rather than on good judicial qualities. It is feared that justices and judges will feel obligated to political leaders and campaign contributors. Finally, it is argued that the nature of modern campaigns, with the necessity of retail politics (i.e., door-to-door solicitations, riding in parades, kissing babies, etc.), and fund-raising, might deter more reticent, but very qualified judicial candidates. Among the major groups who want to eliminate judicial elections are the ABA and the United States Chamber of Commerce.

Those who continue to support elections sometimes claim that it humanizes a judge for him or her to meet large numbers of people of all classes whose problems he or she may be dealing with on the bench. To these defenders of elections, the campaign itself is important to recruiting people of integrity, honesty, and empathy to the role of judge. In other words, these people see the politics as part of a socializing process geared to make a jurist both just and wise. They use the word accountable in a different sense than it is used for other officials. Judges must be accountable not to the wishes or preferences of those who elect them, but to their common good. Unfortunately, this argument is difficult to make when so few elected judges ever really participate in a political process, or at least one resembling that required of a legislator or executive. Elections, in fact, may not increase accountability while still reducing independence. Those groups who want to maintain elections are the American trial lawyers association and the AFL-CIO.

Voter Behavior

The election of judges in the states creates very little interest with the voters. Electing judges does not ensure accountability because voters are apathetic and uninformed. Judicial elections have the lowest voter participation rates. In a typical race where, for example, 1,000,000 votes are cast for governor, there may be only 750,000 cast for a state supreme court justice. Where 100,000 votes are cast for a county commissioner, perhaps as few as 65,000 will be cast for county judge. Voters often know less about the judicial candidates than those for almost any other elected office. Usually, the only time that voters become interested in a judicial race is when there is a scandal or notoriety of some sort.

A large number of state judges reach the bench through what are called interim appointments. In most states that elect judges, the governor may appoint someone to an unexpired term whenever a judge dies or retires. Usually, the governor will accept the recommendation of the local political party organization, even where the elections are technically nonpartisan. Many times a judge will time his or her retirement to give a governor of the same party the opportunity to fill the seat. Sometimes the death of a judge gives the governor a similar opportunity, depending on where in the term a judge passes away.

Furthermore, once elected, or appointed, most judges at the trial and intermediate appeal court levels never have to face a contested election again. Research of elections nationwide has shown that as few as 7 out of 100 judicial elections in the nation were contested. Surveys in states such as California, Nevada, South Dakota, Texas, Ohio,

Maryland, and Virginia have confirmed this trend. Based on many years of research, it would appear that large numbers of judges in nominally elective states are initially appointed. Furthermore, once reaching the bench, they rarely draw a strong opponent, and are almost never defeated.

Voters in those elections that do take place often vote blindly. Although partisan judicial elections provide a party label for voters, nonpartisan elections do not. This lack of party label makes it harder for the voter to acquire information about the candidates. Many simply choose to skip the judicial races. Studies of nonpartisan elections have shown that voters were more likely to have an opinion about a candidate if they were given knowledge of his or her party affiliation. Thus, nonpartisan elections actually tend to reduce participation, and increase the advantage of incumbents. Voters use incumbency as their cue for voting.

One consequence of a lack of available issues in judicial campaigns is that voters are hard-pressed to distinguish between the candidates. Voters, who even under the best of circumstances are rarely willing to engage in the difficult work of informing themselves about the differences between the candidates, simply choose not to vote in judicial races. The difference between the number of voters participating in races such as for president and governor, and the number voting in judicial races, is referred to as roll-off.

These roll-off rates tend to be quite high. One study found that over a fifteen-year period, an average of one person in four who voted in a given state election did not vote for the state supreme court candidate on the same ballot. The situation is much worse in local elections where over a third of those who voted in a given election skipped the judicial candidate altogether.

Low information-level elections, such as judicial elections, cause voters to cue on the candidates' names. Certain names are stereotyped as liberal, and others as conservative.

What's in a Name?

Judicial elections were sleepy, low-key affairs that resulted in the election of pro-civil defense Democratic judges. This did not change until the late 1970s. At that time, a remarkable event in the history of the Texas judiciary occurred: an unknown lawyer named Don Yarbrough ran for the Texas Supreme Court and won. Not only was Yarbrough an unknown, but also numerous ethical complaints had been filed against him. His opponent was a highly respected incumbent who had won the state bar poll by a 90 percent margin.

How did he win the election? Yarbrough was a well-known political name in Texas.

Voters probably confused him with either the long-time U.S. Senator Ralph Yarbrough, or with another Don Yarbrough, who had twice run for governor. Regardless, this episode demonstrated that literally anyone could be elected to the Texas Supreme Court if they had a popular name. Yarbrough served only a few months before criminal charges and the threat of legislative removal led to his resignation.

Source: Champagne, Anthony, and Kyle Cheek. 2002. "Judicial Independence: The Cycle of Judicial Elections: Texas as a Case Study." *Fordham Urban Law Journal* 29: 907–940.

Thus Democrats and liberals might be more likely than Republicans and conservatives to vote for candidates who are easily identifiable by name as women and/or minorities. Most troubling of all is that voters often confuse names and vote in judicial elections for familiar sounding names.

If this were not such an important matter, the results would appear humorous. In Ohio, anyone named Brown or Celebreeze seemed to have a good chance of being elected to a judgeship, no matter what his or her qualifications. In another case, a candidate with spare qualifications, but blessed with the name "Gene Kelly," had no trouble winning a seat on the bench.

It is, therefore, quite difficult to conclude that elections achieve the accountability that their proponents suggest. At most, judicial elections may merely allow public control over the broad outlines of judicial selection, or act only as a kind of safety valve in extreme cases.

The lack of contested elections, however, should not be interpreted as evidence of the divorcement of the judiciary from politics. Quite to the contrary; the political system itself dictates the desirability, and sometimes necessity of allowing judges to remain in office without electoral challenge. First there are the obvious practical reasons. It is difficult to unseat a judge who has not committed any egregious errors on the bench, even though it is surprisingly easy to unseat one who has. Second, there are limited party resources to wage judicial campaigns, especially where judges must officially run on a nonpartisan ticket. Political parties may endorse and support candidates for an open seat but are less likely to devote money and time to unseating an incumbent. Without party backing, winning a contested election against an incumbent is even more difficult, and few attempt it.

There are also cultural reasons involved. Some believe that an attorney who has given up his or her practice for the bench ought to be treated with some respect and not made to campaign for office. Potential challengers may also fear reprisals in later appearances before the judge. Incumbent judges have greater name recognition and the ability to raise more campaign funds.

There are indications that this may be changing as the number of contested judicial elections appears to be on the rise, at least in some states. A fifty-state study of courts of last resort found that, between 1980 and 1995, state supreme court incumbents were challenged 44.2 percent of the time in nonpartisan election states and 61.1 percent of the time in partisan election states (Brace and Hall 2003). It should be noted, however, that because these data include any challenger, regardless of strength, they tend to overestimate the extent to which judicial incumbents face serious challenges.

Judicial Elections and the First Amendment

But even if all of these other factors were not present, there would still be the single most important reason that judicial elections are not comparable to other elections:

state attempts to limit the speech of judicial candidates. Historically it has been recognized that judicial elections differ from those of legislators and executives. There has been a perceived conflict between preserving an impartial judiciary, and allowing candidates their right to free speech. For more than eighty years, the ABA has been adopting and revising canons of judicial ethics, severely restricting what a candidate for judge may say in a campaign. States, in turn, have been adopting these canons into election law.

The original attempts were somewhat crude. The so-called announce clause stated that a judge "should not announce in advance his conclusions of law on disputed issues to secure class support" (ABA 1924). The canons also declared that judicial candidates should avoid making political speeches.

In 1972, the ABA adopted the committee's Code of Judicial Conduct. Canon 7 stated that a candidate, including an incumbent judge, "should not . . . announce his views on disputed legal or political issues" (Canon 7[B] of the 1972 American Bar Association Model Code of Judicial Conduct). In the 1980s, the ABA tried to clarify the code, and in 1990 it issued a redrafted Model Code of Judicial Conduct. Canon 5A(3)(d) declares that a judicial candidate shall not "make pledges or promises of conduct in office other than the faithful and impartial performance of the duties of the office; make statements that commit or appear to commit the candidate with respect to cases, controversies or issues that are likely to come before the court; or knowingly misrepresent the identity, qualifications, present position or other fact concerning the candidate or an opponent" (quoted in Ogunro 2003).

The 1990 Model Code attempts to replace the broad language of the 1972 Model Code with a narrow rule against making statements that appear to improperly commit the candidate to matters likely to come before the court. The ABA promulgated the rule to balance the constitutional guarantee of free speech, with the need to prevent the harm that can come from statements damaging to the appearance of judicial integrity and impartiality. The clause has been adopted by many states.

But recently the U.S. Supreme Court has thrown this entire history of attempting to regulate the speech of judges in their election campaigns into confusion. In the case of *Minnesota v. White*, 536 U.S. 765 (2002), the Court not only threw out the announce clause as modified but basically put judicial campaigns on a level playing field with all other electoral campaigns. It said in part that "the announce clause both prohibits speech on the basis of its content and burdens a category of speech that is 'at the core of our First Amendment freedoms'—speech about the qualifications of candidates for public office." And the opinion goes on to say that "This complete separation of the judiciary from the enterprise of 'representative government' might have some truth in those countries where judges neither make law themselves nor set aside the laws enacted by the legislature. It is not a true picture of the American system. Not only do state-court judges possess the power to 'make' common law, but they have the immense power to shape the States' constitutions as well" (*Minnesota v. White*, 536 U.S. 765 at 784 [2002]).

Money and Judicial Elections

The year 2000 should be remembered as a watershed year for elections in state courts. Many events of that election have cast a shadow upon the whole judicial electoral system, and have raised doubts about the ability of election laws and regulations to balance between electing judges, and insulating them from political pressures. During the 2000 Ohio Supreme Court elections, a special interest group spent much more money than all the candidates combined. The most widely known part of the group was the United States Chamber of Commerce. Such groups are obviously not bound by any canons of judicial ethics, and thus are free to manipulate any election of judges for political gain.

Although judicial campaigns frequently lack issues, one thing that is not lacking, at least in those campaigns in which there is a contest, is a need for funding, often reaching into the hundreds of thousands, if not millions, of dollars. Candidates, consequently, must either be wealthy enough to finance their campaign or must solicit others for contributions. Unfortunately, those most likely to give to judicial candidates are also those most likely to appear in the judge's court: attorneys, developers, insurance companies, and, in Nevada, gaming corporations. Solicitation of, and contributions by, those who are likely to appear before the successful judicial candidate creates, at best, the perception of a conflict of interest and, at worst, a true conflict. A Texas study found that 175 out of 246 attorneys responding to a survey disagreed with the statement that "political campaign contributions do not affect a judge's decision-making" (Jackson and Riddlesperger 1990). Similarly, a study commissioned by the Pennsylvania Supreme Court "found that nine out of 10 voters believed that judicial decisions were influenced by large campaign contributions" (Geyh 2001).

Perceptions of a conflict of interest are widespread. However, links between campaign contributions and judges' decisions have been less common, but nonetheless extant. There have been several studies in this area. For example, an analysis by the *Philadelphia Inquirer* into that city's municipal and common pleas courts found that "defense lawyers who had either worked in or contributed money to judges' campaigns won 71 percent of their cases before those judges. Yet in the same municipal courts, an average of only 35 percent of the defendants won their cases" (Stumpf and Culver 1992).

A survey commissioned by the Texas State Bar found that "30 percent of judges said they knew colleagues who assigned counsel because they contributed to their judicial election campaigns" (Bach 2001). Additionally, an analysis of election campaigns for the Texas Supreme Court between 1994 and 1998 found that the justices were "four times more likely to accept an appeal filed by a campaign contributor" and that "the more money that a petitioner contributed to the justices the more likely that they were to accept a given petition" (Texans for Public Justice 2001).

Furthermore, a study of arbitration law in the Alabama Supreme Court found "a strong correlation between a justice's source of campaign funds and how that justice votes in arbitration cases" (Ware 1999). The study concluded that even "seemingly bland questions of contract formation, interpretation, and waiver are apparently battle-grounds between the interest groups. Arbitration law in Alabama seems to . . . have no doctrinal integrity that survives the vicissitudes of the interest group battle" (Ware 1999, 685).

Perceptions of conflict of interest and judicial vote buying can be seriously damaging to the prestige and legitimacy of the courts. This perception is held not only by the public but also by attorneys and judges alike. The cost of elections and the necessity to solicit contributions from prospective litigants may have consequences beyond the creation of a perceived conflict of interest. It is likely that they may serve to discourage competent and highly ethical individuals from running for judicial positions. Not only is the amount needed to run a campaign often staggering, but also many might find the notion of soliciting potential litigants and their attorneys for contributions to be ethically distasteful.

The State Courts and Electoral Disputes

It has been established that state courts are intimately connected to the political system through elections. But there is another way in which elections draw courts into the political arena. Because these bodies have the natural role of settling legal disputes, they will be asked, in due course, to settle such disputes arising from the elections of other branches of government. Thus state courts play an important role in settling disputes in the electoral systems in the states.

If there is one lesson above all others that should be taken from the 2000 presidential election, it is that choosing officials is not an exact science. It is at best an approximation, and it often leads to disputes, which puts the courts of the states in a very difficult political position. The best that a state judge can hope for is an election in his or her jurisdiction that is not close. But even if the margin of victory is large, there are still allegations of voter fraud, denial of the franchise, and other election-law violations that will often come up.

For judges who are elected or appointed in a partisan manner these cases can be a nightmare. No matter how circumspect, no matter how strong the case, a judge who finds in favor of his or her own political party will always be in a difficult situation. Thus it was with the Florida Supreme Court, partisan appointees all, who had to decide the whys and wherefores of counting, and recounting the results in Bush versus Gore. Some might have regarded it as a good outcome that the U.S. Supreme Court would decide the case on federal grounds. Just as many people might think the U.S. Supreme Court lost some credibility by doing so.

It is not just that these cases are so difficult; it is that they are becoming more frequent. Perhaps because there are more close elections, or at least more closely contested elections, there are more irregularities, more people watching for irregularities, and more complaints about both the fairness and openness of elections in the states. It

Examples of Recent Election Irregularities That State Supreme Court Had to Resolve

- In Hawaii, Representative Patsy Mink died just three days after the deadline for the Democratic Party to name a replacement for her on the ballot. They petitioned the Hawaii Supreme Court to permit replacing Mink with a new candidate. The court denied the petition.
- In Minnesota, incumbent Democratic Senator Paul Wellstone died in a plane crash five days before the election. Absentee ballots containing Wellstone's name had already been sent out. The Democratic Party named former Vice President Walter Mondale to replace Wellstone on the ballot. The Minnesota Supreme Court ratified the replacement and established rules for the handling the absentee ballots.
- In several counties from Texas, New Jersey, Florida, and Maryland, new electronic voting machines failed, in some cases, to record votes properly, throwing the election into state courts.
- In Illinois, a federal district court and a state appellate court disagreed as to whether state standards for canvassing ballots satisfied the consistency requirements of *Bush v. Gore*.
- In Georgia, supporters of an incumbent beaten in a primary alleged in court that improper crossover voting by white Republicans violated the Voting Rights Act and the constitutionally protected rights of association.

Paul Wellstone (U.S. Senate)

Source: Adapted from Gardner 2003.

is the unusual term when a number of elections are not rehashed, one way or another in the courts. The coming revolution in electronic voting in the wake of the Florida hanging chads and butterfly ballots made famous in the 2000 presidential election will undoubtedly thrust the courts into even more political thickets

It is unlikely that the number of such controversies will decrease. Many of the electoral rights that will be disputed are federal in nature, guaranteed either by federal legislation, such as the Voting Rights Act, or by the Constitution itself. These rights can be, and often are, adjudicated in state courts. Although the overwhelming majority of elections in the states are held without challenge, judges are still often asked to make decisions that will essentially pick a winner in a contested, partisan election. The best the judge can do, in order to preserve both the image and reality of judicial independence, is to make the decision on clear statutory authority and to make its basis as narrow as possible, not on some general principle of fairness or justice.

In a related area, courts and judges often find themselves involved in political disputes relating to citizen initiatives and referenda. In most states, it is possible to put issues to a direct vote of the people. These issues may be new laws, amendments to the state constitution, or changes to actions taken by the state legislatures. The process itself has become very controversial politically. On the one side, proponents of this exercise in direct democracy say that allowing citizens to vote directly on policy questions will increase citizen participation and trust in government, while opponents say that the initiative weakens state legislatures and threatens minority groups.

In most cases there are both constitutional and statutory guidelines governing the initiative and referendum process in a state. The California Constitution states that "the legislative power of this State is vested in the California Legislature . . . but the people reserve to themselves the powers of initiative and referendum" (Cal. Const., Art. IV, Section 1). Sometimes preelection judicial review is required, in other states only a requisite number of signatures is required for an issue to reach the ballot. But judges are loath to show disrespect for the initiative, as it remains very popular. Many say that greater deference must be paid to initiatives than to ordinary legislation.

In all cases, whether before the election or afterward, the court is the place where disputes are ultimately to be settled. And most of the time, by far, it is in the courtrooms of elected state judges that the case is joined. This puts some obvious pressure on the state judges and justices, especially if they have to review a particularly popular initiative. Still, many of the measures die in court in one way or another.

Two examples of states where review is seen in very different contexts are Florida and Arizona. In Florida there is direct amendment of the constitution, but no way for citizens to place ordinary legislation directly on the ballot. As a consequence, the Florida Constitution has been amended to include the creation of high-speed trains, to regulate the size of fishing nets, and to guarantee the humane treatment of pigs. Judges in that state are forced to interpret often poorly worded citizen-written amendments to the constitution. One commentator likened the document to a junkyard.

In Arizona, on the other hand, judges play a key role in vetting a citizen initiative, not only holding it strictly to the procedural rules in terms of signature gathering but also making sure it does not violate any cannons of legislative construction. As an example, the Arizona Supreme Court prevented the certification of a ballot initiative that would have severely restricted that state's important Citizen Clean Elections Act by preventing public funding of campaigns.

California is not only the largest state but also the largest user of the initiative and referendum process. Most critics of the system of direct ballot access point out that the recent rise in its use is directly related to the fact that individuals and political action groups with the money to sell an idea directly to the voters are able to avoid the delib-

An Example from California: Court Reviews Voter Initiative

A case in California illustrates how a judge can become embroiled in a controversy when interpreting the power of the people to engage in legislating. The case involved the very bitter and contentious issue of Indian casinos. It arose in the city of Rohnert Park, California, which calls itself "The Friendly City."

One of the oldest contracts between Native Americans and Europeans in the United States was Dutch Representative Peter Minuit's purchase of Manhattan Island from "Indians" for 60 guilders worth of goods in 1626.

Times change. Over 377 years later, Native Americans, in a reversal of roles, reached an agreement with city representatives that resulted in this litigation. The . . . Indian tribe . . . announced plans to build a casino, 300 room hotel, spa and entertainment resort on land located west of the City of Rohnert Park (City). When the City approved an agreement with the Tribe . . . a citizens' group filed a petition . . . to place a referendum on the ballot . . . An ad hoc committee authorized the mayor and a council member to meet with the Tribe.

. . . The Tribe and the City entered into a voluntary contractual arrangement with the City to make contributions and community investments to mitigate impacts of the casino project. The [deal] provided for payments of over $200 million to the City over 20 years, considerably more than 60 guilders . . . [T]he City Council passed [an approving] resolution . . . [P]laintiffs . . . sought to place a referendum on the ballot to compel submission of the issue to the voters. The City refused . . .

The City's action in negotiating with the Tribe concerns matters that are regulated solely by federal law . . . The City has merely bargained for some benefit for the community, it has not legislated in this highly regulated field. Consequently, its action is not subject to the referendum process.

—From the Opinion of Judge James Marchiano, California Court of Appeals, in *Worthington v. City Council of Rohnert Park,* 131 Cal. App. 4th 1594 (2005).

Soon after this opinion, the friendly city of Rohnert Park saw the narrow failure of a recall initiative intended to remove two city council members who supported plans for the casino. There was even a well-received documentary made about the entire controversy. Fortunately, the judge in this case was from a larger jurisdiction than just the city, and did not have to face the wrath of the Rohnert Park objectors.

erate, slow, and clumsy legislative process with sound bites and thirty-second commercials. Before 1980 Californians approved about one-third of all ballot initiatives. From 1980 to 1990 voters approved almost half. In November 1996 voters cast ballots on more initiatives than in all of the elections of the 1960s combined. In the 1990s, the initiative became a major way of creating state policy.

Often these initiatives reach the ballot and are voted on with little voter education. As a consequence, many of the resulting laws and amendments wind up being litigated in state court, throwing judges who must stand for reelection in the middle of powerful political interests on both sides of the issue. One judge described the pressure as "like finding a crocodile in your bathtub when you go to shave in the morning. You try not to think about it, but it's hard to think about much else" (Reidinger 1987).

POLITICS AND THE STRUCTURE OF STATE COURTS

There are three types of courts in the states: courts of limited jurisdiction, courts of general jurisdiction, and appellate courts, with appellate courts further subdivided into intermediate appeals courts and courts of last resort. Each type of court relates to the political system in a different way. The factors influencing these different relationships are three in number. The first, and most important, is the method of selecting the judges of the court. The second is the history of the creation of the court. And the third is the current issue set that the court is most involved with. Thus, although every court in the state has a definite relation to the political system, that relationship may vary widely over region and over time, depending on how each of the three factors evolve or change from place to place or time to time.

Limited Jurisdiction

The courts of limited jurisdiction, those that deal exclusively with cases from a defined area or a specific subject matter, have the most overt ties to the state political system. These courts range all the way from justices of the peace, mayor's courts and others staffed by so-called lay judges, to traffic, small-claims, domestic relations, municipal, housing and, most often, juvenile courts. In addition several courts of general jurisdiction have special dockets or sessions that deal with specific problems such as narcotics violations.

Sometimes these courts arise directly out of the political culture of the state or municipality where they are located. It might be due to the rural nature of the setting, or the particular ethnicity of a city, or even because of a tradition of extreme political individualism. In other words, it is the politics of the place that will sometimes determine the structure of these specialized courts.

Other times these courts might be created or abolished as a result of some particular political struggle taking place in other areas of government. They are often created because some interest group feels it is being underserved, or because the costs of general jurisdiction courts are too high, or because there is a perceived need for a completely different judicial system to deal with a particular social problem. In any case, these institutions cannot be understood apart from the struggle for power in the communities they serve.

One of the most instructive examples is the creation, development, and crisis of the juvenile justice system. At one time in this country, a juvenile defendant was treated no differently from an adult. Any special treatment that a child got in court would be entirely dependant on the mercy of a judge. Punishment was often meted out exactly as if the offender was an adult. One of the original intents of juvenile court was to treat and rehabilitate rather than to punish underage defendants. It took decades of political struggle to create the modern juvenile courts. Now there is political pressure to adjudi-

Michigan State Political Struggles

A few years ago, a Michigan Circuit Court jury found a thirteen-year-old named Nathaniel Abraham guilty of second-degree murder. He was convicted of killing another child. When he committed the crime he was only eleven years old. He was tried in an adult court, but the judge sentenced Abraham to a juvenile facility. This means he can be incarcerated only until he is twenty-one, when he must be released according to the law.

This case is a good illustration of the current dilemma in dealing with juvenile offenders. Violent crime among juveniles went up dramatically in the late 1980s and early 1990s. One out of six arrests in 1999 involved a juvenile. Recent crimes committed by juveniles are much more serious, and brutal, than the system was designed to deal with. The public has demanded much harsher treatment of juveniles and this demand is fed by intense media coverage of the issue. Many politicians have vowed to get tough on juvenile crime. State legislatures have sometimes enacted laws making it easier to try juveniles as adults. In Michi-gan, the Abraham case had been transferred from a juvenile court to an adult court using a 1997 law allowing prosecutors to request that a juvenile be tried as an adult for certain offenses regardless of age.

There are many who believe that juvenile offenders can be rehabilitated if treated as juveniles rather than as adults. To these people, getting tough will not work on juvenile crime. The judge in the Abraham case is one of those people. Abraham was tried in an adult court, and the judge believed that Abraham should be sentenced as a juvenile. He even made a statement saying that he remained confident in the ability of the juvenile justice system to reform people like Abraham. He also criticized the law, which allowed the youngster to be tried as an adult.

The judge was not alone in his feelings toward such laws. World organizations have also criticized them. Amnesty International, for one, said that they violated "international human rights standards for the protection of children" (Vandervort and Ladd 2001).

cate more juvenile offenders as adults, as what once was called delinquency is often indistinguishable from violent adult crime.

Sometimes the political impetus that originally created a court leads to unintended consequences. One example of this is the small-claims courts. These simplified versions of civil court have been around for the better part of a century. Even today, states trumpet them as tribunes of the people, where the ordinary person has a chance for a day in court. Many of them are huge. In California there are more than 100,000 cases filed in small-claims court every year. New York City alone handles over 1,000 cases a week in its small-claims courts. Others are quite modest and have very light caseloads such as South Dakota and other rural areas, but all operate much the same. There is a low dollar limit (some say too low), the pleadings and rules are nontechnical, and the "judge" is often a part-time employee, usually a lawyer given a few days or weeks of training in handling these cases.

But these courts have not always delivered on their promise. Many of them have evolved into little more than collection agencies for businesses—a quick way to get a civil judgment against a debtor. In almost every court, the great majority of plaintiffs are businesses, not victimized individuals. Defendants are at a distinct disadvantage as they almost always lose. Some of the procedures have often become more complicated so that people retain an attorney anyway, at least where it is allowed. Yet small-claims courts have become a huge bureaucracy themselves, with employees dependent on them for work and politicians who love the idea of claiming credit about their existence.

Housing courts are another example of limited jurisdiction courts that are clearly political. These courts, which usually exist in high-rent cities like Boston and New York, were originally created to give tenants leverage to force landlords to make necessary or legally required repairs. Now, landlords demanding unpaid rent bring 90 percent of cases. Most tenants believe they are victims in the process. About 90 percent arrive in court without lawyers because they can't afford one. Because housing is part of civil court, not of criminal court, the state is not obligated to provide tenants with legal counsel. On the other hand, landlords are almost always represented by attorneys.

Yet landlords have their own complaints about the courts. They say the judges are prejudiced against them. Some claim the tenants don't need lawyers because they already have the judge on their side. Statistics seem to support that view in part since judges evict tenants in fewer than 10 percent of the cases. Many of the judges are former legal-aid attorneys and tenant lawyers. Housing court is politically seen as a last

---

Housing Courts in Three Cities

The impetus, structure, and processes of housing courts follow the political culture of the jurisdiction within which they reside. In Minneapolis housing court was created as a specialty court to provide an accessible and efficient forum for litigants with landlord and tenant disputes. Housing court there provides a legal way for a landlord to remove or evict a tenant from a rental unit, and also provides remedies for tenant rights.

Part of the Cleveland Housing Court's mission is to provide education to the people of Cleveland. As well as meetings in the community, the court has developed a number of video programs for citizen information. The Selective Intervention Program (SIP), instituted in July of 1998, is an alternative dispute resolution mechanism for homeowners, many of whom are indi-

gent and elderly defendants who come before the court. Participants who successfully complete the program will have their cases dismissed by the court, avoid a criminal conviction, and pay only a minimal fee to offset court costs. Complaints filed by the city of Cleveland for alleged violations of the city's health, housing, building, fire, or safety codes are criminal, misdemeanor cases.

Kansas City's housing court, which is a separate division of the Kansas City Municipal Court, was established by a charter amendment approved by the voters in 1987. Its docket is exclusively devoted to housing code prosecutions of all kinds, including cases brought under the nuisance, property maintenance, building, and zoning codes, and the illegal dumping ordinance.

barrier to homelessness. It is not organized to resolve disputes quickly. It is a true political court. Slumlords and rent gougers are not public favorites. Politicians attacking them can make great political capital. Housing courts are really more like an extension of the enforcement mechanism for health departments and rent-control agencies rather than true courts.

General Jurisdiction

Courts of general jurisdiction appear less overtly political in their formation and operation than limited jurisdiction courts, but they share many of the same characteristics. They are single-member courts and are deeply affected by the political culture of the local area in which they have jurisdiction, whether it is a county or a smaller district. They are also more visible and accessible to the electorate and interest groups than the appellate courts.

Two things set them off from the specialized courts and make them generally less political. The first is the relatively higher status that the judges enjoy and the second is that much more of their work is done in private, outside the courtroom. Their higher status allows them to be somewhat more insulated from both public opinion and press scrutiny. They are generally better educated and trained than limited jurisdiction judges. They must take any case that comes their way and thus cannot afford to be severely typecast as one kind of judge or another.

Limited jurisdiction judges do most of their work in their courtrooms. General jurisdiction judges do not. For example, once an accused is indicted and arraigned, the next time he or she is likely to see the judge in a courtroom is at a sentencing hearing. Once a civil complaint is filed, it is most likely neither party in the case will ever see the inside of a courtroom, unless they wish to accompany their attorneys to on-the-record motion hearings.

It is clear, though, that these courts, and the judges who preside over them are tuned into the local political culture, especially in the recruitment of judges. In some districts the connection is very direct, as where there are partisan elections for judge and one party is dominant. In these courts, there will be no judges who have not been cleared by the local party organization. But even where there are nonpartisan elections, parties often endorse candidates and help campaigns with money and volunteers. Few judges ascend to the bench without prior political experience or a connection of some sort. It would strain credulity that these judges would not be aware, at least, of the general attitudes of the local political organizations, and would not, when possible, take these into account in their decision-making processes.

One obvious example is in the area of sentencing. The sentencing of convicted criminals varies widely across the country and there is a demonstrable connection between the needs and wishes of the local communities and the sentences handed down by the judges. In ethnically and economically diverse communities, sentencing has tended to be more lenient, with greater emphasis on probation and diversion. Similar relationships have also been shown to exist in civil cases depending on whether the plaintiff's bar or the defense bar is better connected politically. Some areas have even been targeted by class-action lawyers because of their receptivity to plaintiffs' claims.

Appellate Courts

There is an irony involved with state appellate courts and politics, especially when it comes to courts of last resort. Appellate courts are the most removed from local politics, the most insulated from scrutiny, of the highest status, and yet they can be labeled the most political of all the court structures. Here a distinction must be made between the input and output sides of politics. Where trial courts, whether general or specialized, are generally concerned with processing a variety of inputs, demands, and supports from the community they serve, appellate courts are more concerned with the outputs. These are often interpretations of law that have a substantial impact on government policy. The work of appellate courts is much more likely to attract the attention of interest groups, large and small businesses, and political officials than the work of trial courts. The fact that only a small fraction of lower court decisions are appealed only increases the political importance of appeals.

Courts of last resort are by this analysis clearly the most political courts of all. Their decisions become the law of the state, subject only to legislative overturning in cases where the state or federal Constitution is not being interpreted. What this means is that these courts have become major actors in the policy-making process, once seen as the province of the other two branches. There are many reasons for this relatively recent development, but the policy-making role of courts in general has a long provenance.

In the first place, interpreting a constitution, whether it is the federal Constitution or one of the fifty state constitutions, always involves some element of government policy. Perhaps the issue is the regulation of private property as in zoning. Perhaps it is police procedure such as search and seizure. One of the most obvious examples is state and local control over education.

Second, there is a long history of marginalized groups seeking relief in the courts, historically federal courts, when they could not succeed with the legislature and the executive branches. The most obvious example is the long struggle to gain equal rights for African American citizens. But other examples of turning to the courts include nontraditional religious groups, pariah political organizations, and even news media, seeking protection from libel laws. More recently, not only marginalized groups but well-funded mainstream groups such as labor unions and chambers of commerce have seen the advantages of litigating to policy, or taking advantage of a third political branch of government.

The attention of interest groups has turned to the state courts especially during the last two decades. Of course even where there is a federal issue involved, only about 2 percent of state cases are ever appealed to the U.S. Supreme Court. Far fewer than that receive a review by that Court. Some of this state activity is the result of a more restrained U.S. Supreme Court following the revolutionary decisions of the Warren Court during the 1950s and 1960s. Scholars who have studied the changes have even dubbed this greater reliance on state supreme courts the new judicial federalism. The U.S. Supreme Court itself recognized the practice by saying that it would not displace a decision of a state supreme court that contained a plain statement that the decision was based on the state, and not the federal, constitution.

Several states took advantage of their ability to go beyond the rights guaranteed by the federal Constitution. California first required equal school funding even though the U.S. Supreme Court said the equal protection clause of the Constitution did not require it. That state also outlawed the death penalty based on provisions of its state constitution (this was later overturned on a citizen initiative that amended the California Constitution, an event repeated in other states as well). Both Ohio and North Carolina found provisions in their state constitutions to call for overhauls in their respective school funding systems. In one ironic decision, the state Supreme Court of Georgia found that the privacy clause of its state constitution forbade the enforcement of anti-sodomy laws, even though the U.S. Supreme Court had years earlier allowed such laws in a case from Georgia. Finally, in the most celebrated or condemned decision of all, the Massachusetts Supreme Court said that its state constitution required the state to allow gay and lesbian marriages, a decision that may have had an effect on the outcome of the 2004 presidential election.

For instance, in the crucial state of Ohio, an initiative to ban gay marriage was on the ballot, thus attracting more conservative and religious voters to the polls. These voters were far more likely to vote Republican. Thus the decision of a state court in Massachusetts had a potentially decisive impact on a national election.

The justices of these courts are not only the most politically active of any judicial personnel, but the most important to other political actors in the state. Potential litigants have come to realize that since these courts can make policies that they like or abhor, involvement in the nomination and election of state supreme court justices has become highly charged and highly financed. Candidates for the office often spend millions of dollars, much of it contributed by individuals, businesses, and groups likely to have business before the court. This has set up an explosive situation in which calls for reform of the electoral system are louder than ever. Some justices have even run for office with the clear, albeit unstated, promise of favorable outcomes in specific cases. An example is the candidate for the state supreme court who all but promised to cast the deciding vote to reverse a five-to-four decision on workers' compensation that was opposed by business interests.

In one recent situation, five of the seven members of the Ohio Supreme Court had to recuse themselves from deciding a case since they had all taken campaign contributions from one of the litigants. In the opinion of some, courts of last resort have been almost completely politicized in many states, casting doubt on their ability to remain truly independent as well as accountable.

RELATIONSHIPS AMONG COURTS

As stated earlier, the relationship between and among courts is informed by the political systems in which they operate. Many of those relationships are, in themselves, apolitical. That is to say that there is no necessary political element to them. For example there is a hierarchical relationship between the appellate courts and trial courts within each state. It is taken for granted that lower courts will follow the precedents established by higher courts, and that they will follow the rules established by those higher courts in their supervisory capacity over the entire court system of the states. When a precedent is not followed, either new law will have been made by the lower court (a rarity), or the appellate court will overrule the lower court (more common).

However, there are differences among states in the number of cases that are appealed, the proportion that are overturned, and the alacrity with which the appeals are finalized. There are also gross differences in the way in which the courts handle different subject matter. Many of these differences are due to the influence of politically active groups on the legal system, as the outcome of the appealed cases often holds great interest for them. For example in the West the issues of land use and water rights are never far from court scrutiny. In the Midwest agricultural and environmental issues receive a lot of attention, while in the Northeast, labor, housing, and welfare issues are more likely to stir the political actors to affect the courts.

Differences among the states are also related to the kinds of appellate systems that the political culture creates between the upper and lower courts. The National Center for State Courts reports that there are at least ten different models for structuring communication between trial and appellate courts in the fifty states. Some appellate courts have mandatory jurisdiction, meaning they must hear appeals. Some have discretionary jurisdiction, picking which cases they wish to hear. In some states the lower courts still operate as independent fiefdoms, with considerable latitude in decision making. In others they are on a short leash, with great numbers of appeals filed. Sometimes these differences are quite striking.

For example, adjusted for population, there are twice as many appeals filed in Florida as there are in New York, even though the rate of criminal trials is about the same. Neither Wyoming nor North Dakota have an intermediate court of appeals, yet they have only half the number of cases in their courts of last resort as West Virginia, which is structured the same way. California has only one-third the rate of criminal cases at the trial level than Texas does; yet each state has the same rate of initial appeals. However, Texas has twice the rate of appeals to its two courts of last resort.

Clearly, there is nothing resembling a national system of appeals in the state courts.

State Courts and Federal Jurisdiction

The political relationship between the federal and state courts is extremely complex and controversial. To begin with, the Constitution limits the jurisdiction of the federal courts to federal issues, while the state courts are free to deal with all the issues that remain. This system differs from some federations where the units are delegated powers and the central government retains the residue. Second, all federal judges and justices are appointed by the president for life, and are confirmed by the Senate. This means that they are much more independent of the short-term political processes than are state judges and justices. Third, state courts of last resort are the final authorities on the laws of the states and of the meaning of the state constitutions. Last, over the last seventy-five years, using a variety of clauses in the federal Constitution, the federal government and the federal courts have preempted a significant portion of the areas where the states in the past had complete control.

There used to be a slang expression that said "don't make a federal case out of it." At that time, federal cases were rare, big, and important. Now the federal courts are inundated with things that years ago would have been restricted to state courts. Chief among these are cases dealing with narcotics. The federal government has so boldly moved into the area of criminal justice that almost any drug crime, and its ensuing punishment, can be a federal matter. The political impact on state courts and state judges is unclear, but the indisputable facts are that both state and federal prisons are bursting with inmates, and sentences for offenses are getting longer. This puts both courts and legislatures in precarious positions, as citizens demand safety from crime but recoil at the high cost of law enforcement. Judges who either try to deviate from strict sentencing guidelines or who propose alternative courses of action risk political reprisals at the polls.

On the other hand, more liberal states, such as Oregon, which adopted a right-to-die law, found its doctors being pursued by the federal authorities for prescribing harmful drugs. Other states that adopted more lenient laws regarding marijuana, especially for medicinal purposes, were similarly in conflict with the federal government. Recently, the Supreme Court said that federal congressional commerce jurisdiction over drugs trumped state power to allow medicinal uses of marijuana.

In the civil law area, the most controversial and politically charged issue is that of diversity jurisdiction. As was noted previously, federal courts are generally restricted to hearing cases involving federal issues. Ordinary disputes over land, contracts, torts, and the like are left to the states. There is one important exception. In the early days of the republic it was feared that persons defending a suit in a state other than their own might be unfairly treated by the court as an outsider. Therefore, written into the Constitution was what has come to be known as the diversity clause. In essence it says that if you are being sued in an out-of-state court, you can, under certain circumstances, have the case heard by a federal court, even though the subject may have nothing to do with federal law.

As the economy of the United States has grown and diversified, almost all businesses have some out-of-state presence. The number of such suits moved to federal courts has grown apace. This puts a burden on the federal courts to hear the cases and on the state courts to keep up with the decisions made by the federal judges, who are supposed to be applying state laws when possible. Needless to say the importance of this political issue will only increase with time.

Still a third area where there is an intersection of interests between the federal judiciary and the state courts is the Eleventh Amendment and the interpretation of the doctrine of sovereign immunity. The idea of sovereign immunity is a kind of vestigial organ in U.S. law, being a holdover from the colonial era when it went without saying that the king, whose word was law, could not be sued. The Framers at Philadelphia did not mention this in the Constitution, and the states, and the federal government, just assumed that they would be in the same posture as the king vis-à-vis their citizens. That is, one cannot sue them without their permission. Of course states do sometimes give permission. Many create special courts of claims where citizens can litigate disputes with state agencies. However, in general, sovereign immunity is alive and well and living in every state.

The Eleventh Amendment was ratified shortly after the founding of the republic. Several states were angered that the diversity clause allowed them to be sued in federal courts, as long as the plaintiff was from out of state. The amendment responded by making an exception to the diversity clause when it came to states, forbidding suits against a state by foreign citizens in federal court. Almost from its adoption, the courts have interpreted the Eleventh Amendment to also bar suits in federal court by citizens against their own states. However, federal court decisions have carried things a step further, complicating the political positions of the state courts.

Congress always had the power to create a federal cause of action in court. Traditionally a citizen can go to any court, federal or state, to press any federal claim. The U.S. Supreme Court has severely limited those areas where Congress can give a citizen the right to sue his or her state government. This has come to mean that state courts are often powerless to grant relief to their own citizens based on federally created right. This greatly affects the political situation between the state courts and the political branches, which are trying to create remedies for problems such as violence against women, gun regulations, and workplace discrimination.

The U.S. Supreme Court and State Court Reform

The federal courts changed many state court practices through their decisions in civil rights and criminal process cases, requiring them to meet minimum federal due process and equal protection standards. Among the hundreds of cases decided by the federal courts the most important were those granting a right to an attorney in criminal cases, the right to be free from abusive interrogations, and the right to be protected from the illegal seizure of evidence. All these had profound impact on state judicial systems, and on the political system as well, as the wisdom and/or necessity of each was debated in legislatures and city halls around the country.

The New Judicial Federalism

At this point, mention should be made of the growing phenomenon of state constitutionalism, opening up the possibility of state courts raising certain rights above a federal floor. The idea that states should look into their own constitutions was famously suggested by the late U.S. Supreme Court Justice William Brennan, many say out of the frustration of the Burger, and later Rehnquist, Courts to protect individual rights to Brennan's liking. The idea is based on the fact that the state supreme court is the final word on what the state constitution means and cannot be overruled by a federal court. So far the most dramatic example of this process has been the decision of the Georgia Supreme Court to overturn that state's sodomy laws based on the privacy clause of the Georgia Constitution just a few years after the U.S. Supreme Court refused to do so on federal constitutional grounds.

Parity and Forum Shopping

Finally, the politically important issue of parity between state and federal courts, and the related phenomenon of forum shopping, ought to be considered. For at least the last forty years, the conventional wisdom has held that the federal courts were superior to the state courts not only in terms of protecting individual rights but also in the general level of talent on the bench. This belief was based both on the experience of trial lawyers who practiced in both forums, and on anecdotal evidence from accounts of events in state courts by observers such as reporters and students. This led many to prefer the federal courtroom to the state courtroom, especially when the issue was emotionally charged. There is no doubt, for example, that a preference for the federal courts was reasonable when racial justice was difficult to secure in certain areas of the country.

Although the federal courts have higher prestige, access to greater resources, and judges are blessed with the life appointments, subsequent empirical attempts to document the disparities in outcomes have not been very successful. In other words, there is no reason to say that the state courts are less committed to fairness and justice than the federal courts, or that a litigant in state court will receive inferior treatment to one in federal court. This is especially true today with an even greater commitment of many groups and organizations dedicated to improving and reforming the state judiciary.

In summary, there are three keys to understanding the relationship between the structure of courts and state and local political systems. First, isolation and high status are no guarantee that a court or the justices who sit on it will be apolitical. Often the stakes are just too high. Second, there are clear connections between the structure of the court and the way that the court affects, and is affected by, politics. This is true in the pure localism and interest group politics of the limited jurisdiction courts and in the statewide, policy-driven courts of last resort. And third, none of this is cause for regret or alarm. Being political is not the same as being corrupt. In short, it may be possible to take the courts out of politics, but more difficult to take politics out of the courts.

REFORMING THE STATE JUDICIARY

In the study of judicial politics, the word *reform* plays a large and long-running role. The word itself long ago came to mean to change for the better. As with most words, the true meaning lies buried in the context. Juvenile detention centers were once called reform schools. The context was clear. The children in the schools had either been unruly, or had committed a criminal offense. Keeping them from repeating their behavior would certainly be making them better. On the other hand, there could never be agreement on whether, for example, the reform of the tax code in 1965 made the code any better. In a sense, reform is sometimes merely a marketing method rather than a true descriptor.

A more politically sophisticated definition of reform, in the context of the judiciary, would mean to change the courts to take political advantage of doing judicial business a different way.

Any person or organization that adopts the word reform in its program has attempted to seize the moral high ground. Reform, like motherhood and patriotism, is one of those things that has become very difficult to oppose. So simply naming something a reform gives the proponent a big advantage in any debate. To attribute base, or self-serving motives to a reformer may appear rude or churlish. Nevertheless, the process of reform is always political, as it is likely to advantage one group and disadvantage another.

Judicial reform in particular involves both procedural and substantive aspects. Among the former are things such as judicial selection and training, processes of appeals, jurisdiction, budgeting, administration, and rules of evidence. The substantive areas include legal representation, bail, sentencing, public access, and limits on court awards. To begin with, it is important to note that judicial reform usually generates significant political energy on both sides of the issue. Some may think that reformers are making things better while others, just as fervently, believe that they are bent on destruction. It is the rare reform indeed that comes about because the entire legal community has a sudden epiphany that something is the right thing to do.

The state courts in the early twentieth century were very disorganized. They had been created to serve many local needs and ambitions and did not have much organizational coherence. Judges tended to run their courtrooms as fiefdoms in isolation even from judges in the same court. Administrative systems and skills were nonexistent. Many judges, spurred on by state bars, and law professors began to call for reform of state court systems. They did this most of all because they believed that state courts were unprofessional and poorly managed. This led to a crisis of public confidence in the existence of justice in these courts.

Over a period of several decades, state courts dramatically changed the way they did business. Among the most important reforms was the creation of central administrative office systems and judicial councils to do planning for the courts. These councils made recommendations on legislation, and thus began a process of centralization of control of state courts in state capitols.

During this period, court administration emerged as a distinct profession. The first court administrator was hired as recently as 1950, but twenty-five years later two-thirds of the courts in the United States had professional administrators. The fiefdoms were crumbling. As is always the case, a national organization of court administrators soon followed, and this group became a powerful political lobby for still more reforms, and incidentally to promote the profession. In 1965, the National Association of Trial Court Administrators and a parallel organization, the National Association of Court Administration, were created. In 1985 these two organizations were merged to form the National Association for Court Management (NACM).

In both the state court systems, the 1960s was a period of rapid growth in the field of judicial education. Judicial educators formed organizations to provide support, networking, and training. Almost seventy different state-based organizations provide continuing judicial education. Many states require judges, by law, to continue their education.

In 1971, Chief Justice Warren Burger was the prime mover behind the creation of the National Center for State Courts. This is a research and consulting arm of the state courts and has been deeply involved in improving court administration.

Most of the reforms have a legislative component to them. Acting under broad constitutional principles, state legislatures have great power over the work of the courts by regulating jurisdiction and providing funding. The state legislature can even attempt to change the structure and personnel of the court if it does not like the decisions that are being made. A recent example comes from Florida, where a state representative introduced legislation to create a whole new level of appellate court and force the current supreme court members into retirement by threatening their retirement funds. The bill did not become law, but if it had, the governor could have created an entirely different court of last resort in that state.

Legislatures most often respond to pressure from outside when attempting judicial reform. The pressure comes from several sources. Among them are actors in the judicial system itself, narrowly focused interest groups, and more neutral good government groups. Throughout history the first group has included bar associations, judicial conferences, and the courts themselves. The second category ranges all the way from the United States Chamber of Commerce to the Southern Poverty Law Institute. Preeminent among the third category are the League of Women Voters, the American Law Institute, and the American Judicature Society.

Some reform proposals deal with issues that have, or could, put the judiciary in a bad light. Preeminent among these issues are the process for choosing judges and the behavior of judges while in office. Category two reform proposals come from more narrowly focused groups. Among these issues are legal training and performance.

An example of the type of reforms is the Civil Justice Reform Initiative of the National Center for State Courts. The initiative includes a long series of projects to improve such areas as case management, rules of discovery, settlement, and trial practice.

Among the more important parts of the initiative are studies of mass tort cases and complex litigation. As with all reforms, interested parties such as trial lawyers who specialize in the latter kinds of cases are watching developments very closely. A lot of effort is also going into applications of new technologies to improve, simplify, and speed up civil court processes. Other projects include better ways to evaluate the performance of trial judges in the states.

Over the last 100 years enormous strides have been made in improving the quality of the state judiciary. What was once seen as the dumping ground for political hacks and cronies of elected politicians has emerged as one that is well trained, well managed, and quite independent.

STATE COURTS AND POLICY

The notion of policy is one of the most studied aspects of American life. Policy can be defined as a consistent, officially sanctioned set of behaviors by government actors to deal with public problems or objectives. Its range is limited only by the imagination of the political institutions that make it. Its subjects range from the most banal, such as sanitation, to the most exalted, such as space travel. Politics is the science of managing power, but policy is its product. Policy is governing.

Policy follows the law, thus all courts, at one time or another, are capable of making policy. Although a trial court can conceivably make policy, for example by failing to follow a precedent and not being overruled, this is the rare exception rather than the rule. Trial courts are basically the enforcers of existing norms. Although their decisions may reflect some minor local differences, their policy-making role is small. Policy making by courts leads to one of the most contentious areas of American politics, one that has been with us almost from the founding of the country. The issue is framed this way: Policy should be made by the people through their representatives, the legislature and the executive. Judges are not representative and sometimes not even elected. Policy should be the result of a particular legislative process. It requires a broad base of knowledge and experience, and ample opportunity for all sides to weigh in on the policy.

Courts operate in a much more limited universe. They can only hear the cases brought before them, and the evidence they consider is restricted to that introduced by the parties. Those parties do not have common good as their goal but only their parochial interests. Therefore for the judges to make policy based on individual cases is to subvert the entire policy process.

The problem with this type of analysis, one that is frequently voiced in the media, is that it assumes judges are intentionally trying to make policy, rather than to fashion remedies in individual cases, and making policy as a by-product of their decisions. But even if appellate judges scrupulously tried to avoid making policy, they would often find themselves doing just that. The reasons for this are clear. Policies are almost always the result of political compromises. This is especially true of what might be referred to as constitutional policies. Compromise, as well as the necessity to leave the details to administrators and experts, often leads to vague wording, or at least to wording that is not self-explanatory. There is no closed set of procedures, for example, that comprises due process. Yet courts are called on every day to give real-life meaning to that term. Much the same can be said for terms such as equal protection, reasonable, disability, and even hostile work environment.

Another point, which is often overlooked about courts, is that they have to act, while legislatures may stall, or even be deadlocked indefinitely. When litigants come before a judge they have every right to expect a decision and a remedy in that case. Sometimes that results in the courts getting out ahead of the other branches of government in making policy, but it is hardly fair to criticize the courts for doing their duty.

Because state supreme courts are the last word on state law, a policy-making decision by that court becomes state policy, unless and until overruled by legislation or state constitutional amendment. In recent years these courts have become the font of many state policies on such subjects as education, workers' compensation, capital punishment, privacy, marriage, land use, and water rights. As legislative battles continue to result in lack of action, the policy palette is likely to include even more colors.

This is not to say that all state supreme courts are alike. There are gross differences in the subjects handled and fine differences in the way personnel are chosen and socialized. Some courts are labeled as activist or liberal while others are deemed conservative or restrained. Even to the trained eye these differences are hard to quantify. One usually labels a court activist when he or she disagrees with some policy-making decision, and claims the court is merely following the clear intent of the law when in agreement with the decision.

Interest Groups and Judicial Policy Making

Normally conservatives are more critical of the state courts for their activism, but in recent days, both liberal and conservative interest groups have found it to be advantageous to seek policy help from the courts. Thus one not only sees a wide variety of public interest litigators arising, but also will find many amicus curiae (friend of the court) briefs filed by a wide political spectrum.

The literature on interest group involvement with court policy making usually concentrates on the activities of national groups in the federal courts. Among the better known are the American Civil Liberties Union and the National Association for the Advancement of Colored People. The American Center for Law and Justice, which was formed in 1990, has argued successfully on behalf of Christian evangelicals in recent years.

THE POLITICAL IMPACT OF COURTS

Up to this point, the discussion has centered on the courts as political institutions, judges as political actors, and attempts to come to grips with this fact. Ultimately, the question must be asked: What difference does it all make? What is the result of the fact that courts are political institutions? As with so many things in life, there are basically two views that predominate among the observers of the court, and as it turns out those less knowledgeable about the workings of the court, the public at large, largely share these views.

The first view is that the courts are, and ought to be, conservative institutions. By conservative in this context is meant that they favor the status quo over change. Such a view is a natural outgrowth of the history and tradition of the Anglo-American legal system, sometime referred to as the common law system of courts. In this tradition courts are expected to follow the rule of *stare decisis,* meaning that they must follow precedent. Only for the most serious reasons should courts depart from prior rulings of the same court, or another court in the same state.

According to this view, individuals and businesses can plan their activities with the assurance that courts will back them up if a dispute arises. Lawyers can advise their clients on the proper course of action in any given situation. Citizens are well aware of their obligations and rights vis-à-vis the government, and can thus minimize the possibility of running afoul of the law. In short, to use a modern term for an ancient idea, the status quo is the default position, and those who would innovate bear a heavy burden.

The other, contrasting view of state courts is that they are in place to protect the rights of individuals against those, both private and public, who would interfere with them. The basis for this view is the fact that courts are constitutional institutions, sworn to uphold a higher law, no matter what the views or actions of the majority of the people might be. This is the so-called counter-majoritarian view of courts. Judges are seen as tribunes of the people against the onslaught of the masses who might bury them in discriminatory legislation, or of big businesses that might thwart their economic ambitions. In this view the beneficiaries of the court system are minorities of any kind, sometimes referred to as discrete and insular minorities, as well as small businesses, individual entrepreneurs, and nonconformists.

This second, more liberal view of the courts is nurtured in large part not by the performance of the state courts in general, but by the popular image, largely incorrect, of the federal courts, especially the U.S. Supreme Court, as the primary protectors of civil rights and civil liberties in this country. And it is true that when faced with clear constitutional violations, or patently illegal behavior on the part of businesses or government, the courts serve to protect individual rights. But innovative and liberal results in the courts are rare and exceptional rather than routine. And aside from cases such as some of those noted earlier in the Georgia and Oregon Supreme Courts, they do not define what can be called typical behavior in the state courts.

This conservative bent of the courts is not the result of any conspiracy. It is a result of both the nature of the law itself, and of those who practice law in the courts. About thirty years ago Marc Galanter, who was then a young law professor, described this situation, in what have become epigrammatic terms (Galanter 1974). In that seminal article Galanter divides the litigants of the world into "one-shotters" and "repeat players." The former are those who only occasionally seek help from the courts. These are the people who initiate the overwhelming majority of cases in the courts. They have been injured in an automobile accident, want a divorce, or are seeking some benefit from government. Repeat players are characterized as those involved "in many similar litigations over time." Examples would be insurance companies, landlords, government agencies, large corporations, and, as noted above, criminal prosecutors. Because one-shotters as individuals have few resources, and they need quick results from the courts, they are in a distinctly inferior bargaining position.

Repeat players, who tend to be relatively wealthy and larger, can have a longer view of the world and of the law. They become proficient in the law, helped by specialists. Repeat players are well positioned to go to court, not just for immediate gains, but for creating or changing the legal rules themselves, if they have not already done so through the legislature using lobbyists. The one-shotter inevitably is interested only in his or her particular case, not in legal rules. Little does the one-shotter realize that he or she is playing by the repeat player's rules.

Finally, repeat players have, in general, much better, and better funded, lawyers. Lawyers or law firms who have them as clients can develop long-term relationships, while lawyers whose clients are individuals may represent them but once. Early settlement becomes the norm, as there is no incentive for either protracted trials or worry about the rules of the game. In common parlance, plaintiffs' lawyers tend to be on the lower economic scale of the profession while defense lawyers (in civil cases) tend to come from the rich and established firms.

Little wonder then that the state courts favor the status quo, the rich, the large, and the powerful in most cases. Studies continue to support the notion that the haves do maintain the advantage, sometimes overwhelmingly, sometimes more subtly. This is true not because of the attitudes of the judges, or because of the electoral system and its corruption, but simply because of the nature of the judicial process in common-law countries. Courts are a conservative political force, and will tend to remain so, absent some radical change. And, contrary to much that has been written, if elements for liberalizing changes in society are to have any success, they would be better off concentrating their political efforts on the other elected branches of government.

REFERENCES AND FURTHER READING

American Bar Association (ABA). 1924. "Canon of Judicial Ethics 30."

———. 2004. "Model Code of Judicial Conduct," http://www.abanet.org/judicialethics/2004_CodeofJudicial_Conduct.pdf (accessed March 26, 2006).

Bach, Amy. 2001. "Justice on the Cheap." *The Nation* 272, no. 20 (May 21): 25–29.

Brace, Paul, and Melinda Gann Hall. 2003. "Predicting Challengers in State Supreme Court Elections: Context and the Politics of Institutional Design." *Political Research Quarterly* 56 (September): 337–349.

Chamberlin, Christine. 2001. "Not Kids Anymore: A Need for Punishment and Deterrence in the Juvenile Justice System." *Boston College Law Review* 42, no. 2: 391–419.

Champagne, Anthony, and Kyle Cheek. 2002. "Judicial Independence: The Cycle of Judicial Elections: Texas as a Case Study." *Fordham Urban Law Journal* 29 (September): 907–940.

Dubois, Phillip L., ed. 1982. *The Politics of Judicial Reform.* Lexington, MA: Lexington Books.

Easton, David. 1953. *The Political System.* New York: Knopf.

Galanter, Marc. 1974. Why the "Haves" Come Out Ahead: Speculation on the Limits of Legal Change." *Law and Society Review* 9, no. 1: 95–160.

Gardner, James A. 2003. "Forcing States to Be Free: The Emerging Constitutional Guarantee of Radical Democracy." *Connecticut Law Review* 35, no. 4: 1467–1507.

Geyh, Charles Gardner. 2001. "Publicly Financed Judicial Elections: An Overview." *Loyola of Los Angeles Law Review* 34, no. 4 (June): 1467–1487.

Glick, Henry R. 1993. *Courts, Politics and Justice,* 3rd ed. New York: McGraw-Hill.

Jackson, Donald W., and James W. Riddlesperger Jr. 1990. "Financing Partisan Campaigns for Judicial Office: The 1988 Election of the Chief Justice of the Texas Supreme Court." Paper presented at the annual meeting of the Western Political Science Association, Newport Beach, CA.

Justice at Stake Campaign. 2001. "Frequency Questionnaire, October 30–November 7, 2001," http://faircourts.org/files/JASNationalSurveyResults.pdf (accessed March 26, 2006).

———. 2002. "The New Politics of Judicial Elections 2002: How the Threat to Fair and Impartial Courts Spread to More States in 2002," http://faircourts.org/files/NewPoliticsReport2002.pdf (accessed March 26, 2006).

———. 2004a. "March 2004 Survey Highlights: Americans Speak Out on Judicial Elections," http://faircourts.org/files/ZogbyPollFactSheet.pdf (accessed March 26, 2006).

———. 2004b. "The New Politics of Judicial Elections 2004: Report on State Supreme Court Elections," http://www.justiceatstake.org/contentViewer.asp?breadcrumb=3,570,633 (accessed March 26, 2006).

Lasswell, Harold D. 1958. *Politics: Who Gets What When How.* New York: P. Smith. (Orig. pub. 1936.)

Meister, Dick. 2004. "The Courage of Rose Bird." *International Labor Communications Association Online,* http://www.ilcaonline.org/print.php?sid=444 (accessed March 26, 2006).

Morehouse, Sarah McCally, and Malcolm E. Jewell. 2003. *State Politics, Parties and Policy,* 2nd ed. Lanham, MD: Rowman and Littlefield.

Ogunro, Bola. 2003. "How Can the Integrity of Judicial Elections Be Safeguarded After *White?*" *Communications Lawyer* 21, no. 4: 19–24.

Reidinger, Paul. 1987. "The Politics of Judging." *ABA Journal* 73 (April): 52–58.

Solimine, Michael E., and James L. Walker. 1999. *Respecting State Courts: The Inevitability of Judicial Federalism.* Westport, CT: Greenwood Press.

Stumpf, Harry P. 1998. *American Judicial Politics,* 2nd ed. Upper Saddle River, NJ: Prentice-Hall.

Stumpf, Harry P., and John H. Culver. 1992. *The Politics of State Courts.* New York: Longman.

Texans for Public Justice. 2001. "Pay to Play: How Big Money Buys Access to the Texas Supreme Court," http://www.tpj.org/docs/2001/04/reports/paytoplay/index.htm (accessed March 26, 2006).

Vandervort, Frank E., and William E. Ladd. 2001. "The Worst of All Possible Worlds: Michigan's Juvenile Justice System and International Standards for the Treatment of Children." *University of Detroit Mercy Law Review* 78: 203.

Von Klemsmed, Rufus B. and Mrs. Duncan S. Robinson. 1934. "California Voter's Pamphlet." California Federal of Women's Clubs. N.p.

Ware, Stephen J. 1999. "Money, Politics, and Judicial Decisions: A Case Study of Arbitration Law in Alabama." *Journal of Law and Politics* 15, no. 4: 645–686.

Worthington, Chip, et al., Plaintiffs and Appellants v. City Council of the City of Rohnert Park, 130 Cal. App. 4th 1132; 31 Cal. Rptr. 3d 59; 2005 Cal. App. Lexis 1047.

6

THE JUDICIARY

STATE BY STATE

ALABAMA
• • • • • • • • • • • • •

On March 3, 1817, the Alabama Territory was created when Congress passed an act allowing a division of the Mississippi Territory and the admission of the state of Mississippi into the Union. During July 5–August 2, 1819, a constitutional convention was held in Huntsville. On the days of September 20 and 21, the first general election for governor, members of Congress, legislators, court clerks, and sheriffs was held as specified by state constitution. On December 14, 1819, Alabama entered the Union as the twenty-second state. On May 8, 1920, the Alabama Supreme Court, composed of Alabama's circuit court judges, convened for the first time.

Alabama Supreme Court

The court of last resort, the Alabama Supreme Court, consists of nine justices who sit in panels of five or en banc. A unique organizational feature of the Alabama Supreme Court is that it operates with two sections. Each section is composed of four justices, with the chief justice a member of both groups. Each section reviews cases separately. If the vote is unanimous by all five of the justices, it does not go before the entire court. If there is a dissenting vote in case, then the case goes before the entire court.

Only a handful of cases go directly to the state supreme court. The Alabama Supreme Court has exclusive jurisdiction over civil appeals greater than $50,000. The Alabama Supreme Court disposed of 2,022 cases between October 1, 2003 and September 30, 2004 (Alabama Administrative Office of the Courts 2004, 5). The court handed down 1,949 decisions without an opinion and 357 cases with an opinion.

In addition to possessing the power of judicial review, the supreme court may give advisory opinions on constitutional questions. Either the governor or the state legislature may ask the questions.

The Alabama Supreme Court's regular term begins on the first Monday in October and continues until the following June. The court may hold special sessions, as it deems necessary.

The chief justice of the Alabama Supreme Court is also the chief administrator of Alabama's judicial system. The Alabama Supreme Court has authority to make rules and procedures for all courts in Alabama.

Appellate Courts

Alabama has two appellate courts, the Alabama Civil Court of Appeals and the Alabama Criminal Court of Appeals. Both courts handle cases appealed directly from circuit courts. The court of civil appeals has jurisdiction over all civil matters not exceeding $50,000. The court also hears appeals from administrative agencies except for the Public Service Commission. The court of criminal appeals hears appeals of all felony criminal cases, misdemeanor cases, and violations of city ordinances. Each appellate court has five judges who sit in panels.

Once petitions and briefs are filed, oral arguments can be heard if requested by the parties or the appellate courts. Decisions of appellate courts are final unless the case is appealed to the Alabama Supreme Court. Cases decided by appellate courts may be taken to the supreme court only by petition for a writ of certiorari. This process is almost entirely at the discretion of the supreme court. The only

time a grant of certiorari is considered to be a right is when a case involves the death penalty.

The court of criminal appeals reported a caseload of 3,217 cases for the 2004 term. Sixty-eight percent of those cases (2,178) were new filings. This represented a 5 percent reduction in filings over the 2003 term and an 18 percent reduction over the past five years. The court of criminal appeals disposed of 2,184 cases and issued 1,452 decisions (Alabama Administrative Office of the Courts 2004, 6–7). The court of civil appeals had a caseload of 2,047 cases during the same time frame, of which 1,182 were new filings. This caseload represents an 18 percent reduction in caseload since 2000 (Alabama Administrative Office of the Courts 2004, 8).

Circuit Courts

Circuit courts are general jurisdiction courts in Alabama. Alabama has 41 circuit courts, with 142 elected judges. These courts have civil and criminal jurisdiction plus some appellate jurisdiction. Appeals from lower courts are appealed *de novo* (a new trial at the circuit court level). Some appeals from lower courts can be appealed directly to the appeals court if there is an adequate record.

Limited Jurisdiction

Alabama has three types of limited jurisdiction courts: probate court, municipal court, and district court. The state has 68 probate courts with 68 elected probate judges. Also, Alabama has 67 district courts with 102 elected district court judges. Finally, there are 263 municipal courts with 315 appointed judges.

Lower courts have jurisdiction that is designated by a geographically drawn district. District courts have exclusive jurisdiction over small civil claims less than $3,000, and they share jurisdiction for claims ranging between $3,000 and $10,000. These courts also handle traffic offenses, misdemeanors, and conduct preliminary hearings.

Each municipality has the option of having a municipal court. These courts are limited to traffic offenses, misdemeanors, and city ordinances. Each year more than a half million cases are filed in municipal courts. A large percentage of these cases are traffic offenses (Alabama Administrative Office of the Courts 2004).

Probate courts are also limited in their jurisdiction. These courts have exclusive jurisdiction over mental health, estates, real property rights, and adoption. All courts of limited jurisdiction are limited to bench trials. Bench trials are tried by a judge alone and without a jury.

Associated Agencies

Alabama's court of the judiciary with its nine judges hears complaints filed by the Judicial Inquiry Commission. The court of the judiciary is comprised of one appellate court judge (who acts as the chief judge of the court), two circuit court judges, one district court judge, two members of the bar, two non-attorneys appointed by the governor, and one person appointed by the lieutenant governor.

The three appointees are subject to senatorial confirmation. The court of the judiciary has authority to censure, suspend, remove, and retire judges. This court can also apply other appropriate and prescribed discipline.

Judicial Selection and Removal

All judges and justices in Alabama, except for municipal judges, are elected in partisan elections to six-year terms. Most elections do not receive a great deal of media attention. Often incumbents run for reelection unopposed. After the 2000 elections, eight of the nine justices, including the chief justice, were Republicans. Municipal judges are appointed by their respective municipal governing bodies for two- or four-year terms. The positions are part- or full-time, depending on the municipality's needs. Vacancies in elected judgeships are filled by appointment by the governor.

As with judges in many states, Alabama judges and justices are governed by canons of judicial ethics. Alabama's provides methods to investigate judicial misconduct and incapacity. The nine-member Judicial Inquiry Commission investigates complaints of judicial misconduct or professional wrongdoing. If upon investigation the commission finds merit to the complaint, it files a complaint with the Alabama Court of the Judiciary. The court of the judiciary holds a public hearing and renders a decision based on the evidence presented at the hearing. The court then makes its decision based on the evidence. The court has authority to apply appropriate sanctions up to removal from office.

The fiscal year (FY) 2004 budget for the state's judiciary was about $137.4 million. The budget represents an $8.7million decrease from FY 2003 due to state financial problems. The unified judicial system accounts for the largest portion of the budget ($121 million). The supreme court's annual budget is about $7.9 million; the court of criminal appeals annual budget is $3.6 million; and the court of civil appeals is slightly less with a budget of $3.1 million.

James A. Newman
Idaho State University

Doug Goodman
Mississippi State University

References and Further Reading

Alabama Administrative Office of the Courts. 2004. *The Unified Judicial System of Alabama: 2003 Annual Report and Statistics.* Montgomery, AL: Administrative Office of the Courts.

Alabama Judicial System Online. 2004. "Alabama Judicial System Online," http://www.judicial.state.al.us/ (accessed August 6, 2004).

Alabama State Constitution, http://www.legislature.state.al.us/CodeOfAlabama/Constitution/1901/Constitution1901_toc.htm (accessed March 29, 2006).

Martin, David. 1985. *Alabama's State and Local Governments.* Tuscaloosa, AL: University of Alabama Press.

Rottman, David B., et al. 2000. *State Court Organization 1998.* Washington, DC: United States Department of Justice.

Thomas, James, and William Stewart. 1988. *Alabama Government and Politics.* Lincoln, NE: University of Nebraska Press.

United State Bureau of Census. 2004. "Alabama QuickFacts," http://quickfacts.census.gov/qfd/states/01000.html (accessed August 6, 2004).

ALASKA

The Territory of Alaska did not have a court system until Congress passed the First Organic Act in 1884. Until then, Alaskan cases were heard in the state and federal courts in Washington, Oregon, and California. The First Organic Act created the District of Alaska and extended the laws of Oregon to the territory. Section 3 of the act established a district court for the District of Alaska with the civil and criminal jurisdiction of district courts of the United States. A district judge was to be appointed and the court was to meet at least once a year at Sitka starting in May and once a year in Wrangel starting in November. The president of the United States appointed the district judge.

The gold rushes at the end of the nineteenth century brought large numbers of people to Alaska. By 1900, Congress decided that it needed to establish civil and criminal codes for Alaska. These new laws resembled those in effect in Oregon. Alaska was granted a district court, and the territory was divided into

Judge James Wickersham (center row, third from right) in council with Alaska native leaders in the early 1900s. President William McKinley appointed Wickersham district judge of the Third Judicial District in 1900, becoming the first judge to sit in the interior of Alaska. Wickersham's district covered 300,000 square miles, accessible by ferry and dogsled. (Library of Congress)

three judicial districts. In 1909, Congress provided for a fourth judicial district. These four judicial districts are still in effect today. Alaska became a state in 1959.

The state of Alaska operates under the constitution written in 1956, in preparation for statehood. Because it is relatively new the Alaska Constitution retains much of its original content. The document was written by the constitutional convention to be a model constitution with relative simplicity, conciseness, and establishing a good government

Alaska Supreme Court

The Alaska Supreme Court is the state's highest court hearing appeals. The five justices, by majority vote, select one of the members to be the chief justice for a single three-year term. The court must accept appeals from final decisions by the superior court in civil cases. It has discretionary jurisdiction to hear criminal appeals from decisions of the court of appeals and interlocutory petitions from the superior court in civil cases. The Alaska Supreme Court also has discretionary jurisdiction over matters involving membership in the Alaska State Bar and attorney discipline matters. As the administrative body of the court system, the supreme court makes rules for the administration of all courts in the state. The Alaska legislature may change the court's procedural rules by passing an act. The court hears cases monthly in Anchorage, approximately quarterly in Fairbanks and Juneau, and as needed in other communities. It prefers to hear cases in the city where the case was heard in the trial court.

The Alaska Supreme Court has expanded the protection of individual rights in three areas. In civil law, the court evaluates the importance of the interests affected, rather than just considering whether a suspect class was involved. The court has expanded the right to privacy as protected by the state constitution. The court also applies the state's constitutional protections to criminal defendants. The Alaska Constitution has stringent evidence requirements and procedures for search warrants. Like most courts, the Alaska Supreme Court occasionally changes direction as the justices change.

In 2002, 258 cases were filed under mandatory jurisdiction and 157 discretionary petitions were filed in the Alaska Supreme Court. The court granted twenty-one of the discretionary petitions.

Court of Appeals

The Alaska Court of Appeals is a three-judge panel, a chief judge and two associate judges. In 1980, the legislature created the court of appeals to help the supreme court with its workload. The chief judge is appointed by the chief justice of the supreme court to serve a two-year term in that position. The court regularly meets in Anchorage and it meets in Fairbanks as required by the caseload. The court of appeals has jurisdiction to hear appeals in cases involving criminal prosecutions, juvenile delinquency, extradition, habeas corpus, probation and parole, bail, and the excessiveness or lenience of a sentence. It must hear appeals from decisions by the superior court or the district court. These appeals can be merit appeals—issues concerning the merits of a conviction, or sentence appeals—issues concerning the sentence. The court of appeals has discretionary jurisdiction over petitions of nonfinal decisions from the superior court or the district court. The court of appeals received almost 290 mandatory cases and 35 discretionary petitions in 2002. It granted six of the petitions.

Superior Court

The superior court is Alaska's trial court of general jurisdiction. There are thirty-four superior court judges located throughout the state. The state is divided into four judicial districts. These districts determine the boundaries for the retention elections at which voters indicate their approval or rejection of judges. Each January, the chief justice of the supreme court selects a superior court judge from each of the four districts to serve as presiding judge for one year. The presiding judge is responsible for the administration of the district courts within his or her district as well as his or her regular judicial duties.

The superior court is a trial court for criminal and civil cases, but it does not hear cases that may be brought to a district court. It serves as an appellate court for appeals in civil and criminal cases that have been tried in the district court. The superior court hears cases involving children who have committed crimes or who have been abused or neglected as well as cases involving the property of deceased or mentally incapacitated people. It also handles domestic relations cases. In 2002, superior courts heard 11,900 civil cases, or 1,800 cases per 100,000 total population. The courts heard 3,550 criminal cases, or nearly 800 per 100,000 total population.

District Courts

The Alaska Constitution grants the legislature the power to create any lower courts it deems necessary. In 1959, the legislature created a district court for each of the four judicial districts and it delegated to the supreme court the power to increase or decrease the number of district court judges in each district. There are currently seventeen district court judges. The district court has limited jurisdiction. A district court judge may hear misdemeanor cases and violations of city and borough ordinances. The judge also may issue summonses, arrest and search warrants, and preside over preliminary hearings in felony cases. District courts hear civil cases in which the judgment is no more than $50,000 as well as small claims. In some parts of the state, district court judges also record vital statistics. In 2002, there were 26,320 civil cases and 31,780 criminal cases filed in district courts.

Magistrates

Magistrates are the lowest-level judicial officers in Alaska. They are a remnant of territorial days when they were very important officials at the local level of government. The magistrate may be the only judicial official in a rural area. Some magistrates serve several court locations. In urban areas, magistrates help ease the workload of district court judges. The presiding superior court judge in a judicial district appoints the magistrates for that district. Magistrates hear small claims with a $7,500 maximum award. They may issue writs of habeas corpus, perform marriages, serve as notary publics, record vital statistics, handle cases involving children on an emergency basis, and hear domestic violence cases. Magistrates also hear cases involving violations of municipal ordinances, state traffic infractions, and misdemeanors if the defendant agrees in writing to be tried by a magistrate. They issue summonses, search and arrest warrants, and may preside over preliminary hearings in felony cases.

Associated Agencies

The Alaska Judicial Council is a citizen's agency created by the Alaska Constitution. It has three functions. The council solicits applications for judicial vacancies, screens the applicants, and sends a list of nominees to the governor for appointment. It evaluates judges up for retention and publicizes information about those judges to voters. The council also conducts research to improve the administration of justice in Alaska. The Alaska Judicial Council is comprised of the chief justice, three attorneys appointed by the Alaska Bar Association, and three non-lawyers appointed by the governor and confirmed by the legislature. Council members serve six-year terms.

The Commission on Judicial Conduct is an agency created by the Alaska Constitution to be in the judicial branch, but separate from the court system. The commission is comprised of nine members: three state court judges or justices; three lawyers with at least ten years legal practice in Alaska; and three persons who are not judges or lawyers. The commission investigates complaints of misconduct by state judges and justices. After investigating a complaint, the commission may recommend that the supreme court punish a justice or judge.

Judicial Selection and Removal

Since statehood, Alaska has used a merit selection system, commonly referred to as the Missouri Plan, to select judges. The governor appoints supreme court justices, and court of appeals, superior court, and district court judges from lists of qualified candidates screened by the Alaska Judicial Council. Magistrates are not appointed by the governor and the judicial council does not review their qualifications. Magistrates are appointed by the presiding judge of the judicial district and at that judge's pleasure. All judges and justices must be licensed attorneys who are United States citizens and have lived in Alaska for at least five years before appointment. Magistrates do not have to be attorneys. They are required to have lived in Alaska for six months prior to appointment.

All judges and justices, except magistrates, must run for retention by the voters. Supreme court justices and court of appeals judges are required to run for retention at the first general election held more than three years after appointment. Supreme court justices must seek retention every ten years while court of appeals judges seek retention every eight years. Superior court judges must seek retention at the first general election held more than three years after appointment and every six years after that. District court judges must run in a retention election at the first general election held more than two years after appointment and every fourth year thereafter. The judicial council provides evaluation information to the public on each judge or justice running for retention.

Judges in Alaska may be removed from office in one of two ways. After investigating complaints, the Alaska Commission on Judicial Conduct may recommend to the supreme court that a judge be suspended, removed from office, retired, or censured. Judges also are subject to impeachment. The process requires that the state senate impeach a judge by a two-thirds vote and the Alaska House of Representatives convicts the judge also by a two-thirds vote.

John David Rausch Jr.
West Texas A&M University

Further Reading

Alaska Bar Association, http://www
.alaskabar.org/.

Alaska Judicial Council, http://www
.ajc.state.ak.us/.
Alaska State Law Library, "Alaska Court System," http://www.state.ak.us/courts/.
McBeath, Gerald A., and Thomas M. Morehouse. 1994. *Alaska Politics and Government.* Lincoln, NE: University of Nebraska Press.
State of Alaska Department of Law, http://www.law.state.ak.us/.

ARIZONA

On the frontier of New Spain and later Mexico, present-day Arizona was lightly governed. The region had few apparent mineral resources and it was located distant from both Santa Fe and Los Angeles. With the end of the Mexican War and the signing of the Treaty of Guadalupe Hidalgo in 1848, the region came under the authority of the United States. From 1850 to 1863, Arizona was part of the Territory of New Mexico. In the mid-1850s, residents of Tucson began a movement asking Congress to create a separate territory because Santa Fe was located too far away to provide adequate security. In 1858, President James Buchanan observed that Arizonans were practically without a government. He recommended that Congress grant the region separate territorial status. Spurred in part by a Confederate Army skirmish in Arizona, Congress finally created the Arizona Territory in 1863. Territorial supreme court judges were appointed by the president. Probate

judges and justices of the peace were appointed locally. Arizona attained statehood in 1912.

The Arizona Constitution was written after Congress passed and President William Howard Taft signed the Arizona Enabling Act in 1910. The act called for a convention to be called to draft a constitution in preparation for statehood. In writing the act, Congress included numerous provisions that had to be placed in the constitution including provisions guaranteeing freedom of religion, prohibiting plural marriages, and forbidding the sale of intoxicating liquors to Indians. The act further specified that the constitution had to be approved by the president of the United States as well as Congress before the state's first general election. In writing the Arizona Constitution, convention delegates looked to the constitutions of Oregon and Oklahoma and incorporated a number of progressive measures found in them. The final document included provisions on direct democracy, the direct primary, and the direct election of many administrative officials. There are three ways to amend the Arizona Constitution. By a simple majority vote, the legislature can refer amendments to a vote of the people. The legislature also may call a constitutional convention that meets after the voters approve the call. The recommendations of the convention are added to the constitution if approved by the voters. Constitutional amendments also may be enacted through the citizen initiative process.

Arizona Supreme Court

The Arizona Supreme Court is the state's court of last resort. The original supreme court established by the 1911 state constitution consisted of three justices, two less than the number of justices in the final territorial days. The legislature increased the number of justices to the current five in 1947. The court's primary duties are to review appeals and to provide rules of procedure for the courts in Arizona. The supreme court has discretionary jurisdiction in that it may refuse to review the decision of the lower courts. Decisions in death penalty cases automatically go directly to the supreme court for review. The court also regulates the activities of the State Bar of Arizona and oversees the admission of new attorneys to the practice of law in the state. Charges of misconduct against attorneys are reviewed by the court, which has the authority to

suspend or disbar attorneys. The supreme court serves as the final decision-making body when disciplinary recommendations are filed against judges by the Commission on Judicial Conduct. The five justices serve six-year terms. One justice is selected by the other justices to serve as the chief justice for a five-year term. The chief justice handles casework like the other justices in addition to being the administrative head of the entire Arizona court system. Justices must retire when they reach seventy years of age. There were 1,190 cases filed in the Arizona Supreme Court during fiscal year 2003.

The Arizona Supreme Court has slowly adopted the position of looking at the Arizona Constitution to find a higher level of equal protection than that provided by the U.S. Constitution. In considering issues of free speech, the court also looks to the state constitution first to identify protections. The court has a mixed record in cases involving the establishment of religion. In some cases, the court looks to the state constitution while in other cases, the court adopts positions more consistent with federal authority. The Arizona Supreme Court does not have a consistent approach in terms of considering the state constitution first.

Court of Appeals

The court of appeals is the state's intermediate appellate court. It was created by the legislature in 1965. The court has two divisions: division one in Phoenix with sixteen judges and division two in Tucson with six judges. Judges in both divisions serve six-year terms. The court hears and decides cases in three-judge panels. It has jurisdiction over all matters appealed from the superior court. It also has to review all lower court decisions appealed to it. Division One of the court of appeals has the responsibility to hear appeals from the Industrial Commission, unemployment compensation rulings from the Department of Economic Security, and rulings by the tax court. In fiscal year 2003, Division One of the court of appeals received 2,676 appeals. Division Two received 964 appeals.

Tax Court

The tax court was established in 1988 and has exclusive jurisdiction over all questions relating to disputes involving the imposition, assessment, or collection of Arizona taxes. The tax court is physically located in the superior court in Maricopa County, but it handles cases across the state. A special department in Division One of the court of appeals hears appeals from the tax court. In certain instances, a taxpayer may choose to use the small-claims division of the tax court. The small-claims division hears disputes concerning property tax appeals, valuation or classification of residential property, or those in which the full cash value of all real and personal property is less than $300,000. In addition, the small-claims division judges hear all tax cases in which the amount of taxes, interest at the time of assessment, and penalties are less than $5,000. There is

no right to appeal the decision of the tax court's small-claims division. There were 1,050 cases filed in tax court during fiscal year 2003.

Superior Court

The superior court is Arizona's trial court of general jurisdiction. It is a single entity with locations in each county. Each county has at least one superior court judge. Counties are eligible for an additional superior court judge for every 30,000 county residents. The superior court has jurisdiction over civil cases where the judgment is $1,000 or more, felony criminal cases and misdemeanors not under the jurisdiction of other courts, probate matters, and divorces. The superior court hears appeals from justice and municipal courts. The superior court also supervises adults and juveniles on probation. Superior court judges serve four-year terms. In 2004, there were more than 100 Arizona superior court judges, most of whom serve in Maricopa and Pima counties. There were 192,100 cases filed in superior court in fiscal year 2003.

Juvenile Court

Counties with more than one superior court judge also have a special juvenile court. One or more superior court judges are assigned to hear all juvenile cases involving delinquency and dependency. Juvenile traffic cases may be heard by a court other than juvenile court, if allowed by the presiding juvenile court judge.

Municipal Court

Incorporated cities and towns may have a municipal court, which may be known as a city court or a magistrate court. Municipal courts have criminal jurisdiction over misdemeanors and petty offenses committed in the municipality. They share jurisdiction with justice courts over violations of state law. Municipal court judges may issue restraining orders and search warrants. Qualifications for these judges are defined by the city charter or ordinances. Some cities do not require judges to be attorneys. City governments in every city, except Yuma where the municipal court judges are elected, appoint municipal judges. There were 1.5 million cases filed in municipal courts in fiscal year 2003.

Justice of the Peace Courts

Justices of the peace are county judicial officers who serve geographical divisions of their counties, called precincts. They hear traffic cases and have limited criminal and civil jurisdictions. Their civil jurisdiction is limited to cases involving claims less than $10,000. They issue search warrants and they also conduct preliminary hearings in felony criminal cases. Justices of the peace are elected to four-year terms. A justice's precinct may not be abolished until he or she has completed the four-year term to which he or she was elected. In fiscal year 2003, 862,500 cases were filed in justice of the peace courts.

Associated Agencies

The Arizona Judicial Council was established in 1990 by the chief justice to assist the supreme court in managing the court system. The judicial council helps develop the central direction for managing all state courts and coordinating court services. The council has a large membership including: the chief justice of the supreme court; the chief judges from both divisions of the court of appeals; two presiding judges of the superior court in urban counties; two presiding judges of the superior court in rural counties; a magistrate; a justice of the peace; the administrative director of the court; the president of the State Bar of Arizona or a designee; nine public members; a clerk of the superior court; the chair of the Committee on the Superior Court; and the chair of the Limited Jurisdiction Committee.

The Administrative Office of the Courts is authorized by the Arizona Constitution. Under the direction of the chief justice of the supreme court, the office provides the necessary support to allow for the supervision and administration of all state courts.

The Commissions on Judicial Appointments, also know as Judicial Nominating Commissions, are responsible for screening and nominating individuals to fill judicial vacancies in the appellate courts and in the superior court in Maricopa and Pima counties. The commissions submit at least three names to the governor for each judicial appointment after reviewing the applicants' resumes, references, and taking public comment. The commissions also vote in public.

The Commission on Judicial Performance Review was established by a 1992 constitutional amendment. The commission reviews the performance of appointed judges to provide information to voters before each general election.

The Commission on Judicial Conduct is authorized in the Arizona Constitution to review and investigate complaints against state and local judges and other judicial officers. The commission has eleven members. Six members are judges appointed by the supreme court. Two members are attorneys appointed by the State Bar of Arizona. Three public members who are not attorneys are appointed by the governor. Commission members serve six-year terms. The commission may discipline a judge informally and issue a private punishment, or the commission may initiate a formal hearing and submit a recommendation to the supreme court that it censure, suspend, or remove a judge for serious misconduct.

proved a citizen initiative in 1992 that called for the adoption of a judicial performance evaluation process. Arizona is the only state with a constitutionally mandated program for evaluating judicial performance. The review process is intended to provide voters with information about judges who are running for retention and to encourage judicial self-evaluation and improvement.

There are three methods for removing a judge in Arizona. Judges may be impeached by a simple majority vote of the Arizona House of Representatives and convicted by a two-thirds vote of the Arizona senate. After investigating complaints, the Commission on Judicial Conduct may recommend to the Arizona Supreme Court that a judge be censured, suspended, removed, or retired. The supreme court takes final action on the commission's recommendation. In Arizona, judges also are subject to recall elections.

John David Rausch Jr.
West Texas A&M University

Judicial Selection and Removal

Arizona uses a combination of methods to select judges. Appellate judges and superior court judges in Maricopa and Pima counties are chosen through merit selection. After a two-year term, these judges must run for retention. Superior court judges in smaller counties are chosen in nonpartisan elections. Arizona voters ap-

Further Reading

Arizona Attorney General, http://www.ag .state.az.us/.

Arizona Supreme Court, "Arizona Judicial Branch," http://www.supreme .state.az.us/.

Berman, David R. 1998. *Arizona Politics and Government: The Quest for Autonomy, Democracy, and Development.* Lincoln, NE: University of Nebraska Press.

State Bar of Arizona, http://www .azbar.org/.

ARKANSAS
• • • • • • • • • • • •

Arkansas became the twenty-fifth state on June 15, 1836. In 2000, Arkansas's population was 2,673,400. The state is twenty-ninth in size geographically with 53,182 square miles.

Along with Mississippi and Tennessee, Arkansas (until recently) remained one of the few states with dual-system courts for law (circuit court) and for equity (chancery court). However, the origin of Arkansas's dual system stemmed from politics more than it did from justice. Efforts to consolidate these courts through constitutional reform have failed over the years, but in 1979 general jurisdiction courts were realigned into circuits, thus giving them boundaries similar to the circuit and chancery courts. However, by 1985, there were only eight circuits that had only one judge acting as both a circuit court judge and a chancellor.

In November 2000, voters approved the Eightieth Amendment to the Arkansas Constitution after thirty years of attempting to reform the court system. This amendment dissolved jurisdictional lines that previously required similar cases to be artificially divided and litigated separately in different courts. Also, the amendment resulted in structural changes that unified the courts of general and limited jurisdiction, allowed for new members on the appeals court, and granted the Arkansas Supreme Court greater discretion in taking cases.

Arkansas Supreme Court

The state constitution authorizes the elected, seven–member supreme court to review those cases that have been appealed from trial courts and the court of appeals. Arkansas's constitution also provides the supreme court with administrative and supervisory control over all lower courts. Amendment 80 altered the court's jurisdiction. It gave the supreme court original jurisdiction for initiative and referendum petitions and proposed constitutional amendments. The supreme court has the authority to call cases up from the court of appeals prior to the appeals court hearing or deciding on the case. The supreme court disposes of about 350 cases per year.

Court of Appeals

The Arkansas Constitution allows citizens one appeal either to the supreme court or to the court of appeals depending on where the case is assigned. In 1978, voters approved Amendment 58 that authorized the general assembly to establish the court of appeals under the supervision of the supreme court. A dozen appellate court judges are elected from seven districts throughout the state. The court hears cases en banc. The court of appeals hears cases appealed from circuit courts, and it has mandatory appellate jurisdiction over civil, noncapital criminal, administrative agency, and juvenile cases.

The court of appeals disposes of more than 1,000 cases each year.

General Jurisdiction

Arkansas's court system had many reforms, particularly with the court of general jurisdiction, since its creation in 1874. The most recent reform was Amendment 80 that voters passed in 2000. The new constitutional amendment resulted in merging chancery and probate courts into one circuit court. Thus, chancery and circuit-chancery judges became circuit judges. The supreme court mandated that each circuit establish five divisions to include civil, criminal, juvenile, probate, and domestic relations.

The civil division encompasses contract, issuance of injunctions, tort, and real estate. The juvenile division handles cases concerning abuse and neglect, delinquency, and families in need of services. The domestic relations division receives cases regarding custody, divorce, and paternity matters. The probate division reviews and makes decisions on adoptions, guardianships, and decedents' estates matters. Claimants have the right to a jury trial in circuit court.

District Courts

Currently, Arkansas has two types of limited jurisdiction courts, district courts and municipal courts. The constitution of 1874 provided for six different types of courts of limited jurisdiction (e.g., municipal courts, city courts, county courts, justice of the peace courts, courts of common pleas, and police courts). Prior to 2001, each of these courts possessed overlapping jurisdictions. With the adoption of Amendment 80, all these limited jurisdiction courts became consolidated into the district court by 2005. As part of the reorganization, the courts of common pleas, municipal courts, police courts, and justices of the peace were merged to form district courts.

District courts are the main courts of limited jurisdiction. They provide countywide jurisdiction over issues of preliminary felony cases, misdemeanor, and civil cases involving less than $5,000. The small-claims division of the district courts handles minor civil matters, and individuals can represent themselves in small-claims proceedings. The municipal courts operate in smaller communities in areas where district courts do not exist and their jurisdiction is more limited than the other courts. Furthermore, complainants do not have a right to a jury trial in limited jurisdiction courts.

Selection and Removal of Judges

Prior to the enactment of Amendment 80, all judges were chosen through partisan elections. Arkansas was one of eight states that used partisan election for the selection of its appellate judges, and one of eleven states that used the same approach in selecting trial judges. However, the change in selection processes was controversial. The Arkansas Bar Association preferred the use of a merit selection system, while political parties opposed the merit process, in part, for fear of losing revenues generated from the fees paid by judicial candidates.

In 2001, the general assembly enacted the new election law to set out the process for nonpartisan elections. Supreme court justices and court of appeals judges are elected in nonpartisan elections to eight-year terms. These justices and judges must be practicing members of the Arkansas bar for eight years prior to their election. Circuit court judges must be members of the Arkansas bar for six years, and they are elected in nonpartisan elections to six-year terms. District court judges are elected to four-year terms in nonpartisan elections. They must also be practicing attorneys for four years.

In 1988, Amendment 66 authorized the creation of the Judicial Discipline and Disability Commission. The commission encompasses members who are residents of Arkansas. Three of the members are judges appointed by the supreme court and three are lawyers who are authorized to practice in the state, but who are not judges. The attorney general appoints one member; the president of the state senate and the speaker of the House also appoint one member each. The governor appoints three other members to the commission who are neither lawyers nor judges. The general assembly expanded the provision of Amendment 66, which authorizes the supreme court to make provisions for the removal or suspension of judges as well as provisions concerning length of terms on the commission. Judges are also subject to impeachment by the Arkansas House of Representatives and trial by the state senate.

The Arkansas judiciary is funded through state and local appropriations. In fiscal year (FY) 2001, the state's judiciary budget was about $73.6 million. These appropriations are used to fund the salaries, the courts, administrative offices of the courts, court reporters, prosecuting attorneys, and defense attorneys.

La Shonda Stewart
Mississippi State University

Doug Goodman
Mississippi State University

References and Further Reading

Administrative Office of the Courts. 2004. *Arkansas Judicial Elections.* Little Rock: Administrative Office of the Courts, http://courts.state.ar .us/pdf/ar_judicial_elections2004.pdf (accessed August 26, 2004).

Arkansas Judiciary. 2002. "Arkansas Judiciary Annual Report 2001," http:// www.courts.state.ar.us/2001_annual_ report/court_structure.html (accessed August 9, 2004).

———. 2003. "Statistical Court Data," http://courts.state.ar.us/02cal_report/ stats.html (accessed August 6, 2004).

Blair, Diane D. 1983. *Arkansas Politics and Government: Do the People Rule?* Lincoln, NE: University of Nebraska Press.

Greenebaum, Edwin. 1973. "Arkansas' Judiciary: Its History and Structure." In *Readings in Arkansas Government,* ed. Walter Nunn. Little Rock, AK: Rose Publishing Company.

Stevenson, C. R. 1946. *Arkansas Territory—State and Its Highest Courts.* Little Rock, AK: Clerk, Supreme Court.

CALIFORNIA

The Spanish settled California in the late eighteenth century, and held to its Spanish governing system well into the middle 1800s. California became a Mexican territory when it gained independence in 1821. In 1846, the Mexican-American War began and the United States quickly occupied California. Mexico formally ceded it to the United States by treaty in the spring of 1848, at a time when gold was discovered in the San Francisco area. President Polk set up a military government in California after the U.S. occupation.

By treaty the United States was to respect the customs, language, and traditions of the Mexicans who remained after the war. The U.S. military government intended to retain the Mexican alcalde system of government, but few of the Anglo-American immigrants understood the system. The military governors altered the alcalde system in response to the changing demographics of the territory. In the Spanish colonial tradition, the alcalde was elected, but in Spain he was a royal appointee. The alcalde in Spanish-America was a locally elected justice of the peace, in other parts of the Spanish empire he was a royal appointee. The alcalde held broad legislative, judicial, administrative, and law enforcement powers. U.S. military governors grafted a U.S. form of government onto the Spanish system, but by 1849, the influx of gold-seekers created local governments in the mining camps independent of the military government. Confused about the alcalde system and disgusted with the military government, the writers of the constitution of 1849 rejected both systems and instead looked to other state constitutions for guidance.

A constitutional convention met in 1849, put the document up for a popular vote, and then submitted it to the United States Congress for its approval. The document was written in an era of little trust in state legislatures as exemplified in the 1849 constitution's provisions limiting legislative power. The legislature was prohibited from enacting legislation dealing with certain subjects including divorces, lotteries, and banks.

John Geary, the last alcalde of San Francisco under Spanish rule and then the American mayor of the city. (Library of Congress)

The legislature was allowed to meet in annual sessions. The constitution provided for a limited government that protected individual rights and sought to develop the common welfare of the new state.

In 1878, the legislature enacted a bill calling for a constitutional convention to meet to write a new constitution to serve a rapidly growing and modernizing state. The convention wrote a document that reflected the anti-immigrant sentiments of the population as well as the economic miseries caused by the railroads and corporations. The new constitution sought to protect Californians from corrupt politicians, included provisions to prevent high rates of taxation, reduced the power of corporations, and restricted the fundamental rights of immigrant Chinese.

The California Constitution may be amended in several ways. The legislature by a two-thirds vote of each chamber may propose amendments to be approved by a vote of the people. The legislature, also by a two-thirds vote of each chamber, may ask voters to approve a call for a constitutional convention. Voters also have the ability to amend the constitution through the initiative process. The ease of making amendments and the willingness of the people to limit their state government, has created one of the longest constitutions in the world. It has been amended over 500 times since 1879. In 1994, a Constitutional Revision Commission attempted to make California government more efficient. The commission was unsuccessful in its work.

Supreme Court of California

As the state's court of last resort, the seven–member Supreme Court of California sits atop the largest court system in the United States. Article VI of the 1849 constitution provided for a supreme court consisting of a chief justice and two associate justices. The justices were to serve six-year terms. The first three members of the court were selected by the legislature with the provision that the voters would select future justices. In 1862, the California judiciary was reorganized. The number of supreme court justices was increased to five and their terms of office were extended to ten years. Californians called for a state constitutional convention in 1877. Meeting in 1878 and early 1879, the new constitution expanded the size of the court to include a chief justice and six associate justices. The terms of office were increased to twelve years and all opinions were required to be in writing.

The court has mandatory jurisdiction in death penalty cases as well as reviewing the recommendations concerning the discipline of judges and attorneys for misconduct. Death penalty cases are appealed directly from the trial court. The supreme court has the authority to review decisions of the courts of appeal. It uses its discretion to select cases that raise important legal questions. During fiscal year 2001–2002, 8,917 cases were filed in the California Supreme Court. Almost 59 percent (5,255) were petitions for review of decisions of the courts of appeal. The court granted the petitions in 136 cases.

The California court was one of the leaders in the new judicial federalism movement. In 1972, the court relied on the California Constitution's prohibition against cruel and unusual punishment in declaring the death penalty unconstitutional and to require a more uniform system of public-school funding.

As in many states, the California Supreme Court also has seen its power to apply the state constitution limited by constitutional amendment. Voters approved an amendment to eliminate a line of judicial interpretation that went beyond federal limits on the subject of busing to create more racially diverse public schools. Members of the California Supreme Court who supported expanded protection under the state constitution faced well-financed and organized campaigns to remove them from the bench in retention elections. The most well known of these campaigns was the 1986 election in which three sitting justices, including the chief justice, were voted out of office. The willingness of the California Supreme Court to look to the state constitution to grant additional protections not afforded by the U.S. Constitution has become dependent on the ideological composition of the court.

Courts of Appeal

The courts of appeal were created by a constitutional amendment in 1904, in an attempt to manage the delay and congestion in the court system. California is divided into six appellate districts, each with at least one division. There are 19 divisions with 105 justices statewide. Additional court of appeal districts and divisions can be created by the legislature as necessary. Each division has a presiding justice and two or more associate justices.

Three-judge panels decide cases. Decisions are published if they establish a new rule of law, if the decision makes a significant contribution to legal literature, or if the case involves a question of continuing controversy. More than 22,000 cases were filed in the courts of appeal during 2001–2002. Almost 14,000 of these filings were mandatory cases. About 6 percent of the decisions met the requirements to be published. Courts of appeal have appellate jurisdictions over trial decisions coming from superior courts. The courts of appeal receive appeals from decisions of the Workers' Compensation Appeals Board, the Agricultural Labor Relations Board, and the Public Employment Relations Board.

Superior Courts

Superior courts are the trial courts in California. Prior to June 1998, trial courts consisted of the superior and municipal courts. The jurisdiction and number of judges in each court was established by the legislature. In 1998, voters approved a constitutional amendment permitting the judges in each county to merge superior and municipal courts into a single superior court. By 2001, all of California's fifty-eight counties voted to unify their trial courts. The superior courts have 1,499 judges and 437 commissioners and referees. The number of judges in each court is established by the legislature.

Superior courts have trial jurisdiction over criminal cases including felonies, misdemeanors, and traffic. They also have jurisdiction over civil matters including family law, probate, juvenile cases, and general civil matters. Appeals are allowed in limited civil cases (where the controversy involves $25,000 or less). The appellate division of the superior court hears appeals in these cases and in misdemeanors. In fiscal year 2001–2002, superior courts heard 8,092,631 cases. More than 19 percent of these filings were civil cases.

Associated Agencies

The California Constitution provides for several judicial agencies to serve the court system. The chief justice of the Supreme Court of California chairs the Judicial Council, which serves as the governing body of the court system. It provides policy guidelines to the courts and adopts and revises the California Rules of Court. The Commission on Judicial Appointments confirms the governor's appointments to the supreme court and the courts of appeal. The commission consists of three members: the chief justice, the attorney general, and the senior presiding justice of the court of appeal of the affected appellate court. In cases of a vacancy on the supreme court, the third member of the commission is the state's senior presiding justice of the courts of appeal.

Judicial Selection and Removal

All judges in California were selected by popular election until 1934. Constitutional amendments since then have produced the current system that is sometimes called the California Plan. Supreme and appellate court judges are appointed by the governor and confirmed by the Commission on Judicial Appointments. The ability of the commission to veto the governor's selection is the innovation that distinguishes the California Plan. Justices in their first term must run for retention by the voters at the next gubernatorial election. Justices also must seek retention at the end of their twelve-year terms.

Superior court judges are elected in nonpartisan elections to serve six-year terms. Most superior court judges reach the bench by gubernatorial appointment to fill a vacancy and incumbents are rarely challenged in their reelection bids.

Judicial retention elections tend to be low-key affairs in most states. California is the exception. In 1986, groups supporting the death penalty targeted three justices, including Chief Justice Rose Elizabeth Bird, for nonretention. After the state reinstituted capital punishment in the late 1970s, Bird never voted to uphold the death penalty. She vacated the sentences of sixty-one inmates sentenced to death. About $11.5 million was spent campaigning on behalf of and against these justices, a record amount for retention campaigns. Republican Governor George Deukmejian, a vocal opponent of

Bird, was able to appoint three conservative justices.

Since 1986, other appellate judges have been targeted in their retention attempts, largely because of their decisions on abortion cases. These efforts have been unsuccessful. The American Judicature Society reports that the margin of approval for state appellate justices in retention elections declined from an average of 77 percent in the 1980s to 60 percent in 1994. Superior court judges are elected by county voters in nonpartisan elections to serve six-year terms. The governor fills vacancies. A superior court judge must have been an attorney practicing law in California or have served as a judge in a court of record for at least ten years immediately before being elected or appointed.

Judges in California may be removed in one of three ways. Judges may be impeached by the California Assembly and convicted by a two-thirds vote of the California senate. Judges also are subject to recall elections. Since 1911, California voters have been able to remove elected public officials from office before their terms have expired. The Commission on Judicial Performance recommends discipline for judges and commissioners for misconduct. In 1994, a constitutional amendment was approved permitting the commission itself to remove, retire, or censure a judge, without automatic review by the supreme court. The commission is comprised of eleven members including judges, attorneys, and public citizens who are not attorneys.

John David Rausch Jr.
West Texas A&M University

Further Reading

Grodin, Joseph R. 1989. *In Pursuit of Justice: Reflections of a State Supreme Court Justice.* Berkeley, CA: University of California Press.

Judicial Council of California, "California Courts," http://www.courtinfo.ca.gov/.

Office of the Attorney General, California Department of Justice, http://caag.state.ca.us/.

COLORADO

The Colorado judiciary has its origins in two separate, but related settlement processes. In 1858, gold was discovered in a creek south of the present-day Denver. The news of the discovery brought settlers to a region that had previously only been lightly governed. As the population grew, so did the need for some sort of government. Miners' districts, organized wherever a large enough group of miners settled, were created in the mountains. These districts established boundaries, defined property rights, elected officers, and set up courts to try criminals and settle lawsuits. The first miners' districts were created in 1859.

The second process of settlement and government developed in a more conventional manner along the Front Range east of the Rockies. Prior to 1861, most of what is now Colorado was part of Arapahoe County in the Territory of Kansas. The Kansas Territorial Legislature appointed a probate judge for the region in 1855, but he never served. In March 1859, the first probate court was established in Pike's Peak Country, the widely used name for the region. The settlers began to call for secession from Kansas and in October 1859, an election created the Territory of Jefferson in what is now Colorado without the consent of the federal government or the Kansas territorial government. The new territory's government created a supreme court with a chief justice and two associate justices. After Kansas became a state in 1861, the people living in the Territory of Jefferson saw the need for recognition by the federal government. Congress agreed, and in February 1861, the Territory of Colorado was created. The new territory was divided into three judicial districts, each served by a member of the Territorial Supreme Court. President Abraham Lincoln appointed the justices. Colorado, the Centennial State, was admitted to statehood in 1876.

Colorado government operates under a constitution written in 1876. A constitutional convention, the territory's third by this time, was called after Congress enacted an enabling act for Colorado Territory. The convention first met in 1875 and produced a document that relied on the Declaration of Independence and various provisions from other states' constitutions. Among other provisions, the Colorado Constitution more explicitly protects freedom of speech than does the U.S. Constitution. Among the innovations that appear in the document is a provision that the supreme court may issue advisory opinions.

Colorado Supreme Court

The Colorado Supreme Court is the court of last resort and its decisions are binding on all other state courts. While the original Colorado Constitution established a supreme court with three justices, over time the court came to have seven justices. The justices serve ten-year terms. The justices select one of their colleagues to serve as chief justice who remains in the position at the pleasure of the other justices.

Most of the cases heard by the court are discretionary appeals that come to the court from the court of appeals. The supreme court has direct appellate jurisdiction over cases in which a statute has been challenged as being unconstitutional. Cases involving decisions of the Public Utilities Commission, writs of habeas corpus, and cases involving water rights claims also are directly appealed to the court. In 2003, about 1,400 cases were filed in the Colorado Supreme Court.

The court establishes the rules governing practice and procedure in all state courts. The supreme court also licenses and disciplines attorneys in Colorado. The chief justice is the administrative head of the court system. The chief judge of the court of appeals and the chief judge of each of the twenty-two judicial districts are appointed by the chief justice.

Court of Appeals

The first court of appeals was created in 1891 by the legislature to assist the supreme court with its case volume. The statute creating the three-member court did not specify a length of its term. It was abolished in 1904. In 1913, a second court of appeals was created. It had five judges and the legislature specified that it would be in operation for only four years. This court ceased operation in 1917. The current court of appeals, the third in the state's history, was established in 1970. It initially had six judges, a number increased to ten in 1974. On January 1, 1988, the number was increased to thirteen. Since July 1, 1988, the court of appeals has had sixteen judges who served eight-year terms.

The sixteen judges sit in three-member panels to decide cases. The chief judge is appointed by the chief justice and is responsible for assigning judges to the panels. Because the court was created by statute, its jurisdiction can be found in state statutes. The court of appeals has jurisdiction over appeals from the district courts, the Denver Probate Court, and the Denver Juvenile Court. The Colorado Supreme Court also has appellate jurisdiction over cases coming from decisions made by a number of state administrative boards and agencies. District court decisions may be appealed to the court of appeals. There were about 2,500 cases filed in the court of appeals during the fiscal year that ended in 2003.

District Courts

Colorado is divided into twenty-two judicial districts. The districts consist of one county in urban areas and more than one county in more rural areas. Each district court has at least one judge who serves a six-year term. The chief justice appoints a chief judge to administer the district. The chief judge serves as an administrator while also handling a normal district court caseload.

District courts have limited appellate authority and general original jurisdiction in felony criminal cases and in civil cases involving amounts over $5,000. District courts also hear cases related to mental health, divorce, child custody, adoption, juvenile delinquency, dependent and neglected children, and probate matters. Losers in county courts may make an appeal to the district court. In 2003, 169,460 cases were filed in district court (excluding cases involving water rights). Of these, 26 percent were civil cases, 24 percent were criminal cases, and 21 percent involved juveniles. Just over one-quarter of the cases were appeals from county courts.

County Courts

All sixty-three counties have a county court with at least one judge. The legislature determines the number of judges in each county. County court judges serve four-year terms. County courts try misdemeanors and handle civil cases involving amounts less than $5,000. Most of the cases heard in county courts were traffic cases, until 1975 when the legislature allowed all but the most serious traffic fines to be paid by mail. Judges in larger counties must be attorneys. In smaller counties, judges are only required to have high school diplomas. These judges must attend educational programs conducted under the supervision of the supreme court. Decisions may be appealed to the district court of the district in which the county lies. In 2003, 498,500 cases were filed in county court. Civil cases comprised 33 percent of the cases and traffic infractions comprised 30 percent. The balance were appeals from the municipal courts.

Municipal Courts

Cities and towns are permitted to establish municipal courts to try cases involving municipal ordinances. Municipal courts hear traffic cases, except for the most serious driving offenses that are heard in county courts. Municipal court judges are not required by state law to be lawyers, but some cities have enacted ordinances requiring judges to have law degrees. Judges are paid a salary set by the city government. Municipal court decisions may be appealed to the county court.

Specialized Courts

Colorado has seven water courts, one in each of the major river basins in the state. Water courts are a division of district court. The supreme court appoints a district court judge from within the water division to act as the water judge. Water court has exclusive jurisdiction over cases involving water rights. All appeals of water court decisions go directly to the Colorado Supreme Court.

Small-claims courts are a division of county court. Individuals are allowed to argue their own cases on civil cases involving less than $5,000. Sometimes a magistrate hears cases instead of a judge. Plaintiffs are only allowed to file two cases per month and no more than eighteen cases per year. The city of Denver has its own court system in part because Denver is both a city and a county. The Denver County Court is both a municipal court and a county court. It is funded by Denver taxes and not state taxes. The mayor of Denver appoints Denver County Court judges. Denver has a separate juvenile court and a separate probate court. These courts are state courts and are funded by the state government.

Associated Agencies

To assist with the administration of the Colorado judicial branch, the chief justice of the supreme court appoints the state court administrator. The state court administrator's office provides administrative support to keep the trial and appellate courts operating efficiently.

A 1966 constitutional amendment led to the creation of the Commission on Judicial Discipline. The commission investigates complaints that a judge is not properly performing his or her duties. The commission may meet with the judge to work out a solution to the problem, privately or publicly reprimand the judge, or recommend to the supreme court that the judge be removed. The commission does not have jurisdiction over Denver county or municipal court judges. Ten members serve on the commission: four citizens; two attorneys, two district court judges; and two county court judges. The members serve four-year terms.

In 1988, the Colorado legislature created commissions on judicial performance. These commissions evaluate the judges seeking retention and provide the information to voters. The State Commission on Judicial Performance evaluates district and county judges, supreme court justices, and judges on the court of appeals. Each judicial district also has a Judicial Performance Commission.

In 1970, the Colorado legislature reorganized the state court system, giving control over state courts to the state government. The state assumed responsibility for the indigent defense system. The legislature also created the Office of the State Public Defender. Initially, the Colorado state public defender was appointed by the supreme court. In 1979, the legislature created the Public Defender Commission to oversee the public defender's office including appointing and removing the state public defender.

Judicial Selection and Removal

Judges were popularly elected under the original Colorado Constitution. In 1966, voters approved a merit selection process. The governor appoints judges from a list of names submitted by the Judicial Nominating Commission. Appointees then must run for retention at least two years after their initial appointment. To help voters decide which judges to retain, the Colorado legislature in 1988 created Judicial Performance Commissions to evaluate judges.

The Colorado Constitution provides two methods of removing judges from office. The Commission on Judicial Discipline investigates complaints against judges and submits its recommendations to the supreme court. The court may remove, retire, suspend, censure, reprimand, or find another method of disciplining a judge. Judges also may be impeached by a majority vote of the Colorado House of Representatives and then are convicted by a two-thirds vote of the Colorado senate. Voters in Colorado may remove judges using the recall process.

John David Rausch Jr.
West Texas A&M University

Further Reading

Colorado Bar Association, http://www .cobar.org/.

Colorado Department of Law, http:// www.ago.state.co.us/.

Colorado Supreme Court, "Colorado State Judicial Branch," http://www.courts .state.co.us/.

Cronin, Thomas E., and Robert D. Loevy. 1993. *Colorado Politics and Government: Governing the Centennial State.* Lincoln, NE: University of Nebraska Press.

Office of the State Public Defender, http:// www.state.co.us/defenders/.

CONNECTICUT
• • • • • • • • • • • • •

Connecticut became the fifth state on January 9, 1788, and is frequently referred to as the "constitution state" based on claims by nineteenth-century historian John Fiske who asserted that the *Fundamental Orders of 1638/1639* were the first written constitution in history. Connecticut has a strong history of patriotism, being home to figures such as Nathan Hale who proclaimed "I regret that I have but one life to lose for my country" before being hanged by the British and General Israel Putnam who cried: "Don't fire until you see the whites of their eyes!" during the battle of Bunker Hill. Today, Connecticut is home to 3,405,565 residents governed by a general assembly comprised of 36 senators and 151 representatives. Interestingly, the state does not have any counties as unit of government but has only cities or towns, of which there are 169 municipalities.

Organization of the State Judiciary

Like other jurisdictions, Connecticut's arbiter of last resort is the supreme court. Organizationally speaking, cases are transmitted to the supreme court from the appellate court. The state's superior court exercises general jurisdiction while probate court has limited jurisdiction. Supreme, appellate, and superior court justices are all nominated by the governor (from a list compiled by the Judicial Selection Commission) and are ap-

pointed to eight-year terms by the general assembly. The state's constitution stipulates that judges must retire at age seventy whereupon they become eligible to serve as referees for the remainder of their terms. They remain eligible for reappointment as referees for life. The composition, organization, jurisdiction, and unique characteristics of each are enumerated in the discussion that follows. For fiscal year (FY) 2002–2003, the Connecticut judiciary operated on a budget of $333,657,764 drawn from the state's general fund. The budget for FY 2003–2004 increased to $334,133,557, allowing the system to support 196 justices and a permanent, full-time staff of 3,923 employees. During the 2002–2004 biennium, a total of 1,667,691 filings were received across all levels of the judiciary.

Supreme Court

The Connecticut Supreme Court was created in 1784 and was originally referred to as the Supreme Court of Errors. Prior to this, the state's general assembly or executive branch (governor) handled all claims of judicial error. Separation between the three branches of government was reinforced in 1818 when the state's first constitution was adopted, allowing the legislature to create additional levels of the judiciary on an as-needed basis. Today, the court consists of one chief justice and six associate justices. It exercises mandatory jurisdiction over capital cases and judicial disciplinary proceedings involving judges. The court retains discretionary appellate jurisdiction in civil, noncapital, and administrative law cases.

During FY 2002–2003, the supreme court received 234 filings. Of these, 160 were civil matters with the remaining 74 being of a criminal nature. A total of 198 appeals were disposed of during this period. For the 2003–2004 period, the state's supreme court received 202 cases—140 of which were civil with the remaining 62 being criminal in nature. A total of 237 cases were disposed of during this time frame.

Appellate Court

The state's appellate court consists of ten justices. It exercises mandatory appellate jurisdiction over civil, noncapital, juvenile, and administrative cases. It also has original jurisdiction in disciplinary proceedings involving attorneys. Finally, the court retains discretionary appellate jurisdiction in zoning cases.

During the 2002–2003 fiscal year, the appellate court received a total of 1,172 filings. Of these, 945 were civil with an additional 227 being criminal in nature. For the 2003–2004 fiscal period, 1,221 cases were accepted of which 995 were civil and 226 were criminal. A total of 1,227 cases were disposed of during FY 2002–2003 with an additional 1,162 being disposed of in FY 2003–2004, resulting in a total of 2,389 dispositions for the 2002–2004 biennium.

Superior Court

The 179 justices of the superior court system exercise original jurisdiction over all criminal and traffic offenses.

This level of the judiciary also has broad jurisdiction over cases involving child support, custody, divorce, domestic violence, real estate, property rights, civil suits, and juvenile offenders. As a general rule, all proceedings at this level are by bench trial—jury trials are accommodated only in limited instances (as noted later). The state is divided into thirteen judicial districts, twenty-two geographical areas, and fourteen juvenile districts.

The superior court system consists of four divisions: civil, criminal, housing, and family. Of these, the civil division is itself split into five areas: administrative appeals, civil jury, civil nonjury, landlord/tenant disputes, and small claims (less than $2,500). The criminal division consists of four parts: Part A hears capital felonies and unclassified felonies punishable by sentences of more than twenty years; Part B hears class B felonies and unclassified felonies punishable by sentences of ten to twenty years; Part C hears class C felonies and unclassified felonies punishable by sentences of five to ten years; and Part D hears class D felonies and all other crimes, violations, and motor vehicle violations, and infractions. The housing division hears evictions proceedings, small claims, and administrative appeals, among others. The family division consists of three parts: juvenile matters, support and paternity actions, and all other family matters.

With regard to juvenile matters, the superior court system disposed of 15,654 cases during FY 2002–2003. It resolved 16,549 juvenile cases during FY 2003–2004. Statewide, superior courts also disposed of 10,169 child protection cases in FY 2002–2003, with an additional 11,831 resolved for FY 2003–2004. With regard to criminal cases, superior courts resolved 3,102 matters during FY 2002–2003. An additional 3,144 cases were disposed of in FY 2003–2004. For FY 2002–2003, the criminal division resolved a total of 200,453 motor vehicle (traffic) cases. For FY 2003–2004, 190,100 motor vehicle (traffic) cases were moved from the docket. The civil division of superior court disposed of 50,192 cases during FY 2002–2003. An additional 50,807 were resolved during the 2003–2004 fiscal year. Small-claims courts disposed of 72,237 cases in FY 2002–2003 as compared to 73,257 in FY 2003–2004. The family division resolved a total of 30,494 filings in FY 2002–2003. It disposed of an additional 30,958 cases in FY 2003–2004. The system's housing division resolved 20,244 cases in 2002–2003. For FY 2003–2004, the housing division disposed of 17,909 cases.

Probate Court

This level of the state's judiciary is staffed by 133 justices from 123 districts and is colloquially referred to as neighborhood or family courts because they most frequently hear cases involving child support, custody, miscellaneous do-mestic relations, and mental health. Justices are elected to four-year terms but are not required to have any formal legal training as attorneys and are paid for their service from court fees. Statistical data regarding the workload and disposition of cases are not readily available for probate courts.

Judicial Support

The workload of the state's judiciary is supported through the efforts of a chief court administrator who is responsible for ensuring that the system functions in an effective fashion. To this end, several administrative divisions have been created. These include administrative services; affirmative action and employment discrimination, external affairs; information technology, and superior court operations divisions.

R. Alan Thompson
Old Dominion University

Further Reading

State of Connecticut Judicial Branch. 2005. *Connecticut Judicial Branch: Biennial Report and Statistics 2002–2004.* Hartford, CT: State of Connecticut Judicial Branch.
———. 2005. "Connecticut Courts," http://www.jud.state.ct.us/courts.htm. (accessed May 2, 2005).

DELAWARE
•••••••••••••

Despite sizable loyalist presence and support, Delaware voted for independence at the Continental Congress and became a state in 1776. Eleven years later, in 1787, it became the first state to ratify the new U.S. Constitution, subsequently adopting a new constitution of its own in 1792. Despite its loyalty to the Union during the Civil War, Delaware not only rejected President Lincoln's Emancipation Proclamation, but also refused to ratify the Thirteenth, Fourteenth, and Fifteenth Amendments until 1901. As the second-smallest state, Delaware is home to approximately 783,000 residents governed by a general assembly comprised of 21 senators and 41 representatives.

Organization

Like other jurisdictions, Delaware's arbiter of last resort is the supreme court. Organizationally speaking, cases are transmitted to the supreme court by one of three intermediate tribunals—family, superior, or chancery court. Of these, the superior court hears appeals from the court of common pleas, which, in turn, receives cases from either justice of the peace or alderman's courts. The composition, organization, jurisdiction, and unique characteristics of each are enumerated in the paragraphs that follow. Selection and eligibility for judgeships is different in each of the courts, so they are treated under each court's heading.

For fiscal year (FY) 2005, the Delaware judiciary operated on a budget of $78,591,100, which constituted only 2.71 percent of the state's general fund. This budget allows the system to serve a population of approximately 783,000 residents By comparison to operating costs, the judiciary as a whole collected $22,297,683 in revenues for the state during FY 2004. During this same period, the Delaware judiciary accepted a total of 620,909 filings. Of these, 619,591 were disposed of in some form or fashion at various levels of the state's judicial system.

Supreme Court

Article IV, Section 1 of the state's constitution created the supreme court. The court exercises final appellate jurisdiction on the record over all criminal and civil matters on appeal from lower chancery, family, and superior courts. It also has the authority to issue orders such as writs of certiorari, mandamus, prohibition, and quo warranto.

The supreme court is comprised of one chief justice and four associate justices nominated by the governor and confirmed by the senate to twelve-year terms. Justices must be learned in the law and citizens of the state. Interestingly, three of the justices must be of one of the major political parties while the remaining two must be of the other major party. Responsibilities of the chief justice include administration of all courts within the state. An administrator, appointed by the chief justice, oversees the nonjudicial aspects of court administration. Clerks, attorneys, law clerks, and secretaries staff the court.

During FY 2004, the court received a total of 564 cases. Of these, 268 were criminal matters, 264 civil cases, and 32 original applications. During the same period, the court disposed of 586 cases by opinion, order, or dismissal. The average time to disposition was fifty-nine days—an increase of roughly eighteen days from FY 2003. Over the ten-year period from 1995–2004, the number of cases accepted by the court ranged from a low of 530 (1995) to a high of 715 (2002). The number of cases disposed of during this same time ranged from a low of 495 (1995) to 726 (2003). Assuming a ten-year base, the court projects an increased filing caseload fluctuating from 670 (2005) to 727 (2009).

Chancery Court

Also a product of Article VI, Section 1, chancery courts possess authority to resolve all matters and causes in equity. More simply stated, they routinely deal with cases involving trusts, estates, corporations, titles, commerce, contracts, and various fiduciary matters.

The chancery court is comprised of one chancellor and four vice-chancellors who are nominated by the governor and confirmed by the senate for twelve-year terms. The chancellor and vice-chancellors must be learned in the law and citizens of the state. Operation of the chancery court system is supported by a register (clerk) and chief deputy register (assistant clerk).

During FY 2004, the chancery courts received a total of 4,112 filings from the state's three counties. A total of 3,391 cases were disposed of. Data regarding the average time to disposition was not readily available. Over the ten-year period from 1995–2004, the number of cases filed with the chancery ranged from a low of 3,853 (1996) to a high of 4,442 (2000). The number of cases disposed of during this same period ranged from a low of 3,391 (2005) to a high of 4,367 (2000). Assuming a ten-year base, the chancery courts project a fairly stable filing caseload with minor fluctuations ranging from 4,350 (2005) to 4,517 (2009).

Superior Court

Similarly originated, superior courts exercise original jurisdiction over all criminal and civil cases except for those involving domestic matters (handled by family court) or equity issues (handled by chancery courts). The scope of its authority encompasses cases involving personal injury, libel/slander, malpractice, foreclosures, liens, condemnations, and involuntary commitments. It also exercises original jurisdiction over felony and drug offenses. Last, superior court hears appeals on the record from the family and common plea courts as well as fifty-plus state administrative agencies.

A maximum of nineteen justices may be appointed by the governor and confirmed by the senate to serve as superior court judges for twelve-year terms. One of the nineteen justices is appointed as president and is charged with administrative responsibility for the courts that are situated in each of the state's three counties. Three of the justices are appointed as resident judges and must be residents of the county over which they preside. No more than a bare majority of the judges may be of a single political party. Those remaining must be affiliated with the other major party. Superior court operations are supported by an appointed prothonotary (clerk), court reporters, law clerks, bailiffs, presentence officers, and secretaries on an as-needed basis.

During FY 2004, superior courts received a total of 20,387 filings from the state's three counties. A total of 19,398 cases were disposed of. Data regarding the average time to disposition was not readily available. Over the ten-year period from 1995–2004, the number of cases filed with the superior courts ranged from a low of 14,328 (1995) to a high of 20,387 (2004). The number of cases disposed of during this same period ranged from a low of 13,595 (1996) to a high of 24,367 (2000). Assuming a ten-year base, the superior courts project an increased filing caseload fluctuating from 20,587 (2005) to 23,019 (2009).

Family Court

Title 10, Chapter 9 of the Delaware Code authorized creation of the state's family court. As expected, it exercises jurisdiction over cases involving juvenile delinquency, child neglect, dependency, abuse, crimes against juveniles, child and spouse support, paternity, custody, visitation, adoption, termination of parental rights, divorces/annulments, guardianship, and protection orders, among others. Excluded from this context, however, are cases involving adults or juveniles charged with first- or second-degree mur-

der, rape, kidnapping, and first-degree assault or robbery.

A maximum of fifteen judges are appointed by the governor and confirmed by the senate to serve twelve-year terms. One justice is appointed as chief judge and is charged with administrative responsibilities. To qualify for appointment, judges must have been admitted to the state bar and have five years of prior legal experience in addition to having a knowledge of the law with an interest in family and child issues. Judges are not allowed to practice law during their tenure on the bench and may be reappointed at the end of their twelve-year term. Operation of the family court system is supported by the use of commissioners who are appointed by the governor and approved by the senate to hear specific types of cases. The system also has a staff of approximately 300 personnel including court administrators, directors, clerks, specialists, accountants, assistants, arbitration officers, intake officers, program coordinators, and volunteers.

During FY 2004, family courts received a total of 55,959 filings from the state's three counties. A total of 55,056 cases were disposed of. Data regarding the average time to disposition is not readily available. Over the ten-year period from 1995–2004, the number of cases filed with the family courts ranged from a low of 51,187 (1995) to a high of 58,203 (1999). The number of cases disposed of during this same time ranged from a low of 51,031 (1995) to a high of 58,850 (1998). Assuming a ten-year base, the family courts project a fairly stable filing caseload with minor fluctuations ranging from 55,692 (2005) to 55,774 (2009).

Court of Common Pleas

Title 10, Chapter 13 of the Delaware Code, created the court of common pleas system. These courts exercise original jurisdiction over all misdemeanor offenses (except for certain drug-related crimes) and conduct all preliminary hearings. Common plea courts share concurrent jurisdiction with the superior court in civil matters where the amount at issue does not exceed $50,000. Last, the common plea system has jurisdiction over appeals from justice of the peace and alderman's courts in both civil and criminal instances as well as administrative appeals from the Department of Motor Vehicles.

This level of the judiciary is comprised of seven judges with five representing New Castle, two representing Kent, and two representing Sussex counties. All are nominated by the governor to twelve-year terms with consent by the senate and must have at least five years of prior experience practicing law within the state. A majority of no more than one judge can be from the same political party. A chief judge, appointed by the governor, is responsible for appointing a court administrator and clerk for each of the three counties. Bailiffs, reporters, law clerks, secretaries, presentence officers, and other staff are appointed on an as-needed basis.

During FY 2004, common plea courts received a total of 100,232 filings from the state's three counties. A total of 95,611 cases were disposed of. Data regarding the average time to disposition is not readily available. Over the ten-year period from 1995–2004, the number of cases filed with the common plea courts ranged from a low of 34,658 (1995) to a high of 110,232 (2004). The number of cases disposed of during this same period ranged from a low of 26,622 (1996) to a high of 95,611 (2004). Assuming a ten-year base, the common plea courts project an increased filing caseload fluctuating from 112,511 (2005) to 142,627 (2009).

Justice of the Peace Court

Article IV, Section 1 of the Delaware Constitution created the state's system of justice of the peace (JP) courts which exercise jurisdiction over various criminal and civil matters. For example, they are authorized to hear certain misdemeanors and motor vehicle cases and share subject matter jurisdiction with the court of common pleas. Jurisdiction in civil cases is limited to $15,000.

State law authorizes a maximum of sixty justices of the peace. Of this total, twenty-nine can serve in New Castle, twelve in Kent, and nineteen in Sussex counties. All justices are appointed by the governor and confirmed by the senate. To be eligible, one must be at least twenty-one and a resident of the state and the county in which he or she serves. A chief magistrate is appointed by the governor to oversee operations of the system with the assistance of an administrator, two operations managers, an administrative officer, and a fiscal administrative officer. The state provides clerks, constables, and other personnel on an as-needed basis.

During FY 2004, JP courts received a total of 421,156 filings. Of these, 390,097 were criminal in nature with the remaining 31,059 being of a civil nature. A total of 427,798 cases were disposed of. Data regarding the average time to disposition was not readily available. Over the ten-year period from 1995–2004, the number of cases filed with JP courts ranged from a low of 297,079 (1996) to a high of 421,156 (2004). The number of cases disposed of during this same time ranged from a low of 293,946 (1996) to a high of 427,798 (2004). Assuming a ten-year base, the JP courts project an increased filing caseload fluctuating from 439,391 (2005) to 496,596 (2009).

Alderman's Court

Authorized by their respective town charters, alderman's courts typically exercise limited jurisdiction over traffic offenses, parking violations, and minor civil matters. Appeals are heard de novo by common plea courts within fifteen days of adjudication.

The selection, number, qualifications, and length of service for judges at this level are determined by the towns that have created the courts. There is no requirement that the judges be practicing attorneys or learned in the law, nor is there widespread standardization regarding required full- or part-time employment status.

During FY 2004, alderman's courts received a total of 18,499 filings. A total of 17,751 cases were disposed of. Data regarding the average time to disposition was not readily available. Over the ten-year period from 1995–2004, the number of cases filed with alderman's courts ranged from a low of 14,678 (2000) to a high of 30,501 (1995). The number of cases disposed of during this same period ranged from a low of 15,161 (2000) to a high of 30,668 (1995). No projections regarding future caseload trends are readily available for alderman's courts.

Selection of Judges

Delaware's general jurisdiction judges are selected through a method similar to the federal courts. The governor appoints judges from a list generated by a nominating commission. The state senate either confirms or rejects the nomination. The state constitution holds that no more than a simple majority of judges on any court can be identified with a single political party. Judges typically serve for twelve-year terms. To be eligible, one must be licensed to practice law in the state and a resident of the district one would represent on the court.

On the court of common pleas and family court, judges are to be licensed to practice law and have a minimum of five years experience as a lawyer. On the alderman's and JP courts, regulations are made locally. All of these judges are appointees; alderman judges are appointed by mayors and the others are selected by the governor. Legislative consent follows each, with city councils voting on mayoral appointees to the alderman's courts and the senate voting on gubernatorial appointees.

Removal of Judges

Judges on the Delaware general jurisdiction courts may be removed in one of two ways: Judges may be impeached by a majority of the Delaware House of Representatives and convicted by two-thirds of the senate. Judges may be removed, retired, or disciplined by a two-thirds vote of the court on the judiciary.

R. Alan Thompson
Old Dominion University

Further Reading

Administrative Office of the Courts. 2005. "2004 Annual/Statistical Report of the Delaware Judiciary." Wilmington, DE: Administrative Office of the Courts.

Delaware Judicial Information Center. "First State Judiciary–Delaware State Courts," http://courts.state.de.us/ (accessed April 25, 2005).

FLORIDA

The Florida court system, with roots in English law, has gone through a series of changes since its inception. The state supreme court was created with Florida's statehood in 1845. Though state legislators dubbed the court as the highest judicial power in the state, they failed to provide for justices to serve on the court. Between the years of 1846 and 1851, circuit judges who had been appointed by the legislature were also periodically appointed to serve as justices of the supreme court.

The state constitution was amended in 1851 to give the legislature the authority to appoint a chief justice and two associate justices, and then again in 1853 to choose justices by popular elections. After this amendment nine other changes were made to the structure of the court and selection process of justices through a series of newly rewritten state constitutions and constitutional amendments. During that time, Florida's court system went from one of the most convoluted judicial systems to a very streamlined judiciary system. The Florida judiciary system today consists of the supreme, appellate, district, and county courts.

Though Florida's judicial history is filled with many unique cases, most memorable perhaps is its involvement in the 2000 presidential election between Democrat Al Gore and Republican George W. Bush. Nationally, the presidential election was among the closest in history and the Florida election ended in a virtual tie. At stake in Florida were fewer than 1,000 ballots that would determine the presidency. Florida's secretary of state declared Bush the winner, but Gore filed suit in Leon County Circuit Court. Gore argued that thousands of votes needed to be recounted by hand. Judge N. Sanders Sauls sided with Bush, ruling that there was no need for a manual recount. Gore appealed to the Florida Supreme Court. The Florida Supreme Court ruled in a 4–3 decision that only the ballots that did not read a presidential vote when ran through the counting machine should be recounted by hand. This decision would

Florida Supreme Court Chief Justice Charles T. Wells questions a lawyer on December 7, 2000, in Tallahassee, Florida. The Florida Supreme Court was at the center of controversy over counting fewer than 1,000 disputed votes that determined the 2000 presidential election. (Charlie Archambault/AFP/Getty Images)

have given Gore the presidency. Bush appealed to the U.S. Supreme Court and on December 13, 2000, the Court reversed the Florida Supreme Court, resulting in Bush ascending to the presidency.

Supreme Court

Florida's court of last resort, the Florida Supreme Court, has seven justices (one chief justice and six associates) appointed by the governor and retained at a popular election. Florida's constitution defines the supreme court's jurisdiction, though the legislature has some discretion in deleting or adding certain types of cases to the court's jurisdiction. The court has

mandatory appeal on final orders imposing death sentences, district court decisions exercising judicial review, bond validations, and certain orders of the Public Service Commission on utility rates and services. In 2002, there were 2,780 cases filed with the Florida Supreme Court. The court gives full consideration to fewer than 150.

In addition to its appellate duties, the Florida Supreme Court is one of a few in the country that issues advisory opinions at the request of the governor. The court also disseminates rules and procedures for the state's judicial system. The supreme court regulates admission to the state's bar, and it has exclusive jurisdiction for disciplining members of the bar. The court also disciplines members of the judiciary on recommendation by the Judicial Qualification Commission.

Some of the chief justice's responsibilities include assigning justices and judges to serve in courts that require temporary assistance, swearing in other state officials, presiding over impeachment hearings in the senate, and supervising the compilation of the judicial budget.

Appellate Courts

Florida's intermediate appeals courts are the five district courts of appeals with sixty-two judges who sit in three-judge panels. District courts of appeals are located in Tallahassee, Lakeland, Miami, West Palm Beach, and Daytona Beach. The district courts of appeals were created by constitutional amendment in 1957. They have mandatory jurisdiction in civil, noncapital criminal cases, administrative agency, and juvenile cases. Generally, these courts' decisions are final since the Florida Supreme Court accepts very few appeals. In 2002, 20,600 cases were filed with the district courts of appeals. These courts hear a vast majority of all cases appealed in Florida.

Trial Courts

District courts of appeals are located in Tallahassee, Lakeland, Miami, West Palm Beach, and Daytona Beach. Florida's courts of general jurisdiction are the circuit courts. Florida has 20 circuits with 527 judges. Finally, county courts are courts of limited jurisdiction. There are 37 county courts with 280 judges.

The general jurisdiction circuit court system was developed during the 1970s. The state currently has twenty circuit courts. The circuit courts have general trial jurisdiction for all cases except for those assigned to the county courts. Also, circuit courts are the lowest appeals court. These courts hear appeals from county courts. Circuit courts have criminal, civil, probate, juvenile, and domestic divisions.

In fiscal year (FY) 2002–2003, 183,000 defendants were accused of felony crimes in circuit courts in Florida. In the same time frame, Florida circuit courts disposed of 181,713 felony cases. Only 3 percent of the cases went to a jury trial. A large percentage (79 percent) of cases were disposed of through plea bargaining. Another 185,000 civil cases were filed in circuit courts. These courts disposed of 173,200 civil cases. Approximately 277,000 cases were filed in domestic rela-

tions divisions, 101,700 cases were filed in probate divisions, and 135,000 cases were filed in juvenile divisions.

The limited jurisdiction courts county court's jurisdiction extends to include civil disputes involving $15,000 or less, misdemeanors, traffic violations, and preliminary hearings. The majority of nonjury trials in Florida take place before one of these judges. Jury trials are allowed except for minor traffic offenses. In 2002–2003, nearly 2.7 million cases were filed in county courts: 489,400 criminal cases (misdemeanors and ordinances), 460,000 civil cases, and 1.7 million traffic offenses.

Selecting and Removing Judges

Justices of the Florida Supreme Court and judges of the five district courts of appeals must be residents of the judicial jurisdiction to which they are appointed. Appointees must be active members of the Florida bar for ten years or more. Appellate court judges and supreme court justices are appointed by the governor from a list of three to six nominees provided by the appropriate judicial nominating commission to six-year terms. Judges and justices face voters every six years for retention elections.

Florida's circuit courts have 527 judges who are elected in contested, nonpartisan elections to six-year terms. The number of judges who serve each court depends on the population. To be eligible to serve the court, judges must be an elector of the county within the circuit and must have been a member of the Florida bar for at least five years. The governor appoints judges to fill vacancies. The governor selects a name from a list of three to six nominees provided by the judicial nominating commission for the circuit. Judges must be elected in the next primary/general election cycle provided that they have been in office for at least one year prior to the election. A majority of voters in a county have the option of selecting circuit judges by merit and retention instead of through contested, nonpartisan elections. In 2000, the option was placed on the ballot in all of Florida's sixty-seven counties.

County court judges are selected in the same manner as circuit court judges. In counties with fewer than 40,000 people, county judges do not need to be a member of the Florida bar for five years. In some counties, county court judges fill in for circuit court judges as needed.

The Judicial Qualifications Commission investigates allegations of judicial misconduct and makes recommendations to the supreme court for discipline. The commission also investigates incapacitation allegations. The commission is comprised of two district courts of appeals judges selected by the appellate judges; two circuit court judges selected by other circuit judges; and two county court judges selected by other county court judges. The Florida Bar Association selects four lawyers, who also must be registered to vote. Finally, the governor appoints five citizens who are not members of the bar or the judiciary.

The Judicial Qualifications Commission has jurisdiction over investigating and recommending cases involving judicial misconduct and competency disciplinary action to the Florida Supreme Court. The supreme court then schedules arguments and has several options for disciplining judges. Discipline can range from no discipline to removal from office. The supreme court can also involuntarily retire disabled judges.

Florida's constitution also gives the legislature the authority to impeach justices and judges.

Supporting Agencies

Other judicial offices or agencies supporting the courts include the Board of Bar Examiners whose members are appointed by the supreme court. The board assists the supreme court in regulating and admitting members to the bar. The Office of State Courts Administrator is the business office of the court. The office also acts as the liaison between the court and the legislature. The clerk, the marshall, the library, and the state courts administrator are offices that fall under the direction of the Florida Supreme Court.

Florida's judicial system budget for FY 2005 stands at $1.04 billion. The state courts system accounts for $391.6 million of that budget. State attorneys ($322.5 million) and public defenders ($177.2 million) also receive a large portion of the budget. The balance is for other administrative programs. Florida's FY 2006 budget will see a modest increase to $1.07 billion with $405 million of that going to the state courts system.

Doug Goodman and Barbara Patrick
Mississippi State University

Further Reading

Hilden, Julie. 2000. "Reading the Florida Supreme Court's Opinion: The usual, the unusual, and the extraordinary," http://writ.news.findlaw.com/hilden/200 01211.html.

Office of the State Courts Administrator. 2003. *The 2002 State Courts System Annual Report*. Tallahassee, FL: Office of State Courts Administrator.

———. 2004. "Florida's Court System," http://www.flcourts.org/index.html (accessed August 9, 2004).

Rottman, David B., et al. 2000. *State Court Organization 1998*. Washington, DC: United States Department of Justice.

Stickland, Shauna M. 2003. *State Court Caseload Statistics*. Williamsburg, VA: National Center for State Courts.

GEORGIA
• • • • • • • • • • • • •

Georgia was the first Southern state to join the Union and the fourth overall on January 2, 1788. However, it was not until 1835 that the state constitution authorized its supreme court and another ten years before the legislature gave its approval. Prior to the establishment of the state supreme court, another jury generally retried cases that were appealed. For years, the state legislature was reluctant to empower a supreme court out of suspicion toward the judicial branch, especially after an unfavorable ruling in *Chisholm v. Georgia* (1793). That ruling held that citizens of one state could sue states they were not residents of in federal court. The uproar led to swift passage for the Eleventh Amendment.

Georgia Supreme Court

Georgia's supreme court has seven justices who sit en banc and are elected statewide to six-year terms. In addition to being the court of last resort in the state of Georgia, the supreme court has the authority to hear all cases where a death sen-

tence is imposed. The supreme court also has exclusive jurisdiction in disciplinary matters, original proceeding cases, and certified questions from federal courts. Article VI of Georgia's 1983 constitution outlines the supreme court's exclusive jurisdiction: "all cases involving the construction of a treaty or of the Constitution of the State of Georgia or of the United States and all cases in which the constitutionality of a law, ordinance or constitutional provision has been drawn in question; and all cases of election contest" (Georgia Constitution, 37). The supreme court has appellate jurisdiction over other matters of law and equity. The supreme court also promulgates rules and procedures for the administration of Georgia's judicial system. In 2003 1,882 cases were filed before the supreme court; the court disposed of 1,832 that same year.

Appellate Courts

Georgia, as many other states, has two levels of appellate courts. The court of appeals was created in 1906 as the intermediate appellate court. It began hearing cases in 1907. The court of appeals has four divisions and is composed of twelve judges who sit either in panels of three or en banc. It has one chief judge and four presiding judges (one over each division). The court of appeals has statewide appellate jurisdiction of all cases not falling within the expressed jurisdiction of other courts. The court hears arguments in every month except August and December. Each year more than 3,000 petitions pass through these courts.

Superior Courts

Superior courts are both an appellate court and Georgia's general jurisdiction trial courts. Unless otherwise provided, superior courts have jurisdiction over all trial-level cases in Georgia. This jurisdiction includes felonies, civil case, property rights issues, and domestic relations cases. These courts also have criminal appellate jurisdiction from lower limited jurisdiction courts.

There are 49 superior court circuits with 188 judges. Each county seat has a superior court. Georgia's forty-nine judicial circuits cover at least one county and as many as eight. Each judicial district is presided over by a chief judge who supervises the administration of each circuit court.

Limited Jurisdiction Courts

Georgia has myriad limited jurisdiction courts. There are three civil courts, one municipal court, 70 state courts, 159 probate courts, 159 juvenile courts, four county recorder courts, 159 magistrate courts, and the City Court of Atlanta (Atlanta's magistrate court) with its 307 judges in approximately 380 courts.

The state court was established by a 1970 legislative act that designated certain existing countywide courts of limited jurisdiction as state courts. State courts may exercise jurisdiction over misdemeanor violations, traffic cases, and civil actions, regardless of the amount claimed, unless the superior court has exclusive jurisdiction. State courts have authority to review lower court (magistrate courts) decisions. The general assembly creates state courts and determines the number of judges and whether the judges are to be full- or part-time. Part-time judges may practice law, but not in the courts where they are judges.

Magistrate court jurisdiction includes: civil claims of $15,000 or less; minor criminal offenses; and county ordinance violations. Magistrates may also grant bail in some cases. A chief magistrate presides over each of Georgia's magistrate courts. No jury trials are held in magistrate court. The chief magistrate has administrative duties in the county where he or she presides.

Another limited jurisdiction court is juvenile court. These courts are charged with protecting children. Juvenile courts have exclusive jurisdiction over children younger than seventeen years of age and in some instances children under the age of eighteen. They share jurisdiction with superior courts in capital felonies, custody, and emancipation cases. The superior courts have original jurisdiction over juveniles who commit violent felonies.

County probate courts have exclusive, original jurisdiction over mental health issues, estates, the probate of wills, and guardianship. Probate judges can also preside over traffic violations and game and fish violations.

Approximately 400 local courts are also part of the Georgia court system. These special courts and courts serving municipalities operate under various names with varying jurisdictions.

Judicial Selection

Supreme court justices and appeals court judges are elected in nonpartisan elections to six-year terms. Appellate court judges and justices must be residents of Georgia and be members of the bar for at least seven years. Most other Georgia judges are elected to four-year terms in nonpartisan, countywide elections. Superior court judges are elected in nonpartisan elections to a four-year term. These judges must be residents of their respective courts' jurisdictional boundaries and must have practiced law in Georgia for at least seven years. Most probate court judges are elected in countywide, partisan elections to a four-year term. A probate judge must be an attorney. Most chief magistrates are elected in partisan, countywide elections to four-year terms. Terms for other magistrate judges run concurrently with that of the chief magistrate who appointed them. A magistrate court judge may also serve as a judge of another limited jurisdiction court in the same county. Superior court judges appoint juvenile court judges to four-year terms. Municipalities set qualifications and terms of office for municipal courts. The governor appoints judges to fill vacancies on the supreme court, court of appeals, and superior courts from a list of qualified candidates provided by the Judicial Nominating Commission. The appointed judge may then stand for retention.

Associated Agencies

The Judicial Qualifications Commission is charged with investigating complaints against judges. The commission consists of seven members: two judges, selected by the supreme court; three attorneys who have practiced law in Georgia for at least ten years, and been elected by the Board of Governors of the State Bar; and two citizens who are not members of the state bar, appointed by the governor.

If a complaint is found to have merit, the commission holds a formal hearing. If at the hearing a violation (or disability that makes the judge unable to perform his work) is found, the commission makes a recommendation of discipline—retirement, censure, suspension, or removal from office. The state supreme court then votes on the recommendation. The state legislature also has constitutional authority to impeach and remove judges and justices from office.

The fiscal year (FY) 2005 Georgia judiciary budget was approximately $165.2 million. The largest outlay is for the superior court for $50.4 million. Money for superior court district attorneys accounts for the second-largest expenditure ($46 million). The supreme court and the court of appeals receive $7.5 million and

$11.8 million, respectively. The balance is divided between lower level courts and various judicial councils and administrative offices.

James A. Newman
Idaho State University

Doug Goodman
Mississippi State University

Further Reading

Administrative Office of the Courts. 2004a. "Supreme Court of Georgia," http://www2.state.ga.us/Courts/Supreme/index.html (accessed August 13, 2004).
———. 2004b. "Judicial Branch of Georgia," http://www.georgiacourts.org/ (accessed August 13, 2004).

Council of Superior Court Judges of Georgia. 2004. "The Superior Court of Georgia," http://www.cscj.org/ (accessed August 13, 2004).
Fleischmann, Arnold, and Carol Pierannunzi. 1997. *Politics in Georgia.* Athens, GA: University of Georgia Press.
Georgia Constitution, http://www.sos.state.ga.us/elections/constitution.htm.
Harris, John B. 1948. "The Supreme Court of Georgia: An Account of its Delayed Birth." In *A History of the Supreme Court of Georgia, A Centennial Volume,* ed. John B. Harris. Macon, GA: J. W. Burke.
Saye, Albert. 1970. *Constitutional History of Georgia, 1732–1968.* Athens, GA: University of Georgia Press.

HAWAII
• • • • • • • • • • •

Admitted to the Union in 1959, Hawaii is the youngest state in the United States. Its court system dates back to before the arrival of Europeans to the islands, however. Hawaiians were governed by custom and traditions in a system called kapu. Kapus were things that were physically dangerous, restricted, prohibited, forbidden, and to be avoided. Many individuals and physical objects were considered kapu. The traditional punishment for touching an item considered kapu was death.

The first court system with Western characteristics was established by the constitution of 1840. It created a supreme court comprised of the king, the prime minister, and four other judges appointed by the legislature. The court was an appellate court. District courts were created on the islands with judges appointed by the island governors. There also was a system of tax courts and tax judges, appointed by the king and the prime minister. The 1852 constitution replaced the original supreme court with a supreme court comprised of a chief justice and two associate justices. All judges were royal appointees. Hawaii became a territory in 1900. The Hawaiian Organic Act provided that the U.S. president appoint all judges.

In an effort to become a state, the Territory of Hawaii held a constitutional convention in 1950. The document was called the "hope chest" constitution because it was drafted before congressional action on statehood. At 14,000 words, it was praised for being relatively brief. It did not include the detailed restrictions on legislative action found in many state constitutions. Among the document's innovations was a provision prohibiting segregation in any state military organization and another provision setting the voting age at twenty when other states established the voting age at twenty-one. The convention also included a provision calling for periodic voter consideration of whether the constitution should be reviewed by a constitutional convention. Constitutional conventions have been held in 1968 and 1978, but voters rejected the call for another convention in 1986.

Hawaii Supreme Court

The judicial branch in Hawaii is a unified court system under one administrative head, the chief justice of the Hawaii Supreme Court. The supreme court is comprised of the chief justice and four associate justices who serve ten-year terms. As the state's highest court, the decisions of the supreme court are binding on all other state courts.

The court hears appeals in decisions coming to it from lower courts or from state government agencies. It has original jurisdiction in cases involving questions of law reserved to it by trial courts or remanded to it by a federal court. It also hears original cases in questions of writs of mandamus and habeas corpus. The court also is responsible for formulating court rules, licensing and disciplining attorneys, and determining the competency of judges. The caseload of the Hawaii

Supreme Court has been variable over the past decade. During the 1996–1997 court year, 822 primary cases were filed with another 2,440 supplemental proceedings filed. Supplemental proceedings are cases that are filed as part of primary cases, including motions, and applications for certiorari. During the 2002–2003, 730 primary cases were filed with 2,550 supplemental proceedings filed in the court.

In the early 1980s, the Hawaii Supreme Court regularly looked to the state constitution to provide its citizens with protections from infringements on their civil liberties. The court ruled in 1993 that the state constitution prohibited the state from limiting the right to marry to opposite-sex couples. Opponents of same-sex marriages were able to block the court's action by enacting a limit on the right to marry in the constitution.

Intermediate Court of Appeals

The intermediate court of appeals (ICA) is Hawaii's second-highest court. Its main function is to take some of the workload off the supreme court. The supreme court assigns cases to the ICA. Usually the ICA reviews trial court decisions for errors in procedure while the supreme court reviews matters involving the formulation of the law. The ICA is comprised of four judges who serve ten-year terms. The ICA was the result of a compromise after the 1978 constitutional convention rejected a proposal to expand the size of the supreme court. The sitting chief justice recommended that an intermediate appeals court be created to relieve the supreme court.

The judges hear cases in panels of three. During 2002–2003, 231 primary cases and 166 supplemental cases were filed in the ICA. The supreme court assigns primary cases while supplemental cases may come directly to the ICA from lower courts or be assigned by the supreme court.

Trial Courts

Hawaii's trial courts are comprised of circuit courts and district courts. The state is divided into four judicial circuits, one for each county. The first judicial circuit serves the island of Oahu, including the city and county of Honolulu. The circuit is comprised of twenty-one districts, each presided over by a circuit court judge, fourteen district court judges, and ten family court judges. The second circuit is made up of the County of Maui, which includes the islands of Maui, Molokai, and Lanai. This circuit has three circuit, three district, and two family court judges. The third judicial circuit, divided into districts for the cities of Hilo and Kona, covers the Big Island of Hawaii. Three circuit, three district, and two family court judges serve it. The fourth judicial circuit is no longer in existence. It merged with the third circuit in 1943. The fifth judicial circuit services the County of Kauai, including the islands of Kauai and Nihau. It has one circuit court judge and two district court judges.

All jury trials are held in the circuit courts. These courts have general jurisdiction in civil and criminal cases. They also have exclusive jurisdiction in probate, guardianship, and felony cases, as well as civil cases with judgments exceeding $20,000. In civil cases with judgments between $10,000 and $20,000, the circuit courts share jurisdiction with the district courts. Circuit courts also hear misdemeanor cases that require juries.

The district courts have jurisdiction over civil matters in which the judgment is $10,000 or less, criminal cases that are punishable by a fine or imprisonment of one year or less, and violations of county ordinances. The district courts also have exclusive jurisdiction over traffic cases. The chief justice of the supreme court appoints district court judges to six-year terms. Prior to 1966, district courts were the responsibility of the county governments.

During the 2002–2003 fiscal year, 11,952 cases were heard in the circuit courts. Of these, 35 percent were civil cases and 42 percent were criminal cases. During the 2002–2003 fiscal year, 499,941 cases were filed in the district courts. At 84 percent of the cases, traffic cases were the bulk of the district courts' workloads. Approximately 4 percent of the cases were civil, 11 percent were criminal, and 1 percent involved other violations.

Specialized Courts

The land court, tax appeal court, and family courts are found within the circuit courts. The land court is a statewide court with exclusive jurisdiction over issues within the state involving land titles, easements, or rights to land. The decisions of the land court may be appealed.

In 2002–2003, thirty-nine cases were filed in the land court.

The tax court is a statewide court that hears property tax assessments appeals and disputes concerning property, excise, liquor, income, and insurance taxes. The court is located in Honolulu and meets in the other circuits at least once each year. In 2002–2003, 200 cases were filed in tax court.

State law established the family courts in 1965 to handle virtually all legal issues affecting families and children. The family courts hear all cases involving children, such as delinquency, child abuse and neglect, termination of parental rights, adoption and guardianship, and juvenile detention. In the area of domestic relations, the family courts hear cases involving divorce, child support, paternity, and other custody matters. The courts also review requests for civil restraining orders involving family members. The family courts hear civil commitment cases, guardianships of adults, and adult abuse cases. A total of 36,000 cases were filed in the Hawaii family courts in fiscal year 2002–2003. Family court judges are appointed to six-year terms by the chief justice.

Associated Agencies

The Judicial Council is a citizen's group that provides advice about the administration of justice in the state. The Commission on Judicial Conduct is an independent panel created by the supreme court in 1979 to investigate allegations of judicial misconduct and disability. The commission has jurisdiction over all state justices and judges. The Judicial Selection Commission evaluates applications for all judicial vacancies. The names of the nominees are forwarded to the appropriate appointing authority, either the governor or the chief justice. The commission also decides if justices and judges should be retained at the expiration of their initial term of office. Before making retention decisions, the commission solicits opinions from the public and other interested parties. The Judicial Selection Commission has nine members who serve staggered six-year terms. The governor and the legislature appoint the members according to a formula. No more than four of the members may be lawyers.

Judicial Selection and Removal

Judges in Hawaii are selected using a merit selection process and they serve ten-year terms. The governor appoints appellate court judges and circuit judges from a list of names submitted by the Judicial Selection Commission. The chief justice appoints district and family court judges from a list compiled by the Judicial Selection Commission. The state senate must confirm all appointees. At the end of their terms, judges may be retained in office by a majority vote of the Judicial Selection Commission.

Prior to constitutional changes in 1978, the governor appointed all judges with the advice and consent of the senate. The constitutional convention of 1978 created the Judicial Selection Commission to remove political patronage from the selection process. The voters approved the constitutional change in the fall of 1978. The commission began its work in 1979.

All judges must retire by age seventy. Other forced removals can be initiated by the Commission on Judicial Conduct, which investigates complaints of judicial misconduct or disability against judges. If the allegations warrant, the commission may recommend to the supreme court that a judge be reprimanded, disciplined, suspended, retired, or removed.

John David Rausch Jr.
West Texas A&M University

Further Reading

Department of the Attorney General, http://www.hawaii.gov/ag/index.html.
Hawai'i State Judiciary, http://www.courts.state.hi.us/index.jsp.
Pratt, Richard C., with Zachary Smith. 2000. *Hawai'i Politics and Government: An American State in a Pacific World.* Lincoln, NE: University of Nebraska Press.

IDAHO
• • • • • • • • • • • •

Idaho was made a territory in 1860 and President Abraham Lincoln appointed the first three justices of the territorial supreme court. The territory was divided into three judicial districts in which a district court was to be held periodically by each of the supreme court justices. In 1863, the first Idaho Territorial Legislature met in Lewiston and finalized the judicial district boundaries and assigned judges to the districts. The opening of the territorial supreme court was delayed by the inability to bring the three justices together in one place. The court did not officially open until May 31, 1866, four months after the legislatively mandated opening date, because one of the justices was delayed by winter weather. When Idaho became a state in 1890, the new constitution provided for a supreme court comprised of three justices.

Idaho has operated under the same constitution since statehood in 1890. In the original document, women were granted the right to vote and to hold school offices. However, Mormons and naturalized Chinese immigrants were prohibited from voting. The constitution limited the power of the state government by implicitly specifying individual rights that were to be protected. There have been two failed attempts to thoroughly revise the constitution. Despite the failure of these attempts, the Idaho Constitution has been amended around 125 times.

Supreme Court of Idaho

Idaho has a unified court system. According to Article 5, Section 2 of the Idaho Constitution, all state courts are administered and supervised by the Supreme

Court of Idaho. While the supreme court is the head of the judicial branch, the lower courts are funded in part by the state government and in part by city and county governments. Judges are paid by the state, and clerks and other staff are paid out of county funds. The other courts in the system include a three-judge court of appeals, and seven district courts with magistrates divisions.

The first Idaho Constitution (ratified in 1890) provided for a supreme court consisting of three justices. A constitutional amendment in 1919 expanded the court to its current composition of one chief justice and four justices. The court has original jurisdiction in claims against the state and disciplinary actions involving attorneys. The court hears appeals of decisions from the district courts, the State Public Utilities Commission, and the Industrial Commission. The supreme court received 757 cases in 2002.

Idaho Court of Appeals

The court of appeals consists of a chief and two associate judges. Created in 1981 to relieve the backlog of appeals from the district courts to the supreme court, the court of appeals hears cases assigned to it by the supreme court. The supreme court is prohibited from assigning cases involving claims against any state, death penalty appeals, or appeals from the Public Utilities Commission or the Industrial Commission. In 2002, the Idaho Court of Appeals received 491 cases. While a decision of the court of appeals may be appealed to the supreme court, most cases stop at the court of appeals.

District Courts

The state is divided into seven judicial districts, with four to ten counties in each district. Each county has a district court, which includes a magistrate division. There are thirty-nine district judges and eighty-three magistrate judges in the state. District courts have civil and criminal jurisdiction. Judges decide cases involving felonies as well as civil cases where the amount in controversy is greater than $10,000. District judges may also hear family law cases, but magistrates usually hear cases of this type. District courts heard 20,019 cases in 2003. About 61 percent of the cases were criminal. The civil caseload is rapidly growing. In 1996, district courts heard 5,332 civil cases. In 2003, the courts heard 7,198 civil cases for an increase of 35 percent. District court judges also hear appeals from magistrate judges.

The district judges in the district choose an administrative district judge. The administrative district judge performs a number of administrative duties as well as maintaining a judicial caseload. The administrative district judge compiles the budget for local courts and facilities and participates in personnel decisions. The administrative district judge also serves as chair of the district magistrates commission, a body of county commissioners, mayors, citizens, and attorneys, that appoints magistrates to their positions.

Magistrate judges hear misdemeanors and decide civil cases where the amount of money involved is less than $10,000. Magistrates also are responsible for preliminary hearings and issue arrest and search warrants. Magistrates handle probate, juvenile, and family law cases. Magistrate judges also sit as a small-claims court deciding civil disputes where less than $4,000 is in question. Most of these cases are heard informally without attorneys or juries. In 2003, magistrate judges heard 459,497. Of those, 126,462 cases were criminal and 221,848 were infractions. Infractions and misdemeanors brought to the magistrate judges are primarily traffic violations. Magistrate judges heard 27.3 percent more civil cases in 2003 than in 1996, but actually saw an 11.7 percent decrease in the number of criminal cases.

Judicial Selection

The selection process for supreme court justices, court of appeals judges, and district judges is the same. When a vacancy occurs, the Idaho Judicial Council advertises the vacancy to all attorneys licensed in Idaho and solicits applications. After the time period for submitting applications has expired, the council surveys members of the bar about their opinions of the applicants. The general public also is allowed to provide input on individual applicants. The data collected by the surveys are used in the interview process. After the council has completed its interviews, it submits the names of at least two but up to four qualified persons to the governor. The governor then appoints a justice or judge to complete the unexpired term.

Supreme court justices, court of appeals judges, and district judges run for election on a subsequent nonpartisan ballot. Justices and appellate court judges run statewide while district judges run in their districts. Any qualified lawyer can challenge a sitting justice, appellate court judge, or district judge at election time.

Despite the nonpartisan nature of Idaho judicial elections, a number of campaigns were charged with party politics. In 1998, an election was held for an open supreme court seat, the first open-seat election in twenty-five years. One of the candidates, former Attorney General Wayne Kidwell, identified himself as a Republican and presented his positions on issues like abortion, gun control, and capital punishment. Both of these tactics violated tradition, if not the code of judicial conduct. Kidwell's opponent, Michael Wetherell, tried to keep the fact that he was a Democrat to himself. Kidwell was elected.

In the 2000 election, Justice Cathy Silak was targeted because of a ruling on an environmental case. Silak's defeat by District Judge Daniel Eismann was the first time in fifty-six years that Idaho voters ousted an incumbent supreme court justice. The Eismann campaign focused attention on Silak's majority opinion on a case that upheld federal water rights in Idaho wilderness areas. Silak's campaign funds came from Democrats and trial lawyers, while Eismann received support from Republicans, resource industries, and agricultural interests. The campaign was the most expensive in Idaho history. Silak spent $149,000 on her campaign while Eismann spent about $140,000. Eismann, the challenger, was assisted by tens of thousands of dollars spent by an independent expenditure campaign.

Starr Kelso challenged Chief Justice Linda Copple Trout in 2002. The race became particularly vitriolic when Idahoans for Tax Reform called Trout "very liberal" and Kelso "conservative" in last-minute independent expenditure advertisements. Trout was reelected by a wide margin despite the attacks. After the election, Trout began advocating a merit selection system with retention elections to replace the nonpartisan popular elections.

Magistrate judges are initially selected by the district magistrates' commission. The new magistrate judge serves an initial eighteen-month term after which the commission reviews the new magistrate's performance. The commission may extend the probationary period or remove the magistrate from office. The magistrate judge must run in a retention election every four years to remain in office.

There are two methods for removing judges in Idaho. They may be impeached by a simple majority vote of the Idaho House of Representatives and convicted by a two-thirds vote of the senate. Judges also may be punished by removal after the Idaho Judicial Council investigates complaints and issues a recommendation to the supreme court. The supreme court may review the council's recommendation and take additional evidence. The court may then reject the council's recommendation, or order the discipline, removal, or retirement of the judge.

Associated Agencies

The Idaho Judicial Council investigates allegations of judicial misconduct or disability. It consists of three citizen members, two attorneys, one district judge, and the chief justice. Using the report of the judicial council investigation, the supreme court acts on complaints made against judges. The council also serves as a clearinghouse of information on judicial vacancies.

The supreme court maintains a project called the Court Assistance Office (CAO) project. The CAO is a one-stop clearinghouse of information on legal services and other resources for those involved in family law cases and other civil court matters. As of 2004, there are CAOs in twenty-three courthouses around the state of Idaho. The CAO also maintains a website from which visitors may download court forms, instructions, and attorney rosters.

John David Rausch Jr.
West Texas A&M University

Further Reading

Court Assistance Offices Project, http://www2.state.id.us/cao/.
Idaho Judicial Council, http://www2.state.id.us/ijc/.
Idaho State Bar and Idaho Law Foundation, http://www2.state.id.us/isb/.
Idaho State Law Library, http://www.isll.idaho.gov/.
Idaho Supreme Court, http://www.isc.idaho.gov/.
State of Idaho, Office of Attorney General, http://www2.state.id.us/ag/.

ILLINOIS

Illinois was among the six states affected by the Northwest Ordinance of 1787. Until 1800, at which time Ohio Territory had sufficient population for self-government, the entire Northwest Territory was ruled by a military governor and a general court of three judges. The judiciary, along with the governor, also acted as a legislature. In 1800, the Indiana Territory was created by Congress, and in 1809 was split into the Indiana and Illinois territories. The Illinois Territory initially included the present states of Illinois and Wisconsin. Both territories were divided into three districts, and the territories were governed by a governor and by three judges, who also as a group, assumed legislative powers. In 1812 a general assembly was created, and in 1814, the Supreme Court of the Illinois Territory was established. County courts were also created, but criminal and civil jurisdiction to hear cases was given to the supreme court justices, who were required to ride circuit. In 1818, Illinois became a state.

The 1818 Illinois Constitution provided for a judiciary that included a supreme court of four judges who had original and appellate jurisdiction. Judges were selected by the general assembly and judicial tenure was based on good behavior; judges could be removed by a two-thirds vote of the general assembly. It also allowed the general assembly to establish inferior courts. During the period from 1824 through 1848, the legislature created circuit courts and circuit court judges but legislated them out of existence on multiple occasions. In 1848, Illinois adopted a new constitution. It established a supreme court of three justices, elected by the people to nine-year terms. It also established nine circuits, each staffed by a judge elected by the people to a term of six years. Subsequent legislation also created county courts in each county with a county court judge who served a four-year term. Justices of the peace were also elected in the counties, serving terms of four years.

In 1870, Illinois adopted yet another new constitution. It created a detailed and complex judicial system. This judicial system included a supreme court consisting of seven members, each elected from one of seven supreme court districts in the state. It also gave the legislature the power to establish an appellate court, which the legislature did in 1877. The constitution also provided for circuit courts, county courts, police magistrates, and justices of the peace. This court system remained in place until the voters ratified the Judicial Article of 1964, providing Illinois with a unified court system. Under the Judicial Act of 1964, the judicial power of Illinois was vested in a supreme court, an appellate court, and circuit courts. All trial-level courts except for the circuit courts were abolished. The supreme court and the appellate court were organized around five judicial districts while the circuit courts were organized into twenty-two circuits. The new constitution adopted by Illinois in 1970 essentially refined the Judicial

Act of 1964. The structure of the judiciary was retained. Modifications involved a reduction in the mandatory caseload of the supreme court, increased the supervisory powers of the supreme court, and adjusted how judges were selected.

Organization of State Courts

The supreme court, the highest court in Illinois, has seven justices. In 2004, the justices on the court were Chief Justice Mary Ann G. McMorrow, and associate justices Charles E. Freeman, Thomas R. Fitzgerald, Robert R. Thomas, Thomas L. Kilbride, Rita B. Garman, and Lloyd A. Karmeier. Illinois has five appellate court districts served by forty-two judges. Eighteen are elected to the first district, with six each elected from the remaining four districts. Judges hear cases in panels of three. Illinois trial courts and courts of general jurisdiction are the circuit courts. The state is divided into twenty-two judicial circuits that are staffed by 509 circuit court judges and 391 associate judges. Each of the twenty-two circuits elects its own chief judge.

Supreme Court

The supreme court has discretionary appellate jurisdiction over cases brought to it from appellate and circuit courts. The supreme court must hear cases, as a matter of right, if a question under the state or U.S. Constitution is raised for the first time. The court has mandatory review of death penalty cases, which in recent years has amounted to about one-third of the court's total workload. The supreme court has original jurisdiction over cases relating to revenue, mandamus, prohibition, or habeas corpus. The supreme court has exclusive original jurisdiction in cases involving redistricting of the general assembly and to the ability of the governor to serve or resume office. In 2003, 2,967 cases were filed with the Illinois Supreme Court. This is down from 3,231 cases in 1999, 3,122 cases in 2000, 3,145 cases in 2001, and 3,310 cases in 2002.

In addition to its original and appellate jurisdiction, the supreme court has administrative responsibilities. The court has supervisory authority over all state courts, and the supreme court has the authority to appoint an administrative director and staff who serve at the pleasure of the court. The court also has the power to assign temporarily judges to other circuits as needed. The supreme court also provides for an annual judicial conference to design improvements to the administration of justice and to the courts in Illinois.

The seven justices on the supreme court sit en banc for all decisions. Three supreme court judges come from Cook County, and one judge each from the remaining four districts.

Appellate Court

The Illinois Appellate Court is divided geographically into five regions. The appeals court hears appeals from the circuit courts on final judgments and mandatory interlocutory appeals on procedural issues that are either irreversible or would affect the outcome of a trial. The appellate court also has power of direct review of administrative action, as provided by law. The Appellate Court of Illinois saw 8,903 case filings, 4,857 of which were civil and 4,046 of which were criminal.

Appeals courts are advised to publish opinions only where there is some precedent-setting potential. Otherwise justices sit in panels of three judges to review cases, and occasionally sit en banc. In Cook County, with the court's headquarters in Chicago, the appeals court is further divided into subdivisions for administrative convenience.

Trial Courts

The state is divided into twenty-two judicial circuits, and all circuits, except for the first circuit in Cook County, are divided into fifteen subcircuits. The Illinois circuit courts are the courts of general jurisdiction and have original jurisdiction over all matters except those given exclusively to the supreme court. Circuit courts also have the power of direct review of administrative action, as provided by law. Associate circuit judges are not allowed to preside over criminal cases where an individual is facing a sentence of one or more years. The circuit courts saw 4.1 million case filings in 2003. This included more than 2.7 million traffic cases, 737,557 civil cases, 89,020 felony criminal cases, and 42,867 juvenile cases.

Selection and Removal of Judges

Supreme court, appellate court, and circuit court judges are all publicly elected in partisan elections. In the case of vacan-

Illinois Supreme Court Chief Justice James Heiple faced impeachment and state judicial disciplinary commission charges in 1997. He was accused of abusing his power to get out of traffic citations. The proceedings prompted Heiple to step aside as chief justice, but he stayed on the court until the end of his term in 2000. (AP/Wide World Photos)

cies, primary elections in the spring will determine who among several candidates will become each party's candidate in a fall general election.

A judge in Illinois is required to be a U.S. citizen, a resident of the unit from which they are selected, licensed to practice law in the state, and under the age of seventy-five. Supreme court and appellate court judges are elected to terms of ten years and circuit court judges are elected to terms of six years. After serving their terms, judges who wish to serve an additional term are placed on the ballot for retention. A judge stands in an uncontested retention election and must receive 60 percent of the vote to be retained for an additional term. In the event of interim vacancies due to death, resignation, retirement, or removal of a judge at any level, the supreme court appoints the replacement, and that person will serve until the next general election, unless the next general election is less than sixty days away.

The state is divided into five appellate districts for the purpose of selecting supreme court and appellate court judges. Eighteen appellate court judges are selected from the first judicial district with six judges each selected for each of the remaining four districts. Circuit court judges are elected at the subcircuit level. Circuit courts are served by 391 associate judges who are appointed by the judges of each circuit. Associate judges serve four-year terms. These judges generally try misdemeanors, set bail in felony cases, and handle divorces or smaller civil actions.

The chief justice is selected by a majority vote of the supreme court and serves a term of three years. By courtesy, selection of the chief justice usually comes on a seniority basis, with justices taking turns from senior to junior justices over the course of a ten-year period.

The chief judge of the appellate court is chosen by a majority vote of appellate court judges in each appellate district and serves a term of one year. The chief judge of each circuit is chosen by a majority vote of the judges in that circuit and serves at the pleasure of the court.

Article IV of the Illinois Constitution provides for a Judicial Inquiry Board, comprised of two circuit judges selected by the supreme court, and three lawyers and four nonlawyers, chosen by the governor. No more than two of the lawyers or two of the nonlawyers can be from the same political party. Board members serve terms of four years, and no board member can serve more than eight years. The board has the authority to "conduct investigations, receive or initiate complaints concerning a Judge or associate judge, and file complaints with the Courts Commission."

The Independent Courts Commission, also provided for in the constitution, consists of one supreme court justice (selected by that court as a member) and one alternate, as well as two appellate court judges (selected by the supreme court as members), and three alternates, and two citizens selected by the governor as members. Appellate court members must be from different districts and circuit court members must be from different circuits. The commission meets to hear complaints filed by the Judicial Inquiry Board. The commission has the authority to reprimand a judge, censure a judge, suspend a judge without pay, or to remove a judge from office.

Judges may also be impeached by a majority vote of the House of Representatives and removed by a two-thirds vote of the senate.

Ruth Ann Watry
Northern Michigan University

Further Reading

American Judicature Society, "Center for Judicial Selection," http://www.ajs.org /selection/index.asp.

Gove, Samuel Kimball, and James D. Nowlan. 1996. *Illinois Politics and Government: The Expanding Metropolitan Frontier.* Lincoln: University of Nebraska Press.

Supreme Court of Illinois, http://www.state.il.us/court/.

INDIANA
●●●●●●●●●●●●●

Indiana was among the six states that had territory impacted by the Northwest Ordinance of 1787. Until 1800, at which time Ohio Territory had sufficient population for self-government, the entire Northwest Territory was ruled by a military governor and a general court of three judges. The judiciary, along with the governor, also acted as a legislature. In 1800, the Indiana Territory was created by Congress, and in 1809 was split into the Indiana and Illinois Territories. In 1816, Indiana became a state.

The Indiana Supreme Court was created by the new state constitution. It consisted of three judges appointed by the governor for terms of seven years. The supreme court had appellate jurisdiction over cases arising under state law, as well as original jurisdiction in capital cases, cases of chancery, or cases where the president of a circuit court had a conflict of interest. The constitution also allowed for circuit courts and such other inferior courts that the general assembly chose to create. The state was divided into three circuits, each of which had three judges (one was circuit president) appointed by the governor for terms of seven years. A new constitution in 1851 modified the appearance of the judiciary. The judiciary was still made up of a supreme court, circuit courts, and inferior courts created by the general assembly. The supreme court was set at having three to six members, elected for terms of six years. The general assembly set the size of the supreme court at four justices in 1853, and increased it to five in 1872. Circuit courts, consisting of one judge, were to have criminal and civil jurisdiction. Judges were elected by the voters for a term of six years.

The constitution was amended in 1881, most recently, and for purposes of the judiciary, again in 1970. The judicial power of Indiana now lies in one supreme court, one court of appeals, circuit courts, and other courts that the general assembly chooses to create. Judges of the supreme court and the court of appeals are selected using a merit selection plan while other judges are elected.

Indiana Supreme Court

Indiana has three constitutional courts. The Indiana Supreme Court is comprised of five justices, including a chief justice who is chosen by the Judicial Nominating Commission. In 2005 justices on the Indiana Supreme Court included Chief

Justice Randall T. Shepard and associate justices Brent E. Dickson, Frank Sullivan Jr., Theodore R. Boehm, and Robert D. Rucker.

The Indiana Supreme Court has exclusive original jurisdiction over admission to the practice of law; discipline and disbarment of lawyers; unauthorized practice of law; discipline, removal, and retirement of judges; supervision of the exercise of jurisdiction by other courts; issuance of writs necessary in aid of its jurisdiction; appeals from judgments imposing the death sentence; appeals from denial of post-conviction relief where the death penalty has been imposed; appealable cases where a state or federal law has been declared unconstitutional; and cases involving substantial questions of law, great public importance, or emergency. In fiscal year 2003, 1,097 cases were filed in the Indiana Supreme Court. Of these, majority opinions or published dispositive orders were issued in 198 cases.

Court of Appeals

The appeals court is divided into five geographic districts, each served by three judges. The fifteen judges select a chief judge, and each of the five districts elects a presiding judge. All cases are considered by a panel of three judges.

The appeals court has no original jurisdiction, except where the supreme court has given it authority to directly review final actions of administrative agencies. The appeals court has appellate jurisdiction over all cases not taken directly to the supreme court. During the same year, the Indiana appeals court saw 2,299 cases

filed. The court affirmed lower court decisions 76.5 percent of the time. Oral arguments were held in only fifty-nine cases.

Trial Courts

Trial courts of general jurisdiction are the circuit courts. Indiana has 90 circuits employing 102 judges. Eighty-eight of the ninety-two counties in the state make up eighty-eight of the circuits, while the remaining four counties make up two circuits.

The superior court is a court created by the general assembly. There are currently 71 superior courts employing 193 judges. An additional court in Indiana is the St. Joseph Probate Court, which is served by one judge. Although county courts still operate in Indiana, the majority of them have been converted into superior courts. As of December 31, 2003, only four county courts remained in Indiana. City and town courts can be created by local ordinance. As of December 31, 2003, there were forty-seven city courts and twenty-seven town courts in Indiana. Finally, Marion County has a small-claims court served by nine judges.

Circuit courts have unlimited trial jurisdiction over all cases, except where other courts have been given exclusive or concurrent jurisdiction. They also have appellate jurisdiction over cases coming from city and town courts. Circuits in counties without superior or county courts maintain small-claims divisions. Circuit courts may also have a division that deals with minor offenses, some felonies, misdemeanors, infractions, and ordinance violations.

Superior courts are generally courts of general jurisdiction, and often have appellate jurisdiction over appeals from city and town courts. As with circuit courts, superior courts in counties without county courts often have a small-claims division. County courts have original and appellate jurisdiction in class D felonies, misdemeanor and infraction cases, violations of local ordinances, and in all civil cases where damages do not exceed $10,000. Appeals from county courts go directly to the court of appeals.

Town and city courts have jurisdiction over ordinance violations, misdemeanors, and infractions. They also have jurisdiction over city civil cases involving less than $500. Cases from these courts are appealed to a circuit court or a superior court. The small-claims court in Marion County has jurisdiction over civil cases where the damages do not exceed $6,000.

The Indiana Tax Court had 342 cases on its docket during the same time period. Included are cases involving the Board of Tax Review, the Department of Revenue, and county elections.

The majority of cases dealt with by the Indiana judiciary are within the trial courts. In Indiana's circuit, superior, probate, and county courts, over 1.3 million cases were filed in fiscal year 2003. This included 1.1 million criminal cases, 68,577 juvenile cases, almost 300,000 small-claims cases, over 215,000 civil cases, and almost 26,000 probate and adoption cases. This reflects a decrease in the number of cases from fiscal years 2001 and 2002. These numbers do not include cases decided by town and city courts.

Selection and Removal of Judges

Supreme court and court of appeals judges in Indiana are chosen through the merit selection method. The Commission on Judicial Qualifications acts as the state Judicial Nominating Commission. The commission is comprised of the chief justice of Indiana, who is an ex-officio member and chairman of the commission, three lay citizens appointed by the governor from three geographic districts, and three attorney members elected by lawyers from each of the three respective districts. Lay and attorney members serve three-year terms. The commission recruits and interviews applicants for vacancies, and then forwards three names to the governor. The governor then chooses one of those individuals for the judicial vacancy. At the next general election, after the judge has served at least two years, the judge stands for an appointment election. If the judge receives a majority of the vote, he or she serves a term of ten years, after which the judge once again has an appointment election. In the event that an interim vacancy occurs, it is filled in the same manner. Judges must be citizens of the United States, a resident of the state, admitted to state practice of law for ten years, or served as a judge of a trial court for five years, and under the age of seventy-five. Judges of the tax court are also chosen in this manner and serve terms of ten years. Judges of the tax court must be citizens of the United States, a resident of the state, admitted to state practice of law for five years, and must be under the age of seventy-five.

Circuit court and superior court judges are selected through partisan elections, with the exception of Vanderburgh County, where elections are nonpartisan. In addition, in Lake and St. Joseph counties, superior court judges are selected using the merit selection method, discussed earlier. Superior court judges in Allen County are selected using nonpartisan elections, while vacancies are filled by the Judicial Nominating Commission. Circuit court and superior court judges serve terms of six years. In the event that an interim vacancy occurs, it is filled by gubernatorial appointment, and the individual stands for election at the next general election. Judges in these two courts must be a resident of the circuit in which they serve, must have been admitted to the Indiana bar for at least five years, and must be under the age of seventy-five.

Judges of the probate court in St. Joseph County, county courts, town courts, city courts, and the small-claims court in Marion County are also selected through partisan elections. Judges of the probate court in St. Joseph County must be admitted to practice law in the state while judges of the county court must be a U.S. citizen, a county resident, and admitted to practice law in the state. Some town and city courts require judges to be attorneys while others do not. Judges of the small-claims court in Marion County are required to be U.S. citizens, residents of the county, admitted to practice law in

the state, and residents of the township for at least one year.

The Commission on Judicial Qualifications has authority over discipline of judges in Indiana. The commission is comprised of the chief justice of Indiana, who is an ex-officio member and chairman of the commission, three lay citizens appointed by the governor from three geographic districts, and three attorney members elected by lawyers from each of the three respective districts. Lay and attorney members serve three-year terms. On recommendation of the commission, the supreme court may discipline, suspend, retire, or remove a judge. Judges may also be impeached by the house of representatives and convicted by the senate. Finally, judges may be removed by a joint resolution of the general assembly, upon agreement of two-thirds of the members of each house.

Ruth Ann Watry
Northern Michigan University

Further Reading

American Judicature Society, "Center for Judicial Selection," http://www.ajs.org/selection/index.asp.

Harmon, Robert B. 1990. *Government and Politics in Indiana: A Selected Guide to Information Sources.* Monticello, IL: Vance Bibliographies.

Indiana Courts, http://www.in.gov/judiciary/ (accessed March 29, 2006).

Indiana Courts Annual Report, http://www.in.gov.judiciary/admin/.

IOWA

The Territorial Government of Iowa was created on June 12, 1838. The law establishing the territory also established a supreme court, probate courts, district courts, and justices of the peace. The supreme court, appointed by the president, consisted of a chief justice and two associate justices, each serving terms of four years. In 1846, Iowa became the twenty-ninth state. The Iowa Constitution provided for a supreme court whose justices were elected by a joint vote of both houses of the general assembly, to six-year terms. A new constitution in 1857 vested the judicial power in a supreme court, district courts, and such lower courts as established by the general assembly. The supreme court had three justices who were elected to six-year terms. District court judges were also elected by the people. The number of judicial districts increased as the population of the state increased. Likewise, as the size of the state increased, the number of supreme court justices also increased, going from four in 1864, to six in 1894, to eight in 1927, and to nine in 1929.

In 1962 voters in Iowa adopted a constitutional amendment requiring merit selection system for the selection of judges (explained later). In 1965 a mandatory retirement age of seventy-two was set for all judges. In 1969, a system of eighteen chief judges was established to supervise the judicial districts, although in 1972, the eighteen judicial districts were consolidated into eight, each with a chief judge who serves a two-year term. These chief judges, along with the chief justice of the supreme court, make up the judicial council, which advises the supreme court on administrative matters.

The Unified Trial Court Act of 1973 abolished justices of the peace, and mayor's, municipal, and police courts and, instead, created a unified trial court known as the Iowa District Court. The establishment of judicial magistrates, who are not required to be attorneys, freed many district court judges from having to process simple misdemeanor cases, small-claims cases, and other simple matters.

Iowa got its first intermediate appellate court in 1976 with the creation of the Iowa Court of Appeals, a court with five members. In 1983 the Court Reorganization Act shifted the expense of operating the court system from the counties to the state. Funding for juvenile court officers, bailiffs, and indigent defense was no longer a responsibility of the county. In 1998 the legislature approved the Appellate Restructuring Plan which increased the number of Iowa Court of Appeals judges from six to nine, and reduced the number of supreme court judges to seven. This change came because the supreme court had been hearing cases that should have been heard at the court of appeals, which was working above capacity while the supreme court was working below capacity. The 1998 plan seems to have fixed that problem.

Organization of State Courts

The Iowa court system is led by a seven–member supreme court. The chief justice of the supreme court is elected by a majority of the members of the court. The Iowa Court of Appeals has nine members. The chief judge is also elected by a majority of the members of the court. The trial level of the Iowa court system is its district courts. There are eight judicial districts, employing in 2002, 116 district judges, 35 senior judges, 135 magistrates, 12 associate juvenile judges, 1 associate probate judge, and 81 district court clerks.

Powers of State Courts

The supreme court has general appellate jurisdiction over civil and criminal cases, appellate jurisdiction over all final judgments and interlocutory orders, and has original jurisdiction over cases involving reapportionment and cases involving bar discipline. All appeals go directly to the supreme court, which then has the power to transfer cases to the nine–member Iowa Court of Appeals. The supreme court also has supervisory and administrative responsibilities. As the leader of the Iowa judiciary, the supreme court oversees a staff of approximately 1,900 individuals as well as a budget of $100 million. The court is assisted in this task by the office of the state court administrator. The Iowa Court of Appeals has the power to hear only those cases transferred to it by the supreme court.

The district court is the court of general jurisdiction. It has exclusive jurisdiction over civil, domestic, and probate cases as well as juvenile, criminal, and traffic violation cases. This court also hears appeals from magistrate court and district associate courts. Judicial magistrates hear simple cases within their counties of residence. This includes civil suits for money judgments involving less than $5,000 and simple misdemeanors. Associate juvenile judges have authority over orders, findings, and decisions in juvenile cases involving neglect, abuse, delinquency, and termination of parental rights. Associate probate judges have jurisdiction over probate matters such as conservatorships, trusts, and estates, and district associate judges have the jurisdiction of judicial magistrates as well as the jurisdiction to hear aggravated misdemeanor cases and civil suits involving $10,000 or less.

Selection of Judges

Prior to 1962, judges in Iowa were selected by the voters. In 1962, voters approved a constitutional amendment that established a merit selection process for Iowa judges. Selection of judges begins with a nonpartisan commission of lawyers and nonlawyers. It is the commission's job to review the qualifications of applicants for judicial office. The commission selects a group of names and advances that list to the governor. The governor then makes his or her appointment from that list of names. A judge is subject to a retention election as he or she nears the end of the term. If the judge receives the majority of the vote in the retention election, another term can be served. Since Iowa began using retention elections, only four judges have lost.

There is some variation in how judges for the different courts are chosen. All judges, with the exception of judicial magistrates, must be lawyers admitted to practice law in Iowa. Nominees for all appointments must be of such an age that they can serve out their full term prior to reaching age seventy-two. Appellate court judges (including the supreme court) are selected by the State Nominating Commission, which is composed of a chair, as well as one lawyer commissioner and one nonlawyer commissioner from each of the seven congressional districts that existed in 1962. Within sixty days of receiving notice of a vacancy from the secretary of state, the commission must advance a list of nominees (three names for supreme court and five names for court of appeals) to the governor. The governor must make the appointment from this list of names. Supreme court justices serve terms of eight years, while court of appeals judges serve terms of six years.

District nominating commissions are responsible for screening and selecting nominees for district court judgeships. There is a nominating commission for each of Iowa's judicial election subdistricts. Each commission has eleven members, including the most senior district court judge in the district who acts as the chair, five lawyer members chosen by the lawyers in the district, and five nonlawyer members, chosen by the governor. Commissioners serve six-year terms.

When a vacancy occurs, the commission provides the governor with a list of two names from which to make the appointment. District court judges serve terms of six years.

The County Magistrate Appointing Commission assists with the selection of district associate judges, associate juvenile judges, associate probate judges, and magistrates. The commission is made up of a district court judge chosen by the chief judge of the judicial district, up to three nonlawyer judges selected by the board of supervisors, and up to two attorneys selected by attorneys in the county. Within thirty days of receiving notice of a vacancy, the commission advances a list of three nominees to the chief judge of the district from which the district judges make a final selection. These judges serve terms of six years each.

Discipline

The state supreme court and the Judicial Qualifications Commission are responsible for disciplining judges and other employees of the judicial branch. The Iowa Code of Judicial Conduct creates the standards that all Iowa judges are expected to maintain. It includes seven canons, covering everything from maintenance of the integrity and independence of the judiciary to compensation for quasi-judicial and extra-judicial activities. If a judge is accused of violating one of these canons, his or her case will be heard by the Judicial Qualifications Commission. The commission will make a recommendation to the supreme court concerning appropriate discipline.

Workload

In 2002, there was a combined total of 2,129 cases filed in the Iowa Supreme Court and the Iowa Court of Appeals. This was a slight increase (2 percent) from the previous year. There were over one million cases filed in the district courts (1,065,328), including 75,615 civil cases, 87,921 criminal cases, 12,329 juvenile cases, 17,019 probate cases, and 89,171 small-claims cases.

Ruth Ann Watry
Northern Michigan University

Further Reading

American Judicature Society, "Center for Judicial Selection," http://www.ajs .org/selection/index.asp.

Harmon, Robert B. 1990. *Government and Politics in Iowa: A Selected Guide to Information Sources.* Monticello, IL: Vance Bibliographies.

Iowa Code of Judicial Conduct, http://judicial.state.ia.us/judges/ conduct.asp.

Iowa Judicial Branch, http://www .judicial.state.ia.us/.

KANSAS
• • • • • • • • • • • •

Congress created the Kansas Territory on May 30, 1854, and at the same time it created a supreme court for the territory. The supreme court consisted of one chief justice and two additional justices. The president appointed them for a term of four years each. The Kansas Territory was made up of three judicial districts, and each of the three supreme court justices also served as a district court trial judge for one of the districts.

On January 29, 1861, when Kansas became a state, the state constitution created a supreme court as well as district courts (trial courts). The supreme court was still made up of three justices, though they would now be elected at large, for a six-year term. In 1885 voters rejected an amendment that would have increased the size of the supreme court. The legislature then went and created commissioners of the supreme court, who were selected by the governor (with consent of the senate) to serve three-year terms and to help the supreme court with its large number of pending cases (this legislation was later extended beyond the three years). Commissioners had the same power to decide cases as the justices. Between 1887 and 1893, the commissioners were handling as many cases as the supreme court, but the legislature was still unsuccessful in increasing the number of justices on the court.

During this time, the size of the population, and the subsequent number of cases being heard in the courts, was increasing rapidly. In 1895, the legislature created the Kansas Court of Appeals, but this was just a temporary solution. The legislation was set to expire in 1901, and then another solution for the heavy appellate caseload would have to be found. Any permanent change in the structure of the

Kansas courts required a constitutional amendment, which needed voter approval. In 1900 voters approved an amendment that increased the size of the supreme court to seven members (its current size). The judges were still elected for six-year terms, although the chief justice was now the justice on the court with the longest term of service on that court.

In 1958, the method of selecting Kansas judges changed from elections to a merit appointment method (explained later). In 1977 the court of appeals was reestablished as a seven-member court, and in 1987 it was expanded to eleven judges (ten judges plus one chief judge). With the introduction of this court of appeals, the supreme court has discretion concerning which appeals it chooses to hear.

State Supreme Court

The supreme court is the highest court in Kansas. It is made up of seven justices. The chief justice has the longest continuous service.

The supreme court functions primarily as a discretionary appellate court, reviewing the decisions of lower courts. It hears cases heard previously by the court of appeals and also has the power to transfer a case from another court to the supreme court. In the fiscal year ending June 30, 2004, almost 507,500 cases were filed in the Kansas courts with 118 filed in the supreme court.

The supreme court has administrative authority over all Kansas courts, oversees admission of attorneys to the state bar, sets forth a code of professional responsibility for attorneys, and governs the conduct of judges. The personnel plan governing all nonjudicial employees in the Kansas court system was adopted and is administered by the supreme court. The Office of Judicial Administration oversees payroll and personnel records of these employees. The supreme court also prepares the budget for the entire judicial branch and presents it to the Kansas legislature.

Court of Appeals

The court of appeals, which has existed since 1977, has ten members and serves as an intermediate appellate court. The court typically sits in three-judge panels, but it can also hear cases en banc.

The court of appeals hears appeals from the State Corporation Commission, appeals of civil and criminal cases heard in the district courts, and also has discretionary jurisdiction to hear original actions in habeas corpus. During 2004, 1,695 cases were brought before the appellate courts.

Trial Courts

District courts, the trial courts of Kansas, were created by the 1861 constitution. The state is currently divided into six judicial departments—geographic divisions, each of which includes multiple districts. A district court judge is assigned by the supreme court to head each of these departments. There are 31 judicial districts comprised of 234 district court judges. All except eight of the districts also employ magistrate judges. These individuals, who are not required to be lawyers, are able to reduce the workload of the district court judges.

Municipal courts exist to settle cases involving violations of city ordinances that occur within the city limits. These often include traffic violations and other minor offenses. A person is not given the right to a jury trial, and if a person is unhappy with the outcome in this court, he or she may appeal the case to the district court of the county in which the municipal court is located.

Kansas's district courts have original jurisdiction over all civil and criminal cases. This includes (but is not limited to) small claims, juvenile cases, family matters (divorce, custody, etc.), and probate cases. Although municipal courts have the jurisdiction to hear cases involving the violation of city ordinances, the district courts also have jurisdiction over these cases. If a person is not satisfied with the outcome in a municipal court, he or she can appeal the case to the district court. In 2004, 505,650 cases were filed in the district courts. At the district court level, this resulted in an average annual caseload of 2,790 cases per judge in districts that did not have magistrate judges, and 1,900 cases per judge in districts with magistrate judges. This difference is explained by the fact that magistrate judges are able, among other things, to preside over traffic cases, removing those cases from the pool of cases in the district courts judge caseload.

Selection and Removal of Judges

Like many states, Kansas selects its judges using the Missouri Plan or a merit selection and retention vote. When a vacancy occurs on the supreme court, the Supreme Court Nominating Commission provides the governor with a list of three qualified candidates. The Supreme Court Nominating Commission is comprised of four lawyer members (one from each congressional district), four nonlawyer members (one from each congressional district), and one additional lawyer to act as the chairperson. Commission members serve four-year terms. Once the governor receives the list of three names, the governor appoints one of these individuals to the supreme court, and after he or she has served as a justice for one year, that person is subject to a retention vote at the next regularly scheduled election (the justice up for retention is the only name on the ballot). If the justice is retained he or she serves a six-year term, and is then again subject to a retention vote. Appellate judges are selected in a similar manner. The governor receives the list of three names from the Supreme Court Nominating Commission, selects one name, and then that individual is subject to a retention election after one year. Court of appeals judges serve four-year terms and are then again subject to another retention election. Supreme court justices and appellate judges must be at least thirty years old, no older than seventy years old, a state resident, and a practicing attorney in the state for at least ten years.

District court judges and district magistrate judges are selected in two different ways. In some districts, voters have chosen to select district judges by merit selection and retention vote. In these districts, district magistrate judges are selected by the Supreme Court Nominating Commission, without participation by the governor. In other districts, district judges and district magistrate judges are selected in partisan elections. In either case, judges serve a four-year term. District court judges must be a resident of Kansas, a member of the Kansas bar in good standing for at least five years, and less than seventy years old.

Disciplinary powers over judges within the Kansas judiciary rest within the supreme court. The supreme court has the power to discipline attorneys, judges, and nonjudicial employees. Kansas state law, most recently amended in 1995, lays out a code of judicial conduct. The code addresses integrity and independence of the judiciary, appearance of impropriety, impartial and diligent performance of duties, extra-judicial activities, and political activity. The law also provides guidelines concerning the investigation process, the elements and procedural rights during the hearing (if one is held), and the possible outcomes if a judge is in violation of the code. If a judge is unhappy with the decision made by the Commission on Judicial Qualifications, he or she can request to have the case heard by the supreme court.

Ruth Ann Watry
Northern Michigan University

Further Reading

American Judicature Society, "Center for Judicial Selection," http://www.ajs.org/selection/index.asp.

Harmon, Robert B. 1990. *Government and Politics in Kansas: A Selected Guide to Information Sources.* Monticello, IL: Vance Bibliographies.

Kansas Judicial Branch, http://www.kscourts.org/.

KENTUCKY
• • • • • • • • • • •

As a border state, Kentucky has been a battleground for conflicting national political forces. Kentucky was the first American frontier west of the Appalachians; its frontier period lasted into the 1850s. Individuals with the traditionalistic political culture of Virginia and the Carolinas settled the new frontier. These early settlers also brought with them their elitist orientation toward the power of state government and politics. Kentucky was admitted to the Union in 1792 as the fifteenth state. Since then Kentucky has had four constitutions. The first three were in 1792, 1799, and 1850, respectively. The fourth and current constitution was adopted in 1891.

Prior to the unified court of justice, Kentucky had many types of courts. These included the police and county courts, quarterly courts, and justices of the peace with overlapping jurisdiction. In November 1975, voters affirmed the unification of the state's judicial system. The need to revise the current constitution began in 1964 when the Constitutional Revision Assembly (CRA) was created. After initial proposal rejections, the final draft, which included a unified court system, was approved by voters. The chief justice now serves as the chief executive and administrator of the unified court of justice. The court of justice includes the supreme court, court of appeals, circuit courts, and district courts. Only 35 of Kentucky's 120 counties voted in favor of unification with support coming from the largest metropolitan areas.

Kentucky Supreme Court

The Kentucky Supreme Court is the court of last resort and the final interpreter of state law. Though it hears appeals of decisions from the lower state courts, cases that involve the death penalty, life imprisonment, or imprisonment for twenty years or more go directly from the trial court to the supreme court for review. A case that comes before the supreme court for review is not retried. There are no witnesses, juries, or testimony. Attorneys present the supreme court with written briefs and oral arguments addressing the legal issues to be decided by the court. Seven justices review cases as a panel and issue written decisions. In 2002, the supreme court alone had 1,155 filings and 1,123 dispositions.

Seven justices from seven appellate districts are elected to the court for eight-year terms in nonpartisan elections. To qualify for election to the supreme court, one must have been licensed to practice law for eight years and have lived in the appellate district for at least two years. Supreme court justices choose a chief justice who serves for a four-year term. This person becomes the administrative head

of the state's court system and is responsible for its management and operation. The supreme court promulgates rules of practice and procedure for the entire court of justice, for the conduct of attorneys and judges, and for procedures to be followed by all state court officials.

Court of Appeals

The court of appeals reviews decisions of the trial-level circuit court. Most cases go to the court of appeals on appeal of a trial decision of the circuit court or a district court judgment. The court of appeals reviews the original trial record with attorneys presenting the legal issues to the court for a decision. The court of appeals has fourteen judges who sit in panels of three or en banc. The panels travel throughout Kentucky to hear appeals. The court of appeals occasionally publishes its rulings on cases. Those rulings become the governing case law for all similar cases in the trial courts of Kentucky. In 2002, the court of appeals disposed of nearly 2,900 petitions (Strickland 2003, 108–109).

Trial Courts

In 1975 voters passed a constitutional amendment that replaced the commonwealth's fragmented judicial system with its current unified system. The circuit court is Kentucky's general jurisdiction court. The commonwealth is divided into fifty-six judicial circuits with ninety-six circuit judges. There also are circuit family courts with thirty-three judges. Each circuit judge is elected to an eight-year term in nonpartisan elections. A judge may serve one or more counties. Similarly, a judicial circuit may contain one or more counties with several judges. The number of judges in any circuit depends on its population and caseload.

Circuit courts hear civil cases with values of more than $4,000 and other civil matters. It has exclusive jurisdiction over felonies (including capital offenses). Circuit courts also have appellate jurisdiction from district courts. The circuit courts have the power to issue injunctions, writs of prohibition, writs of mandamus, and to hear appeals from both district courts and administrative agencies. The newly created circuit family court has thirty-three judges in forty-two counties. Kentucky will make family courts accessible to all its citizens within ten years.

Recent caseload statistics show that 103,200 cases were filed in Kentucky's circuit courts and 103,801 cases were closed. Of those cases filed, 29,900 were criminal cases, 46,600 were civil cases, and 17,200 were family cases. The remaining filings were appeals, administrative boards, and other miscellaneous filings.

District Courts

The district courts, referred to as "the people's courts," have limited jurisdiction. Kentucky has 60 district courts and 129 district judges who serve those courts. Districts with a large population and relatively heavy caseloads may consist of only a county but will have several judges. Rural and less populated districts may cover more than one county. The district courts have jurisdiction over property cases less than $4,000, estate, mental health issues, small claims less than $1,500, paternity, probate of wills, and misdemeanors (exclusive of traffic offenses and juvenile offenses), and these courts also conduct preliminary hearings. Nearly 830,000 cases were filed in district courts in 2004. A large number of those cases involved traffic offenses (384, 800). District courts cleared somewhat fewer cases than were filed, 818,800. The appeals court dealt with 2,600 filings and 2,900 dispositions.

Associated Agencies

The Administrative Office of the Courts, established in 1976, provides support services to the commonwealth's chief justice. The administrator also manages the court of justice under the direction of the chief justice. The Division of Accounting, the Division of Information Distribution, the Division of Printing, and the Division of Purchasing provide support services to the courts. The Research and Statistics unit of the Administrative Office of the Court has the primary responsibility of collecting data on judiciary cases in the state.

The Judicial Conduct Commission investigates complaints and if necessary disciplines judges. The commission judges include one judge from each of the courts of appeals, circuit courts, and district courts.

Judicial Selection and Removal

The supreme court justices and appellate court judges are elected in nonpartisan elections from seven appellate districts to their respective courts. Kentucky has strict laws prohibiting judges from engaging in partisan activities. It is against state law for both incumbent judges and candidates for judicial offices to participate in partisan political functions. Though individuals can speak at political gatherings they are not to identify themselves as belonging to any one particular political party. Judicial candidates including judges are prohibited from becoming officers in political organizations, or from soliciting money for political parties or organizations. Additionally, they are not to raise money for their own campaigns, but could establish committees to raise funds for their campaigns.

To qualify to become a supreme court justice, a court of appeals judge, or a circuit court judge one must be a citizen of the United States, at least thirty-five years of age, and licensed to practice law in the state for at least eight years. Those interested in becoming a district court judge must be licensed to practice law for two years prior to seeking office. Supreme court justices select a chief justice to serve a four-year term. In the case of a vacancy, the governor appoints a judge from a list of three qualified names provided by the Judicial Nominating Commission. If the governor does not make an appointment within sixty days of the vacancy, the chief justice can fill the position.

A Judicial Retirement and Removal Commission holds hearings upon complaints that a judge behaves unprofessionally. This commission may reprimand, suspend, or remove a judge from office.

The operating budget for Kentucky's unified court of justice is approximately $234.6 million for fiscal year (FY) 2005 and $243 million for FY 2006. The legislature uses program budgeting and is not specific as to the particular programs except for designation of certain expenditures.

Kwame Badu Antwi-Boasiako
Stephen F. Austin State University

Doug Goodman
Mississippi State University

References and Further Reading

Administrative Office of the Courts. 2000. "Justice in Our Commonwealth 2000" (Reader No. P-1). Frankfort, KY: Administrative Office of the Courts.

Barker, Thomas G. 2002. "Official Immunity in Kentucky: The New Standard Under *Yanero v. Davis*." *Kentucky Law Journal* 90 (Spring): 635.

Channing, Steven A. 1977. *Kentucky: A Bicentennial History*. New York: Norton Publications.

Kentucky Court of Justice, http://www .kycourts.net/ (accessed October 31, 2005).

———. Office of Budget and Policy, http://www.kycourts.net/AOC/BPR/ Budget/Budget.shtm (accessed October 31, 2005).

Lancaster, Nancy. 1985. "Judicial Reform in Kentucky." *Accent on Courts* 7 (4).

Miller, Penny M. 1993. *Kentucky Politics and Government: Do We Stand United?* Lincoln, NE: University of Nebraska Press.

Stickland, Shauna M. 2003. *State Court Caseload Statistics*. Williamsburg, VA: National Center for State Courts.

LOUISIANA

The French initially claimed Louisiana, but turned it over to Spain in 1763. Louisiana's early settlers were Spanish, French, and Acadian (French Canadians from Nova Scotia). In 1800, Spain ceded Louisiana back to the French who then sold it to the United States in 1803. After the Louisiana Purchase, the Territorial Legislature of Orleans formally based its law in Roman and Spanish civil code. Territorial Governor Claiborne vetoed the civil law system, but two years later the civil code was adopted. After statehood in 1812, Louisiana readopted this form with the civil code of 1825. Its third civil code was adopted after the Civil War, in 1870, which is still in use today. Over the years, English common law has crept into the civil law system.

The primary difference between civil law and common law is the civil code. In civil law, the legislature is supreme. Judges must base their decisions on legislative intent—based on the civil code—instead of judicial precedent. Judicial precedent is not binding in civil law. Furthermore, civil law is deductive in nature. The civil code provides the bases for decisions.

Supreme Court

Housed in New Orleans, the Louisiana Supreme Court has one chief justice and six associate justices who sit en banc. The chief justice is the chief administrative officer of Louisiana's judicial system. The state's constitution creates six supreme court districts, with at least one judge elected from each of the districts.

The supreme court's reviewing authority in civil cases extends to both law and facts. In criminal matters, its appellate jurisdiction extends only to questions of law. The supreme court has mandatory jurisdiction if a law or ordinance has been declared unconstitutional, the defendant has been convicted of a capital offense and a penalty of death actually has been imposed, regarding judicial disciplinary actions, and in administrative agency cases. In 2004, there were 3,228 filings with the Supreme Court. The filings represent a 9 percent decrease in filings from 2003. The Supreme Court handed down nearly 314 opinions in 2004.

The supreme court supervises all other courts in the state. It promulgates rules and procedures. It may assign a sitting or retired judge to any court. The supreme court has sole authority to provide, by rule, for appointments of attorneys as temporary or ad hoc judges of city, municipal, traffic, parish, juvenile, or family courts. The supreme court also has exclusive original jurisdiction for disciplinary proceedings against a member of the bar. The supreme court includes other officers such as the clerk of the supreme court and the Office of the Judicial Administrator.

Court of Appeals

The state is divided into five appellate circuits, with one court of appeal in each circuit. Louisiana has fifty-three appellate judges. The first, third, and fourth circuits each have twelve judges. The second circuit and fifth circuits have nine and eight judges, respectively. In 2003, more than 9,500 appeals were filed with the courts of appeal. Like many intermediate appellate courts, the courts of appeal in Louisiana have mandatory cases they hear and discretion over other cases. These courts have mandatory jurisdiction in civil, noncapital criminal cases, administrative agency, and juvenile cases. Each court sits in panels of at least three judges. A majority of the judges sitting in a case must concur to render judgment. If there is a dissent in a civil matter that overturns or modifies a district court ruling, the case must be reargued before at least five judges.

General Jurisdiction Courts

Louisiana's main court of general original jurisdiction is the district court. District courts also have appellate jurisdiction from courts of limited jurisdiction. Louisiana has 40 judicial districts with more than 200 judges statewide. There are also four juvenile courts and one family court. Louisiana has four juvenile courts with jurisdiction over juveniles, adoption, interstate support, and mental health. There is also one family court in East Baton Rouge that handles mental health issues, juveniles, domestic violence, marriage, dissolution, support and custody issues, and paternity cases.

District courts have jurisdiction over all civil and criminal matters and exclusive jurisdiction over felony cases and es-

tate matters. District courts also hear election disputes, probate, marriage, divorce, and other matters of equity unless otherwise stated by the legislature. Each district court selects a chief judge who performs administrative functions prescribed by rule. In 2004, there were more than 740,000 cases filed in district courts in Louisiana.

Limited Jurisdiction Courts

Louisiana has several limited jurisdiction courts, of limited dollar value, misdemeanor criminal complaints, and some family relations cases. Justice of the peace courts hear civil and small-claims cases (less than $2,000), and traffic cases. Mayor's courts hear traffic cases and misdemeanors. City and parish courts hear civil cases less than $15,000, small claims (less than $2,000), paternity and domestic relations cases, misdemeanor, traffic, and some juvenile cases. These courts also conduct preliminary hearings for felony cases. City and parish courts also have appellate jurisdiction over civil appeals from justice of the peace courts. These courts hear cases from the bench rather than by a jury.

Selection and Discipline of Judges

All judges in Louisiana are elected. Elections are held during the regular congressional election. Supreme court justices and courts of appeal judges are elected in nonpartisan elections to ten-year terms. Qualifications for all judges of the supreme court, courts of appeal, district court, family court, parish court, or court having solely juvenile jurisdiction are that they have to be licensed to practice law in Louisiana for at least five years prior to election. They also must live in the respective jurisdiction for the two years preceding election. Judges may not practice law while on the bench.

Vacancies are filled by special election. The supreme court appoints an interim judge or justice to serve until the special election. The interim judge is not eligible for election to the position. Often these vacancies are filled with retirees, willing to perform short-term services. Judges cannot run for election after their seventieth birthday. A judge who attains seventy years of age while serving a term of office is allowed to complete that term of office. The chief justice and chief judges are selected based on seniority.

The judiciary commission investigates complaints against judges and justices. It then gives a disciplinary recommendation to the supreme court. Penalties may include censure, suspension with or without salary, removal from office, or involuntary retirement. Judges may be penalized for willful official misconduct, persistent failure to perform their duties, persistent and public conduct prejudicial to the administration of justice, behavior that brings the judicial office into disrepute, or felony criminal activity.

The nine-member judiciary commission consists of one appellate judge and two district court judges selected by the supreme court, two licensed attorneys with ten years' experience, one attorney with at least three to ten years' experi-ence, and three citizens selected by the Louisiana District Judges' Association.

Associated Offices

In addition to the Louisiana Judiciary Commission, the court system is supported by the Judicial Council of Louisiana and the Louisiana Judicial College, which are associations that lobby and network judges. The Louisiana Attorney Disciplinary Board and the Bar Admissions Committee are concerned with admitting and disciplining lawyers. The Office of the Judicial Administrator is part of the supreme court's administrative arm.

The Louisiana fiscal year (FY) 2004 judicial budget was $112 million. The budget does not fund the state's entire judicial system. The state funds the supreme court and the district courts of appeals. The state also funds the salaries of supreme court justices and appellate court and district court judges. It also partly funds parish and city court salaries (Supreme Court of Louisiana 2005).

Doug Goodman
Mississippi State University

James A. Newman
Idaho State University

References and Further Reading

Labbe, Ronald. 1982. "The Judiciary." In *Louisiana Politics: Festive in a Labyrinth*, ed. James Bolner. Baton Rouge, LA: Louisiana State University Press.

Louisiana First Circuit Court of Appeal. 2004. "A Brief History of the Louisiana Appellate Court System," http://www.la-fcca.org/history.htm (accessed August 18, 2004).

Supreme Court of Louisiana. 2004. "The Louisiana Supreme Court," http://www.lasc.org/index.asp (accessed August 18, 2004).

———. 2005. *The Supreme Court of Louisiana: Annual Report 2005 of the Judicial Council of the Supreme Court.* New Orleans: Judicial Administrator's Office, http://www.lasc.org/press_room/annual_reports/reports/2004_ar.pdf (accessed November 21, 2005).

Willard, Valerie S., ed. 2004. *The Supreme Court of Louisiana: Annual Report 2003 of the Judicial Council of the Supreme Court.* New Orleans: Judicial Administrator's Office.

MAINE

Originally part of Massachusetts, Maine was admitted as a free state in 1820 as part of the Missouri Compromise. Historically more conservative than its neighbors, politics in the twenty-third state were dominated by Republicans after Democrats expressed reluctance to take a firm antislavery stance during the 1850s. Another hot-button issue involved prohibition—Maine was the first state to adopt such a law in 1851 that was later incorporated into its constitution in 1884 and then not repealed until 1934. The state's supreme court was called on to settle a heated political debate in 1879 when it seated a Republican legislature after uncovering evidence of election fraud by Democrats. The state remained largely controlled by Republicans through the 1950s. In the intervening years, Maine has contributed several prominent leaders to national politics. Today, the state has an estimated population of 1.3 million residents who are governed by a bicameral legislature comprised of 35 senators and 151 representatives, all of whom serve two-year terms.

Organization of the State Judiciary

There are three levels to the Maine judiciary—the supreme court, trial courts (district and superior), and county courts. The composition, organization, jurisdiction, and unique characteristics of each are enumerated in the discussion that follows.

For fiscal year 2004, the Maine judiciary operated on a budget of $51,503,196, which constituted only 1.9 percent of the state's general fund. This budget allows the system to serve the population through its 49 courts in 41 locations occupied by 56 justices, 8 family case management officers, and 398 support personnel. By comparison to operating costs, the judiciary as a whole collected $38,917,688 in revenues for the state during fiscal year 2004—an increase of just over $7 million (22 percent) from the previous period.

Supreme Court

Also referred to colloquially as the "law court," the Maine Supreme Court was created in 1820 when Maine seceded from Massachusetts and was admitted to statehood as part of the Missouri Compromise. Consisting of one chief justice and six associate justices, it is the court of final appeal. The principal task of the court is to resolve criminal and civil appeals arising from lower levels of the state judiciary. In addition to being the final arbiter of state legal matters, the court issues advisory opinions when requested by the executive or legislative branches. It oversees admission to the state's bar and, where necessary, disciplines judges and attorneys. Other tasks include hearing appeals from the Public Utilities Commission and the Workers' Compensation Board. Last, the supreme court establishes operational procedures for all lower-level courts.

With regard to workload, the court received 753 filings in 2004. Of these, the largest portion were civil in nature (270), followed by those of a criminal nature (228). Workers' compensation cases comprised another 126 cases, with the remaining filings arising from the family/divorce context (85) or child protection (44).

Superior Court

The superior court system was created in 1930 and situated in each of the state's counties. The sixteen superior courts hear criminal and civil cases with the exception of those involving family matters and juvenile offenses. A superior court chief justice, appointed by the supreme court chief justice, is responsible for overseeing the daily administrative affairs at this level of the judiciary. A deputy chief judge assists in these and other duties. A unique aspect about the superior court is that it is the only one to employ trial by jury. In civil cases where the plaintiff seeks monetary damages, he or she can file in either superior court (and request trial by jury) or district court (as a matter of convenient location). Consequently, it hears a wide variety of cases ranging from murder to low-level class E misdemeanors. For 2004, superior courts received 15,381 filings. The largest portion of these (12,051) were criminal in nature while the remaining 3,366 were civil matters.

District Court

Created by the state legislature in 1961, there presently exists thirteen districts with a total of thirty-one courts occupied by thirty-three justices situated throughout the state. The primary task of these courts is to resolve sundry criminal, civil, and familial cases by bench trial—no jury trials are conducted at this level of the judiciary. Cases involving familial matters are heard by a special family division that was created in 1988 and is staffed by case management officers—specially trained quasi-judicial officers with limited authority to issue protective and child support orders. Cases involving small claims not to exceed $4,500 also fall under the jurisdiction of the district court. The chief judge sets aside special dates on the docket to hear cases where parties appear without legal representation under relaxed procedures. Class D and E offenses as well as all traffic violations are heard at the district level.

District courts received 129,071 filings for 2004. Of these, the clear majority were criminal (61,862) followed by civil (17,618) cases. Other matters presented to superior courts for resolution included civil violations (15,171), protective petitions (11,958), familial disputes (divorce—8,963), small claims (8,884), and juvenile adjudications (4,615). Additionally, 138,673 traffic violations were forwarded to the district courts. These cases generated $17.7 million in revenue for fiscal year (FY) 2004. This amount constituted 48 percent of all fines and fees collected by the entire state judiciary.

County Courts

Also referred to as probate courts, county courts were created by the state's constitution in 1820 and are situated in each of the sixteen counties with one judge assigned to each. The primary task of these courts is to resolve estate, trust, adoption, and guardianship cases by bench trial (no jury). Judges are elected and serve in a part-time capacity. Although not technically under control of the state court system, county courts are included in this description because they preside over many proceedings central to the judiciary. Information regarding the workload and resources of county courts is not readily available given the decentralized nature of their administration.

Administrative Support

As noted earlier, probate courts are administered at the county level, independent of the state's larger judicial structure. However, operation of the district and superior courts, as well as the supreme court are supported by the Administrative Office of the Courts. The administrator and staff are responsible for collecting statistical data on workload, managing financial resources, maintaining facilities, and conducting relevant in-service training for court personnel.

Selection of Judges

With the exception of probate courts, Maine judges are selected through a federal method. The governor appoints judges to seven-year terms with senate confirmation. Probate judges are locally elected on a partisan ballot. For the supreme and superior courts, appointees must be learned in the law; however, on the other courts judges are expected to hold a license to practice law.

Discipline and Removal of Judges

Maine judges may be removed in one of three ways: First, judges may be impeached by the House of Representatives and convicted by a two-thirds vote of the senate. Second, judges may be removed upon the address by the governor of both houses of the legislature. Finally, the supreme judicial court may remove, retire, or discipline judges with the recommendation of the Committee on Judicial Responsibility and Disability.

R. Alan Thompson
Old Dominion University

References

Administrative Office of the Courts, "State of Maine Judicial Branch: Courts," http://www.courts.state.me.us /mainecourts/index.html (accessed April 25, 2005).

Coogan, W. H. 2004. "Citizen's Guide to the Maine Courts." Portland, ME: Administrative Office of the Courts.

Maine Constitution. 2004. Art. VI, Section 3.

———. Duties of Chief Judge. 4 Maine Revised Statutes, Section 164.

———. Duties of State Court Administrator. 4 Maine Revised Statutes, Section 17.

———. Superior Court; Civil Jurisdiction. 4 Maine Revised Statutes, Section 105.

MARYLAND
● ● ● ● ● ● ● ● ● ● ● ●

The colony of Maryland had one of the first American feudal charters issued by the king of England. George Calvert is commonly known as the father of Maryland, but died before he could implement his plans for the charter. Maryland, named after Queen Henrietta Maria, was thereafter chartered to Calvert's son, Cecilius Calvert. Cecilius transformed Maryland into a prosperous colony where those who had previously suffered from religious oppression could avoid persecution. The first settlers arrived in 1634 and prospered from the Calvert administration as well as the lack of Native American attacks. However, Virginia was a formidable enemy for many years. At one point, the governor of Virginia took possession of Maryland. During the Virginian occupation, the Maryland Toleration Act was enacted. The Maryland Toleration Act required anyone who did not believe in the Holy Trinity to be put to death. However, Calvert soon regained control of Maryland and sent his son, George Calvert, to be the lord. Maryland remained in the control of the Calvert family until the colony obtained independence following the Revolutionary War (Elson 1904).

Maryland Court of Appeals

The Maryland Court of Appeals is possibly the oldest appellate court in the country. During settlement, Maryland created a general assembly that consisted of a legislature as well as the court. However, in 1650, the assembly was divided, resulting in the court of appeals. The ratification of the Maryland Constitution in 1776 transformed the court of appeals by allowing the governor to appoint the judges with the advice and consent of the executive council.

The court of appeals has undergone many improvements throughout the years. The full court has been sitting in Annapolis since 1851. Presently, the court of appeals consists of seven justices from seven judicial districts, who are initially nominated by the governor and subject to confirmation by the senate. Justices serve ten-year terms, but may be removed from the bench by the governor with agreement from two-thirds of the House and the assembly.

The chief justice of the court of appeals is selected by the governor with the advice and consent of the senate. Five justices constitute a quorum, but the court may designate additional justices to hear the case. If the case is equally divided in a three-to-two vote, the entire court may be convened to hear the case on the petition of the losing party (Maryland Constitution 1776).

The court of appeals is the primary appellate court and retains exclusive jurisdiction over redistricting, death penalty cases, and the removal of officers. Since the creation of the court of special appeals in 1966, the court of appeals, with the exception of those matters over which it has exclusive jurisdiction, uses discretionary review to determine which cases it will hear. Thus, parties aggrieved by the decision of the court of special appeals can file a petition for writ of certiorari pending, or following, a decision of the court of special appeals. Petitions are granted and writs issued if the case involves significant legal issues.

In addition to functioning as the highest appellate court, the court of appeals is also responsible for bar admissions and disciplinary actions against judges or attorneys. In 2004, the court admitted 1,408 persons to practice law within Maryland. Within that same fiscal year the court of appeals heard 136 docketed cases, 664 petitions for certiorari, and conducted 85 attorney grievances.

The chief justice of the court of appeals earns an annual salary of $151,352. Associate judges earn annual salaries of $132,352. An appellate court judge must retire by his or her seventieth birthday.

Maryland Court of Special Appeals

The court of special appeals also sits in Annapolis. This court was created in 1966 to ease the workload of an overburdened court of appeals. The court of special appeals sits three-judge panels. If a majority of the incumbent judges feels it is necessary, the court may sit en banc. With the exception of death penalty cases, the court has jurisdiction over appeals from the circuit courts. The court also hears postconviction matters typically raised by criminal defendants, who, by virtue of the entry of a guilty plea, are unable to file a direct appeal. During the 2004 fiscal year, the special court of appeals rendered 1,360 opinions and disposed 1,936 appeals.

The court of special appeals consists of thirteen judges. Seven are appointed by the governor with the consent of the senate, one from each judicial district, with the remaining six to be selected at large. The judges serve ten-year terms. When the appointed term expires, judges may be elected and returned to the bench (Management Analysis and Research 2004).

The chief judge of the court of special appeals is chosen by the governor. The chief justice currently earns an annual salary of $127,552. Associate judges earn an annual salary of $124,552. All are required to retire at age seventy.

Maryland Circuit Courts

There are eight circuit court districts throughout Maryland that are comprised of twenty-four circuit courts in the twenty-three counties and one court in Baltimore City. Circuit courts have general jurisdiction in major civil cases, serious criminal matters, domestic relations, juvenile matters, and orphans' court matters. Circuit courts function as an appellate court in cases involving appeals from decisions of administrative agencies and certain appeals from the district courts.

In addition, circuit courts are responsible for recording and maintaining land records and transactions. Circuit courts also issue business and marriage licenses. Given their broad jurisdiction and administrative responsibilities, it is not surprising that circuit courts reported approximately 290,000 filings for fiscal year 2004. Of that number, approximately 90,000 were family matters, 75,000 were general civil matters, 78,000 were criminal matters, and 36,000 were matters involving juveniles.

There are approximately 146 circuit court judges throughout the state of Maryland. The most senior judge within each circuit serves as the chief judge for that circuit. In addition to the judicial duties, the chief judge performs administrative functions for the circuit court district. Circuit judges earn an annual salary of approximately $120,352.

Juvenile Courts

Each of the twenty-three counties and Baltimore City has a juvenile court. Juvenile courts are a division of the circuit court system and are vested with jurisdiction over individuals under the age of eighteen. Juvenile courts may retain jurisdiction over a child until the child attains the age of twenty-one and hear cases involving abused and neglected children, status offenders, alcohol violations, runaways, adoptions, delinquencies, and terminations of parental rights.

Orphans' Court

The orphans' court was developed in 1777 to handle probate matters. It, along with the circuit court, has jurisdiction over estate and guardianship matters. Three judges preside over the orphans' court. These judges are elected to serve ten-year terms or until the judge's mandatory retirement at age seventy.

Maryland District Court

There are twelve district court districts throughout Maryland. Currently, there are thirty-four district courts. Each county has at least one judge presiding, and one presides in Baltimore City. The court hears civil claims involving less than $25,000 in damages, landlord-tenant issues, criminal misdemeanors, certain felonies, requests for protective orders, and traffic violations. Jury trials are not used in the district courts. In fiscal year 2004, the district court reported

2,466,774 filings. Of that number, 214,321 were criminal matters and 158,697 were traffic cases.

With the advice and consent of the senate, the governor appoints the district court judges for ten-year terms. District court judges must retire on reaching the age of seventy. The chief judge of the court of appeals appoints a chief judge of the district court who earns an annual salary of $124,552 (Constitution of Maryland 1776; Maryland Judiciary). District court judges earn approximately $112,252.

District court headquarters assists with the administrative functions of the district courts. Under the direction of the chief clerk, headquarters is home to four administrative departments including Operations, Administrative Services, Engineering and Central Services, and Finance.

Maryland Tax Court

The Maryland Tax Court was created in 1959 to hear matters involving income, sales, and property taxes. The tax court can also hear cases that challenge the constitutionality of certain legislative acts involving taxation. Taxpayers may proceed either pro se or with legal counsel.

The tax court consists of five judges that are appointed by the governor for six-year terms. The judges must reflect representation of the major political parties. The chief judge of the tax court is appointed by the governor. The chief judge and at least one other member of the court must be members of the Maryland bar. Judges of the tax court may but are not required to sit in panels. In fact, tax court cases may be determined by single judges.

Administrative Office of Courts

Created by the Maryland legislature, the Administrative Office of Courts is responsible for providing administrative assistance and support to the chief judge of the court of appeals. The Administrative Office of Courts functions under the leadership and supervision of the state court administrator who serves at the will and pleasure of the chief judge of the court of appeals. The office performs the following functions: human resources, research and planning, administration of family divisions, case management, data collection, and analysis and budgeting.

Maryland's Commission on Judicial Disabilities

In 1966, the Commission on Judicial Disabilities was established by constitutional amendment. The eleven-member commission investigates and conducts proceedings in cases involving complaints against judges. Three members of the commission must be judges serving on the circuit court, district court, and court of special appeals. Remaining panel members consist of three attorneys and five laypersons. Commission members are appointed by the governor for terms ranging from two to four years.

Selection and Removal of Judges

With the exception of the orphans' court, Maryland's judges are selected through a Missouri method. There is a selection commission, which refers eligible nominees to the governor. This commission, though, is a creation of the governor's executive order, which a governor may rescind at his or her discretion. The governor chooses a name for nomination and the state senate votes to ratify. Orphans' court judges are chosen by partisan election. Appellate and circuit court judges are retained by election, while district court judges are reappointed. Judges must be U.S. and state citizens; registered to vote in state elections; and state residents for at least five years by the time of taking office. They must be between thirty and seventy years of age and licensed to practice law.

Judges must retire by the age of seventy. They also may be removed from office in one of four other ways. First, judges may be removed by the governor on the address of the general assembly with the concurrence of two-thirds of the members of each house. Second, judges may be retired by the general assembly with a two-thirds vote of each house and the governor's concurrence. Third, judges may be impeached by a majority of the house of delegates and convicted by two-thirds of the senate. Finally, judges may be removed or retired by the court of appeals on the recommendation of the Commission on Judicial Disabilities.

Vicki Lindsay and Lisa S. Nored
University of Southern Mississippi

References

Constitution of Maryland, http://www .mdarchives.state.md.us/msa/mdmanual /43const/html/const.html (accessed April 4, 2005).

Elson, H. W. 1904. *History of the United States of America.* New York: Macmillan.

Management Analysis and Research. 2004. *Annual Report of the Maryland Judiciary—2003–2004,* http://www .courts.state.md.us/publications/annualr eport/arstats0304.pdf (accessed April 4, 2005).

Maryland Archives. 1999. "Archives of Maryland Historical List: Maryland Court of Appeals," http://www .mdarchives.state.md.us/msa/speccol/ sc2600/sc2685/html/ctappeals.html (accessed April 4, 2005).

Maryland Judiciary, http://www.courts .state.md.us (accessed March 29, 2006).

Maryland Judiciary Court of Appeals, http://www.courts.state.md.us/coappeals /coaoverview.html (accessed March 29, 2006).

Sandler, Paul Mark, and Andrew D. Levy, eds. 2001. *Appellate Practice for the Maryland Lawyer: State and Federal.* Baltimore: Maryland Institute for Continuing Professional Education of Lawyers.

MASSACHUSETTS
• • • • • • • • • • • •

In 1620, the Pilgrims set sail for North America seeking religious freedom and soon established the colony of Plymouth. The Mayflower Compact established a democratic government and bound all colonists to the will of the majority. The colony prospered and in 1621 the Pilgrims celebrated the first Thanksgiving. In 1628, a royal charter was granted to the Massachusetts Bay Company to promote the settlement of the territory. The charter served as the foundation of the government of the Massachusetts Bay Colony and specifically provided for a general court, governor, and a deputy governor.

By 1684, the Massachusetts Bay Colony charter was revoked when the colonists resisted stricter control by the British monarchy. In 1691, the Massachusetts Bay Colony became a royal province. The Crown appointed a governor and approved the establishment of two legislative houses.

Massachusetts experienced significant population growth and was thriving economically while England was involved with the Second Hundred Years' War. However, in need of revenue, England enacted a series of acts that inflamed the bay settlers beginning with the Sugar Act (1764), the Stamp Act (1765), and the Tea Act (1773). Following the Boston Massacre (1770) and the Boston Tea Party (1773), the American Revolution began.

In 1780, nine years before the American Constitution was ratified, the Mass-achusetts Constitution was ratified. The Massachusetts Constitution is the oldest functioning written constitution in existence. The Massachusetts Constitution provided for three branches: executive, legislative, and judicial. John Hancock was elected the first governor under the new constitution.

Massachusetts Supreme Judicial Court

The Massachusetts Supreme Judicial Court (SJC) is the highest court in the Commonwealth of Massachusetts. The formerly named superior court of judicature was established in 1692. SJC is the oldest continuously running appellate court in the Western Hemisphere. The name of the superior court of judicature was changed to Massachusetts Supreme Judicial Court with the ratification of the constitution in 1780. The court consists of six associate justices and a chief justice. Each justice is appointed at the pleasure of the governor with approval by the executive council. Judicial appointments are held until the mandatory retirement age of seventy. The court sits from September through May, and hears over 800 cases annually. The single justices render over 600 decisions, while the full bench renders about 200 written decisions a year.

The SJC hears civil and criminal appeals. Aside from appellate matters, additional duties of the court include advising the governor and the legislature on legal questions, making rules for the operation of all courts, and supervisory functions over the judiciary and the bar. Each associate justice sits singly hearing appellate motions, bail reviews, petitions for admission to the bar, and bar disciplinary proceedings. They perform their duties singly on a monthly rotation schedule (Supreme Judicial Court). In 2000, the chief justice of the SJC received a salary of $132,000, with the associate justices receiving $127,000 (National Center for State Courts).

The Massachusetts Supreme Judicial Court is one of the most reputable state supreme courts in the United States. The court has handed down both contentious and progressive rulings in the past 300 years. Landmark cases rendered by this court include *Commonwealth v. Jennison* (1783), *Roberts v. Boston* (1850), and *Goodridge et al. v. Department of Public Health* (2003) (Supreme Judicial Court).

In *Commonwealth v. Jennison* (1783), the Massachusetts Supreme Judicial Court held that slavery was unconstitutional and the Massachusetts Constitution had in fact granted rights to individuals that were inconsistent with slavery. Jennison had been charged with assault and battery against Walker, his former slave. The attorney general argued that Jennison had assaulted a free man, while Jennison's attorney argued that the Massachusetts Constitution did not specifically forbid slavery. The jury found Jennison guilty, thereby allowing slaves to sue their masters for freedom and thus ending slavery in the state of Massachusetts (Slavery in the North).

Lemuel Shaw was one of the most influential jurists of the nineteenth century. He was chief justice of the Massachusetts Supreme Judicial Court for almost 30 years, and many of his decisions remained valid law for a century or more. (Library of Congress)

In *Roberts v. Boston* (1850), the Massachusetts Supreme Judicial Court led by Chief Justice Lemuel Shaw established the now infamous separate-but-equal doctrine. The court had before it the case of a five-year-old girl, Roberts, who was attending the Smith School. The Smith School was a feebly supported "colored" school. The court concluded that Roberts had not proven that the Smith School was inferior to those schools for white children. Furthermore, the fact that the

Smith School was racially segregated was not a violation of the rights of African American students. As a result, the *Roberts* decision authorized the school board to assign students to schools based on race, if necessary. This case was later cited in the infamous U.S. Supreme Court decision *Plessy v. Ferguson* (1896).

In *Goodridge et al. v. Department of Public Health* (2003), the Massachusetts Supreme Judicial Court held that the denial of marriage licenses to same-sex couples violated the Massachusetts Constitution. Seven gay and lesbian couples who were denied marriage licenses at their local towns or city halls sued the Department of Public Health. Attorneys for the plaintiffs argued that the Massachusetts Constitution afforded gay and lesbian couples the right to marry. Moreover, the basic protections of equality and liberty guaranteed by the Massachusetts Constitution were not being afforded to gay and lesbian couples in denying them the right to marry. The court agreed and found that gay and lesbian couples were not prohibited from marrying according to the Massachusetts Constitution.

Massachusetts Appeals Court

The Massachusetts Appeals Court is a general appellate court created in 1972. The court hears appeals from the trial court. In addition to hearing appeals from the seven departments of the trial court, the Massachusetts Appeals Court also hears appeals from the Appellate Tax Board and the Labor Relations Commis-

sion. The appeals court has concurrent appellate jurisdiction with the Massachusetts Supreme Judicial Court. The appeals court consists of a chief justice and twenty-four associate justices. The appeals court sits in panels of three justices. In addition, single justices sit for a month at a time. They have the authority to hear interlocutory orders, motions for stays in civil and criminal proceedings, and orders for injunctive relief. The court hears cases in Boston every month from September through June. In addition, the court holds session in locations outside of Boston throughout the year (Administrative Office of the Trial Court). In 2000, the chief justice of the appeals court received a salary of $122,000, with the associate justices receiving $117,000 (National Center for State Courts).

Administrative Office of the Trial Court and the Massachusetts Trial Courts

The Administrative Office of the Trial Court was created in 1978 to manage the trial court. The Office of the Trial Court oversees seven judicial departments. These include the Housing Court Department, the Boston Municipal Court Department, the Land Court Department, the Superior Court Department, the District Court Department, the Juvenile Court Department, and the Probate and Family Court departments. In addition, the Administrative Office of the Trial Court has supervisory authority over the Office of the Commissioner of Probation and the Office of the Jury Commissioner. In 2000, the state court administrator received a salary of $122,000 (National Center for State Courts).

In 1978, the Massachusetts legislature created the Massachusetts Trial Court. Prior to 1978, the county or local courts administered all trial courts. Currently, there are 362 judicial positions in the trial court system. The trial courts are the largest part of the Massachusetts judiciary.

Housing Court Department

The housing court has jurisdiction over cases involving landlord-tenant disputes, violations of housing codes, and evictions. Further, the housing court has concurrent jurisdiction with the district and superior courts regarding civil matters including torts, discrimination, contracts, and small claims. The court has six primary locations. The housing court consists of a chief justice and nine associate justices (Administrative Office of the Trial Court). In 2000, the chief justice of the housing court received a salary of $117,000, with the associate justices receiving $113,000 (National Center for State Courts).

Boston Municipal Court Department

The Boston Municipal Court has civil and criminal jurisdiction. In addition, the court shares concurrent jurisdiction with the superior court over felonies. The court's civil jurisdiction includes torts, contracts, small claims, mental health commitments, and paternity and domestic abuse actions. The court consists of a chief justice and twenty-nine associate justices. In 2004, 505,008 criminal charges were filed in the court. In addition, there were 16,443 civil matters filed (Massachusetts Trial Courts 2004). In 2000, the chief justice of the Boston Municipal Court received a salary of $117,000, with the associate justices receiving $113,000 (National Center for State Courts).

Land Court Department

The land court is designed to hear cases involving real property. The court has statewide jurisdiction and has original jurisdiction over the registration of titles to real property and over title disputes. The court has a chief justice and five associate justices. In 2004, there were 79,559 new and pending cases (Administrative Office of the Trial Court). In 2000, the chief justice of the land court received a salary of $117,000, with the associate justices receiving $113,000 (National Center for State Courts).

Superior Court Department

The superior court has jurisdiction in civil actions over $25,000 and matters where equitable relief is sought. In addition, the court hears labor disputes and medical malpractice matters. The court consists of a chief justice and eighty-one associate justices. In 2004, there were 1,145 new and pending cases (Administrative Office of the Trial Court). In 2000, the chief justice of the superior court received a salary of $117,000, with the associate justices receiving $113,000 (National Center for State Courts).

District Court Department

The district court has jurisdiction over a variety of matters. The court hears civil matters with no monetary limit, including small claims. The court's criminal jurisdiction includes all felonies punishable up to five years in prison and all misdemeanors. The district court consists of a chief justice and 157 associate justices. In 2004, there were 764,415 new and pending cases (Administrative Office of the Trial Court). In 2000, the chief justice of the district court received a salary of $117,000, with the associate justices receiving $113,000 (National Center for State Courts).

Juvenile Court Department

The juvenile court has jurisdiction over all matters concerning juveniles, including delinquent juveniles, children in need of supervision, adoption, guardianship, and termination of parental rights. The court consists of a chief justice and forty associate justices. In 2004, there were 45,135 new and pending cases (Administrative Office of the Trial Court). In 2000, the chief justice of the juvenile court received a salary of $117,000, with the associate justices receiving $113,000 (National Center for State Courts).

Probate and Family Court Department

The probate and family court has jurisdiction over family matters, including divorce, paternity, child support, child custody, adoption, and abuse prevention. The court also has jurisdiction over probate matters, including wills, conservator-ships, and guardianships. The court consists of a chief justice and fifty associate justices. In 2004, there were 149,786 cases filed with this court (Administrative Office of the Trial Court). In 2000, the chief justice of the probate and family court received a salary of $117,000, with the associate justices receiving $113,000 (National Center for State Courts).

Selection and Removal of Judges

Judges in Massachusetts are chosen by a nominating commission and gubernatorial appointment with legislative approval. There is no retention election. A judge must be a U.S. citizen, state resident, and state bar member in good standing. To be eligible to assume a place on the court a judicial nominee must have ten years legal experience and training.

Massachusetts judges may be removed in one of three ways. First the Commission on Judicial Conduct investigates complaints of judicial misconduct. Following a formal hearing, the commission may recommend to the supreme judicial court removal, retirement, or reprimand of a judge. The governor, with consent of the governor's council, may remove judges on the joint address of both houses of the general court. The governor, with consent of the governor's council, may also retire judges because of advanced age or mental or physical disability. Judges may be impeached by the House of Representatives and convicted by the senate.

Sara Buck
University of Southern Misssissippi

References and Further Reading

Administrative Office of the Trial Court, http://www .mass.gov/courts.

National Center for State Courts, http:// www.ncsonline.org.

Slavery in the North, http://www.slavenorth.com.htm.

Supreme Judicial Court, http://www .mass.gov/courtssupremejudicalcourt .html.

The Supreme Judicial Court Historical Society, http://www.sjchs-history.org.

Cases

Commonwealth v. Jennison (1783), *Proceedings of the Massachusetts Historical Society*, Vols. 1873–1875: 292–295, http://www.lexisnexis .com/academic/1univ/hist/aa/aas_case .asp (accessed March 26, 2006).

Goodridge et al. v. Department of Public Health (2003), 440 Mass. 309.

Plessy v. Ferguson. 1896. 163 U.S. 537.

Roberts v. Boston (1850), 59 Mass (5 Cush.).

MICHIGAN

• • • • • • • • • • •

The judiciary is a product of the 1963 Michigan Constitution and the Revised Judiciary Act of 1961, and its subsequent amendments. Michigan's first constitution was adopted in 1835, and was revised in 1850, 1908, and 1963. The 1835 Constitution of Michigan (territory) provided that "The judicial power shall be vested in one supreme court, and in such other courts as the legislature, may, from time to time, establish" (Article VI, Section1). Justices of the supreme court were to be appointed by the governor, approved by the senate, and to serve terms of seven years. The constitution also mentions a court of probate to be organized in each county, with terms of four years for "Judges of all County Courts, Associate Judges of circuit courts and judges of Probate," who were to be elected by qualified voters. The constitution also allowed for each township to elect four justices of the peace, each of whom would hold office for four years, allowing the legislature to

increase the number of justices of the peace when necessary.

The 1850 Constitution of Michigan, adopted on receiving statehood, was very explicit about the judiciary (Article VI, which dealt with the judiciary, had thirty-five sections). It provided that "The judicial power is vested in one supreme court, in circuit courts, in probate courts and in justices of the peace. Municipal courts and courts of civil and criminal jurisdiction may be established by the Legislature in cities" (Article VI, Section 1). The supreme court would originally be made up of circuit court judges, and would eventually be comprised of one chief justice and three associate justices. There were six circuits, one judge was assigned to each, and the term of a circuit court judge was six years. The constitution addressed everything from terms of the court to clerks of the court to rights of the accused and bail and due process.

In 1908, Michigan once again ratified a new constitution. The courts discussed in section 1 of the judiciary article are the same as those in the 1850 constitution. The size of the supreme court, as well as the terms of the justices, was set by the legislature. The legislature also created judicial circuits, each of which would have one judge. The constitution provided that each county could have a probate judge, holding office for a term of four years, and each organized township would have no more than four elected justices of the peace.

Michigan once again adopted a new constitution in 1963. It is this constitution, as well as the Revised Judiciary Act of 1961, that has created the judiciary operating in Michigan today.

Organization of State Courts

The Michigan Constitution reads that "the judicial power of the state is vested exclusively in one court of justice which shall be divided into one supreme court, one court of appeals, one trial court of general jurisdiction known as the circuit court, one probate court, and courts of limited jurisdiction that the legislature may establish by a two-thirds vote of the members elected and serving in each house" (Article VI, Section 1).

The supreme court is at the top of the Michigan judicial system. A court of last resort, the supreme court consists of seven justices.

The Michigan Court of Appeals is comprised of four appellate districts, each of which is assigned seven judges. Districts are constructed to be relatively equal in population, and judges hear cases in various locations in the state. Cases are heard by three-judge panels.

The trial court of general jurisdiction is the circuit court. Michigan is divided into 57 circuits, staffed by 210 judges. A second layer of trial courts is the district court. Michigan is divided into ninety-six districts. Additionally, each Michigan county has a probate court, with the exception of ten counties that have combined to form five probate court districts.

As of January 1, 2005, Michigan circuit courts have the power to create drug treatment courts. This court would involve collaboration with the prosecuting attorney and the criminal defense bar, as well as representatives of community treatment providers. The family division of the circuit court also has the power to create a juvenile drug treatment court. Once again, Michigan law requires that collaboration occur among various groups in the judiciary and the community.

Powers of State Courts

The Michigan Supreme Court is Michigan's court of last resort. The supreme court annually reviews approximately 2,000 applications seeking review. The majority of cases come from the Michigan Court of Appeals. The court has discretion as to which cases it will hear, although it issues an order or opinion in all cases, whether or not oral argument occurred. The supreme court is also responsible for the general administration and supervision of all state courts, and establishes rules for practice and procedure in the courts.

The Michigan Court of Appeals is an intermediate appellate court. In 2003, 54 percent of the cases that came to the court of appeals were decided by order, while 46 percent were by opinion. The court mainly hears cases coming from circuit courts.

Michigan's fifty-seven circuit courts have jurisdiction over criminal cases involving felony or serious misdemeanors, civil cases involving over $25,000, family division cases (divorce, paternity actions, juvenile proceedings, and adoptions), and appeals from administrative agencies and other courts. Circuit courts also act as supervisors over other courts in their circuit.

Michigan's ninety-six district courts are Michigan's courts of limited jurisdiction. They have jurisdiction over civil claims involving less that $25,000 including small claims, landlord-tenant disputes, civil infractions, and land contract disputes. They also handle a large range of criminal cases including misdemeanors where the maximum penalty is less than one year in jail. District courts also assist circuit courts in felony cases by conducting preliminary examinations. Most district courts also have a probation department, which follows an individual sentenced to probation. District court judges also have the power to appoint district court magistrates who can hear small-claims cases, issue arrest and search warrants, arraign, and set bail.

Probate courts have jurisdiction over admission of wills, administration of estates and trusts, guardianships, conservatorships, and treatment of mentally ill and developmentally disabled persons. In many districts, probate judges also assist with the family division caseload.

Selection of Judges

Supreme court justices are elected for eight-year terms. The method of election is a combination of partisan and nonpartisan election. Political parties select candidates for supreme court justices in their primary elections, but in the general election, there is no indication of a candidate's party on the ballot. Supreme court justices' terms are staggered, with two justices elected every two years (every fourth election, only one justice is elected). The two candidates with the largest number of votes are elected. Candidates for the supreme court, as well as for the court of appeals, the circuit courts, the district courts, and the probate courts, must be licensed to practice law in Michigan for at least five years and must be under seventy years of age. Every two years, the justices elect the chief justice among themselves.

Selections of Michigan's twenty-eight court of appeals judges are conducted in a similar manner. Court of appeals judges serve six-year terms. There are seven judges assigned to each of the four appellate districts, and two judges are elected every two years (every third election, three judges are elected) for a six-year term. Michigan's 57 circuit courts are staffed by 210 circuit court judges, who serve terms of six years. Michigan's approximately 260 district court judges also serve terms of six years, as do probate judges. All are elected with a partisan primary election and a nonpartisan general election. If a judicial vacancy occurs between elections, the governor appoints a judge, choosing the nominee from names provided by the standing Committee on Judicial Qualifications of the State Bar of Michigan.

Discipline

The Judicial Tenure Commission oversees complaints concerning the conduct of judges in Michigan. The commission investigates complaints regarding judicial misconduct. After completing the investigation, the commission can dismiss the charges, admonish the judge, recommend private censure by the supreme court, or file a complaint to initiate formal proceedings. When the commission decides to file a complaint to initiate formal proceedings, the proceedings become open to public inspection. At the end of formal proceedings, the commission can recommend dismissal of the complaint, discipline, removal, retirement, or suspension of the judge. The initial investigatory stage is confidential.

In addition to being removed by the Judicial Tenure Commission, judges in Michigan can also be removed by impeachment, with a majority vote from the House of Representatives and a conviction by two-thirds of the senate. In addition, the governor can remove a judge with a concurrent resolution from two-thirds of both houses of the legislature.

Workload

In 2003, 2,256 cases were filed with the Michigan Supreme Court, while the court of appeals had 7,445 filings. Michigan circuit courts saw 335,571 case filings, while the district courts saw over three-and-a-half million cases. Finally, in 2003, the probate court saw 64,964 cases filed.

Ruth Ann Watry
Northern Michigan University

References and Further Reading

American Judicature Society, "Center for Judicial Selection," http://www.ajs .org/selection/index.asp.

Browne, William P., and Kenneth Verburg. 1995. *Michigan Politics and Government.* Lincoln, NE: University of Nebraska Press.

Michigan Courts, http://www.courts .michigan.gov/.

Michigan Supreme Court. *2003 Annual Report,* http://www.courts.michigan .gov/scao/resources/statistics/2003/2003 execsum.pdf.

Revised Judicature Act of 1961, http://michiganlegislature.org.

MINNESOTA
• • • • • • • • • • • •

The Territorial Act of 1849 that established the Minnesota Territory also created the Minnesota Supreme Court. The original supreme court had three justices who acted as both trial court and appellate judges. The judges would individually hold trials throughout the territory and would then reassemble to sit as a supreme court to review those decisions. On adoption of the state constitution in 1857 (actually adopted in 1858), Minnesota had a supreme court and district courts. The constitution also allowed for probate judges, justices of the peace, and other inferior courts. An 1875 amendment to the constitution allowed for an indefinite number of district judges in each judicial district while two 1883 amendments to the constitution changed the terms of supreme court justices and district judges from seven years to six years. Proposed amendments in 1914 and 1926 attempted to change and set the number of supreme court justices but failed.

In 1956, and again in 1972, the constitution was amended to permit the state legislature to reorganize the judicial power of the state. This was possibly in response to the American Bar Association urging state court reform such as centralization and consolidation (Elazar 1999). By 1974, the Minnesota Constitution allowed for a supreme court consisting of one chief judge and between six and eight associate justices. The legislature has chosen to put the size of the supreme court at seven. The constitution also allowed for a district court and other such courts and judicial officers as the legislature may establish. The legislature has established 10 judicial districts employing a total of 275 district court judges. A constitutional amendment approved in 1983 allowed for a court of appeals. Originally comprised of twelve judges, the court now has sixteen judges who hear cases in three-judge panels. In 1991 the Minnesota Supreme Court became the first state supreme court to be majority female.

State Supreme Court

Minnesota's judiciary is led by a seven–member supreme court. In 2004, the chief justice was Kathleen Blatz, and associate justices included Alan Page, Paul Anderson, James Gilbert, Russell Anderson, Helen Meyer, and Sam Hanson.

The supreme court hears appeals from the appellate court, the workers' compensation court of appeals, and the tax court. The supreme court is not required to hear all cases appealed to it, and often lets the lower court decision stand. It also hears appeals from the district courts involving convictions of first-degree murder as well as disciplinary matters concerning attorneys and judges. The supreme court has original jurisdiction over legislative election contests as well as writs of prohibition, habeas corpus, and mandamus. The Minnesota Supreme Court has discretionary jurisdiction. In 2003, the seven justices of the Minnesota Supreme Court dealt with 732 filings, 530 of which they did not accept for review. Supreme court justices also oversee the administration of the judicial branch and act as liaisons for the state's ten judicial districts.

The supreme court also has oversight powers over the Minnesota judiciary. Supreme court justices act as liaisons to the state's judicial districts, regulate the practice of law, and serve on various boards, task forces, and committees.

Court of Appeals

Below the supreme court is a court of appeals, made up of sixteen judges. The appellate court was created in 1983 to help reduce the supreme court's caseload, which had approached 1,800 cases per year. All cases are considered by a three-judge panel. In cases where oral argument is not heard, the court issues its opinion within ninety days of the scheduled conference day; in cases where oral argument is held, the court issues its opinion within ninety days of oral argument. The court has always met these goals.

The appellate court has jurisdiction over administrative agency decisions (with the exception of tax court and workers' compensation cases) and all trial court decisions (except for first-degree murder and decisions of the Commissioner of Economic Security). It also has original jurisdiction over writs of mandamus or prohibitions that order a trial judge or public official to perform a specified act. The appellate court disposed of 2,186 cases in 2003.

Trial Courts

The trial court level is comprised of 10 judicial districts, staffed by 275 district court judges. District courts hear juvenile, probate, criminal, civil, and family cases, as well as appeals from conciliation courts. This is the trial court of general jurisdiction in Minnesota. Conciliation courts, which are located in the district courts, are small-claims courts that can hear cases involving civil matters in amounts up to $7,500. Parties are not allowed to have attorneys, and decisions of this court can be appealed to the district courts. Finally, more than 2 million cases were filed in Minnesota's district courts in 2003. Each district court judge handles approximately 8,000 cases per year.

Limited Jurisdiction Courts

Recent additions to the Minnesota court system are seven drug courts that were created in 2003. The courts currently operate in Hennepin County (adult), Ramsey County (adult and juvenile), Dodge County (adult and juvenile), Stearns County (adult), and St. Louis County (adult). Six additional counties are planning for drug courts. There are also conciliation courts, located within the district courts, that hear civil matters in amounts up to $7,500.

Administrative Courts

Minnesota has two nonjudicial branch courts. These are the Minnesota Tax

Court and the workers' compensation court of appeals. The three judges of the tax court hear tax-related cases, while the five judges of the workers' compensation court of appeals hear cases coming from the Office of Administrative Hearings and the Workers Compensation Division of the Department of Labor and Industry.

Selection and Removal of Judges

Article VI, Section 7 of the state constitution provides that trial (district) and appellate (court of appeals and supreme court) court judges in Minnesota are to be elected for terms of six years. The constitution also allows that in the event of a midterm vacancy, the governor may appoint a judge. As a result, the majority of judges in Minnesota are initially appointed by the governor.

Judicial elections are nonpartisan at all stages of the campaign. In addition, a rule issued by the supreme court prevents candidates from seeking endorsement from political parties and from personally soliciting contributions for their campaigns, and it restricts what candidates can say during the campaign. Candidates can campaign on "integrity, maturity, health (if job related), judicial temperament, diligence, legal knowledge, ability, experience, and community service" (Minnessota Judicial Branch).

Since 1979, Minnesota governors have used a commission to assist them in appointing district court judges. In 1991, the legislator made it a requirement that the governor use the Judicial Merit Selection Commission in selecting district court judges. The commission is comprised of forty-nine members, chosen by the governor and the supreme court. It is the job of the commission to evaluate potential district court judges. The commission forwards a list of nominees to the governor; however the governor has the right to ignore the commission's recommendations. The governor acts on his or her own when appointing appellate court and supreme court positions.

The supreme court oversees the state's court system. This includes the oversight of judicial behavior and discipline, suspension, or removal of judges who have violated ethical standards. The court performs this oversight task with the assistance of the Board of Judicial Standards, an independent state agency created by the legislature in 1971. The board investigates allegations of misconduct of Minnesota judges, as well as referees and child support magistrates. It can issue private warnings or public reprimands, or it can recommend discipline to the supreme court. This discipline includes censure, suspension, retirement, or removal of judges. The board is comprised of ten members including one judge from the court of appeals, three trial judges, two lawyers with ten years of experience with the state, and four public members. Board members are limited to two full four-year terms.

Ruth Ann Watry
Northern Michigan University

References and Further Reading

American Judicature Society, "Center for Judicial Selection," http://www.ajs.org/selection/index.asp.

Elazar, Daniel Judah. 1999. *Minnesota Politics and Government*. Lincoln, NE: University of Nebraska Press.

Krueger, Christine. 1994. *Three Paths to Leadership: A Study of Women on the Minnesota Supreme Court*. St. Paul, MN: Hamline University Press.

Minnesota Guidebook to State Agency Services, http://www.yellowpages.state.mn.us.mnyp/twllowpages.nsf/.

Minnesota Judicial Branch, http://www.courts.state.mn.us/.

Minnesota Judicial Branch 2003 Annual Report, http://www.courts.state.mn.us/documents/CIO/annualreports/2003/.

MISSISSIPPI

● ● ● ● ● ● ● ● ● ● ● ●

The Mississippi Territory, organized in 1798, initially consisted of Mississippi and parts of Alabama. With the forced relocation of the Native Americans, the fertile territory was settled by white settlers from the eastern United States. The primary interest was cotton that soon became "King" in the Deep South (Skates 1973). Using slave labor, many plantation owners were able to transform cotton farming into a fortune. Mississippi became the twentieth state on December 10, 1817. The Civil War brought widespread devastation. With ratification of the Fourteenth and Fifteenth Amendments to the U.S. Constitution, Mississippi was readmitted in 1870.

With popularly elected judges, there has been growing concern about the amounts of money needed to run successful judicial campaigns. In response to the problematic 2001 supreme court elections, then-Chief Justice Edwin Pittman created the Mississippi Judicial Advisory Study Committee to evaluate judicial elections in Mississippi. Chief Justice Pittman proposed significant reforms to the process including alternative methods to select judges. Current (2006) Chief Justice James W. Smith Jr. has vowed to maintain the committee as well as the scrutiny of campaign contributions and judicial elections.

Mississippi Supreme Court

The Supreme Court of Mississippi is the only appellate court created by the Mississippi Constitution. However, review panels have been created by legislation. The supreme court has nine justices who serve eight-year terms following a nonpartisan election. Three justices are chosen from each of the three supreme court districts, the Northern District, the Central District, and the Southern District. Decisions are made by panels of three justices or the full court. In 2003 the supreme court disposed of 297 cases on merit, 204 of them were civil, and 93 criminal, and 100 more cases were motions of various sorts.

The supreme court has three primary responsibilities. First is reviewing lower court decisions; second is promulgating rules of legal practice and procedure; the last is serving as arbiter in judicial performance and proceedings. While the supreme court is authorized to assign cases to the court of appeals, it may not delegate death penalty cases, election contests, utility rate regulation, public bond issues, and cases of first impression or judicial review. Other cases the supreme court must resolve include any issues of fundamental or urgent public importance and cases involving inconsistency or conflict between the decisions rendered by the court of appeals and supreme court. In other cases, the court has discretionary review. The chief justice is designated as the chief administrative officer of all courts in the state.

Mississippi Court of Appeals

In 1993, the legislature created the court of appeals to alleviate a backlog of appeals going to the supreme court. The court of appeals hears those cases assigned to it by the supreme court. The court of appeals is comprised of ten elected judges. Like the supreme court, the court of appeals may hear cases while sitting in panels of three or en banc. In 2003, the court of appeals disposed of 543 cases on merit, 374 were civil and 169 were criminal.

Courts of General Jurisdiction

There are two courts of general jurisdiction within the Mississippi legal system. Each is a trial court and was created by the 1890 constitution. However, the division of general jurisdiction of these courts reflects the common law distinction between law and equity.

Circuit Courts

Circuit courts are trial courts of general jurisdiction. There are twenty-two circuit court districts throughout the state with forty-nine judges. Six of the districts are further divided into subdistricts. Circuit court districts are reconsidered following each federal census. Circuit courts are courts of general jurisdiction and civil and criminal matters. Circuit courts are authorized to hear civil matters where $200 or more is in controversy and they hear all felony criminal cases involving adults. Moreover, circuit courts possess appellate jurisdiction over appeals from justice or municipal courts and certain administrative proceedings.

Chancery Courts

Chancery courts are courts of equity established by the Mississippi Constitution. These courts are similar to family or probate courts that are commonly found in the majority of other states. There are forty-five chancery court judges serving twenty chancery court districts. These jurisdictions do not mirror or necessarily include the same geographic area as the circuit court districts.

Chancery courts have jurisdiction over a variety of civil matters including all matters in equity; family matters; matters testamentary and of administration; involuntary hospitalization for mental health reasons; and real estate actions. Chancery courts also possess concurrent jurisdiction with the circuit courts over certain matters involving business and financial law. If no county court exists, the chancery court serves as the juvenile court for the district.

Courts of Limited Jurisdiction

Courts of limited jurisdiction include county courts, justice courts, and municipal courts. These courts have concurrent jurisdiction over many civil and criminal matters. Appeals from the same may be taken to the appropriate circuit or chancery court.

County Courts

County courts once held the charge of enforcing the slave code and conducting felony trials involving slave defendants. Now, county courts are an interesting hybrid of appellate and trial court. Like justice courts, county courts have jurisdiction over adult misdemeanor offenses as well as noncapital felony cases transferred by the circuit court. County courts also possess jurisdiction over civil matters involving amounts not exceeding $200,000 and possess exclusive jurisdiction over matters involving eminent domain, the partition of personal property, and unlawful entry and theft.

County courts also serve as the appellate court for appeals from justice and municipal courts. Appeals from justice or municipal courts to the county court are de novo and as such, occur as an entirely new proceeding.

County courts are required in counties with populations greater than 50,000, but are optional in counties with fewer than 50,000 residents. There are currently nineteen Mississippi county courts and twenty-six county court judges.

Juvenile Court

In those counties with a county court, the courts function as the youth court. However, if there is no county court in the jurisdiction, the chancery court serves as the youth court. In Mississippi, youth courts hear cases involving juveniles including delinquency, abuse and neglect, dependency, and cases involving children in need of supervision. The youth court is a civil court whose primary focus is the protection of the best interest of the child.

Justice Courts

The justice court is the only court of limited jurisdiction that is constitutionally created. While the constitution requires that justice courts hear civil cases in excess of $500, the legislature has expanded the jurisdiction of justice courts to include civil actions under $2,500. Typically, justice courts adjudicate misdemeanor criminal offenses that occur in the county, as opposed to those that occur within the city limits, conduct initial and preliminary hearings in felony cases, make bail decisions, and entertain requests for search-and-arrest warrants.

There are currently eighty-two justice courts in Mississippi, which corresponds to the number of counties in the state.

Municipal Courts

Municipal courts are widely known as city or police courts. These courts are present in all cities, towns, and villages with a population greater than 10,000. Municipal courts hear matters involving violations of municipal ordinances and misdemeanor criminal offenses and traffic violations that occur within the city limits. In limited cases, the municipal court serves as the juvenile court. While municipal courts do not hear civil matters, municipal judges may perform marriages.

Municipal court judges are attorneys and appointed by municipal authorities, typically the mayor and/or city council, and serve at the will and pleasure of those authorities. Municipal court judgeships are considered part-time positions and most municipal judges practice law.

Selection and Removal of Judges

Mississippi selects judges by popular, nonpartisan election. The justice court elections are the exception with partisan elections. Gubernatorial appointment of judges occurs only to fill vacancies. All but county court judges must be licensed to practice law, reside, and be eligible to vote in the jurisdiction from which they are chosen. Once convicted of a felony, an individual is usually ineligible for service as a judge. Supreme court justices and appellate court judges must be at least thirty years of age, and others must be twenty-six. Supreme court justices serve ten-year terms, while appellate court judges serve eight-year terms. While the supreme court justices are chosen from unique districts, appellate judges are chosen from each of Mississippi's congressional districts. Trial court judges are elected in nonpartisan elections to four-year terms and must be licensed to practice law. Justice court and municipal court judges need have only a high-school diploma. They may be either elected or appointed by the local governing body. Most justice court judges are not lawyers. Repeated efforts to increase the required level of education for justice court judges have failed.

The Mississippi Commission on Judicial Performance is created by the Mississippi Constitution. The commission is composed of seven members and includes judges, practicing attorneys, and lay citizens. Following review of complaints, the commission submits a recommendation to the Mississippi Supreme Court. Possible recommendations include removal from office, suspension, imposition of a fine, public censure, or reprimand.

Associated Agencies

The Administrative Office of Courts was established in 1993 to coordinate research, maintain statistical and financial data, create and disseminate court forms, and make recommendations regarding the improvement of the court system.

Legal-aid services are offered by Legal Services offices throughout the state. However, these offices do not exist in every jurisdiction. Criminal defense services for the indigent are provided by county public defenders. The state lacks a uniform or statewide system of public defenders and relies on each county to determine the structure and funding of these services. In 2000, the Mississippi legislature established and funded the Office of Capital Defense Counsel.

Mississippi's fiscal year (FY) 2006 judiciary budget was approximately $79.4 million. The largest portion of the budget goes to state trial judges ($16.6 million) followed by $16.1 million for state district attorneys.

Lisa S. Nored
University of Southern Mississippi

Doug Goodman
Mississippi State University

Further Reading

Hoffheimer, Michael H. 1995. "Mississippi Courts: 1790–1868." *Mississippi Law Journal* 65: 99–169.

Mississippi Judiciary Home Page, http://www.mssc.state.ms.us/.

Robertson, James. 2003. "Constitutional Law." In *Encyclopedia of Mississippi Law*, eds. Jeffrey Jackson and Mary Miller. Eagen, MN: West Publishing.

Sansing, David G. 1986. "Mississippi's Four Constitutions." *Mississippi Law Journal* 56: 3–15.

Skates, John R., Jr. 1973. *Mississippi's Present and Past.* Fenton, MI: K.E. McRoberts.

State of Mississippi, "Joint Legislative Budget Committee." 2005. *State of Mississippi Budget Fiscal Year 2006*, http://www.dfa.state.ms.us/bdgtfund/EnactedBudget.pdf (accessed November 21, 2005).

MISSOURI

The supreme court of the Territory of Missouri was created in 1820 with the adoption of Missouri's first constitution. The size of the court was three justices. In 1872 the court was expanded to five justices and in 1890, to seven. Circuit courts were established as trial courts. Missouri has operated under four different constitutions, the most recent of which was adopted in 1945. Prior to 1940, judicial selection in Missouri was accomplished through partisan elections. Party politics were so intense in Missouri that from 1918 through 1941 only two supreme court justices were successful in their reelection bids (AJS). Missouri's Nonpartisan Selection of Judges Court Plan, better known as the Missouri Plan, was adopted in 1940 and added into the state constitution in 1945. Thirty-four other states have modeled their judicial selection for some or all judicial vacancies on the Missouri Plan.

Organization of State Courts

Article V of the constitution states that there will be a supreme court composed of seven members. In 2005, the justices of the Missouri Supreme Court are Ronnie L. White (chief justice), Michael A. Wolff, Laura Denvir Stith, William Ray Price Jr., Richard B. Teitelman, Stephen N. Limbaugh Jr., and Mary Rhodes Russell. The constitution allows for three court of appeals districts, each to have at least three judges. There are currently thirty-two court of appeals judges in the three districts.

Missouri's trial courts of general jurisdiction are its circuit courts. Missouri has 45 circuit courts (there is a court in every county), employing 135 circuit court judges, as well as 175 associate circuit judges, and 331 municipal judges. Within each of the circuits, there are various divisions including probate, small claims, family, criminal, and juvenile. Municipal courts are subdivisions of circuit courts and have jurisdiction over cases concerning city ordinances.

Powers of State Courts

The supreme court is the highest court in the state. It has exclusive appellate jurisdiction over all cases involving the validity of a U.S. treaty or statute as well as cases involving a statute or provision of the state constitution or the construction of state revenue laws. The court also has exclusive appellate jurisdiction over cases where the death penalty has been imposed and in cases involving title to a state office. In all other cases, it has discretionary appellate jurisdiction. Under its discretionary jurisdiction, it accepts less than 10 percent of the cases decided by the court of appeals. The supreme court also has supervisory control over the Missouri judiciary, as well as the power to appoint a state courts administrator and any appropriate staff to aid in the administration of the supreme court. Finally, the supreme court may establish rules for the day-to-day operation of the courts, as well as having oversight over the legal profession in the state.

The court of appeals has appellate jurisdiction in those cases where the supreme court does not have exclusive appellate jurisdiction. The court of appeals has discretion as to whether to hear oral arguments in a case. Although it is a court of first appeal and must therefore consider all cases, in 2003 it provided a written opinion in less than 60 percent of cases it considered. A three-judge panel may review briefs in a case, and without holding oral arguments, dismiss the case.

Missouri circuit courts are the courts of original jurisdiction in Missouri. They hear cases including, but not limited to, criminal, civil, family, probate, and juvenile matters. This is the court in which trials occur. In some circuits, cities have created municipal courts that have jurisdiction over cases involving city ordinances. The municipal courts are subdivisions of the circuit courts.

Selection of Judges

Supreme court justices and court of appeals judges are selected through what is widely known as the Missouri Plan. The Appellate Judicial Commission, comprised of the chief justice of the supreme court, three lawyers chosen by the Missouri bar (one from each court of appeals district), and three citizens selected by the governor (one from each court of appeals district), accepts and reviews applications for supreme court justices, and nominates three candidates to fill any vacancy. The governor then chooses one of those candidates to fill a vacancy. After the justice serves one year on the bench, he or she is placed on the ballot at the next general election for retention, and if he or she is retained, the judge holds the seat for twelve years, at which time his or her name is once again placed on the ballot. Supreme court justices and court of appeals judges must be at least thirty years of age, licensed to practice law in Missouri, a U.S. citizen for at least fifteen years, and a qualified voter in the state for at least nine years. Court of appeals judges must also be residents of the court of appeals district in which they will serve.

In some parts of the state circuit court judges are selected using the Missouri Plan, while in other parts of the state they are selected in nonpartisan elections. In Clay, Jackson, Platte, and St. Louis counties, as well as the city of St. Louis, the Missouri Plan is used. The Circuit Judicial Selection Commission is comprised of the chief judge of the court of appeals district in which the circuit is located, two lawyers selected by the bar, and two citizens selected by the governor. The commission reviews applications and presents a list of three candidates to the governor. The governor then chooses one of those candidates to fill a vacancy. After the judge serves one year on the bench, he or she is placed on the ballot at the next general election for retention, and if re-

tained, holds the seat for six years, at which time his or her name is once again placed on the ballot.

In all other parts of the state, circuit court judges are elected in nonpartisan elections. If an interim vacancy occurs, the vacancy is filled through gubernatorial appointment. Interim appointments are placed on the ballot in the next general election for a retention vote. A circuit court judge must be at least thirty years of age, licensed to practice law in Missouri, a U.S. citizen for at least ten years, and a qualified voter in the state for at least three years. The judge must also be a resident in the circuit in which he or she will serve for at least one year. Associate circuit judges must be qualified voters, residents of the circuit, and must be twenty-five years of age. Associate circuit judges serve terms of four years. Missouri also has municipal judges who are elected or appointed to terms of at least two years, depending on city ordinance. All judges and justices must retire at the age of seventy.

Discipline

The Commission of Retirement, Removal, and Discipline of Judges is comprised of six members: one circuit judge, one court of appeals judge, two lawyers, and two nonlawyers. The commission is responsible for investigating alleged misconduct of judges and commission members, as well as investigating requests for retirement of judges due to disability. The commission informally investigates complaints. If four members of the commission believe there is probable cause to believe the person may be guilty of actions constituting grounds for discipline, a formal investigation is conducted. The commission then provides a report to the supreme court with recommendations for discipline, including removal from office, suspension, or other action. The supreme court then makes the final ruling on the case.

disposed of 116 cases by opinion. The court of appeals disposed of 3,660 cases in 2003. This included 3,212 appeals and 448 writs. Of the 3,212 appeals, 1,855 were disposed of by opinion and 1,183 were dismissed. In 2003, circuit courts in Missouri disposed of 842,431, including civil, criminal, juvenile, and probate cases.

Ruth Ann Watry
Northern Michigan University

Workload

In 2003, the Missouri State Supreme Court disposed of 889 cases. These cases included appeals, writs, applications to transfer, and supervisory matters. The supreme court is a discretionary court of appeals, and does not accept every case brought to it. In 2003, the supreme court

References and Further Reading

American Judicature Society, "Center for Judicial Selection," http://www.ajs .org/selection/index.asp.

Hardy, Richard J., Richard R. Dohm, and David A. Leuthold, eds. 1995. *Missouri Government and Politics.* Columbia, MO: University of Missouri Press.

Missouri Judiciary, http://www .courts.mo.gov/.

MONTANA
● ● ● ● ● ● ● ● ● ● ● ●

Carving off a portion of Idaho Territory, Congress created the Territory of Montana on May 26, 1864. Section 9 of the Organic Act created a three-member supreme court, and district, probate, and justice of the peace courts. President Abraham Lincoln appointed two associate justices on June 22, 1864. One of the associate justices declined to move to Montana and was replaced by another Lincoln appointee in March 1865. Lincoln appointed Hezekiah L. Hosmer the first chief justice on June 30, 1864. Each justice also presided over one of the three judicial districts. This arrangement usually meant that when a case was appealed

to the supreme court, one of the justices personally had tried the case in district court. This changed in 1886 when Congress authorized the appointment of a fourth supreme court justice. The territorial court system continued in operation until Montana became a state on November 8, 1889.

Montana government operates under the state's second constitution ratified in 1972. The new constitution continued the basic structure of Montana government found in the older constitution. While the basic structure is patterned after the three branches found in the U.S. Constitution, there are significant differences. The grant of constitutional power to the Montana government is general and nonspecific. The constitution includes a Declaration of Rights of which seventeen provisions are not found in the Bill of Rights in the U.S. Constitution. Among these are the right of participation in governmental decision making, the right of individual privacy, and the unlimited right to sue government entities and their agents. The 1972 constitution also has strong environmental protections not found in other state constitutions. The Declaration of Rights states that all persons have an inalienable right to a clean and healthful environment.

Supreme Court of Montana

Article VIII of the 1889 constitution established the Supreme Court of Montana. There were three justices who were elected to six-year terms. In 1903, the Montana legislature provided the appointment of a three-member Court Commission of Legal Learning and Personal Worth to assist the justices. All three commissioners resigned in 1905 and were not replaced. The legislature increased the number of justices on the supreme court to five. In 1979, the supreme court was expanded to seven in order to handle the increased case volume.

The court has jurisdiction over appeals from all the district courts. Appeals from the workers' compensation court and the water court also proceed directly to the supreme court. The constitution gives the court original jurisdiction to hear and decide habeas corpus claims and applica-

tions for control over actions not finalized by the district courts. In 2002, 472 civil cases and 326 criminal cases were filed in the Supreme Court of Montana.

The supreme court also has the authority to discipline attorneys, develop rules governing appellate procedure and practice, and create the procedures that govern the other state courts.

District Courts

There are fifty-six district courts, divided into twenty-two judicial districts and served by forty-two district court judges. The district courts have general jurisdiction and hear felony cases, probate cases, most civil cases, civil actions that may result in a finding against the state for the payment of money, naturalization proceedings, and some narrowly defined ballot issues. The district courts also have limited appellate jurisdiction over cases from the courts of limited jurisdiction in their districts. There were 10,673 civil cases and 7,046 criminal cases filed in Montana's district court in 2002.

Workers' Compensation Court

In 1975, the Montana legislature created the workers' compensation court to provide an efficient method for handling the resolution of disputes arising under the Workers' Compensation Act and the Occupational Disease Act. The court's jurisdiction has been expanded to include disputes involving independent contractor exemptions from the acts and reemployment preferences. The courts also decide requests for judicial review from final orders of the Montana Department of Labor and Industry. The workers' compensation court heard 243 cases in 2002. Appeals from the workers' compensation court go directly to the supreme court.

Water Court

The water court was created by the legislature in 1979 to handle cases from the over 219,000 state law–based water rights and federal and Indian reserved water rights claims. The court has exclusive jurisdiction over water rights claims. The chief water judge is appointed by the chief justice from a list of nominees provided by the Judicial Nomination Commission. There is a water judge appointed for each of Montana's four major water regions. These judges are elected by a majority vote of a committee composed of the district court judge from each single-judge judicial district and the chief district judge from each multiple-judge judicial district within each water region. Until 2009, the water court may not hear federal or Indian reserved water rights claims while the state, federal, and tribal authorities continue negotiations over reserved water rights.

Courts of Limited Jurisdiction

There are three types of courts of limited jurisdiction in Montana: justice, city, and municipal courts. There are sixty-six justices courts, eighty-one city courts, and five municipal courts. Courts of limited jurisdiction have jurisdiction over criminal misdemeanors, civil cases involving amounts up to $7,000, small claims involving amounts up to $3,000, landlord/tenant disputes, local ordinances, protection orders, and certain cases involving juveniles. In 2002, there were 109 judges in courts of limited jurisdiction. Some judges serve as both justices of the peace and city judges. When a Montanan goes to court, he or she is most likely to appear in a court of limited jurisdiction. In 2002 there were 568 civil cases and 31,076 criminal cases filed in city courts; 31,206 civil cases and 56,201 criminal cases filed in justice courts; and 1,155 civil cases and 57,798 criminal cases filed in municipal courts.

Associated Agencies

The Montana legislature authorized the Office of the Court Administrator in 1977. The court administrator works with the chief justice to supervise the operation of the Montana court system. The court administrator prepares the judicial branch budget for presentation to the legislature, studies and recommends changes in the judicial branch to the supreme court, and administers state funding for the district court.

The Judicial Standards Commission was created by a constitutional amendment in 1973. The commission investigates complaints of judicial competency and can censure, suspend, or remove a judicial officer. The commission is composed of two district court judges elected by the district court judges, one attorney appointed by the supreme court, and two lay members appointed by the governor.

The Judicial Nomination Commission reviews potential appointees to vacancies on the supreme, district, the workers' compensation courts, and the chief water court judge. In the case of vacancies, the governor appoints supreme court justices, district court judges, and workers' compensation court judges, while the chief justice appoints the chief water judge.

The Montana Supreme Court created the Commission on Courts of Limited Jurisdiction. The commission supervises educational programs that result in judge certification. The commission is comprised of six judges from limited jurisdiction courts, a district court judge, a representative of a city and a county government, the president of the limited jurisdiction clerks' association, and a member of the State Bar of Montana. The supreme court appoints members to four-year terms.

Judicial Selection and Removal

Supreme court justices and district court judges are elected statewide on a nonpartisan ballot to eight-year terms. When a vacancy occurs, the governor makes an appointment from a list submitted by the Judicial Nomination Committee. The Montana senate must confirm appointees. Montana's 1889 constitution provided that the members of the supreme court would be elected to six-year terms and district court judges would be elected to four-year terms. In 1909, the legislature passed a law requiring nonpartisan judicial elections and

that citizen petitions nominate judicial candidates. The Montana Supreme Court found this law unconstitutional in 1911 since it did not provide a means for nominating candidates for newly created judgeships.

In 1935, the legislature again enacted legislation calling for nonpartisan judicial elections by prohibiting political parties from endorsing, contributing to, or making expenditures to support or oppose judicial candidates. A 1972 constitutional amendment increased the length of supreme court justice terms to eight years. District court judge terms were increased to six years. The amendment also called for the creation of the Judicial Nomination Commission that began operation in 1973. Beginning in 1974, voters would be asked whether an incumbent judge who is running unopposed should be retained. The governor, on the recommendation of the Judicial Nomination Commission, appoints the workers' compensation court judge. Justice court and municipal court judges are elected, but can be appointed to fill vacancies. Judges who are appointed to fill a vacancy must run for the position at the end of the term to which they were appointed. City court judges may be elected or appointed. Justice court and city court judges are not required to be attorneys. The supreme court provides training conferences and certification for these judges. Municipal court judges are required to be attorneys.

Montana judges may be removed using one of two methods. Judges may be impeached by a two-thirds vote of the House of Representatives and convicted by a two-thirds vote of the senate. The second method empowers the Judicial Standards Commission, based on investigations of misconduct complaints, to issue a recommendation to the supreme court. On that recommendation, the court may retire, censure, suspend, or remove a judge from the bench.

John David Rausch Jr.
West Texas A&M University

Further Reading

Montana Department of Justice, http://doj.state.mt.us/.
State Bar of Montana, http://www .montanabar.org/.
State Law Library of Montana, "Montana Courts and Judicial Districts/Announcements," http://www .lawlibrary.state.mt.us/dscgi/ds.py/View/ Collection–45.

NEBRASKA
● ● ● ● ● ● ● ● ● ● ● ●

Nebraska was organized as a territory on May 30, 1854, and was admitted as a state on March 1, 1867. Under the Organic Act, which created the Nebraska Territory, there was to be "a Supreme Court, District Courts, Probate Courts and Justices of the Peace." The supreme court was comprised of one chief and two associate justices, each holding office for four years, and the territory was divided into three districts, each staffed by one of the supreme court justices. Probate courts and justices of the peace could be created by the territorial legislature. When Nebraska became a state in 1867, the state was operating under an 1866 constitution that had been hurriedly written by the territorial legislature. It was soon replaced with a new constitution in 1875. The 1875 constitution provided for "a Supreme Court, District Courts, County Courts, Justices of the Peace, Police Magistrates and other courts inferior to District Courts as may be created by law for cities and incorporated towns" (Article VI, Section 1).

The supreme court consisted of three justices elected for terms of office of six years, with the chief justice being the individual with the shortest amount of time left in his or her term. The state was divided into six judicial districts, each served by one judge elected to a four-year term. County courts were to have original jurisdiction over "matters of probate, settlement of estates of deceased persons, appointments of guardians, and settlement of their accounts, in all matters relating to apprentice; and such other jurisdiction as may be given by general law." Each county would have one judge elected to a two-year term. Justices of the peace and police magistrates were to be elected as provided for by local law.

Until 1970, the system of courts in Nebraska remained virtually unchanged. A 1970 amendment to the constitution, along with 1972 legislation, allowed the legislature to revamp the local and regional courts. As a result of this, local and district courts were included in a more unified system. A 1990 amendment to the state constitution made possible the creation of the court of appeals in 1991.

Organization of State Courts

The Nebraska Supreme Court is comprised of a chief justice and six associate justices. The chief justice represents the state at large, while each of the associate justices represents one of six districts. In 2005 the justices of the supreme court were Chief Justice John Hendry and associate justices Michael McCormack, John Gerrard, Kenneth Stephan, Lindsey Miller-Lerman, John Wright, and William Connolly.

The court of appeals has only been in existence since 1991. It is comprised of six members, each representing one of six districts. The chief justice is chosen by the supreme court to serve a one-year renewable term. For the convenience of the citizens of Nebraska, the court travels around the state to hear appeals, although its primary courtroom is in the state capitol in Lincoln.

The state of Nebraska has been broken into twelve district courts that are served by fifty-five district court judges. The three smallest districts are served by two judges each, while the most populous district has sixteen judges assigned to it. Each county in the state has a clerk of the district court who performs the administrative duties associated with that court.

Nebraska's ninety-three counties are also organized into twelve judicial districts for the purpose of organizing county courts. Each judicial district is comprised of one to nine counties, and fifty-nine judges staff the county courts. The four smallest districts are served by three judges each, while the most populous district is served by twelve judges.

Nebraska has two courts not created by the constitution. Three Nebraska counties have separate juvenile courts. These courts, located in Douglas, Lancaster, and Sharpy counties, are staffed by ten judges. These courts have the same juvenile jurisdiction and procedures as county courts. The workers' compensation court consists of seven judges who have statewide jurisdiction.

Powers of State Courts

The supreme court is the administrative leader of the Nebraska court system as well as an appellate court and a court of limited original jurisdiction. The court can be the original court under certain limited circumstances. It is the court of first appeal in death penalty cases, sentences of life imprisonment, and cases in which constitutional questions are raised (the state constitution requires the vote of five justices to hold a legislative act unconstitutional). The supreme court also hears appeals from the court of appeals and the workers' compensation court, as well as from the various trial courts and from administrative agencies. The administrative responsibility of the supreme court includes oversight of the Nebraska bar, oversight of the Administrative Office of the Courts, membership on various state committees, and appointment of attorneys to serve on local committees of inquiry. Supreme court justices serve on each of the judicial nominating commissions, and the supreme court has oversight over the discipline of judges.

The court of appeals has jurisdiction to hear all appeals (except death penalty cases, sentences of life imprisonment, and cases in which constitutional questions are raised) coming out of state trial courts and administrative agencies. The court is divided into two panels of three judges each who decide cases. Composition of panels are changed over time so that all judges have an opportunity to work with each other. The supreme court has the power to grant a petition asking that a case bypass the court of appeals and go directly to the supreme court. In 2003 the supreme court received fifty-one such petitions and granted twenty-two.

Nebraska district courts are the courts of general jurisdiction. District courts have concurrent jurisdiction with county courts. They mainly hear felony criminal cases, equity cases, and civil cases involving more than $45,000. They also act as an appellate court for some cases coming out of county courts and coming out of administrative agencies. County courts are also courts of general jurisdiction. They hear misdemeanor cases, traffic and municipal ordinance violations, preliminary hearings in felony cases, some divorces, small claims, civil suits involving less than $45,000, probate, guardianship, conservator and adoption proceedings, and juvenile matters. In Douglas, Lancaster, and Sharpy counties there are separate juvenile courts to hear juvenile matters.

The Nebraska Workers' Compensation Court has statewide jurisdiction over cases arising under the Nebraska Workers' Compensation Act. Judges are expected to travel throughout the state to hold hearings. All industrial accidents must also be reported to this court.

Selection of Judges

Nebraska judges are selected through the merit selection system. Nebraska has thirty-three judicial nominating commissions; one for the chief justiceship (one), one for each district of the supreme court (six), court of appeals (six), district court (twelve), and for courts of limited jurisdiction (eight). In four of the judicial districts there is a separate nominating commission for circuit court judges; in the remaining eight, one commission acts on both district and circuit court judges. There are also separate nominating commissions for each of the three county juvenile courts, as well as the workers' compensation court. Each commission is made up of four lawyers chosen by the state bar association as well as four non-lawyers appointed by the governor. No more than two lawyers and two non-lawyers on each commission can be from the same political party. The commission is chaired by a supreme court justice who is a nonvoting member of the committee. Commission members serve staggered four-year terms.

When a judicial vacancy occurs the appropriate commission holds public hearings to interview applicants. The commission advances a list of the two most qualified candidates to the governor who then chooses one to fill the judicial vacancy. If the governor does not act within sixty days, the chief justice of the supreme court makes the appointment. A judge must run for retention in the first general election held three or more years after the judge was appointed. After the first retention election, judges must run in a retention election every six years. There is no mandatory retirement age for judges.

To be a judge in Nebraska, an individual must be at least thirty years of age, a citizen of the United States, have practiced law in Nebraska for at least five years, and must be a current member of the Nebraska State Bar Association. In addition, justices of the supreme court must have resided in Nebraska for three years and must be a resident of the district they are appointed to, effective the date of appointment. Court of appeals judges must be residents of Nebraska, and district, county, and juvenile judges must be residents of the district in which they are serving, effective the date of appointment.

Discipline

The conduct of Nebraska judges is governed by the state constitution and the Nebraska Code of Judicial Conduct, which is based on the ABA Model Code of Judicial Conduct. The Judicial Ethics Committee, the Commission of Judicial Qualifications, and the supreme court all have roles in judicial discipline. The Judicial Ethics Committee interprets the Nebraska Code of Judicial Conduct at the request of a court or at the request of the Nebraska Commission of Judicial Qualifications. If a complaint is made against a judge, the Nebraska Commission of Judicial Qualifications conducts an informal

inquiry. If the commission determines that there is sufficient evidence to proceed, a formal hearing is held. If the commission determines that there is probable cause that a judge or justice should be subject to discipline, it can issue a reprimand or order a further hearing to consider reprimand, discipline, suspension, removal, or retirement. If a further hearing is held, it is held in front of a special master, who after additional hearings, issues a report of master to the commission. After allowing the accused judge/justice to respond to the report, the commission makes its decision. The commission then files a certified copy of the recommendation with the supreme court that then makes its decision concerning the recommendation of the commission.

Workload

The Nebraska Supreme Court processes approximately 300 cases per year (311 cases were disposed of in 2002, 282 in 2003). These cases come from many levels of the Nebraska courts, including the court of appeals; district, county, and juvenile courts; and administrative agencies. The Nebraska Court of Appeals disposed of 1,131 cases in 2002 and 1,269 cases in 2003. Cases were disposed of in many ways including transfer to the supreme court, a petition for further review, and disposition by opinion.

In 2003, Nebraska district courts saw over 41,000 case filings. This ranged from a low of 1,005 cases in Nebraska's eighth district to a high of 14,398 cases in Nebraska's fourth district. In 2003, county courts saw over 400,000 case filings. This ranged from a low of 14,637 cases in Nebraska's eighth district to a high of 96,867 filings in Nebraska's fourth district.

Nebraska has two additional courts; separate juvenile courts in Sarpy, Lancaster, and Douglas counties; and the workers' compensation court. In 2003, the three county juvenile courts handled 4,472 cases while the workers' compensation court handled 1,424 cases.

Ruth Ann Watry
Northern Michigan University

References and Further Reading
American Judicature Society, "Center for Judicial Selection," http://www.ajs.org/selection/index.asp.
Andreas' History of the State of Nebraska, http://kancoll.org/books/andreas/.
Miewald, Robert D. 1984. *Nebraska Government and Politics.* Lincoln, NE: University of Nebraska Press.
Nebraska Judicial Branch, http://court.nol.org/.

NEVADA

The first government to come to the area that is now Nevada was the provisional State of Deseret, established by Mormon pioneers in the Salt Lake Valley of present-day Utah. The United States had acquired the area with the signing of the Treaty of Guadalupe Hidalgo in 1848, ending the Mexican War. Much of the area that is now the state of Nevada was Carson County, Utah Territory, organized in 1854 by the Utah territorial legislature. The legislature granted Governor Brigham Young the power to appoint probate judges for the county. Located 500 miles west of the Utah territorial seat of government, residents called on Congress to split Nevada off from the Utah Territory. In 1861, Congress passed, and President James Buchanan signed, the Organic Act creating the Territory of Nevada from Carson and Humboldt counties of Utah Territory. President Abraham Lincoln appointed the first three justices to the Nevada Territorial Supreme Court. The three justices also rode the circuit as the judges in the three district courts created by the Organic Act. Local authorities appointed probate court judges and justices of the peace. Nevada attained statehood in 1864.

The Nevada Constitution is nearly twice as long as the United States Constitution, but it is of average length compared to the constitutions of the other states. The California Constitution of 1849 served as a model for Nevada's constitutional drafters. For this reason, the Nevada Constitution includes a list of limitations on the power of the legislature. No constitutional convention has ever been called. Nevada voters also have the ability to change the constitution through the initiative process. A proposed amendment must receive a majority of the vote in two successive general elections. Voters rejected judicial merit selection in 1972. In 1976, voters approved a constitutional amendment creating the Commission on Judicial Selection to screen candidates for midterm vacancies on the supreme court and the district court. The amendment also created the Commission on Judicial Discipline. In 1996, Nevada voters rejected a proposed constitutional amendment by a seventy to thirty margin. The amendment would have imposed term limits on Nevada judges. Had the amendment succeeded, judges would not have been able to be elected to the same court more than twice, or more than once if the judge had previously served on that court. Voters had approved the amendment in 1994 by a seventy to thirty margin. Nevada voters must approve of a constitutional amendment in two consecutive elections

Supreme Court of Nevada

The Supreme Court of Nevada is the court of last resort in the Nevada judicial branch. From statehood in 1864 until 1967, the court consisted of three justices. In 1967, the legislature increased the size of the court to five justices. Additional expansion occurred in 1997, when the legislature increased the number to seven in recognition of the court's sizable case volume. In fiscal year 2003, 1,850 cases were filed in the supreme court. Of these cases, 1,500 were appeals. The number of cases filed in the supreme court has remained level since 2000. The court hears appeals from the decisions of the district courts. All cases appealed to the court must be reviewed. Beginning in

January 1999, the court began to decide cases by meeting in three-justice panels, with one panel meeting in Carson City and one panel in Las Vegas. Panel membership rotates every twelve months. The move to a panel system was an attempt to dispose of cases more rapidly. The full court still meets in Carson City twice yearly for those cases that must be heard by the entire panel.

The most senior justice becomes chief justice and serves a two-year term in that position. If two justices are equal in seniority, the chief justice is selected by lot. The chief justice is the administrative head of the Nevada court system and the supreme court writes the rules and procedures governing all other courts in the state. The court also determines who may practice law in Nevada.

Intermediate Appellate Court

In 2004, Nevada was one of ten states that did not have an intermediate appellate court. During its 2004 session, the Nevada legislature approved a proposal that would create an appeals court between the district courts and the supreme court, if the legislature determined that the appeals court was needed. The proposal would have had to be approved by the Nevada legislature in 2005 and then by Nevada voters in 2006. The proposal was withdrawn from consideration in 2005 when a report found that filings in the supreme court had not increased much from the year before. The proposal may be reintroduced during future sessions of the legislature. If an intermediate appellate court were established, two seats would be removed from the supreme court. The new court would be given space within the existing supreme court building.

District Court

The district courts have general jurisdiction. The courts may hear felony criminal cases and civil cases where the amount in dispute is more than $7,500. They also have jurisdiction for all family and juvenile cases. The seventeen counties in Nevada are divided into nine judicial districts, presided over by sixty judges. Five of the judicial districts include multiple counties. District court judges may hear cases anywhere in the state, even though they are elected by voters in the judicial district they generally serve. In 2003, 12,000 criminal cases and 28,100 civil cases were filed in district courts. There also were 52,260 family cases filed.

Justice Court

Justice courts are courts of limited jurisdiction with their caseload restricted by Nevada statutes. Justice courts determine whether enough evidence exists in felony criminal cases to have a district court trial. Preliminary hearings are the bulk of the work done by justice courts. They hear misdemeanor non-traffic cases as well as civil cases in which the amount in dispute is less than $7,500. They also hear small-claims, summary eviction cases, and requests for temporary protective orders. Justice courts have jurisdiction over traffic cases and parking infractions in some communities. They may hear cases in other parts of their county or as temporary judges in townships in other counties. There were 76,100 criminal cases and 106,600 civil cases filed in justice courts during 2003. Justice courts allow residents to access justice in places other than their county seats, which may be located at some distance.

Municipal Court

Each incorporated city in Nevada is required to have a municipal court presided over by a municipal judge. Because some smaller cities do not have the financial ability to support a full-time municipal judge, the legislature has allowed the justice of the peace, whose territory includes the city, to serve as a municipal judge with the consent of both the county commission and the justice of the peace. The jurisdiction of municipal courts is limited to only violations of city ordinances. Much of their caseloads are traffic cases and in some cities, parking infractions. Municipal courts also may handle civil cases in very limited situations. In 2003, a municipal court had civil filings for the first time since data collection began in 1999. The Caliente Municipal Court had three small-claims filings. The city was seeking payment through the courts for unpaid municipal utility bills. In 2003, 73,600 non-traffic misdemeanor cases and 240,600 traffic and parking infractions were filed in municipal courts.

Associated Agencies

The Judicial Council of the State of Nevada is the administrative arm of the judiciary that develops policies for the improvement of the court system and makes recommendations to the Nevada Supreme Court. There are sixteen judges from across the state at every level of court. The chief justice of the supreme court is the ex-officio chairperson of the council. Five regional judicial councils meet independently to discuss issues of more local concern. Each regional judicial council is composed of one district court judge and one limited jurisdiction judge. In recent years, the council has examined problems facing a court system in the unevenly populated and growing state. The Commission on Rural Courts was established to examine the problems facing the smaller courts and communities in the state and to propose solutions to those problems.

A constitutional amendment approved by voters in 1976 created a Commission on Judicial Discipline. This commission has the power to censure, retire, or remove a supreme court justice or district court judge. The commission consists of two justices or judges appointed by the supreme court, two attorneys appointed by the State Bar of Nevada, and three nonlawyers appointed by the governor. The members appoint one of the nonlawyers to serve as chair.

The court administrator heads the Administrative Office of the Courts. The office performs administrative functions for the supreme court. It also assists lower court staffs with training and new technology.

Judicial Selection and Removal

Each supreme court justice is elected to a six-year term. Any midterm vacancies are filled by gubernatorial appointment. Judges are selected in nonpartisan elections. Nevada voters have an unusual choice when voting for judge. They are able to select "none of the above." In a 2002 supreme court race, nearly 78,000 voted for "none of these candidates." Prior to 1976, the governor had sole responsibility to appoint judges to fill vacancies. By constitutional amendment, a judicial selection commission, made up of a supreme court justice, three attorneys appointed by the State Bar of Nevada, and three nonlawyers appointed by the governor advises the governor on nominations. The governor makes appointments from among the three nominees screened by the commission. Justices of the peace are elected within the townships they serve. They serve six-year terms.

There are four ways that a Nevada judge may lose his or her seat. The Commission on Judicial Discipline may investigate complaints and issue an order disciplining, censuring, retiring, or removing a judge. The commission's decisions may be appealed to the supreme court. Second, judges may be impeached by a simple majority of the assembly and convicted by a two-thirds vote of the Nevada senate. Third, judges may be removed by a legislative resolution approved by two-thirds of the members of both houses. Finally, Nevada voters also have the ability to recall judges between regularly scheduled judicial elections.

John David Rausch Jr.
West Texas A&M University

Further Reading
Driggs, Don W., and Leonard E. Goodall. 1996. *Nevada Politics and Government: Conservatism in an Open Society.* Lincoln, NE: University of Nebraska Press.
Office of the Attorney General, "Nevada Department of Justice," http://ag.state.nv.us/.
State Bar of Nevada, http://www.nvbar.org/.
Supreme Court of Nevada, http://www.nvsupremecourt.us/index.html.

NEW HAMPSHIRE

New Hampshire, also known as the Granite State, was one of the thirteen original colonies. New Hampshire was settled three years after the Pilgrims arrived at Plymouth, Massachusetts, and was the ninth state to ratify the United States Constitution. Interestingly, New Hampshire is responsible for casting the deciding vote in favor of the U.S. Constitution.

New Hampshire is one of the six states that constitute New England and is the seventh-smallest state in the United States. New Hampshire was named by Captain John Mason who received a land grant from England for modern-day New Hampshire. New Hampshire is bordered on the north by Quebec, Canada, on the east by Maine and the Atlantic Ocean, on the south by Massachusetts, and on the west by Vermont.

New Hampshire currently operates under its second constitution, which was adopted in 1784 making it five years older than the United States Constitution. New Hampshire is the only state without a general sales or state income tax. When necessary, the state has used limited sales taxes on specific items.

Like Massachusetts, the legislative function in New Hampshire is performed by an executive council. The executive council is a five-member elected body with significant veto power over the governor. The governor of New Hampshire is elected to two-year terms and makes all executive appointments with the exception of the secretary of state and the state treasurer. The third branch of government is an interesting blend of traditional and modern and has four primary courts: the New Hampshire Supreme Court, and superior, district, and probate courts. These courts operate from a budget of approximately $61 million.

New Hampshire Supreme Court

Prior to the adoption of the first New Hampshire Constitution, the court of appeals served as the highest court. The governor and the executive council served as the judges for the court of appeals. However, with the adoption of the first constitution, the legislature abolished the court of appeals and created the superior court of judicature to serve as the appellate court for the state. The original court had four justices.

In 1876, the legislature created what is now the supreme court. The supreme court has one chief justice and four associate justices. Justices are nominated by the governor and subject to the approval of the executive council. Once confirmed, justices receive lifetime tenure. Judicial salaries are determined by the legislature. In 2005, the chief justice received an annual salary of $128,488 and associate justices $124,593. Justices also receive reimbursement for allowed expenses.

In an interesting turn, the supreme court recently modified its process of appellate review. Prior to January 2004, the supreme court used a system of discretionary review, which required screening by the court prior to granting the right to be heard. At that time, the court heard approximately 40 percent of appealed cases. In response to growing concerns regarding the right of litigants to a final appellate review, the court modified its approach and after January 2004, began hearing all appeals from decisions of the trial courts.

Despite the modification of appellate review, the court did not experience a significant change in its caseload. In 2004, 1,244 were pending before the supreme court. Of that number, 898 were new filings and 346 were pending or reinstated matters. During 2004, the court disposed of 721 cases. Annual expenditures of the supreme court are approximately $6.7 million or 11 percent of the total budget allocated to the judicial branch.

In 1978, by constitutional amendment, the supreme court was authorized to promulgate rules of practice and procedure for the operation of all courts. The 1978 amendment also designated the chief justice as the administrator of the New Hampshire judicial system. In 1983, the administrative responsibilities of the chief justice increased significantly when the legislature centralized state funding of all courts, including those that had historically been funded at the county level. Thereafter, the administrative duties of the chief justice included the preparation and submission of the budget as well as personnel administration for all courts within the New Hampshire judicial system.

Administrative support for the supreme court is the responsibility of the Administrative Office of Courts (AOC). Led by an executive director, the AOC is responsible for the daily administration of New Hampshire courts. Moreover, the AOC provides services including the preparation and administration of the judicial budget as well as oversight and administration of personnel matters.

In addition to the AOC, a host of supreme court committees have been created to carry out the variety of functions required of the court. For example, committees exist for topics such as judicial conduct, judicial ethics, attorney discipline, bar admission and examination, character and fitness, rules of practice and procedure, and court accreditation.

Superior Courts

In 1901, the legislature formally distinguished between trial and appellate courts and delineated the jurisdiction, which had, until that time, been vested primarily in the supreme court. With the stroke of a pen, the legislature designated the supreme court as the appellate court and the superior courts as trial courts.

Superior courts are courts of general jurisdiction, which are located throughout the state. Superior courts have jurisdiction over civil and criminal matters. Superior courts have concurrent jurisdiction with district courts over civil cases that involve a minimum of $1,500 in controversy and exclusive jurisdiction over cases involving damage claims in excess of $25,000, domestic relations and domestic violence cases, felony criminal matters, and appeals of misdemeanor criminal matters. The superior courts are the only courts that provide a jury trial for litigants.

The superior courts are staffed with one superior court judge and twenty-eight associate justices. The chief justice of the superior court receives an annual salary of $124,593, and associate justices receive $116,806. Like supreme court justices, superior court justices may receive reimbursement for allowed expenses. Annually, the superior courts hear approximately 50,000 cases, one-half of which are domestic relations matters. Expenditures for the operations of the superior courts were approximately $18 million in the 2004 fiscal year, which is approximately 30 percent of the total budget for the judicial branch. At 30 percent, the operation of the superior court system requires the greatest proportion of the budget for the judicial branch when compared to other courts.

District Courts

District courts are located in thirty-six cities and towns throughout New Hampshire. Like superior courts, district courts have jurisdiction over civil and criminal matters involving juveniles, small claims, landlord-tenant disputes, and misdemeanor criminal offenses. District courts have concurrent jurisdiction with superior courts over civil matters involving less than $25,000 in damages.

District court judges may be part-time or full-time positions. District court justices who are prohibited from practice receive an annual salary of $116,806. Use of a weighted scale assists with the determination of the proper salary for part-time district court judges. When compared to other courts, the district courts process the greatest number of cases. For example, in fiscal year (FY) 2004, the district courts of New Hampshire disposed of 182,461 cases and in FY 2003, the courts disposed of 174,020 cases. Second only to the superior courts, the operation of the district courts requires 25.6 percent of the total budget for the judicial branch.

Probate Courts

Probate courts are located throughout the state. Probate courts hear cases involving domestic relations, adoptions, terminations of parental rights, wills and estates, trusts, guardianships of incapacitated persons and minors, and certain cases involving matters affecting real estate. In FY 2004, probate courts disposed of approximately 9,700 cases. The operation of the probate courts requires 6.9 percent (FY 2004) of the total budget for the judicial branch.

Probate court judges may be full-time or part-time depending on the needs and caseload in the county. Full-time probate judges earn an annual salary of $116,806. The use of a weighted scale assists in the determination of the proper salary for part-time probate court judges. Part-time salaries range from $2,500 to $43,700. Ongoing efforts within the probate court system are directed at efficient and effective resolution of cases involving families in conflict. These efforts culminated with the development and implementation of the Family Division Pilot Project in 1995. Family divisions are currently in operation in two New Hampshire counties. The chief justice of the New Hampshire Supreme Court has proposed statewide expansion of the family division concept. Expansion of the use of family divisions will be accomplished through the reduction in number of superior court judges and those funds used for the provision of services through the family division. To facilitate the expansion, the chief justice has created the Judicial Branch Family Division Implementation Committee, which has recommended the addition of at least twenty-one additional family division sites over a three-year period.

The family division concept is unique and is specifically designed to meet the needs of families in conflict. If present, the family division hears cases involving divorce and child custody, domestic violence, child abuse and neglect, juvenile delinquency and status offenses, adoptions, and guardianship of minors and termination of parental rights. Specific objectives of the family division include timely resolution of cases, consolidation of all matters involving the same family before one judge, the use of case managers to facilitate resolution of cases involving pro se litigants, and the use of mediation to reduce the adversarial nature of family court proceedings.

Judicial Selection and Removal

New Hampshire's selection process is unique. The governor nominates judicial appointments and an elected executive council makes the final determination. The council is a five-member body charged with advising the governor. Council members are chosen every two years in partisan elections. The qualifications for supreme, superior, and probate courts are not specified; however, district judges must be members of the state bar.

New Hampshire's judges may be removed involuntarily in one of three ways: One, the governor, with the consent of the executive council, may remove judges for reasonable cause upon the joint address of both houses of the general court. Second, judges may be impeached by the House of Representatives and convicted by the senate. Finally, judges are forced to retire when they reach the age of seventy.

Lisa Nored
University of Southern Mississippi

References
"Justice Moving Forward: A Time For Change." 2003–2004. Report of the Judicial Branch of New Hampshire, http://www.courts.state.nh.us.

New Hampshire Constitution, http://nh.gov/constitution/constitution.html.

NEW JERSEY

In 1664 the Duke of York gained control of the Dutch colony known as New Netherland. He granted this land to his friends Lord Berkley and Sir George Carteret. Sir George was once the governor of an island called Jersey in the English Channel and this new colony became known as New Jersey. The two men intended to use this land as a real estate venture. A royal charter was granted to the colony in 1702. New Jersey went on to become the third state to ratify the U.S. Constitution and the first state to ratify the Bill of Rights.

The state of New Jersey has had three constitutions. The first was written in 1776, the second in 1844, and the third in 1947. The constitution of 1947 had a substantial impact on the court structure. Prior to this constitution there was a disjointed mass of courts where the court of errors and appeals was at the top. According to the New Jersey Bar Association, a judicial council was established between 1921 and 1930 by the New Jersey legislature to assess the problems that plagued the court system. This council proposed several laws dedicated to the consolidation and systemic improvement of the judiciary.

The current court structure is the product of the 1947 constitution and legislative efforts. One of the most significant changes was the replacement of the court of errors and appeals with a supreme court. Today the organizational structure of the judiciary has been significantly streamlined and includes the supreme court, the superior court, the tax court, and municipal courts. While a few county courts remain, the superior courts have jurisdiction over most matters formerly under the jurisdiction of county courts. Approximately 7 million cases are filed in New Jersey annually, with the majority of these cases filed in municipal courts.

New Jersey Supreme Court

The New Jersey Supreme Court is the highest court in the state. Currently, there are six associate justices and one chief justice. The supreme court serves as the highest appellate court for the lower courts in the state. The New Jersey Supreme Court, like the U.S. Supreme Court, has the authority to interpret state laws and ensure that they are in agreement with the New Jersey and United States Constitutions. The supreme court considers approximately 3,000 cases per year.

Judicial salaries in New Jersey are set by the legislature and codified in New Jersey law. The chief justice earns an annual salary of $164,250 and associate justices earn $158,500 a year. In addition to their base salary, justices receive reimbursement for expenses incurred in the fulfillment of their duties.

The New Jersey Constitution mandates that the chief justice of the supreme court oversee the administration of the state judicial system. The Administrative Office of Courts (AOC) was established to provide administrative assistance and support to the chief justice. As such, the AOC, headed by an administrative director, manages the daily operation of the judicial system. The AOC performs the following functions: human resources; budgeting; and data collection, analysis, and dissemination. In 2005 the New Jersey judicial system comprised 400 judges and approximately 9,000 support staff.

The Superior Court

Each of the twenty-one counties within the state has a superior court and there are currently approximately 360 superior court trial judges. The New Jersey Superior Court has two primary divisions: an appellate division and a trial division. The trial division conducts trials over those cases for which it possesses jurisdiction, including criminal, civil, and family matters. The trial division uses a twelve-member jury in serious criminal matters and a six-member jury for civil cases.

Civil cases where the amount in controversy exceeds $15,000 are heard in the civil division of superior court. If the amount is less than $15,000 but more than $ 3,000, the case is assigned to the Special Civil Part of the Civil Division. Cases involving claims less than $3,000 are considered to be small claims and are also assigned to the Special Civil Part. The civil divisions of the superior courts hear more than 500,000 cases each year.

The Civil Division also hears civil cases, which do not involve claims for monetary damages. These matters are assigned to the General Equity Division of the superior court and include cases involving trade secrets, labor matters, foreclosures, restraining orders, and other types of emergency relief. Jury trials are not available within the General Equity Division.

Matters involving the family are assigned to the Family Division of the superior court. The Family Division is a trial court that possesses jurisdiction over matters involving divorce, domestic violence, juvenile delinquency, child support, foster-care placements, and termination of parental rights. The Family Division hears approximately 400,000 cases annually. To assist families in crisis and strengthen the effectiveness of the family courts, this division uses a host of committees including those devoted to family practice, judicial education, domestic violence, and juvenile justice.

The Appellate Division of the superior court hears appeals filed from lower courts. Like the supreme court, this division does not conduct proceedings de novo but is limited to review of lower court rulings for error. When functioning as an appellate court, the superior court sits in panels of two or three judges. The Appellate Division currently hears approximately 7,000 appeals and 7,500 motions annually.

In an attempt to strengthen judicial independence the state has developed a system of tenure for superior court judges. These individuals are appointed by the governor and approved by the state senate to serve an initial term of seven years. If the judge is reappointed after the initial seven-year period he or she is granted tenure until reaching the mandatory age of retirement, seventy. Judges who serve in the Appellate Division earn an annual salary of $150,000. Those judges serving as an assignment judge of the superior court will earn an annual salary of $146,750.

Tax Court

The tax court has jurisdiction over cases involving tax disputes. The tax court has twelve judges who review decisions of county boards of taxation and the State Division of Taxation. Cases involve disputes regarding business, property, sales, and state income tax. The tax court handles approximately 15,000 cases per year.

Tax court judges are appointed by the governor and approved by the state senate to serve an initial term of seven years. If the judge is reappointed after the initial seven-year period, he or she is granted

tenure until reaching the age of seventy. At the age of seventy, judges are required to retire. Tax court judges earn an annual salary of $141,000.

Municipal Courts

Municipal courts are courts of limited jurisdiction and primarily hear cases involving minor criminal offenses; violations of city ordinances; and hunting, fishing, and boating laws. In 2005 there were 539 municipal courts in the state of New Jersey. Approximately 6 million of the 7 million cases filed in New Jersey each year are filed in municipal courts.

Municipal judges are appointed by the municipal government for 3-year terms. While municipal judges may be reappointed, they are ineligible for tenure. In order to serve as a municipal court judge, an individual must be a resident of New Jersey and an attorney-at-law. In addition, the individual must be admitted to practice in New Jersey for at least five years prior to the judicial appointment. Municipal judges are compensated by their respective municipalities and as such salaries vary among jurisdictions.

Associated Agencies

The New Jersey Board of Bar Examiners was established in 1969 to preside over the administration of the bar examination as well as the review of bar applications for admission to the New Jersey bar. Members of the board are appointed by the New Jersey Supreme Court to serve three-year terms. Members are limited to four successive appointments. One member will be designated the chair of the board by the supreme court. The chair will appoint a secretary who is not a member of the committee itself. The actual number of committee members is decided by the supreme court and may change as deemed necessary.

The judiciary also relies on the work of juvenile conference committees (JCCs), which operate throughout the state. These committees consist of six- to nine-member panels of trained volunteers who hear cases involving juvenile offenders. Committee members make recommendations to a judge. Committees monitor the progress of juveniles and work to ensure compliance with court-ordered dispositions. In the mid-1990s there were approximately 296 committees operating statewide with more than 2,000 volunteers. Committees are present in all New Jersey counties.

Child Placement Review Boards are also used by the judicial system. These boards assist with foster-care review, reunification of families, and permanency planning. Review boards monitor the provision of services to children and families with the goal of achieving a permanent home for the child within one year.

The number of review boards in each county is based on the number of reviews conducted in the previous calendar year. However, the law suggests a 1:200 ratio between board and number of reviews. Each board has five members and two alternates who the presiding judge appoints. Members must be residents in the county served by the board.

The presiding judge appoints a committee chairperson.

The initial appointment term for new committee members is one year, but they may be reappointed for three-year terms thereafter. The Child Placement Advisory Council is composed of one member from each Child Placement Review Board who is appointed by their chairperson to advise the supreme court in matters concerning a budget that will help the board reach its goals.

For purposes of ensuring ethical behavior throughout the bench and the bar, the New Jersey Supreme Court created disciplinary districts defined by geographical areas and appoints an ethics committee to serve in each district. Each committee must have at least eight members. Four committee members must be attorneys admitted to practice in New Jersey. Two committee members must be lay persons. All committee members must either reside or work in the district or county in which they serve. The supreme court appoints members for four-year terms.

The Office of Attorney Ethics manages the seventeen district ethics committees and fee arbitration committees. This was an agency established by the New Jersey Supreme Court to help investigate and prosecute attorney misconduct occurring in the state. Possible sanctions include admonition, reprimand, censure, suspension from practice, or permanent disbarment. The New Jersey Lawyers' Fund for Client Protection was established to reimburse clients who have suffered a loss due to dishonest conduct of a member of the New Jersey bar.

Selection and Removal of Judges

In an attempt to strengthen judicial independence, the state has developed a system of tenure for supreme court justices. Justices are appointed by the governor and approved by the state senate to serve an initial term of seven years. If the justice is reappointed after the initial seven-year period, he or she is granted tenure until reaching the age of seventy. Judges may be removed from office by legislative impeachment and trial. A Judicial Standards Commission may hear complaints about misbehavior of judges and investigate, dismiss, or recommend further action to the supreme court. Only the court, or legislative impeachment, can force a judge from office.

Elizabeth Corzine McMullan
University of Southern Mississippi

References and Further Reading

New Jersey Judiciary, "New Jersey Courts Overview," http://www.judiciary.state
.nj.us/index.html.
New Jersey Judiciary, "Office of Attorney Ethics," htto://www.judiciary.state.nj.us.
New Jersey State Bar Association, "History," http://www.njsba.com/.

NEW MEXICO

As a part of New Spain and later Mexico, present–day New Mexico was lightly governed under the Spanish alcalde system. The alcaldes were government officials operating in a manner similar to justices of the peace, with broad legislative, administrative, and judicial responsibilities. In 1846 during the Mexican War, U.S. General Stephen Kearny marched his army into Sante Fe and took possession of the territory. He issued the Organic Law of the Territory of New Mexico in September 1848. Known popularly as the Kearny Code, government was divided into the U.S.-style three branches. Judicial power was granted to a superior court consisting of three judges appointed by the U.S. president. Additional courts were to be established by statute. The vestiges of the alcalde system remained as many became justices of the peace.

The war with Mexico ended in 1848 and a civil government met under the terms of the Kearny Code. Congress debated the issue of territorial status or statehood for two years, in part due to the national debate over slavery. Territorial status was finally granted in 1850 and a three–justice supreme court was appointed. The justices also served as district court judges. Working toward statehood for sixty years, New Mexico finally was admitted to the Union in 1912.

The framers of the New Mexico Constitution designed a detailed document to provide for every contingency. At its drafting, the document was about 21,000 words long. Most of the changes since 1912 have been through legislatively referred amendments, though there was one attempt at a complete revision through a constitutional convention. In

1968, the voters approved the legislature's call for a constitutional convention. The convention met in 1969, but its recommendations were rejected by the voters.

New Mexico Supreme Court

The New Mexico Supreme Court consists of five justices who hears cases as one panel and three justices must be present for a quorum. The court has original jurisdiction in cases involving conflicts between officials from different branches of government or between different officials within the executive branch. The court's appellate jurisdiction is determined by statute. It involves hearing appeals from lower courts. Death penalty cases from the district court are directly appealed to the supreme court, instead of the normal path through the court of appeals. In 2002, 59 mandatory cases were filed in the supreme court and 515 discretionary petitions. The court granted the petitions in fifty-two cases.

The supreme court was an early leader in recognizing the role of the state constitution in protecting individual civil liberties, applying the New Mexico Constitution to criminal cases as early as 1976. In 1997, the court established a procedure for invoking the state constitution in a claim. The party making the claim must clearly present the issue and show how the New Mexico Constitution is the controlling authority on that issue.

Every January in even-numbered years, the justices select one of their own by majority vote to serve as chief justice.

Court of Appeals

The court of appeals was created in 1965 by voter-approved constitutional amendment. The judges sit in panels of three to hear appeals. It only has appellate jurisdiction and reviews appeals in all cases except death penalty cases. It also rules on appeals from decisions, regulations, and rules of various state boards, commissions, and administrative agencies. There were 866 cases filed in the appeals court in 2002. In 2002, district courts heard 68,953 civil cases and 20,649 criminal cases. The court has ten judges in all and two offices, one in Santa Fe and one in Albuquerque. In 2004, six judges were headquartered in the Santa Fe office and four judges were headquartered in Albuquerque.

District Court

District courts are the state's trial courts of general jurisdiction. They hear criminal cases ranging from major felonies to misdemeanors. They also hear civil cases, including divorce, property damage, and property disputes. These judges are able to specialize in juvenile matters, domestic relations, or civil cases. District courts can receive appeals from lower magistrate or municipal courts. They supervise the lower courts within the district, and administer the children's court and the Juvenile Probation Office. The state is divided into thirteen judicial districts served by seventy-two full-time judges. Depending on population, a judicial district may include one to four counties.

Bernalillo County (Albuquerque) makes up the Second Judicial District and has twenty-two judges.

Magistrate Court

The magistrate court was created by a 1966 constitutional amendment to replace the justice of the peace courts and the fee system. Magistrate court judges are paid by the state based on case volume. In 2002, 23,600 civil cases and 24,250 criminal cases were filed in magistrate courts. Magistrates have original jurisdiction in civil cases with judgments under $7,500. Magistrates also hear criminal misdemeanor cases and may conduct preliminary hearings on felony cases. The magistrate court is not a court of record, meaning that if a case is appealed to district court, it involves a de novo proceeding. Magistrates do not have to be attorneys, but they must take legal education training. Each county has at least one magistrate and more populous counties have several.

Municipal Court

There is a municipal court in every incorporated city and town, except Albuquerque with its metropolitan court. The municipal court has jurisdiction over all violations of municipal ordinances. Most of the cases are misdemeanors such as traffic infractions. There were 18,096 civil cases and 15,450 criminal cases filed in Bernalillo County Metropolitan Court in 2002.

Bernalillo County Metropolitan Court

Since July 1, 1980, the Bernalillo County Metropolitan Court has existed in Albuquerque. The metropolitan court consolidated the Bernalillo County Magistrate Court, Small-Claims Court, and the Albuquerque Municipal Court. Metropolitan court judges are elected to four-year terms. Vacancies are filled by the governor until the next general election. Judges must be licensed attorneys. There is a chief metropolitan judge who supervises the administration of the metropolitan court. The metropolitan court has the same jurisdiction as a magistrate court with jurisdiction over all offenses and complaints involving ordinances of the county and any municipality within Bernalillo County.

Probate Court

The probate court shares jurisdiction with the district courts over informal proceedings for decisions relating to the disposition of a person's property after his or her death, referred to as probate matters. There is a probate judge in each county. The probate judge is a part-time position and the judge holds court when needed.

Associated Agencies

The Administrative Office of the Courts was created in 1988 by the supreme court to ensure that all courts have the resources and technologies necessary for the effective and efficient administration of justice. The office also collects data and statistics relating to the work of the courts and compiles a report submitted to the supreme court and the legislature.

The Judicial Standards Commission is an independent commission that investigates complaints of judicial misconduct and makes recommendations to the supreme court regarding the removal, retirement, and discipline of any state justice, judge, or magistrate. The commission consists of two justices or judges of the supreme court, appellate court, or district court, one magistrate, two attorneys, and six nonlawyer citizens. The supreme court appoints the judicial members of the commission. The Board of Bar Commissioners appoints the attorneys. The governor appoints the nonlawyers. Judicial and attorney members are appointed for four-year terms. The nonlawyers are appointed for five-year terms. Each year, one of the nonlawyers is selected chair.

The New Mexico Public Defender Department provides legal representation to those clients who cannot afford to hire an attorney. The governor appoints the chief public defender, who is the administrative head of the department. The chief public defender serves at the pleasure of the governor.

Judicial Selection and Removal

Justices of the supreme court and the ten appellate court judges are elected statewide in a partisan election to serve eight-year terms. District court judges are elected in partisan elections to six-year terms and they must live in the judicial district they serve. Magistrates are elected in partisan elections to serve four-year terms. Municipal court judges are elected for four-year terms at regular municipal elections. In cities with populations greater than 30,000 people, additional judges may be elected if the city government thinks the caseload warrants more than one judge.

From statehood in 1912 until 1988, all judges were elected in partisan elections. In 1988, New Mexico voters approved a constitutional amendment that established the hybrid system of judicial selection. The governor, from a list submitted by a nominating commission, would fill midterm vacancies. Appointees would run in contested partisan elections in the next general election and in retention elections thereafter. Voters rejected a more complete system of merit selection in 1951 and 1982.

The state constitution provides two methods for punishing and removing judges from office. The first method involves the Judicial Standards Commission. After investigating complaints against a judge, the commission issues a recommendation to the supreme court. The court may discipline, retire, or remove a judge. Judges also may be impeached by a simple majority vote of the House of Representatives and removed from office by a two-thirds vote of the senate.

John David Rausch Jr.
West Texas A&M University

Further Reading

Garcia, F. Chris, Paul L. Hain, and Gilbert K. St. Clair, eds. 1994. *New Mexico Government.* Albuquerque, NM: University of New Mexico Press.

New Mexico Administrative Office of the Courts, "New Mexico Courts Information Center," http://www.nmcourts.com/.

New Mexico Attorney General, http://www.ago.state.nm.us/.

New Mexico Public Defender Department, http://www.state.nm.us/nmpdd/.

State Bar of New Mexico, http://www.nmbar.org/.

NEW YORK

• • • • • • • • • • • • •

European explorers came to the New York region in 1524, leading up to Henry Hudson's explorations of 100 years later. Soon after Dutch settlements sprang up in what then was called New Netherland. After English conquest of the Dutch territory in 1664, the colony was renamed New York in honor of the Duke of York. After a century of British rule, New York declared its independence on July 9, 1776, becoming one of the original thirteen states of the American Revolution. New York was a significant battleground of the Revolutionary War, with about one in every three of the war's battles being fought there. It was from New York City that General George Washington commanded the Continental Army and bade farewell to his officers at the end of the war. Many of the founders of the U.S. Constitution came from New York. These include: President John Adams, Governor George Clinton, Treasury Secretary Alexander Hamilton, and John Jay, the first chief justice of the United States.

New York's economic power gave it the name Empire State. It was home to innovations in transportation such as the Erie Canal, which opened much of New York and opened the interior of the state to maritime commerce. New York continues to make strides in international commerce. The New York Stock Exchange has been a pillar of capitalism and investment for not only New York's trade, but for the world. With this commerce, New York also would become renowned for its Broadway plays, art museums, legendary sports figures, and the Stature of Liberty, which is the symbolic gateway to the New World for millions of immigrants and their descendants. Today New York State is the third most populous in the country and New York City is the most populous city in the United States.

The Supreme Court of the State of New York may be traced to its colonial origins. The state's first constitution established the court for the trial of impeachments and the correction of errors. This was the highest court, with eight appellate tribunals holding intermediate jurisdiction. Constitutional revisions following the Civil War called for the election of judges to the court of appeals. A 1977 amendment brought about the gubernatorial appointment process. Ostensibly a unified court, New York's judicial system is, in the words of Chief Judge Judith Kaye, "the most cumbersome, complicated trial court structure in the entire country," (1998).

Court of Appeals (Court of Last Resort)

Today, the court of appeals is the highest court in the state of New York. It is composed of a chief judge and six associate judges. Each is appointed to a fourteen-year term. New York's highest appellate court has discretion over most every case brought before it. Its purpose is to clarify law, and so of the 3,900 petitions filed each year only 140 or so appeals merit the court's attention. About three-fourths of the decided cases are civil, and the balance are criminal in nature. The court issues decisions on another 1,200 motions. Though there is a right to appeal capital cases in New York, none were filed in 2004, the most current available statistics.

The court sits en banc to review all cases and answer certified questions. The court meets for two-week-long sessions throughout the year to hear cases. Justices return to their communities to draft decisions and to prepare for the next session. The court operates on a $13.5 million budget and an additional $14 million for its ancillary agencies.

This court has long been counted among the most influential in the country. From here judicial luminaries such as Justice Benjamin Cardozo were appointed to the U.S. Supreme Court after writing

Before being appointed to the U.S. Supreme Court, Benjamin Cardozo served as chief judge of the New York Court of Appeals. There he wrote one of the country's most important personal injury decisions, McPherson v. Buick Motor Co. *(1916). (Library of Congress)*

McPhearson v. Buick Motor Co. (1916), a consumer-rights case that shaped manufacturer's liability law for the rest of the twentieth century.

In New York the intermediate court is called the Appellate Division of the Supreme Court of New York. There are fifty-six judges on this court, which receives approximately 10,000 cases annually. The Appellate Division is divided into four geographic departments, which are further divided into a total of twelve geographic terms. There are 15 judges on each of the terms, each responsible for approximately 134 cases per year. Appeals may proceed from a term to a division and on to the court of appeals. The judges of the Appellate Division are chosen from the supreme court's judges, so they also serve as senior trial court judges.

In civil matters, two layers of the divisions of the supreme court review cases prior to court of appeals review. The First and Second departments hear appeals from civil and criminal cases originating in the civil and criminal courts of New York City. The Second Department has jurisdiction over appeals from lower courts from outside New York City as well. In department hearings between four and five judges will review a case, while between two and three judges hear cases in the term hearings.

Supreme Court (General Jurisdiction Trial Courts)

The Supreme Court of New York is the statewide trial court. It is divided into twelve regional jurisdictions, with authority to hear all cases except those brought against the state government. This court has exclusive jurisdiction in matters of matrimony, annulment, and divorce. Justices, as they are called, hear cases from the jurisdiction in which they reside.

Court of Limited Jurisdiction

The court of claims has only one function: to review cases brought against the state government. Judges are selected by the governor and are approved by the senate to serve nine-year terms. Family court

has jurisdiction in most family matters, except matrimony and divorce. It has jurisdiction in juvenile delinquency cases and child support, adoption, and child custody. Family judges serve ten-year terms and are elected to office, except in New York City, where the mayor appoints them. The surrogate court handles probate and wills for any deceased property owner in the state. Judges in this court serve ten-year terms. County courts are the most local courts, with elected judges serving ten-year terms. County courts have general jurisdiction in criminal matters, but they are limited in civil cases to those with monetary values of less than $25,000. In smaller counties a single judge may preside in county court, family court, and surrogate court, while in New York City judges practice solely in a single type of limited jurisdiction court. City courts are even more local and they handle misdemeanor cases, preliminary hearings for felony cases, landlord-tenant cases, and small claims. City judges serve ten-year terms and are appointed by the mayor in New York City, while they are elected elsewhere. In New York local judges are appointed based on residency in their boroughs.

Judicial Selection and Removal

New York's court system uses a variety of methods for judicial selection. Local courts are either mayoral nominees or locally elected. The court of appeals judges are appointed by the governor, who makes his selections from a list of qualified candidates prepared by a nomination commission. Judges of the Appellate Divisions are chosen by the governor from among sitting supreme court justices, however, supreme court justices are chosen through partisan elections to serve fourteen-year terms.

In the New York City metropolitan area judges in these courts are chosen by the chief administrator of the court with approval from the chief judge of the Appellate Division. Supreme court judges are chosen in general elections to serve fourteen-year terms.

A judicial conduct commission is authorized by the state constitution to review matters related to the fitness of judges to continue in office. It reviews claims of illegal or unethical activity. This commission has authority to exonerate the accused judge, impose reprimands, and cause his or her termination. It may remove judges who become disabled while in office. The appellate court may review this commission's work.

R. Alan Thompson and Sean O. Hogan

References and Further Reading
Historical Society of the New York State Courts, http://www.nycourts .gov/history/.
Kaye, Judith S. 1998. "The State of the Judiciary 1998," http://www.courts .state.ny.us/admin/stateofjudiciary/ stofjud8/stofjud98.htm (accessed March 26, 2006).
Office of the Chief Judge, New York Court of Appeals. 2005. "The State of the Judiciary, 2004." Albany, NY.
Office of the Clerk of the Court of Appeals. 2004. "2004 Annual Report of the Clerk of the Court." Albany, NY.

NORTH CAROLINA

English, French, and Spanish colonial explorers made their ways to what is now North Carolina during the 1500s. At the time, more than two-dozen Indian tribes, belonging to three large nations, had inhabited the region. They were the Iroquoian, Siouan, and the Algonquian families. These native peoples shared language and customs. The Carolina colony fell under English influence as Virginians began exploring the southern reaches of their colony. During the mid- to late 1500s English and Spanish imperial forces vied for control. In 1663 King Charles established colonial rule there under the control of his eight Lords Proprietor for the Carolina colony, named for his predecessor, Charles I. For the Crown, John Locke wrote documents on which the Carolinians and later the American revolutionaries, would base their political ideals and the U.S. Constitution.

Until 1712 North and South Carolina seemingly existed as a single entity with a single governor but separate assemblies. In 1729 seven of the lords sold their interests in the colony and the division was complete; North Carolina became a Crown colony under royal charter and control. North Carolina was among the original thirteen colonies, some say the first officially, to call for independence.

Later, North Carolina joined the Confederacy and seceded from the United States. It was readmitted in 1868 upon ratifying both the U.S. Constitution and its own. It is somewhat ironic that a North Carolina native, Andrew Johnson, was president at the time of the post–Civil War Reconstruction period.

Under colonial rule, the eight lords sat as the general court and appointed justices of the peace to manage general civil and criminal disputes. After Reconstruction judges were elected officials. The state constitution had been ratified multiple times, including a complete overhaul of the court system in 1966 when the current system came into being. These reforms centralized budgeting and administration, unified the local courts, and eliminated justices of the peace and vestiges of colonial custom. A new state constitution was put in place in 1970, leaving this court structure largely as the 1960s reforms envisioned.

John Locke was a seventeenth-century political philosopher who gave the Western world the first distinctly modern theory of human nature. (Library of Congress)

Court of Last Resort

The supreme court is the state's highest court and sits in the state capitol of Raleigh. This court has a chief justice and six associate justices elected to eight-year terms. It receives and disposes of about 200 cases per year. This court considers questions of legal procedures or interpretation of the law. The supreme court's caseload consists primarily of cases involving questions of constitutional law, legal questions of major significance, and appeals from convictions imposing death sentences in first-degree murder cases. Rate-making decisions from regulatory agencies also bypass the appellate court and are reviewed immediately by the supreme court. The constitution provides mandatory appeal in cases where a party loses on a constitutional question at appeal and any case involving a dissenting opinion on the appellate court. Its only mandatory original jurisdiction is in cases of judicial discipline.

The chief justice of the supreme court has responsibilities that include appointing the senior executives of the Administrative Office of the Courts, designating a chief judge for the court of appeals, and selecting a chief district court judge for each of the state's district courts. The chief justice also assigns superior court judges to the scheduled sessions of superior court.

Appellate Court

The fifteen-judge court of appeals, created in 1967, is North Carolina's intermediate appellate court. Like the supreme court, the court of appeals decides only questions of law. It hears about 1,700 cases per year. A majority of the appeals originate in the state's trial courts. The appeals court also may hear disputes arising from decisions of state regulatory agencies including employment matters. Judges of the court of appeals are elected by popular statewide vote for eight-year terms. The chief justice of the supreme court designates a chief judge for the appellate court. Panels of three judges hear cases with the chief judge responsible for assigning members of the court to the five panels.

Superior Court

The superior courts, with 106 judges statewide, are the general jurisdiction trial courts for the state. This level of the court handles more than 300,000 cases per year, with felonies making up nearly one-third of the court's work. All felony criminal cases, civil cases involving more than $10,000, and misdemeanor and infraction appeals from district court are tried in superior court. Cases involving constitutional questions start in the superior courts, as do eminent domain, contested state-agency decisions, and most injunctions.

A jury of twelve hears the criminal cases. In the civil cases, juries are often waived. The superior court is divided into eight divisions and forty-six districts across the state. Judges are elected to eight-year terms and rotate every six months between the districts within their division.

District Court

The district courts handle the vast majority of the trial-level cases, nearly 2.8 million cases per year. Nearly 1.5 million of these cases are traffic violations of some sort. The 235 judges have exclusive jurisdiction over civil cases involving less than $10,000, almost all misdemeanors, probable-cause hearings in felony cases, juvenile proceedings, mental health hospital commitments, and domestic relations cases. North Carolina has 40 district court districts, and 235 district court judges, elected to four-year terms.

Other Judicial Agencies

The eighteen-member State Judicial Council consists of court officials from every court function. The governor, chief justice, legislature, and court and bar associations appoint council members. The Judicial Council is largely an advisory body. It makes recommendations to the chief justice about finances, benefits, and compensation of judicial officials; judicial administration and access to justice; alternative dispute resolution; boundaries of the judicial districts; and other matters.

The seven-member Judicial Standards Commission is responsible for the investigation of complaints concerning the qualifications of any justice or judge of the general court of justice. The commission was created in 1972 after a constitutional amendment was approved by the voters.

The Administrative Office of the Court (AOC) provides support services for the courts, including information technology, human resources, financial, legal research, and planning. The AOC prepares annual reports and other information for the public and other governing agencies.

The Commission on Indigent Defense Services has 155 lawyers who represent poor criminal defendants at trial. The Office of the Appellate Defender defends the poor on appeal.

Judicial Selection and Removal

Judges on the appellate and supreme court are elected in partisan elections. Superior court judges are nominated locally and stand for statewide election. They serve eight-year terms. District judges are elected in local partisan elections and serve four-year terms. Magistrates are appointed by the superior court judges to serve two-year terms. The governor fills vacancies. They are subject to review by the Judicial Standards Commission. This commission makes nonbinding recommendations to the supreme court, which has final authority to dismiss a case or the judge if he or she is found guilty of an infraction. The state assembly also may remove a judge through an impeachment process. Judges also are removed from office on reaching the age of seventy-two years.

Sean O. Hogan

References and Further Reading

Administrative Office of the Courts. 2005. "Fiscal Year 2003–04 Annual Report for the North Carolina Courts." Raleigh, NC.

State Library of North Carolina, "Information Services Branch, State History," http://statelibrary.dcr.state.nc.us/nc/cover.htm.

NORTH DAKOTA
● ● ● ● ● ● ● ● ● ● ● ●

In 1861, the supreme court of the Dakota Territory was established. Originally staffed by three justices, by 1888 the court had eight justices. In 1889 the constitution of the state of North Dakota provided for a supreme court with three justices to be elected by the people for terms of seven years. The constitution also created six judicial districts, each of which would be served by one judge, who would be elected for four-year terms. Within six years a new judicial district was created and eight years later, another judicial district (with one judge each). In 1908, a constitutional amendment increased the size of the supreme court from three to five justices. This is still the size of the court. However, a 1930 amendment to the constitution increased the length of a supreme court justice's term from six to ten years.

The number of judicial districts increased to ten in 1907. In 1909, the legislature passed a statute requiring that district court judges be elected on a nonpartisan ballot. Although the legislature created eleventh and twelfth judicial districts in 1911, in 1919 it reduced the number of judicial districts to six, although they now allowed for multijudge districts. The six districts were staffed by fifteen judges. A 1930 amendment to the constitution increased the length of a district court judge's term to six years.

In 1979, the legislature completely reorganized the district court system. The state was divided into seven judicial districts, staffed by a total of twenty-four judges. In 1991, the legislature abolished county courts, giving North Dakota a unified system of trial courts. Legislation in 2001 increased the number of district court judges to forty-two.

Organization of State Courts

The North Dakota court system is led by a five–member supreme court. In 2005 Gerald W. VandeWalle was the chief justice, and associate justices were William A. Neumann, Dale V. Sanderstrom, Mary Muchlen Maring, and Carol Ronning Kapsner. Since 1987, North Dakota has had a court of appeals. It is important to note that this is a temporary court, in part because legislation creating it runs out in 2008, and in part because it has no permanent judges assigned to it. Moreover the court of appeals does not meet every year. It is made up of three judges chosen by the supreme court, from active and retired district court judges or retired supreme court justices.

The trial-level courts in the North Dakota judiciary have district court judges. There are currently seven judicial district courts, staffed by forty-two district court judges. Finally, there are municipal courts that employ seventy-seven municipal court judges.

Powers of State Courts

The supreme court has adjudicatory as well as administrative powers. The chief justice is chosen by the supreme court justices and the district court judges, and he or she serves a term of five years. The chief justice presides over the supreme court, represents the judiciary at state functions, and serves as head of the judicial branch. The supreme court is required to hear all appeals arriving from the district courts. The supreme court also decides which, if any, cases to assign to the court of appeals. In its administrative role, the supreme court is responsible for the efficient operation of all nonfederal courts in the state, as well as the supervision of the legal profession. The chief justice appoints a clerk of the supreme court who supervises the administrative activities involved in the smooth operation of the supreme court.

The court of appeals has very limited powers. Judges are assigned to this court at the discretion of the supreme court, and cases are assigned to it at the discretion of the supreme court. Although this court has heard approximately seventy-five cases since its inception, it has not convened in recent years.

District courts are the courts of general jurisdiction in North Dakota. They act as juvenile courts and they also have jurisdiction over civil cases, criminal felony cases, and criminal misdemeanor cases. Each of the seven judicial districts is served by a court administrator or administrative assistant.

Finally, North Dakota has municipal courts, staffed by seventy-seven municipal court judges. These courts have jurisdiction over municipal ordinances, both criminal and civil. The majority of cases heard in municipal courts are administrative traffic cases. When hearing class B misdemeanors, the municipal courts are able to provide a jury trial. Criminal appeals from the municipal courts go to the district court.

Selection of Judges

All judges in North Dakota are elected in nonpartisan elections. Supreme court justices are elected for ten-year terms, district court judges are elected for six-year terms, and municipal court judges are elected for four-year terms. Midterm vacancies on the supreme court and on the district courts can be filled either through special elections or through gubernatorial appointment. If the governor replaces a judge through appointment, the governor must choose from a list of potential judges provided by the Judicial Nominating Committee. Any position filled through a special election or appointment must go before the voters during the general election following a minimum of two years after the judge/justice takes the bench. Vacancies in the munic-

ipal courts are filled by the executive officer of the municipality in which the vacancy occurred with the consent of the governing body of the municipality. Justices of the supreme court, district court judges, and municipal court judges in cities with populations over 5,000 must be licensed attorneys. In cities with populations smaller than 5,000, municipal court judges must be a qualified elector in the city.

Discipline

All judges are subject to discipline or removal for misconduct. The Judicial Conduct Commission was established in 1975. Its job is to handle complaints involving judges and other state judicial officers. The commission has the power to discipline or to remove judges. Complaints heard by the commission in 2003 involved abuse of authority, improper decisions or rulings, and improper conduct on the bench, among other things. Of the forty-nine complaints disposed of by the commission in 2003, forty-one were summarily dismissed, five were dismissed, one resulted in admonishment by the Judicial Conduct Commission, and only two resulted in formal charges. The majority of the 2003 complaints involved district court judges. A complaint is summarily dismissed when the material included in the complaint would not construe misconduct or incapacity, even if it were true. A dismissal, on the other hand, occurs after an investigation has taken place, when charges could construe misconduct or incapacity but are not supported by evidence.

Workload

During the 2002 term of the North Dakota Supreme Court there were 353 cases filed, and in 2003, there were 361. Since North Dakota does not have a traditional intermediate appellate court, the supreme court generally hears all appeals coming from the district courts. The state constitution requires that a justice not agreeing with the majority of the court must write a dissenting opinion. As a result of this, in 2003, each justice wrote an average of forty-six majority opinions and fifty-eight concurrences or dissents. In addition to hearing oral argument and writing opinions, the court also had its administrative responsibilities, which included management of the state court system and supervision of the legal profession.

The North Dakota Court of Appeals was established in 1987 to assist the supreme court in managing its caseload. Although the court of appeals disposed of seventy-five cases during its history, it has not heard any cases in recent years.

North Dakota's forty-two district court judges, in its seven judicial districts, disposed of 168,036 cases in 2002 and 174,786 cases in 2003. It is worth noting that approximately 90,000 of the cases are administrative traffic cases. There has been a slight decline in the number of cases filed between 2002 and 2003. This included a decrease of almost 12 percent in small-claims case filings. During 2003 there were 301 jury trials held in the district courts.

Ruth Ann Watry
Northern Michigan University

References and Further Reading

American Judicature Society, "Center for Judicial Selection," http://www.ajs.org/selection/index.asp.

Harmon, Robert B. 1990. *Government and Politics in North Dakota: A Selected Guide to Informational Sources.* Monticello, IL: Vance Bibliographies.

North Dakota Courts Annual Report 2003, http://www.ndcourts.com/court/news/AnnualReport2003/.

North Dakota Supreme Court, http://www.court.state.nd.us/.

OHIO
● ● ● ● ● ● ● ● ● ● ● ● ●

Ohio was among the six states that had territory impacted by the Northwest Ordinance of 1787. Until 1798, at which time the Ohio Territory had sufficient population for self-government, Ohio was ruled by a military governor and three judges. In 1802 Ohio became eligible for statehood, and its first constitution was adopted. The constitution provided that all judicial power would rest in "a Supreme Court, in Courts of Common Pleas for each county, in Justices of the Peace, and in such other courts as the legislature may, from time to time, establish" (Article III, Section 1).

The supreme court was made up of three judges, appointed by a joint ballot of both houses of the general assembly, with terms of seven years. The state was divided into three circuits, each of which had a court of common pleas, with one president and two associate judges, selected in the same manner as the supreme court judges. The constitution also provided that justices of the peace, whose powers and duties would be set by law, would be elected for terms of three years. The supreme court was a court of original as well as appellate jurisdiction. In 1807, less than five years after its creation, the supreme court established the power of judicial review, ruling part of a state law to be in violation of the state constitution. The legislature responded by attempting to impeach the two justices who participated in the case, but failed.

Because of significant changes occurring during its first fifty years as a state, Ohio found the need to create a new constitution in 1850. The new constitution, ratified in 1851, changed the structure of the judiciary. The constitution provided that judicial power would be vested in "a Supreme Court, in District Courts, Courts of Common Pleas, Courts of Probate, Justices of the Peace, and in such other courts inferior to the Supreme Court, in one or more counties, such as the General Assembly, may, from time to time, establish" (Article IV, Section 1).

The size of the supreme court was increased to five justices, the number of common pleas districts (previously called circuits) increased to nine, and the number of judges in each district would be determined by law. District courts were composed of judges of common pleas and well as one supreme court judge. Each county would also now have a probate court staffed by one judge. All judges were to be elected by the voters for five-year terms for supreme court and common pleas court judges, and three years for probate judges and justices of the peace. In 1912 the constitution was amended to increase the number of supreme court judges to seven, to create the position of chief justice, and to change the length of term of office to six years.

During this period, there was a woman making many firsts in the Ohio courts. In 1920, Florence Allen became the first woman ever elected to be a judge when she was elected to a court of common pleas judgeship. In 1922, she was elected as the first woman to sit on any state supreme court.

An amendment in 1968 gave the supreme court the power to adopt rules governing all Ohio courts, as well as giving all supreme court judges the right to be called "justice." In 1977 the Office of Disciplinary Counsel was created to undertake investigations of misconduct by attorneys and lawyers, and the court of appeals was created in 1995.

Organization of State Courts

There are many layers to the Ohio court system. At the top is the supreme court, comprised of seven justices. In 2005 the justices of the Ohio Supreme Court were Chief Justice Thomas J. Moyer and associate justices Terrence O'Donnell, Evelyn Lundberg Stratton, Maureen O'Connor, Judith Ann Lanzinger, Alice Robie Resnick, and Paul E. Pfeifer. The next level of the Ohio court system is the courts of appeals, comprised of twelve districts and sixty-eight judges. The number of judges in each appellate district ranges from three to twelve.

The court of general jurisdiction in Ohio is the court of common pleas. There are eighty-eight courts; one for each county. This is the only trial court created in the state constitution. These courts are staffed by 376 judges. In all but seven counties, within the courts of common pleas, there are general, domestic relations, probate, and juvenile divisions.

Ohio has many courts of limited jurisdiction. The court of claims was created to handle civil actions filed against the state of Ohio. Judges are temporarily assigned to this court. There are also 118 municipal courts staffed by 203 judges, 47 county courts staffed by 55 judges, and 428 mayors courts, staffed by said mayors.

Powers of State Courts

The supreme court is the court of last resort as well as the leader of the Ohio courts. Original jurisdiction of the supreme court includes the issuance of extraordinary writs as well as admission to the practice of law and related disciplines. The supreme court has appellate jurisdiction over cases involving the Ohio or U.S. Constitution, cases originating in courts of appeals, and cases where two courts of appeals are in conflict on some question of law. The supreme court is required to hear appeals in all cases involving imposition of the death penalty, and since 1995, has heard those cases as the court of first appeal. The supreme court also has appellate jurisdiction over certain administrative agencies, including the Board of Tax Appeals and Public Utilities Commission. Much of the appellate jurisdiction is discretionary, and the supreme court does not hear many cases that come to it. In addition to its judicial powers, the supreme court is also the head of the Ohio judiciary. The supreme court oversees the rules of practice and procedure in all state courts, oversees the bar, and has disciplinary power over judges found guilty of ethics violations.

The courts of appeals are the court of first appeal for most appeals in Ohio. Sitting in three-judge panels, judges hear appeals from the common pleas, municipal, and county courts. The court can also hear appeals from the Board of Tax Appeals. In addition to their appellate jurisdiction, the courts of appeals also have original jurisdiction to grant writs of habeas corpus, mandamus, procedendo (a higher court's order directing a lower court to determine and enter judgment in a previously removed case), prohibition, and quo warranto.

The court of common pleas is the only trial court created in the constitution. The court has original jurisdiction over civil and criminal cases, divorces and dissolutions, support and custody of children, probate cases, adoption cases, mental illness cases, paternity actions, and offenses involving minors. The court has civil jurisdiction in all cases involving more than $500.

Municipal courts, which are created by law, have jurisdiction over misdemeanor offenses, traffic offenses, and civil actions up to $15,000. County courts, created when municipal courts do not have countywide jurisdiction, have the same jurisdiction. Mayors courts have jurisdiction over misdemeanor cases and traffic offenses. The court of claims has statewide jurisdiction over cases involving a civil action filed against the state.

Selection of Judges

Judges in Ohio are selected through a combination of partisan and nonpartisan elections. Judicial candidates are initially nominated through partisan primary elections, thus receiving endorsement from a political party. During the general election, candidates run on a nonpartisan ballot. Supreme court, court of appeals, court of common pleas, county court, and municipal court judges are elected to six-year terms. When a vacancy occurs during a judge's term, the judge is replaced by gubernatorial appointment and then stands for election for the remainder of the term during the next general election. Although it is not required by law, when a judicial vacancy has occurred, the governor has asked party leadership in the appropriate county for a list of possible candidates and has chosen the appointee from the list. All judges must have practiced law for at least six years and must be under the age of seventy. With the exception of supreme court justices, judges must be residents of the district, county, or municipality in which they will serve. The court of claims judges are assigned to the court by tem-

porary assignment by the chief justice of the supreme court.

Discipline

Conduct of Ohio judges is governed by the Ohio Rules of Court for the Government of the Judiciary of Ohio. The Office of Disciplinary Counsel and the Board of Commissioners on Grievances and Discipline oversees discipline of Ohio lawyers and judges. The twenty-eight-member commission is comprised of seventeen attorneys, seven active or retired judges, and four nonlawyers, all serving three-year terms. The board conducts hearings and makes final recommendations to the supreme court in disciplinary cases involving ethical misconduct charges concerning judges and attorneys. Decisions of the commission can be appealed to the supreme court. Judges may also "be removed from office, by concurrent resolution of both houses of the general assembly, if two-thirds of the members, elected to each house, concur therein; but, no such removal shall be made, except upon complaint, the substance of which shall be entered on the journal, nor, until the party charged shall have had notice thereof, and an opportunity to be heard" (Article IV, Section 17).

Workload

In 2003, there were over 3.3 million cases filed in Ohio courts. The Ohio Supreme Court saw 2,237 cases filed. This included 1,686 jurisdictional appeals, 433 merit cases, and 118 cases involving the practice

of law. Of the 1,686 cases involving jurisdictional appeals, 1,547 were discretionary appeals. Of the jurisdictional appeals, 229 were accepted for review. In
the courts of appeals, 10,905 cases were
filed. The number of cases ranged from
303 in the fourth district to 1,128 in the
eighth district. The average caseload per
judge was 160 cases, ranging from an average of 116 cases per judge in the fourth
district to 206 cases per judge in the fifth
district. Additional caseloads included
211,376 cases filed in the courts of common pleas general division; 79,527 cases
in the domestic relations courts; 95,338
cases in the probate courts; 264,897 cases
in the juvenile courts; 2,447,108 cases in
the municipal courts; 256,045 cases in
the county courts; and 1,134 cases in the
Ohio Court of Claims.

Ruth Ann Watry
Northern Michigan University

References and Further Reading

American Judicature Society, "Center for
    Judicial Selection," http://www.ajs.org/
    selection/index.asp.
Lieberman, Carl, ed. 1995. *Government,
    Politics and Public Policy in Ohio.*
    Akron, OH: Midwest Press.
Ohio History Central, http://www
    .ohiohistorycentral.org/.
Ohio House of Representatives, http://
    legislature.state.oh.us/.
Ohio Judicial Conference, http://
    ohiojudges.org/.
Supreme Court of Ohio, http://
    sconet.state.oh.us/.
Walter, Janis L. 2005. *Ohio Courts.* Upper
    Saddle River, NJ: Prentice-Hall.

OKLAHOMA
• • • • • • • • • • • • •

Oklahoma initially petitioned Congress
as two separate states. The eastern half
was highly populated with Native Americans. White settlers dominated the western half of the state. After settlers in the
western part of the state petitioned for
statehood, the Five Civilized Tribes held
a convention and wrote a constitution
hoping to petition for statehood for the
Indian Territory. Congress rejected the
Five Civilized Tribes' petition. Oklahoma
was admitted to the United States as a
single state on November 16, 1907. In
1967 Oklahoma's judicial system was
overhauled. The overhaul abolished superior courts, courts of common pleas, justices of the peace, and magistrates, and
consolidated them into district courts.

Oklahoma is one of two states with two
courts of last resort: the supreme court
and the court of criminal appeals.

Article VII of the Oklahoma Constitution established Oklahoma's judiciary.
The constitution authorizes the senate as
the court of impeachment, a supreme
court, the court of criminal appeals, the
court on the judiciary, the state workmans' compensation court, the court of
tax review, appellate courts as may be
provided by statute, and district courts.

Oklahoma's judiciary budget is about
$66.2 million for fiscal year (FY) 2006.
This budget represents a 5.3 percent increase over the FY 2005 budget. A majority of the budget funds Oklahoma's
district courts ($45.6 million). The

supreme court operates on a $13.7 million budget.

Courts of Final Resort

In Oklahoma there is a right to at least one appeal. The Supreme Court of Oklahoma and the court of criminal appeals are the two final courts in the Oklahoma appeal process.

Civil Appeals

The court of last resort for civil matters is the Oklahoma Supreme Court. The supreme court consists of nine justices appointed from nine separate judicial districts. In Oklahoma all cases except criminal cases are appealed directly to the supreme court. Though all civil matters are appealed directly from district court to the supreme court, the supreme court assigns almost all appeals to the court of civil appeals.

The Oklahoma Supreme Court has appellate jurisdiction from trial courts, agencies, boards, and commissions. The supreme court will act on a writ of certiorari on limited occasions. Certiorari may be granted when the court of appeals does not conform with a decision by the Oklahoma Supreme Court or the U.S. Supreme Court; the court of civil appeals divisions have conflicting opinions; or when the court of civil appeals' decision is a substantial departure from the usual course of judicial proceedings.

The supreme court does not have appellate jurisdiction from the court of the judiciary and courts of impeachment. Decisions of those courts are final. Decisions of the Oklahoma Supreme Court based on the Oklahoma Constitution are final.

Once a case is appealed to the Oklahoma Supreme Court it is assigned to the court of civil appeals. From time to time the Oklahoma Supreme Court may take the case itself rather than assigning it to the court of civil appeals. The Oklahoma Supreme Court also decides on writs of certiorari. The Oklahoma Supreme Court has full discretion on which cases it grants certiorari. When the Oklahoma Supreme Court accepts a case it receives the transcripts, the records, and briefs. The case is then assigned to an individual justice for review. If the Oklahoma Supreme Court receives a petition of certiorari it also requires the court of civil appeals' opinion. A referee reviews the opinion along with the petition and its reply. He or she then makes a recommendation to an individual justice for review. That justice then makes a recommendation to the court. If the court decides to accept the case it is assigned to an individual justice to write an opinion.

The Oklahoma Supreme Court rarely hears oral arguments. If the Oklahoma Supreme Court rejects the case, the opinion of the court of civil appeals becomes final. Once the individual justice researches and writes an opinion, it is circulated among the other justices and voted on. If five justices agree with the opinion it becomes the opinion of the court. Other justices can write concurrent or dissenting opinions if the opinion is not unanimous. The supreme court disposes of about 1,600 cases each year.

The supreme court also administers the judicial system in Oklahoma. The court establishes operating rules and procedures for other courts in the state. It also establishes rules of conduct for attorneys throughout Oklahoma.

Criminal Appeals

The court of criminal appeals is the court of last resort for criminal matters. The court of criminal appeals consists of five judges who sit en banc. Criminal cases are appealed directly from the district court to the Oklahoma Court of Criminal Appeals. The 1907 constitution provided for the court of criminal appeals. A year later the legislature created the court with three judges. In 1959, the name was changed to the court of criminal appeals. In 1988 the court was expanded to its current five judges. The court hears appeals directly from trial. There is no intermediate court of appeals for criminal cases in Oklahoma. The court of criminal appeals disposes an average of 1,600 to 1,800 cases each year. In cases where there is a jurisdictional question between the court of criminal appeals and the supreme court, the supreme court makes the final decision on where the case is assigned.

The Oklahoma Court of Civil Appeals has twelve appointed judges who serve in four divisions. The courts sit in three-judge panels either in Oklahoma City or Tulsa. It hears cases referred by the supreme court. It disposes of most appeals that end up before the supreme court.

District Courts

Oklahoma has twenty-six judicial districts that include seventy-one district judges, seventy-seven associate judges, and seventy-three special judges. District courts have original jurisdiction over all criminal and civil matters. These courts also have appellate jurisdiction from municipal courts that are not of record. They hear appeals de novo. Many of the districts and counties have special judges. These judges conduct preliminary hearings, and hear small-claims cases and uncontested family matters. They can also be asked to hear other matters.

Other Courts

Workers' compensation court handles matters concerning on-the-job injuries. The workers' compensation court has evolved over the years. Initially, the State Industrial Commission handled workmans' compensation cases. It currently has ten judges, with one selected by the governor to act as the presiding judge for a two-year term.

Judges hear cases individually. If the parties do not agree with the judge's decision, they can appeal the case to a panel of three judges who act as the court en banc. No new evidence is introduced at this point. The parties can bypass the court en banc and appeal directly to the state supreme court.

Associated Offices

Several judicial offices assist the court in Oklahoma. These offices include the clerk of the supreme court, the administrator for the courts, and central staff for the courts. Nine presiding judges are elected by their peers to oversee the administration of the state's judicial system. They meet monthly with members of the supreme court and the court of criminal appeals to discuss judicial matters and trends in the state. The forum provides a bridge between the trial and appellate courts.

Selection of Judges

Appellate court justices and judges are appointed on a modified Missouri Plan. Lower court judges are elected.

For appellate-level openings, the governor chooses judges from a list of three recommendations made by the Oklahoma Judicial Nominating Commission to twelve-year terms. The supreme court justices select a chief justice and vice chief justice from among their ranks to serve in those positions for two years. There are nine supreme court districts in Oklahoma, and one justice from each district.

Justices must be at least thirty years old, qualified to vote prior to the appointment, and have been a licensed attorney or judge of a court of record for five years before. The justices must maintain their status as licensed attorneys while holding office. Justices and appellate court judges face retention elections every six years.

District court judges and associate judges are elected in nonpartisan elections every four years. The governor fills vacancies. District court judges must have at least four years experience as a practicing attorney or judge in Oklahoma, and associate judges must have two years of experience. A judge must also be a registered voter and reside in the county and district six months prior to the beginning of the election cycle.

Discipline and Removal of Judges

Judges can be disciplined and removed from office for incompetence, crimes of moral turpitude, gross partiality in office, oppression, gross negligence, habitual drunkenness, or other grounds established by the legislature. The court of the judiciary has exclusive jurisdiction in removal of judges. The legislature can also impeach and fire judges and justices. The court of the judiciary is limited in its scope to judicial disciplinary matters. The court of the judiciary has two divisions—trial and appellate—with exclusive jurisdiction involving corruption, incompetence, malfeasance, and so on in the state's judicial system. The trial division has nine judges, eight of whom are senior district judges and one an active lawyer. The appellate division has nine judges, two are supreme court justices, one is from the court of criminal appeals, and five are senior district court judges. The court of the judiciary's decisions are final, and they are not appealed to the supreme court.

Doug Goodman
Mississippi State University

References and Further Reading

Adkison, Danny M. 2002. "Oklahoma." In *Legal Systems of the World*, vol. 3, ed. Herbert M. Kritzer. Santa Barbara, CA: ABC-CLIO, 1227–1230.

Office of State Finance. 2005. "FY 2006 Executive Budget," http://www.osf .state.ok.us/bud06.pdf (accessed November 21, 2005).

Oklahoma Bar Association. 2004. "Judges and Courts," http://www.okbar.org /judges/ (accessed July 21, 2004).

Oklahoma State Courts Network, http:// www.oscn.net/.

State of Oklahoma. 2004. "Your Oklahoma," http://www.oklahoma.gov (accessed July 21, 2004).

OREGON

• • • • • • • • • • • •

Prior to 1841, Oregon's judicial system relied on the British Hudson's Bay Company justices of the peace. American settlers refused to recognize British jurisdiction. The Methodist missionaries in the region appointed their own justices of the peace. In 1841, a series of meetings was held to set a procedure for dealing with the property of a wealthy American entrepreneur, Ewing Young. Young had left no will and he did not have any known heirs. The region needed a civil government to decide who would get Young's sizable estate. Ira Babcock, a physician, was appointed supreme judge with probate powers. Justices of the peace, constables, and an attorney general were also appointed at the mission meetings.

In 1843, meetings were held at Champoeg to form a provisional government for Oregon. Under the provisions of the laws established at these meetings, a three-member supreme court was created. The court had original jurisdiction in cases of treason, felonies, breaches of the peace, and all civil actions exceeding $50. The law was changed in 1844 to provide for the election of new judges. Additional laws provided for a system of county circuit courts and justices of the peace, who relieved the supreme court of many trial responsibilities. Congress granted territorial status to Oregon in 1848. Three judicial districts were created, with one of the three justices of the supreme court serving each district. The supreme court remained largely unchanged until statehood in 1859.

The Oregon state government has operated under the same constitution since statehood in 1859. The document includes provisions taken from earlier state constitutions, especially the constitutions of Indiana, Maine, and Iowa. The Oregon Constitution, at slightly more than 26,000 words, is roughly average in length when compared with other state constitutions. Besides allowing the legislature to amend the constitution, an amendment approved by the voters in 1902 provided for the citizen initiative. The constitution has been amended over 220 times. The document includes numerous spelling and punctuation errors.

Oregon Supreme Court

The Oregon state courts are organized into a unified system called the Oregon Judicial Department. The highest court in Oregon is the supreme court. The court has seven elected justices.

The supreme court has the discretion whether to hear an appeal from the appellate court. Usually the court will only hear those cases that raise significant questions of law or that may have widespread impact. In addition to cases from the appellate court, death penalty appeals and tax court appeals bypass the appellate court. The supreme court also has direct appeal in cases involving contested titles on state ballot questions and the discipline of judges and lawyers. In 2002, there were 231 petition for review filed with the supreme court. The court agreed to review fifty-seven of the cases.

The supreme court also plays a significant role in the Oregon legal system. The justices are responsible for admitting new lawyers to the practice of law, following the recommendations of the Board of Bar Examiners. The supreme court may remove, suspend, or censure judges for misconduct, based on the recommendations of the Oregon Commission for Judicial Fitness and Disability. Justices choose one of their own to serve a six-year term as chief justice. The chief justice supervises the state court system, makes rules, and issues orders to carry out the duties of the office, appoints the chief judge of the court of appeals and the presiding judges of the state trial courts, adopts rules that establish procedures for

Oregon Supreme Court Justice Hans Linde served on the Oregon Supreme Court from 1977 to 1990. He was a pioneer of the "new judicial federalism," arguing that state constitutions were "first in law and first in logic." His influence on Oregon law continues to be felt. He was a member of Oregon's Commission on Constitutional Revision in 1961–1963, and has served on the Oregon Law Commission since its inception in 1997, where he now serves on an ethics panel. (Frank Miller/Willamette University)

all state courts, and supervises the statewide fiscal plan and budget for all state courts.

The Oregon Supreme Court is recognized as one of the early leaders in the new judicial federalism movement. A member of the court from 1977 through 1990, Justice Hans Linde has been attributed as the father of the principle of state constitutional primacy. As a law professor and before being appointed to the court, Linde published an article in the *Oregon Law Review* advocating the process of looking to the state constitution for civil liberties protections. According to Professor Linde, a state judge should consult the state constitution first, giving only a secondary consideration to federal law. Although the Oregon Supreme Court acknowledged this theory, the justices rejected it in their opinions. When Linde joined the court in 1977, he was able to apply his theory to supreme court rulings. In 1984, he sought reelection to a second six-year term. Supreme court elections are usually quiet, low key affairs. Linde faced two opponents in 1984 in part because law-and-order interest groups saw his rulings limiting police searches and the death penalty as being soft on crime.

Oregon Court of Appeals

Until 1969, all appeals from trial courts went directly to the Oregon Supreme Court. The Oregon legislature created the court of appeals to allow the supreme court to focus on very important cases. Originally, the appellate court had jurisdiction over criminal, domestic relations, and administrative appeals. The legislature broadened the court's jurisdiction during the 1970s. The court has jurisdiction to hear all civil and criminal appeals from circuit courts, except death penalty cases, and to review most state administrative agency actions. There were 3,277 cases filed in the court of appeals in 2002.

The appellate court has ten judges. The court's chief judge is appointed by the chief justice of the supreme court. The judges divide into three panels of three judges each to consider appeals. The chief judge does not serve on any panel but is available to substitute for another judge who is not available or has a conflict of interest. A panel's decision can be considered further when requested by three judges and a majority agrees to the reconsideration.

Circuit Courts

Circuit courts are the state's trial courts of general jurisdiction. Until January 1998, Oregon had limited jurisdiction trial courts called district courts to hear small civil cases and misdemeanors. The district courts were merged into the circuit courts in 1998.

The state is divided in twenty-seven judicial districts, each of which has one or more counties. State law determines the number of judges elected in each district based on population and case volume. Counties with small populations and case volumes are combined into multicounty judicial districts. Each county has a circuit court, even those in multicounty districts. The chief justice appoints a presiding judge in each district to provide administration and supervision over the district.

Each case is heard in the county in which it originated. Circuit courts hear cases regardless of subject matter, amount of money involved, or the severity of the crime. Circuit courts are courts of record. Decisions appealed from circuit court go directly to the appellate court, except for death sentences. Death penalty appeals go directly to the supreme court. Oregon circuit courts heard 644,800 cases in 2002.

Oregon Tax Court

The Oregon Tax Court is a trial court whose jurisdiction is limited to cases involving Oregon's tax laws, including income taxes, corporate excise taxes, property taxes, timber taxes, cigarette taxes, local budget laws, and property tax limitations. The legislature created the tax court to encourage the uniform application of tax laws. The tax court hears most cases in Salem. There are no jury trials and appeals go directly to the supreme court. In 2002, the Oregon Tax Court decided 1,167 cases.

The tax court has two divisions, a regular division and the magistrate division. The magistrate division tries or mediates all tax appeals unless the case has been assigned to the regular division. A magistrate's decision may be appealed to the tax court judge.

Local Trial Courts

Municipal, county, and justice courts are local courts outside the state-funded court system. Their jurisdiction is limited to violations, lesser crimes, and some other less serious cases. The Oregon Judicial Department has no administrative control over those local courts. In nine eastern Oregon counties, those to the east of the Cascade Mountains, county voters elect a county judge who chairs the Board of Commissioners and spends some time on judicial duties. The county judge does not have to be an attorney. Most cities have municipal courts. The judges on these courts usually are appointed by the city councils. These courts deal with violations of city ordinances. Oregon also has thirty justice courts. They serve districts established by the County Boards of Commissioners in nineteen counties. Justice courts share jurisdiction within their county with the circuit court in all criminal prosecutions except felony trials. Justice courts have jurisdiction over traffic, boating, wildlife, and other violations occurring in their county. Justices of the peace also perform weddings at no charge if performed at their offices during regular business hours. Justices of the peace are elected on a nonpartisan ballot.

Associated Agencies

The Office of the State Court Administrator oversees the state-funded court system. The chief justice of the supreme court appoints a chief administrative officer whose title is state court administrator, a position created by statute. The Public Defense Services Commission is an independent commission in the judicial branch but outside the state court system. The commission is responsible for establishing a cost-effective public defense system that satisfied constitutional and statutory requirements.

Judicial Selection and Removal

Oregon judges have been chosen in nonpartisan elections since 1931. The governor makes appointments to fill vacancies, and the appointee must run for election at the next general election. In recent years, approximately 85 percent of Oregon judges have first been appointed rather than elected to office, and the vast majority are unopposed in elections to retain their seats.

In 2002, voters rejected two judicial selection proposals. The first would have given voters a "none of the above" option when voting for judge and would have required appointed judges to run for election at the next available election, rather than the next available general election. The second would have provided for the election of appellate judges from geographic districts rather than statewide.

Circuit court judges are elected in the judicial districts in which they serve. The supreme court may appoint any elected judge or other eligible person to serve as a temporary judge on any circuit court. A person must be a resident of Oregon who has been a member of the Oregon State Bar for at least three years.

The Oregon Constitution provides for two methods for removing judges from the bench. First, voters may initiate a recall process to remove a judge before his or her term has expired. Second, the Commission on Judicial Fitness and Disability reviews complaints and can recommend that the supreme court censure a judge or suspend or remove the judge from office. The supreme court makes the final decision. The commission is comprised of three lay members appointed by the governor and confirmed by the senate, three lawyers appointed by the Oregon State Bar, and three judges appointed by the supreme court. Commission members serve four-year terms.

John David Rausch Jr.
West Texas A&M University

Further Reading

Office of the State Court Administrator, http://www.ojd.state.or.us/osca/index.htm.

Oregon Judicial Department, "Oregon Courts," http://www.ojd.state.or.us/.

Oregon State Bar, http://www.osbar.org/.

State of Oregon, "Department of Justice," http://www.doj.state.or.us/.

PENNSYLVANIA
• • • • • • • • • • • •

The state now known as Pennsylvania changed hands from the Duke of York (who later became King James II) to William Penn on March 4, 1681. The land was given to Penn by King Charles II of England in exchange for forgiving an unpaid loan in the amount of £16,000. In a time of religious intolerance Penn secured the land to offer a safe haven for those who wished to practice the beliefs of the Society of Friends, also known as the Quakers. Although Penn was granted the land, England still maintained control and provided protection for its people with English laws. A true cultural melting pot, Pennsylvania has been the home to settlers since its creation. The Indians were the first to inhabit Pennsylvania followed by the English, Germans, Scots-Irish, African Americans, and many others.

Despite its many inhabitants, England provided the largest influence on the government and judiciary system. The court structure here began as a disjointed mass of municipal courts headed largely by part-time nonlawyers, appointed and controlled by the governor. In 1684 England agreed to allow Pennsylvania to establish its own provincial appellate court, but until 1722 England remained the final court of appeal for Pennsylvania. It was not until the Judiciary Act of 1722 that Pennsylvania began to resemble a unified judicial system.

Today, the Pennsylvania judicial system consists of the supreme court, superior court, commonwealth court, common pleas courts, and special courts. The special courts are the lower-level courts and are composed of the magisterial district judges, Philadelphia Municipal Court, Philadelphia Traffic Court, and the Pittsburgh Municipal Court. All judges serving in the supreme, superior, commonwealth, and common pleas courts are elected to serve ten-year terms. Vacancies occurring before an election year are temporarily filled with a gubernatorial appointment with senate confirmation until the next election. All judges must meet basic citizenship and residency requirements before being elected. Those judges serving above the special courts level must also be members in good standing of the bar of the Pennsylvania Supreme Court.

Pennsylvania Supreme Court

The Pennsylvania Supreme Court was originally created with the Judiciary Act of 1722. This act provided for one chief justice and two justices who would sit for supreme court cases biannually. In 1895, the general assembly responded to the supreme court's overwhelming workload by creating the superior court. The superior court would also serve as an appellate court but would have separate legal jurisdiction from the supreme court. In 1980, the powers of the superior court were increased to help the supreme court manage its docket.

The modern Pennsylvania Supreme Court uses the writ of certiorari to determine which cases to hear. The Pennsylvania Supreme Court is the state's highest judicial authority. This court is the last resort for cases heard in the commonwealth court. The supreme court also has the responsibility and authority to oversee all other courts within the state.

Superior Court

In 1895, the superior court was created to hear appeals from the courts of common pleas of the commonwealth. Absent the supreme court granting a petition for writ of certiorari, the superior court becomes the final arbiter of appeals in Pennsylvania. The superior court hears appeals from the commonwealth court involving children and families, criminal cases, and certain civil appeals.

The superior court began with seven judges who heard every case together. However, in 1978 the supreme court allowed the superior court to hear cases in three-judge panels. Each panel would consist of a supreme court justice, a superior court judge, and a common pleas judge. Today the superior court is comprised of fifteen judges who are elected by the public. The president judge is determined on the basis of seniority of continuous service. In the event there are several judges who began service at the same time, the members of the court will vote for a president judge to serve a five-year term.

Commonwealth Court

The commonwealth court originated with the constitution of 1968 in an attempt to reduce the workload being experienced by the superior and supreme courts. This court hears original civil cases that are either initiated by or against the commonwealth. The court serves as an appellate court for decisions of the courts of common pleas and also reviews decisions rendered by state agencies. Cases appealed to the commonwealth court must include the commonwealth or a state agency as a party. All other appeals go to the superior court.

Court of Common Pleas

The Pennsylvania Court of Common Pleas was created in the Pennsylvania Constitution of 1776. Originally there

was a court in every county, but today there are sixty judicial county districts, seven of which are composed of two counties. The court of common pleas has jurisdiction over cases involving criminal and civil crimes deemed too serious to be heard at the special courts level. This is similar to the county courts established in many other states that hear all major criminal cases. The court of common pleas has legal jurisdiction over all major criminal and civil cases, and most matters involving children and families. This court also hears appeals from the special courts regarding civil, criminal, and traffic matters. Today there are three major divisions of this court: trial, orphans' court, and the family court.

The orphans' court division of the court of common pleas was once a separate entity. A constitutional amendment in 1969 abolished the once-separate orphans' court and merged it with the court of common pleas. Although its name may be deceptive, the orphans' court handles a wide range of cases involving both minors and adults. This branch of the court of common pleas has jurisdiction over cases that involve individuals who cannot necessarily handle their own affairs. The orphans' court division of the court of common pleas hears a wide range of cases including, but not limited to, disputes involving inheritance and tax on estates, appointing executors of wills, and appointing guardians to both minors and persons deemed incapacitated.

Another division of the court of common pleas is the family court. The family court is further subdivided into the juvenile division and the domestic relations division. The juvenile division has jurisdiction over delinquency cases, dependency cases involving abused, neglected, or incorrigible youth, criminal cases with a juvenile victim, and both termination of parental rights and adoption proceedings. The domestic relations division handles cases involving custody, divorce, domestic violence, paternity, support, and visitation.

Special Courts

The special courts include the magisterial district judges, Philadelphia Municipal Court, Philadelphia Traffic Court, and the Pittsburgh Municipal Court. The Pittsburgh Municipal Court judges are appointed by the mayor to serve a four-year term. All other judges within the special courts are elected to serve six-year terms. They are the lowest level of courts within the judicial hierarchy. These courts handle the bulk of judicial traffic for the state. The special courts handle primarily misdemeanor or less serious civil cases that do not require a jury, all traffic cases, and make all decisions regarding bail. This court also determines whether or not more serious cases should go to the court of common pleas.

Judicial Selection and Removal

All judges except those who serve in the Pittsburgh Magistrates Court are elected by the residents of Pennsylvania. Judges serving in the Pittsburgh Magistrates Court are appointed by the mayor to serve a four-year term. The election process begins with new candidates listing their political affiliation. Those judges seeking reelection are voted in or out on a "yes-no" basis absent political affiliation on the ballot. Elections are held in odd-numbered years. The number of years a person is appointed depends on which tier of the judicial system they work in. Special court judges are elected to serve six-year periods. All other judges and justices serve a period of ten years on election or reelection. To be eligible, a candidate must be a member of the state bar between the ages of twenty-one and seventy years.

Judges can be removed involuntarily from office in a number of ways. The mandatory retirement age for judges in Pennsylvania is seventy. Those retired judges can be approved by the Pennsylvania Supreme Court to continue to serve as senior judges within the commonwealth. Judges can be forced from office. The Judicial Conduct Board investigates complaints regarding judicial conduct filed by individuals or initiated by the board. The board determines whether probable cause exists to file formal charges, and presents its case to the court of judicial discipline. The disciplinary court has the authority to impose sanctions ranging from a reprimand to removal from office if the formal charges are sustained. Judges also may be impeached by the House of Representatives and convicted and fired by a two-thirds vote of the senate.

Associated Agencies

In 2005 there were fifteen supreme court committees for the state of Pennsylvania. In alphabetical order the committees are: Appellate Courts Procedural Rules Committee, Board of Law Examiners, Civil Procedural Rules Committee, Committee for Proposed Standard Jury Instructions, Committee on Rules of Evidence, Continuing Legal Education Board, Criminal Procedural Rules Committee, Disciplinary Board of the Supreme Court, Domestic Relations Procedural Rules Committee, Juvenile Court Procedural Rules Committee, Minor Court Rules Committee, Minor Judiciary Education Board, Orphans' Court Procedural Rules Committee, Pennsylvania Interest on Lawyers Trust Account Board, and the Pennsylvania Lawyers Fund for Client Security. All committees were created by the Pennsylvania Supreme Court. Each committee serves a distinct function stemming from some need within the Pennsylvania judicial system. The committees are typically composed of a specific number of committee members and a few staff members.

Judicial Salaries

Judicial salaries in Pennsylvania are established by the legislature and are codified in Pennsylvania law. In 2005 there were six justices and one chief justice serving the supreme court. The chief justice earns an annual salary of $123,000. The other six justices earn $119,750 a year. The superior court currently has fourteen judges, eight senior judges, and one president judge. The president judge for the superior court earns an annual salary of $117,750 while the other judges earn $116,000.

The Commonwealth Court of Pennsylvania in 2005 was composed of eight judges, six senior judges, and one president judge. The president judge for the commonwealth court earns an annual salary of $117,750 and all other judges serving this court earn $116,000. The courts of common pleas are composed of many judges serving many districts within Pennsylvania. The annual salary for judges who serve the courts of common pleas are based on either the district they serve in or the number of judges serving in their district. Judges in Allegheny County earn an annual salary of $106,000. Judges in Philadelphia County earn $106,500 a year.

All other judges, including administrative judges for Allegheny and Philadelphia counties, serving the courts of common pleas earn an annual salary based on the number of judges who serve in their district. Judicial districts that have six or more judges pay their judges an annual salary of $105,000. A judge serving a judicial district composed of three to five judges will earn $104,500 a year. Judges serving a judicial district composed of one or two judges will earn an annual salary of $104,000. The other judges of the courts of common pleas, not described earlier, will earn an annual salary of $104,000. The president judge of the Philadelphia Municipal Court earns an annual salary of $103,000. All other judges of this court earn $101,250 a year. The presiding judge of the Philadelphia Traffic Court earns an annual salary of

$55,000. All other judges serving this court earn $54,500 a year. Senior judges earn $315.00 per day.

Elizabeth Corzine McMullan
University of Southern Mississippi

Further Reading
Pennsylvania's Unified Judicial System, http://www.aopc.org/ (accessed March 29, 2006).

RHODE ISLAND

Officially the State of Rhode Island and Providence Plantations, Rhode Island is the smallest state in the United States. The state is approximately 60 miles long and 40 miles wide at it longest and widest points, respectively. This tiny state, however, has played a major role in the history of the United States. Rhode Island was the first state to declare independence from England and the last colony to ratify the Constitution of the United States.

Although there are five counties in Rhode Island—Washington, Providence, Kent, Bristol, and Newport—they do not have independent governments. Instead, the counties represent state judicial districts. Local government is divided among the state's thirty-nine contiguous municipalities of thirty-one towns and eight cities. Rhode Island has a unified court system that consists of six courts: the supreme court, superior court, district court, family court, workers' compensation court, and traffic tribunal. Some of these courts also offer specialized court processes. Rhode Island receives some 101,600 cases for the state's court system each year (NCSC 2004).

The state judiciary offers several educational and community interest programs.

The supreme court has revived the tradition of "riding the circuit" by hearing cases in different locations in the state two times each year. In 2005, a live call-in television program called *Justice Matters* allows viewers to comment and ask questions of Chief Justice Frank Williams. The program *Justice Rules* is designed to teach students from kindergarten to the twelfth grade about the legal system.

Supreme Court

The supreme court is the highest court in Rhode Island. This court hears appeals from cases decided by the superior and family courts and may hear certain cases decided by the district and workers' compensation courts. The supreme court also supervises the administration of the other state courts and routinely advises the legislative and executive branches regarding constitutional issues.

There are five supreme court justices, one chief justice and four justices. The chief justice is also responsible for overseeing the administration of the state judicial system and the budget of the state judiciary. The Administrative Office of State Courts is responsible for assisting the chief justice with the budgetary and administrative tasks of the court.

In 2003 the supreme court received about 400 discretionary appeals and heard about 130 (NCSC 2004). Just under 300 mandatory cases are filed each year.

Superior Court

The superior court is Rhode Island's court of general jurisdiction. It has original jurisdiction in all felony cases, civil cases involving claims for monetary damages in excess of $10,000, and concurrent jurisdiction with the district court in civil cases of claims ranging between $5,000 and $10,000. This court has appellate jurisdiction in cases decided by the district, municipal, and probate courts. Appeals of superior court decisions are heard by the state supreme court. About 16,000 incoming cases were filed in 2003 (NCSC 2004).

The highest judge of the superior court is the presiding justice of the superior court, who also serves as the chief administrator of the court. In addition to the presiding justice, there are twenty-one associate justices and four magistrates.

District Court

District courts have jurisdiction over small claims, municipal ordinance violations, and misdemeanors when the defendant's right to a jury trial has been waived. About 76,000 incoming cases were presented to this court in 2003. If the defendant asserts this right, the case is referred to the superior court. Appeals of decisions of the district court are heard

by the superior court in de novo proceedings. The jurisdiction of the court also includes all state housing code violations, local housing code violations where there is no municipal court with this authority, and appeals of the ruling and orders of the state tax administrator and other regulatory agencies. Matters related to involuntary hospitalization for mental health or substance abuse reasons, including alcoholism, are also within the jurisdiction of the district court. Appeals in these areas are heard by the supreme court.

There are thirteen judges who preside over cases in the district court: one chief judge, one administrative judge, eleven associate judges, and two magistrates. The district court is divided into four geographic divisions, one in each county of Providence, Kent, Washington, and Newport.

Family Court

From 1935 to 1961, family relations cases in Rhode Island were handled by the domestic relations division of the superior court. The state became the first to have a statewide family court when, in 1961, the state general assembly enacted legislation that created the family court. The goal of family court is to help and protect families involved in divorce proceedings or having other types of domestic relations problems. Its jurisdiction extends to include any matter related to family domestic relations and juveniles. There are twelve judges of the family court: the chief judge and eleven associate judges; and six magistrates—a general magistrate and five magistrates. About 23,000 cases are brought to the family court each year. Appeals of family court decisions are heard by the state supreme court.

Workers' Compensation Court

In 1991, the state general assembly created this court, consisting of one chief judge and nine associate judges, to handle disputes about workers' compensation benefits between injured employees and their employers, as well as other matters related to workers' compensation. During a pretrial conference, an associate judge may issue orders concerning issues disputed by the parties involved. These orders may be appealed to the appellate division of the court by filing a claim for trial, and a trial judge will schedule an initial hearing. A full evidentiary hearing on the record of the issues is conducted during the trial. Appeals of the decisions of the trial judge are heard by a panel of the appellate division. About 9,000 cases come into the workers' compensation court each year. Further appeal of the decision of the appellate panel occurs only if the supreme court issues a writ of certiorari.

Traffic Tribunal

This court was created by statute in 1999 to replace the previous system for handling traffic offenses that had become ineffective. Most traffic violations in Rhode Island were decriminalized in 1975, and these are now under the jurisdiction of the traffic tribunal. The chief judge of the district court supervises the operation of the traffic tribunal, and there are currently four associate judges and four magistrates serving in this court. The four judges were carried over from the previous system. On their retirement, they are to be replaced with magistrates appointed by the district court chief judge with the senate's approval. Appeals within the tribunal are heard by a panel of three judges, and decisions of the tribunal are appealed to the district court.

Specialized State Court Processes

The state judiciary system offers a number of special court processes to ease the courts' caseloads, expedite case resolution, and provide special services to both victims and offenders. The supreme court offers an appellate mediation program for civil cases appealing final judgment. The office of alternative dispute resolutions administers this program with retired state judges mediating the cases participating in the program.

Adult, juvenile, and family substance-abuse problems are addressed by court programs geared for these three areas. The superior court's adult drug court provides rehabilitation opportunities and accountability for adults charged with drug and alcohol offenses and adults with a history of substance abuse charged with nonviolent offenses. Juveniles with substance-abuse problems receive assistance from the family court's juvenile drug court. Using a system of rewards and sanctions to encourage compliance, this post-adjudication, post-plea program promotes treatment and education. Successful completion of the six- to twelve-month program results in dismissing the charges, vacating the plea, and closing the petitions. Also under the family court, the family treatment drug court addresses the substance-abuse problems of parents with infants and children by providing services to improve parental effectiveness and create a safe, stable home for the children.

Family court offers additional programs to benefit families and juveniles. The divorce mediation program focuses on amicable resolution of child custody and visitation issues during separation and divorce. Domestic violence cases in which there are children in the home are handled by the domestic violence court. While focusing on protecting the victim and other family members, this court also holds abusers accountable for their behavior, as well as providing rehabilitation services for abusers to help them change their behavior. Juvenile offenders who are sentenced to the state training school may request to participate in the reentry, or "going home early," court, a program of court review and supervision by the juvenile probation and parole agency to facilitate early release and community reintegration of these juveniles. Another juvenile program, truancy court, is a collaborative effort between the court, school officials, community mental health professionals, and families to promote regular school attendance by juveniles.

Municipal and Probate Courts

Municipal courts have jurisdiction over violations of ordinances of the city or town in which they are located. Judges are appointed by the city or town council or by the mayor with the approval of the council. Appeals of municipal court decisions are heard by the superior court.

Each city and town has a probate court with jurisdiction over matters related to the probate of wills. The city or town council appoints the probate court judge, except in one town where the town council is the probate judge.

Selection of Judges

Until 1994, Rhode Island Supreme Court justices were elected by the general assembly meeting in grand committee, with a majority of the members of the senate and of the House of Representatives present. The governor appointed lower court judges subject to senate approval. Then in 1994, the state constitution was amended and legislation passed that created the merit selection system the state uses today (Jenks 1996). All state court vacancies, except those of the traffic tribunal, are now filled by gubernatorial appointment, subject to appropriate legislative approval.

The new system allows the governor to appoint a judge chosen from a list of between three and five candidates submitted to the governor by the judicial nominating commission. This commission consists of nine members—four practicing attorneys, four laypeople, and one additional member who may be an attorney or layperson. The members are appointed by the governor, although only three of the attorney positions and one of the non-lawyer positions are completely within the governor's discretion. The remaining positions are filled based on the governor's choice from a list of candidates nominated by the general assembly. Members of the commission serve staggered terms of four years (Jenks 1996).

Once the governor has notified the commission of a vacancy or potential state court vacancy, the commission advertises the vacancy to solicit candidates. The commission chooses the required three to five qualified candidates and gives these names to the governor, who then chooses his or her nominee. Appointments to the supreme court are subject to the approval of both the senate and the House of Representatives. Lower court appointments must be approved by the senate. All state judicial appointments are for life, barring bad conduct; judges are also prohibited from practicing law while they serve on the bench.

Discipline and Removal of Judges

The Commission on Judicial Tenure and Discipline was created by statute in 1974 to provide an avenue for complaints regarding the conduct of any state judge or magistrate. The fourteen-member commission consists of six gubernatorial appointees approved by the senate, at least three of whom are practicing attorneys, five judges selected by the supreme court, two appointed by the speaker of the house, and one appointed by the senate majority leader. Complaints of serious violations of the code of judicial conduct are reviewed by the commission. After a formal hearing with at least eight of the commission members present and the determination by the commission that the charges were sustained, the findings are reported to the supreme court, along with recommendations for the appropriate disciplinary action.

Melissa Montgomery

References and Further Reading

Jenks, Barton P., III. 1996. "Rhode Island's New Judicial Merit Selection Law." *Roger Williams University Law Review* 1: 63–85.

National Center for State Courts. 2004. "State Court Caseload Statistics, 2004," http://www.ncsconline.org/D_Research/csp/2004_Files/2004_SCCS.html (accessed March 26, 2006).

Rhode Island Bar Association, http://www.ribar.com.

Rhode Island Information, http://www.info.state.ri.us.

Supreme Court of Rhode Island, http://www.courts.state.ri.us.

SOUTH CAROLINA
● ● ● ● ● ● ● ● ● ● ● ●

One of the original thirteen colonies, South Carolina became the eighth state of the Union when it ratified the Constitution on May 23, 1788. In early statehood, South Carolina demonstrated its dissatisfaction with the Union. South Carolina was particularly upset with the tariffs of 1828 and 1832. The public felt that the tariffs unfairly hurt their well-being. South Carolina's political leaders were among the first to advocate the theory of "nullification," which means states could nullify acts of Congress they do not agree with. The 1832 election pitted Unionists against Nullifiers in South Carolina, with Nullifiers gaining ground in the elections. On November 24, 1832, the general assembly declared the tariffs "null and void" in South Carolina. South Carolina eventually relented when Congress altered the tariffs and President Andrew Jackson threatened military action.

South Carolina was the first state to secede from the Union on December 20, 1860. South Carolina, as many other Southern states, was devastated by the Civil War. About 20 percent of South Carolina's white male population was killed during the conflict, and its economy was devastated. It took decades before South Carolina's economy recovered. During this time the state's judiciary underwent several overhauls. The 1868 constitution established a supreme court and other inferior courts, but did not establish an intermediate appeals court. It was in 1979 that the general assembly created a forerunner to the current court of appeals. That became bogged down in litigation since four of the five judges selected by the legislature were sitting members of the legislature at the time of their selection. The courts found that the four judges could not be seated on the court of appeals because they were members of the legislature when the court was created. It would not be until 1983 when the four vacancies were filled and the court of appeals finally began hearing cases. In 1985, the court of appeals became a constitutional court when the voters amended the state's constitution.

Article V of South Carolina's constitution says, "The judicial power shall be vested in a unified judicial system, which shall include a Supreme Court, a Court of Appeals, a Circuit Court, and such other courts of uniform jurisdiction as may be provided for by general law." Like other states, South Carolina's judicial system has three general levels of courts: appellate courts, court of general jurisdiction, and courts of limited jurisdiction.

Supreme Court

The South Carolina Supreme Court has five justices elected by the state legislature who sit en banc. The South Carolina Supreme Court possesses both appellate and original jurisdiction. As an appellate court, the supreme court has exclusive appellate jurisdiction over criminal cases where the death penalty was imposed; constitutionality issues of state law or local ordinances; issues involving public bonds and indebtedness; appeals over utility rates set by the circuit court; appeals over election issues; and appeals involving a minor and abortion. In addition, the supreme court may call up a case pending before the court of appeals. The supreme court has discretion for granting writs of certiorari for appeals from the court of appeals. In 2002, the supreme court disposed of more than 1,550 cases and petitions.

The supreme court is responsible for publicizing rules governing conduct, practice, procedures, and administration of all the courts of this state. The supreme court also develops and publishes rules governing the practice of law and conduct of attorneys and other court personnel. The chief justice is the administrative head of the statewide judiciary.

Court of Appeals

The court of appeals was created to hear appeals from the circuit court and the family court. The court of appeals hears all appeals except in cases where the supreme court has exclusive jurisdiction. The court of appeals was organized in 1983; it has nine judges who sit in panels of three or en banc and one chief judge and eight associates. The court of appeals workload is similar to the supreme court; it disposed of more than 1,450 cases in 2002.

Circuit Court

Circuit courts are South Carolina's general jurisdiction trial courts. The state is divided into sixteen judicial circuits with forty-eight judges who rotate between circuits. Each circuit has one chief administrative judge and each county has a resident judge who maintains an office in his or her home county. These courts also have twenty-two masters-in-equity.

The circuit court is the state's court of general jurisdiction. Circuit courts include a civil court—the court of common pleas—and a criminal court known as the court of general sessions. The circuit court also has limited appellate jurisdiction over appeals from the probate, magistrate's, and municipal courts, as well as appeals from the Administrative Law Judge Division, which hears matters relating to state administrative and regulatory agencies.

Masters-in-equity hear cases referred to them by the circuit courts. They have the power of the circuit court sitting without a jury. They may regulate all proceedings in every hearing before them.

Limited Jurisdiction Courts

South Carolina has four limited jurisdiction courts. Each of South Carolina's forty-six counties has a family court. There are fifty-seven family court judges. In 2005 South Carolina had roughly 300 magistrates who preside in magistrate courts. These courts exist in each of South Carolina's counties. Each county also has a probate judge. City governments in South Carolina can establish municipal courts at their discretion. A city council may establish a municipal court and/or contract with the county governing authority for the services of a magistrate to serve as its municipal judge. There are approximately 300 municipal court judges in South Carolina.

Each county has a probate judge who has jurisdiction over legal matters such as wills, estates, and trusts, as well as having concurrent jurisdiction with circuit courts over powers of attorney.

Magistrates generally have criminal trial jurisdiction over misdemeanors. In addition, they are responsible for setting bail, conducting preliminary hearings, and issuing arrest and search warrants. Magistrates have civil jurisdiction when the amount in controversy does not exceed $7,500.

Municipal courts have jurisdiction over cases arising under ordinances of the municipality, and over misdemeanor offenses occurring within the municipality. The powers and duties of a municipal judge are the same as those of a magistrate with regard to criminal matters. Municipal courts have no civil jurisdiction. The term of a municipal judge is set by the municipality but cannot exceed four years. Approximately 200 municipalities in South Carolina have chosen to create municipal courts.

The family court has exclusive jurisdiction over all matters involving family relationships. The family court is the sole forum for the hearing of all cases concerning marriage, divorce, legal separation, custody, visitation rights, termination of parental rights, adoption, support, alimony, division of marital property, and change of name. In most cases, the court also has exclusive jurisdiction over minors under the age of seventeen. Serious criminal charges may be transferred to the circuit court.

Associated Offices

The Office of Disciplinary Counsel screens and investigates complaints against judges and lawyers. The office also receives complaints through the Commission on Judicial Conduct and the Commission on Lawyer Conduct. The Commission on Judicial Conduct is comprised of twenty-four members: eighteen judges, four lawyers, and two citizens (nonlawyers). The Commission on Lawyer Conduct is comprised of forty-two attorneys and two citizens. The

South Carolina Court Administration assists the supreme court with its administrative duties. The Office of Information Technology and an Office of Budget and Personnel exist in the judicial branch. There are several boards and commissions that also assist the judiciary. The commissions and boards oversee education, the bar exam, alternative dispute resolution, and certification for magistrates and municipal court judges.

Selection and Removal of Judges

South Carolina's general assembly is deeply involved in selecting judges. In fact, South Carolina is one of two states (the other is Virginia) where the legislature elects many of the judges. The general assembly elects the chief justice and associate justices to staggered ten-year terms. The general assembly also elects court of appeals judges to staggered six-year terms.

Like court of appeals judges, circuit court judges and family court judges are elected by the general assembly to staggered six-year terms. Governors can appoint people to fill vacancies if there is less than a year left in the term. The governor appoints magistrates who also have to be confirmed by the senate. Probate judges are elected in partisan elections to four-year terms. Masters-in-equity are appointed by the governor to six-year terms with approval of the general assembly.

The Commission on Judicial Standards, formed in 1976, accepts complaints on judicial misconduct and investigates permanent mental and physical disabilities that might impair a judge's abilities to perform his or her duties. The commission is now called the Commission on Judicial Conduct. The commission has one panel that investigates allegations and another that conducts hearings if warranted. The disciplinary counsel screens complaints and prosecutes cases assigned by the commission. Once a panel hears the case it makes recommendations to the supreme court. The supreme court can dismiss that case, censure, suspend, remove, or retire judges.

The South Carolina General Assembly also reserves the right to impeach judges. The House of Representatives impeaches state officials, including judges, by a two-thirds vote, and the senate tries all of those impeached. The official is convicted and removed with a two-thirds vote of those elected to the senate.

South Carolina's budget for fiscal year (FY) 2006's judicial department was approximately $54 million. This amount represents a slight increase over the FY 2005 budget ($2.25 million). Circuit courts represent the largest expenditures with a budget of $12.6 million. Family courts consume nearly $11 million of the judicial department's budget.

Doug Goodman
Mississippi State University

James A. Newman
Idaho State University

References and Further Reading

Cureton, Jasper M. "Coming of Age: The South Carolina Court of Appeals," http://www.judicial.state.sc.us/appeals/history.cfm (accessed August 18, 2004).

Morgan, Mary L. 2001. "A Brief History of South Carolina," http://www.state.sc.us/scsl/brfhist.html (accessed August 17, 2004).

Rottman, David B., et al. 2000. *State Court Organization 1998.* Washington, DC: United States Department of Justice.

South Carolina Legislature. 2005. "South Carolina Legislature Online," http://www.scstatehouse.net/html-pages/research.html (accessed November 21, 2005).

Supreme Court of South Carolina. 2004. "South Carolina Judicial Department," http://www.judicial.state.sc.us/ (accessed August 16, 2004).

SOUTH DAKOTA
• • • • • • • • • • • •

When the Dakotas became a territory on March 2, 1861, it had a governmental structure including an executive branch, legislative branch, and judicial branch. The judicial branch was comprised of a supreme court, district courts, probate courts, and justices of the peace. The Dakota Territory continued under this governmental structure until South Dakota became a state in 1889. During that time, thirty presidential appointees served as judges of the Territorial Supreme Court. With statehood in 1889, South Dakota adopted its first constitution, a constitution that has since been amended but remains in use. The constitution provided for a judicial branch that would consist of a supreme court, circuit courts, county courts, and justices of the peace. Initially, there were three justices on the supreme court, one chosen from each of three districts within the state. The supreme court held its first session on October 13, 1891, and had sixty-two cases on its calendar.

Changes have occurred over time in the structure of South Dakota courts, both through constitutional amendments and through changes in state law. In 1972, amendments were proposed to the constitution that influenced the supreme court, circuit courts, and district courts. Included was a change in the manner in which judges were selected in South Dakota. Over time, changes in state law has resulted in the elimination of municipal courts (1973), the elimination of justices of the police and police magistrates (1973), the elimination of district county courts (1973), and a change in the number of justices on the supreme court (1972). These are just some of the changes made in the 1970s.

Organization of State Courts

Since 1973, South Dakota has had a unified judiciary. The judiciary consists of a supreme court and seven circuit courts. The South Dakota Constitution requires that the supreme court consist of a chief justice and four associate justices; however it allows the legislature the discretion to increase the size of the court to seven. in 2005, members of the supreme court included Chief Justice David Gilbertson, and justices Richard W. Sabers, John K. Konenkamp, Steven L. Zinter, and Judith Meierhenry. Each justice is assigned a secretary and a law

clerk. The circuit courts are the next level of courts. There are a total of thirty-eight circuit judges assigned to the seven circuits. These are the trial courts of general jurisdiction. In addition, there are twenty-seven magistrates and magistrate judges also assigned to the seven circuits. Magistrate courts are an additional tier in the Unified Judicial System and are a court of limited jurisdiction.

In addition to courts, South Dakota's judicial system also consists of the Judicial Qualifications Commission (discussed later in the "Selection of Judges" section), presiding circuit judges (one presiding judge for each circuit), the state court administrator, the clerk of the supreme court, and the chief of legal research. The state court administrator oversees human resources, budget and finance, trial court services, information and technology, and public information and education. The clerk of the supreme court is appointed by the court and is responsible for indexing, filing, and preserving all court records. The chief of legal research acts as secretary to the Board of Examiners, supervisor for the court's staff attorneys, and as manager of the supreme court's law library.

Powers of State Courts

The primary function of the supreme court is that of an appeals court. The supreme court may on occasion issue original or remedial writs or act as an advisor to the governor. The justices of the supreme court have the power to elect the chief justice of the supreme court. The supreme court is South Dakota's primary appellate court, so it is required to hear every case. The supreme court is also the administrator of the state judicial system. The chief justice is the administrative head of the Unified Judicial System. The court also prepares and submits an annual budget, supervises the work of the circuit courts, appoints necessary court personnel, and makes rules concerning practice and procedure, administration of the courts, and discipline of members of the bar.

Circuit courts are South Dakota's courts of general jurisdiction for civil and criminal cases. They have original jurisdiction over all felony cases and all civil cases involving $10,000 or more. They also have jurisdiction over appeals coming from magistrate courts.

Magistrate courts are courts of limited jurisdiction. They have jurisdiction to receive depositions, issue warrants, conduct preliminary hearings, set bail, appoint counsel, and hold trials for criminal misdemeanors, small-claims actions involving less than $8,000, and civil actions involving less than $10,000.

Selection of Judges

Judges in South Dakota are selected using the merit selection plan. There is a Judicial Qualifications Commission made up of seven members. Two members are circuit court judges elected by the judicial conference, three members are lawyers (no more than two can be from the same political party) appointed by the president of the state bar association, and two members are nonlawyers, not of the same political party, appointed by the governor.

Commission members serve four-year terms, and are limited to serving two terms. When a judicial vacancy occurs, the commission recommends nominees to the governor to fill the vacancy. The commission submits at least two names to the governor for each vacancy, and the governor must appoint one of those individuals. At the first general election following three years of service, the judge is subject to a retention election. So long as a judge is retained, he or she serves an eight-year term, and is then again subject to a retention election. The state is divided into five appointment districts, and one supreme court justice is appointed from each of the districts. Circuit court judges must be residents of the circuit from which they are appointed. Supreme court and circuit court judges serve terms of eight years.

In order to serve as a judge in South Dakota an individual must be a U.S. citizen, a resident of the state, a voting resident of the district or circuit in which he or she is serving, and licensed to practice law in the state. In addition, South Dakota has a mandatory retirement age of seventy for its judges and justices.

Magistrate judges are chosen in a different manner than supreme court and circuit court judges. Magistrate judges, who must be licensed attorneys, are appointed by a presiding circuit judge and approved by the supreme court for a term of four years. Lay magistrate judges, who must be high school graduates, are appointed by the presiding circuit judge and serve at the pleasure of the presiding circuit judge. A magistrate judge must be a U.S. citizen, a resident of the state, and a voting resident of the circuit in which he or she is serving.

Discipline

The Judicial Qualifications Commission, working along with the supreme court, has the power to censure, remove, or retire a judge. The commission investigates complaints against justices or judges, and when necessary conducts confidential hearings concerning punishment of a justice or judge. The commission then makes a recommendation to the supreme court that has the power to censure, remove, or retire a judge. In addition, judges may be impeached by a majority vote of the House of Representatives and convicted by a two-thirds vote of the senate.

Workload

In 2004, 439 cases were filed with the South Dakota Supreme Court. There has been an annual decrease in filings over the past five years with 508 cases filed in 2000, 494 in 2001, 457 in 2002, and 447 in 2003. Since it is the only appellate court in South Dakota, it is required to act on all appeals since the appeal is a matter of right. In 2004, circuit courts saw 75,520 civil cases and 169,462 criminal cases. Of the civil cases, slightly more than 9,000 were juvenile cases, almost 34,000 were small claims, less than 5,000 were miscellaneous, and around 13,400 were child support cases. Of the criminal cases, over 142,000 were class 2 misdemeanors and petty offenses, 20,542 were class 1 misdemeanors, and only 6,895 were felonies.

Ruth Ann Watry
Northern Michigan University

References and Further Reading
American Judicature Society, "Center for Judicial Selection," http://www.ajs .org/selection/index.asp.
Harmon, Robert B. 1991. *Government and Politics in South Dakota: A Selected Guide to Information Sources.* Monticello, IL: Vance Bibliographies.
Oviatt, Ross H. 1989. *South Dakota Justice: The Judges and the System.* Watertown, SD: Tesseract.
South Dakota Unified Judicial System, http://www.sdjudicial.com/.

TENNESSEE
• • • • • • • • • • • •

The Watauga Association, formed about 1771, organized the first government for the frontier region that is now Tennessee. Tennessee became the sixteenth state in 1796. Its first constitution included justices of the peace, the court of common pleas, and quarter sessions as inferior courts. The superior court of law and equity served as the general and appellate jurisdiction courts until 1809 when the legislature formed circuit courts in each county and renamed the superior court the Superior Court of Errors and Appeals—giving it appellate jurisdiction. Tennessee's justice system evolved to what it is today with the help of the constitution of 1870, constitutional amendments, and legislative acts.

Tennessee Supreme Court

The Tennessee Supreme Court has the final say in all questions of state law. It is composed of five justices, not more than two of whom can live in any one of the state's three grand geographical divisions. As dictated by the state constitution, the court must meet in Knoxville, Nashville, and Jackson. While in each city, the court hears appeals from that division of the state.

The only cases for which the supreme court must grant review are those involving the death penalty, disciplinary actions against attorneys, and the right to hold public office. Because of the high amount of autonomy given to the supreme court, its caseload is lower than in most other states.

The supreme court may assume jurisdiction over undecided cases in the court of appeals or court of criminal appeals when there is special need for a speedy decision. The court also has appellate jurisdiction in cases involving state taxes, the right to hold public office, and issues of constitutional law. In fiscal year (FY) 2004, 1,290 cases were filed with the Tennessee Supreme Court. The court disposed of 1,278 cases that same year (Supreme Court of Tennessee 2004, 37–38). A unique characteristic of the Tennessee Supreme Court is that the court chooses the state's attorney general.

Appellate Courts

Tennessee has two intermediate appellate courts: the court of appeals and the court of criminal appeals. These appellate courts are composed of twelve judges each. Panels of three judges sit monthly in Jackson, Nashville, and Knoxville. One unique feature of the Tennessee court system is the divided structure of intermediate appellate courts. One is for civil cases and the other is for criminal cases. A result of this is a division of labor in the courts that separates trial courts into two classifications. One group often referred to as major courts considers felonies and other serious civil and criminal matters.

The court of appeals meets in Jackson, Nashville, and Knoxville. The court of appeals has jurisdiction over most noncriminal cases such as civil matters, administrative agency decisions, and juvenile cases. The court of criminal appeals hears all felony, misdemeanor, and juvenile criminal appeals. The court of criminal appeals also sits in Knoxville, Nashville, and Jackson. Intermediate appellate court decisions are final unless appealed to the Tennessee Supreme Court.

In FY 2004 there were 1,312 cases filed for appeal in the criminal court of appeals; that court disposed of 1,366 cases that same year. Another 1,191 cases for appeal were filed in Tennessee's court of appeals in FY 2004. The court of appeals disposed of 1,395 cases in 2004 (Supreme Court of Tennessee 2004, 39–40).

Courts of General Jurisdiction

Tennessee has thirty-one judicial districts covering its ninety-five counties with four types of trial courts: circuit, probate, chancery, and criminal. Each district has a chancery court (thirty-five chancellors) and circuit courts (eighty-five judges). Some counties have criminal courts (thirty-five judges), and there is one probate court.

In 1809, circuit courts were created and the superior court of law and equity was renamed the supreme court of errors and appeals. Tennessee's second constitution in 1834 added chancery courts to the state's judicial system. This created the distinction between courts of law and equity. The court of common pleas and quarter sessions became county courts. These courts handled minor cases.

Tennessee's circuit courts are courts of general jurisdiction, which means they hear both civil and criminal cases. In thirteen of the state's thirty-one judicial districts, separate criminal courts relieve the circuit courts from hearing criminal cases. These courts hear not only felony, but also misdemeanor criminal charges. Chancery courts are exclusively civil courts. In FY 2003–2004, 69,121 cases were filed with Tennessee chancery courts. These same courts disposed of 66,376 cases in FY 2003–2004. Another 67,581 cases were filed and 63,208 cases were disposed of in circuit courts (Supreme Court of Tennessee 2004, 47–48). Probate court handles estates and administrative appeals. Only two counties in Tennessee have probate jurisdiction, Shelby and Davidson. In 1998, the Davidson County Probate Court became a circuit court with probate jurisdiction.

Limited Jurisdiction Courts

There are three limited jurisdiction courts in Tennessee. The most important of the courts of limited jurisdiction is the court of general sessions. The general sessions courts were created by the state legislature in 1960 to replace the justice of the peace system. Under the old system, the justices of the peace presided over limited jurisdictional courts and often did not have any formal legal training. There are 154 general sessions judges.

General sessions courts function in all of Tennessee's ninety-five counties. The jurisdiction of the general sessions courts varies from county to county, based on acts of the general assembly. The primary purpose of general sessions courts is to handle preliminary matters in major criminal cases. They also possess jurisdiction over minor criminal and civil matters. They have the authority to issue search and arrest warrants, set bond, and conduct hearings before a grand jury. General sessions courts also hear cases involving juveniles, except where there are separate juvenile courts.

Other courts, which have limited jurisdiction, hear misdemeanors and small civil claims. Often these "minor" courts will conduct preliminary hearings in cases that will be tried in the courts of general jurisdiction.

Municipal Courts

Tennessee has approximately 300 municipal courts with 170 judges. The vast majority of the cases they hear are violations of city ordinances. In general, the jurisdiction of these courts is limited to hearing only these violations. Each municipality has the authority to create these courts and set the requirements for the judges.

Juvenile Courts

Juvenile courts have exclusive jurisdiction over proceedings involving minors. Their jurisdiction is also concurrent with other state courts in some matters. The first juvenile court was established during the early twentieth century. Established in each county, Tennessee has approximately 100 juvenile courts. There are seventeen juvenile judges and ninety-five general sessions judges with jurisdiction over juvenile matters.

Until the 1980s, judges who were not required to undergo formal legal training ran juvenile courts. The judges also possessed a great deal of discretion in assigning punishment. After an increase in violent crimes by juveniles in the 1970s and 1980s, many of the serious offenses committed by juveniles were sent to other courts where the juvenile was tried as an adult.

Associated Agencies

The Administrative Office of the Courts provides support and services to all state courts. Tennessee's disciplinary tribunal for members of the judiciary is the fifteen-member Tennessee Court of the Judiciary that is composed of nine judges, three attorneys, and three laypeople.

The fifteen-member Judicial Selection Commission consists of appointments from the governor, the legislature, and the Tennessee Bar Association. At least three members must be nonlawyers.

Selection and Removal of Judges

The state constitution requires Tennessee judges to be elected to eight-year terms. The general assembly determines a process under which the elections take place.

Until the 1970s, all state judges were elected on partisan ballots. Partisan elections still exist at the trial court level. State law requires candidates to be lawyers and meet certain residency requirements.

In 1971, the state of Tennessee began selecting judges through a modified Missouri Plan, aptly labeled the Tennessee Plan. Under Tennessee's plan, when a vacancy occurs in the appellate courts, the governor appoints a replacement from a list of applicants provided by the Judicial Selection Commission. When that judge's term has expired, he or she runs unopposed in a retention election. If the majority votes to retain the judge, that judge serves another eight-year term and is subject to another retention vote at the end of that term. If the incumbent does not win the election, the merit selection process begins again.

In 1994, the general assembly extended merit selection to cover the Tennessee Supreme Court. Initially, justices were up for retention one at a time. The first justice up for retention soundly lost the election. Some believed that voters were not aware of, or did not understand, the new system and thought the judge was being recalled. In 1996, each justice of the state supreme court came up for retention. This time, all justices were retained by comfortable margins.

All other trial court judges and limited jurisdiction judges are elected in partisan elections to eight-year terms. Municipalities can determine the manner of appointment for municipal court judges.

Tennessee's judicial department's budget for FY 2004 was $92.4 million. About half ($43.6 million) of the budget is used to fund appellate and trial courts. The next largest expenditure is for indigent representation ($17.9 million) (Supreme Court of Tennessee 2004).

James A. Newman
Idaho State University

Doug Goodman
Mississippi State University

References and Further Reading

Bergeron, Paul H., Stephen V. Ash, and Jeanette Keith. 1999. *Tennesseans and Their History*. Knoxville, TN: University of Tennessee Press.

Greene, Lee Seifert, David H. Grubbs, and Victor C. Hobday. 1982. *Government in Tennessee*. Knoxville, TN: University of Tennessee Press.

Lyons, William, John M. Scheb II, and Billy Stair. 2001. *Government and Politics in Tennessee*. Knoxville, TN: University of Tennessee Press.

Netstate, http://www.netstate.com/states /index.html (accessed August 9, 2004).

Sherrill, Charles A. 1998. Tennessee Court System Prior to 1870, http://www .tngenweb.org/law/courtsys.htm (accessed August 16, 2004).

Supreme Court of Tennessee. 2004. *Annual Report of the Tennessee Judiciary*. Nashville, TN: Administrative Office of the Courts, http://www.tsc .state.tn.us/geninfo/Publications/Annual Report/2003-2004/2003-04annrptCD.pdf (accessed November 21, 2005).

Wilson, Richard. 1976. *Tennessee Politics: A Program for Research*. Dubuque, IA: Kendall/Hunt.

TEXAS

• • • • • • • • • • • •

The Texas court system can be dated from 1822 when Stephen F. Austin appointed Josiah Bell as provisional justice of the peace for the province of Texas. Austin's appointment was revoked by the Mexican provisional governor's appointment of three alcaldes. The alcaldes had both administrative and judicial duties and applied Spanish law in the colony. Attempts to reform the alcalde system ended with the Texas revolution. In 1836, the constitution of the Republic of Texas established a judicial system that was predominantly Anglo-American. There was one supreme court with jurisdiction over appeals only, and such inferior courts as the Congress might establish. The supreme court was comprised of a chief justice and the judges of several judicial districts. Both houses of Congress elected the chief justice and district judges. Each county had a county court and justice of the peace courts. The judges of these lower courts were selected by popular election.

The first Texas state constitution was written in 1845 and maintained the general structure of the judicial system established in the constitution of the republic. This structure was continued in the constitutions of 1861, 1866, and 1869. The 1845 constitution removed the district judges from the supreme court and replaced them with two associate justices. The governor, with the consent of the senate, selected the justices. In 1850, a constitutional amendment made the offices elective. An increasing workload after Reconstruction led the writers of the 1876 constitution to include a second court of last resort, the court of appeals. The court of appeals was renamed the court of criminal appeals in 1891. A constitutional amendment approved in 1891 established intermediate courts of appeals.

The Texas court system is one of the most complex in the United States. There are three levels of trial courts—district, county, and inferior—without uniform jurisdiction. To determine a court's jurisdiction, the statute establishing the court must be consulted. There are two levels of appellate courts: the courts of appeals; and the two courts of last resort, the court of criminal appeals and the supreme court.

Texas's constitution, drafted by a constitutional convention, took effect in 1876. It was written in an era of distrust of centralized governmental power and it was written specifically to protect citizens against the powers of the kind of strong governor that existed during Reconstruction. The document is one of the longest state constitutions. It also is one of the most detailed and most frequently amended. Since 1876, the Texas Constitution has been amended almost 475 times. The detail and frequent amendments have created a document with almost 93,000 words. Texas voters do not have the citizen initiative; all amending is done by the legislature with the proposed amendments needing to be ratified by a simple majority vote of the people. Such constitutional amendment elections usually have voter turnout rates of 15 to 20 percent. In 1975, voters rejected a proposed revision of the constitution that would have reduced the number of articles from seventeen to eleven and the number of words from 80,800 to 17,700.

The Courts of Last Resort

Texas is one of two states with two courts of last resort. The court of criminal appeals hears appeals from death-penalty convictions and denials of bail. It has discretion to review decisions in criminal cases appealed from the courts of appeal, but the court has the power to refuse to hear an appeal without explanation. Decisions of the court of criminal appeals may be appealed to the U.S. Supreme Court; there is no procedure for appealing to the Texas Supreme Court.

The Texas Supreme Court is the court of last resort in civil and juvenile cases. A 1980 constitutional amendment also gave the court the authority to regulate the state's legal profession. In 2002, 7,200 mandatory cases were filed in the court of criminal appeals. The court grants about 150 of 1,950 discretionary petitions filed each year. In 2002, 6 mandatory cases were filed in the supreme court while 1,300 discretionary petitions were filed. Only about 110 discretionary petitions are granted. The Texas Court of Criminal Appeals regularly looks to the Texas Constitution, but it usually does not find an expansion of rights for criminal defendants. The Texas Supreme Court also has turned to the Texas Constitution to find rights not identified in the U.S. Constitution. The court's decisions regarding public school financing are some of its most notable. In its 1989 decision in *Edgewood v. Kirby*, the court ruled that the state's educational funding system violated the Texas Constitution because it did not provide an efficient system of funding public schools.

Courts of Appeals

Fourteen courts of appeals hear appeals in both civil and criminal cases from the district- and county-level courts in their regions. Death penalty appeals go directly to the court of criminal appeals. The state is divided into fourteen districts, each with a court of appeals with a chief justice and at least two other justices and a statewide total of about eighty. During the annual reporting period ending August 31, 2002, 12,000 mandatory cases were filed in the appellate courts, a number that averages to 150 cases per justice.

Trial Courts

There are three levels of trial courts. The inferior courts are the justice of the peace courts and municipal courts. Both courts have similar jurisdiction in that most of their cases involve traffic violations. Justices of the peace are county officials; the Texas Constitution requires at least one justice of the peace precinct in each county. The least populous counties may have only one precinct. Counties with populations of 30,000 or more must have from four to eight precincts. Justice courts are not courts of record, requiring that appeals to county-level courts are de novo proceedings. Justice courts have jurisdiction over criminal offenses that are punishable by fine only (not more than $500), and over small civil claims (not more than $5,000). The courts function as magistrates issuing arrest and search warrants in felony and misdemeanor cases. They also serve as coroners in counties that do not have a medical examiner. There were nearly 3 million cases filed in justice of the peace courts in 2002. Nine percent of those cases were civil and 91 percent were criminal filings.

Incorporated cities and towns establish municipal courts. The courts' organizations and status are identified in a city's charter or municipal ordinances. Municipal courts have the sole jurisdiction to try violations of city ordinances. Their jurisdiction extends to class C misdemeanors, those violations for which the punishment is a fine of $500 or less and does not include a jail sentence. Municipal courts share this jurisdiction with justices of the peace. Most of the cases heard in municipal courts involve traffic violations. City governments have the option to determine if their municipal court will be a court of record; most are not. In 2002, there were 7.5 million cases filed in municipal courts. Of that number, 88 percent were traffic cases.

Appeals in such a situation are heard de novo by county courts. Municipal court judges must meet the qualifications specified by the city government and most are appointed by the city.

The county-level trial courts are the constitutional county courts and the statutory county courts. There is a constitutional county court in all 254 counties. The constitutional county court hears appeals from the inferior courts as well as having jurisdiction over higher-level misdemeanors, probate matters, and civil claims in which the amount in controversy is between $200.01 and $5,000. This civil jurisdiction overlaps with the justice of the peace courts. The county judge also serves a legislative function as the presiding officer of the county commissioners' court and an executive function exercising power over all county business.

Since the county judge also has legislative and executive functions, the judge may have little time to exercise judicial functions. For this reason, the legislature established county courts-at-law in certain counties. There are 195 statutory county courts in 74 counties. For example, Dallas County has fifteen statutory county courts while Harris County (Houston) has nineteen. These judges are elected to four-year terms. Statutory county courts have either civil or criminal jurisdiction, as determined by the legislative act that established them. Civil jurisdiction is over cases involving less than $100,000. Criminal jurisdiction includes serious misdemeanors with a punishment of a jail sentence or a fine over $500. According to data available from the National Center for State Courts, 725,000 cases were filed in county-level trial courts in the annual reporting period ending August 31, 2002. Almost 30 percent of those cases were civil filings. Qualifications for statutory county judge depend on the statute that created the court and usually include at least four years experience as a practicing attorney.

The district courts are the chief trial courts of the state. The names of the courts and their jurisdictions vary across the state. There are 418 district courts. Each court has one judge, who must be at least twenty-five years of age, a resident of the district for at least two years, a U.S. citizen, and a licensed attorney or judge for four years.

District court have general jurisdiction including felony criminal cases and misdemeanors involving official misconduct, divorce cases, election contests, and civil cases in which the matter of controversy exceeds $200. Felony cases make up about one-third of district courts' workload while civil cases constitute most of the workload. Juvenile cases are usually tried in district courts. In district court, 740,000 cases were filed. The courts were able to dispose of about 95 percent of those cases. Over 70 percent of the cases were civil. The geographic area of most district courts is one county. More populous counties have many district courts while some judicial districts in sparsely populated areas include more than one county. District courts in metropolitan areas tend to specialize in criminal, civil, or family law matters.

Associated Agencies

The Texas Office of Court Administration (OCA) provides administrative support and technical assistance to all Texas courts. The OCA was created in 1977 and operates under the direction of the chief justice of the Texas Supreme Court. The OCA researches innovative court programs and technologies that promote more efficient judicial administration. The agency also gathers judicial statistics and other data from judges and court officials in the state. This data is reported to national judicial agencies as well as the state legislative and executive branches.

The Texas State Commission on Judicial Conduct is an independent agency created by an amendment to the Texas Constitution in 1965. The commission is responsible for investigating allegations of judicial misconduct or judicial disability, and for disciplining judges. The body consists of eleven members who each serve six-year terms. It has jurisdiction over all judges in the state, including municipal judges, and retired and former judges who are sitting on the bench by assignment. The commission enforces the Texas Code of Judicial Conduct.

Judicial Selection

Since 1876, the people have elected judges at all levels through partisan elections. Until the 1980s, Democrats filled most judicial positions. With the growing influence of the Republican Party, more judicial elections were contested and judicial campaigns became more costly. In 1988, there were six open seats on the Texas Supreme Court. The candidates spent over $10 million. Between 1992 and 1997, the seven winning candidates for the Texas Supreme Court raised almost $9.2 million with more than 40 percent of that amount coming from lawyers or law firms with cases before the court. In 1995, the Texas legislature passed the Judicial Campaign Fairness Act. The act limits individual contributions to candidates in statewide judicial campaigns to $5,000 from individuals and $30,000 from law firms.

Public opinion indicates the weak support in Texas for an elected judiciary. A 1990 poll revealed that 71 percent of Texans supported electing judges; by 1997 that figure had dropped to 52 percent. In addition, leaders of racial and ethnic minority communities criticize the selection process because of a lack of representativeness among judges. In 1997, only eight of the ninety-eight appellate judges were Hispanic and two were African American. Only 11 percent of 396 district judges were Hispanic or African American.

In the courts of last resort, the presiding judge (or chief justice) and associates serve six-year terms. Appellate judges serve six-year terms and district judges, justices of the peace, and municipal judges are elected to four-year terms.

Retirement and removal provisions were added to the constitution in 1965. District court judges and judges and justices of the appellate courts must retire when they reach age seventy-five.

Judges may be removed from office, suspended, censured, or disciplined by the State Commission on Judicial Conduct for incompetence, violation of the code of judicial conduct, violation of the rules of the Texas Supreme Court, or actions that discredit the judiciary or the administration of justice. The commission submits a recommendation to the Texas Supreme Court. When the commission recommends removal or retirement, the court selects a review tribunal from among appellate court judges to verify the commission's findings and reach a judgment. Judges may appeal decisions of the review tribunal to the supreme court.

Another removal method is for the governor to remove a judge at the request of two-thirds of the members of the House of Representatives and the senate. Judges may be impeached by the House of Representatives and removed by a two-thirds vote of the senate, even without the governor's approval. Finally, the supreme court may remove a judge from office.

John David Rausch Jr.
West Texas A&M University

Further Reading
Attorney General of Texas, http://www .oag.state.tx.us/.
Edgewood v. Kirby, 777 S.W.2d 391 (TX 1989).
Office of Court Administration, "Court Structure of Texas," http://www.courts .state.tx.us/publicinfo/crt_stru.htm.
Texas Judiciary Online, http://www .courts.state.tx.us/.

UTAH
• • • • • • • • • • • • •

The Utah court system has its origins in the State of Deseret, the quasi-government established by the Mormon pioneers in the Salt Lake Valley in 1847. At the time, the region was part of Mexico. With the signing of the Treaty of Guadalupe Hildalgo in 1848, the region came under the control of the United States. The Mormon leadership petitioned for territorial status, and then quickly changed their minds and asked for statehood. While waiting for a response from Congress in Washington, the pioneers began developing their State of Deseret. The constitution of 1849 outlined a government, including a supreme court made up of three justices. The constitution also specified that the general assembly could create additional courts.

Deseret was formally dissolved by the general assembly in April 1851. Congress had created the Utah Territory in 1850. The Organic Act created a territorial supreme court with three justices, appointed by the president. The justices also served three judicial districts. The act provided for local justices of the peace. The territorial legislature created probate courts in each county to conduct hearings on matters related to estates, divorces, and guardianships, as well as hear appeals from justice courts. Utah was admitted to statehood in 1896.

The current Utah Constitution was drafted at a convention meeting in Salt Lake City in 1895. Voters ratified the constitution in November 1895 and it took effect on January 4, 1896, when Utah became a state. The document is one of the shorter state constitutions with slightly more than 11,000 words. It has been amended only about 100 times since 1896. The Utah Constitution includes an unusual provision added in 1993 that declares, "It is the policy of the state that a free market system shall govern trade and commerce in this state to promote the dispersion of economic and political power and the welfare of the people."

Utah Supreme Court

The Utah Supreme Court's five justices serve ten-year terms. The supreme court has appellate jurisdiction to hear appeals in felony and death penalty cases from the district court. The court also hears appeals in civil cases except for those involving domestic relations. Administrative decisions from the Public Service Commission; Tax Commission; School and Institutional Trust Lands Board of Trustees; Board of Oil, Gas, and Mining; and the state engineer may be appealed to the supreme court. The court has discretionary jurisdiction over appeals of decisions from the court of appeals. In fiscal year 2003, 596 cases were filed in the Utah Supreme Court. About 49 percent of the cases were appeals in civil cases, 11 percent criminal appeals, and 14 percent came to the supreme court on writs of certiorari from court of appeals decisions.

The chief justice is elected by a majority vote of the other justice to serve four years. An associated chief justice is elected to serve for two years. As the administrative head of the Utah court system, the supreme court adopts the rules of civil and criminal procedure for use in the state courts. It also governs the practice of law in Utah, including the conduct and discipline of lawyers.

The Utah Supreme Court has used the state constitution to decide cases, especially in areas in which the U.S. Constitution is silent. For example, the Utah Constitution includes an original equal rights provision that includes religion as one of the categories on which discrimination is forbidden. In the 1970s Utah also amended its constitution to include an equal rights amendment.

Court of Appeals

The Utah Court of Appeals was created by the state legislature to assist the supreme court with its caseload. The appellate court hears all appeals from the juvenile and district courts, except for small claims. It also hears appeals from the district court involving domestic relations cases and criminal matters except for death penalty cases. The court also reviews administrative decisions by state agencies including the Utah Industrial Commission and the Department of Employment Security Career Service Review Board. The appellate court has jurisdiction to review cases sent to it by the supreme court. There were 830 cases filed in the court of appeals in 2003. Of those, 39 percent were criminal appeals, 29 percent were civil appeals, 9 percent were appeals in cases involving juveniles, and 9 percent were appeals from administrative agency decisions.

The appellate court consists of seven judges who serve six-year terms. The presiding judge is elected by a majority vote of the other judges and serves two years. Prohibited by statute from sitting as one panel of seven members, the court sits and decides cases in rotating panels of three judges.

District Court

The district court is the trial court of general jurisdiction. Utah is divided into eight judicial districts. The seventy full-time district court judges serve those districts. The district court has original jurisdiction in all civil cases, all felony criminal cases, and certain misdemeanors. One of the largest categories of cases to come to the district court are domestic relations cases, including divorces, child custody and support, adoption, and probate matters. The district court also has appellate jurisdiction to review informal proceedings from administrative agencies. In 2003, 264,188 cases were heard in Utah's district courts. Of these cases, 40 percent were civil, 29 percent were traffic offenses, and 16 percent were criminal cases.

Juvenile Courts

The juvenile court is a specialized court with twenty-two full-time judges. The judges are divided into eight judicial districts. The juvenile court has status equal to the district court. The court has exclusive jurisdiction over youths under eighteen years of age who violate federal, state, or municipal laws, and any child who has been abused, neglected, or is dependent. The court determines child custody, support, and visitation, and it is able to terminate parental rights and to authorize treatment for mentally ill or retarded children. It also has jurisdiction over truants and runaways. The juvenile court has exclusive jurisdiction over traffic offenses involving minors, including automobile homicide, driving under the influence of alcohol or drugs, reckless driving, joy riding, and fleeing a police officer. It shares with the district and justice courts jurisdiction over adults contributing to the delinquency of a minor and neglect of a minor. During 2003, the juvenile courts heard 47,726 cases. This number included 60 percent misdemeanors, 14 percent status cases, 8 percent dependency/neglect/abuse cases, and 7 percent felony criminal cases.

The juvenile court administers a probation department to serve the juveniles who have been placed on probation by the court. Appeals from the juvenile courts go to the appellate court.

Justice Courts

Counties and municipalities establish justice courts to hear lower misdemeanors, ordinance violations, and small claims. The judges are hired by the local government entity. Some justice courts judges are county judges who are initially appointed by a county commission and then must run for retention every four years. Other justice courts judges are municipal court judges who are appointed by city governments to serve a four-year term. Some justice courts judges are both county and municipal judges. Justice court judges do not need to be attorneys, although they receive continuing legal training. There are 128 justices in 147 county and municipal courts. In 2003, justice courts heard 539,457 cases, with over 80 percent of the volume resulting from traffic offenses.

Associated Agencies

The Utah Judicial Council makes policy for the judicial branch of state government. It was created by a constitutional amendment. The council adopts rules for the administration of all courts in the state. It also sets standards for judicial performance, court facilities, support services, and judicial and nonjudicial staffing. The Judicial Council has fourteen members. The chief justice of the supreme court is the chair. The other members include a supreme court justice, an appellate judge, five district judges, two juvenile judges, three justice judges, a representative from the Utah State Bar, and the state court administrator. The judges and the state bar representative all serve three-year terms.

In 1973, the Utah legislature passed the Court Administrator Act to provide for the appointment of a state court administrator who manages the administrative office of the courts. This office serves as the staff for the judicial council, the nominating commissions, and provides support to court clerks throughout the state.

Judicial Selection and Removal

All judges, except for those on justice courts, are chosen through a merit selec-

tion process. The governor fills vacancies from a list of candidates submitted by a judicial nominating commission. The Utah senate must then confirm all appointees. In the senate, a seven-member confirmation committee first considers the appointees. The confirmation committee votes whether to send the appointees to the full senate. Recently adopted senate rules require the confirmation committee to thoroughly investigate each appointee rather than basing its recommendation solely on the candidates' resumes. Candidates are interviewed, the written materials used by the governor in making the appointment are reviewed, and public comments and evaluations are solicited. The public comments are not shared with the appointee.

From statehood until 1945, judges were elected through partisan elections. A 1945 constitutional amendment specified the merit selection process to be used in filling judicial vacancies. Incumbent judges were still required to run in partisan elections to retain their seats. In 1951, retention elections became nonpartisan. The legislature amended the laws governing the judicial nominating commissions in 1994. The governor was given the power to appoint all members of the commissions and to name the chairs of the new commissions. From 1945 until 1994, the Utah State Bar appointed the attorneys who served on the commissions.

The Utah Constitution provides two methods for removing judges. The Judicial Conduct Commission is an independent agency that investigates complaints alleging misconduct of judges. The commission consists of two state senators and two state representatives, three members of the public, two attorneys, and two judges. The commission determines whether a judge's conduct violates the code of judicial conduct. It may reprimand, censure, suspend, or remove a judge from office. The supreme court reviews all decisions of the Judicial Conduct Commission. Judges also may be impeached by a two-thirds vote of the Utah House of Representatives and convicted and removed from office by a two-thirds vote of the Utah senate.

John David Rausch Jr.
West Texas A&M University

Further Reading
Administrative Office of the Courts, "Utah State Courts," http://www .utcourts.gov/.
Utah Attorney General, http://attygen .state.ut.us/.
Utah State Bar, http://www.utahbar.org/.

VERMONT
• • • • • • • • • • • • •

The first Vermont republic constitution was signed in 1777 and required each county in Vermont to have a court. Vermont became a state in 1791 and signed the official Vermont Constitution in 1793. The legislature organized the first courts during the year of 1778 until the superior court could be created. However, decisions rendered by the superior court could be overturned by the governor and the legislature.

By 1782, each county had a court in place that was staffed with one chief judge and five assistant judges. Shortly thereafter, the Supreme Court of Vermont was established and the superior court dissolved. In 1797, the decisions of the supreme court were required to be recorded in writing. In 1825, supreme court judges were required to hear cases at the county level. This practice continued until 1906 when the legislature increased the number of supreme court judges to four and thereafter delineated duties among the justices. In 1908, the number of supreme court judges increased to five.

Vermont Supreme Court

The Supreme Court of Vermont consists of one chief justice and four associate justices. All are selected by the governor from a list of nominees provided by the judicial nominating board. The governor's decision is subject to the approval of the senate. Once approved, justices serve six-year terms in office. Justices retain their seats through a process of affirmation that occurs every two years.

Interestingly, the chief justice of the supreme court serves an entire six-year period. In order to qualify for a supreme court judgeship, an individual must be an attorney or judge who has worked in Vermont for longer than five years. The Supreme Court of Vermont uses a mandatory retirement age of seventy for those serving as judges.

The supreme court reviews appeals from lower courts in the state of Vermont as well as cases involving original jurisdiction, administrative state agencies' appeals, interlocutory (provisional) decisions, appeals from juvenile cases, and civil and criminal appeals. Review by the supreme court is discretionary and at least three justices must agree that a case be considered. Moreover, three out of the four justices must agree in order for the court to render a final decision. The number of appeals to the supreme court for the fiscal year 2002 was the lowest to date, around 500.

In addition to its appellate jurisdiction, the supreme court is vested with the authority to promulgate rules of practice and procedure for the entire judicial branch. The court also possesses ultimate control over administrative matters for the entire judicial branch. The court oversees disciplinary matters involving attorneys as well as the admission of new attorneys to the Vermont bar.

Superior Court

Vermont superior courts are trial courts that are present in each county. Fourteen superior courts hear civil cases involving personal injury, contract disputes, small claims involving less than $3,500 in damages, and certain appeals from lower courts. Jury trials are available in superior courts.

Currently, there are fifteen superior court judges who are selected in the same manner as supreme court justices. Superior court judges serve a six-year term and are retained with the approval of the legislature. An administrative judge is appointed by the supreme court to serve a four-year term. Individuals who serve as superior court judges must be either a lawyer or judge and have worked within the state for at least five years. At least two of the superior court judges are assistant judges who are elected officials within each county. Despite the expiration of a term, judges are allowed to hear any remaining cases that are assigned to them.

By statute, rulings of the superior court have precedential value. Moreover, if a county adopts rules in conflict with the precedent of the superior court, the precedent of the superior court has priority.

District Court

Like superior courts, district courts are also trial courts and function at the county level throughout Vermont. The difference between superior and district courts is largely jurisdictional. The district courts hear the majority of criminal cases and a limited number of civil matters. Civil matters include traffic and wildlife violations, license suspension, and violations of ordinances.

There are currently seventeen district court judges who are selected in the same manner as superior court judges and supreme court justices. District court judges serve six-year terms and retain their seats by a majority vote of the legislature. An administrative judge is selected by the Supreme Court of Vermont and serves in that position for a four-year term. Requirements for appointment as a district court judge include serving as an attorney or judge within the state for a period of five years or more.

Criminal defendants in district court may proceed with counsel or pro se. Legal representation is available for those who are indigent. Absent waiver of the right to a jury trial, criminal matters are determined by jury; however, sentencing decisions are made by the district court judge. Vermont, like other states, has seen an increase in felony cases.

Family Court

Family courts are trial courts with limited jurisdiction and are located in the fourteen Vermont counties. Family courts hear cases involving domestic relations, domestic violence, paternity, juvenile delinquency and dependency, and mental health issues. The family courts also hear a small number of appeals.

Family court judges are chosen from the ranks of superior and district court judges by the administrative judges. Family court judges serve six-year terms. Currently, there are twenty-eight assistant family court judges and five magistrates who handle child-support matters. To qualify for service as a family court judge, an individual must be a lawyer or judge who has worked in the community for at least five years

Family courts have reported a decrease in most categories of cases. However, the courts have experienced an increase in the numbers of cases involving divorce, juvenile delinquency, and child abuse and neglect.

Probate Court

Probate courts handle cases involving adoptions, wills and estates, guardianships, name changes, and gifts to minors. Currently, there are eighteen probate judges serving fourteen Vermont counties. However, four counties have two probate courts located inside their parameters.

Probate court judges are selected in partisan elections. Probate court judges are elected for four-year terms. Interestingly, probate judges are the only Vermont judges who may serve without benefit of a formal legal education.

Vermont Judicial Bureau

The Vermont Judicial Bureau hears cases arising from complaints filed by officers of the law. The judicial bureau hears cases involving traffic violations, violations of municipal ordinances, violations of fish and wildlife laws, and alcohol-related violations. The bureau has reported an increase in all types of cases except municipal ordinances. There are four hearing officers who are appointed by the administrative judge. The only requirement to serve on the judicial bureau is passing the state bar exam. Bureau judges serve a six-year term.

Environmental Court

There is one environmental court with one sitting judge. The environmental court reviews decisions relating to the regulation of natural resources and zoning. The environmental court also hears appeals relating to Act 250 which regulates land-use permits.

Judges are nominated by the judicial nominating committee, selected by the governor, and thereafter subject to approval by the senate. Nominees must be lawyers who are admitted to practice before the Vermont Supreme Court. Environmental court judges serve six-year terms.

Associated Agencies

The Judicial Nominating Board was formed in 1966 for the purpose of selecting appropriate judicial nominees for the three highest Vermont courts. The board has eleven members, five of whom must be attorneys. Four of the five attorneys are selected by the legislature. Remaining members are laypersons, two of whom are selected by the governor. The remaining four members are chosen by the legislature.

The Joint Committee on Judicial Retention assists the legislature by preparing a summary and report regarding the service of judges while on the bench. Committee members are selected on the recommendations of four senators and four representatives. Performance assessment requires members of the committee to communicate with the judge in person, provide opportunities for the public to express their impressions of the judge and his or her service, and conduct a hearing regarding the service of the judge. Committee members may also disseminate surveys to gauge public opinion regarding the service of judges. Votes of committee members are not recorded or known to one another; the majority vote is forwarded as the final recommendation to the legislature.

The Office of the Court Administrator assists the supreme court with fulfilling its role as administrative head of all courts. This office is responsible for hiring personnel, training, identifying long-term management needs, obtaining governmental appropriations, and creating evolving rules and regulations of the courts. There are four departments located within the office of the court administrator.

The Division of Administrative Services provides a variety of services for the judiciary. These include financial services, needs assessment, caseload management, and generally working to insure that the judiciary is operating in an efficient and effective manner. The Division of Court Operations is responsible for conducting research on bills that impact or involve the judicial system, investigating complaints, and cooperating with external agencies to improve the overall functioning of the judicial system. The divisions assist the family and district courts and provide some assistance to the superior court.

The Division of Judicial Education is responsible for providing educational and training opportunities for employees of the judicial branch. Additional responsibilities of this division include orienting new employees as well as facilitating mentoring relationships between employees. The judicial education division is also in charge of scheduling forums based on the latest legal issues as well as obtaining external funding for expanded educational opportunities.

The Division of Research and Information Services is the technological center for the judicial system. This division implements and maintains technology used throughout the judicial system. The division also gathers, provides, and presents statistical information regarding the operation of the judicial system.

Selection and Removal of Judges

Judges on the general jurisdiction courts are selected by the governor with input from a nomination commission. The state senate votes to confirm judges to an initial six-year term. At that time, the state assembly votes on retention. To qualify, a nominee must have been licensed to practice law in the state for at least five years. Each of the limited jurisdiction courts have differing selection methods. Probate court judges are chosen by partisan election; family court judges are assigned by judges on the superior and district courts; environmental court judges are appointed like general jurisdiction judges, and judicial bureau judges are appointed by an administrative judge. Judges may be relieved of their duties when they reach age seventy, or through two disciplinary processes. Judges may be impeached by a two-thirds vote of the House of Representatives and convicted by a two-thirds vote of the senate. Also a judicial conduct board investigates complaints of judicial misconduct or disability and recommends action to the supreme court. Disciplinary actions range from public reprimand of the judge, to suspension for a part or the remainder of the judge's term of office. This commission may also cause the retirement of a judge found to be physically or mentally incapable.

Lana McDowell and Lisa S. Nored
University of Southern Mississippi

References and Further Reading

American Judicature Society, "Judicial Selection in the States," http://www.ajs.org/js/VT.htm (accessed April 3, 2005).

Office of the Court Administrator, "State of Vermont Judicial Statistics: Year ending June 30, 2002," http://www.vermontjudiciary.org.

Vermont State Historic Sites, "Vermont Timeline," http://www.dhca.state.vt.us/HistoricSites.

VIRGINIA
• • • • • • • • • • • • •

The Virginia judicial system is the oldest court system in the United States. Its judicial system has its foundation in the Jamestown Charter of 1606. In 1623, the Virginia Houses of Burgesses created the five-man appellate court. The court was required to meet quarterly. In 1661, the quarterly court became the general court and was given both original and appellate jurisdiction. The Virginia General Assembly created four superior courts— the supreme court of appeals, admiralty, general, and chancery. The supreme court included justices from the other three courts. In 1788, the general assembly separated the supreme court from other courts. It divided the state into five judicial districts, required written opinions, and specified that justices be elected to life-long terms by popular vote.

The 1850 constitution limited judicial terms to twelve years. The 1870 constitution limited justices to twelve years and moved their selection to the general assembly. A 1928 constitutional amendment increased the size of the supreme court to seven and renamed the president of the supreme court to the chief justice of the supreme court. In 1970 the court received its current name, the Supreme Court of Virginia. Virginia's constitution vests judicial power in the supreme court and any other courts (original jurisdiction and appellate jurisdiction) that are inferior to the supreme court as the general assembly dictates.

Virginia Supreme Court

Virginia's court of last resort is the supreme court. Although the supreme court has both original and appellate jurisdiction, its primary purpose is hearing appeals. The supreme court has original jurisdiction over habeas corpus petitions, mandamus, and prohibition. The supreme court also has original jurisdiction for judicial conduct cases filed by the Judicial Inquiry and Review Commission related to judicial discipline and other personnel issues. The Supreme Court of Virginia receives nearly 3,000 petitions each year.

The Virginia Supreme Court has one chief justice and ten associate justices. They are elected by the general assembly to twelve-year terms. The supreme court includes other officers such as the clerk of the supreme court, the executive secretary of the supreme court, the court reporter, the chief staff attorney of the supreme court, and the law librarian. Each of these positions serves at the pleasure of the supreme court. The court reporter must be a distinguished law professor at one of Virginia's law schools. Each justice also appoints his or her law clerk.

The chief justice of the supreme court is also the administrator of the judicial system in Virginia. The supreme court promulgates rules for judicial procedure in Virginia, and the chief justice sits on other policy-making committees.

Court of Appeals

There is one intermediate appellate court in Virginia with eleven judges who are elected to eight-year terms by the general assembly. The court of appeals in Virginia was created in 1985. Criminal and traffic offenses are appealed through petition and all other appeals are a matter of right. The court of appeals also has original jurisdiction to issue writs of mandamus, prohibition, and habeas corpus in any case over which the court would have appellate jurisdiction. The court of appeals hears cases in panels of three. The court can sit en banc if the panel hands down a split decisions and three other justices vote to hear the case en banc. It will also sit en banc when a panel's decision conflicts with other decisions of the court; and in a case where a majority of the court votes to hear the case en banc. The court of appeals receives about 3,300 petitions each year.

Circuit Courts

Virginia has 31 circuits with 150 circuit judges who are elected to eight-year terms by the general assembly. Circuit courts are Virginia's only general jurisdiction trial courts. These courts have jurisdiction over civil claims over $15,000; criminal felony cases and misdemeanors indicted by a grand jury; and equity issues such as divorce, wills, trusts, and so on. Circuit courts also have appellate jurisdiction from general district courts and juvenile and domestic relations district courts. Appeals are heard de novo (retried in their entirety from the beginning).

District Courts

Virginia has thirty-two judicial districts for its district courts. District courts include general district courts and juvenile and domestic relations district courts. These courts exist in each city and county in Virginia. Virginia has 124 general district court judges and 110 juvenile and domestic relations district court judges. District court judges are elected by the state's general assembly to six-year terms.

General district courts have limited jurisdiction; these courts hear minor civil cases (under $15,000). In fact, they have sole jurisdiction for claims under $4,500. These courts also have jurisdiction over minor criminal offenses (misdemeanors and petty offenses) and traffic offenses. The district court also conducts preliminary hearings in felony cases.

Juvenile and domestic relations district courts have jurisdiction over cases involving juvenile delinquency, juveniles accused of traffic offenses, children in need of services, abused and neglected children, spousal abuse, other domestic abuse cases, custody issues, child support, abandonment, and foster care, to name a few. These courts are also responsible for keeping the confidentiality of juvenile offenders. The aim of these courts is to rehabilitate rather than punish.

Magistrates

Finally, magistrates exist in each of the districts. Magistrates are not judges, but they are judicial officers. Virginia's current magistrate system grew out 1974 reforms that phased out justices of the peace and replaced them with a statewide magistrate system. A magistrate is usually the first contact a person has with the court system in Virginia. Magistrates conduct initial appearances, hold bond hearings, collect fines for traffic offenses and misdemeanors, issue search and arrest warrants, and subpoenas. Each of Virginia's thirty-two districts includes a chief magistrate and a number of magistrates who serve under the direction of the chief magistrate. Most magistrates are not lawyers, but they are specially trained officials.

Selection of Judges and Other Important Officials

Virginia is one of two states (the other is neighboring South Carolina) where judges are elected by the legislature. Judgeships are seen as a reward for legislative service. Since the general assembly elects all judges of record, the process favors sitting or former legislators. Many are elected to the legislature with the intent of a future judicial election (Bowman and Kearney 2002). If the legislature is not in session the governor appoints judges to serve in the interim until the general assembly reconvenes. Both houses of the general assembly must elect appointed judges within thirty days of the beginning of the session. The judge serves a full term once he or she is elected by the general assembly. All district court judges are elected by the general assembly. Interim appointments are filled by circuit court judges of the relevant circuit. Chief circuit court judges appoint magistrates to four-year terms. They serve under the direction of the circuit court chief judges.

Virginia's constitution says the Judiciary and Inquiry Commission investigates "members of the judiciary, the bar, and the public," and it has "power to investigate charges which would be the basis for retirement, censure, or removal of a judge" (Office of the Executive Secretary 2004). In other words, the commission investigates misconduct complaints and competency matters of all judges, justices, and members of the special state panels. If the commission finds credible evidence of malfeasance or misconduct it files a complaint with the supreme court. The supreme court holds a hearing and decides what actions to take. If the court finds there was misconduct it can censure the judge or remove him or her from office.

The seven judiciary and inquiry commissioners are elected by the general assembly to a four-year term. The commission is composed of one circuit court judge, one general district court judge, one juvenile and domestic relations district court judge, two lawyers, and two members of the public (Office of the Executive Secretary 2004).

The Virginia judicial system fiscal year (FY) 2005 budget was $270 million. This budget was about 3.2 percent more than FY 2004. About 60 percent of the budget is used to pay salaries and benefits for judges and staff. The Supreme Court's annual budget is $18.3 million. The court of appeals budget is $5.9 million; circuit courts spend another $69.3 million. Finally, district courts have the largest share of Virginia's judicial system budget—$157.1 million (Supreme Court of Virginia 2005, A13-A15).

Doug Goodman
Mississippi State University

References and Further Reading
Bowman, Ann O'M., and Richard C. Kearney. 2002. *State and Local Government*, 5th ed. Boston: Houghton Mifflin.
Judicial Council of Virginia. 2003. *Report to the General Assembly and Supreme Court of Virginia*. Richmond, VA: Judicial Council of Virginia.

Office of the Executive Secretary, Supreme Court of Virginia. 2004. "Virginia Courts in Brief," http://www.courts.state.va.us /cib/cib.htm (accessed March 29, 2006).

Rottman, David B., et al. 2000. *State Court Organization 1998*. Washington, DC: U.S. Department of Justice.

Supreme Court of Virginia. 2005. *Virginia 2004 State of the Judiciary Report*, http://www.courts.state.va.us/reports/ 2004/home.pdf (accessed November 21, 2005).

Virginia Courts, http://www.courts.state .va.us/courts/courts.html.

WASHINGTON

Washington's court system can be divided into three historic periods. From 1848 through 1853, the Oregon Territory included land south of the 49th parallel, west of the Rockies, and north of California. The U.S. president primarily appointed territorial officials, including judges. These officials had the responsibility of governing a large territory. In 1853, the area north of the Columbia River and east to the Continental Divide was separated from Oregon and became the Washington Territory. For Washington Territory, Congress established a court system that consisted of a supreme court, district courts, probate courts, and justice of the peace courts. The three judges on the supreme court were to be appointed by the president. They also served as the district court judges. Congress had divided the territory into three judicial districts. The territorial legislature was permitted to select probate court judges and justices of the peace using any method that did not violate the U.S. Constitution or federal law. In 1883, the territorial legislature asked Congress to create a fourth judicial district, an action taken by Congress. This solved the problem of having one of the supreme court judges hearing an appeal to the supreme court from the judicial district of which he was district judge. Washington was admitted to the Union at the same time as Montana, North Dakota, and South Dakota.

The current Washington Constitution was drafted in July and August 1889, in Olympia. Voters approved the document that fall, while rejecting separate measures that would have given women the right to vote and prohibited the sale and manufacture of alcoholic beverages in the state. The constitution took effect when Washington became a state on November 11, 1889. With more than 29,000 words, the Washington Constitution is of average length. The state was one of the first states to limit government through instruments of direct democracy: the initiative, referendum, and recall processes. The constitution has been amended more than 100 times since 1889.

Supreme Court

The supreme court is the state's highest court and the state government finances its functions. The court has original jurisdiction and appellate jurisdiction in cases where people have appealed a decision of a state officer. The supreme court has direct appellate jurisdiction when a trial court has ruled a statute or ordinance unconstitutional, if there are conflicting statutes or rules of law involved, or if the issue requires a prompt and final determination. The supreme court directly reviews all cases involving the death penalty. The court may choose to review appellate court decisions. The court also may review decisions of lower courts if the judgment involves more than $200. This limit does not apply if the case involves the legality of a tax, duty, assessment, toll, or municipal fine, or the validity of a statute. In 2002, 1,540 cases were filed in the supreme court. Of these 680 were petitions for review, 430 were discretionary reviews, and 160 cases involved attorney admission to the bar and discipline matters. There was one death penalty case.

Five justices hear motions and petitions for review of court of appeals decisions. In the case the five-member panel is not unanimous, all nine members must consider the matter. The chief justice is the administrative head of the judicial branch. Since 1995, the justices have selected a member of the court to be chief justice. The supreme court is the final rule-making authority for Washington's courts. Local courts may make their own rules of procedure, but these rules may not conflict with the rules established by the supreme court. The court also has responsibility over certain activities of the Washington State Bar, including issues related to disciplinary matters.

Court of Appeals

To reduce the workload on the supreme court, the legislature created the court of appeals in 1969. Most cases appealed from the superior courts go to the appellate courts. They must accept all appeals filed with them. Some specific types of cases go directly to the supreme court without being heard in the appellate courts. The appellate court is divided into three divisions. Division I is based in Seattle and has ten judges. Division II in Tacoma has seven judges. Division III has five judges and is located in Spokane. The three divisions are further divided into three geographic districts and a specific number of judges must be elected from each district.

A presiding chief judge is selected to a one-year term as administrator for all three divisions. Each division also elects a chief judge to be the administrator at the division level. The state government finances the activities of the appellate courts. The appellate courts received 4,323 cases in 2002: Division I (Seattle) received 1,830 cases; Division II (Tacoma) received 1,569 cases; and Division III (Spokane) received 924 cases. Only a small number (about 9.2 percent) of these cases were discretionary appeals. Slightly over half of the appeals were from criminal cases.

Superior Courts

Superior courts are trial courts of general jurisdiction. There is no limit on the type of civil or criminal cases heard by superior courts. This level of courts also has the authority to hear appeals from courts of limited jurisdiction. Superior courts are courts of record. In most cases, appeals go to the appellate courts, but specific types of cases may be appealed directly to the supreme court. Superior courts handled 300,000 cases in 2003, an increase of 4.7 percent over 2002. Civil cases made up 42.8 percent. About 16 percent were criminal cases, while the remainder were domestic relations cases, cases involving juvenile offenders or juvenile dependency, probate cases, adoption and paternity issues, mental illness cases, and guardianships.

The state government finances half of a superior court judge's salary and benefits. All superior courts are grouped into thirty single or multi county districts based on population. Counties with large populations usually form one district. Less-populated counties are joined together to form a district. While each of Washington's thirty-nine counties has a superior court, judges in rural districts rotate between their counties as needed. There is a presiding judge in each county or judicial district who serves as the administrator. Juvenile court is a division of the superior court. This court was established to deal with youth offenders and youth who are abused or neglected.

Courts of Limited Jurisdiction

There are two types of courts of limited jurisdiction. District courts serve counties. Cities and towns create municipal courts. District courts have jurisdiction over criminal and civil cases. They hear misdemeanors and criminal traffic cases, including driving under the influence, hit-and-run, and driving with a suspended license. District courts also hold preliminary hearings for felony cases. Jurisdiction in civil cases is limited to those cases in which judgment is less than $50,000. District courts have jurisdiction over traffic infractions, including those cases involving a monetary penalty but no jail sentence. Municipal courts or traffic violation bureaus hear violations of municipal ordinances. In some areas, cities contract with the district court to serve as a municipal court. Judges may impose fines up to $5,000 or a year in jail, or both. Traffic violation bureaus have jurisdiction provided by city law. Appeals are heard in superior court. If the lower court did not record a case, the appeal is heard anew in superior court. More than 2 million cases were filed in Washington's courts of limited jurisdiction in 2003.

Associated Agencies

The Washington State Commission on Judicial Conduct investigates complaints about a judge's misconduct or disability. The commission is made up of two lawyers, three judges, and six citizens who are not lawyers or judges. Any person, organization, or association may file a complaint with the commission. The commission then investigates to determine if the code of judicial conduct was violated. If misconduct is identified, the commission may reprimand or censure the judge or it may recommend to the supreme court that the judge be suspended or removed. A judge may appeal the commission's decision to the supreme court. The Administrative Office of the Courts was established by the legislature in 1957. It operates under the direction of the chief justice of the supreme court to improve the efficiency of the Washington court system.

Judicial Selection and Removal

The Washington Constitution stipulates that judges are to be elected, and in most cases licensed to practice law. Municipal court judges are the exception, and they may be selected either by election or appointment. Judicial elections are nonpartisan according to statute. In 1907, the Washington legislature established a direct nonpartisan election system for nominating judges, replacing the party conventions used since statehood. Nonpartisan ballots also were established by general elections.

The nine supreme court justices and appellate court judges are elected to six-year staggered terms. A candidate for the review-level courts must have five years practicing law and have lived for at least a year in the district from which that judgeship is drawn. The governor fills vacancies with the appointee serving until the next general election. A candidate must be a practicing attorney in the state.

The Walsh Commission, a twenty-four-member committee of citizens, judges, and attorneys, reviewed judicial selection in Washington and proposed a modified merit plan for selecting judges. The governor was to appoint judges based on recommendations from a judicial nominating commission. Judges would run in contested elections after one year in office, and in retention elections thereafter. The legislature never considered the proposal, but the supreme court adopted a recommendation for the distribution of a judicial voter guide.

Despite the nonpartisan nature of judicial elections, some elections have involved partisanship. Political observers described a 2002 supreme court race as one of the most partisan nonpartisan races in the state's history. The state Republican and Libertarian parties endorsed one candidate. This candidate also had the endorsement of conservative business and other interest groups. The other candidate was endorsed by the state Democratic Party and liberal interests like organized labor and environmental groups. The candidate supported by the Democratic Party, attorney Mary Fairhurst, was elected, giving women a majority on the supreme court for the first time.

There are two ways to remove a judge from the bench in Washington. A joint resolution of the legislature, approved by three-fourths of the members of each house, may be enacted to remove a judge. The Commission on Judicial Conduct investigates complaints of judicial misconduct or disability and submits a recommendation to the supreme court. The commission may recommend that a judge be suspended, removed, or retired. The supreme court makes a final decision after reviewing the recommendation and holding a hearing on the matter.

John David Rausch Jr.
West Texas A&M University

Further Reading
Administrative Office of the Courts, "Washington Courts," http://www .courts.wa.gov/.

State of Washington, Office of the Administrator for the Courts. 2001. *A Citizen's Guide to Washington Courts*, 9th ed. Olympia, WA: Office of the Administrator for the Courts.
Washington State Commission on Judicial Conduct, http://www.cjc.state.wa.us/.
Washington State Office of the Attorney General, http://www.atg.wa.gov/.
Washington State Bar Association, http://www.wsba.org/.

WEST VIRGINIA

West Virginia became a state on June 20, 1863, after breaking with Virginia over secession. The first constitution of West Virginia placed the judicial power of the state in a supreme court of appeals, in circuit courts, and various inferior panels. In 1880, the first constitution was displaced by a new constitution, but some provisions of the old constitution (e.g., the judicial powers) remained. However, it did increase the number of judges for the supreme court of appeals. In 1902, an amendment to the constitution further increased the number of judges and reinstated the county court into the county government.

On November 5, 1974, voters ratified the Judicial Reorganization Amendment. Under this amendment, justices of the peace were eliminated and all other courts, with the exception of municipal courts, were integrated into one court system with administrative and oversight functions of the supreme court of appeals by 1976. The amendment further created three levels (the supreme court of appeals, circuit court, and magistrate courts) for which the court was to be organized. In November 2000, a constitutional amendment resulted in the creation of family courts that were put into effect on January 1, 2002.

Supreme Court of Appeals

The supreme court of appeals was established in 1863 with three justices. In 1902, an amendment to the constitution further increased the number of justices to five. The supreme court of appeals is deemed the court of last resort and West Virginia is one of eleven states that has a single appellate court. The court has two terms each year. The first term commences in January and ends in July. The second term starts in September and ends in December. While in session, the court has appellate jurisdiction over civil cases equal or in excess of $300, cases concerning matters of the constitution, felonies, and misdemeanor issues appealed from the circuit court. It hears appeals of family court decisions provided that both parents are in agreement that they will not appeal first to the circuit court. Moreover, it hears workers' compensation appeals that are appealed to the court by the state administrative agency. The court also has original jurisdiction in proceedings of habeas corpus, certiorari, mandamus, and prohibition.

Unlike the lower trial courts, which have a jury and testimonies, oral arguments are presented and attorneys submit briefs to the judges. Thereafter, the judges issue a written decision or opinion that may be appealed to the U.S. Supreme Court.

In 2004, West Virginia received 2,449 new petitions representing a 15 percent decline from the previous year. This figure is nearly double the number of petitions filed in 1985 to suggest a steady increase in caseload over the years. Other similar states (e.g., Nevada, Delaware, Maine, North Dakota, and Rhode Island) have also received an increase in case filing and have established intermediate appellate courts to deal with the caseload. West Virginia has a caseload of 147 cases per 100,000 people. In 2000, West Virginia's caseload was almost 1.5 times that of Nevada. When comparing West Virginia to other states, the caseload that the state receives is more than Delaware, Maine, North Dakota, and Rhode Island combined.

Circuit Courts

Circuit courts are the only trial courts of general jurisdiction. They have jurisdiction over cases involving amounts equal or in excess of $300, felonies, misde-

meanors, and juvenile matters. The courts have the authority to hear and make decisions for habeas corpus proceedings, quo warranto, mandamus, certiorari, and prohibition. Moreover, they receive appeals from family courts provided they are not appealed directly to the supreme court of appeals, magistrate courts, municipal courts, and administrative agencies, with the exception of workers' compensation appeals that are directly appealed to the supreme court of appeals. Circuit courts are also recipients of recommendations from the judicial officers regarding juvenile and mental issues.

Mental Hygiene Commissioners

There is a mental hygiene commissioner in each of the circuits. The commissioners are lawyers who preside over guardianship, conservatorship, and involuntary hospitalization matters.

Family Courts

In November 2000, voters of West Virginia passed a constitutional amendment establishing family courts. These courts began operations on January 1, 2002. The court has jurisdiction over separate maintenance, divorce, annulment, family support, paternity, child custody, visitation, and issue protective orders in domestic violence cases.

Magistrate Courts

At least two magistrate courts exist in each county. Some counties have as many as ten magistrate courts. Magistrates have jurisdiction over civil cases disputing issues involving $5,000 or less, issue search-and-arrest warrants, conduct preliminary hearings in felony cases, and hear misdemeanor cases. They also issue emergency protective orders for matters regarding domestic violence.

Juvenile Referees

Juvenile referees hold detention hearings when matters concern a child being arrested or detained. Only three counties (Wayne, Kanawha, and Cabell) use two full-time and one part-time juvenile referee. But in most counties, the magistrate serves as the juvenile referee.

Municipal Courts

Municipal courts are created and operated at the local level. The state provides the municipality with a charter to include provisions for the creation and regulation of these courts. The charter designates who presides over police courts. The mayor, a police judge, or another authorized person acts as a police court judge. Over time, municipalities have been able to secure lawyers to serve as judges. The courts have jurisdiction over ordinance and traffic violations.

Selection and Removal of Judges

Supreme court of appeals justices are elected in partisan elections and serve twelve-year terms. The constitution requires that the judges be at least thirty-

years of age, a citizen for five years, and able to vote. Like the U.S. Constitution, the West Virginia Constitution makes no requirement that judges have legal training or experience. However, state law mandates that they must have practiced law for at least ten years. The chief justice position rotates each year depending on the seniority of the judges. In instances where a vacancy occurs, it is the responsibility of the governor to appoint a judge to serve until the next election. Those appointees seeking to maintain their positions must participate in the next general election.

Circuit court judges are elected in partisan elections and serve eight-year terms. These judges must have legal experience in law for five or more years. In the case of a vacancy, the governor appoints a circuit court judge to complete the remainder of the term. Appointees seeking to maintain their positions must run in the next general election. These judges must have practiced law for at least five years.

West Virginia has 158 magistrates who are elected in partisan elections to four-year terms. Magistrates are not required to be lawyers. The circuit judge has the responsibility of filling vacancies and those magistrates seeking to remain in office must participate in the next election.

The Judicial Investigation Commission determines whether sufficient evidence exists to charge a judge with violating the code of judicial conduct administered by the court. The Office of Disciplinary Counsel investigates all complaints of code violations. It may also conduct investigations at the request of the Judicial

Investigation Commission or may initiate its own investigations. A written report is completed for each complaint and submitted to the Office of Disciplinary Counsel (which prosecutes violators) recommending whether there is sufficient evidence to charge a judge with violating the code. The Office of the Judicial Hearing Board conducts a hearing on official charges and imposes sanctions for violations.

The budget of West Virginia's judicial system for fiscal year (FY) 2006 is about $82.4 million. The largest expense is for personnel ($46.6 million). The director of administrative services for the supreme court of appeals administers the judiciary budget.

La Shonda Stewart
Mississippi State University

Doug Goodman
Mississippi State University

References and Further Readings

Lambert, Oscar Doane. 1951. *West Virginia and Its Government.* Boston: D. C. Heath.

Netstate, http://www.netstate.com/states/index.html (accessed August 13, 2004).

Rice, Otis K. 1985. *West Virginia: A History.* Lexington: University Press of Kentucky.

State of West Virginia Legislature. 2005. "Digest of the Enrolled Budget Bill: Fiscal Year 2005–2006," .http://www.legis.state.wv.us/Budgetdigest/budget%20digest%202005-2006.pdf (accessed November 21, 2005).

West Virginia Supreme Court of Appeals. 2004a. "Supreme Court of Appeals of West Virginia: 2004 Annual Report," http://www.state.wv.us/wvsca/clerk/statistics/2004StatRept.pdf (accessed November 21, 2005).

———. 2004b. "West Virginia Court System," http://www.state.wv.us/wvsca/ (accessed November 21, 2005).

Williams, John Alexander. 1976. *West Virginia: A Bicentennial History.* New York: Norton.

WISCONSIN

In 1848, the Wisconsin Constitution created a judiciary that included a supreme court, circuit courts, courts of probate, and justices of the peace. The legislature was also given the power to establish inferior courts and municipal courts. The state was originally divided into five judicial circuit districts, each presided over by one judge. These five judges also met once a year as a supreme court. In 1853, the legislature established a separate supreme court, staffed by the justices, chosen in statewide elections. In 1877 a constitutional amendment increased the size of the supreme court to five justices, and in 1903, an amendment to the constitution increased the size of the supreme court to seven justices, the size of the court today. In 1889, an amendment to the constitution changed the original practice of electing a person to the position of chief justice, to the current practice of having the member of the court with the longest service become chief justice.

Over the years, there were various county and municipal courts, as well as other special courts, created by the state legislature. In 1959 the Wisconsin legislature began court reorganization, eventually resulting in the trial court system currently in place. The 1959 law left the supreme court and circuit courts relatively unchanged, but abolished the county, municipal, and other special courts that had been created by the legislature. The chief justice of the supreme court was also given the authority to reassign circuit court judges to other circuits with the goal of balancing the amount of work done by each circuit judge. Two constitutional amendments in 1959 abolished justices of the peace and permitted municipal courts. A 1977 amendment to the constitution, along with a 1978 law, created the courts of appeals.

Organization of State Courts

The Wisconsin judiciary is headed by a seven–member supreme court. The court of appeals, which is staffed by sixteen judges, is divided into four districts. Cases are heard by three-judge panels. The next level is the circuit court. With the exception of six counties that are paired together (Buffalo/Pepin, Florence/Forest, and Shawano/Menominee), each of Wisconsin's seventy-two counties has a circuit court. The circuit courts, staffed by 241 circuit court judges, are organized into 10 judicial administrative districts. Finally, there are the municipal courts that as of September 2003, were 225 in number, staffed by 227 judges.

Powers of State Courts

The Wisconsin Supreme Court has appellate jurisdiction over the entire Wisconsin judiciary and has discretion as to which cases it will hear. The supreme court also has the power to hear original actions, at its own discretion. Article VII, Section 4 of the Wisconsin Constitution states that "The chief justice of the supreme court shall be the administrative head of the judicial system and shall exercise this administrative authority pursuant to procedures adopted by the supreme court. The chief justice may assign any judge of a court of record to aid in the proper disposition of judicial business in any court of record except the supreme court." Administrative duties of the chief justice include, but are not limited to, budgeting, long-range planning, juror use and management, and rules of pleading and practice. The supreme court also oversees the legal profession (bar).

Wisconsin's court of appeals is an intermediate court of appeals. Its primary function is to correct errors occurring at the circuit court level. A single judge of the court can hear cases stemming from small-claims actions, municipal ordinance violations, traffic regulation violations, and mental health, juvenile, contempt, and misdemeanor cases. All other cases are heard by a three-judge panel. The court issues a written opinion with every case, although not all are published opinions. The court has discretion as to whether it will allow oral arguments in a case, and in 2003, only heard oral arguments in forty-eight cases.

The circuit courts are Wisconsin's trial courts. Each circuit has a clerk of the court, an elected official, responsible for the various record-keeping functions of the court. This includes keeping records of proceedings, jury management, and court finances and administration. In each of the ten judicial administrative districts, the chief justice of the supreme court appoints a chief judge. The chief judge of each judicial district appoints a deputy chief judge. The responsibilities of the chief judge include administration of the district. The circuit courts have trial-level jurisdiction over all cases arising under state law, as well as under municipal ordinances in municipalities without a municipal court. This includes civil cases, criminal cases, cases involving family law, and juvenile and probate cases. Funding for a circuit court comes from both the state and the county in which it is located. The state pays for judicial salaries, salaries of court reporters, reserve judges, and travel and training of judges. The state also uses formula grants to assist with the expense of providing guardians ad litem (court-appointed attorneys), court-appointed witnesses, interpreters, and jurors. All other expenses are paid for by the county.

Municipal courts have exclusive jurisdiction over ordinance violations (when a municipal court does not exist, these cases go to the circuit court). Cases heard by municipal courts frequently involve traffic violations, juvenile matters such as truancy and underage drinking, and ordinance matters. Municipal courts do not have the authority to hold jury trials ex-cept in first-offense drunken driving cases. Municipal court decisions can be appealed to circuit courts either for a new trial or for review of the record. Since 1996, a person choosing to have a case heard in a circuit court where a municipal court with jurisdiction exists faces a fine of $48 to $55 or more than the amount of the citation. If a municipality does not have a court it must pay the circuit court $5 per municipal ordinance case it hears.

Selection of Judges

Judges in Wisconsin are elected in non-partisan elections. The exception to this is that when a midterm vacancy occurs, the replacement can be appointed. Supreme court justices are elected to ten-year terms, with no more than one justice being elected in any given election. Court of appeals judges serve six-year terms, as do circuit court judges. Interim vacancies are filled by the governor and a judicial selection committee. A list of potential candidates is created by the judicial selection committee, a committee comprised of nine attorneys appointed by the governor. Although the committee makes recommendations to the governor, the governor is not bound by the committee's recommendation. Judges must be a resident of the state, licensed to practice in the state for at least five years, and under the age of seventy.

Municipal judges serve terms of two, three, or four years, depending on which term of office the municipality chose when creating the court. Municipal judges are elected in nonpartisan elections. Municipal court judges must be licensed to practice law in Wisconsin.

Discipline

State law in Wisconsin includes a code of judicial conduct, which is overseen by the Judicial Conduct Advisory Committee, a nine-member committee appointed by the supreme court. The committee provides informal advice and formal advisory opinions concerning compliance with the code. In addition, the Wisconsin Constitution provides that "[e]ach justice or judge shall be subject to reprimand, censure, suspension, removal for cause or for disability, by the supreme court pursuant to procedures established by the legislature by law. No justice or judge removed for cause shall be eligible for reappointment or temporary service" (Article VII, Section 11). Judges may also be removed by a two-thirds vote of both chambers of the legislature.

Workload

Wisconsin's supreme court receives approximately 1,000 petitions per year. The supreme court is a discretionary court, and chooses to accept 100–120 cases per year. In 2003, the supreme court provided written opinions in 141 cases. The supreme court justices are also involved in administrative oversight of the Wisconsin judiciary. The Wisconsin Court of Appeals was initially designed to hear 1,200 cases per year. In 2003, the court of appeals had 3,453 appeals filed. Of these, only 35 percent received a full opinion, while 31 percent were disposed of with summary disposition and 27 percent received memo opinions. The majority of cases coming to the court of appeals fall under mandatory jurisdiction, meaning that the court must hear cases appealed to it. Wisconsin's 241 circuit court judges in its 72 circuit courts disposed of over 1 million cases in 2003; Wisconsin's 225 municipal courts judges disposed of 572,594 cases.

Ruth Ann Watry
Northern Michigan University

References and Further Reading

American Judicature Society, "Center for Judicial Selection," http://www.ajs .org/selection/index.asp.

Gray, Trine E., ed. 2003. *Portraits of Justice: The Wisconsin Supreme Court's First 150 Years.* Madison, WI: Wisconsin Historical Society.

Harmon, Robert B. 1991. *Government and Politics in Wisconsin: A Selected Guide to Information Service.* Monticello, IL: Vance Bibliographies.

Wisconsin Court System, http://www .wicourts.gov/.

WYOMING
• • • • • • • • • • • • •

The Wyoming court system began with organization of Laramie County in Dakota Territory in 1867. The coming of the Union Pacific Railroad brought rapid population growth and necessitated a government. Cheyenne was 800 miles from the territorial capital in Yankton, so county residents, calling their home "Wyoming," began to lobby for the creation of a new territory. Congress granted Wyoming territorial status through the Wyoming Organic Act in 1868. While the territory waited for Congress to approve President Andrew Johnson's appointments, Dakota law remained in effect. Since the creation of Laramie County in 1867, no Dakota judges traveled to the region to hold court. Territorial officials did not arrive in Cheyenne until May 1869.

While the president appointed members of the territorial supreme court, local judgeships were created and filled by the territorial legislature. In 1870, Ester Hobart Morris became the first woman to be appointed justice of the peace. President Benjamin Harrison appointed Willis Van Devanter to be chief justice of the Wyoming Territorial Supreme Court in 1889. Van Devanter eventually was appointed to the U.S. Supreme Court. Wyoming was granted statehood in 1890.

After working for twenty-five days, a constitutional convention proposed a constitution to the voters who approved the document on November 5, 1889. It took effect on statehood in July 1890. With about 32,000 words, the Wyoming Consti-

Willis Van Devanter served as chief justice of the Wyoming Territory and on the federal Eighth Circuit Court of Appeals. He served as an associate justice of the U.S. Supreme Court from 1911 to 1937. (Library of Congress)

tution is slightly longer than average. It has been amended more than sixty-five times since 1890. The original document included a provision allowing women the right to vote. Utah was the only other state to provide this right to women in its original constitution. Because of the importance of mineral extraction on the Wyoming economy, the constitution includes provisions relating to mines and mining. The constitution allows

Wyoming voters to participate in government through direct democracy. The citizen initiative may be used to propose and enact laws as long as the laws do not dedicate revenues, make or repeal appropriations, create courts, define the jurisdiction of courts, enact local or special legislation, or take actions that are prohibited to the legislature by the constitution.

Supreme Court of Wyoming

The five–member Supreme Court of Wyoming is the court of last resort in the state. Most cases filed in the supreme court are appeals from the decisions of district courts. When the supreme court issues its decisions in these cases, the decisions are binding an all Wyoming courts and state agencies unless overturned by legislative action. In 2001, 283 cases were filed in the supreme court.

The Supreme Court of Wyoming also administers the legal profession in the state by supervising the Wyoming State Bar. The state court administrator who serves at the pleasure of the court assists the court. The chief justice of the supreme court is elected by the other justices to a four-year term.

The Supreme Court of Wyoming has considered the role of the state constitution in broadening individual rights of citizens. After a lively debate in the 1990s, the court decided to use a criteria approach for applying the state constitution. Using this approach, the court identifies a list of circumstances under which it will feel justified in interpreting the state constitution more broadly than the U.S. Constitution.

District Courts

The district courts are the trial courts of general jurisdiction in Wyoming. District judges hear felony criminal and civil cases as well as juvenile and probate matters. Appeals from lower courts also are heard in district courts. There are seventeen district court judges organized into nine districts. District court is held in each county seat, requiring some judges to travel to different counties to hear cases from that county. District court judges are appointed by the governor on the recommendation of the Judicial Nominating Commission and serve six-year terms.

Circuit Courts

There are twenty-five circuit courts organized into nine circuits. The circuits are the same areas served by the judicial districts for the district courts. Circuit courts hear civil cases in which the amount does not exceed $7,000. The circuit courts also hear cases involving family violence. The criminal jurisdiction includes all misdemeanors. The circuit courts may act as a municipal court over ordinance violations if a municipality makes a request that is granted by the supreme court. Circuit courts set bail amounts for the accused and hold preliminary hearings in felony criminal cases. A part-time position, magistrates with law degrees may perform all the duties of circuit court judges. Magistrates who do not have law degrees may perform functions limited by statute.

Justice of the Peace Courts

The first judge to serve the area that was to become Wyoming was a justice of the peace appointed to Laramie County by the Dakota territorial legislature in 1897. The office of justice of the peace ceased to exist on January 6, 2003, when the last six counties to operate justice courts abolished them. In 1971, the Wyoming legislature created the county court system that was subsequently replaced in 2000 with the circuit court system. With each county having its own court, there was little need for justices of the peace. Counties abolished their county-funded justice courts to be replaced by the state-funded circuit court system.

Municipal Courts

All incorporated cities and towns in Wyoming have municipal courts. These courts of limited jurisdiction hear cases of ordinance violations. Municipal courts have no jurisdiction to hear civil cases. Municipal court judges are appointed by the mayor with the approval of the municipal council. Most municipal court judges serve part-time and about one-half are lawyers. There were 11,875 civil cases and 2,158 criminal cases filed in district courts in 2001.

Associated Agencies

The Judicial Nominating Commission is a key component of the merit selection process in Wyoming. The commission consists of seven members: the chief justice of the supreme court; three members of the Wyoming State Bar; and three voters, appointed by the governor with the approval of the senate. The Judicial Nominating Commission reviews applications for vacant judgeships and submits a list to the governor from which he or she appoints a judge.

The Judicial Planning Commission operated from 1998 until 2002. The job of the commission was to reorganize the Wyoming judicial branch.

The Office of the State Public Defender was established by the Wyoming legislature in 1978. The public defender represents any needy person who is under arrest for or formally charged with having committed a serious crime. The office also is responsible for representing juveniles charged as delinquents, individuals facing revocation of their probation or parole, and individuals being extradited to other states. The Office of the State Public Defender is part of the executive branch in Wyoming.

Judicial Selection and Removal

Supreme court justices, district court judges, and circuit court judges are chosen using the merit selection process. The governor appoints a judge from a list of three names submitted by the Judicial Nominating Commission. After at least one year in office, the judges must run for retention. Circuit court judges, however, are allowed to appoint magistrates with the consent of the county commissioners in the county in which magistrates will serve. If retained, the supreme court justice serves eight-year terms, district court judges serve six-year terms, and circuit court judges serve four-year terms. The supreme court's justices must have at minimum nine years legal experience, be at least thirty years of age, and have lived in Wyoming for at least three years prior to appointment to be eligible to serve. Judges must retire when they reach seventy years of age. Wyoming voters approved a constitutional amendment implementing merit selection in 1972. Since then, five judges were denied retention by the voters, including a supreme court justice whose bid for retention failed in 1992.

There are three methods for removing a Wyoming judge from the bench. The Wyoming Constitution provides for the Commission on Judicial Conduct and Ethics. The commission investigates complaints of misconduct on the part of Wyoming Supreme Court justices, district court judges, circuit court judges and magistrates, municipal court judges, and other judicial officers. The commission may recommend censure, suspension, removal, or retirement of the offending judge. Acting on the commission's recommendation, the supreme court may take the proposed action against the judge. The supreme court, of its own volition, may censure, suspend, retire, or remove a judge. Judges may be impeached by a simple majority vote of the Wyoming House of Representatives and be convicted by a two-thirds vote of the senate.

John David Rausch Jr.
West Texas A&M University

Further Reading

Office of the Wyoming Attorney General, http://attorneygeneral.state.wy.us/.

Wyoming Judiciary, http://www.courts .state.wy.us/.

Wyoming Public Defenders Office, http:// wyodefender.state.wy.us/.

Wyoming State Bar, http://www .wyomingbar.org/.

GLOSSARY OF COMMON JUDICIAL TERMS

Acquittal: A decision by a judge or jury determining that a person charged with a crime is not guilty.

Advisory opinion: A nonbinding opinion of a court, which suggests how the court might react if the constitutionality of a particular law was challenged. While federal courts do not issue advisory opinions, some state courts are required to provide legislatures or governors such input on request.

Affidavit: A statement made both voluntarily and under oath.

Amicus curie: Literally, "friend of the court." A party not involved in litigation that presents an appellate court with an opinion on a case before that court.

Appeal: The process of asking a higher court to review and overturn the ruling of a lower court.

Appellant: The party initiating an appeal to overturn the lower court ruling.

Appellate jurisdiction: The authority of a higher court to review the decisions of a lower court.

Appellee: The party resisting the appeal.

Arraignment: The stage in the criminal process during which a judge formally informs the defendant of the charges against him or her. The defendant enters a plea during this hearing.

Bail: The money, bonds, or other valuable deposit put forward as security to allow a defendant to be released from jail during the trial process.

Bench trial: A trial decided by a judge rather than a jury.

Brief: (a) A written summary of a specific court decision. This type of brief reports the name and year and citation of the case, circumstances of the case, the disputed legal question, a summary of arguments, the vote of the court's members, and the court's rationale, any novel legal principles announced or applied, and dissenting opinions. (b) A legal argument, written to inform and persuade a court. These follow format guidelines required by the court.

Certiorari, writ of: Literally, an order to "make us informed." The order issued by an appellate court to a lower court calling for transcripts and documents relating to a case. The grant of a writ of certiorari means the higher court has voluntarily agreed to review a case.

Civil law: Law governing private rights of individuals and relationships between individuals, as opposed to criminal law.

Common law: Decisions of courts on points of law. Common law has evolved from English custom.

Contempt of court: The deliberate disobedience of a court order, or the disruption of a court proceeding.

Criminal law: Law concerned with the relationship between the community and the individual.

Defendant: A person charged with a crime in a criminal case, or the party responding to a civil complaint.

Deposition: Testimony taken under oath, but outside of court.

Directed verdict: The determination of a judge that a jury should provide a certain decision; the decision by a judge made prior to the conclusion of trial testimony that the prosecution's case is too weak to sustain charges against a defendant.

Discovery: The pretrial period where lawyers for opposing sides provide each other with the information, names of witnesses, and the evidence that will be used at trial.

Dissenting opinion: The written rationale explaining the vote of the justices on an appellate court who disagrees with the majority's decision.

Docket: The schedule of cases coming before a court.

Due process: The steps government must follow to ensure citizens, including criminal suspects, are afforded fundamental fairness before being denied life, liberty, or property. States are required to follow fair decision-making procedures under the Fourteenth Amendment of the U.S. Constitution.

En banc: A proceeding at which all members of an appeals court, as opposed to a three-judge panel, review a case.

Equal protection clause: The provision of the Fourteenth Amendment of the Constitution that says government should not discriminate against individuals or classes of people.

Equity law: Legal principles based on ideals of fairness, rather than written laws.

Exclusionary rule: The legal principle, under the Fifth and Fourteenth Amendments, that judges may forbid prosecutors from presenting improperly acquired evidence at a criminal trial.

Executive order: The commandments, rules, or regulations issued by the authority of the highest administrative officer of some unit of government, such as a mayor, governor, or the president. Executive orders often provide details on how an administration will implement a statute or court order.

Felony: The most serious type of criminal offenses, eligible for punishments of more than 365 days in prison.

Grand jury: A group of laypersons who review and hear police evidence to decide if there is enough evidence to press charges. This group usually has twenty-three people and it may review many cases.

Habeas corpus: Literally, "you have the body." A writ of habeas corpus is used by courts to determine whether the government is properly, or improperly, detaining someone.

Hung jury: A jury unable to reach a verdict.

In camera: Literally, "in chambers," or in private. Judicial proceedings between the judge and opposing lawyers, outside public view.

Indictment: The written charges issued by a grand jury against a criminal defendant.

Injunction: A decision by a judge forbidding someone from doing something.

Interlocutory appeal: A proceeding brought to an appellate court before a trial is finished. These decisions affect temporary disposition of money, children, or progress on something until the trial verdict can be rendered.

Judicial activism: A philosophical approach that says courts are duty-bound to correct perceived injustices, even when there is no grant of authority in statute or established legal principle for the court to do so.

Judicial restraint: (a) The philosophical approach that says courts are duty-bound to adhere to established legal principles and remain within the boundaries of their authority when making decisions, even when doing so allows a perceived injustice to occur. (b) The belief that judges should not express personal views or emotions in court.

Jurisdiction: The subject matter or geographical area in which a decision maker has authority to act.

Justiciable: A case that can be resolved by a court.

Litigant: A party to a lawsuit.

Litigator: A lawyer representing a litigant in court.

Magistrate: A low-level judge, with restricted authority.

Mandamus: Literally, "we command." The court order compelling a governmental official to carry out some action.

Mandatory jurisdiction: The requirement of a court to decide a case.

Misdemeanor: A minor criminal offense, usually punishable by fewer than 365 days in jail or fines less than $5,000.

Motion: A request made of a court.

Natural law: Those obligations that are placed on all persons, or rights recognized for all people, because of human nature.

Order: The decision of a court commanding someone or some organization to do something.

Ordinance: The rules and regulations enacted by a city or county legislature.

Original jurisdiction: The authority to hear the initial proceedings in a case. A court of origin is the court in which a case originates. Appellate courts do not have original jurisdiction, except in exceptional cases.

Per curiam: Literally, "for the court." An unsigned decision of an appeals court; usually a unanimous decision.

Petit jury: A trial jury, usually with between six and twelve individuals, authorized to hear a trial and decide the facts of a case.

Plea bargain: A negotiated settlement in a criminal case. Usually a prosecutor agrees to reduce a charge or seek a reduced sentence and the defendant agrees to plead guilty.

Police power: The authority of government to protect the health, safety, well-being, and morals of a community.

Positive law: Rights and obligations created by governments, as opposed to those thought to be inherent in human nature.

Precedent: An appellate court's reasoning that will, or does, govern decision making on similar matters that come after it.

Recusal: The decision of a judge to disqualify him- or herself from participating in a case. This usually occurs when a judge has a personal stake in the outcome, or otherwise believes he or she has a diminished ability to sit as a neutral decision maker.

Remand: An order that returns a case from a higher court to a lower court for further proceedings.

Standing: The legal prerogative of an individual or organization to sue or be sued in a particular situation. To have standing, a party must have a direct stake in the outcome of a case.

Statute: The formal rules created by legislatures.

Stay: A court order to postpone a particular decision from taking effect.

Strict construction: The narrow interpretation of statute, precedence, or a constitutional provision.

Subpoena: A court order to provide testimony or evidence.

Temporary restraining order: A decision compelling someone to discontinue some action, usually until judicial proceedings have been exhausted in a case.

Venire: Literally, "to appear at court." The panel of citizens from which a petit jury will be selected.

Voir dire: Literally, "tell the truth." The process of interviewing prospective jurors and selecting a petit jury.

Warrant: A written court order permitting police to arrest a specific individual, or authority to search for and seize evidence from a particular place.

Writ: A court document giving some kind of commandment to the party named in the order.

ANNOTATED BIBLIOGRAPHY

Anderson, Terry L., and Peter J. Hill. 2004. *The Not So Wild, Wild West: Property Rights on the Frontier.* Stanford, CA: Stanford University Press.

The not-so-violent story of how the West was won. Rather than being a legacy of the spoils of gunslingers, the settlement of the West is seen by the authors as a triumph of entrepreneurship and the protection of property rights in frontier court systems. Cooperation and the rule of law overcame violence among free people acting in their economic rights.

Baum, Lawrence. 1994. *American Courts: Process and Policy.* Boston: Houghton Mifflin.

An excellent series of essays examining the work of state and federal courts, with insights into the history and workings of U.S. courts. Baum's offering is primarily descriptive and explanatory in nature, with the focus largely on processes. Generally avoiding normative discussions and details about outcomes, Baum instead provides careful and succinct discussion of the various theories of judicial behavior.

Gates, John, and Charles Johnson, eds. 1990. *The American Courts: A Critical Assessment.* Washington, DC: Congressional Quarterly Press.

The strength of this text is its focus on how state courts shape the policy-making process. Separate entries (particularly those by Henry Glick and Lynn Mather) identify the different ways in which courts make policy. The work highlights the frequency with which state courts use the power of judicial review, the ways in which state court precedent is diffused to other states, and the means by which plaintiffs get access to state courts.

Kritzer, Herbert M. 1990. *The Justice Broker: Lawyers and Ordinary Litigation.* New York: Oxford University Press.

Relying on interviews with nearly 1,400 lawyers practicing in state and federal courts, along with other case outcome data, Kritzer pulls together a picture of ordinary litigation and the role played by the conceptions of the lawyers who argue these cases. This book is rich in detail about lawyers' relationships to one another and to clients, the types of cases lawyers handle, fee arrangements, and time involved.

Nagel, Robert F., ed. 1995. *Intellect and Craft: The Contributions of Justice Hans Linde to American Constitutionalism.* Boulder, CO: Westview Press.

Linde is one of the most significant figures in modern judicial theory in America. A scholar, diplomat, and jurist, Linde may be most remembered for advancing the idea of new judicial federalism by finding within the Oregon Constitution libertarian principles not to be found in parallel language of the U.S. Constitution. Linde's work remains current in its consideration of models of interpretation for judges and the bounds that federalism place on the federal government in interfering in the prerogatives of the states. This collection of Linde's writing can be appreciated by readers with a firm footing in legal theory.

National Center for State Courts, http://www.ncsconline.org/ (accessed April 6, 2006).

The National Center for State Courts oversees the Court Statistics Project (CSP; http://www.ncsconline.org/d_research/csp/CSP_Main_Page.html), which collects an enormous amount of data on the workload of state courts. The CSP monitors what type of cases are filed, which types of courts do the most work, and changes in this data over time. The center also provides detailed diagrams highlighting the structure and jurisdictional make-up of every state court system. Its information was the basis for the "The Work of State Courts" section in Chapter 2.

Pinello, Daniel R. 1995. *The Impact of Judicial Selection Method on State Supreme Court Policy: Innovation, Reaction and Atrophy.* Westport, CT: Greenwood Press.

This book is a rare find: a systematic and intellectually rigorous analysis of the role the judicial selection method has on the nature and decisions of state courts. Pinello uses quantitative and qualitative approaches to uncover the extent to which selection method used (election, legislative selections, and the Missouri Plan) affects the demographic composition of courts and the extent to which each method seems variously to favor business interests, the individual, or government, as illustrated by selected cases.

State Supreme Court Data Project, http://www.ruf.rice.edu/~pbrace/statecourt/ (accessed April 6, 2006).

A collaborative project between Rice University and Michigan State University and sponsored by the National Science Foundation, the State Supreme Court Data Project provides this database with information on State Supreme Court decisions in all fifty states.

Tarr, G. Alan, ed. 1996. *Constitutional Politics in the States: Contemporary Controversies and Historical Patterns.* Westport, CT: Greenwood Press.

This edited volume highlights many of the emerging developments in state constitutional law and provides case studies illuminating how state courts are addressing these new issues, offering insight into the complicated nature of judicial federalism and how state and national court systems simultaneously—although not necessarily cooperatively—create law.

———. 1998. *Understanding State Constitutions.* Princeton, NJ: Princeton University Press.

Tarr here provides an excellent overview of the structure and historical development of state law, state courts, and state constitutions. The text also addresses why state constitutions, and therefore state courts, are so different from the U.S. Constitution and federal courts.

Tarr, G. Alan, and Maria Cornelia Aldis Porter. 1988. *Supreme Courts in the State and Nation.* New Haven: Yale University Press.

This in-depth and qualitative study of the decision-making practices and political environments of the state supreme courts in Alabama, Ohio, and New Jersey is also one of a few attempts to provide a comparative analysis of the situations and personalities that give rise to monumental decisions. The book begins with an overview of the notion of judicial federalism and the role of state supreme courts in state government. Then the three state courts and their leading judicial actors are described in rich detail. This book is accessible to general readers but also informative for advanced legal scholars.

INDEX